Using Quattro Pro® 5.0, Special Edition

PATRICK J. BURNS

Using Quattro Pro 5.0, Special Edition

Library of Congress Catalog No.: 93-85043

ISBN: 1-56529-257-X

95 94 93   4 3 2 1

Interpretation of the printing code: the rightmost double-digit number is the year of the book's printing; the rightmost single-digit number, the number of the book's printing. For example, a printing code of 93-1 shows that the first printing of the book occurred in 1993.

Using Quattro Pro 5.0, Special Edition, is based on Quattro Pro through Version 5.0.

Publisher: David P. Ewing

Associate Publisher: Rick Ranucci

Managing Editor: Corinne Walls

Publishing Plan Manager: Thomas H. Bennett

Marketing Manager: Ray Robinson

For Mom:

Thanks for sitting me down in front of your typewriter all those years ago.

CREDITS

Title Manager
Don Roche Jr.

Acquisitions Editor
Sherri Morningstar

Product Development Specialists
Shelley O'Hara
Robin Drake

Production Editor
Susan M. Dunn

Editors
Elsa M. Bell
Joy M. Preacher
Kathy Simpson

Technical Editors
Michael Watson
Cathy Kenny

Book Designer
Amy Peppler-Adams

Production Team
Jeff Baker
Angela Bannan
Diana Bigham
Danielle Bird
Katy Bodenmiller
Brad Chinn
Meshell Dinn
Howard Jones
Heather Kaufman
Tom Loveman
Beth Rago
Carrie Roth
Marc Shecter
Greg Simsic
Tina Trettin

Indexer
Michael Hughes

Composed in *Cheltenham* and *MCPdigital* by Que Corporation.

Patrick J. Burns is an established author, an expert in spreadsheet development, and a university lecturer. His work in the computer field also includes beta-site testing, confidential review, and program development of software packages for major publishers.

Author of the books *I Hate Excel* and *I Hate 1-2-3*, both published by Que Corporation, Burns has written and contributed to 18 other books about using Quattro Pro, Quattro Pro for Windows, Windows, Word, Excel, 1-2-3, and WordPerfect.

Burns holds a bachelor of science degree in finance with a minor in economics. A native of Pennsylvania, he has traveled worldwide and has lived in Europe and Asia. He is a founder and principal of Burns & Associates, a professional consulting firm based in San Diego, California.

ACKNOWLEDGMENTS

To Don Roche and Robin Drake: My sincere thanks for your patience, considerate guidance, and consistently competent editing throughout the development of *Using Quattro Pro 5*, Special Edition. Also, many thanks to the development and editing team from the previous edition of this book: Shelley O'Hara, Diane L. Steele, Kelly Currie, Kelly D. Dobbs, Robin Drake, Jeannine Freudenberger, Lori A. Lyons, Susan Shaw Dunn, and Betty White.

Trademarks

CONTENTS AT A GLANCE

TABLE OF CONTENTS

II Printing and Graphing

III Advanced Spreadsheet Features

Appendixes

Introduction

Today's electronic spreadsheet programs replace the manual accounting worksheets of yesteryear. The electronic spreadsheet, in fact, combines the best features of the accountant's multicolumn worksheet with the number-crunching power of today's PCs. Every spreadsheet program performs the same mathematical operations—addition, subtraction, multiplication, and division—easily and efficiently. The best spreadsheet programs, however, offer you much more than that.

Quattro Pro is one of the most powerful electronic spreadsheet programs available for PCs. Version 5.0 is a crowning achievement in the ongoing development of Borland International's best-selling Quattro program. The adoption of a multipage notebook feature in Version 5.0 demonstrates Borland's continuing commitment to integrating the newest available technologies into the Quattro Pro environment.

In a Quattro Pro 5.0 *notebook*, each page is the equivalent of one spreadsheet. Because every notebook has 256 pages, you can create complex reports and store them together in a single location. You can turn a notebook into a multiperiod income statement, a monthly calendar, a written paragraph, a database, or a pie graph. You can use Quattro Pro to record your personal financial budget, do regression analysis for economic forecasting, or store an inventory list of your favorite computer software programs. With Quattro Pro Version 5.0, you can reach more ambitious spreadsheet goals faster and more easily.

Using Quattro Pro 5.0, Special Edition, teaches you how to install, operate, and master the operation of Quattro Professional (Pro) Version 5.0. The step-by-step instructions in each chapter clearly show you Version 5.0's potential for building elegant computer solutions to meet specific personal management and business reporting needs.

This book also teaches you how to install, operate, and master the operation of Version 5.0. Released in September 1993, Version 5.0 offers multipage notebook technology, a WYSIWYG (what-you-see-is-what-you-get) graphical user interface and several new SpeedBar buttons, enhanced data analysis and file translation capabilities, new and revised @functions, new macro commands, and many other new features.

Using Quattro Pro 5.0, Special Edition, is a unique book for many reasons. In this book, you find 16 chapters of targeted, easy-to-follow tutorial text. Realistic examples sprinkled throughout each chapter help you envision your own uses for Quattro Pro.

Each chapter in this book offers a comprehensive look at one aspect of using Quattro Pro, such as enhancing notebook style. Tips, notes, and cautions guide you through some of the more complex and interesting aspects of using the program.

A Questions & Answers section appears at the end of each chapter. These special troubleshooting sections cover many common problems and their solutions to help you maintain uninterrupted Quattro Pro work sessions.

Three detailed appendixes provide you with invaluable coverage of additional user topics such as installing the program, operating Quattro Pro in a network environment, and creating and using printer setup strings.

The inside front and back covers offer a quick reference to the most commonly used Quattro Pro commands.

Using Quattro Pro 5.0, Special Edition, will help you discover that Quattro Pro Version 5.0 does everything that Version 4.0 can do—and more.

The Evolution of Quattro Pro

When Borland released Quattro in November 1987, the company took the software industry by surprise. Quattro was the first functional, affordable, and fully 1-2-3-compatible spreadsheet program. With Quattro on the market, anyone could afford to enter the electronic number-crunching arena.

With the release of Quattro Pro Version 5.0, Borland demonstrates the company's commitment to keeping pace with changing hardware and software technologies. Throughout this evolution, each version of Quattro Pro still runs under the DOS 2.0 (or later) operating system, yet also can take full advantage of the newest PC hardware. Spreadsheet users who own older, slower computer systems, however, also can take advantage of Version 5.0's power.

Whether you are a beginning spreadsheet user or a dedicated "Quattrophile," you will appreciate Quattro Pro's power, professional look, compatibility, and functionality—qualities that make Quattro Pro *the* premier electronic spreadsheet program in the DOS environment:

- *Quattro Pro is powerful.* With Version 5.0, you can create and move quickly between 256 unique pages per notebook, link data between multiple notebooks, open and view up to 32 windows at the same time, transform a notebook into a flat-file database, and permanently record repetitive notebook formatting steps into macros for future use. Version 5.0 can operate on an IBM XT, a 486-class machine, and everything in between. With Borland's Virtual Real-time Object-Oriented Memory Manager (VROOMM), you also can load and run Quattro Pro with only 512K of RAM.

- *Quattro Pro is professional.* Version 5.0 offers 14 typefaces and an advanced WYSIWYG graphical user interface (GUI) that enables "real-time" development of original, professional-looking, presentation-quality reports. *WYSIWYG notebook development* means that what you create and see on-screen is what you get on a printed page, including customized fonts, shaded cells, drawn lines, and other stylistic enhancements. With Quattro Pro, you also can insert graphs directly onto your notebooks.

■ *Quattro Pro is compatible.* Quattro Pro 5.0 automatically translates files created with earlier versions of Quattro Pro. Version 5.0 also enables you to access the data stored in many popular program formats. Quattro Pro uses files created with 1-2-3 Releases 1A, 2.x, and 3.x; Lotus Allways and Impress; Symphony Versions 1.2 and 2.0; Surpass; Paradox Versions 3.x and 4.x; dBASE II, III, III Plus, and IV; Reflex Versions 1 and 2; and VisiCalc, Multiplan, and Harvard Graphics. With complete 1-2-3 (Release 2.01) macro, file, and keystroke compatibility, you know that your 1-2-3 data is preserved when you switch to Quattro Pro.

■ *Quattro Pro is functional.* You immediately feel at home with Quattro Pro. Version 5.0 offers pull-down menus, a SpeedBar, and keystroke shortcuts for command execution. Because Quattro Pro can use Logitech, Mouse Systems, PC Mouse, and Microsoft-compatible mice, operating a notebook is easy.

Some of Quattro Pro 5.0's less conspicuous—but equally welcomed—enhancements include an installation program that automatically detects the hardware on your system, an Undo option, expanded printer controls, and a larger library of @functions and macro keywords. With Quattro Pro you also can create multiple hardware configurations, which you can invoke and cancel from the command menu, to hide notebook borders and columns, to present notebooks and graphs on-screen, and to print a graph without leaving the program.

What's New in Version 5.0?

Some of the new features in Version 5.0 are as follows:

■ *Multipage notebook structure.* Quattro Pro Version 5.0 replaces the basic spreadsheet with a much more powerful data-entry medium called the notebook. A single notebook contains 256 unique pages, making it simple to group together the various documents, graphs, databases, and macros for any project into a single file. Every data-manipulating command that can work on a single page now can work across several pages at once—saving you literally thousands of keystrokes each time you create a complex document.

■ *Group mode editing.* Never before has creating, producing, and publishing groups of reports been so easy. Version 5.0 enables you to associate pages within a single notebook into a group, and then simultaneously modify the same block of cells in each page. When you enter data into one page, you even can "drill" the entry into the same cell in every other page in the group. Group mode editing is the ultimate time-saving productivity tool.

■ *New SpeedBar buttons.* Quattro Pro Version 5.0 enables you to reproduce the most popular notebook operations by clicking the appropriate button on the SpeedBar, the sculpted horizontal panel appearing at the top of the WYSIWYG screen display. You can toggle between WYSIWYG and text display mode, for example, by clicking a single SpeedBar button, which enables you to develop applications more easily in either display mode. Look for the SpeedBar icons throughout this book to point out the quickest methods for using Quattro Pro.

■ *Enhanced data analysis capabilities.* Version 5.0 offers several new options that offer you greater flexibility and help you attain your objectives more quickly when using the Optimizer data modeling tool.

■ *New printing features for notebooks.* Version 5.0 offers new printing features to match the special needs of the notebook environment. You can identify 3-D print blocks that span several pages in the same notebook, eliminating the need for issuing the same printing commands over and over again for each notebook page you want to print.

■ *New spreadsheet commands and features.* Quattro Pro has several new commands and features to help you manage your work sessions better. The Consolidate command enables you to consolidate into a single notebook all spreadsheets associated with a file-linking application that you created with a previous version of Quattro Pro. Version 5.0 does away with the FontTable command and integrates all its functions into the Font command, enabling you to manage all font enhancement features from a single location.

■ *Updated file translation support.* Version 5.0 keeps pace with the ever-changing software industry by updating its file translation utility to support the most current versions of Paradox, dBASE, Harvard Graphics, and Quattro Pro for Windows.

Who Should Read This Book?

This book is designed for beginning, intermediate, and advanced Quattro Pro users. This book teaches the beginner how to design and build notebooks and coaches more experienced users through the process of recording notebook formatting steps and selecting macro language commands for use in macro programs. For the advanced user, this book shows how to handle many computational tasks at one time and how to control every operation to produce logical, well-organized, and up-to-the-minute reports.

Users at every level learn how to install and configure Quattro Pro so that they can delegate simple tasks (such as data input) to others without worrying about compromising the integrity of the business, the program, or the notebook application.

How This Book Is Organized

Using Quattro Pro 5.0, Special Edition, shows the reader how to create and use notebooks from the first step to the last. All the important rules and programming procedures are emphasized throughout the book to create an efficient, self-paced curriculum leading to the successful creation of Quattro Pro notebooks. The book is divided into three major sections, each covering techniques that progress in difficulty.

Part I: Using Quattro Pro Notebooks

Part I, "Using Quattro Pro Notebooks," consists of Chapters 1 through 8 and covers basic Quattro Pro operations. Novices who have selected Quattro Pro as their first electronic spreadsheet program will benefit from the Quick Start material presented in Chapter 1. This tutorial chapter enables users of all levels to jump in and use Quattro Pro. If you want to create a notebook quickly, see Chapter 1.

Beginners also benefit from the fundamental basics presented in Chapters 2 through 4. Detailed discussions show you how to get Quattro Pro up and running, and supporting examples show the best ways to design, create, edit, and improve your Quattro Pro notebooks.

Part I includes suggestions for using @function commands in your notebooks, improving the style of your notebooks, analyzing notebook data, and effectively managing your notebook files.

If you are an intermediate user who already knows how to use an electronic spreadsheet program, you can skip the initial chapters. Instead, you quickly can get up to speed by scanning Chapters 5 through 8 to get a feel for Version 5.0's new and different features. When you have the time for more detailed reading, begin reading Chapter 5 to learn about Quattro Pro and specific ways to enhance your existing library of notebooks.

The chapters in Part I are summarized as follows:

■ Chapter 1, "Quick Start: Using Quattro Pro," presents the basics for building and using Quattro Pro notebooks.

■ Chapter 2, "Getting Started," introduces the Version 5.0 notebook and the proper way to begin and end a Quattro Pro work session. Chapter 2 then shows how Quattro Pro interacts with a keyboard and mouse. The chapter progresses into specific discussions of the Version 5.0 screen display: the pull-down menu bar, the SpeedBar, the input and status lines, and the notebook area. An overview of using the on-line help feature concludes the chapter.

■ Chapter 3, "Entering and Editing Data," shows how to enter, edit, move, and view data on the Quattro Pro notebook. The discussion addresses the rules for entering numbers, formulas, and @function commands. Chapter 3 also explains how to correct errors in formulas and use the Undo feature. The discussion then turns to the procedures for creating and managing page groups within a notebook. This chapter concludes with a review of the different Quattro Pro display modes. These basics give you the logical and most ideal methods for consistently using Quattro Pro to build useful notebook applications.

■ Chapter 4, "Manipulating Data," teaches you how to manipulate cell data to create the most logical, organized notebook presentation. You learn how to copy, move, and delete cell data in a single page—and from page to page—within the notebook. You also learn how to create and manage groups of pages, and techniques for extending the power of the menu commands by using two- and three-dimensional blocks of notebook data. The chapter concludes by showing you how to search for and replace data on a notebook. These fundamental Quattro Pro commands are among the most used during every notebook work session.

■ Chapter 5, "Formatting Data," presents a comprehensive review of the Quattro Pro **S**tyle menu. Use the commands found on this menu to enhance the look of a notebook. You learn how to change the way Quattro Pro displays data in a cell, set the numeric format, and format text labels. This chapter also covers how to change and reset the width of columns and how to hide columns. The chapter concludes with directions for creating presentation-quality notebooks using fonts, line drawing, and shading.

■ Chapter 6, "Using Functions," defines and explains how to use Quattro Pro's built-in @function commands in your notebooks. From basic mathematical operations to applying logical and string functions, this chapter shows you how to turn notebooks into statistical, scientific, and financial analysis tools.

■ Chapter 7, "Analyzing Notebooks," shows how to monitor the construction of notebook formulas by using the **T**ools Au**d**it command. This chapter explains how to identify formula dependencies, how to locate circular, blank, label, and ERR references, and how to monitor external formula links to other notebook files. Chapter 7 concludes with a presentation of using the Version 5.0 **T**ools **S**olve For command to solve formulas backwards.

■ Chapter 8, "Managing Files and Windows," covers multiple notebook operations. Quattro Pro notebooks easily can consolidate information from several sources onto one notebook, or arrange the same information into a group of pages within the same notebook. This chapter explains why, how, and when you should use multiple notebooks. Topics covered in this chapter include inserting text, moving between notebooks, and viewing multiple notebooks. Examples clearly illustrate several techniques for linking files with formulas. Finally, the steps required to consolidate linking applications from earlier versions of Quattro Pro into a Version 5.0 notebook are provided.

Part II: Printing and Graphing

Part II, "Printing and Graphing," consists of Chapters 9 through 12 and illustrates the two methods for presenting Quattro Pro notebooks: on a printed page or in graph form. These chapters include tips for placing live graphs on your notebooks, enhancing the look of your graphs, analyzing graph data, and preparing your printed output for use in other programs. The chapters are summarized as follows:

■ Chapter 9, "Printing," provides you with the tools, techniques, and instructions you need to print notebook reports and graphs in Quattro Pro. In this chapter, you generate an unformatted snapshot of data in the current window and examine your output on-screen before you print, using the Screen Preview feature. You learn the procedures and rules for creating print files with a PRN extension, and about printing draft-quality copy and final presentation-quality versions of your notebook reports and graphs.

■ Chapter 10, "Creating Graphs," introduces you to one of the program's most appealing aspects: envisioning, designing, and displaying graphs. In this chapter, you learn about the utility and anatomy of the Quattro Pro graph, how to quick-create a basic graph, and how to build a custom graph from the ground up. Throughout this chapter, figures show how to enhance the appearance of a basic graph. Finally, you learn how to manage graph files so that you can recall, update, and review these files during other work sessions.

■ Chapter 11, "Customizing Graphs," picks up where the preceding chapter leaves off. Although Chapter 10 offers many good suggestions for improving the appearance of a basic graph, this chapter introduces techniques for creating customized graphs that locate important trends and point out problem areas better than basic graphs. Customized graphs also leave a viewer with more than just a general feeling about notebook data. By using the Graph Annotator tool, you learn how to add boxed text, geometric figures, and clip art to your graphs to create presentation-quality visual aids.

■ Chapter 12, "Analyzing Graphs," introduces the Version 5.0 /Graph **A**nalyze commands. With this group of commands, you can analyze a graph without altering the notebook from which the graph derives. The material in this chapter illustrates advanced methods for analyzing graph data: in aggregate time periods, by moving averages, and in exponential and linear form.

Part III: Advanced Spreadsheet Features

Part III, "Advanced Spreadsheet Features," consists of Chapters 13 through 16. Advanced Quattro Pro users and experienced programmers will benefit from Part III's presentation of notebook concepts you use to develop complicated applications. Chapters 13, 14, and 15 address the creation and management of databases, macro programs, and advanced macro applications. Chapter 16 offers complete coverage of how to customize Version 5.0, including start-up options, colors, printers, SpeedBar buttons, display mode, and much more.

The chapters in Part III are summarized as follows:

■ Chapter 13, "Managing Your Data," demonstrates that as an electronic notebook program, Quattro Pro is a flat-file database manager. This chapter focuses on how to transform a notebook into a database so that you can sort, extract, and delete records like you can with other database programs.

■ Chapter 14, "Analyzing and Manipulating Data," provides instructions for using Quattro Pro's data analysis tools. You learn how to perform regression analysis, do optimization modeling, build sensitivity tables, and conduct frequency distribution analysis.

■ Chapter 15, "Creating Macros," shows you how to record macro programs so that you can replicate keystrokes and menu commands. These macros can assume many of the repetitive formatting steps that you perform each time you load a new, blank notebook into Quattro Pro. Later chapter material familiarizes you with advanced macro topics such as macro program management, macro debugging, and manually writing macros to meet specific needs.

■ Chapter 16, "Customizing Quattro Pro," stresses the importance of mastering the commands found on the **O**ptions menu, because these commands determine how Quattro Pro interacts with computer peripherals such as printers, expanded memory, and mice. Chapter 16 addresses how to create customized global notebook settings to meet the unique needs of the user. Topics covered in this chapter include choosing the right printer and using display mode, fonts, colors, the date and time display, SpeedBar settings, and initial start-up options. With the **O**ptions menu commands, you also determine how Quattro Pro recalculates, protects data, and interacts with data files from other programs.

Appendixes

Appendixes A through C address advanced user issues such as how to install and customize Quattro Pro so that the program uses your hardware in the most efficient manner. Users operating Quattro Pro on a local-area network (LAN) will find Appendix B particularly useful for learning about installing and managing the program in a LAN environment.

The appendixes are summarized as follows:

- Appendix A, "Installing and Customizing Quattro Pro," shows you how to build the ideal computer environment for Quattro Pro. This appendix presents a step-by-step review of the installation process and rules for reconfiguring and enhancing an installed copy of the program.

- Appendix B, "Using Quattro Pro on a Network," shows you how to install and manage Quattro Pro on a local area network (LAN). Because Version 5.0 arrives "network-ready," the discussion concentrates on the steps you take to prepare your network for program installation.

- Appendix C, "Using ASCII Characters," contains a table of control characters and printable characters as presented by the American Standard Code for Information Interchange (ASCII). The table lists 255 characters and their decimal and hexadecimal equivalents.

Conventions Used in This Book

The conventions used in this book have been established to help you learn to use the program quickly and easily. As much as possible, the conventions correspond with those used in the Quattro Pro documentation.

Italic type emphasizes an important point or introduces a new concept.

Boldface type highlights the keyword that appears in a menu or command name and, in step-by-step instructions, indicates a word or phrase that you should type. To execute the /**F**ile **S**ave **R**eplace command, for example, you type /**FSR**.

A digital typeface example denotes on-screen messages or text.

Tips provide insider clues to many of the Quattro Pro features. The tips offer time-saving advice and suggestions that help you develop power-user skills.

Notes clarify topics and offer additional material about the use and application of a particular program feature.

Cautions warn you about the potential negative consequences of an operation or action.

The small figure next to this paragraph is the kind of icon used to point out notebook operations that you can perform using a button on the Version 5.0 SpeedBar.

The following Quattro Pro elements appear in uppercase:

- Range names, such as PROFIT

- @Function commands, such as @SUM

- Mode and status indicators, such as POINT and READY

- Cell references, such as A1..D10

The following Quattro Pro conventions regarding macro programs also apply to this book:

- Macro names are formed with a backslash (\) followed by a lower-case letter, such as \a. This naming convention also indicates that you can execute this macro program by pressing Alt+a.

- Quattro Pro menu keystrokes in a macro program, such as /fsr, are lowercase letters.

- Range names in a macro program, such as /ecPROFIT, are upper-case letters.

- The tilde (~) represents the action of pressing the Enter key in a macro, as in /fsBUDGET~.

All screen shots appearing throughout the book are in WYSIWYG display mode, except when noted otherwise.

PART

I

Quick Start: Using Quattro Pro

This chapter introduces you to the basic methods for using Quattro Pro Version 5.0. The material here covers five activities fundamental to using Quattro Pro.

The following topics correspond to a chapter in the first part of this book. When you come across a topic that you want to explore, refer to the corresponding chapter for complete coverage.

- Loading and exiting the program (Chapter 2)
- Creating and viewing a notebook (Chapter 3)
- Using @function commands (Chapters 3 and 6)
- Improving notebook style (Chapter 5)
- Saving a notebook (Chapter 8)

This chapter also shows you how to build a sample notebook from the ground up. Along the way, you will come across features that you have encountered in other programs as well as features that are new to you. In either case, after completing this hands-on exercise, you should be able to create notebooks that you can use to meet many personal management and business reporting needs.

Beginning a Quattro Pro Work Session

After you install your copy of Quattro Pro, you are ready to initiate a work session. (For information on installation, see Appendix A.) Perform the following steps to begin a new work session:

1. At the DOS command prompt, type **cd \qpro** and press Enter.

Unless you specified otherwise during the installation (discussed in Appendix A), the Quattro Pro program files are stored in a directory called QPRO.

2. Type **q** and press Enter to load Quattro Pro into your computer's memory.

NOTE

If you are operating in the Microsoft Windows environment, double-click the Quattro Pro icon to load the program.

Unless you specify otherwise, each time you load the program into your computer's memory, Quattro Pro displays a blank notebook, NOTEBK1.WQ2, that is ready for input (see fig. 1.1).

Executing a Command

After this notebook is on-screen, you can enter data or execute commands. To execute a Quattro Pro command, you need to activate one of the nine pull-down menus. To activate a menu, press the forward slash key (/) to enter Quattro Pro's MENU mode. The word MENU replaces the word READY on the status line. Each menu contains a list of commands that perform various notebook and file activities.

To open the **F**ile menu, for example, follow these steps:

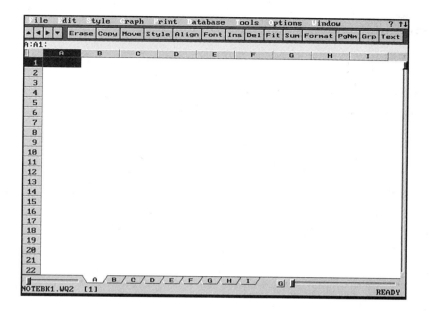

Fig. 1.1

The Quattro Pro screen display.

1. Press the forward slash key (/). By default, Quattro Pro highlights File in the menu bar.

2. Press Enter to pull down the File menu. You also can use the mouse to click File in the menu bar. Quattro Pro displays a list of commands that help you manage your notebook files (see fig. 1.2).

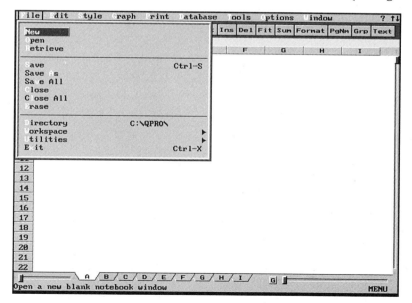

Fig. 1.2

The pull-down **F**ile menu.

Each command name appears at the left margin of the menu. Notice that one letter in each name appears in boldface. To choose a command when a menu is pulled down, press the letter that appears in boldface or click the command name.

3. To practice choosing a command, press D to choose **D**irectory. You can use this command to change directories.

4. Press Esc twice to close the menu and return to READY mode.

Entering and Editing Notebook Data

With the remaining material in this chapter, you build a sample notebook application for J. Dunn & Company, an industrial goods manufacturer. The finished application appears in figure 1.3.

Fig. 1.3

The J. Dunn & Company purchasing report.

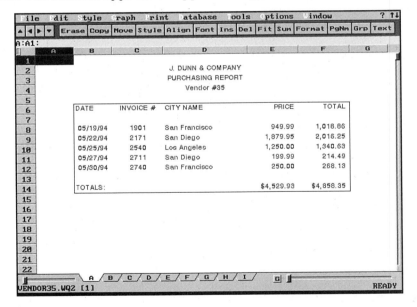

Entering Different Data Types

Quattro Pro accepts two types of data as valid entries: labels and values. A *label* is a text entry; a *value* can be a number, a formula, or a date-and-time entry.

Quattro Pro looks at the first character in an entry to decide whether that entry is a label or a value. When you enter a label into a cell, the mode indicator on the status line displays the word LABEL; when you enter a value, the mode indicator displays the word VALUE.

By default, Quattro Pro places an apostrophe in front of every label entry. A value entry must begin with a number (0 through 9) or with one of the following value symbols:

> + − . ($

Quattro Pro assumes that the value of all numbers is positive unless you specify otherwise.

Building the basic form of the notebook shown in figure 1.3 is a three-step process, as follows:

1. Enter the report titles.

2. Enter the column and row headings.

3. Enter data into the notebook.

Entering the Report Titles

At the top of your notebook, you want to add a title that explains what the notebook contains. For the example, follow these steps to add a title:

1. Use the arrow keys to move the selector to cell A1 or click cell A1 with the mouse.

2. Type **J. DUNN & COMPANY** and press Enter to record the main report title.

TIP

Rather than press Enter to complete an entry, you can press the down-arrow key or click cell A2 with the mouse to record the entry and move to cell A2.

3. Press the down-arrow key to move the selector to cell A2, type **PURCHASING REPORT**, and press Enter to record the secondary report title.

4. Press the down-arrow key to move the selector to cell A3, type **Vendor #35**, and press Enter to record the third and final report title.

Entering the Column and Row Headings

Each column in your notebook contains a certain type of data. The DATE column, for example, contains dates. To enter descriptive headings for each of your columns, follow these steps:

1. Move the selector to cell A5, type **DATE**, and press Enter to record the column A heading.

2. Move the selector to cell B5, type **INVOICE #**, and press Enter to record the column B heading.

3. Move the selector to cell C5, type **CITY NAME**, and press Enter to record the column C heading.

4. Move the selector to cell D5, type **PRICE**, and press Enter to record the column D heading.

5. Move the selector to cell E5, type **TOTAL**, and press Enter to record the column E heading.

Add a row heading by following these steps:

1. Move the selector to cell A13.

2. Type **TOTALS:** and press Enter to record the row heading.

Your notebook should look like figure 1.4.

Notice that the CITY NAME descriptive heading shown in figure 1.4 doesn't display in full. Column C isn't wide enough to accommodate it. You fix this display later in the section "Changing Column Widths."

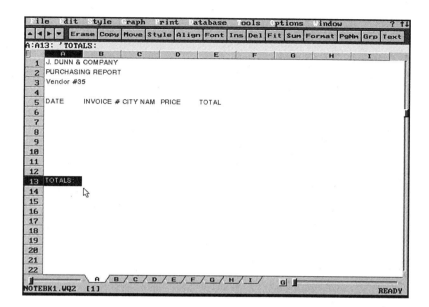

Fig. 1.4

The notebook report with titles and column and row headings.

Entering Data

After you set up your column and row headings, you can begin to enter data. For the sample notebook, you enter dates, invoice numbers, city names, prices, and totals. Follow these steps:

1. Move the selector to cell A7 to begin entering the dates.

2. Press Ctrl+D to enter DATE mode. While in DATE mode, you can format cells to display numbers as dates.

3. Type **05/19/94** and press Enter to record the first date.

4. Move the selector to cell A8 to enter the second date.

5. Repeat step 2 for the following dates: **05/22/94**, **05/25/94**, **05/27/94**, and **05/30/94**. Move the selector down one cell after each entry.

To enter the invoice numbers, follow these steps:

1. Move the selector to cell B7 to enter the first invoice number.

2. Type **1001** and press Enter to record the first invoice number. Move the selector down one cell for the next entry.

3. Repeat step 2 for the remaining four invoice numbers, moving the selector down one cell each time. Type the following numbers: **2171**, **2540**, **2711**, and **2740**.

To enter the city names, follow these steps:

1. Move the selector to cell C7 to begin entering the locations.

2. Type **San Francisco** and press Enter to record the purchase location for the first invoice. Move the selector down one cell.

3. For the rest of the invoices, type the following locations: **San Diego**, **Los Angeles**, **San Diego**, and **San Francisco**. Move the selector down one cell after each entry.

To enter the prices, follow these steps:

1. Move the selector to cell D7 to begin entering the price data.

2. Type **949.99** and press Enter to record the purchase price for the first invoice. Then, move the selector down one cell.

3. Type the remaining four prices, moving the selector down one cell after each price: **1879.95**, **1250**, **199.99**, and **250**.

Your notebook should look like figure 1.5.

Fig. 1.5

The purchasing report with dates, invoice numbers, city names, and prices.

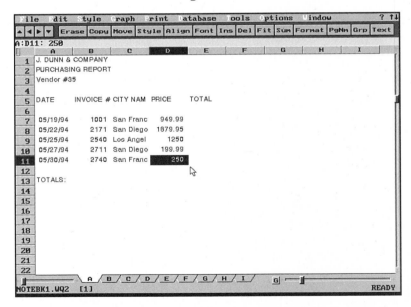

Notice that the San Francisco and Los Angeles city names shown in figure 1.5 do not display in full. Column C isn't wide enough to accommodate them. The section "Changing Column Widths" covers this subject later. For now, turn your attention to creating formulas that complete the basic form of this notebook report.

Entering Formulas

Quattro Pro evaluates notebook formulas and returns answers in the cells in which the formulas reside. You can create simple arithmetic formulas to add a column of figures, to multiply values, and to return percentages.

To create a formula in cell E7 to add 7.25 percent sales tax to the value appearing in cell D7, follow these steps:

1. Move the selector to cell E7.

2. Type **+D7*1.0725** and then check the input line to ensure that you typed the correct formula.

> You also can press the plus sign (+), move the selector to cell D7, and then finish typing the rest of the formula beginning with the asterisk (*).

TIP

3. Press Enter to record the formula.

Quattro Pro displays the value 1018.864 in cell E7. Notice that this value is not rounded properly. You learn how to format numbers later in the section "Formatting Numbers." For now, concentrate on copying this formula so that all the prices in column D display in column E with tax included.

Copying Formulas

Although you can repeat steps 2 and 3 from the preceding exercise to create the same formulas for cells E8 to E11, you easily can copy the formula in cell E7 so that Quattro Pro calculates the tax-included totals for cells E8 to E11. Follow these steps:

1. Move the selector to cell E7. (If you completed the preceding exercise, you are already there.)

2. Type **/EC** to activate the **Copy** command on the **Edit** menu, or press the shortcut key Ctrl+C.

3. Press Enter to choose cell E7 as the source cell.

4. Move the selector to cell E8, which becomes the destination cell on the input line.

5. Press Enter to copy the formula. Quattro Pro moves the selector back to cell E7.

   Now move the selector to cell E8. Look at the input line at the top of the notebook to check that Quattro Pro has entered the formula +D8*1.0725.

6. Using cell E7 as the source cell, move the selector back to cell E7 and repeat steps 2 and 3 to copy the tax-included formula to cells E9, E10, and E11.

Your notebook should look like figure 1.6.

TIP

You also can copy the formula to all the cells at once. As soon as you choose E7 as the source cell, move the selector to cell E8 and press the period key (.) to anchor the selector. Use the down-arrow key to highlight cells E8 to E11 and then press Enter to copy the formula.

Fig. 1.6

The purchasing report with tax-included invoice totals.

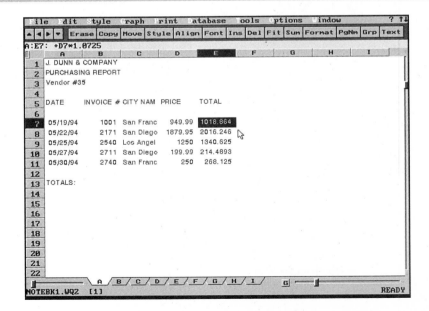

Using @Functions

Quattro Pro's built-in formulas, called *@function commands* (pronounced "at function"), perform basic and advanced mathematical operations. The formula +A1+A2+A3, for example, returns the same answer as the @function formula @SUM(A1..A3). The greatest benefit of @function commands is that when created in POINT mode, they greatly simplify the process of adding formulas to a notebook.

When you are creating a formula in a cell and you move the selector away from that cell (using the keyboard or the mouse), Quattro Pro changes to POINT mode. Place the selector at the cell address you want to include in the formula, and then press an operator key or the closing parenthesis. The selector returns to the cell with the formula, the cell address automatically appears in the formula, and the mode returns to READY.

To display a list of the Quattro Pro @function commands, press Alt+F3 from anywhere on the notebook.

To create a formula (while in POINT mode) that totals the column D data, follow these steps:

1. Move the selector to cell D13.

2. Type **@SUM(** and press the up-arrow key six times to make cell D7 the active cell. Quattro Pro enters POINT mode.

3. Press the period key (.) to anchor cell D7 as the first cell in the range to be summed.

4. Press the down-arrow key four times to make cell D11 the active cell.

5. Press the closing parenthesis key. Quattro Pro moves the selector back to cell D13.

6. Press Enter to record the formula in cell D13.

To create a formula that adds the values in the TOTAL column, you can repeat steps 1 through 5 for the values in column E. Instead, copy the formula in cell D13 to cell E13 so that Quattro Pro totals the data appearing in column E. Follow these steps:

1. Move the selector to cell D13. (If you completed the preceding exercise, you are already there.)

2. Type **/EC** to activate the **C**opy command on the **E**dit menu or press the shortcut key Ctrl+C.

3. Press Enter to choose cell D13 as the source cell.

4. Move the selector to cell E13. This cell becomes the destination cell on the input line.

5. Press Enter to copy the formula. Quattro Pro moves the selector back to cell D13.

Now move the selector back to cell E13. Look at the input line at the top of the notebook to be sure that Quattro Pro has entered the formula @SUM(E7..E11).

Your notebook should look like figure 1.7.

Fig. 1.7

The purchasing report with formulas that display total purchases for May 1994.

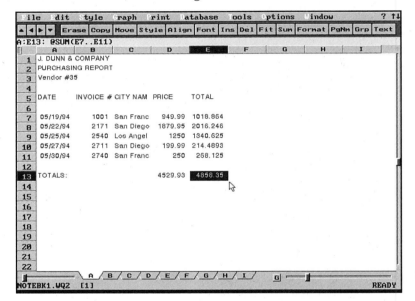

Editing Data

Quattro Pro enables you to edit data as you enter the data on the input line or after you press Enter to place the text into a notebook cell. You can reverse the effects of many menu-command operations by choosing /**E**dit **U**ndo, which is discussed in the section "Using the Alt+F5 Undo Key" later in this quick-start chapter.

Changing Data in EDIT Mode

To edit the contents of a notebook cell, press F2 to enter EDIT mode. If you have a mouse, click the cell you want to edit and then click the input line just below the pull-down menu bar. Quattro Pro displays the unformatted cell data on the input line. When you finish editing, press Enter to record the changes.

To see how easy editing data is, change an invoice number appearing on the notebook shown in figure 1.7. Follow these steps:

1. Place the selector in cell B7.

2. Press F2 to enter EDIT mode.

3. Press the left-arrow key three times to place the edit cursor on the first 0.

4. Press Del.

5. Enter **9** and then press Enter to record the new invoice number.

Using the Alt+F5 Undo Key

With the /**E**dit Undo command, you can undo the most recent edit performed or command executed. By default, the Undo feature is disabled (turned off). To use this feature, you first must choose /**O**ptions **O**ther Undo Enable. After you enable Undo, save this setting for future work sessions by choosing Update and then **Q**uit to return to READY mode.

To reverse the edit operation you just performed, follow these steps:

1. Type /**EU** (or press Alt+F5) to activate the **U**ndo command on the **E**dit menu.

Quattro Pro displays the original invoice number, 1001, in cell B7.

2. Type /**EU** again (or press Alt+F5) to reinstate the edited invoice number, 1901, in cell B7.

Your notebook should look like figure 1.8. In this figure, the selector is in cell B7, showing that the edited invoice value has been reinstated.

Fig. 1.8

The purchasing report notebook, complete with formulas and cell edits.

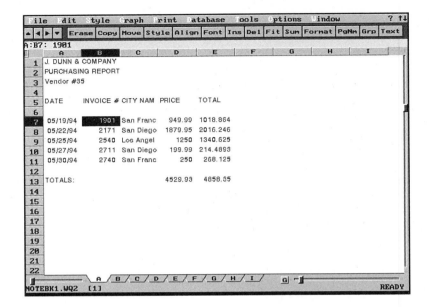

Improving Notebook Style

Another look at figure 1.8 reveals that although the data is complete, the format leaves much to be desired. The data in certain cells appears crowded and/or aligned improperly. The invoice amounts also don't have dollar symbols.

The following sections describe how to improve the appearance of your data.

Moving Data

You can relocate data from one area of the notebook to another by choosing /Edit Move. To move the report titles to a more central location on the J. Dunn & Company notebook, for example, follow these steps:

1. Type **/EM** to execute the /Edit Move command, or press the shortcut key Ctrl+M.

2. When prompted, type **A1..A3** and press Enter to choose the source block.

TIP

Alternatively, you can press Esc to unanchor the cell. Then move the selector to cell A1, press the period key (.) to reanchor the cell, move to cell A3, and then press Enter.

3. Type **C1** when prompted for a destination block.

4. Press Enter to move the report titles to column C.

Your notebook should look like figure 1.9. In this figure, the titles formerly in A1..A3 now appear in C1..C3.

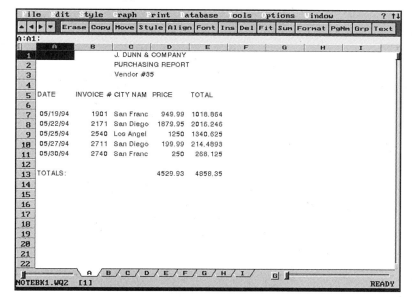

Fig. 1.9

Relocated titles on the purchasing report.

Changing Column Widths

By default, each notebook column is nine characters wide. To enter data longer than nine characters, use the /**S**tyle **C**olumn Width command to change the width of a column.

After you change a column width, the new entry on the input line for any cell in that column is [W#]. Here, # represents the number of characters that can display in the column.

To change the widths of columns B, C, D, and E on the J. Dunn & Company notebook, for example, try each of the following techniques:

Technique 1:

  1. Place the selector in cell B1.

  2. Type **/SC** to execute the **/S**tyle **C**olumn Width command.

  3. Type **12** and press Enter to make column B 12 characters wide.

  4. Place the selector in cell C1.

  5. Type **/SC** to execute the **/S**tyle **C**olumn Width command.

  6. Type **20** and press Enter to make column C 20 characters wide.

Technique 2:

  1. Place the selector in cell D1.

  2. Press Ctrl+W, the Ctrl+*key* shortcut for the **/S**tyle **C**olumn Width command.

  3. Press the right-arrow key 3 times and then press Enter to make column D 12 characters wide (3 characters wider than the default 9-character width).

Technique 3:

  1. Place the selector in cell E1.

  2. Click and hold the mouse button on the column letter E and drag to the right until 12 appears next to the prompt display on the input line.

  3. Release the mouse button to make column E 12 characters wide.

Your notebook should look like figure 1.10, which reflects the new width settings for columns B, C, D, and E.

Aligning Data in Cells

Uniformly aligned headings make identifying the values that belong to a particular heading easier. To center-align the report title, for example, follow these steps:

  1. Place the selector in cell C1.

  2. Type **/SAC** to execute the **/S**tyle **A**lignment **C**enter command.

  3. Press the down-arrow key twice to extend the highlight block to cell C3.

4. Press Enter to center-align the title labels.

To right-align the last two column headings on row 5, follow these steps:

1. Place the selector in cell D5.

2. Press Ctrl+A, the Ctrl+*key* shortcut for this command.

3. Enter **R**, the boldface letter for the **R**ight option.

4. Press the right-arrow key to extend the highlighted block to cell E5.

5. Press Enter to right-align both labels.

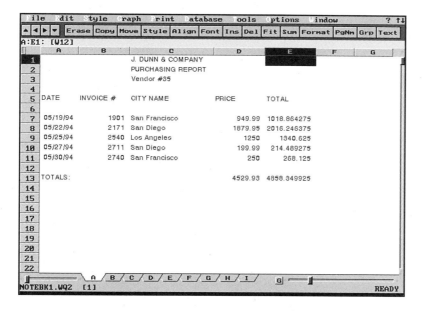

Fig. 1.10

Changed column widths on the purchasing report.

The input line now displays a quotation mark (") rather than an apostrophe (') at the beginning of each label to indicate that the label is right-aligned.

To center-align the heading and invoice numbers in column B, follow these steps:

1. Place the selector in cell B5.

2. Press Ctrl+A, the Ctrl+*key* shortcut for this command.

3. Enter **C**, the boldface letter for the **C**enter option.

4. Press End to enter END mode.

5. Press the down-arrow key to extend the highlighted block to cell B7.

6. Press End and then the down-arrow key to extend the highlighted block to cell B11.

7. Press Enter to center-align all values in column B.

NOTE

Values don't display the caret (^) to indicate center alignment—only labels do, such as the one in cell B5.

Your notebook should look like figure 1.11. This figure displays the new title, heading, and data alignments.

Fig. 1.11

Aligned data on the purchasing report.

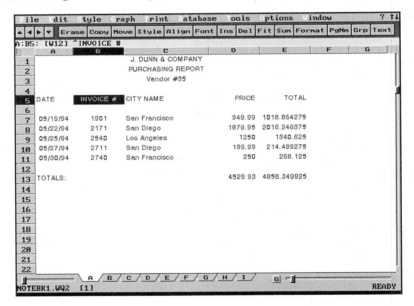

Formatting Numbers

Properly formatted numbers tell more about the values on a notebook and make it easier to read. Formatting a number changes only how the number displays, not the number itself: the underlying number appears on the input line, and the formatted number appears in the notebook.

Format the PRICE and TOTAL column numbers so that they display commas and two decimal places by following these steps:

1. Place the selector in cell D7.

2. Type **/SN** to execute the /**St**yle **N**umeric Format command.

3. Press the comma key (,) to choose the comma format.

4. Press Enter to accept the default setting of two decimal places.

5. Press the right-arrow key, press End, and then press the down-arrow key to highlight cell block D7..E11.

6. Press Enter to format the numbers in the highlighted block.

Now format the numbers on the TOTALS row to display a dollar sign and commas with two decimal places. Follow these steps:

1. Place the selector in cell D13.

2. Press Ctrl+F, the Ctrl+*key* shortcut for this command.

3. Enter **C** to choose the **C**urrency format.

4. Press Enter to accept the default setting of two decimal places.

5. Press the right-arrow key to highlight cell block D13..E13.

6. Press Enter to format the numbers in the highlighted block.

Your notebook should look like figure 1.12. This figure displays the numeric formats of the values appearing in the report.

Drawing Lines

Drawing lines around your notebook data transforms a basic notebook document into a professional-looking report. You can add a few final stylistic touches to the J. Dunn & Company report.

To draw a line around the data area, follow these steps:

1. Type **/SL** to execute the /**St**yle **L**ine Drawing command.

2. When Quattro Pro prompts you for the block to draw lines, type **A5..E13** and press Enter to choose the source block.

3. When Quattro Pro displays the Placement submenu, enter **O** to choose the **O**utside line option.

4. When Quattro Pro displays the Line Types submenu, enter **S** to choose the **S**ingle line option.

5. Enter **Q** to choose the **Q**uit option and return to the notebook.

Your notebook should look like figure 1.13, which shows the addition of lines around the purchasing report.

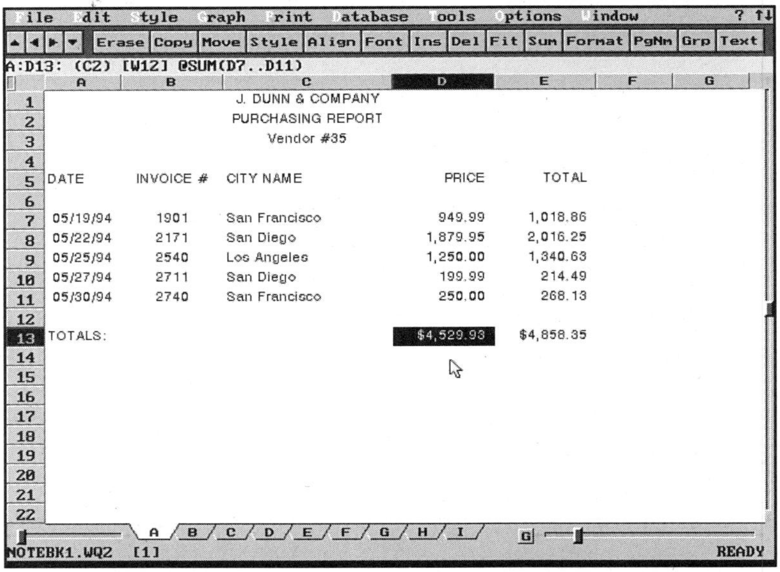

Fig. 1.12

Formatted numeric data on the purchasing report.

> **TIP**
>
> To remove lines, type **/SL** and indicate the block from which you want to remove the lines. Choose the line type you want to remove from the block, or choose **A**ll to remove all lines and then choose **N**one as the line type.

Inserting Rows and Columns

To conclude this exercise, add some finishing touches to the J. Dunn & Company purchasing report. First, insert a column before column A to center the report on the notebook by using the following steps:

1. Press the Home key to place the selector quickly in cell A1.

2. Press Ctrl+I, the Ctrl+*key* shortcut for the /**E**dit **I**nsert command.

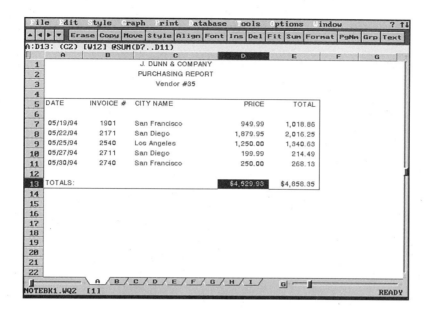

Fig. 1.13

Drawn lines around the
purchasing report.

3. Enter **C** to insert **Columns**.

4. When Quattro Pro prompts you for a column insert block, press
Enter to accept the single-column default, A1..A1.

To conclude, insert one row on top of the first title line in the report by
following these steps:

1. Press Ctrl+I, the Ctrl+*key* shortcut for the /**E**dit **I**nsert command.

2. Enter **R** to insert **R**ows.

3. When Quattro Pro prompts you for a source block, press Enter to
accept the single-row default.

Figure 1.14 shows the finished form of the sample report for J. Dunn &
Company.

Managing Documents

Managing documents is an important part of each Quattro Pro work
session. Without the **S**ave, create (**N**ew), **R**etrieve, and **O**pen notebook
files capabilities, Quattro Pro is useless.

Fig. 1.14

A presentation-quality version of the J. Dunn & Company purchasing report.

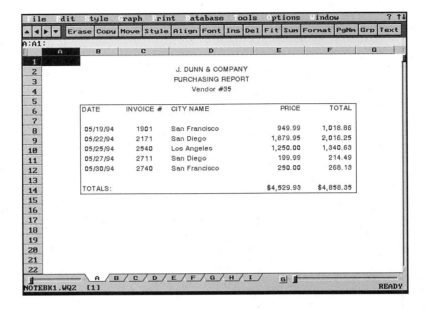

Saving a Notebook to a Hard Drive

To save the J. Dunn & Company notebook as a file with the name VEN-DOR35, perform the following steps:

1. Type **/FS** to execute the /**F**ile **S**ave command.

2. Type **vendor35** when prompted to enter a save file name.

3. Press Enter to save the file with the new name to the current directory on the hard disk drive.

NOTE

When you use the /**F**ile **S**ave command to save this file during future work sessions, Quattro Pro automatically uses the same file name.

Saving a Notebook to a Floppy Disk

If you want to save the J. Dunn & Company notebook to a drive other than the default drive, include a drive designator in the file name. To save the file on a disk in drive A, for example, follow these steps:

1. Type **/FA** to execute the /**F**ile Save **A**s command.

2. When prompted to enter a file name, press Esc until the cursor appears at the beginning of the input line inside the file name prompt box.

3. Type **a:\vendor35** for the file name.

4. Press Enter to save the new file name to the disk in drive A.

Ending a Work Session

To end a Quattro Pro work session and save all files open in Quattro Pro's memory, follow these steps:

1. Type **/FX** to execute the /**F**ile E**x**it command.

Alternatively, if you have a mouse, click **F**ile (on the menu bar) to pull down the menu and then click the E**x**it command to exit Quattro Pro; or press Ctrl+X, the shortcut key for ending a work session.

If you have not made any changes to the open notebooks since the last save operation, Quattro Pro clears the screen display and returns to the DOS command prompt.

If you have made changes, Quattro Pro displays the following prompt:

```
Lose your changes and Exit?
```

2. To exit the program without saving open files, enter **Y** to choose **Y**es; to remain on the active notebook, enter **N** to choose **N**o; enter **S** to choose **S**ave & Exit if you want to save all open notebooks before returning to DOS (see fig. 1.15).

If you choose **S**ave & Exit, one by one, Quattro Pro activates each open notebook as it saves it and displays the following prompt:

```
File already exists:
```

3. When prompted, enter **C** to **C**ancel and remain on the active notebook; enter **R** to **R**eplace the active notebook's file with the on-screen information and then display the next notebook; or enter **B** to **B**ackup an open file before exiting the program (see fig. 1.16).

Fig. 1.15

The File Exit command prompt.

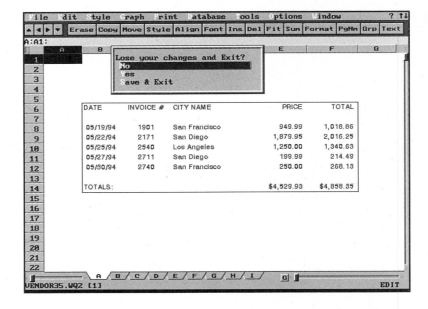

Fig. 1.16

The Save & Exit command prompt.

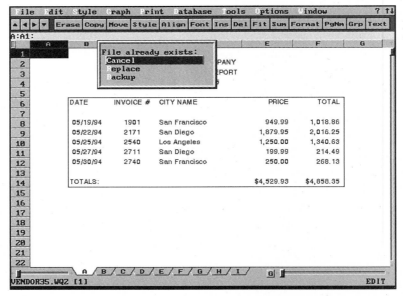

Summary

After completing this quick start, you should be familiar with the following concepts:

- Beginning and ending a work session
- Pulling down a menu and executing a command
- Entering values and labels into notebook cells
- Editing, copying, and moving data and formulas on the notebook
- Using the Undo feature to reverse operations
- Creating a basic notebook report that contains a title, column heading, formatted data, and drawn lines
- Saving notebook files to a hard and floppy disk

Chapter 2 expands on the information you became acquainted with in this quick start and broadens the scope of coverage to help you get started with Quattro Pro.

Getting Started

This chapter helps you envision how to use a notebook for a wide range of simple tasks. Read this chapter carefully, because the terminology and ideas in later chapters rely heavily on the concepts presented here. If you master the basics outlined in this discussion, you can begin to tackle the Quattro Pro notebook basics presented in Chapter 3, "Entering and Editing Data."

For first-time electronic spreadsheet program users, this chapter discusses the basics of working with Quattro Pro. You see how a notebook is more than just rows and columns of numbers and letters. You learn how to begin and end a work session. You also review how to use a keyboard and mouse.

The chapter also presents an in-depth, feature-by-feature review of the Quattro Pro WYSIWYG ("what-you-see-is-what-you-get") screen display. You learn how to switch between WYSIWYG and character (text) display modes.

The chapter concludes with a discussion of the Quattro Pro built-in help windows. This final section shows you how to get general and context-sensitive help from any location on a notebook.

Learning about Notebooks

Basically, Quattro Pro is a large electronic worksheet with millions of cells of storage area. You can enter data into these cells and enter formulas that perform mathematical operations on a group, or *block*, of cells.

Whether you are adding 2 numbers or 2,000 numbers, Quattro Pro calculates an answer in seconds. If you change a number on a manual accounting worksheet, you must take the time to add the numbers over again. After you change a number in a Quattro Pro formula, however, the program recalculates the new answer in a few seconds.

Quattro Pro remembers all the cell relationships that you define on a notebook. A formula that adds values appearing in two cells, such as +D8+D9, creates the most common type of cell relationship. If you design a notebook to record your monthly business expenses, for example, you must do the work only once. For subsequent months, you retrieve and modify the original notebook file by entering new numbers into the cells storing the current month's expenses.

FOR RELATED **INFORMATION**

▶▶ "Entering Numbers," p. 96.
How to enter numbers into notebook cells.

▶▶ "Entering Formulas," p. 98.
How to enter the three basic types of formulas into notebook cells.

Understanding Notebooks and Pages

When you start Quattro Pro, you initially see a two-dimensional worksheet made up of columns and rows. This worksheet, though, is just one component of a much larger tool called a *notebook*. Each Quattro Pro notebook contains 256 individual worksheets, formally called *spreadsheet pages* (or *pages*, for short).

Figure 2.1 shows cell D10 on the first page in a notebook. The name of each page appears in a tab that extends down from the bottom of the notebook. Initially, you can see the first nine page tabs, lettered A through I. The first 26 pages in a Quattro Pro notebook are named A through Z. Pages 27 through 52 are named AA, AB, AC, AD, and so on. Pages 53 through 79 are named BA through BZ. This naming scheme continues through page 256, or page IV.

The notebook is an ideal medium for creating, formatting, and organizing groups of related information. In other spreadsheet programs, you must create a unique file for each report, and sharing information among the reports is often cumbersome. In Quattro Pro 5.0, you can create and store up to 256 unique reports in a single notebook by placing each report on its own page. When the reports you create use an identical structure, you even can organize the reports into a group and then format all the pages at once.

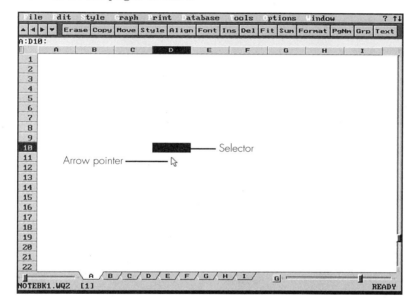

Fig. 2.1

The Quattro Pro notebook, with the selector in cell D10 on page A.

Quattro Pro makes quickly moving back and forth between notebook pages easy for you. To display the next page in the active notebook, press Ctrl+Page Down or click the page tab. To display the preceding page, press Ctrl+Page Up or click the page tab.

For several useful keyboard techniques for navigating through a notebook, see the section "Using the Arrow Keys" later in this chapter.

FOR RELATED INFORMATION

▶▶ "Managing Pages," p. 181.
How to work with notebook pages, including how to name a page, move a page, and create a group of pages.

Understanding Columns and Rows

Columns and rows make up each page in a notebook. You can enter numbers, letters, and formulas into a notebook *cell*, which is the intersection of any column and row.

The active cell on a Quattro Pro notebook appears as a highlighted rectangle—the *selector* (refer to fig. 2.1). Notice that the row number on the left and column letter on top at this intersection also are highlighted.

Finally, observe the arrow pointer in the middle of the screen. This pointer appears if you have a mouse connected to your computer. If you use a mouse in text display mode, Quattro Pro displays a small rectangle rather than the arrow pointer.

Each notebook cell has a unique name. A *cell address* combines the page name and the column and row locations into one description. The cell in figure 2.1 is named A:D10, which describes the intersection of column D and row 10 on page A.

TIP

Pages and columns always use letter descriptions, and rows always use number descriptions. A cell named A:10D, then, isn't correct; cell B:D10 is correct.

Each page in a Quattro Pro notebook contains 256 columns and 8,192 rows. A single page contains 2,097,152 unique cells. One Quattro Pro notebook, therefore, contains 536,870,912 unique cells.

The rows on each Quattro Pro notebook page are numbered from 1 to 8,192; the columns are labeled from A to IV. The columns use the same naming scheme used by the notebook pages: the first 26 columns are named A through Z; columns 27 through 52 are named AA, AB, AC, AD, and so on. This naming scheme continues through column 256, or column IV. Figure 2.2 shows the last cell on the last page in a Quattro Pro notebook—cell IV:IV8192.

Using multiple windows is a powerful Quattro Pro capability that enables you to work with up to 32 notebook windows simultaneously. The multiple-windows feature, therefore, places approximately 17 million notebook cells at your disposal. Imagine how many accounting ledger worksheets you need to equal that much calculation space.

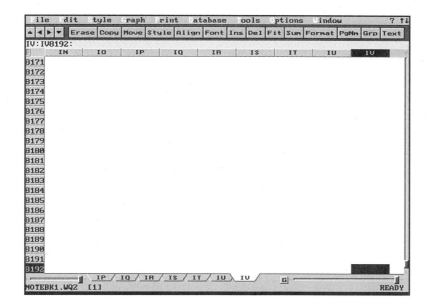

Fig. 2.2

The Quattro Pro notebook, with the selector in IV:IV8192.

FOR RELATED **INFORMATION**

▶▶ "Working with Notebook Windows," p. 389.
How to organize and display multiple notebook windows
and tile, stack, move, and size windows.

Reviewing the Uses of a Notebook

The Quattro Pro notebook is more than a collection of pages, rows, columns, and cells. With a little imagination, you can turn a notebook into a presentation-quality graph, a database application, or a macro program. In fact, the name *Quattro* (the number four in Italian) derives from these four main program features.

Constructing a Notebook

The easiest way to design a Quattro Pro notebook is to re-create the appearance of the original document. Figure 2.3 shows how easily you can duplicate on a spreadsheet page a simple multiplication exercise from a paper worksheet. The formula in cell C7 multiplies the value in C4 by the value in C5. The formula in cell C7 appears on the input line below the menu bar.

Fig. 2.3

A Quattro Pro notebook.

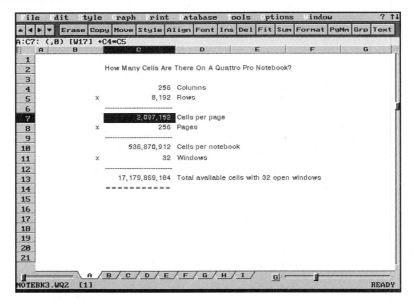

When you design a notebook, you must follow a few basic rules:

- Duplicate the organization and structure of the original document as closely as possible. You typically create notebooks to assume the duties of a written document or manually calculated report. Use this written document or report as a guide.

  To design a three-month income statement report, for example, you can place the ledger account titles in column B, the month descriptions in row 2, and the numbers in cells C3 through F10 (see fig. 2.4).

- Avoid mixing numbers and letters in the same cell until you are familiar with the rules for data entry (covered in Chapter 3, "Entering and Editing Data"). For now, remember that when you enter a number into a cell, Quattro Pro stores the number as a value. When you enter a word into a cell, Quattro Pro stores the word as a label by placing an apostrophe (')—not a prime—before the first letter.

- Quattro Pro can perform mathematical operations only on numbers. If you try to add two text labels, for example, Quattro Pro returns the value 0.

■ Gather related reports into a single notebook. Be sure to create each report on a separate page so that you can create custom formats for each report. When creating a group of reports whose structure and layout is essentially identical, use the Group mode feature to simplify your creation and design efforts.

By creating the report shown in figure 2.4 while in Group mode, for example, you simultaneously can create and format the reports for the second, third, and fourth quarters as well. Quattro Pro stores each report on its own page in the notebook. You even can change the page names from A, B, C, and D to 1st Q, 2nd Q, 3rd Q, and 4th Q to help you remember what information is found on each page.

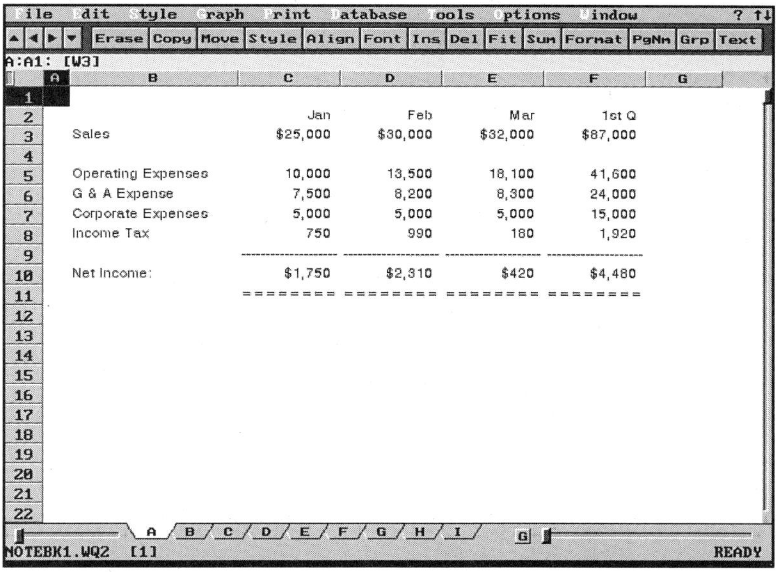

Fig. 2.4

A logically designed notebook.

You can perform mathematical operations on the data in cells C3 through F10 (refer to fig. 2.4). If you try to add or subtract the labels appearing in column B, Quattro Pro displays the value 0 because the program finds no numbers to add or subtract.

The real purpose of the electronic spreadsheet program is to ask questions and get acceptable answers. Examples of some typical what-if questions follow:

■ What happens to profits if expenses rise by 10 percent?

■ What happens to sales if a company loses three salespeople?

■ What happens to the average height figure if Mark's height is removed from the sample?

Because Quattro Pro enables you to define and store numeric relationships, you can play out an infinite number of what-if scenarios with Quattro Pro notebooks. Figure 2.5 shows how easily you can turn the notebook in figure 2.4 into a what-if analysis tool.

Fig. 2.5

A report transformed into a financial analysis tool.

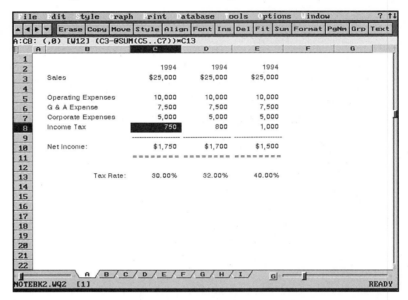

The notebook in figure 2.5 follows a yearly format and shows only 1994 data. Except for the Income Tax row (row 8), columns D and E contain the same information as column C. The formula in cell C8 calculates income tax by multiplying pre-tax net income—C3–@SUM(C5..C7)—by the tax rate appearing in cell C13.

To perform a what-if analysis, alter the Tax Rate entry and watch how net income changes. Imagine that you want to see what net income would be under three different tax rate assumptions. By changing the tax rate values in cells C13, D13, and E13, you can create different scenarios in which net income rises and falls.

TIP

Quattro Pro goes one step further by supplying you with the **W**hat-If command on the **T**ools menu. With this powerful command, you can create one-way and two-way sensitivity tables. A *sensitivity table* lists a wide range of possible solutions to a problem that you define. Rather than change cell values to test the effect on the results displayed in other cells, you create one table that lists all the possible results. This approach to asking what-if questions is more flexible and accurate and provides you with better information than ever before.

Designing a Graph

With Quattro Pro, you easily can turn your notebook data into an attractive, presentation-quality graph that you can view or print. Figure 2.6, for example, shows a stacked-bar graph of crop yields for a California orange grower.

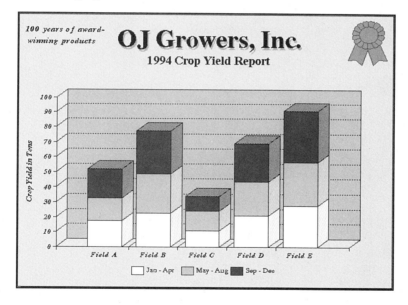

Fig. 2.6

A Quattro Pro stacked-bar graph.

Quattro Pro graphs are smart: each time you change numbers on the notebook, the graph adjusts to reflect the new data. Chapters 10, 11, and 12 provide for complete coverage of graphs.

Building a Database

You also can turn a Quattro Pro notebook into a flat-file database by using the commands found on the **Database** menu. After you enter your data records, you can sort them, extract records that meet specified criteria, and build new databases with the extracted data.

When you set up a database using Quattro Pro, you define rows as records and columns as fields. Figure 2.7 shows a database that inventories computer software. See Chapter 13, "Managing Your Data," for complete coverage of database operations.

Fig. 2.7

A Quattro Pro database.

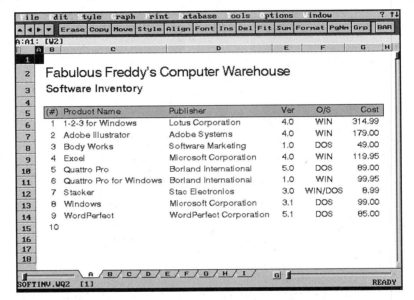

Creating a Macro Program

Certain notebook operations are repetitive. Each time you create a notebook, for example, you must format, name, enter data into, save, modify, and print the notebook. A macro program can do many of these operations for you.

After you create a macro program, you give the program an Alt+*key* shortcut name. To run the macro program, press the Alt+*key* shortcut and then watch Quattro Pro duplicate each menu command that you want executed. Figure 2.8 shows a macro that opens a notebook, changes the column width, and saves the notebook under a new file name. See Chapter 15, "Creating Macros," for complete coverage of macro programming.

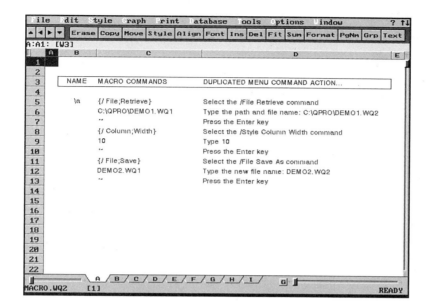

Fig. 2.8

A Quattro Pro macro.

Organizing Information Logically

The multiple-page notebook is revolutionary in the manner in which it handles information. Rather than require you to create many separate files for your reports, graphs, databases, and macros, Quattro Pro now enables you to consolidate easily all documents associated with a single project onto separate pages within one notebook. Then, by giving each page a plain-English name, you quickly can locate and display any individual document at the click of a mouse (see fig. 2.9).

Notebook pages are extremely versatile tools. In a basic application, each page can contain a unique report with original stylistic formatting. Alternatively, you can create formulas in one page that summarize information contained in several other pages. You even can group pages so that you can create and format several reports simultaneously. Explanations of different ways to work with notebook pages are offered in Chapter 3, "Entering and Editing Data"; Chapter 4, "Manipulating Data"; and Chapter 5, "Formatting Data."

Fig. 2.9

A multipage application that organizes two financial reports, a database, and a macro.

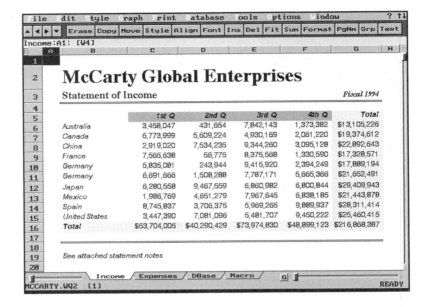

File	Edit	Style	Graph	Print	Database	Tools	Options	Window	? ↑↓

▲ ◄ ► ▼ | Erase | Copy | Move | Style | Align | Font | Ins | Del | Fit | Sum | Format | PgNm | Grp | Text

Income:A1: [W4]

	A	B	C	D	E	F	G	H
1								
2		**McCarty Global Enterprises**						
3		Statement of Income					*Fiscal 1994*	
4								
5			*1st Q*	*2nd Q*	*3rd Q*	*4th Q*	*Total*	
6		Australia	3,458,047	431,654	7,842,143	1,373,382	$13,105,226	
7		Canada	6,773,999	5,609,224	4,930,169	2,061,220	$19,374,612	
8		China	2,919,020	7,534,235	9,344,260	3,095,128	$22,892,643	
9		France	7,565,638	66,775	8,375,568	1,330,590	$17,328,571	
10		Germany	5,835,081	243,944	9,415,920	2,394,249	$17,889,194	
11		Germany	6,691,666	1,508,288	7,787,171	5,665,366	$21,652,491	
12		Japan	6,280,558	9,467,559	6,860,982	6,800,844	$29,409,943	
13		Mexico	1,986,769	4,651,279	7,967,645	6,838,185	$21,443,878	
14		Spain	8,745,837	3,706,375	5,969,265	9,889,937	$28,311,414	
15		United States	3,447,390	7,081,096	5,481,707	9,450,222	$25,460,415	
16		*Total*	$53,704,005	$40,290,429	$73,974,830	$48,899,123	$216,868,387	
17								
18								
19		See attached statement notes						
20								

Income / Expenses / DBase / Macro /   G

MCCARTY.WQ2 [1]   READY

Starting and Ending a Work Session

Q.EXE is the name of the program file that loads Quattro Pro into your computer's RAM memory. Quattro Pro's installation utility copies this file into the \QPRO directory on your hard disk drive. (See Appendix A, "Installing and Customizing Quattro Pro," for a step-by-step look at the Quattro Pro installation process.) To start a new work session, first load Quattro Pro, as discussed in the next section.

Starting Quattro Pro

To load Quattro Pro from the DOS command level, type **cd \qpro** and press Enter to move to the QPRO directory. Enter **q** and then press Enter to load Quattro Pro.

If you are working in a Microsoft Windows operating environment, double-click the Quattro Pro icon to load the program.

When loaded, Quattro Pro displays a blank notebook with the default file name NOTEBK1.WQ2. You now can enter data into the active notebook page, load a different notebook file, or end the current work session. To load an existing notebook into Quattro Pro, choose /**F**ile **R**etrieve, type the name of the file you want to edit, and then press Enter.

Using Special Start-Up Parameters

You can load Quattro Pro with special start-up parameters that further clarify how the program should work with your hardware. The /X start-up parameter, for example, tells Quattro Pro to load with extended memory code-swapping enabled. This setting is recommended if you have a 286-based AT computer with 1M of RAM.

The /IM start-up parameter tells Quattro Pro to load in text display mode with a monochrome palette rather than the default WYSIWYG display mode with a multicolored palette. To use the /IM start-up parameter, type **q /im** at the DOS command prompt and then press Enter.

> For Microsoft Windows users, you can enter the Quattro Pro start-up parameters in the **O**ptional Parameters field of your program information file (PIF). To load Quattro Pro with a monochrome palette for each new work session, for example, type **/im** in the **O**ptional Parameters field.

TIP

FOR RELATED INFORMATION

▶▶ "Setting Start-Up Options," p. 790.
How to specify start-up information that Quattro Pro uses each time you load the program into your system or create a new notebook file.

Returning to the Operating System

You can conclude a successful Quattro Pro work session in many ways, some of which you may not want to use. The worst possible outcome of any computer work session is that you quit a program before saving your work.

Quattro Pro helps ensure that you save your work before you exit the program. After you choose /**File** Exit, the program displays a dialog box that asks the following:

```
Lose your changes and Exit?
```

Enter **N** to continue with the current work session, **Y** to exit without saving, or **S** to save your changes and exit the program.

Get in the habit of saving your notebook several times during each work session to guard against the possibility of losing all your work if your system crashes or the power fails.

To save your notebook and continue with your current work session, choose **S**ave from the **File** menu (type /**FS**, click **S**ave on the File menu, or press Ctrl+S).

Working with a Keyboard

You can use one of three accepted keyboard standards with your PC. Each keyboard has three sections in common: the function keypad, the alphanumeric keypad, and the numeric keypad (see figs. 2.10, 2.11, and 2.12). The extended keyboard in figure 2.12 also has two extra sections: a command keypad and an arrow-direction keypad.

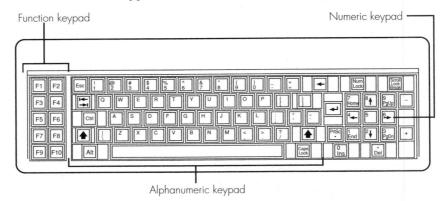

Fig. 2.10

The IBM PC keyboard.

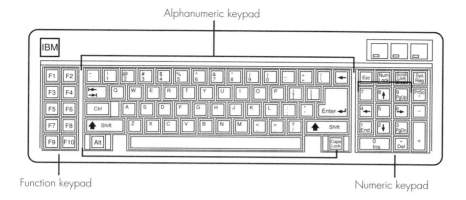

Fig. 2.11

The IBM AT keyboard.

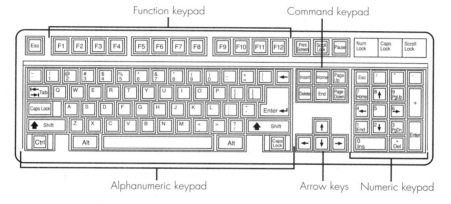

Fig. 2.12

The IBM AT extended keyboard.

Using the Alphanumeric Keyboard

The alphanumeric keyboard is located in the center of the keyboard. Except for the eight keys in table 2.1, the keys on the alphanumeric keyboard have the same functions as those on a typewriter.

Table 2.1 Special Keys on the Alphanumeric Keyboard

Key	Function
Tab	Moves selector one screen to the right; Shift+Tab moves selector one screen to the left
Alt	Invokes keyboard macros; when combined with one character, executes macro programs (see Chapter 15)

(continues)

Table 2.1 Continued

Key	Function
Shift	When pressed, enables you to use the numeric keypad to enter numbers, like a temporary Num Lock
Backspace	Deletes from right to left, one character at a time, while you are in EDIT mode
Slash (/)	Enters MENU mode so that you can choose a menu command; also is the division symbol used for mathematical operations
Period (.)	Separates cell addresses like A1..D10 and anchors cell addresses when in POINT mode; also is the decimal point in mathematical operations
Tilde (~)	Represents the action of pressing Enter once in macro programs
Ctrl	Executes menu commands quickly when combined with one character

Using the Numeric Keypad

You use the keys on the numeric keypad primarily to move the selector or the cursor. Ten keys and four combination keystrokes, however, enable you to perform other actions when using Quattro Pro (see table 2.2).

Table 2.2 Special Action Keys on the Numeric Keypad

Key	Function
Esc	Cancels a menu or command selection. Also enables you to interrupt and cancel any command selection sequence that ends with Enter by pressing Esc before Enter.
Num Lock	Dedicates the numeric keypad to only numeric entry. When you press Num Lock again, reactivates the special-action keys.
Scroll Lock/Break	Scroll-locks the notebook screen. The screen scrolls one row or column in the direction that you move the cursor. On certain keyboards, functions as the Break key; press Ctrl+Break to return to active notebook from any location in Quattro Pro.

Key	Function
PrtSc*	Shift+PrtSc* prints the contents of the active notebook window. If Shift+PrtSc* doesn't work, use the Print Screen key, without the Shift key.
Home	Moves to the first item on an activated menu. With no active menu, relocates the selector to the home position (cell A1).
End	Moves to the last item on an activated menu. To enter END mode, make sure that no menus are active; then press End and an arrow key to move to the last block of data in that direction, or press End and then Home to move the cursor to the lower right corner of the last data block on the notebook.
Page Up	Scrolls the notebook up one full screen at a time.
Page Down	Scrolls the notebook down one full screen at a time.
Ctrl+Page Up	Activates the preceding page.
Ctrl+Page Down	Activates the next page.
Ctrl+Home	Activates the first page, page A.
Ctrl+End	Activates the last page, page IV.
Ins	Toggles between the insert and typeover modes. In insert mode, each typed character moves the character under the cursor to the right one space.
Del	Deletes the contents of the active cell. In EDIT mode, deletes the character at the current cursor position.

Using the Arrow Keys

The four arrow keys enable you to move around the active notebook page in the directions that they point. You also can use these keys to position the cursor when you edit the contents of a cell in EDIT mode, to highlight commands on a menu, or to page through the help windows.

The End and Ctrl keys extend the power of the arrow keys by enabling you to take giant steps around the notebook. Table 2.3 explains how to use the arrow keys.

Table 2.3 Extending the Power of the Arrow Keys

Key	Function
←	Moves the selector one cell to the left
→	Moves the selector one cell to the right
↑	Moves the selector up one cell
↓	Moves the selector down one cell
Ctrl+←	Moves the selector one screen to the left
Ctrl+→	Moves the selector one screen to the right
End+↑	Moves the selector up to the next non-blank cell below a blank one if the current cell contains an entry, or up to the next non-blank cell if the current cell is blank
End+↓	Moves the selector down to the next non-blank cell above an empty cell if the current cell contains an entry, or down to the next non-blank cell if the current cell is blank
End+→	Moves the selector right to the next non-blank cell followed by an empty cell if the current cell contains an entry, or right to the next non-blank cell if the current cell is blank
End+←	Moves the selector left to the next non-blank cell preceded by an empty one if the current cell contains an entry, or left to the next non-blank cell if the current cell is blank

TIP

When you type data into a cell and press Enter to record the data, the selector remains in the current cell. To move to another cell, press any arrow key, and Quattro Pro moves to the next cell in that direction. If you type data into cell A5 and then press the down-arrow key without first pressing Enter, for example, Quattro Pro enters the data into cell A5 and makes A6 the active cell.

NOTE

If you want to use the arrow keys on a non-extended keyboard, the Num Lock key must be toggled off. To dedicate the numeric keypad to only numerical entries, the Num Lock key must be on.

Using the Function Keys

Quattro Pro assigns 1 of 10 often-used notebook commands to each function key found at the top or left of your keyboard. To invoke the Quattro Pro GoTo key and move the selector to a user-specified address, for example, press F5, type the cell address, and then press Enter.

You can access additional Quattro Pro commands by pressing Ctrl, Shift, or Alt and then pressing the appropriate function key. To display a menu of all the open windows, for example, press Shift+F5, the Pick Window key. Table 2.4 lists the Quattro Pro function-key assignments available when you are using a notebook.

NOTE

When you use the File Manager or Graph Annotator, certain keys or key combinations have slightly different functions. The File Manager helps you manage files on your hard disk; the Graph Annotator enables you to customize your graphs. Chapters 8 and 11, respectively, discuss how to use these special secondary functions.

Table 2.4 Quattro Pro Function-Key Assignments

Key	Function
F1 (Help)	Invokes a help window from anywhere on the notebook or during any notebook operation.
F2 (Edit)	Enters EDIT mode so that you can change a cell's contents.
Alt+F2 (Macro Menu)	Displays the Macro submenu.
Shift+F2 (Debug)	Enters DEBUG mode so that you can execute a macro one command at a time.
F3 (Choices)	Displays a list of block name choices when Quattro Pro prompts you for a block of cells; press F3 again to enlarge the display of names. Also enlarges the display of file names when performing a function in the File menu.
Alt+F3 (Functions)	Displays a list of all Quattro Pro @function commands.
Shift+F3 (Macro List)	Displays a list of the macro commands for a notebook.

(continues)

Table 2.4 Continued

Key	Function
F4 (Absolute)	Toggles through the four available cell reference formats; changes the format of the cell address to the left of or below the cursor on the input line.
F5 (GoTo)	Moves the selector to a specified cell or block address.
Alt+F5 (Undo)	Undoes notebook cell operations such as erasures, edits, deletions, and file retrievals.
Ctrl+F5 (Group)	Turns on Group mode so that you can modify multiple pages at the same time; press Ctrl+F5 again to turn Group mode off.
Shift+F5 (Pick Window)	Displays a list of open windows.
F6 (Pane)	Moves the selector between the active and inactive window panes when a notebook window is split.
Alt+F6 (Zoom)	When you are in text display mode, enlarges the active window so that it fills the screen; when the window is fully enlarged, shrinks the window back to its original size.
Shift+F6 (Next Window)	Displays the next open window.
F7 (Query)	Repeats the preceding /**D**atabase **Q**uery command.
Alt+F7 (All Select)	Selects and deselects files in the active File Manager list.
Shift+F7 (Select)	Enters EXT mode so that you can select a block of cells by pressing the arrow keys before performing a function on them. In the File Manager, selects and marks as active the highlighted name in a list.
F8 (Table)	Repeats the last what-if command and recalculates a new sensitivity table.
Shift+F8 (Move)	Removes files marked in the active File Manager list and stores them in temporary memory so that you can paste them in a new location.
F9 (Calc)	Calculates formulas on the active notebook if you are in READY mode. In VALUE or EDIT mode, converts the formula appearing in the input line to the end result.

Key	Function
Shift+F9 (Copy)	Copies files marked in the active File Manager list into temporary memory so that you can paste them to a new location.
F10 (Graph)	Displays a graph of selected data appearing on the current active notebook; press Esc to return to the active notebook.
Ctrl+F10	Toggles between Paradox and Quattro Pro.
Shift+F10 (Paste)	Pastes files stored in temporary memory into the current directory displayed in the active File Manager file list.

Working with a Mouse

With a mouse, you can duplicate any command or action that you can execute with a keyboard. A mouse actually simplifies many Quattro Pro notebook operations. With one click, you can activate a menu; select a menu command; mimic the action of the Esc, Enter, and Del keys; invoke Quattro Pro help windows; select a cell or block of cells; scroll the active notebook window vertically or horizontally; resize the active notebook; and so on.

Learning Basic Mouse-Movement Techniques

Many brands of mice are available. Some devices have one or two keys; others have three or more. To accommodate as many types of mice as possible, Quattro Pro uses only the left and right mouse buttons.

The four basic techniques that you must know to use a mouse with Quattro Pro are described as follows:

Technique	Action
Click	Quickly press once and release the left or right button
Double-click	Press and release the left or right button twice in quick succession

(continues)

Technique	Action
Drag	Hold down the left mouse button while moving the arrow pointer across the screen
Point	Slide the mouse to relocate the pointer to different parts of the display

Switching Mouse Buttons

Quattro Pro enables you to use either mouse button to initiate mouse-related activities in a work session. By default, the left mouse button is the one you press to do such activities as selecting a cell or choosing a command. To switch to the right mouse button—for example, if you are left-handed—choose /Options Hardware Mouse Button, and then choose the Right option. To save this setting as the default for future work sessions, choose Update on the Options menu.

Turbocharging Your Mouse

If your mouse's point-and-drag action seems sluggish, you need to adjust your mouse's tracking speed. The *tracking speed* determines how quickly the mouse pointer responds to your hand movement when you drag the mouse in any direction. A low tracking speed rating causes mouse action to appear sluggish; a high rating appears to turbocharge your mouse.

Many mouse manufacturers enable you to increase and decrease drag sensitivity when Quattro Pro is loaded, without requiring you to reinstall the driver program. For details, see the documentation that came with your mouse.

If you are running Quattro Pro under Microsoft Windows, you can click the Control Panel icon (in the Main group) and then click the Mouse icon to alter your mouse's tracking speed.

Reviewing the Screen Display

The Quattro Pro screen display has five major areas: the pull-down menu bar, the SpeedBar, the input line, the notebook area, and the status line.

By default, Quattro Pro displays in WYSIWYG display mode. The presence of sculpted row and column borders and the horizontal SpeedBar at the top of the screen distinguishes this display mode from other display modes. (In text display mode, the SpeedBar appears as a vertical bar along the right side of the notebook area.)

Figure 2.13 shows the default Quattro Pro screen display. The following sections go into more detail on the individual features.

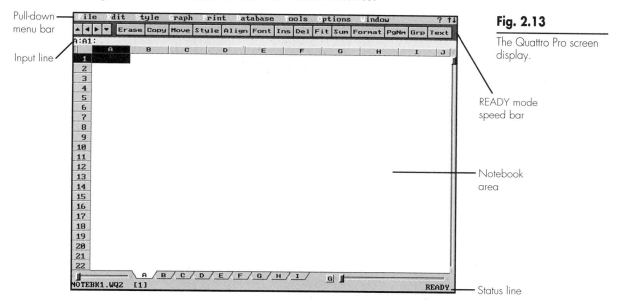

Fig. 2.13

The Quattro Pro screen display.

The Pull-Down Menu Bar

Nine menus are available on the pull-down menu bar: **F**ile, **E**dit, **S**tyle, **G**raph, **P**rint, **D**atabase, **T**ools, **O**ptions, and **W**indow. Each menu has a different function. The **F**ile menu, for example, enables you to perform file operations. To create a file, retrieve an existing file, save and close a file, or do other file activities, you use the commands found on the **F**ile menu. For more information on choosing menu commands, see "Accessing Quattro Pro Menus" later in this chapter.

The SpeedBars

The Quattro Pro Speedbar contains sculpted buttons that enable you to reproduce commonly used keyboard keystrokes with one mouse click.

The SpeedBar gives you instant access to many commands commonly used when creating, editing, and stylizing your notebooks.

After you load a mouse driver into memory, Quattro Pro detects its presence and displays the SpeedBar. If you disconnect the mouse, the SpeedBar doesn't appear the next time you load the program.

When you are in WYSIWYG display mode, the SpeedBar displays horizontally along the top of your screen. When you are in text display mode, the SpeedBar displays on the right side of the screen.

In READY mode, Quattro Pro displays the READY mode SpeedBar. In EDIT mode, the EDIT mode SpeedBar appears. Both SpeedBars are fully customizable (see Chapter 16).

The READY Mode SpeedBar

The buttons on the READY mode SpeedBar duplicate many commands you frequently use when creating and customizing notebooks (refer to fig. 2.13). If you don't see all these buttons on your SpeedBar, use the BAR button, located on the far right in WYSIWYG display mode, to access more buttons. If the BAR button isn't visible, all the buttons defined for your SpeedBar are visible.

Table 2.5 explains the function of each button on the READY mode SpeedBar, from left to right.

Table 2.5 READY Mode SpeedBar Buttons

Button	Function
Four triangles	Each duplicates the action of pressing the End key plus an arrow key, enabling you to move quickly around your notebook
Erase	Erases the cell block currently highlighted in the notebook
Copy	Makes a copy of the current cell block and prompts you to choose a destination for the copy
Move	Prompts you to choose a destination where you want to move the data contained in the current cell block
Style	Displays the /**S**tyle **U**se Style menu, from which you can select a named style to apply to the current cell block
Align	Displays the /**S**tyle **A**lignment menu, from which you can choose one of four data alignment options

Button	Function
Font	Displays the /Style Font menu, from which you can change the font characteristics for the current cell block
Ins	Inserts rows, columns, row blocks, column blocks, and pages
Del	Deletes rows, columns, pages, row blocks, column blocks, and pages
Fit	Adjusts the width of the selected column(s) according to the longest label in the block
Sum	Uses @SUM to total rows, columns, or both
Format	Displays the /Style Numeric Format menu, from which you can choose one of 12 value formatting options
PgNm	Enables you to display a custom name on a page tab
Grp	Enables you to name a group of pages
Text/WYS	Switches to WYSIWYG display mode from text display mode, and vice versa
BAR	Displays more SpeedBar buttons when they are available

The EDIT Mode SpeedBar

The buttons on the EDIT mode SpeedBar give you instant access to many of the commands you use when editing notebooks (see fig. 2.14). With a click of your mouse, you can enter a named block, macro command, or @function on the input line. You also can construct and calculate formulas directly on the input line using your mouse.

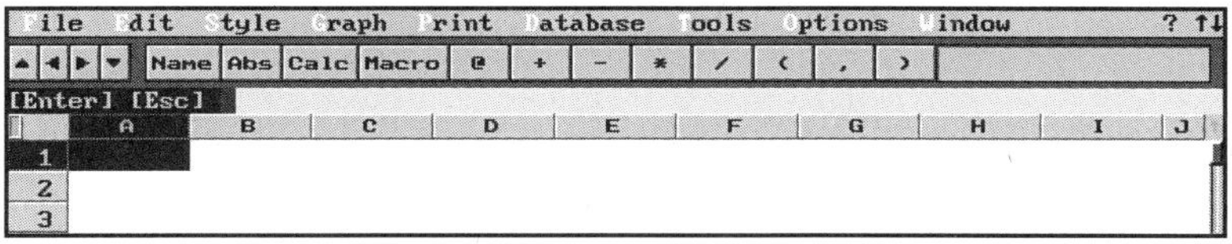

Fig. 2.14

The EDIT mode SpeedBar.

Table 2.6 explains the function of each button on the EDIT mode Speed-Bar, starting at the left. If you don't see all these buttons on your Speed-Bar, click the BAR button located on the far right to access more buttons.

Table 2.6 The EDIT Mode SpeedBar

Button	Function
Four triangles	Each duplicates the action of pressing the End key plus an arrow key, enabling you to move quickly around your notebook.
Name	Displays a list of named blocks. Highlight a name and press Enter to enter it on the edit line (same as pressing F3).
Abs	Toggles cell coordinates between absolute and relative (same as pressing F4).
Calc	Calculates the formula on the input line (same as pressing F9).
Macro	Displays a list of menu-equivalent macro categories (similar to pressing Shift+F3). Choose a main topic to reach a menu of specific actions, and then choose a specific action to place that menu-equivalent command on the edit line.
@	Displays a list of @functions (similar to pressing Alt+F3). Highlight one @function and press Enter to place it on the edit line at the current position.
+	Enters a plus sign on the input line.
−	Enters a minus sign on the input line.
*	Enters a multiplication sign on the input line.
/	Enters a division sign on the input line.
(	Enters an open parenthesis on the input line.
,	Enters a comma (argument separator) on the input line.
)	Enters a close parenthesis on the input line.
BAR	Displays more buttons, when they are available.

FOR RELATED INFORMATION

▶▶ "Customizing the SpeedBar," p. 796.
How to add to the READY and EDIT mode SpeedBars buttons that perform specific tasks.

The Input Line

The input line on the Quattro Pro screen contains seven data fields and presents two kinds of information (see fig. 2.15). The information displayed depends on whether you are in READY or EDIT mode.

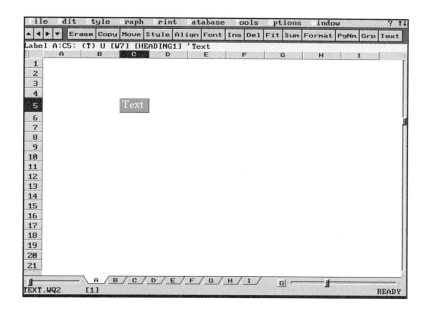

Fig. 2.15

The input line.

You are in READY mode when the active notebook is ready to accept data into any cell. You are in EDIT mode when you press F2 to edit the data in a specific cell. You always can tell what mode you are in by looking at the status line at the bottom of the active notebook. The mode indicator is located in the right corner of the status line.

When you are in READY mode, Quattro Pro displays format data for the active cell on the active notebook. If the selector is in cell C5 and you are in READY mode, for example, the input line may show the format information displayed in figure 2.15. A brief description of each kind of field follows:

- The first field displays Label, Date, or Graph. The field displays Graph when the selector is on an inserted graph. The field displays Date or Label when you use the /Database Data Entry command to restrict acceptable cell entries to dates or labels.

■ The second field displays the name of the active page and active cell, such as A:C5.

■ The third field displays a description of the numeric format and the number of decimal places, when applicable. The description (T) indicates that the cell is formatted to display text. Examples of other numeric formats include (P2) for percent with 2 decimals, (C4) for currency with 4 decimals, and (,0) for comma with 0 decimals.

■ The fourth field displays a description of the cell-protection status. When /Options Protection is enabled, a U indicates that a cell is unprotected, and a PR indicates that a cell is protected.

■ The fifth field displays the width of the active column. Quattro Pro doesn't display this field when set to the default width. The description [W7] indicates that the active column is 7 characters wide.

■ The sixth field displays a description of the named style used in the active cell. The description [HEADING1] indicates that this cell is formatted with a style named HEADING1.

■ The last field displays the unformatted contents of the active cell. This field displays .15, for example, when the formatted cell displays 15.25% on the notebook. In figure 2.15, cell C5 contains a label called Text.

Press F2 to place Quattro Pro in EDIT mode when you want to edit the contents of the active cell. Figure 2.16 shows how Quattro Pro displays the contents of cell C5 on the input line when in EDIT mode. Chapter 3 covers rules for editing the contents of a cell.

The Notebook Area

The notebook area is the largest part of the Quattro Pro screen. The notebook area is the part of the notebook that you can see—the area where your selector is. Figure 2.17 highlights the different elements of the notebook window.

NOTE

Remember, a notebook has 256 pages; each page has 256 columns and 8,192 rows. The part you see on-screen represents just a fraction of the entire notebook.

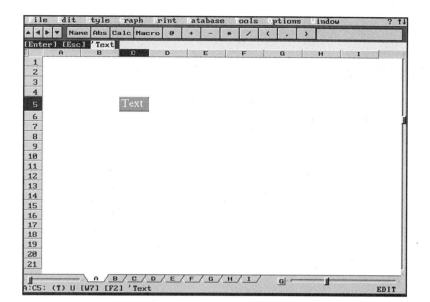

Fig. 2.16

The input line in EDIT mode.

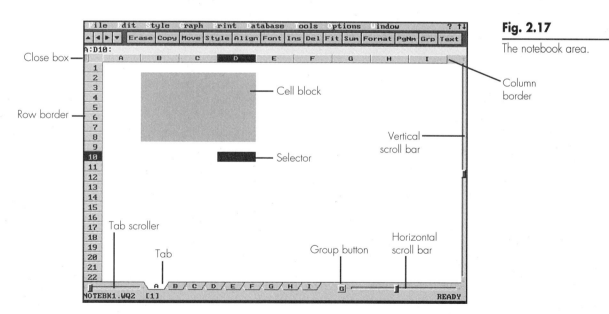

Fig. 2.17

The notebook area.

Close box

Row border

Column border

Cell block

Vertical scroll bar

Selector

Tab scroller

Tab

Group button

Horizontal scroll bar

The Close Box

Click the close box to close the active notebook window. Clicking the close box is the same as selecting the **C**lose command from the **F**ile menu.

The Selector

The selector is the rectangle you use to highlight a cell or a block of cells. You form a block of cells by pressing and holding down the left mouse button while in the active cell and then dragging the selector through the notebook area. Alternatively, in READY mode, you can press Shift+F7 to anchor the selector in the active cell, and then identify the cell in the opposite corner of the block by clicking the cell or moving the selector to the cell by using the arrow keys.

Quattro Pro names a block of cells as follows:

- The first element in the block name is the page name.

- The second element is the location of the upper left cell in the block range.

- The third element is the location of the lower right cell in the block range.

These three items make up the *block name*. Quattro Pro separates the two cell locations with two decimal points, as in A:B2..D8.

TIP

Create cell blocks when you want to perform the same operation on multiple columns and rows. You can select the cell block range A:B2..D2, for example, to change the width of columns B, C, and D on page A.

The Scroll Bars

The horizontal and vertical scroll bars enable you to use your mouse to control the location of the selector on the active window. To move the selector around the active notebook, point the mouse at a scroll box, press and hold down the left mouse button, and then drag the scroll box along the scroll bar; or click anywhere on the scroll bar.

The Column and Row Borders

The column border contains the alphabetic name of each column, and the row border contains the numeric name of each row in the window. Both borders are highlighted or appear in reverse coloring so that they stand out from the rest of the notebook area.

The Tabs and the Tab Scroller

The tabs that project down from the bottom of the notebook area identify the notebook page names. To display tabs for pages that aren't visible, drag the tab scroller to the right.

The Group Button

Click the Group button to activate Group mode. When activated, the Group button appears "pushed in." Click the button again to turn off Group mode.

The Status Line

The status line on the Quattro Pro screen contains four data fields and presents two kinds of information (see fig. 2.18). Like the input line, the type of information that the status line displays depends on whether you are in READY or EDIT mode.

When you are in READY mode, Quattro Pro displays information about the active notebook file. If NOTEBK4.WQ2 is the active notebook, and you are in READY mode, for example, the status line may display the information in figure 2.18. A brief description of each part of the status line follows:

■ *File Name.* The first field displays the name of the active notebook file. Each time you load Quattro Pro, the default file name on the status line is NOTEBK1.WQ2 or the name of the file you have specified as the default file. During any work session, however, you may need to close one notebook and create another. Quattro Pro names the files NOTEBK2.WQ2, NOTEBK3.WQ2, and so on. To change the default name of a notebook, see Chapter 8, "Managing Files and Windows."

- *Window Number.* The second field displays the number of the current window. A single notebook occupies a single window. You can have up to 32 windows open at one time, which means that you can have up to 32 unique notebooks open at a time. In figure 2.18, [1] indicates the first window.

- *Status Indicator.* The status indicators to the right of the window number keep you informed of notebook activity by displaying the current status of certain program features. This field displays NUM, for example, when the Num Lock key is on, CAP when the Caps Lock key is on, and so on. Table 2.7 defines the eight Quattro Pro status indicators.

- *Mode Indicator.* The mode indicator in the right corner of the status line tells you Quattro Pro's current program-execution mode. READY, for example, indicates that the current notebook is ready to accept input. Table 2.8 defines the 15 mode indicators.

Fig. 2.18

The status line.

Table 2.7 Status Indicators

Status Code	Description
CALC	Current notebook requires recalculation because a value referenced in a formula has been changed.
CAP	Caps Lock key is on.
CIRC	Formula in the current notebook contains a circular reference, which occurs when a formula refers to itself or to a cell that refers back to the formula.
END	End key is enabled; key is inoperative in EXT mode.
EXT	Shift+F7 has been pressed to extend a block; status is unavailable when End key is enabled.
NUM	Num Lock key is on.
OVR	Ins key has been pressed and can overwrite data on the input line.
SCR	Scroll Lock key is on.

Table 2.8 Mode Indicators

Status Code	Description
BKGD	Quattro Pro is recalculating notebook formulas in the background, between presses of keystrokes on your keyboard.
DEBUG	Quattro Pro invokes the macro debugger when a macro is started.
EDIT	You are editing a cell on the current notebook.
ERROR	Quattro Pro encountered an operation error. Press F1 to learn more about the error or Esc to cancel ERROR mode and return to the current notebook.
FIND	Quattro Pro is searching for a match to a search string specified in the /Database Query command.
FRMT	You are editing a format line during a parse operation.

(continues)

Table 2.8 Continued

Status Code	Description
HELP	Quattro Pro is displaying a help window.
LABEL	The entry you are typing in the input line is a label.
MACRO	Quattro Pro is executing a macro program.
MENU	A menu is activated.
POINT	You can choose a cell or block with the selector. Press F3 to view a list of the block names on the current notebook.
READY	Quattro Pro is ready for you to make an entry or menu selection.
REC	The macro recorder is turned on and is recording your keystrokes.
VALUE	The entry you are typing in the input line is a value.
WAIT	You must wait until Quattro Pro finishes with the current operation.

FOR RELATED INFORMATION

▶▶ "Using Quattro Pro's Coloring Palette," p. 774.
How to change the color of various elements in the Quattro Pro screen display.

Accessing Quattro Pro Menus

To use Quattro Pro properly, you must familiarize yourself with its menu-command language. Fortunately, Quattro Pro uses simple descriptive names for each menu command that you use to enter, edit, manipulate, and view your notebook data. Each of the nine menus has a unique name, offers a unique set of command options, and requires a unique keystroke action to execute commands.

Activating a Menu

To execute a command, you first must activate a menu. To enter Quattro Pro's MENU mode, press the forward slash (/) key once. This action highlights the name of the **File** menu. If you want to activate the File menu, press Enter. If you want to activate a different menu, use the arrow keys to highlight the menu name you want and then press Enter.

You also can activate a menu by using the boldface letter key assigned to the menu name. The letter E, for example, is the boldface letter key for the **Edit** menu. To activate the Edit menu, type **/E**. The menu shown in figure 2.19 appears.

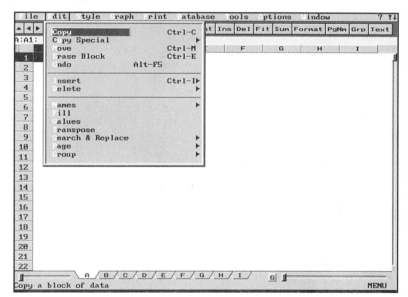

Fig. 2.19

The **E**dit menu.

You can use a mouse to simplify the process of activating and choosing Quattro Pro menu commands. To activate a menu, click the menu name. Then choose a command by clicking the command name.

Choosing a Command

When you activate (pull down) a menu, Quattro Pro displays a list of menu commands. By default, Quattro Pro activates the first command on each menu. To choose this command, press Enter. If you want to choose a different command, use the arrow keys to highlight your choice and then press Enter, or press the boldface letter key in the command name to execute that command.

NOTE

After you highlight a menu or command name, Quattro Pro displays a brief description of the item's purpose on the status line.

When you choose a menu command, Quattro Pro often displays a submenu. To set the page orientation to **L**andscape for printing a graph, for example, you must travel through three "child" menus by choosing /**P**rint **G**raph Print **L**ayout **O**rientation (see fig. 2.20).

Fig. 2.20

The menu and three submenus used to set the page orientation.

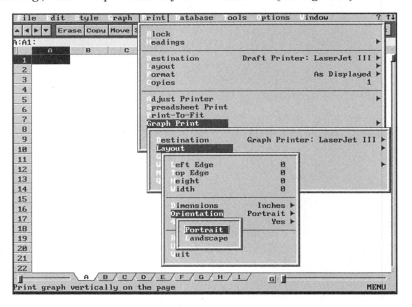

Quitting a Menu Selection

You can cancel a menu selection or command choice in three ways. Most menus have a **Q**uit option, which you can select to return to the preceding menu. You also can press Esc to back up to the preceding menu. To close all menus and revert to the active notebook, press Ctrl+Break. This key sequence is like pressing Esc several times to return to the active notebook.

> **TIP**
>
> Although all extended keyboards have a Break key, many of the earlier keyboards (PC XT and some PC AT) don't have this key. If your keyboard doesn't have a Break key, try substituting the Scroll Lock key for the Break key when you use the Ctrl+Break sequence. If this substitution doesn't work, choose **Q**uit or press Esc to return to the active notebook.

If you use a mouse, you have two additional menu-management techniques at your disposal. Clicking a menu border makes that menu active and closes its submenus. Clicking a notebook while the menu is active—like using Ctrl+Break—closes all menus.

> **TIP**
>
> When the menus you pull down obscure data in the active notebook, rather than quit each menu to return to the notebook, press F6. This function key temporarily hides all open menus. To reveal hidden menus, press F6 again.

Reviewing Data on a Quattro Pro Menu

Figure 2.21 shows the kinds of data you see on a pull-down menu. The menu command names appear at the left margin. Each command has a boldfaced letter key. Certain default settings—such as the default directory C:\QPRO\—appear in the middle of the menu.

Ctrl+*key* shortcuts and submenu arrowheads appear at the right margin of a pull-down menu. A submenu arrowhead resembles a small triangle turned on its right side (▶). This symbol appears next to a menu command whenever the command has another submenu of commands. If you choose /**E**dit **I**nsert, Quattro Pro displays a submenu that asks you to specify what you want to insert—**R**ows, **C**olumns, Row **B**lock, Column **B**lock, or **P**ages (see fig. 2.22).

The **F**ile pull-down menu.

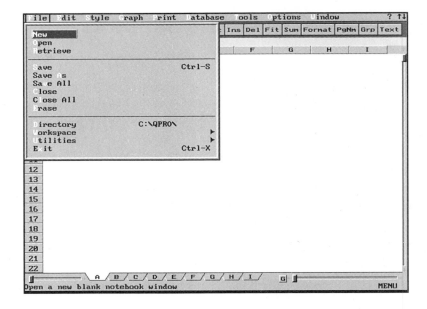

Because none of the commands on the submenu in figure 2.22 contains an arrowhead, choosing any option executes the Insert command.

The **I**nsert submenu of the **E**dit menu.

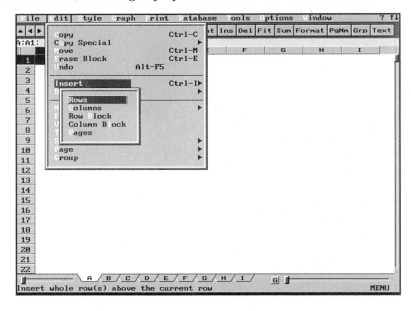

Using Ctrl+*Key* Shortcuts

Most Quattro Pro menus offer Ctrl+*key* shortcuts with which you can execute a command quickly. The shortcuts are the next best thing to a mouse for saving you time because they replace all the steps required to execute a menu command. To exit Quattro Pro, for example, you must activate the File menu, scroll down to Exit, and press Enter. With the Ctrl+*key* shortcut, you can press Ctrl+X from the active notebook and accomplish the same result more quickly.

Remember the following three factors when using Ctrl+*key* shortcuts:

- You must execute Ctrl+*key* shortcuts from the active notebook. When you create a custom Ctrl+*key* shortcut (one that loads a file, for example), you can execute the shortcut only when no menus are active. (The next section describes how to create a custom shortcut.)

- You cannot assign the same Ctrl+*key* shortcut to two different commands.

- Ctrl+*key* shortcuts are menu-tree specific. Quattro Pro can display menu-tree variations on its default menu structure. These trees are accessed with the /Options Startup Menu System command. Suppose that you have created a custom menu tree based on Lotus 1-2-3. If you switch that menu tree, you must create Ctrl+*key* shortcuts that work with the menu names and command names for that menu tree. (See Chapter 16, "Customizing Quattro Pro," for complete coverage of menu trees.)

Creating Custom Ctrl+*Key* Shortcuts

To create your own Ctrl+*key* shortcuts for frequently used menu commands, follow these steps:

1. Activate a menu and highlight the command you want.

2. Press Ctrl+Enter.

3. Press Ctrl and the letter you want to use as the shortcut key.

If another Ctrl+*key* shortcut already uses the letter, Quattro Pro displays an error message. When you perform this operation successfully, the Ctrl+*key* shortcut appears next to the command name on the menu.

Deleting Custom Ctrl+Key Shortcuts

To delete an existing Ctrl+*key* shortcut so that you can reassign its function, follow these steps:

1. Activate a menu and highlight the command you want.

2. Press Ctrl+Enter.

3. Press Del twice.

When you perform this operation successfully, the Ctrl+*key* shortcut next to the menu command disappears.

Table 2.9 lists Quattro Pro's Ctrl+*key* shortcuts. Except for Ctrl+D and Ctrl+F10, you may reassign any of the shortcuts listed to suit your preferences.

TIP

You easily can remember most of these shortcuts because they use the boldfaced letter in the last command to start a notebook operation.

Table 2.9 Ctrl+*Key* Shortcuts

Shortcut Key	Equivalent Menu Command
Ctrl+A	/**S**tyle **A**lignment
Ctrl+C	/**E**dit **C**opy
Ctrl+D	Date Prefix (cannot be reassigned)
Ctrl+E	/**E**dit **E**rase Block
Ctrl+F	/**S**tyle **N**umeric **F**ormat
Ctrl+G	/**G**raph **F**ast Graph
Ctrl+I	/**E**dit **I**nsert
Ctrl+M	/**E**dit **M**ove
Ctrl+N	/**E**dit **S**earch & Replace **N**ext
Ctrl+P	/**E**dit **S**earch & Replace **P**revious
Ctrl+R	/**W**indow **M**ove/Size
Ctrl+S	/**F**ile **S**ave
Ctrl+T	/**W**indow **T**ile

Shortcut Key	Equivalent Menu Command
Ctrl+W	/**St**yle **C**olumn Width
Ctrl+X	/**F**ile **E**xit
Ctrl+F5	/**E**dit **G**roup **C**reate **M**ode **E**nable/**D**isable
Ctrl+F10	/**D**atabase **P**aradox **A**ccess **G**o (cannot be reassigned)

Switching Display Modes

Thus far, the figures in this chapter illustrate the look of Quattro Pro's WYSIWYG display mode. In WYSIWYG display mode, a horizontal SpeedBar—which displays if you have a mouse loaded—appears at the top of the notebook. The WYSIWYG display mode setting is ideal if you prefer to review presentation-quality notebook settings such as custom fonts, drawn lines, and shaded cells as they use them. If you are less concerned with the program's presentation-quality notebook-building capabilities, use text display mode.

Quattro Pro enables you to switch display modes to meet different viewing needs. If you previously used Quattro (Quattro Pro's predecessor) or 1-2-3, for example, you may want to display Quattro Pro in text display mode—the default display mode used by these other programs.

To switch to text display mode, choose the /**O**ptions **D**isplay Mode **A**: 80x25 command. You also can click the Text button on the READY mode SpeedBar to switch to text display mode from WYSIWYG display mode. Quattro Pro immediately switches to text display mode (see fig. 2.23).

```
Text
```

Notice that Quattro Pro's screen in text display mode is slightly different than in WYSIWYG display mode. The SpeedBar buttons lose their sculpted appearance, the SpeedBar itself becomes a vertical bar at the right edge of the notebook, and the mouse arrow becomes a rectangle.

Quattro Pro offers two special features in text mode: the capability to zoom and resize a window and the capability to stack, or layer, windows on-screen so that they overlap each other. These features aren't available in WYSIWYG mode.

Fig. 2.23

A Quattro Pro notebook
in text display mode.

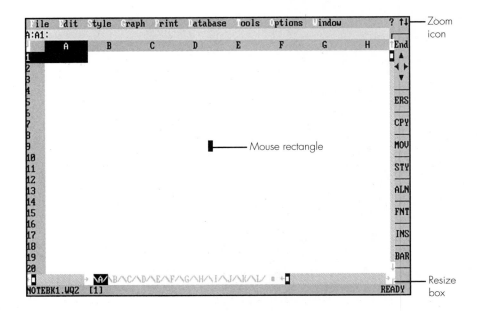

If you own an EGA or VGA graphics display system, you also can access
several extended text display modes. In general, Quattro Pro shows
more rows and columns in extended text display mode than in the
normal text or WYSIWYG display modes. For more information about
extended text display modes, see the section "Setting Display Mode
Options" in Chapter 16.

The Zoom Icon

The Zoom icon—located at the right end of the menu bar, above the
SpeedBar—is a tool specific to text display mode that shrinks or
enlarges the active window. Even though it appears on-screen in
WYSIWYG display mode, the Zoom icon is inoperative. Instead, use
the /Options **W**YSIWYG Zoom % command to shrink and enlarge a
notebook.

To use the Zoom icon, you first must switch to text display mode by
clicking the Text button on the READY mode SpeedBar or using the
/Options **D**isplay Mode **A**: Text 80x25 command. Click the Zoom icon
once to shrink the active window and reveal other windows open behind the active notebook. Click the Zoom icon again to enlarge the
active window so that the window fills the screen.

▶▶ "Using WYSIWYG Zoom %," p. 788.
How to shrink and enlarge the display of Quattro Pro.

FOR RELATED INFORMATION

The Resize Box

The Resize box—at the right edge of the horizontal scroll bar, above the mode indicator—is a text-mode-specific tool that changes the size of a notebook window. Because no menu command is available in WYSIWYG display mode for resizing a notebook, you may want to use the /Window Tile command to approximate the same display effect.

To use the Resize box, first switch to text display mode by clicking the Text button on the READY mode SpeedBar or by using the /Options Display Mode A: Text 80x25 command. Click the Resize box and then drag the lower right edge of the notebook. When the window is the correct size, release the mouse button. Quattro Pro draws the window to the specified proportions.

TIP

If you don't have a mouse and are operating in text display mode, use the /Window Move/Size command to shrink or enlarge a window. This command is inoperative when Quattro Pro is in WYSIWYG display mode.

Getting Help

If you have a question, encounter an error, or forget the purpose of a menu command, Quattro Pro's help window can provide the solution quickly. During most operations, you can press F1 to activate the help window from any location on the notebook.

If you press F1 while in the active notebook, Quattro Pro displays the help window shown in figure 2.24.

NOTE

Pressing F1 at any time invokes a Quattro Pro help window. Press F1 while an error message is displayed, for example, to learn more about the problem. You also can access the Help menu by clicking the ? on the far right of the pull-down menu bar when you are in READY mode.

Fig. 2.24

Quattro Pro's main help window.

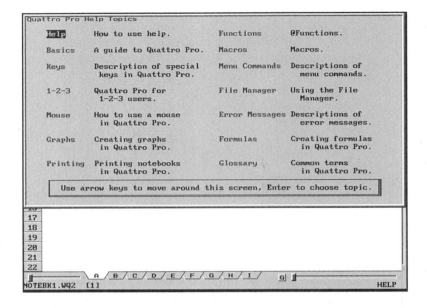

Boldfaced names appearing in a help window are keywords. If you need more information about the topics covered in a help window, look for those keywords. To choose a topic, move the highlight bar to a keyword and then press Enter (or click the keyword).

After help is invoked, you quickly can access a specific help topic by typing the first few letters of the topic or command you want more information about. To use this feature, first press F1 and then press F3. Quattro Pro displays an alphabetical list of help topics.

If you want more information about shading cells, you can enter **S** to reach the first help topic beginning with S, or you can type the first few letters of the topic—**SHA** for example—to get even closer to your topic. After you reach the general area, use the arrow keys to scroll slowly or, if necessary, use the scroll bar to scroll quickly. A text description preceded by an arrow at the top of the index displays the title of the help screen to which the topic leads. To move to a help screen, highlight the topic and press Enter.

Quattro Pro help is context-sensitive. It displays data about the current operation taking place on your notebook.

Figure 2.25 shows the **G**raph menu's help window. To display this window, pull down the **G**raph menu and press F1. The screen displays the 12 graph types, and the four category names appearing at the bottom of the screen are the boldfaced keywords.

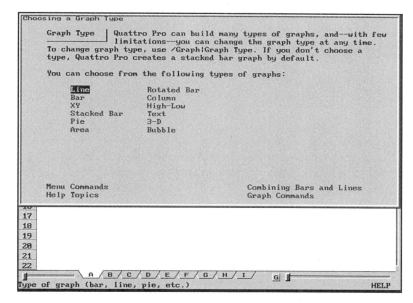

Fig. 2.25

The **G**raph menu's help window.

To exit a help window and return to the active notebook, press Esc.

Using the help window saves time by preventing unnecessary interruptions of work sessions. Using Quattro Pro's help also can save you the time required to flip through reference manuals to find a solution.

You also can get on-line help through another method. When you scroll through a menu's commands, a short description of each command's purpose appears on the status line. Use this feature when you need help understanding the purpose of a menu command.

Questions & Answers

This chapter covers most of the basics you need to get started with Quattro Pro. If you have questions about any topic covered in this chapter and cannot find the right answer by using the help windows, scan this section.

Loading Quattro Pro

Q: What do I do if Quattro Pro will not load onto my computer?

A: Make sure that you are logged onto the proper directory. By default, this directory is called C:\QPRO.

Quattro Pro also may not recognize your display. Try reinstalling the program (see Appendix A). Alternatively, try using the various command-line options described in the section "Using an Auto-load File" in Chapter 16.

Q: What if the computer displays the message Not enough memory to run Quattro when I try to load the program?

A: Quattro Pro may not load because you have terminate-and-stay-resident (TSR) programs loaded into your computer. To see whether the TSRs are causing the problem, temporarily disable the TSR statements in your CONFIG.SYS and AUTOEXEC.BAT files by typing **rem** before the TSR program name. Now reboot your computer.

If the TSR programs aren't consuming too much memory, remove REM from the CONFIG.SYS and AUTOEXEC.BAT files and reboot your computer again. (To check whether the TSR programs are using too much memory, use the DOS CHKDSK command to verify that you have at least 384K of free memory.)

Another possible answer is that your expanded memory may be incompatible with Quattro Pro. Disable the EMS driver in your CONFIG.SYS file. Reboot the system and try again (see Appendix A).

Q: What if I loaded Quattro Pro using the \IM monochrome start-up parameter, but Quattro Pro didn't load the monochrome palette?

A: Precede any special start-up parameters with a *forward slash*. Type **/im**, for example, to load Quattro Pro with a monochrome palette. If you accidentally type **\im**, Quattro Pro loads without the proper palette. Press Ctrl+X to leave Quattro Pro. Restart the program using the /IM parameter. Choose **/O**ptions **U**pdate to save this palette setting for future work sessions.

Working with a Keyboard and Mouse

Q: Why can't I activate a menu when I press the forward slash key (/)?

A: The forward slash cannot activate a Quattro Pro menu unless the program is in READY mode. Check the mode indicator on the status line. If the indicator doesn't say READY, press Esc until you are in the correct mode and then try again.

Q: Why does pressing an arrow key cause my notebook screen to shift up and down rather than move the selector from cell to cell?

A: Press your Scroll Lock key to turn it off.

Q: Why doesn't my mouse work properly with Quattro Pro?

A: When installed, Quattro Pro tries to recognize and configure itself for use with your mouse. Check Appendix A to make sure that your mouse is compatible with Version 5.0.

You also can check the README text file included in your Quattro Pro package. To do so, type **readme** at the DOS command prompt while in the QPRO directory.

Using SpeedBars

Q: I see only the READY mode SpeedBar on my screen. How can I get to the EDIT mode SpeedBar?

A: You must be in EDIT mode to access the EDIT mode SpeedBar. Press F2 to enter EDIT mode and display the EDIT mode SpeedBar.

Q: I selected a column of numbers, clicked the SUM button, and then got the error message `No blank area available for total(s)`. Why?

A: When selecting a column or row to sum, you also must select blank cells beneath or to the right of the block you want to sum. The blank cell indicates where Quattro Pro should display the total.

Accessing Quattro Pro Menus

Q: Why did Quattro Pro enter LABEL mode when I tried to activate a menu by pressing the forward slash key?

A: One of the common mistakes made when activating a menu is confusing the forward slash with the backslash key. The forward slash key (/) is located at the bottom of your alphanumeric keyboard and always is paired up with the question mark key (?). If you type the backslash key, Quattro Pro enters LABEL mode and displays the \ on the input line.

The backslash key is used to enter repeating characters—for example, \– repeats the – across the width of the cell and adjusts as the width of the cell changes. The method of entering repeating characters also saves memory.

Q: Why did nothing happen when I pressed the first letter in a menu command?

A: Not all Quattro Pro commands use the first letter of the command name as the boldface letter key. On the **F**ile menu, for example, the **E**rase and E**x**it commands begin with the letter E, but they both cannot use E as a boldfaced letter key. Always press the letter that corresponds to the boldfaced key in a menu or command name.

Q: Why did Quattro Pro beep when I tried to use a Ctrl+*key* shortcut to execute a menu command?

A: You must be on the active notebook with no activated menus for Ctrl+*key* shortcuts to work.

Alternatively, the Ctrl+*key* shortcut you pressed may not exist. Pull down the menu on which the command resides and verify that you pressed the correct shortcut key.

You also may have deleted the shortcut key you tried to use if you have tried creating and deleting your own shortcut keys.

Getting Help

Q: I pressed F1 for help, but nothing happened. What's wrong?

A: The program couldn't find the file called QUATTRO.HLP in the Quattro Pro directory (C:\QPRO by default). If you don't find the file in this directory, reinstall the program (refer to Appendix A).

Summary

This chapter introduces you to the electronic spreadsheet program. You learned how to get started using Quattro Pro. You now should understand the following basic Quattro Pro concepts:

- Using notebook pages, columns, and rows

- Knowing how Quattro Pro deals with numbers and letters when you enter them into a notebook cell

- Knowing the difference between notebook, graph, database, and macro programs

- Beginning and ending a work session

- Using a keyboard and mouse

- Interpreting the information that appears in the various sections of the Version 5.0 screen

- Switching between WYSIWYG and character (text) display modes

- Getting on-line help during program operation

In Chapter 3, you take the next logical step toward learning how to enter, edit, move, and view data on a Quattro Pro notebook page.

Entering and Editing Data

In this chapter, you learn the skills you need to use Quattro Pro on a daily basis. The material presented in this chapter shows you how to enter, edit, and view data on the Quattro Pro notebook. The chapter also defines some important Quattro Pro terminology used throughout the book.

Learning Notebook Terminology

Before you begin creating notebooks, you should learn the following Quattro Pro terms: notebook, cell address, block address, 3-D block address, file name, file, window, and workspace.

This book uses the term *notebook* to describe the area where data appears.

Chapter 2, "Getting Started," defines a *cell address* as the basic unit of a notebook. The cell address also is part of a *block address*, which contains two coordinates (two cell addresses) that describe the upper left and lower right parts of a group of cells on a notebook. D2 is one of two coordinates, for example, appearing in block address D2..D10.

A cell address also can be part of a *3-D block address*, which is a block address that has been selected on a group of consecutive notebook pages. You can create a 3-D block address by including the first and last page names at the front of a block address. Block address A..C:D2..D10, for example, describes the same block address, D2..D10, on three different pages—pages A through C.

All Quattro Pro menu commands that require you to enter a cell address also can work on a block address, and many can work on a 3-D block address. Working with blocks of notebook data is much more efficient than working with one cell at a time.

After you build a notebook, you assign a *file name* to the notebook and save the file on a disk. To accomplish both steps simultaneously, choose the /**F**ile **S**ave command. Doing so assigns to the notebook a unique file name that you specify so that you easily can locate the notebook the next time you want to review its data. To review the data, choose the /**F**ile **R**etrieve command and retrieve the file in which the Quattro Pro notebook is stored.

Quattro Pro enables you to open and view up to 32 windows at a time. A *window* is an area on-screen where you view a notebook. When you have only one notebook open during a work session, the notebook window fills the entire screen display. When you open a second notebook, Quattro Pro creates a second window. (See "Viewing the Notebook" later in this chapter for more details.)

To display both notebook windows at the same time, choose the /**W**indow **T**ile command. Now, each window occupies one half of the entire screen. The more notebook windows you open, the smaller the program must make the windows so that they all can fit on-screen at the same time. (See "Displaying Tiled Notebooks" later for more details.)

The term *workspace* describes all the notebook files that you have loaded into your computer's memory at one time. Workspaces can be extremely useful when you link notebooks or work with several related notebooks during one work session.

To assign a file name to a workspace, choose /**F**ile **W**orkspace **S**ave. When you assign a workspace file name, you tell Quattro Pro to remember the names of all the files now in memory, and how they are arranged. The next time you need to work with this group of related notebooks, choose /**F**ile **W**orkspace **R**estore, type the name of the workspace file, and press Enter. Quattro Pro loads all the notebooks originally saved as one workspace.

Entering Data

Quattro Pro accepts two types of data as valid entries: labels and values. A *label* is defined as a text entry; a *value* can be a number, a formula, or a date-and-time entry.

To enter data into a notebook cell, follow these steps:

1. Select a cell by using the arrow keys or by clicking it.

2. Type data using any keys on your keyboard.

3. Press Enter to tell Quattro Pro to store the data in the active cell.

4. Press an arrow key to move to a new cell.

> After typing data, rather than press Enter, you can move to a second cell by pressing any arrow key. Pressing an arrow key enables you to store the data you typed and to move to the next cell with one keystroke.

TIP

Quattro Pro looks at the first character in an entry to decide whether the character is a label or a value (see fig. 3.1). When you enter a label into a cell, the mode indicator on the status line displays the word LABEL. When you enter a value into a notebook cell, the mode indicator displays the word VALUE.

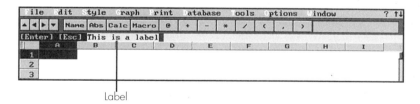

Label

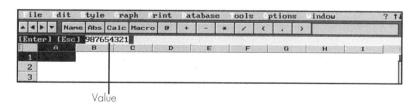

Value

Fig. 3.1

A label and a value on the input line.

TIP

Always check the mode indicator to make sure that Quattro Pro interprets your data correctly. If you accidentally enter a number as text—for example, by typing a letter before you type a number—and the number is used in a notebook formula, the formula cannot calculate an answer correctly.

If you try to enter a label when Quattro Pro is in VALUE mode, the program sounds an error tone. Press Esc, re-enter the data correctly, and then press Enter.

Learning about Labels

The word *label* is just a formal description for text. Label also suggests that you can use text as column-heading labels and row-description labels to describe the data on a notebook.

A text entry can be many things—the word *catch* as well as the words *catch22* or *22skidoo*. Remember, the first character you type tells Quattro Pro how to interpret the rest of the characters in the entry. If the first letter is a number but the entry is actually a label, you must enter a label prefix.

A label prefix has two functions. First, the prefix tells Quattro Pro that an entry is text, regardless of its composition of numbers and letters. Second, the prefix tells Quattro Pro how to align the text entry in a notebook cell. The following table lists label prefixes:

Label	Description
'	Left-aligns text in a cell
"	Right-aligns text in a cell
^	Centers text in a cell
\	Repeats a character or group of characters in a cell until the character fills the entire cell

By default, Quattro Pro places an apostrophe (the left-alignment prefix) in front of every entry initially recognized as text. If you want to change the alignment of text in a cell or enter a label that begins with a number, type one of the other label prefixes shown in the preceding table before you type the first character of the entry. Figure 3.2 shows how each label prefix aligns a text entry in a notebook cell.

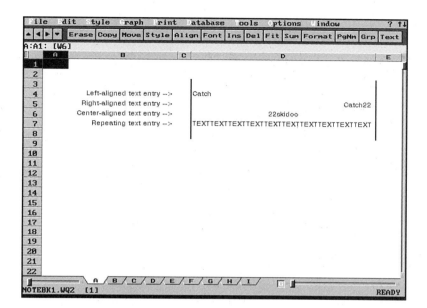

Fig. 3.2

The effects that label prefixes have on your notebook entries.

Quattro Pro enables you to enter up to 254 characters per label. When you enter a label longer than the width of the cell's column, Quattro Pro displays the entire label by extending the text into the next cell on the same row (see cell B4 in fig. 3.3). If the next cell contains data, Quattro Pro cuts off the initial entry, preventing the entry from overlapping onto the contents of the next cell (see cell B6 in fig. 3.3).

Fig. 3.3

An entry cut off when the next cell contains data.

You can deal with the overlapping cell label in cell B6 shown in figure 3.3 in two ways. First, you can leave the entry as is. Although you cannot see the entire label entry, it is stored. Place the selector in the cell to verify that the text displayed on the input line is intact. Second, you can set the column width to equal the width of the entire label entry (like in cell D8). (See "Setting the Width of a Column" in Chapter 5 for information about altering the width of a column.) Figure 3.3 shows both alternatives.

NOTE

Quattro Pro also cuts off an overlapping text entry when you put a box around the entry by using the /**S**tyle **L**ine **D**rawing **O**utside command (see "Drawing Lines and Boxes" in Chapter 5).

Learning about Values

The term *value* encompasses three types of data: numbers, formulas, and date-and-time entries (see fig. 3.4). A *number* is any digit or series of digits. A *formula* is an entry that performs a calculation on two or more digits or series of digits. A *date-and-time entry* enables you to use a notebook cell to display commonly used date-and-time formats.

When you enter a value into a notebook, Quattro Pro right-aligns the value in the cell. Unlike other spreadsheet programs, Quattro Pro enables you to change the alignment of numbers in a cell with the /**S**tyle **A**lignment command (see Chapter 5, "Formatting Data").

Entering Numbers

Although you can enter numbers and letters as text labels, a value entry must begin with a number (0 through 9) or one of the following value symbols:

Value Symbol	Description
+	Indicates a positive value
–	Indicates a negative value
(	Indicates a parenthetical calculation
$	Indicates a number entered with a currency symbol
.	Indicates a decimal value

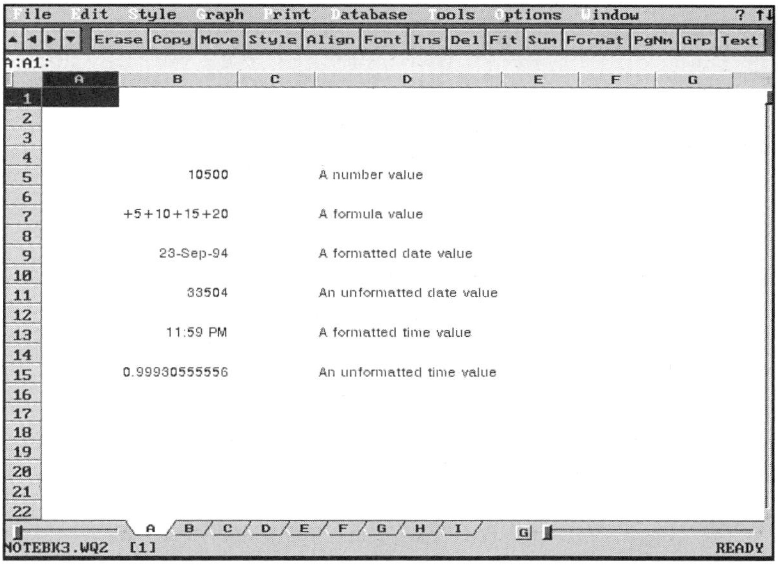

Fig. 3.4

Values as numbers, formulas, and date-and-time entries.

Quattro Pro also accepts a number entry if you follow the entry with a percent sign (%), such as 10%.

> **TIP**
>
> Although Quattro Pro enables you to enter a currency symbol with a number, the program doesn't display the currency symbol in the cell until you choose the /**S**tyle **N**umeric Format **C**urrency command and apply the currency format to that cell.

Quattro Pro assumes that all numbers are positive unless you specify otherwise. If you want to change a number's default value, precede the number with any of the value symbols shown in the preceding table.

When you enter a number longer than the width of the active cell's column, Quattro Pro doesn't overlap the entry into an adjacent blank cell (as the program does with labels). How Quattro Pro treats these "long" numbers depends on how you format the cell. Figure 3.5 shows how Quattro Pro treats a series of three numbers when the cell's numeric format is changed.

To reveal the value pictured in cell C18, choose /**S**tyle **C**olumn Width (Ctrl+W) and press the right-arrow key until numbers appear in place of the asterisks.

Fig. 3.5

The effect of numeric formats on the width of numbers in notebook cells.

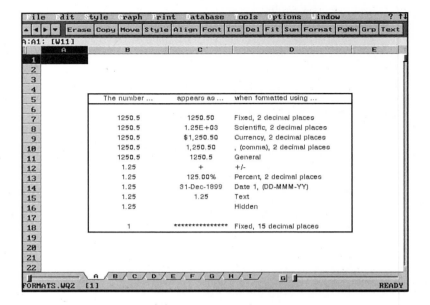

Although entering numbers into a notebook cell is simple, remember the following rules:

- Don't use parentheses to enter a negative number. Precede a negative number with a minus sign.

- Don't enter commas as part of a numerical entry. Instead, format an entry so that it displays commas.

- Don't add spaces or non-numerical characters between numbers. Mix numbers and characters only when you want to make a label entry.

- Be careful that you don't substitute a lowercase letter l for the number 1 or an uppercase letter O for the number 0.

- Use the /**S**tyle **N**umeric Format command to change the displayed and printed format of your notebook numbers (see Chapter 5).

Entering Formulas

A Quattro Pro notebook formula is a powerful tool. In its basic application, the notebook formula adds, subtracts, multiplies, or divides two numbers on a notebook, displaying the answer in a notebook cell that you choose (see fig. 3.6).

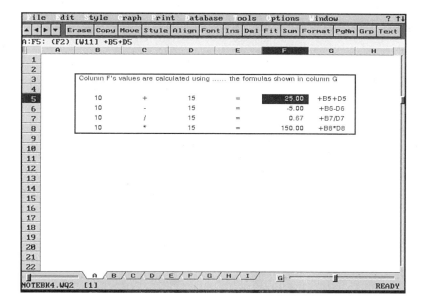

Fig. 3.6

Basic notebook formulas add, subtract, divide, and multiply the data you enter.

Figure 3.6 shows you how to use basic mathematical formulas in a notebook. The formulas shown in this figure contain four parts: a value symbol, the address of a cell containing a number, a mathematical operator symbol, and another cell address.

The formulas in column F perform the mathematical operation indicated by the symbols shown in column C, using the numbers in columns B and D. To enter the formula appearing in cell F5, for example, follow these steps:

1. Place the selector in cell F5.

2. Press the plus sign key (+) to enter VALUE mode.

3. Type **B5**, the cell address of the first value to add.

4. Press + to choose an addition operation.

5. Type **D5**, the cell address of the second value to add.

6. Press Enter to record the formula in cell F5.

After you store the formula in cell F5, Quattro Pro calculates the answer and displays 25.00.

TIP

You can produce this same answer by entering **+10+15** into cell F5.

This formula, however, doesn't recalculate an answer if you later change the value appearing in cell B5 or D5. As a result, you should use cell addresses instead of numbers when you build Quattro Pro formulas.

A Quattro Pro formula can be as complex as you need it to be. A more intricate formula may simultaneously perform mathematical operations on multiple sets of numbers and display an answer in a cell of your choosing.

Figure 3.7 shows how to use more advanced mathematical formulas in a notebook. The formula shown in this figure contains three parts: the @ symbol, a function command name, and a description of a block of cells.

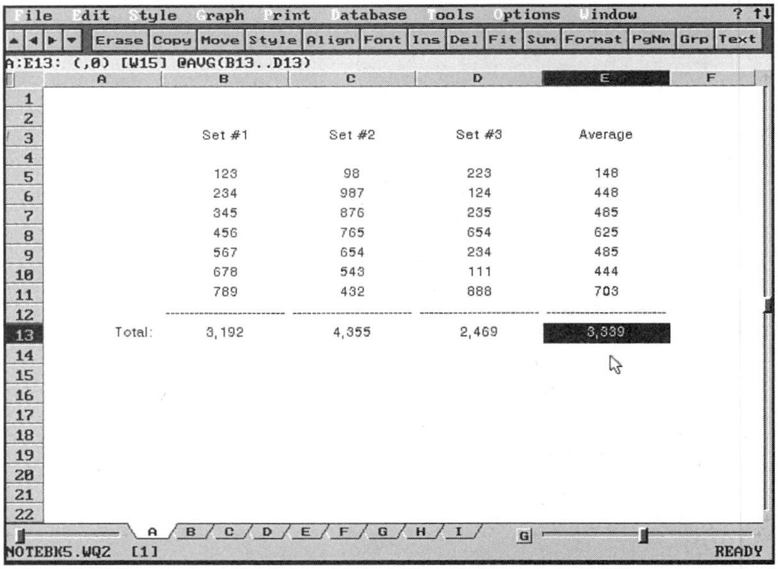

Fig. 3.7

An @function that averages the formula results displayed in B13..D13.

File	Edit	Style	Graph	Print	Database	Tools	Options	Window	? ↑↓

| ▲ | ◄ | ► | ▼ | Erase | Copy | Move | Style | Align | Font | Ins | Del | Fit | Sum | Format | PgNn | Grp | Text |

A:E13: (,0) [W15] @AVG(B13..D13)

	A	B	C	D	E	F
1						
2						
3		Set #1	Set #2	Set #3	Average	
4						
5		123	98	223	148	
6		234	987	124	448	
7		345	876	235	485	
8		456	765	654	625	
9		567	654	234	485	
10		678	543	111	444	
11		789	432	888	703	
12						
13	Total:	3,192	4,355	2,469	3,339	
14						
15						
16						
17						
18						
19						
20						
21						
22						

\ A / B / C / D / E / F / G / H / I /   G

NOTEBK5.WQ2 [1]   READY

The formula in cell E13 averages the values appearing in cells B13, C13, and D13. To enter this formula, follow these steps:

1. Place the selector in cell E13.

2. Press the @ key to enter VALUE mode.

3. Type **avg** to use the built-in average function.

4. Type **(B13..D13)** to specify a block of cells to average.

5. Press Enter to record the formula in cell E13.

After you store the formula in cell E13, Quattro Pro calculates the answer and displays 3,339.

You can choose any of Quattro Pro's built-in formulas, known as *@function commands*, to perform specialized calculations for you. These commands reproduce many types of mathematical operations without requiring you to build long, complex formulas. Chapter 6 shows you how to use @function commands in your Quattro Pro notebooks.

The electronic spreadsheet's capability to create custom formulas makes the program extremely valuable. Quattro Pro manipulates numbers and formulas electronically much more quickly than you can manually.

Valid formula entries can contain up to 254 characters and must begin with a number (0 through 9) or one of the following characters:

. + − (@ # $

When building a formula, you can use any of the five mathematical operators listed in the following table to separate the parts of the formula. Version 5.0 arranges formulas in three groups: arithmetic, text, and logical.

Operator	Description
+	Performs addition
−	Performs subtraction
*	Performs multiplication
/	Performs division
^	Raises a number to the power specified by the number following the operator (5^3, for example, raises 5 to the 3rd power)

Arithmetic Formulas

Arithmetic formulas perform calculations with numbers, cell addresses, and most of the @function commands using mathematical operators.

An operator specifies to Quattro Pro which mathematical operation to perform.

The formulas in figures 3.6 and 3.7 are examples of *arithmetic formulas*, which can use the operators listed in the preceding section.

Quattro Pro makes every attempt to return a value when the program encounters an arithmetic formula. Evaluating formulas is usually a simple and straightforward task. Sometimes, however, Quattro Pro returns an unintended or nonsensical answer. When you enter the formula 10/2 into a cell, for example, Quattro Pro returns the value 5. If you want to display a date such as 9/23/94, and you enter this date as 09/23/94, Quattro Pro thinks it's looking at a two-step division formula—9 divided by 23 divided by 94. Quattro Pro returns the value 0.004163. This value makes no sense when you want to display a date.

To enter a date directly into a cell so that Quattro Pro displays the value as a date, see "Entering Dates or Times" later in this chapter.

Text Formulas

Text formulas enable you to perform specialized tasks that arithmetic formulas cannot. Text formulas perform operations on strings of text enclosed in quotation marks, labels, and @function commands by using the ampersand (&).

Figure 3.8 shows a useful application for a text formula. In this figure, labels appear in three cells: B3, B5, and B7. Using the ampersand operator enables you to *concatenate*, or join, these labels in cell B9.

Briefly, a text formula is made up of three parts: the plus sign (+), the constant, and the variable. The plus sign tells Quattro Pro to expect a formula.

In a text formula, quotation marks must enclose the constant, which doesn't change. Figure 3.8 shows two constants in the formula. Each constant is one blank space surrounded by quotation marks. You use this type of constant to insert a space between labels when they are joined.

The formula also contains three variables: B3, B5, and B7. Text formula variables are much like the ones used in arithmetic formulas—as the cell values change, so do the displayed results.

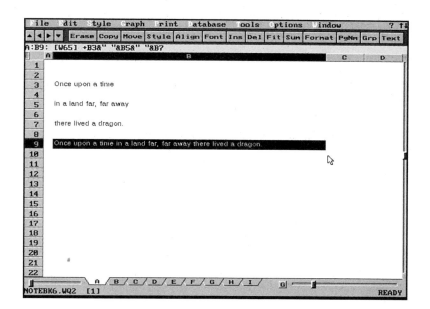

Fig. 3.8

The entries in cells B3, B5, and B7 appear joined in cell B9.

Chapter 6 contains examples that show how to use text formulas in notebooks to accomplish specific tasks.

Logical Formulas

A *logical formula* compares two or more pieces of data and gives the result in the form of true or false conditions (see fig. 3.9). If the result of the comparison is true, Quattro Pro returns the value 1; if the result is false, Quattro Pro returns the value 0. Logical formulas can use @function commands and the following operators: =, <, >, <=, >=, <>, #AND#, #OR#, and #NOT#.

In figure 3.9, cells D5 through D11 contain logical formulas. An expression of the logic that each formula tests appears in cells C5 through C11. Cells B2 and B3 contain the two variables referenced in each formula.

The logical formula stored in cell D5, for example, is B2=B3. This formula determines whether the value in B2 is equal to the value in B3. Because this condition is false, Quattro Pro displays 0. The logical formula stored in cell D6 is B2<>B3. This formula determines whether the value in B2 isn't equal to the value in B3. Because this condition is true, Quattro Pro displays a 1.

Fig. 3.9

Logical formulas
evaluate true and false
conditions.

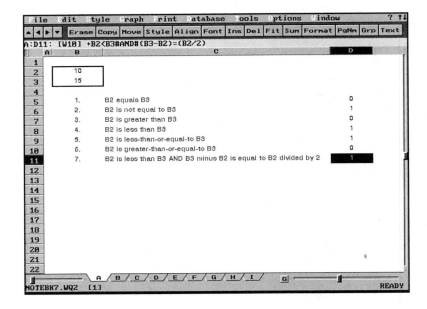

The formula in the highlighted cell in figure 3.9 appears on the input line at the top of the notebook. This logical formula contains the #AND# operator. The #AND#, #OR#, and #NOT# operators have special significance when they appear in logical formulas. The formula in cell D11 determines the following conditions:

- Is B2 less than B3?

- Is the difference between B2 and B3 equal to B2 divided by 2?

- Are expressions 1 and 2 true?

Looking at the first logical expression, you can see that B2 is less than B3. The difference between B2 and B3 is equal to B2 divided by 2. Individually, both expressions are true, and Quattro Pro returns a 1.

Order of Precedence

When Quattro Pro first looks at a formula entry, the program determines which parts of the formula must be calculated first, second, third, and so on. The formulas +10+10 and +10+5+2, on the other hand, have no order of precedence because they perform only one mathematical operation: addition.

Because the formula +10+10/5^2 contains three mathematical operators, each with a different order of precedence, you may get more than
one answer to this problem depending on how you perform the calculation. If you evaluate this formula from left to right, the answer is 16. If
you calculate an answer using Quattro Pro's order of precedence, the
answer is 10.40. Here, Quattro Pro performs the calculation 5^2 first,
divides that answer into 10, and then adds 10 to that result.

Table 3.1 shows the order of precedence that Quattro Pro uses when
evaluating mathematical operators in your notebook formulas.

Table 3.1 Quattro Pro's Order of Precedence

Operator	Operation	Order of Precedence
^	Exponent	1st (highest)
+, −	Positive and negative	2nd
*, /	Multiply and divide	3rd
+, −	Add and subtract	4th
=, <>	Tests of equality	5th
<, >	Tests of relative value	5th
<=	Less-than-or-equal test	5th
>=	Greater-than-or-equal test	5th
#NOT#	Logical NOT test	6th
#AND#	Logical AND test	7th
#OR#	Logical OR test	7th
&	String union	7th (lowest)

Formulas that contain more than one set of parentheses are said to
contain *nested parentheses*. Nested parentheses clarify the way you
want Quattro Pro to evaluate a formula and enable you to create complex formulas by using all the Quattro Pro operators.

When you enter a formula with nested parentheses, Quattro Pro performs the operations enclosed in the innermost parentheses first. The
order of precedence rule holds for multiple operations that appear
within one set of parentheses.

To show how the order of precedence works, the following example uses nested parentheses to clarify the sample formula:

$(10+(10/(5^2)))$

Calculation 1 (5^2) = 25.0

Calculation 2 (10/25.0) = 0.4

Calculation 3 (10+0.4) = 10.4

Quattro Pro evaluates this formula as follows: first the program raises 5 to the 2nd power, resulting in 25; then Quattro Pro divides 10 by 25, resulting in 0.4; finally, the program adds 10 to 0.4 and returns the final result of 10.4.

Entering Dates and Times

Quattro Pro has several built-in @function commands that enable you to store date-and-time formats on a notebook by setting the numeric format of a cell to **D**ate or **T**ime with the **/S**tyle **N**umeric Format command. Because date-and-time formats are considered formulas, you can add and subtract them just like numbers. This feature is helpful in notebook applications that track progress over time.

Figure 3.10 shows a notebook that lists 10 invoices. The formulas appearing in column E use the @NOW function in cell C2 to help you determine the exact age of each invoice for credit collection purposes. The formula in cell E6, +$C$2–B6, for example, subtracts the invoice date from today's date to compute the "age" of the invoice.

NOTE

The presence of the dollar sign ($) within the reference to cell C2 creates what is known as an *absolute reference*. See "Working with Cell References and Blocks" later in this chapter for more details.

The Quattro Pro shortcut key for entering a date or time is Ctrl+D. To use this shortcut, follow these steps:

1. Press Ctrl+D.

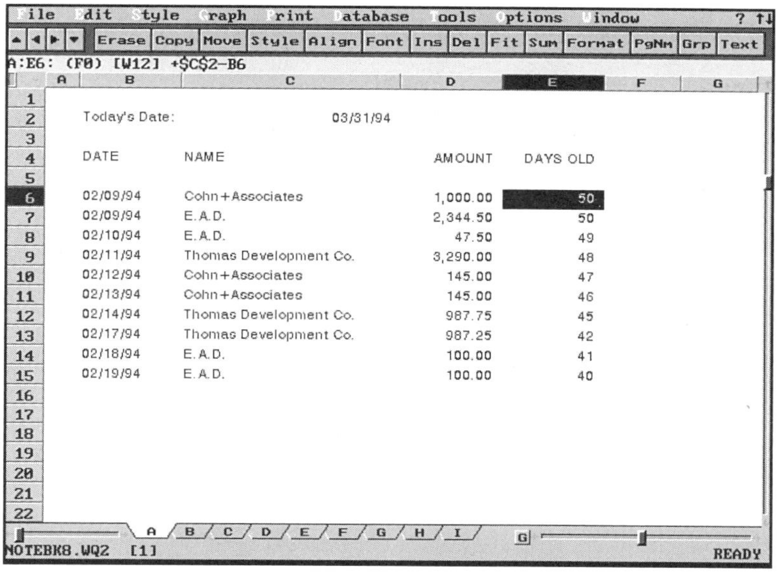

Fig. 3.10

Using date-and-time formats and @NOW to determine the age of each invoice.

2. Type a date using one of the following date formats:

31-Mar-94 (*dd-mmm-yy*)

31-Mar (*dd-mmm*, assumes current year)

Mar-94 (*mmm-yy*, assumes first day of the month)

3. Press Enter.

When you choose the appropriate format using the /**S**tyle **N**umeric Format **D**ate command, Quattro Pro enables you to use short (*mm/dd*) and long (*mm/dd/yy*) international dates. You also can enter a date using the international date formats; just supply the appropriate format in step 2.

▶▶ "Formatting Dates," p. 202.
"Formatting Times," p. 205.
How to format dates and times in several different reporting styles.

FOR RELATED INFORMATION

Entering @Function Commands

The built-in Quattro Pro @function commands enable you to perform advanced mathematical operations and return values. You can use @functions by themselves or embed them inside other formulas (see fig. 3.11). Chapter 5 provides complete coverage of the @functions.

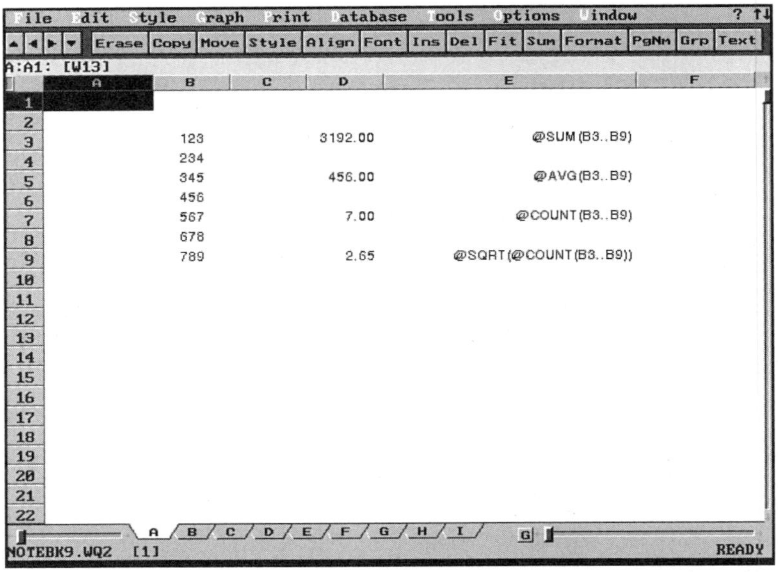

Fig. 3.11

With @functions, you can perform advanced mathematical operations.

In figure 3.11, cells D3, D5, D7, and D9 contain @function commands. Each formula's syntax is listed in column E. The values that the formulas use in their calculations appear in cells B3 through B9.

The formula in cell D3, for example, sums the values appearing in B3..B9; the formula in D5 averages the values; and the formula in D7 counts the values.

The formula in cell D9 is different than the others because this formula contains two @function commands. This formula counts the number of values in cells B3 through B9 and returns the square root of this number.

You can enter an @function onto a notebook in two ways: manually enter the command or choose the command from the @function choice list.

Entering an @Function Manually

To enter an @function manually, press the @ key, type the function name, enter the appropriate arguments, and then press Enter.

An *argument* is a cell reference or a number on which Quattro performs the operation. The first three @function commands shown in figure 3.11, for example, use the same argument: the address of cells B3 through B9. The final @function command shown in figure 3.11 counts the number of values in cells B3 through B9 and passes this value along as the argument in the @SQRT command.

You can type an @function's name in upper- or lowercase text; Quattro Pro recognizes the @function either way. Chapter 6 lists the names and purposes of all @function commands used in Quattro Pro Version 5.0.

Using the Choice List To Enter an @Function

If you press Alt+F3, Quattro Pro displays a list of @functions. Scroll through the list using the up- and down-arrow keys. When you locate the @function you want, press Enter, and Quattro Pro reproduces the @function on the input line, at the cursor position. To complete the @function, type the appropriate cell addresses and mathematical operators called for by the @function, type a close parenthesis, and then press Enter.

To enter an @function that sums cells B3, B4, and B5, for example, highlight the SUM function, press Enter, type **B3..B5)**, and then press Enter to store the @function in the current cell.

You also can use the @ button on the EDIT mode SpeedBar to display a list of @functions. To enter an @function onto the input line, click the @ button, highlight the function name in the list, and press Enter.

Entering Data into Grouped Pages

When you group pages together, anything entered into a cell on one page automatically appears in the same cell on all pages in the group. This data-entry technique—called *drilling* an entry—presents you with many new notebook design possibilities.

Suppose that you want to track sales for five divisions of a company. The column headings, row headings, and cell formulas are essentially the same for each report; only the numbers are different. By grouping five pages together, you can create the framework of the report once on page A and have the same report structure appear instantly on pages B, C, D, and E.

TIP

> When you work in Group mode, creating the framework for a multipage report on page A is common. In reality, you can do your work on any page in a group. Creating the report on page B, for instance, causes it to appear on page A, C, D, and E.

You need to perform two separate tasks when preparing to enter data into grouped pages. First, you create a page group; then you activate Group mode. To create a page group, follow these steps:

1. Choose the /**E**dit **G**roup **C**reate command.

2. At the prompt, type a name for your page group. For this example, type **SALES** and press Enter.

3. Type the name of the first page you want to include in the group. For this example, type **A** and press Enter.

4. Type the name of the last page you want to include in the group. For this example, type **E** and press Enter.

Grp You also can use the Grp button on the READY mode SpeedBar to create a group. The same prompts appear as though you selected the /**E**dit **G**roup **C**reate command.

To activate Group mode so that you can begin entering data into a page group, follow these steps:

1. Choose the /**E**dit **G**roup **M**ode command.

2. Choose the **E**nable option and press Enter.

When Group mode is activated and you are in WYSIWYG display mode, Quattro Pro draws a blue line below the tabs for each page included in the group.

To deactivate Group mode, follow the preceding steps, except highlight the **D**isable option in the step 2.

TIP

The shortcut key for activating and deactivating Group mode is Ctrl+F5. You also can click the Group button on the status line (the small button with the **G** on it) to activate and deactivate.

Entering, or *drilling*, data into a page group is slightly different than entering data into a single page. When you want to drill data into the same cell in every page in a group, type the entry and press Ctrl+Enter.

Keep in mind that pressing Enter stores the entry only on the active page. If you already have entered data on a page and then decide later that you want it drilled into the cells on other pages in the group, put the selector on that cell, press F2 to move the entry into the input line for editing, and then press Ctrl+Enter.

When drilling a formula into a page group, you must *type* the formula into the input line and then press Ctrl+Enter. Each drilled formula then will calculate using the values only on its page.

TIP

Sum To create an @SUM formula that sums the same cell block on different pages in a group, activate Group mode, select the cell block on page A, and then click the Sum button on the READY mode SpeedBar. Quattro Pro writes the formula into each page in the group.

FOR RELATED INFORMATION

▶▶ "Creating Names," p. 161.
  How to assign names to various groups of data so that you can include the name in formulas.

▶▶ "Managing Pages," p. 181.
  How to work with notebook pages in Quattro Pro, including naming a page and moving a page.

Working with Cell References and Blocks

The most common way to enter data is to type the data and press Enter. Quattro Pro, however, has several other data-entry techniques that help you build formulas using single cells and large blocks of cells.

Before you learn these techniques, you need to understand the three types of Quattro Pro cell references and how to enter and modify the references for use in your notebook formulas.

Quattro Pro has three types of cell reference formats: relative, absolute, and mixed. The cell reference format determines how Quattro Pro reproduces a formula when you copy the formula from one cell to another.

Defining Relative Reference Format

By default, Quattro Pro records new cell entries using the *relative reference format*. When you copy a relative reference formula, Quattro Pro changes the addresses to reflect the formula's new location on the notebook. If you copy the formula in cell B7 to C7, Quattro Pro adjusts the formula in a relative fashion (see fig. 3.12). Initially, cell B7's formula references data appearing in column B. When you copy this formula to cell C7, Quattro Pro adjusts the cell addresses in the formula, creating a formula that references data in column C.

Fig. 3.12

When you copy the formula used in cell B7 to cell C7, Quattro Pro adjusts the formula.

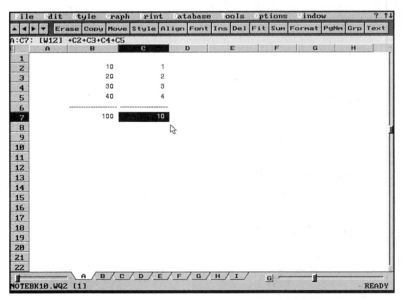

Defining Absolute Reference Format

You use the *absolute reference format* to anchor a cell address in a formula. If you *anchor* a cell address, the address doesn't change when you copy the formula to a different location on the notebook. To format a cell address using an absolute reference format, place a dollar sign ($) in front of the cell address's row number and a dollar sign in front of the column letter.

You can copy the formula shown in figure 3.13 using the absolute reference format. If you copy the formula in cell C7 to cell E7, Quattro Pro doesn't adjust the formula. The formula in cell E7 still sums data appearing in column C and doesn't sum the data in column E. You can copy this formula to cell IV8192, and the result remains 10. This operation is useful for displaying the result of a calculation in several locations on the same notebook report.

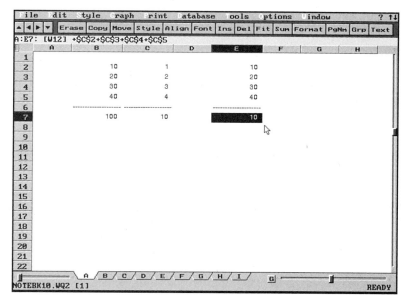

Fig. 3.13

Using absolute reference formats.

Defining Mixed Reference Format

Formulas that have relative and absolute cell references are called *mixed references*. A mixed reference indicates that you are anchoring some mix of row numbers and column letters appearing in a formula (see fig. 3.14).

Fig. 3.14

The mixed reference format for absolute and relative references in a formula.

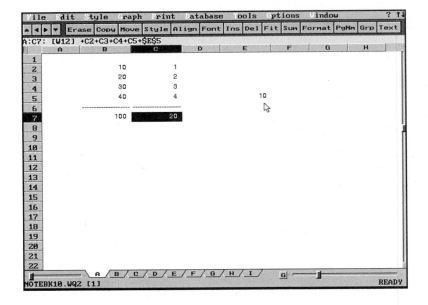

The formula shown in figure 3.14 is a mixed reference formula. The formula in cell C7 adds the value in cell E5 to the summed values in the range C2 through C5. The resulting answer is 20. The last cell address ($E$5) is an absolute reference. The first four cell addresses use the relative reference format. If you copy the formula in cell C7 to cell B7, Quattro Pro adjusts the formula in a relative and absolute reference fashion. The following formula then appears in B7:

+B2+B3+B4+B5+$E$5

Changing the Cell Reference Format

Quattro Pro enables you to change the reference format when you edit a formula on the input line. To change the reference format, place the selector on the target cell and press F2, the Edit key. By using the arrow keys, place the edit cursor on or next to the cell name that you want to edit. Then, by pressing F4, the Abs key, you can view all the possible reference formats until you find the format you need.

The reference formats are as follows:

Reference Formats	Description
$A$1	Absolute column and absolute row
A$1	Relative column and absolute row
$A1	Absolute column and relative row
A1	Relative column and relative row

You also can use the Abs button on the EDIT mode SpeedBar to change a cell's reference from relative to absolute, or vice versa. To change a cell's reference using the Abs button, press F2 to enter EDIT mode, select the cell coordinates, and then click the Abs button. Clicking the Abs button more than once toggles between absolute, relative, and mixed cell references.

Working with Cell References

Chapter 2 mentions using the Quattro Pro notebook as a what-if analysis tool. This type of analysis involves changing the value in one cell and examining its effect on one or more other cells.

The formula in cell C15 in figure 3.15 relies on the data in cells C11 through C13 that shows the cost of goods sold. If you change the value of one or more of the cost accounts, the total cost of goods sold and gross margin values change.

What-if analysis depends on cell referencing. To reference a cell in a formula, include the cell address (instead of a number) in the formula. January's gross margin, for example, equals the difference between total revenues (C8) and total cost of goods sold (the sum of the values in the range C11 through C13). If you replace the formula in cell C17 with the value 2,630, changing the value of any revenue or cost accounts doesn't affect gross margin because cell C17 no longer relies on these values (see fig. 3.16).

What-if analysis requires notebook variables that you can change to test different sets of assumptions.

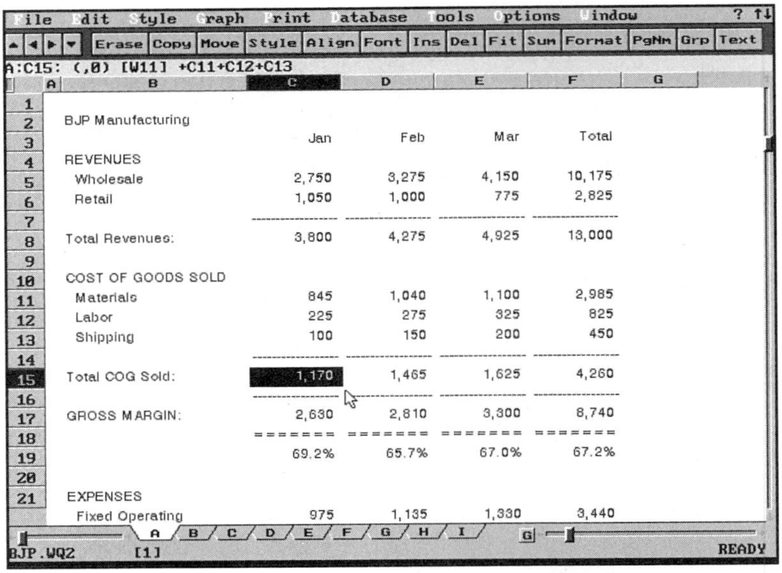

Fig. 3.15

Changes made to the values in C11..C13 affect C15.

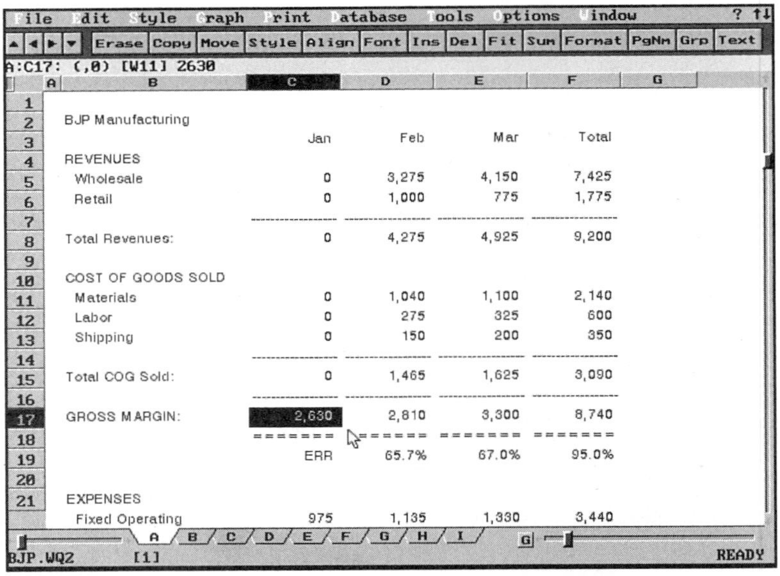

Fig. 3.16

Changes made to the values in C5..C6 and C11..C13 don't affect C17.

You can include cell references in your formulas by using one of two techniques. The basic method used to add the contents of cells C11, C12, and C13 appears in figure 3.15. Follow these steps to create this formula in cell C15:

1. Make cell C15 the active cell by pressing the arrow keys until the selector is in C15, or click the cell.

2. Enter a plus sign (+) to tell Quattro Pro that you are entering a formula value.

3. Type **C11+C12+C13** to complete the formula.

4. Press Enter to record the formula.

You can accomplish this same result by using a technique called *pointing*. This method enables you to build a formula by pointing to the cell addresses that you want in the formula. To point to cell addresses to create a formula, follow these steps:

1. Make cell C15 the active cell by pressing the arrow keys until the selector is in C15, or click the cell.

2. Enter the plus sign (+) to tell Quattro Pro that you are entering a formula value.

3. By using the arrow keys, make C11 the active cell. The cell address, C11, appears next to the plus sign on the input line.

4. Enter the plus sign again to tell Quattro Pro that you are continuing to build the formula.

5. Repeat steps 3 and 4, using cell addresses C12 and C13 (instead of C11) to include them in the formula.

6. Press Enter to record the formula.

You also use a mouse to point to cell addresses, as in the following steps:

1. Click cell C15 to make it the active cell.

2. Enter the plus sign (+) to tell Quattro Pro that you are entering a formula value.

3. Click cell C11.

4. Enter the plus sign again to tell Quattro Pro that you are continuing to build the formula.

5. Repeat steps 3 and 4, using cell addresses C12 and C13 (instead of C11) to include them in the formula.

6. Press Enter to record the formula.

Working with Cell Blocks

If you want to sum the contents of the three cells in the cell block range C5 through E5, you can add each cell address by using the formula C5+D5+E5. Using a cell block range, however, is more efficient. The formula @SUM(C5..E5) uses an @function to sum the values that appear in the cell block range C5..E5.

Pointing to the Block with the Keyboard

You can include a cell block in a formula in two ways: by typing, or by using the selector and the arrow keys.

First, you can type the address of the first cell in the block, type two periods, and type the last cell address in the block. This basic data-entry method is one with which you already are familiar.

The second method uses the selector and the arrow keys to build formulas in POINT mode. In POINT mode, you use the arrow keys to "point out" the cells that you want to reference in a formula. When you point to a cell, Quattro Pro writes the cell address on the input line next to the mathematical operator. To build a formula that adds the values in A1 and A2, for example, you press the plus sign (+), press the appropriate arrow key to move the selector to cell A1, press the plus sign again, press the appropriate arrow key to move the selector to cell A2, and then press Enter to store the formula.

TIP

> The only time you can enter POINT mode while entering data is when you move the selector after a mathematical operator or an open parenthesis.

You can use this pointing method to create the formulas that reside in column F. The formula in cell F5 in figure 3.15, for example, sums the values appearing in block C5..E5.

To build the formula in cell F5, follow these steps:

1. Use the arrow keys to make cell F5 the active cell.

2. Type **@SUM(** to begin the formula.

3. Make cell C5 the active cell. Quattro Pro displays this cell address to the right of the parenthesis in the @SUM command from step 2.

4. Press the period key (.) or the Select key (Shift+F7) to anchor the first cell address and to enter POINT mode. (Check the mode indicator to make sure that you are in POINT mode.)

5. Press the right-arrow key twice to include cells D5 and E5 in the cell block range.

6. Type a closing parenthesis to complete the formula.

7. Press Enter to record the formula.

Pointing to the Block with a Mouse

If you have a mouse, using the pointing technique is easier. To use a mouse to create the formula that sums the values in the range C5..E5, follow these steps:

1. Click cell F5.

2. Type **@SUM(** to begin the formula.

3. Make cell C5 the active cell.

4. While holding down the left mouse button, drag the mouse pointer to cell E5 and release the button. Quattro Pro highlights each cell that you drag through in the cell block range.

5. Type a closing parenthesis to complete the formula.

6. Press Enter to record the formula.

You also can use the following alternative mouse techniques to highlight any cell block range on a notebook:

1. Click the top left cell in the target cell block range.

2. Hold down the mouse button and drag the mouse pointer to the bottom right cell in the target cell block range.

3. Release the mouse button.

Or

1. Click the top left cell in the target cell block range.

2. Put the mouse pointer in the bottom right cell in the target cell block range.

3. Hold down the right mouse button and click the left button.

Working with 3-D Cell Blocks

Working with 3-D cell blocks is similar to working with cell blocks on a single page. Consider the multiple-page notebook report shown in figure 3.17. This report looks similar to the one shown in figure 3.16, with one exception. Rather than use a single page for the report, this version of the notebook summarizes on page A data contained on pages B and C. The formula in cell C7, for instance, sums the data located in cell C7 on pages B and C.

Fig. 3.17

A report that uses three pages to organize sales data.

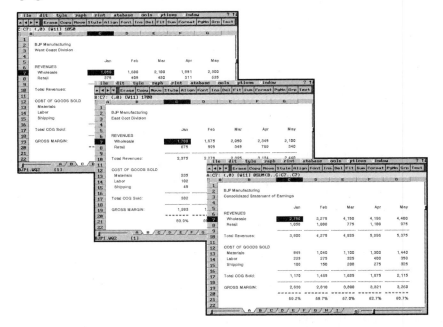

Pointing to a 3-D Block with the Keyboard

The most efficient way to create a formula that operates on a 3-D cell block is to use the POINT mode approach. You "point out" the cell block on each page that contains data you want to include in the formula. You can use this method to create any of the formulas on page A. The formula in cell C7 on page A, for example, sums the values appearing in block B..C:C7..C7.

To build the formula in cell C7, follow these steps:

1. Use the arrow keys to make cell C7 the active cell.

2. Type **@SUM(** to begin the formula.

3. Press Ctrl+Page Down to make page B the active page.

4. Make cell C7 the active cell on page B. Quattro Pro displays this page name and cell address to the right of the parenthesis in the @SUM command from step 2.

5. Press the period key (.) or the Select key (Shift+F7) to anchor the first cell address and to enter POINT mode. (Check the mode indicator to make sure that you are in POINT mode.)

6. Press Ctrl+Page Down to make page C the active page.

7. Make cell C7 the active cell on page C. Quattro Pro displays this page name and cell address to the right of the page B address information from step 4.

8. Type the closing parenthesis key. Quattro Pro returns the selector to page A.

9. Press Enter to record the formula.

Pointing to a 3-D Block with the Mouse

If you have a mouse, using the pointing technique is easier. To use a mouse to create the formula that sums the values in the range B..C:C7..C7, follow these steps:

1. Click cell C7 on page A.

2. Type **@SUM(** to begin the formula.

3. Click the page B tab to make B the active page.

4. Click cell C7 on page B.

5. While holding down the Shift key, click the page C tab. Quattro Pro draws a line underneath the page B and C tabs and extends the 3-D block to include the address for cell C7 on page C.

6. Type the closing parenthesis key. Quattro Pro returns the selector to page A.

7. Press Enter to record the formula.

> **TIP**
>
> Normally, you identify a 3-D cell block by specifying the first and last page names followed by a common block address, as in A..D:F1..F10. Another way of identifying the same 3-D cell block is to specify the first page name and cell address followed by the last page name and cell address, as in A:F1..D:F10. Both styles produce the same results. If you prefer to use the second style when working with 3-D blocks, choose /**O**ptions **S**tartup **3**-D Syntax and then choose the A:A1..**B**:B2 option. Be sure to choose /**O**ptions **U**pdate to save this change for future work sessions.

Drilling Formulas into 3-D Cell Blocks

Drilling labels and values into a page group is fairly straightforward. Entering formulas in Group mode, though, requires some planning. Consider these four rules when entering formulas while in Group mode:

- If you drill formulas such as +D5–D8 or @SUM(Z1..Z10) into a page group by *typing* into the input line and pressing Ctrl+Enter, each drilled formula calculates using the values only on its page.

- When you "point out" a formula that operates on cell blocks, such as @SUM(Z1..Z10), and then press Enter to store it in the active cell, Quattro Pro creates a formula *in the active page* that operates on a 3-D block in the active page group. If the active page group is named SALES, this formula displays as @SUM(SALES:Z1..Z10).

- When you "point out" a basic referencing formula such as +D5–D8 and then press Enter (or Ctrl+Enter to drill the entry), Quattro Pro cannot create formulas that operate on a 3-D block in the active page group. The program beeps and displays the error message `Cannot accept a block here` because the formula +SALES:D5–SALES:D8 is invalid, but @SUM(SALES:D5..D8) is valid.

■ When you "point out" a formula that operates on cell blocks, such as @SUM(Z1..Z10), and then press Ctrl+Enter to drill it into a page group, Quattro Pro creates a formula *on the active page* that operates on a 3-D block in the active page group. If the active page group is named SALES, this formula displays as @SUM(SALES:Z1..Z10).

Quattro Pro also creates formulas on the other pages in the group, but these formulas *don't* operate on the same 3-D block. Suppose that the SALES group consists of pages A through C. In this case, the formula on page B is @SUM(B..D:Z1..Z10) and the formula on page C is @SUM(C..E:Z1..Z10).

Editing Data

Editing cell data is an important function of using a spreadsheet program. Quattro Pro enables you to edit data as you type on the input line or after you press Enter to place data into a notebook cell. Entering new cell data, changing characters or numbers in the active cell, and deleting the contents of a cell are all examples of editing data on the notebook.

To edit the contents of a notebook cell, press F2 to enter EDIT mode. If you have a mouse, click the cell you want to edit and then click anywhere on the input line. When you click the input line, Quattro Pro enters EDIT mode and displays the cell data on the input line in the data's unformatted form.

You also can toggle between EDIT and the default modes (LABEL or VALUE) by pressing F2 (Edit) several times in succession. When you are in EDIT mode, you can use the editing keys listed in table 3.2 to edit the active notebook cell.

Remember, when you are in EDIT mode, the program automatically displays the EDIT mode SpeedBar. The buttons on this SpeedBar give you immediate access to advanced editing features and enable you to move around the notebook by block reference. (See Chapter 2, "Getting Started," for complete coverage of the SpeedBars.)

After you finish editing the data in a cell, press Enter or click the Enter box (at the left edge of the input line) to record the changes.

Table 3.2 Special Keys Available in EDIT Mode

Key	Description
Backspace	Deletes from right to left, one character at a time
Ctrl+Backspace	Erases everything on the input line
Ctrl+\	Deletes everything to the right of the cursor on the input line
Delete	Deletes the character that the cursor is on
End	Relocates the cursor to the end of the input line
Enter	Stores data on the input line in the active notebook cell; press Enter to exit EDIT mode and enter READY mode
Esc	Erases everything on the input line; press Esc a second time to cancel EDIT mode and return to READY mode
F2 (Edit)	Enters EDIT mode and displays the unformatted contents of the active cell on the input line
Home	Relocates the cursor to the first character on the input line
Insert	Toggles between INSERT (default) and Overwrite (OVR) modes
Page Down	Enters data into the active cell, exits EDIT mode, enters READY mode, and moves the selector down one screen
Page Up	Enters data into the active cell, exits EDIT mode, enters READY mode, and moves the selector up one screen
Shift+Tab or Ctrl+←	Moves the cursor five characters to the left on the input line
Tab or Ctrl+→	Moves the cursor five characters to the right on the input line
↑	Enters data into the active cell, exits EDIT mode, enters READY mode, and moves the selector up one cell
↓	Enters data into the active cell, exits EDIT mode, enters READY mode, and moves the selector down one cell

Key	Description
→	Enters data into the active cell, exits EDIT mode, enters READY mode, and moves the selector right one cell
←	Enters data into the active cell, exits EDIT mode, enters READY mode, and moves the selector left one cell

TIP

When in LABEL or VALUE mode, press one of the four arrow keys, the Page Up key, or the Page Down key to enter data into the active cell, move to another cell, and enter READY mode. To enter POINT mode (to continue building a formula on the input line, for example), place a mathematical operator after the last character on the input line before you press one of these six keys.

Using the Alt+F5 Undo Key

Everyone has accidents when working with a notebook—accidentally erasing data, deleting the wrong row or column, or executing a command on the wrong notebook cell. Quattro Pro has a built-in protection mechanism that enables you to reverse the most recent changes made to a cell or the most recent menu-command execution. To undo an operation, press Alt+F5, the Quattro Pro Undo key.

By default, the Undo key is deactivated. Activate the Undo key using the /Options Other Undo Enable command. To make this setting a default for future work sessions, choose /Options Update.

Editing in Group Mode

When working in Group mode, you can edit an entry by retyping it and pressing Ctrl+Enter. This action replaces the entry in the same cell on every page in the group. To delete the same entry from each page in a group, make the cell active and press Ctrl+Backspace.

When you make an entry or editing mistake, you also can press Alt+F5 (Undo) to reverse the effect on every page in the group.

FOR RELATED INFORMATION

▶▶ "Managing Pages," p. 181.
How to work with notebooks pages in group mode, including naming
a page, moving a page, and initiating group mode.

Recalculating Your Notebook Formulas

Quattro Pro recalculates your notebook formulas each time you edit or
erase data referenced in a formula. This activity is called *background
recalculation* because the operation takes place behind the scenes
while you continue to work on your notebook. For small- to medium-
sized notebooks, background recalculation takes only a second or two.
For large notebook applications, background recalculation can take
three or more seconds. When you see BKGD on the status line at the
bottom of the notebook, Quattro Pro is in background recalculation
mode.

You can control how Quattro Pro calculates and recalculates your notebook formulas by choosing /**O**ptions **R**ecalculation **M**ode. The submenu
options for this command are **A**utomatic, **M**anual, and **B**ackground. By
default, this command is set to **B**ackground. If you want Quattro Pro to
pause and recalculate your notebook formulas, choose **A**utomatic.

Choose **M**anual recalculation when you build large notebook applications with formulas that require a great deal of time to recalculate. In
this mode, Quattro Pro does nothing until you press F9, the calculation
key. When you use cell referencing in a formula, such as @SUM(B1..B5),
and then change a value appearing in the range B1..B5, Quattro Pro
doesn't recalculate the formula until you press F9. Quattro Pro displays
CALC on the status line when your notebook formulas require recalculation.

NOTE

Regardless of the way you set the notebook recalculation mode, Quattro
Pro always calculates an answer to every new formula that you enter or
edit on the notebook.

Viewing the Notebook

After you enter and edit data, you can view the data in various ways. The **W**indow and **O**ptions menus contain several commands that enable you to control how Quattro Pro displays your notebooks. By using these commands, you can split a notebook into two vertical or horizontal panes, simultaneously display all open notebooks, or change the display mode.

Quattro Pro's default display setting is one full-screen window. One window displays a small portion of the notebook with approximately 9 columns and 22 rows (in WYSIWYG display mode). You often need more columns and rows than appear in one window. Except for the simplest notebook applications, you want to use the rest of the notebook that exists to the right and below of what you can see in one full-screen window.

The following sections teach you the basic ways to create the on-screen look that you need to enter, edit, and view your notebook data successfully. The **W**indow and **O**ptions menus receive full coverage in Chapters 8 and 16.

Splitting the Screen Horizontally or Vertically

As your notebooks grow, you may need to look simultaneously at two cells in different parts of the notebook. Quattro Pro enables you to split your notebook into two vertical or horizontal panes. To create these panes, place the selector in a location you want to split and choose /**W**indow **O**ptions **H**orizontal (or **V**ertical). To unsplit windows, choose /**W**indow **O**ptions **C**lear.

If your application has more rows than columns, split the notebook horizontally (see fig. 3.18). If your application has more columns than rows, split the notebook vertically (see fig. 3.19).

You can arrange your window panes independently because the cursor movement on one pane doesn't affect the other pane. If you place your selector in the top pane shown in figure 3.18 and press Page Down, only the top pane scrolls down one screen. If you want to synchronize the scroll movement on both window panes, choose /**W**indow **O**ptions **S**ync. Press F6, the Window key, to move between window panes.

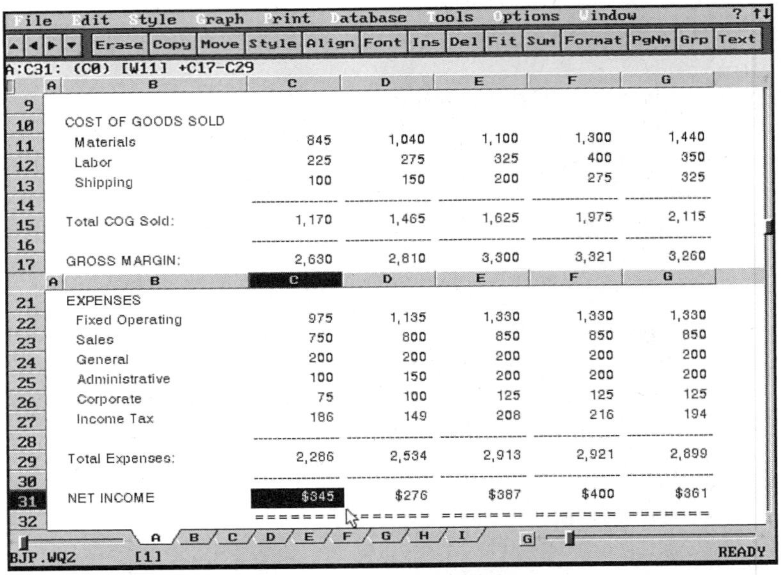

Fig. 3.18

A window split into two horizontal panes.

Fig. 3.19

A window split into two vertical panes.

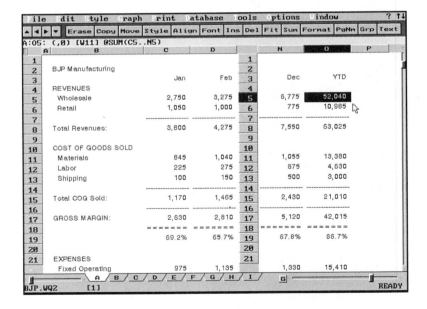

Displaying Tiled Notebooks

As you learn in Chapter 8, "Managing Files and Windows," Quattro Pro enables you to *tile* (display side by side) all open notebooks into one screen display when you select /**W**indow **T**ile (see fig. 3.20). This feature is useful if you have a large workspace application and you need to locate a particular notebook in that workspace.

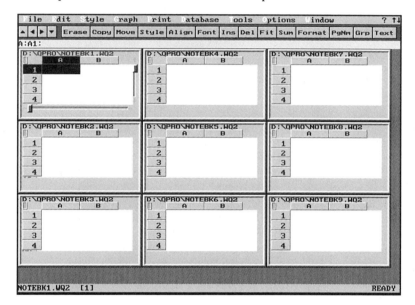

Fig. 3.20

Tiled notebooks.

Selecting the Screen Display Mode

Another way to change the basic look of your Quattro Pro screen display is to select a new display mode using the /**O**ptions **D**isplay Mode command (see fig. 3.21).

If you select the **C**: EGA: 80x43 display option, for example, Quattro Pro can display the entire income statement that appears on the notebooks in figures 3.18 and 3.19.

Quattro Pro supports an extensive list of display mode settings that take full advantage of EGA and VGA graphics display cards. If your graphics card supports extended text mode, you can display up to 132 notebook columns at the same time.

Fig. 3.21

Selecting a new display
mode.

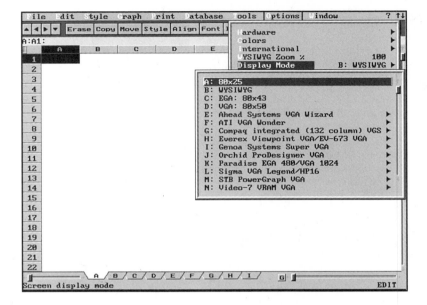

When you select display mode options E through S, Quattro Pro displays a submenu that lists the extended text modes supported by each
graphics card. The number of available display options varies for each
graphics display system. If you select option **H**: Everex Viewpoint VGA/
EV-673 VGA, for example, Quattro Pro displays another submenu listing
six extended text mode display settings (see fig. 3.22).

NOTE

If you choose a display mode that cannot support your mouse, Quattro
Pro will display an error message saying so. Press Esc to return to the
notebook. Your mouse now is disabled. To re-enable the mouse, you
must exit Quattro Pro and load your mouse driver software again. If you
have the driver name included in your AUTOEXEC.BAT file or
CONFIG.SYS file, reboot your computer.

FOR RELATED **INFORMATION**

▶▶ "Working with Notebook Windows," p. 389.
How to organize and display multiple notebook windows.

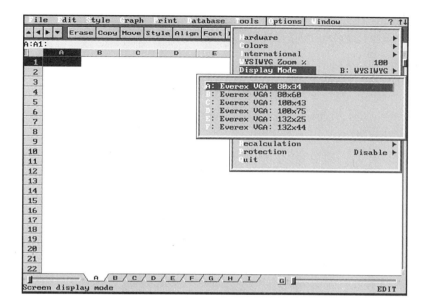

Fig. 3.22

Extended text mode display settings for the Everex Viewpoint graphics card.

Questions & Answers

This chapter covers the basic procedures used to enter, edit, and view data on a Quattro Pro notebook. If you have questions about any of the topics covered in this chapter and cannot find the answer by using Quattro's help windows, scan this section.

Entering Labels

Q: Why doesn't Quattro Pro accept a label I am trying to enter?

A: You must adhere to the data-entry rules outlined in the section "Entering Data" early in this chapter. You must precede labels with a label prefix (', ", ^, or \), enter numbers without commas, press Ctrl+D before typing dates and times, precede formulas with a plus (+) or minus (–) sign, and enter an @function by first typing the @ symbol.

Q: Why did Quattro Pro display the ^ prefix with my label when I tried to center a label that I was entering?

A: When Quattro Pro sees a label character, the program adds the default label prefix (') to the front of the first character. To center a label, type the ^ prefix before the first character in the label.

Q: Why did Quattro Pro display a single hyphen (-) in a cell in which I entered a repeating hyphen label using the \ label prefix?

A: If you try to enter a repeating label into a cell that you previously formatted with the /Style Alignment (Center/Right/Left) command, Quattro Pro ignores the repeating label prefix. To correct this problem, reset the default alignment for that cell with the /Style Alignment General command and re-enter the repeating label.

Entering Values

Q: Why doesn't Quattro Pro accept an @function that I am trying to enter?

A: When you enter an @function, don't place a space between the @ symbol and the command name, always follow the command name by parentheses, and be sure to use the correct syntax and all the appropriate arguments (see Chapter 6). Some @function commands require more information than the cell address or cell block range.

Q: Why is Quattro Pro displaying as a label the formula I entered?

A: You initially typed a character or accidentally typed a label prefix before entering the formula. Press F2 to enter EDIT mode, press Home to move to the beginning of the entry, delete the label prefix, and then press Enter to record the formula.

Q: Why didn't Quattro Pro display a new answer when I changed the value of a notebook cell referenced by a formula?

A: Press F9 to recalculate the active notebook. Choose the /Options Recalculation Mode command and set it to Background or Automatic. In these two modes, Quattro Pro recalculates notebook formulas when you change cell data referenced by the formulas.

Q: Why is Quattro Pro displaying asterisks when I enter values into notebook cells?

A: The values are longer than the width of the cell. To correct this problem, expand the width of the column by using the /Style Column Width command.

Working with Cell References and Blocks

Q: Why did Quattro Pro enter a period on the input line when I pressed the period key to extend a cell block while in POINT mode?

A: The only time you can enter POINT mode while entering data is when you place the selector after an operator or an open parenthesis.

Editing Data

Q: Why did nothing appear on the input line when I pressed F2 to edit a cell?

A: You may be trying to edit overlapping data that actually is in a different cell. Press the left-arrow key a few times until you find the cell containing the label, or press End+left arrow. The selector moves to the first cell to the left that contains data.

Viewing Data

Q: Why can't I split my screen display into two equal panes?

A: Quattro Pro splits a screen at the location of the selector. If you place the selector anywhere in column A and try to split the window vertically, Quattro Pro beeps. If you place the selector anywhere in row 1 and try to split the window horizontally, Quattro Pro beeps. Place the selector in the middle of the screen to split the screen into two equally sized horizontal or vertical panes.

Summary

This chapter introduces you to the basics of entering, editing, and viewing notebook data. Having completed this chapter, you should understand the following Quattro Pro concepts:

- Entering labels and values into a notebook
- Using and changing cell reference formats in formulas
- Using cell blocks and POINT mode to build formulas
- Editing data on the notebook
- Viewing data on the notebook

In Chapter 4, you learn how to build a fully functional notebook application. Chapter 4 also provides full coverage of the **F**ile and **E**dit menu commands. Although these commands represent only a small percentage of all Quattro Pro commands, you use these commands each time you create a notebook. Chapter 4 encourages you to follow along in a notebook-building exercise that demonstrates the best methods for using all the commands on the **F**ile and **E**dit menus.

Manipulating Data

This chapter focuses on the commands found on Quattro Pro's Edit menu. By using the Edit menu commands and your knowledge of entering and editing data, you can manipulate the form and content of your notebook applications.

In a typical notebook-building work session, you load Quattro Pro, and a blank notebook appears. Next, you enter and edit data on the notebook. When you sit back and review the notebook, however, you realize the data makes much more sense in another arrangement. You may need to switch row and column labels or delete one column of data from the notebook.

Each time you must change data in your notebook, you can do one of two things: erase the notebook and start over, or use the Edit menu commands to mold the existing notebook into an organized, logical application.

The Edit menu commands enable you to change the organization, structure, and content of your notebooks. You can use these commands to do the following operations:

- Copy and move cell data and/or cell formatting
- Undo notebook operations when you make a mistake

- Perform copy, move, and erase operations on blocks of cell data
- Insert and delete columns and rows
- Assign unique names to cells and blocks
- Switch or transpose column and row data
- Search for and replace data throughout the notebook

This chapter also introduces the **E**dit menu commands and single-operation topics, such as how to insert a row. Examples of notebook applications built for a fictional company, Speedy Airlines, reinforce your understanding of the purpose and function of each **E**dit menu command.

Reviewing the Edit Menu

Quattro Pro's **E**dit menu commands make copying, moving, erasing, and manipulating cell data extremely easy. You use the 14 **E**dit menu commands to organize and manipulate data on a notebook (see fig. 4.1).

Fig. 4.1

The **E**dit menu.

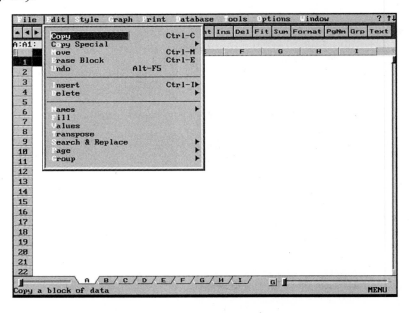

Table 4.1 explains the purpose of the Edit menu commands. Each command's name matches the command's function. You can use Copy, for example, to copy a value or a label to different parts of the notebook.

Table 4.1 Edit Menu Commands

Command	Description
Copy	Copies the contents of one or more cells into another cell or a block of cells
Copy Special	Copies the contents or formatting from one cell or cell block into another
Move	Moves the contents of one or more cells to another location on the notebook
Erase Block	Erases the contents of a block of cells
Undo	Reverses the most recent cell entry or deletion, or any operation you performed using a Quattro Pro menu command
Insert	Inserts a blank row or column, a row or column block, or one or more pages on the notebook
Delete	Deletes a row or column, a row or column block, or one or more pages from the active notebook
Names	Assigns a unique name to a cell or block of cells; used in place of cell references in all Quattro Pro operations
Fill	Enters a sequence of numbers into user-specified block of cells on the notebook
Values	Replaces all cell formulas in a user-specified block of cells with their calculated values
Transpose	Switches the row and column organization of data appearing in a user-specified block of cells
Search & Replace	Searches for a user-specified label or value on the notebook and replaces it with another user-specified label or value

(continues)

Table 4.1 Continued

Command	Description
Page	Renames notebook page tabs and changes the position of one or more pages in a notebook
Group	Creates and deletes page groups and enables and disables Group mode

TIP

Four commands on this menu have Ctrl+*key* shortcuts: **C**opy, **M**ove, **E**rase Block, and **I**nsert. The Ctrl+*key* shortcuts correspond to the bold-faced letters in each command name. When possible, Quattro Pro matches the Ctrl+*key* shortcut and the boldfaced letter key so that you don't have to remember two keys for one command.

The commands on the **E**dit menu perform operations on single cells and on blocks of cells. This section focuses on single-cell operations.

You can use the commands on the **E**dit menu in two ways: choose the command and then type the cell address, or highlight the cell and then choose the command.

Most **E**dit menu commands require two pieces of data to work: a source cell address and a destination cell address. By default, Quattro Pro uses the active cell as the source cell address. To use a different source cell, type the new address after you choose the command or click the cell. When Quattro Pro prompts you, type the destination cell address and then press Enter to complete the operation.

You can execute a menu command more quickly if you preselect the source cell and then choose the command. *Preselecting* a cell means making that cell active, or highlighting it, before executing a menu command. When you preselect a cell before choosing a command, Quattro Pro uses this cell address as the source cell address.

To preselect a block of cells, click the upper left cell in the block, drag the mouse pointer to the lower right cell, and release the button. You also can position the selector in the first cell of block, press Shift+F7 to enter EXT mode, highlight additional cells, and press Enter.

When you preselect a cell or block, the item remains selected after the command is executed. You can perform several formatting operations on the same cell or block without having to reselect each time.

Copying, Moving, and Erasing Cell Data

Copy, Move, and Erase Block are good examples of intuitive Edit menu commands. These three commands are among the most heavily used Quattro Pro menu commands because they meet basic and essential notebook-building needs.

The Copy command leaves the data in the source cell intact while copying the data to a new cell. This way, you easily can reproduce values and labels in several cells on the same notebook page, or on other pages within the same notebook.

The Move command deletes the data from the source cell and shifts the data to a new location. This operation enables you to shift data quickly around the notebook until you create the design you seek.

The Erase Block command deletes the contents of one or more cells on the notebook. This command is useful particularly when you must erase some—but not all—data from a notebook.

To see how these commands work, start by reviewing the items shown in figure 4.2. This figure shows the four starting locations of a text label called HERE: cells C6, C8, C10, and C12.

You can copy or move the text label in four ways: copy one cell to another cell, copy one cell into a block of cells, move one cell to another cell, or move one cell into a block of cells. Each method gives you a different result (see fig. 4.3).

In example 1, when you copy the contents of cell C6, Quattro Pro duplicates the text label HERE in cell E6. In example 2, when you move the contents of cell C8, Quattro Pro relocates the text label HERE to cell E8.

Fig. 4.2

The four starting
locations of the label
HERE.

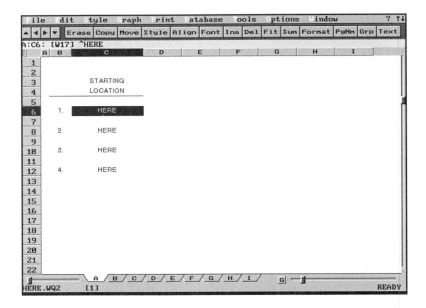

Examples 3 and 4 use the **C**opy and **M**ove commands to perform more
complex operations. In example 3, Quattro Pro copies the text label in
cell C10 into all three cells in cell block E10..G10. In example 4, Quattro
Pro moves the text label from cell C12 into the first address in cell
block E12..G12. Quattro Pro relocates HERE only to the first address in
the cell block because **M**ove is a relocating command and not a duplicating command.

Copying the Contents of a Cell

The **C**opy command saves you time when you build a notebook. If you
plan to use a value or a label many times on the same notebook, enter
the data once and copy it to other parts of the notebook, or copy the
data from one page to another in the same notebook. You also can
copy values and labels to other notebooks in Quattro Pro's memory.
Chapter 8, "Managing Files and Windows," explains how to use multiple
notebooks.

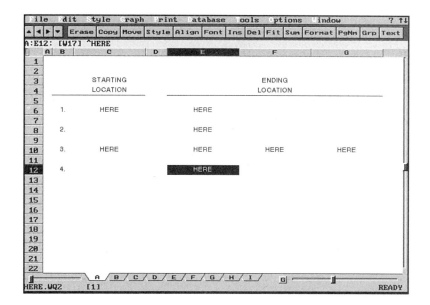

Fig. 4.3

Copying or moving data
four different ways.

You can execute a copy operation more quickly when you preselect the
source cell and then choose the command. To copy the contents of cell
A5 into cell Z5, for example, follow these steps:

1. Highlight A5, the cell you want to copy, by using the mouse or the
arrow keys.

2. Choose **Copy** from the Edit menu. Press Enter after Quattro Pro
displays A5..A5 as the source cell address.

> **TIP**
>
> Press Ctrl+C, the Ctrl+*key* shortcut for the **C**opy command, to execute a
> copy operation quickly.

3. When Quattro Pro prompts you for a destination, type the new
cell location, **Z5**, and press Enter.

Copy

You also can copy data using the Copy button on the READY mode SpeedBar. Highlight the cell or block you want to copy, click the Copy button, and then click [Enter] on the input line. When Quattro Pro prompts you for a destination, click the new location and click [Enter].

The **C**opy command is useful for duplicating formulas. When you copy a relative reference formula, Quattro Pro adjusts the cell addresses in the formula so that they refer to the row and column into which the formula was copied. In figure 4.4, the relative reference formula that sums data in column C is copied into adjacent cells in columns D, E, and F. Quattro Pro adjusts the formula to sum the data in these columns. When you copy an absolute reference formula, Quattro Pro doesn't adjust the cell addresses, which enables you to display a formula result in a different part of the notebook (as discussed in Chapter 3).

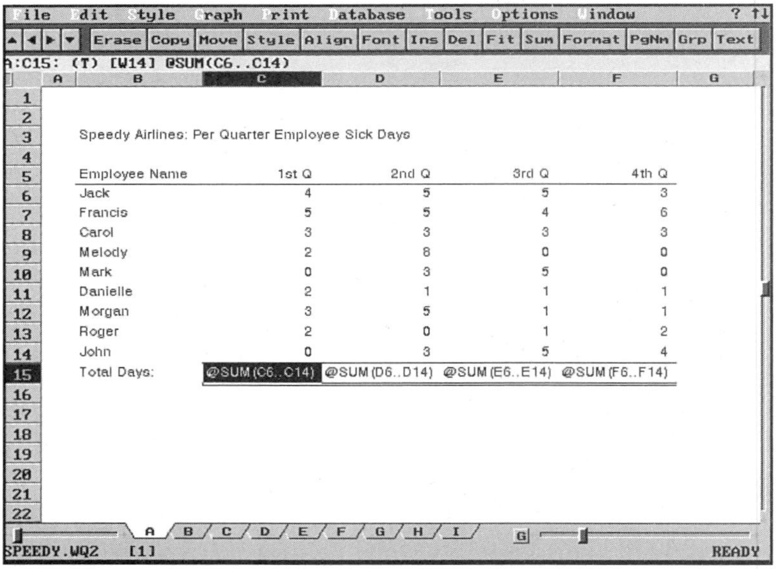

Fig. 4.4

When you copy a relative reference formula, Quattro Pro adjusts the cell addresses.

When you copy a cell, Quattro Pro copies the cell's format—alignment, display format, cell protection, and so on—into the destination cell. Cell C15 in figure 4.4, for example, is formatted to display a formula as text. When you copy the cell to the other columns, the formulas still display as text—you don't have to reformat copied cell data. See Chapter 5, "Formatting Data," for complete coverage of notebook formatting.

Using Copy Special

The /Edit Copy Special command enables you to copy a cell block's contents without copying its formatting or copy a cell block's formatting without copying its contents. This feature is particularly helpful when you want to copy numeric data or formulas but don't want to copy the cell's style attributes, or when you want to reproduce cell formats elsewhere in the notebook without copying the data.

To copy only the format or contents (value, label, or formula) of a cell, follow these steps:

1. Make the cell you want to copy the active cell.

2. Choose /Edit Copy Special.

3. Choose Contents or Format.

4. When Quattro Pro prompts you for a destination block, type the new cell location and press Enter.

If you chose Contents, the data in the source block now also appears in the destination block. If you have chosen Format, the destination block appears empty until you enter data or text into the cells. When you enter data into a cell, the data adopts the format attributes assigned with the Copy Special command.

> **NOTE**
>
> When you copy data using the **F**ormat setting, Quattro Pro doesn't retain the alignment for labels, only for values.

Moving the Contents of a Cell

Like the Copy command, the Move command also saves time when you build a notebook. You can move a label or a value to a different part of the notebook or to other open notebooks in Quattro Pro's memory. You can execute a move operation more quickly when you preselect the source cell and then choose the command.

To move the contents of cell D15 to cell D17, for example, follow these steps:

1. Make D15 the active cell.

2. Choose **M**ove from the **E**dit menu.

3. Press Enter after Quattro Pro displays D15 as the source cell
address.

4. When Quattro Pro prompts you for a destination, type **D17** for
the new location and press Enter.

`Move` You also can move data using the Move button on the READY mode
SpeedBar. To execute a move operation with the Move button, highlight the cell or cells you want to move, click the Move button, and then
click [Enter] on the input line. When Quattro Pro prompts you for a
destination, click the new location and click [Enter].

When you relocate a formula with the **M**ove command, Quattro Pro
doesn't adjust the cell reference formats (relative, absolute, or mixed)
appearing in the formula, as in a copy operation. This way, you can
display a formula result in a different notebook location. In a move
operation, however, Quattro Pro adjusts each formula containing a
reference to the moved formula, reflecting the moved formula's new
notebook location.

In figure 4.5, the formula in cell D15 is moved into cell D17. (Notice that
the formulas now appear formatted as numbers instead of text.) The
formula's original cell addresses and reference formats don't change
(see the input line in fig. 4.5).

When you use the **M**ove command to relocate a value whose cell
address appears as part of a formula, several things can happen, depending on the formula and where you move the value. The following
example illustrates four possible scenarios.

```
 ile   dit   tyle   raph   rint  atabase   ools   ptions   indow        ? ↑↓
▲◄►▼ Erase Copy Move Style Align Font Ins Del Fit Sum Format PgNm Grp Text
A:D17: (,0) [W14] @SUM(D6..D14)
      A      B            C           D          E          F        G
  1
  2
  3          Speedy Airlines: Per Quarter Employee Sick Days
  4
  5          Employee Name       1st Q      2nd Q      3rd Q      4th Q
  6          Jack                  4          5          5          3
  7          Francis               5          5          4          6
  8          Carol                 3          3          3          3
  9          Melody                2          8          0          0
 10          Mark                  0          3          5          0
 11          Danielle              2          1          1          1
 12          Morgan                3          5          1          1
 13          Roger                 2          0          1          2
 14          John                  0          3          5          4
 15          Total Days:          21                    25         20
 16
 17                                          33
 18
 19
 20
 21
 22
        ╲    A / B / C / D / E / F / G / H / I /      G
SPEEDY.WQ2   [1]                                                  READY
```

Fig. 4.5

A formula remains unchanged when moved from one cell to another.

Figure 4.6 displays an abbreviated version of the document appearing in figure 4.5. The formulas in cells C9 and D9 are equivalent to the formulas in cells E9 and F9.

Figure 4.7 shows the results of moving data referenced in notebook formulas. Two types of formulas appear in this figure: individual cell addresses connected by mathematical operators (1st and 2nd Q) and @function commands (3rd and 4th Q). Quattro Pro moves each type of formula differently.

In the 1st Q column in figure 4.7, the 3 in cell C7 is moved to cell C12. Quattro Pro adjusts the original cell reference (C7) in the formula to reflect the new location of the data in cell C12.

In the 2nd Q column in figure 4.7, the 2 in cell D7 is moved to cell D8. Quattro Pro overwrites the data in cell D8, causing ERR to appear in the formula.

Fig. 4.6

The cell address before moving a cell referenced in a formula.

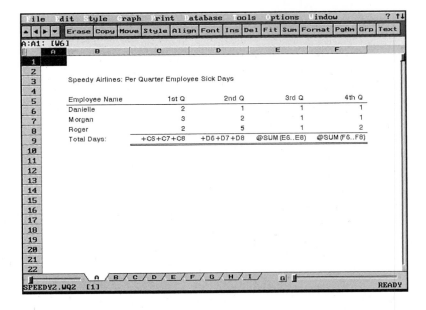

Fig. 4.7

Results of moving a cell referenced in a formula.

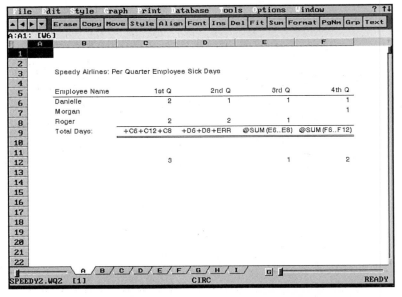

> **NOTE**
>
> When a **M**ove operation causes one cell reference to replace another cell reference in a formula, Quattro Pro displays ERR, indicating an invalid formula. To correct the formula, edit the ERR portion of the formula by retyping the overwritten cell reference.

In the 3rd Q column, the 1 in cell E7 is moved to cell E12. Because cell E7 isn't referenced specifically in the formula, Quattro Pro doesn't adjust this cell reference to reflect the data's new location. The program continues to add the numbers appearing in cell block E6..E8, but the formula result now equals 2 instead of 3.

In the 4th Q column, the 2 in cell F8 is moved to cell F12. Because F8 is one of the two coordinates in the cell block (F6 is the other coordinate), Quattro Pro adjusts the formula to include cell F12. If you move a cell listed in a formula as a coordinate in a cell block, Quattro Pro changes the formula to reflect the new coordinate location.

> **NOTE**
>
> Be careful when using the **M**ove command on a cell address that also is a cell block coordinate in a formula. If you move the cell address in such a way that the adjusted cell block now includes the formula's cell address, you create a circular reference.
>
> In a *circular reference*, the result changes each time you press F9 because the formula includes its own result in the calculation. Quattro Pro displays the CIRC indicator on the status line when the program encounters a circular reference in a formula. To correct this problem, re-enter the formula so that the cells addressed in the formula don't include the address of the formula itself.

Erasing a Cell's Contents

The Erase Block command erases data from one cell, a group of cells, or every cell on the notebook. Erasing data from a cell on a Quattro Pro notebook is like pressing F2 and deleting the characters on the input line. When you erase a value from a formatted cell, Quattro Pro removes only the contents of the cell, not the cell format or alignment settings. If you don't need to save cell formats and want to erase the entire contents of a notebook file, choosing the /**F**ile **E**rase command is easier.

NOTE

You cannot erase cell data when notebook protection is activated with the /**O**ptions **P**rotection command. See Chapter 8, "Managing Files and Windows," for details on how to enable and disable notebook protection.

To erase the contents of a cell, follow these steps:

1. Make the cell you want to delete the active cell.

2. Choose **E**rase Block from the **E**dit menu.

3. When Quattro Pro displays the source cell address, press Enter.

TIP

Press Ctrl+E, the Ctrl+*key* shortcut for the /**E**dit **E**rase Block command, to execute an erase block operation quickly.

You also can press Del to erase data from a cell or a block of cells. Select the cell(s) you want to erase by highlighting them and then pressing Delete.

Erase

You also can erase data by using the Erase button on the READY mode SpeedBar. Highlight the cell or cells you want to erase and then click the button.

Working with Blocks

In addition to working with single cells, the **C**opy, **M**ove, and **E**rase Block commands also operate on blocks of cells on a single page and 3-D cell blocks that span several notebook pages. When you choose one of these commands, Quattro Pro displays the source cell as a cell block (A:A1..A1, for example). As you highlight cells in the same page, the program changes the display to reflect the new block (A:A1..D9, for example). When you highlight cells that span several pages, the program changes the display to reflect the new 3-D cell block (A..C:A1..D9, for example).

Quattro Pro gives you the flexibility to work with one, many, or all cells in the notebook. You can move large chunks of data, copy an entire page onto a new page, or delete large blocks of data from several pages at once.

Copying a Block

When you copy a block of cells, highlight the cell block before choosing the command. To copy the contents of cell block A1..A5 into cell block D1..D5, for example, follow these steps:

1. Make cell A1 active, press Shift+F7 to enter EXT mode, and then use the arrow keys to highlight cell A5. Alternatively, use the mouse to highlight the block.

2. Choose **Copy** from the **Edit** menu.

3. Type **D1..D5** as the destination cell block.

4. Press Enter.

Moving a Block

When you move a block of cells, preselect the cell block before choosing the **Move** command. To move the contents of cell block A1..A5 into cell block D1..D5, for example, follow these steps:

1. Make cell A1 active, press Shift+F7 to enter EXT mode, and then use the arrow keys to highlight cell A5. Alternatively, use the mouse to highlight the block.

2. Choose **Move** from the **Edit** menu (or press Ctrl+M).

3. Type **D1..D5** as the destination cell block.

4. Press Enter.

Erasing a Block

When you erase a block of cells, highlight the cell block before you choose the command. To erase the contents of cell block D1..D5, for example, follow these steps:

1. Make cell D1 active, press Shift+F7 to enter EXT mode, and then use the arrow keys to highlight cell D5. Alternatively, use the mouse to highlight the block.

2. Choose **E**rase Block from the **E**dit menu (or press Ctrl+E).

CAUTION ▶ In an **E**rase Block operation, you have no destination cell block. When you choose this command, Quattro Pro erases the source cell block. If you need to recover data erased accidentally, press Alt+F5 immediately.

Manipulating 3-D Blocks

You can perform copy, move, and erase operations on 3-D cell blocks just as easily as with cell blocks in a single notebook page. When you alter or update the structure of a report that contains similarly designed pages, you want to make sure that any changes you make to one page are made to all pages in the group. (See the section "Managing Pages" later in this chapter for full details about creating a page group.) If you decide to move a row of data on page A, for example, you probably want to do the same for the other pages in the group. This way, you can ensure that the structure of each page in the group remains the same.

The most efficient method is to create a page group for the pages you want to manipulate, enable Group mode, and then copy, move, or erase data on one of the pages in the group. Whatever is done to one page in the group is duplicated on all pages in the group.

Suppose that you want to copy block D1..D5 to E1..E5 on pages A, B, and C. To do so, create a page group that contains pages A, B, and C, and then enable Group mode (choose /**E**dit **G**roup **M**ode **E**nable or click the little Group button on the status line). Now perform the copy operation once on page A; Quattro Pro copies the same blocks on pages B and C. This method works best when you want to manipulate a 3-D block that spans two or more consecutive pages.

Reversing Operations with Undo

If you ever have experienced the horror of accidentally erasing data on your notebook, deleting the wrong row or column, or executing a command on the wrong notebook cell, you may think that all your work has gone down the drain. Fortunately, Quattro Pro's Edit menu has a built-in protection mechanism that in many cases enables you to recall the most recent changes made to a cell or reverse the most recent menu command execution. When you must undo an operation, choose /Edit Undo or press Alt+F5, the Quattro Pro Undo key.

By default, Quattro Pro's Undo key is disabled. Pressing Alt+F5 doesn't affect the active notebook when Undo is disabled. To enable the Undo key, choose /Options Other Undo Enable. After the Undo key is enabled, choose /Options Update to keep the Undo key feature active for future work sessions.

The Undo key is useful for reversing Quattro Pro operations such as copying, moving, and erasing blocks of data. This feature, however, cannot undo every Quattro Pro operation. You cannot undo notebook formats and presentation-quality enhancements added with many of the Style menu commands. You cannot use the Undo key, for example, to remove drawn lines or cell shading after you add them to a notebook. See Chapter 5, "Formatting Data," for a complete list of the Style menu commands that aren't reversible.

TIP

When you need to reverse more than the most recent change or menu command execution, use Quattro Pro's Transcript facility. The Transcript facility retains a history of all keystrokes and mouse clicks for the current work session. By "replaying" your transcript, you can reinstate the current notebook to its condition at any point in its former status—even all the way back to when you first opened the notebook as a new, blank file. See "Playing Back a Transcript Block" in Chapter 15 for more information.

Inserting and Deleting Rows, Columns, and Pages

Use the /**E**dit **I**nsert and /**E**dit **D**elete commands to add and remove rows and columns, row or column blocks, or entire pages from a notebook. When you delete a row or column, you delete all the data in the row or column. Before you use the /**E**dit **D**elete command, scan the target row or column for data you want to keep.

When you delete a row or column, the data in the next row or column moves up or left to fill in the blank row or column. Don't worry if you delete data used in your formulas. Quattro Pro changes formulas to reflect the removed rows or columns.

You can use two methods to scan a row or column for data you may want to keep before executing the **D**elete command. The most direct way is to use the arrow keys or Tab and Page Down to move around a row or column. This method works well when you don't have much territory to cover but becomes tedious when you must look at several screens.

The second method enables you to locate data in a row or column quickly in any part of a notebook. To use this method, follow these steps:

1. Place the selector in row 1 of any column or in column A of any row.

2. Press End on your numeric keypad to enter END mode.

3. Press the right-arrow key to search a row or the down-arrow key to search a column. The selector moves to the first or last piece of data Quattro Pro locates before it encounters a blank cell. If you find yourself at column IV or in row 8,192, Quattro Pro didn't find any data, and you can delete that row or column.

> **CAUTION**
>
> If you have formatted any data with the /**S**tyle **N**umeric Format **H**idden command, be aware that Quattro Pro will not prompt you if you choose to delete that block.

When you choose /**E**dit **I**nsert, a submenu appears, enabling you to select rows, columns, or pages for insertion into the notebook. Quattro

Pro inserts a row above the selector, a column to the left of the selector, and a page before the active page.

When you choose /**E**dit **D**elete, a submenu also appears, enabling you to specify how many rows, columns, or pages to delete from the notebook. Quattro Pro deletes a row, column, or page starting at the selector.

Inserting a Row

To insert rows, Quattro Pro needs to know where to begin inserting and how many rows to insert. To insert one row, follow these steps:

1. Place the selector in the row below where you want to insert a row.

2. Choose /**E**dit **I**nsert **R**ows.

> **TIP**
>
> Press Ctrl+I, the Ctrl+key shortcut for the /**E**dit **I**nsert command, to execute an insert operation quickly.

3. Press Enter.

To insert multiple rows, follow these steps:

1. Place the selector in the row below where you want multiple rows inserted.

2. Choose /**E**dit **I**nsert **R**ows.

3. Press the down-arrow key until you highlight the number of rows you want to insert, highlight the rows using the mouse, or type a valid cell block including all the row numbers you want to insert at the Enter row insert block: prompt. Type **D6..D8**, for example.

> **TIP**
>
> You can preselect an entire cell block quickly with a mouse. Select the first cell in the block and then hold down the left mouse button while you drag the pointer through the source range. When you reach the last cell in the block, release the mouse button. Then choose /**E**dit **I**nsert **R**ows and press Enter.

4. Press Enter. Quattro Pro inserts three rows.

 You also can insert rows by using the Ins button on the READY mode SpeedBar. Place the selector in the row before which you want to insert a row, click the Ins button, and then click **R**ows. If you want to insert a single row, click [Enter] on the input line. If you want to insert multiple rows, highlight the number of the rows you want inserted and then click [Enter].

Deleting a Row

To delete rows, Quattro Pro needs to know where to begin deleting and how many rows to delete. To delete one row, follow these steps:

1. Place the selector in the row you want to delete.

2. Choose /**E**dit **D**elete **R**ows.

3. Press Enter.

To delete multiple rows, follow these steps:

1. Place the selector in the first row you want deleted.

2. Choose /**E**dit **D**elete **R**ows.

3. Press the up- or down-arrow key until you highlight the number of rows you want deleted, use the mouse to highlight the rows, or type a valid cell block including the row numbers, such as **D6..D8**.

4. Press Enter. Quattro Pro deletes three rows.

 You also can delete rows by using the Del button on the READY mode SpeedBar. To execute a delete operation this way, put the selector in the row you want to delete, click the Del button, and then click **R**ows. If you want to delete a single row, click [Enter] on the input line. If you want to delete multiple rows, first highlight the rows you want to delete, click the Del button, click the **R**ows option, and then click [Enter].

Inserting a Column

To insert columns, Quattro Pro needs to know where to begin inserting and how many columns to insert. To insert one column, follow these steps:

1. Place the selector in the column left of where you want a column inserted.

2. Choose /Edit Insert Columns (or press Ctrl+I and then press C).

3. Press Enter.

To insert multiple columns, follow these steps:

1. Place the selector in the column left of where you want columns inserted.

2. Choose /Edit Insert Columns (or press Ctrl+I and then press C).

3. Press the left- or right-arrow key until you highlight the number of columns you want inserted, or type a valid cell block, including the column letters (such as **D6..F6**).

4. Press Enter. Quattro Pro inserts three columns.

You also can use the Ins button on the READY mode SpeedBar to insert columns. Place the selector in the column left of where you want to insert a row, click the Ins button, and then click Columns. If you want to insert a single column, click [Enter] on the input line. If you want to insert multiple columns, highlight the number of columns you want to insert and then click [Enter].

Ins

Deleting a Column

To delete columns, Quattro Pro needs to know where to begin deleting and how many columns to delete. To delete one column, follow these steps:

1. Place the selector in the column you want deleted.

2. Choose /Edit Delete Columns.

3. Press Enter.

To delete multiple columns, follow these steps:

1. Place the selector in the first column you want deleted.

2. Choose /Edit Delete Columns.

3. Press the right-arrow key until you highlight the number of columns you want deleted, use the mouse to highlight the columns, or type a valid cell block including the column letters. Type **D6..F6**, for example.

4. Press Enter. Quattro Pro deletes the columns.

You also can use the Del button on the READY mode SpeedBar to delete columns. Place the selector in the column you want to delete, click the Del button, and then click **Columns**. If you want to delete a single column, click [Enter] on the input line. If you want to delete multiple columns, first highlight the columns you want to delete, click the Del button, click the **Columns** option, and then click [Enter].

Inserting and Deleting Row Blocks and Column Blocks

With Quattro Pro, you can insert and delete blocks of cell data as well as whole rows and columns. Quattro Pro thinks of cell blocks as partial columns and rows. When you insert a block of rows, data previously in the block is pushed downward. When you insert a block of columns, data previously in the block is pushed to the right. Only data in the cells directly below or to the right of the inserted block shifts; data in the whole row or column doesn't shift.

Inserting a Row Block

When you insert a row block of cells, highlight the cell block before choosing the command. To insert blank cells into row block B5..D5, for example, follow these steps:

1. Make cell B5 active, press Shift+F7 to enter EXT mode, and then use the arrow keys to highlight cell D5. Alternatively, use the mouse to highlight the block.

2. Choose /**Edit Insert Row Block**.

Quattro Pro inserts a single empty row into cell block B5..D5 and pushes existing labels and values downward.

You also can click the Ins button on the READY mode SpeedBar to reach the /**Edit Insert** menu and begin an insert row block operation.

Figures 4.8 and 4.9 show a notebook before and after an insert row block operation. In figure 4.8, cell block C17..F17 is preselected and the

/**E**dit **I**nsert menu has been pulled down. The notebook in figure 4.9 shows how Quattro Pro inserts a row block after you choose the Row **B**lock command.

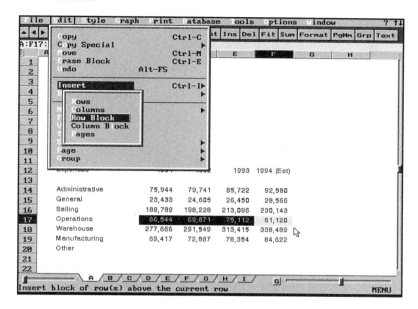

Fig. 4.8

A preselected block of rows on a notebook.

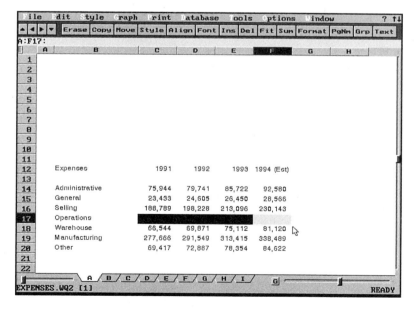

Fig. 4.9

The result of inserting a row block.

Deleting a Row Block

When you delete a row block of cells, highlight the cell block before choosing the command. To delete row block B5..D5, for example, follow these steps:

1. Make cell B5 active, press Shift+F7 to enter EXT mode, and then use the arrow keys to highlight cell D5. Alternatively, use the mouse to highlight the block.

2. Choose /Edit Delete Row Block.

Quattro Pro deletes row block B5..B9 and moves any data below the row block upward.

 You also can click the Del button on the READY mode SpeedBar to reach the /Edit Delete menu and begin a delete row block operation.

Inserting a Column Block

When you insert a column block of cells, highlight the cell block before choosing the command. To insert blank cells into column block B5..B10, for example, follow these steps:

1. Make cell B5 active, press Shift+F7 to enter EXT mode, and then use the arrow keys to highlight cell D5. Alternatively, use the mouse to highlight the block.

2. Choose /Edit Insert Column Block.

Quattro Pro inserts an empty column block in cell block B5..B10 and pushes existing data to the right.

 You also can use the Ins button on the READY mode SpeedBar to reach the /Edit Insert menu and begin an insert column block operation.

Deleting a Column Block

When you delete a column block of cells, highlight the block before choosing the command. To delete cells from column block B5..B10, for example, follow these steps:

1. Make cell B5 active, press Shift+F7 to enter EXT mode, and then use the arrow keys to highlight cell B10. Alternatively, use the mouse to highlight the block.

2. Choose /**E**dit **D**elete Column Block.

Quattro Pro deletes cell block B5..B10 and moves any data right of the column block to the left.

You also can use the Del button on the READY mode SpeedBar to reach the /**E**dit **D**elete menu and begin a column block deletion.

`Del`

Inserting a Page

When you insert a page, place the selector in the page you want moved down a page letter when the new page is inserted. For instance, to insert a page between page D and E, follow these steps:

1. Place the selector in any cell on page E.

2. Choose /**E**dit **I**nsert **P**ages.

3. Press Enter.

Quattro Pro inserts a new, blank page in the position that page E previously occupied. Page E now is in the position previously held by page F, page F moves to the position previously held by page G, and so on.

Inserting more than one page at a time requires a slightly different procedure. To insert two pages between D and E, for instance, follow these steps:

1. Place the selector in any cell on page E.

2. Choose /**E**dit **I**nsert **P**ages.

3. Hold the Shift key down and click the page F tab. Quattro Pro draws a black line under the tabs for pages E and F to signify that you are inserting two pages.

4. Press Enter.

Quattro Pro inserts two pages, which causes pages E through IV to shift as well. When the number of pages you insert forces a page that contains data off the notebook, Quattro Pro beeps and displays an error message telling you so. Try your insert operation again, but this time select fewer pages.

Remember, each notebook has a limit of 256 pages.

NOTE

You also can insert pages by using the Ins button on the READY mode SpeedBar. Make active the page before which you want to insert another page by clicking the page tab. Click the Ins button, and then click **P**ages. If you want to insert a single page, click [Enter] on the input line. If you want to insert multiple pages, highlight the number of the pages you want inserted (as described in step 3 earlier) and then click [Enter].

Deleting a Page

To delete a page, place the selector in the page you want deleted, choose /**E**dit **D**elete **P**ages, and then press Enter. To delete more than one page at a time—for example, to delete pages D and E—follow these steps:

1. Place the selector in any cell on page D.

2. Choose /**E**dit **D**elete **P**ages.

3. Hold the Shift key down and click the page E tab. Quattro Pro draws a black line under the tabs for pages D and E to signify that you are deleting two pages.

4. Press Enter.

Quattro Pro deletes the selected pages and shifts all remaining pages following page E toward the front of the notebook. The data on page F now appears on page D, the data on page G appears on page E, and so on.

You also can delete pages by using the Del button on the READY mode SpeedBar. To execute a delete operation this way, make active the page you want to delete by clicking its tab. Click the Del button and then click **P**ages. If you want to delete a single page, click [Enter] on the input line. If you want to delete multiple pages, first highlight the pages you want to delete, click the Del button, click the **P**ages option, and then click [Enter].

Naming a Block

The **N**ames command assigns text names to cell addresses and cell blocks to create *cell block names*. You can use cell block names instead of cell addresses in Quattro Pro menu commands and formulas. You can remember a cell block name more easily than you can remember a cell block's coordinates. You can create, delete, reset, assign labels as, and make tables of names using the commands found on the **Names** submenu (see fig. 4.10).

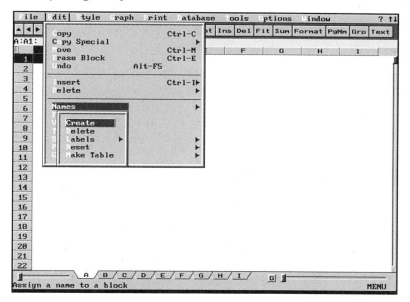

Fig. 4.10

The **N**ames submenu.

When creating or editing a formula in EDIT mode, you can click the Name button on the EDIT mode SpeedBar to display a list of named blocks (similar to pressing F3). For this button to work, the edit cursor must appear after a left parenthesis or a mathematical symbol (such as + or –) before you click Name. If you click a named block, Quattro Pro enters it on the edit line.

Creating Names

When you create cell block names, you must remember five rules:

- A valid name can refer to a cell, a cell block, an entire page, or the entire notebook.

- Valid names can be up to 15 characters long.

- Cell block names can contain any character on your keyboard.

You can use the punctuation characters and the mathematical symbols in a name, but you can remember names more easily if you stick to letters.

■ You can combine names, cell addresses, and cell blocks in a formula; create two or more names for the same cell block; and create names for cell blocks that share cells in common. Figure 4.11 shows examples of valid notebook names.

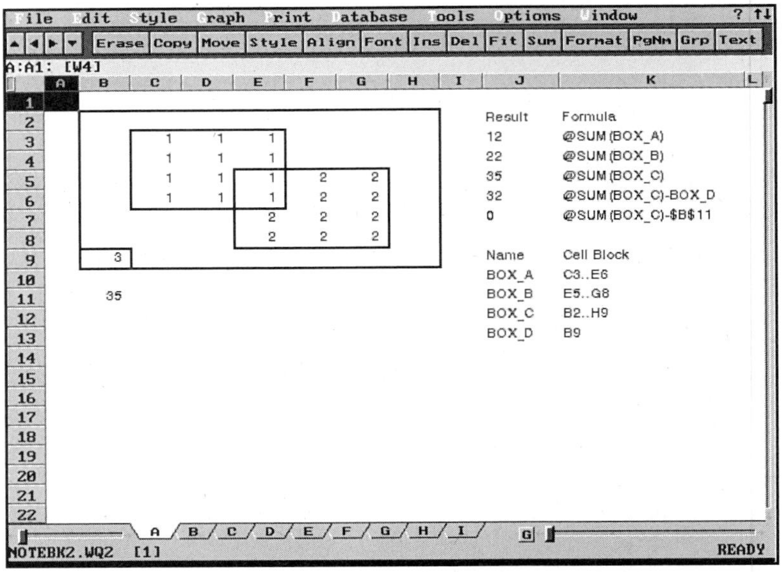

Fig. 4.11

Cell block names can refer to a single cell and cell blocks.

■ Never name cells or blocks with a name that's the same as a cell address. If you create the name Q1 to represent Quarter 1 sales, for example, and then use the name in a formula, Quattro Pro uses the data in cell Q1.

TIP

Intermediate and advanced notebook applications make frequent use of the /Edit Names Create command. You may want to assign a SpeedBar button to this operation. See Chapter 16, "Customizing Quattro Pro," for instructions about assigning menu command operations to a SpeedBar button.

Alternatively, you can create a Ctrl+key shortcut for the command. (Ctrl+N for NAMES works nicely.) See "Using Ctrl+Key Shortcuts" in Chapter 2 for full details about using and creating Ctrl+key shortcuts.

To create a name for cell block C3..E6, follow these steps:

1. Make cell C3 active, press Shift+F7 to enter EXT mode, and then use the arrow keys to highlight cell E6. Alternatively, use the mouse to highlight the block.

2. Choose /**Edit N**ames **C**reate. Quattro Pro prompts you for a block name.

3. Type a valid name and then press Enter.

> Quattro Pro updates a formula when you create a name to replace a cell address or cell block referenced in the formula (see fig. 4.12). If you create the name 1STQ for an existing formula reference such as C6..C8, for example, Quattro Pro substitutes 1STQ for C6..C8 in the formula. If you delete the name 1STQ later, Quattro Pro replaces 1STQ in the formula with the original cell block C6..C8.

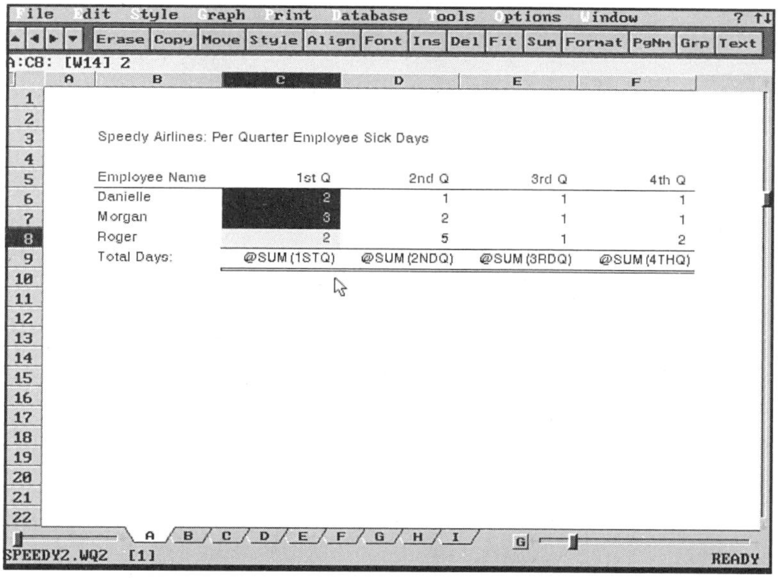

TIP

Fig. 4.12

Quattro Pro substitutes a name for a cell block address.

Each time you create a name, Quattro Pro stores the name with the active notebook. After you create the first name on each notebook or each time you modify an existing name, Quattro Pro shows a dialog box that displays a list of stored names for the active notebook. Only the amount of memory your PC has limits the number of names you can create for a notebook.

Deleting Names

When you modify and update notebooks, you sometimes must delete names. To remove a stored name from a notebook, use the **D**elete command.

If you delete the rows or columns that contain a named cell block, Quattro Pro keeps the name but removes its cell block assignment. If you delete a name assigned to a cell block, Quattro Pro removes the name from the block names list and redisplays the block address in each formula that originally contained the name.

TIP

> When you press F2 to edit a formula containing a name, Quattro Pro displays the cell addresses rather than the stored name on the input line so that you immediately know to which cells the name refers. In EDIT mode, the status line displays the formula with the block name.

To delete a cell block name, follow these steps:

1. Choose /**E**dit **N**ames **D**elete. Quattro Pro displays the block names list and prompts you for a block name (see fig. 4.13).

2. Type a valid name, use the mouse to highlight the block, or press the arrow keys until you highlight the block you want to delete.

TIP

> When you create more block names than Quattro Pro can display on the block names list, you can press F2 and enter a search string. Quattro Pro displays a `Search For *` message on the status line. Press as many letters as necessary to identify the block name. Press Enter to move the highlight bar to the first name on the list that matches the search string. You also can press F3 to expand the block names list to a full-screen display and press the plus sign (+) to display the cell or block of cells for each name.

3. Press Enter.

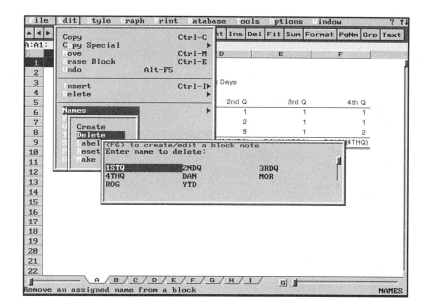

Fig. 4.13

Using the **D**elete command to remove a cell block name.

Adding Notes to Named Blocks

Quattro Pro enables you to add notes to named blocks of data. After you name a block and create a corresponding note, the note appears above the list of block names when the block name list is displayed and the respective block name is highlighted.

You must name a block before you can add a note to it.

NOTE

Use block name notes to remind yourself and others about the information in your notebooks. Notes are helpful particularly for training new users about how macros in a notebook application are designed to work (see fig. 4.14). See Chapter 15, "Creating Macros," for details on how to work with macros.

Fig. 4.14

Adding a block name
note.

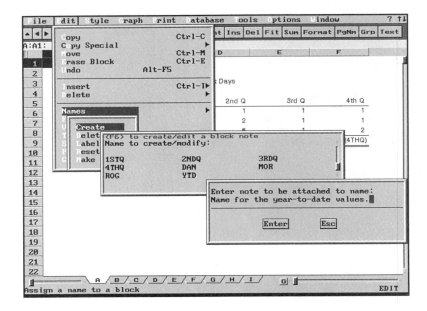

To add a note to a block name, follow these steps:

1. Choose /**Edit N**ames **C**reate.

2. Highlight the block name to which you want to add a note.

3. Press F6 to display a note entry box. Quattro Pro prompts you to
   enter the note you want attached to the name.

4. Type the note and press Enter.

TIP

Name   You also can add notes to named blocks by clicking the
Name button on the EDIT mode SpeedBar, highlighting the
named block to which you want to add a note, and then pressing F6.

Notes can be up to 72 characters long, but Quattro Pro displays only as
many characters as can fit on the line containing the note.

To edit an existing block note, follow these steps:

1. Choose /**Edit N**ames **C**reate.

2. Highlight the block name for the notes you want to edit and then
   press F6. Quattro Pro displays your previously typed note.

3. Make any changes to the note and press Enter.

To delete a note from a block name but to keep the block name, follow these steps:

1. Choose /**E**dit **N**ames **C**reate.

2. Highlight the block name for the note you want to delete and then press F6.

3. Press Ctrl+Backspace and then press Enter.

Using Labels To Create Names

The **L**abels command quickly creates names for rows and columns of data. This command is useful when you want to use labels on a notebook as the names for a group of values appearing in adjacent cells.

The **L**abels command also is useful if you want to create names for the values in cell block G5..G9 by using the labels appearing in adjacent cell block F5..F9 (see fig. 4.15). Here, Quattro Pro assigns the name Sector 1 to cell G5, Sector 2 to cell G6, Sector 3 to cell G7, and so on.

The **L**abels command is similar to the **C**reate command, except that **L**abels operates only on a group of cells appearing in two adjacent columns or rows.

To create names from the labels shown in figure 4.15, follow these steps:

1. Make cell F5 active, press Shift+F7 to enter EXT mode, and then use the arrow keys to highlight cell F9. Alternatively, use the mouse to highlight the block.

2. Choose /**E**dit **N**ames **L**abels.

3. Choose the **R**ight option, which describes the relative location of the cells to the labels.

Quattro Pro assigns each label name in column F to the corresponding value in column G.

Fig. 4.15

Creating names with the **L**abels command.

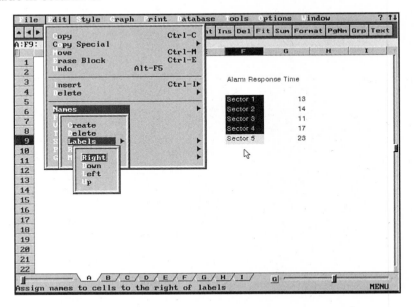

Resetting Cell Block Names

The **R**eset command is like the **D**elete command, except that **R**eset operates on all names in the active notebook. Suppose that you assign 20 names using the **L**abels command. Later, you decide to change the names of the notebook labels. Before you use the **L**abels command to assign new names to the notebook, delete all the old names and start with a clean slate.

To delete all names from the notebook, choose the **R**eset command on the /**E**dit **N**ames menu. When you choose this command, Quattro Pro displays the prompt Delete all block names? Press **N**o to cancel the operation or **Y**es to erase all names from the notebook.

Making a Table of Names

As you build more sophisticated notebooks, using names instead of numbers makes creating and remembering formulas much easier. The formula @SUM(EXPENSE), for example, comes to mind more easily than the formula @SUM(F12..F15). If you frequently use names, you must know how to review all stored names quickly. You can use the **M**ake Table command to copy a list of the current notebook's names, their cell block assignments, and any notes you may have added onto the active notebook in a location that you specify.

Be careful not to overwrite data on the notebook when you execute this command. When determining where to place the table, remember that Quattro Pro requires three columns—one for names, one for cell block assignments, one for block notes—and as many rows as names (see fig. 4.16).

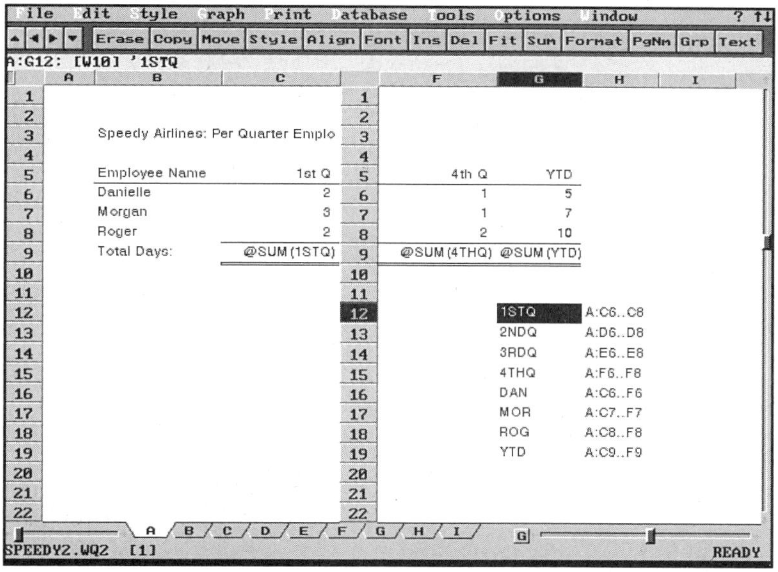

Fig. 4.16

The **M**ake Table command copies cell block names to a designated location.

To make the table of names shown in this figure, follow these steps:

1. Make cell G12 the active cell.

2. Choose /**E**dit **N**ames **M**ake Table.

3. Press Enter to copy the table into the active notebook, beginning in cell G12.

Keep a table of cell block names somewhere in the notebook. When you add or change a name, choose the **M**ake Table command to update your list, because Quattro Pro doesn't perform automatic updates.

Quattro Pro also enables you to view stored names on-screen while you build or edit formulas. To view stored names, follow these steps:

1. In EDIT mode, place the edit cursor next to an open parenthesis or a comma that follows a cell address, or enter a plus sign (+) to begin a formula.

2. Press F3. Quattro Pro displays the block names list (see fig. 4.17).

Fig. 4.17

Displaying a block names list.

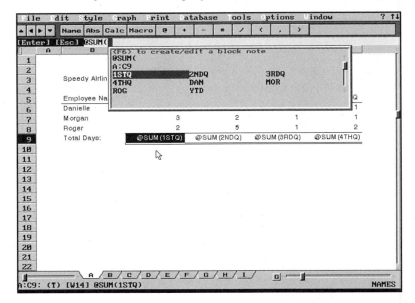

3. Press the Expand key (+) to see the block coordinates for each block name (see fig. 4.18). Press the Contract key (–) to remove this display from your screen.

4. Press F3 again. Quattro Pro displays an expanded version of the stored names.

5. Press Esc to return to the notebook.

Using Names in Formulas

You know that you can substitute names for cell blocks in formulas. Figure 4.17 shows @function commands that contain names instead of cell block coordinates. To create the formula shown in cell C9, follow these steps:

1. Make cell C9 the active cell.

2. Type **@SUM(** and press F3 to display the block names list.

3. Highlight 1STQ on the list.

4. Press Enter to copy the name to the right of the open parenthesis on the input line.

5. Type **)** and press Enter to store the formula in cell C9.

You can use this method to build formulas as long as you define the block names first. If you already know the block name you want to include in the formula, type the name into the formula.

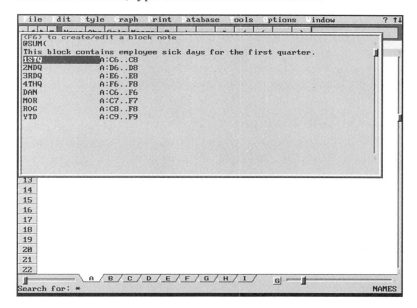

Fig. 4.18

Displaying the block names list with the active block name notes.

FOR RELATED INFORMATION

▶▶ "Understanding Command Syntax," p. 250.
How to use block names instead of block addresses in Quattro Pro's @function commands.

▶▶ "Using Multiple Sort Keys," p. 634.
"Defining the Search Block," p. 640.
How to use block names to simplify the process of sorting and searching for information in a database created in a Quattro Pro notebook.

▶▶ "Naming a Macro," p. 719.
How block names come into play with a Quattro Pro macro.

Filling a Block with Numbers

When you use a notebook as a reporting tool, you probably order your data according to date, transaction number, or invoice number. The /Edit Fill command simplifies the process of entering a large number of sequential values onto a notebook. By using this command, you can enter numbers, formulas, and dates.

To create a check register, for example, use the /Edit Fill command to assign a unique number to each transaction. You also can use the Fill command to create a series of incremental dates.

In a fill operation, the *start value* is the value that Quattro Pro places in the first cell of the destination block. The *step value* is the amount by which Quattro Pro increases or decreases the series values. The *stop value* is the value that Quattro Pro places in the last cell of the destination block.

To fill a cell block with numbers, follow these steps:

1. Choose /Edit Fill. Quattro Pro highlights the active cell as the default destination cell block.

2. Enter a new destination cell block, use the mouse to highlight the cell block, or press the arrow keys to extend the current block. Then press Enter.

3. Enter a start value and then press Enter. If you are entering sequential dates, press Ctrl+D, type a start date (in the form *mm/dd/yy*), and then press Enter.

NOTE

Because Quattro Pro stores dates in serial number form, you must keep two things in mind. First, choose a stop value that is greater than the date serial number (a value greater than 40,000 works well). Second, after you fill a group of cells with date serial numbers, choose /**S**tyle **N**umeric Format **D**ate and format the numbers to display as dates.

4. Enter a step value and press Enter.

5. Enter a stop value and press Enter.

If you define a destination cell block with two or more columns, Quattro Pro fills in each row in the first column before entering data into the second column, and so on. You also can fill numbers in ascending and descending order by altering the step value (see fig. 4.19).

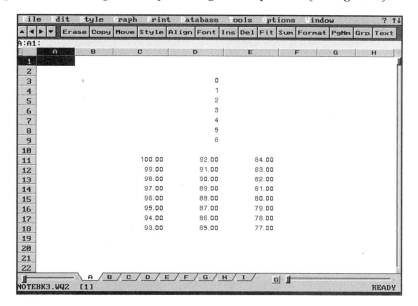

Fig. 4.19

Filling in cell blocks with ascending and descending numbers.

The data appearing in D3..D9 in figure 4.19 shows the results of filling a single column with sequentially increasing numbers. Here, the start value is 0, the step value is 1, and the stop value is 6.

The data appearing in C11..E18 in figure 4.19 shows the results of filling multiple columns with sequentially decreasing numbers. Here, the start value is 100, the step value is –1, and the stop value is 77. First, Quattro Pro fills values into C11..C18. Then, beginning in cell D11, the program fills values into D11..D18. Finally, Quattro Pro fills values into E11..E18.

NOTE

When the block you are filling is a 3-D cell block, Quattro Pro fills the first page with as many values as will fit in the cell block on that page, and then continues filling values into the same cell block on the second page. When that cell block is filled, Quattro Pro moves to the third page, the fourth page, and so on, until all selected pages are filled with values.

Changing Formulas to Values

The /Edit Values command converts a formula into the result, displays the result as a numerical value, and erases the original formula from the notebook. Although the need for this kind of operation may not be obvious, the **Values** command plays an important part in the process of maintaining and modifying your notebook applications.

Notebook formulas calculate answers to problems such as, "What is the value of cell C10 plus the value of cell C11?" If you create a formula that produces one answer, and the answer probably will not change, convert the formula to this value. If the value of C10 plus the value of C11 equals 10 and probably always will equal 10, for example, convert the formula +C10+C11 to the value 10. This conversion frees memory for Quattro Pro to use for other areas of the notebook in which you have ongoing calculations because it releases a cell's dependence on other cells. In this example, you can delete the contents of C10 or C11 without affecting the value 10.

Formulas also pinpoint important relationships among two or more variables such as, "What is the ratio of profits to sales for 1992?" You can use one notebook to process your yearly financial data and another to record year-end historical data. The ratio information appears on a second historical report listing key financial ratios. Because last year's financial data definitely isn't going to change this year, transfer the ratios as values to the second notebook.

To change formulas to values, follow these steps:

1. Make the first cell in the target block active, press Shift+F7 to enter EXT mode, and then use the arrow keys to highlight the last cell in the source block. Alternatively, use the mouse to highlight the block.

2. Choose /Edit Values. Quattro Pro records the location of the source block.

3. Move the selector to the first cell in the destination block.

4. Press Enter to copy the formula results as values into the destination cell block.

Transposing Data in a Cell Block

Another way to manipulate data on a Quattro Pro notebook is by using *transposition*. When you transpose notebook data, you switch the organization of your column and row data. This command is useful after you create a notebook application and decide that the data makes more sense if organized differently.

Figure 4.20 displays an original and a transposed cell block. Notice that the current column width doesn't accommodate the transposed data.

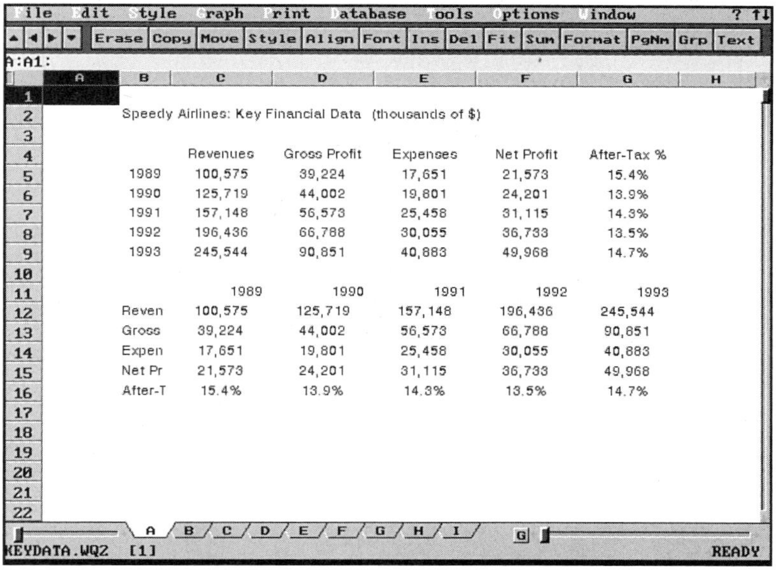

	Revenues	Gross Profit	Expenses	Net Profit	After-Tax %
1989	100,575	39,224	17,651	21,573	15.4%
1990	125,719	44,002	19,801	24,201	13.9%
1991	157,148	56,573	25,458	31,115	14.3%
1992	196,436	66,788	30,055	36,733	13.5%
1993	245,544	90,851	40,883	49,968	14.7%

	1989	1990	1991	1992	1993
Reven	100,575	125,719	157,148	196,436	245,544
Gross	39,224	44,002	56,573	66,788	90,851
Expen	17,651	19,801	25,458	30,055	40,883
Net Pr	21,573	24,201	31,115	36,733	49,968
After-T	15.4%	13.9%	14.3%	13.5%	14.7%

Fig. 4.20

Transposing cell blocks to switch the column and row organization.

Suppose that you want to transpose the contents of cell block B4..G9 into cell B11 in figure 4.20. To do so, follow these steps:

1. Choose /**E**dit **T**ranspose. Quattro Pro prompts you for the source block of cells.

2. Type **B4..G9** and press Enter. Quattro Pro prompts you for the destination cell.

3. Type **B11**, or enter another destination cell block at least one column to the right or one row below the source cell block.

4. Press Enter to transpose information into the destination cell block.

NOTE

When you transpose a 3-D cell block, Quattro Pro transposes each page individually. Information *doesn't* get transposed from one page to another page.

Use the following guidelines to ensure that your cell block data transposes correctly:

- When transposing formatted cell data, you generally should execute the /**E**dit **T**ranspose command before formatting your notebook column width. If you already have formatted your notebook's column width, your transposed data probably doesn't fit neatly into the current cell widths. Press Ctrl+W to change the column widths until all transposed data appears.

- Be sure to transpose a cell block to a different part of the notebook. If you try to transpose a cell block onto itself, Quattro Pro loses the column and row organization and shows a block of garbled numbers. After executing the /**E**dit **T**ranspose command, you can move or copy the transposed block anywhere on the notebook.

- If you try to transpose relative reference formulas, the formulas adjust incorrectly and don't refer to the correct cell addresses. You have two options when you want to transpose blocks containing formulas: change all relative references into absolute references and edit them after transposition; or use the /**E**dit **V**alues command to convert cell block formulas to computed values.

- When you transpose a block of cells, preselect the cell block before choosing the command.

Searching for and Replacing Data

After you enter, edit, display, reorganize, insert, delete, and transpose your notebook data, you may need to search quickly through a large application, replacing letters and numbers with new or updated data. You need Quattro Pro's **S**earch & Replace command.

To use **S**earch & Replace, you must tell Quattro Pro what to look for, where to look, and with what to replace the searched-for item. If you need to create specialized search conditions, you can define the search operation further by setting the commands found in the Options section of the Search & Replace submenu.

Figure 4.21 shows the mission statement for Speedy Airlines. A quick review of this document reveals that a few crucial phrases have been omitted. You can use the Search & Replace command to insert the missing phrases.

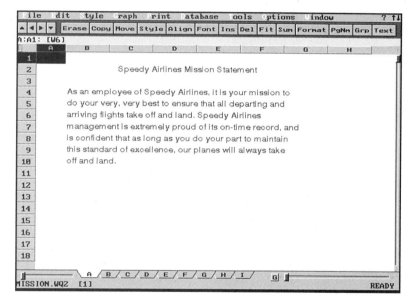

Fig. 4.21

Speedy Airlines' mission statement.

Setting the Search Parameters

With the Search & Replace command, you quickly can update key label descriptions, revise out-of-date numbers, and alter the structure of your notebook formulas. You have complete flexibility to devise the scope of a search-and-replace operation because Quattro Pro enables you to define the parameters explained in the following sections and found on the Search & Replace submenu (see fig. 4.22).

Choosing a Block

By default, Quattro Pro scans the entire notebook for your search data. For large notebook applications, you should restrict the search area to minimize the potential search time.

Fig. 4.22

Settings for Speedy Airlines' search-and-replace operation.

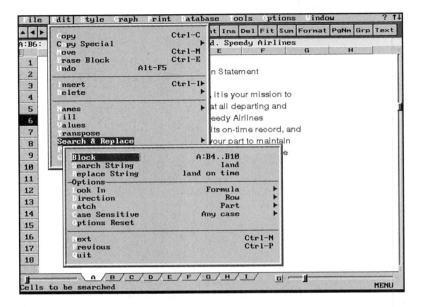

Suppose that you want to search the text appearing in cell block B4..B10 on the active page. To do so, follow these steps:

1. Choose /**E**dit **S**earch & Replace **B**lock.

2. Type **B4..B10** or highlight the block with your keyboard or mouse.

3. Press Enter to store the cell block.

Quattro Pro returns to the **S**earch & Replace submenu so that you can make other choices.

Entering a Search String

A crucial phrase, *on time*, is missing from two sentences in Speedy's mission statement. In both sentences, *land* is the last word after which *on time* should be added; *land*, therefore, becomes the search string.

To enter *land* as the search string, follow these steps:

1. Choose **S**earch String.

2. Type **land** as the search string.

3. Press Enter to store the string.

Quattro Pro returns to the **S**earch & Replace submenu so that you can make other choices.

Entering a Replacement String

To use *land on time* as the replacement string, follow these steps:

1. Choose **R**eplace String.

2. Enter *land on time* as the replacement string.

3. Press Enter to store the string.

Quattro Pro returns to the **S**earch & Replace submenu so that you can make other choices.

Executing the Search Operation

The minimum information needed to execute a search-and-replace operation is the search-and-replace string. With this data, Quattro Pro can begin scanning the notebook. Choose **N**ext from the **S**earch & Replace submenu, and Quattro Pro locates the first occurrence of the string. When Quattro Pro locates a valid matching string, it highlights the string on the notebook. Then the program displays the prompt shown in figure 4.23.

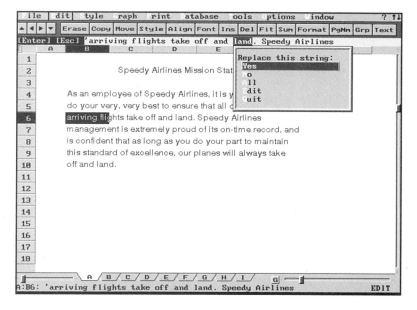

Fig. 4.23

Quattro Pro's prompt to replace the string.

Choose **Yes** to replace the string, **No** not to replace the current string, **All** to replace the current string and all other matching strings without further prompting, **Edit** to edit the current string, or **Quit** to cancel the operation without replacing the current string.

Choose **All** for the Speedy Airlines example to replace both occurrences of the string without further prompting.

> **TIP**
>
> Choose **E**dit to display the located text on the input line, where you can type a different replacement string. Press Enter to store the new data in the cell.

After Quattro Pro finishes the search-and-replace operation, the program returns to the active notebook and makes the first cell address in the defined block (B4) the active cell (see fig. 4.24).

Fig. 4.24

The revised mission statement for Speedy Airlines.

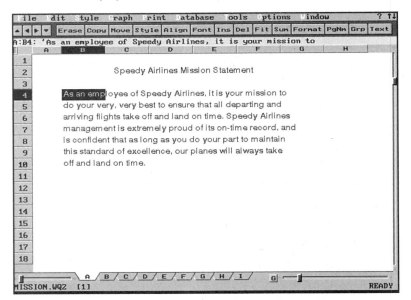

Using Special Search Parameters

The Options area in the middle of the **S**earch & Replace submenu contains the following five special parameters that you can use to delineate further how Quattro Pro evaluates your notebook data in a search-and-replace operation (refer to fig. 4.22):

- Choose **Look** In to tell Quattro Pro to review each **F**ormula or **V**alue, or to set a search string **C**ondition, such as all cell values equal to 100 (? = 100).

- Choose **D**irection to indicate that Quattro Pro should search by **R**ow or **C**olumn.

- Choose **M**atch to tell Quattro Pro whether to locate a search string as part of a **W**hole string or as **P**art of any string containing the search string.

- Choose **C**ase Sensitive to tell Quattro Pro whether to look for a string whose capitalization exactly matches the search string (**E**xact Case) or to accept **A**ny Case.

- Choose **O**ptions Reset to erase all the settings that Quattro Pro stores on the right side of the **S**earch & Replace submenu. Quattro Pro returns to the default search-and-replace settings.

Managing Pages

Quattro Pro provides two commands on the Edit menu for managing the pages in a notebook. The **P**age command enables you to create unique page names, which display on the page tabs. You also can move pages in a notebook with this command. The **G**roup command is used to create and delete page groups, as well as enable and disable Group mode.

Naming a Page

When creating a multipage notebook application, creating plain-English names for each page in a group can be useful. Names such as Sales, Expenses, and Budget are more memorable than A, GZ, or DX. And because Quattro Pro uses page names in 3-D cell block references and in formulas, working with these program features becomes simpler as well.

A page name can consist of a maximum of 15 characters with no spaces. You can use letters and numbers in the name, as well as any of the following characters:

    ~ ' ! % _ | \ ` ?

Page names must be unique in a notebook. You can create two-word names by separating each word with one of these characters, as in the name SALES_1993. To name a page, use the following steps:

1. Activate the page whose name you want to change.

2. Choose /**E**dit **P**age **N**ame. Quattro Pro displays a dialog box with the current name of the page.

3. Press the Backspace key until the current name is deleted.

4. Type in a new name for the page.

5. Press Enter.

Quattro Pro displays the new page name in the page tab and adjusts any formulas in the current notebook that refer to the page by name.

Moving a Page

Quattro Pro enables you to shuffle the position of pages in a notebook. Changing page position is helpful when you want to put the most-often used pages toward the front of a notebook or when you want to arrange several pages consecutively so that you can create a new page group. You can move pages in a notebook in two ways: by dragging and dropping, or by using the keyboard.

The drag-and-drop feature enables you to use your mouse to move pages. To move page D between pages Z and AA, for example, click and drag the page D tab to the right. Notice that the tab becomes a white outline. Now drag the tab until it rests atop the page AA tab, and then release the mouse button. Quattro Pro inserts page D before page AA—in effect, renaming page D as page Z.

TIP

> You can move two or more consecutive pages by clicking the first tab, holding the Shift key down, and then clicking the last page tab. After Quattro Pro puts a black line below each tab, click and drag any tab in the group to the target location, and then release the mouse button.

The second method is accomplished using your keyboard. To move page D between Z and AA, for example, use the following steps:

1. Choose /**E**dit **P**age **M**ove.

2. Type the name of the page to move, followed by a colon. For this example, type **D:** and press Enter.

3. Type the name of the page in front of which you want to move the page, followed by a colon. For this example, type **AA:** and press Enter.

Quattro Pro moves page D between pages Z and AA.

Creating Page Groups

Page groups offer the most efficient way to develop notebook applications that contain two or more similarly designed pages. When you create a page group and then enable Group mode, you can drill entries into the same cell in every page in the group, change column widths and row heights for all pages, and edit and modify the structure of all pages using the **E**dit menu commands. See Chapter 3, "Entering and Editing Data," for full details about drilling entries into a page group.

Suppose that you want to create a quarterly budget for your department. The revenue and expense headings and cell formulas are essentially the same for each report—only the period descriptions and the budget numbers themselves are different. By grouping four pages together, you can create the framework of the budget report once on page A and have the same report structure instantly appear on pages B, C, and D.

To create a page group, follow these steps:

1. Choose the /**E**dit **G**roup **C**reate command.

2. Type a name for your page group. You can use any combination of letters, numbers, and the following characters:

    ~ ' ! % _ | \ ` ?

    You cannot begin the name with a space or the underscore character, nor can you use spaces anywhere in the name. For this example, type **BUDGET93** and press Enter.

3. Type the name of the first page you want to include in the group. For this example, type **A** and press Enter.

4. Type the name of the last page you want to include in the group. For this example, type **D** and press Enter.

| Grp |

You also can use the Grp button on the READY mode SpeedBar to create a group. The same prompts appear as though you selected the /Edit **G**roup **C**reate command.

To activate Group mode so that you can begin entering data into a page group, choose the /Edit **G**roup **M**ode command. Then select the **E**nable option and press Enter.

TIP

The shortcut key for activating and deactivating group mode is Ctrl+F5. The quickest way to activate and deactivate Group mode is to click the little Group button on the status line.

When Group mode is activated and you are in WYSIWYG display mode, Quattro Pro draws a blue line below the tabs for each page in the group. In text display mode, an double underscore (__) connects the page names, which appear on a single page tab.

To deactivate Group mode, click the Group button on the status line a second time, choose /Edit **G**roup **M**ode **D**isable, or press Ctrl+F5 again.

Questions & Answers

This chapter has introduced you to the fundamental Quattro Pro cell block operations and notebook sculpting techniques. If you have questions about any topics covered in this chapter, scan the following sections.

Copying, Moving, and Erasing Cell Data

Q: When do you preselect a cell block?

A: You can preselect cells before choosing any Quattro Pro menu command that performs an operation on a block. If you use a mouse, always preselect cells. If you execute commands from your keyboard, whether you preselect depends on how quickly you can extend a block in EXT mode.

Q: Why did a formula's result change when I copied it to a different part of the notebook?

A: You should have used **M**ove rather than **C**opy. When you move a formula, Quattro Pro doesn't adjust the formula's cell references or change the result. When you copy a formula, Quattro Pro adjusts the cell references in the formula, unless you previously changed the formula to all absolute references.

Q: Why did my formulas display ERR after I moved a cell on the notebook?

A: You probably wrote over data in a cell referenced by other formulas on the active notebook. If you cause one cell to display ERR and that cell's address appears in other notebook formulas, the other formulas also display ERR.

If Undo is enabled, press Alt+F5 to undo the operation and choose a new destination cell for the **M**ove operation. If Undo is disabled, re-enter the overwritten cell data. ERR then disappears, and your formulas display valid results again.

Inserting and Deleting Columns and Rows

Q: Why can't I insert a column or row on my active notebook?

A: Quattro Pro cannot insert a column or row when data is in the last column or row of the notebook; the program has no room.

Q: What do I do if I deleted a column or row containing data I need, and my notebook is displaying ERR everywhere?

A: You deleted a column or row containing a cell block coordinate being used in your notebook formulas.

If Undo is enabled, press Alt+F5 to Undo the operation. If Undo is disabled, insert a column or row at the original point of deletion and re-enter the lost data. Next, replace the ERR portion of the formula with the appropriate cell address (the address of the cell you accidentally deleted). Your formulas now will display valid results.

Naming Cell Blocks

Q: Why won't one of my notebook formulas accept a block name that I created?

A: If you create a name for a block of cells and try to use that name in certain mathematical operations, Quattro Pro displays an error message saying that the block is invalid.

If BLOCK is the name for C5..C10, for example, and you try to enter the formula **+BLOCK+25**, Quattro Pro displays an error message. A cell block name describes an area but doesn't compute a value unless you tell the block name to do so. The same formula is valid when you include BLOCK in an @function command, such as @SUM(BLOCK)+25, for example.

Q: When I copied a named block in the notebook, Quattro Pro didn't copy the block name. Why?

A: Quattro Pro doesn't enable you to duplicate block names on the same notebook. In a copy operation, when the source cell block is also a named block, Quattro Pro copies only the cell data to the destination cell block. The block name remains assigned to the source cell block. The only way to transfer a block name from one part of the notebook to another is to use /**E**dit **M**ove and relocate the cell block.

Q: I used /**E**dit Names **L**abels to create cell block names for a row of data, but when I used the name in a formula, the program didn't return the correct answer. Why?

A: The **L**abels command assigns a name to only one adjacent cell in the direction you specify on the **L**abels submenu. Use the **C**reate command to name a cell block.

Q: Why did nothing happen when I pressed F3 to display a list of stored names for the active notebook?

A: You can display a block names list during two types of Quattro Pro operations: when you are in EDIT mode and the cursor is next to an open parenthesis, a comma, or a mathematical operator (such as + or –); or when you are in POINT mode and Quattro Pro is prompting you for a cell block. When you press F5, the GoTo key, for example, Quattro Pro prompts you to type a cell block. Press F3 to view a list of all names assigned to cell blocks for the notebook.

Filling, Transposing, Searching for, and Replacing Data

Q: Why does Quattro Pro display decimal or negative numbers when I try to fill a cell block with dates?

A: Quattro Pro is evaluating your start value (for example, 10/10/89 or 10-10-89) as a formula. To use this feature properly, press Ctrl+D after you enter the destination cell block and before you enter the start value.

Q: When I transposed a cell block on the notebook, why did Quattro Pro display 0's and ERRs?

A: Your original cell block probably contains formulas. Quattro Pro cannot transpose relative reference formulas correctly. Change the references to an absolute format and edit them after the operation. You also can convert the formulas to their calculated values using /**E**dit **V**alues before choosing /**E**dit **T**ranspose.

Q: Why is Quattro Pro not finding a search string that I know exists on my notebook?

A: Review your option settings on the **S**earch & Replace submenu. You may have specified the wrong **M**atch or **C**ase Sensitive option.

Summary

Chapter 4 explains how to copy, move, and erase cells and blocks of cells on the Quattro Pro notebook. You also learned how to modify an application's organization by adding and deleting columns, rows, and pages. Special cell block operations, such as converting formulas to values, filling in cell blocks with sequential numbers, and searching for and replacing data on the notebook also were discussed.

Having read this chapter, you should understand the following Quattro Pro concepts:

- Preselecting cell blocks on which to perform operations

- Copying one cell into another or into many cells

- Moving one cell or a block of cells to another part of the notebook or to another page in the notebook

- Erasing cells and cell blocks

- Reversing Quattro Pro operations with the **U**ndo command

- Inserting and deleting multiple rows, columns, row blocks, column blocks, and pages

- Creating text names for cell blocks

- Using cell block names in formulas

- Converting formulas to their values, filling a cell block with sequential numbers, and transposing column and row data

- Searching for and replacing data on a notebook

In Chapter 5, you learn how to add the finishing touches to your notebook applications using Quattro Pro's **S**tyle menu commands. The commands on this menu help you fine-tune your notebook data. Choose options from Quattro Pro's **S**tyle menu when you need to display numbers as dollars or percentages, align data in a cell, draw a line around a cell, change fonts, and add shading so that you can create a final, presentation-quality report for an important meeting.

Formatting Data

Although the discussion so far has centered on Quattro Pro's usefulness as a calculating tool, the inherent power of any electronic spreadsheet program lies in its capability to store and remember numerical and formula relationships.

This chapter introduces techniques that enable you to expand the usefulness of a Quattro Pro notebook by turning the notebook into a presentation-quality reporting tool. Although much of the chapter talks about how to create reports that look good, you don't lose sight of the notebook's important role as a mathematical tool.

This chapter introduces you to the 13 **S**tyle menu commands. The commands are organized into three groups: cell-formatting commands, column- and row-adjustment commands, and presentation-quality commands.

The discussion also focuses on how to realign data in a cell; choose the appropriate format for values, labels, dates, and times; and protect important cell data. The chapter continues by showing how to widen and narrow column widths, manage blocks of columns, enlarge and shrink row heights, and hide column data temporarily from prying eyes.

The final section in Chapter 5 examines how to turn a basic notebook application into a presentation-quality report. You learn how to draw lines and boxes around cells to highlight critical data, add shading to cell blocks, use multiple fonts, and insert page breaks to control report printing. You also learn how to create customized styles, apply them to cell blocks on a notebook, and save them in a file for future use.

As you read this chapter, keep two things in mind. First, preselecting cells simplifies the use of Quattro Pro menu commands, because when you preselect a cell block, you can perform multiple operations on that block without having to respecify the block each time. Preselect cells when you use the **S**tyle menu commands because this method is the most efficient for formatting and creating your reports. Second, when formatting the style of similarly designed pages in a notebook, be sure to group the pages and enable Group mode. That way, any formatting done to one page in the group will be done to all pages in the group.

Using Style Menu Commands

After you build the basic form of a notebook application, you can use this form or enhance its appearance to call attention to and clarify important points. Quattro Pro's **S**tyle menu enables you to add stylistic effects to your notebook applications. You can draw, for example, a box around text and values so that they stand out on-screen, draw double lines under financial statement figures, and shade and protect important cell data.

Quattro Pro enables you to use different typefaces to give your reports and graphs a professional look. You may want to select a large Swiss font for a report title; a medium-sized, boldfaced Sans Serif font for the secondary titles and headings; and a smaller, italicized font for account names or other descriptions. You can change the width of a column or a block of columns, or hide columns containing private data. You also can enlarge and shrink the height of a row or a block of rows to accommodate large-sized fonts or to create special effects.

By using the **S**tyle menu commands, you can mold basic notebooks into creative and informative reports and graphs. (See Chapters 10 and 11 for more information on creating and annotating graphs.)

You can use the 13 **S**tyle menu commands shown in figure 5.1 to fine-tune and enhance your notebook's data display. The **S**tyle menu commands are organized roughly in the order that you should use them during a work session. When you align and format cell data, you sometimes must change the column width so that the formatted data fits into a cell. You then add the final stylistic touches—such as lines, shading, and custom fonts—and even define and apply customized styles of grouped attributes. Table 5.1 explains the **S**tyle menu commands.

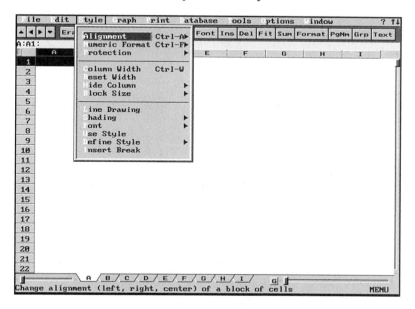

Fig. 5.1

The **S**tyle menu.

Table 5.1 Style Menu Commands

Command	Description
Alignment	Aligns data at the left or right edge, in the center of a cell, or back to the default (**G**eneral)
Numeric Format	Formats the notebook display of values, dates, and times
Protection	Protects and unprotects cell data on the active notebook
Column Width	Widens and narrows the width of the active column
Reset Width	Resets the width of the active column to the default column width setting
Hide Column	Hides columns on the active notebook
Block Size	Widens, narrows, and resets the width and height of multiple columns and rows

(continues)

Table 5.1 Continued

Command	Description
Line Drawing	Draws and removes lines and boxes of various thicknesses around cells
Shading	Adds gray or black shading to notebook cells and removes shading from cells
Font	Assigns different fonts and font styles to cells to enhance printouts
Use Style	Applies a customized style to a cell block
Define Style	Creates, erases, and removes customized styles; saves and retrieves customized styles
Insert Break	Inserts a page break at the selector's location

Undoing Style Menu Commands

Pressing Alt+F5 reverses Quattro Pro notebook operations such as copying, moving, and erasing blocks of data. This feature, however, cannot undo every Quattro Pro operation.

You cannot undo notebook formats created with the following Style menu commands: Alignment, Numeric Format, Protection, Column Width, Reset Width, Hide Column, and Block Size. You also cannot undo presentation-quality enhancements achieved with the Line Drawing, Font, and Shading commands.

You *can* undo data alignments created manually or alter these alignments when in EDIT mode. You also can undo a page break inserted with the Insert Break command. See the section "Using the Alt+F5 Undo Key" in Chapter 3 for full details about enabling and disabling Quattro Pro's Undo feature.

Changing the Default Global Settings

Quattro Pro initially uses global format settings to format your data entries. Quattro Pro uses these format settings each time you load a notebook. The program right-aligns values and left-aligns text in a cell, for example. Consider the income statement notebook shown in figure 5.2. The labels in C3..E3 are aligned with the global default setting. The labels in C10..E10 are right-aligned with the /**S**tyle **A**lignment command.

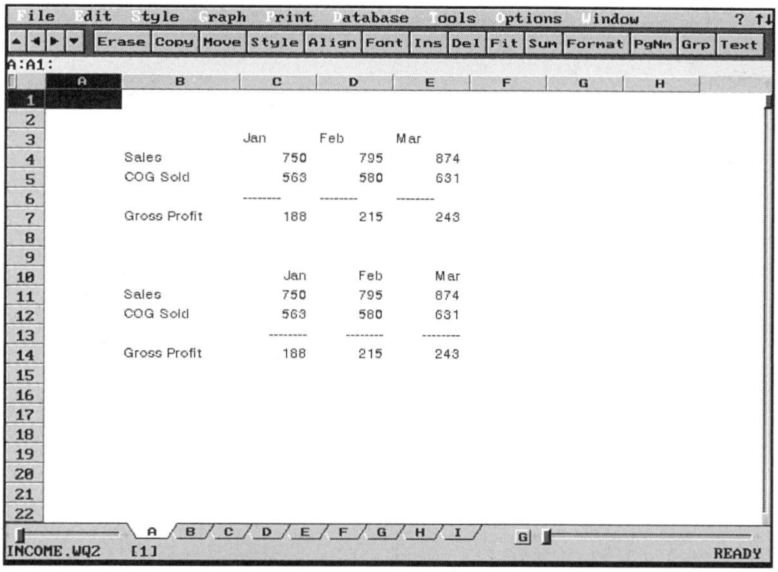

Fig. 5.2

Quattro Pro right-aligns values and left-aligns text by default.

To change one of the global format settings, choose /**O**ptions **F**ormats and choose a command from the submenu shown in figure 5.3. If you always want labels right-aligned in your notebooks, choose **A**lign Labels **R**ight. Quattro Pro uses that global label alignment setting from now on until you exit Quattro Pro.

You also can choose **N**umeric Format to change the global numeric format setting, **H**ide Zeros to tell Quattro Pro whether or not to display zero values on the notebook for the current work session, and **G**lobal Width to set the global column width to a new value.

To change the global currency symbol, punctuation method, or date-and-time settings to conform to international standards, choose /**O**ptions **I**nternational.

When you change any of Quattro Pro's global format settings, choose /**O**ptions **U**pdate before you end the current work session. The next time you load the program, the new default settings will be in effect. (See Chapter 16, "Customizing Quattro Pro," for complete coverage of the **O**ptions menu commands.)

Fig. 5.3

The /**O**ptions **F**ormats default settings.

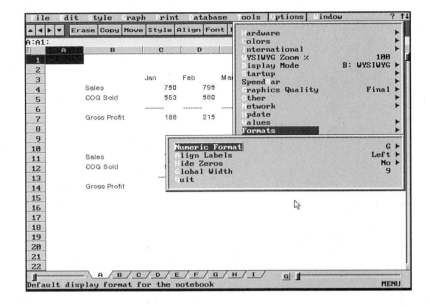

Hide Zeros isn't a global default that can be saved with /**O**ptions **U**p-date; you must set the setting to **Y**es each time you load the program.

FOR RELATED INFORMATION

◄◄ "Using the Alt+F5 Undo Key," p. 125.
How to enable Quattro Pro's Undo key.

►► "Specifying Format Options," p. 806.
All the commands and rules governing Quattro Pro's global notebook and page defaults.

Controlling Data Display

The first three commands on the **S**tyle menu control the display of data within a notebook cell and affect the appearance of data displayed in a printout. These commands enable you to realign data in a cell; format labels, values, dates, and times; and protect and unprotect data in a cell.

Aligning Data

If Quattro Pro didn't provide the capability to align cell data, your notebooks could look like a jumble of numbers and letters. The data shown in figure 5.4, for example, appears disorganized because it hasn't been formatted.

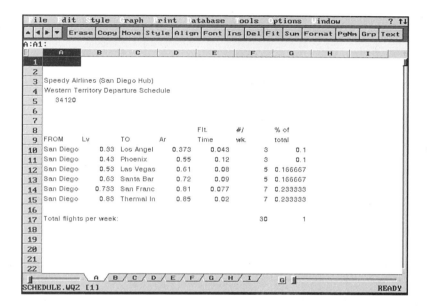

Fig. 5.4

An unformatted Quattro Pro notebook.

When you write a report by hand, you intuitively know how to space numbers, letters, words, and paragraphs so that they make sense. When you enter data into a notebook cell, Quattro Pro decides the type of data (value or label) and aligns that data according to predefined default global settings: labels are left-aligned in a cell, whereas values, dates, and times are right-aligned.

Selecting a New Alignment

Use the /Style **A**lignment command to alter the alignment of values, labels, dates, and times in a cell block. Quattro Pro displays a submenu with four choices: **G**eneral, **L**eft, **R**ight, and **C**enter.

In a typical notebook, report titles are center-aligned, column labels and data are right-aligned, and row headings usually are left-aligned.

The **G**eneral format (the default alignment setting) right-aligns values and dates and aligns labels according to the /**O**ptions **F**ormats **A**lign Labels setting.

To correct the confusing alignment of the data in figure 5.4, follow these steps:

1. Preselect cell block A3..G17.

2. Choose /**S**tyle **A**lignment.

TIP

Press Ctrl+A, the alignment shortcut key, to choose the /**S**tyle **A**lignment command.

3. Choose **L**eft from the submenu.

Quattro Pro aligns the data in each cell block. After your column data is aligned under a column heading, reviewing the report becomes easier. This operation is just the first of several that you perform in this chapter.

TIP

`Align` You also can click the Align button on the READY mode Speed- Bar to change a cell's alignment. When you click the button, Quattro Pro displays the /**S**tyle **A**lignment menu. Choose an alignment, highlight the block you want to align, and then click [Enter] on the input line. Remember, if you preselect the block you want to align before you click the Align button, you need to select only the alignment to complete the operation.

Selecting an Alignment Manually

You can change the alignment of a label in two ways without using the **A**lignment command. You can align a label by preceding it with one of the following label prefix characters:

Prefix	Description
'	Left-aligns text in a cell
"	Right-aligns text in a cell
^	Centers text in a cell
\	Repeats a character or group of characters in a cell until the character fills the entire cell

To center-align the label in cell E8, for example, follow these steps:

1. Make cell E8 active.

2. Type ^ (the caret label prefix).

3. Type the label on the input line.

4. Press Enter to center-align the label.

You also can alter an existing label's alignment while in EDIT mode. To realign the label from the preceding example, follow these steps:

1. Press F2 to edit cell E8.

2. Press Home. Quattro Pro moves the selector to the label prefix at the beginning of the entry.

3. Press Del to delete the prefix.

4. Type a new label prefix and press Enter to realign the label.

> Press Alt+F5 to undo either manual alignment operation.   **TIP**

You cannot adjust the alignment of a value manually because Quattro Pro doesn't store an alignment prefix with values. To align or realign a value, choose **A**lignment from the **S**tyle menu.

Formatting Values, Labels, Dates, and Times

Without the appropriate numeric format, you may not be able to tell whether a value is a percent, dollar, date, or time. Imagine receiving a bill from your credit card company and not knowing whether the bill is for $1,000 or $10.

With the /**S**tyle **N**umeric Format command, you can clarify the display of data on a notebook. By using this command, you can create a monetary value by adding a dollar sign and decimal point, and commas to numbers greater than 999. You also can tell Quattro Pro to display a formula instead of a value, add a percent sign to a financial ratio, or display a date and time in several different formats.

The **N**umeric Format command affects the way Quattro Pro *displays* a value, not how the program stores the value in a cell. To check this setting, pick any formatted cell and look at its value on the input line. You also can press F2 and look at the value on the status line.

Even if you format the number 25.7565 to display as 26, Quattro Pro uses 25.7565 in all calculations. Quattro Pro performs mathematical operations using entire numbers—not their abbreviated, on-screen equivalents.

Another way to change the display of a value is to use the @ROUND function command. The cell entry @ROUND(25.7565,0) rounds the value 25.7565 to 0 decimal places, which displays the value 26. In this case, Quattro Pro performs mathematical operations using the rounded value 26—not the value 25.7565. (Chapter 6, "Using Functions," covers @ROUND and other mathematical @function commands.)

TIP

Quattro Pro stores numbers with up to 16 significant digits. A *significant digit* is any integer except a leading zero. Quattro Pro doesn't count decimals, commas, dollar signs, and percent signs as part of the total.

Selecting the Appropriate Numeric Format

To convey a point clearly, you must choose the most appropriate numeric format for your data. Otherwise, your data can be confusing or completely useless. If you format a percentage as a date, for example, the information is useless. If you format a monetary value with commas and a decimal point but without a dollar sign, the information is incomplete.

When you format a cell, Quattro Pro displays a format code on the input line when the cell is active. This code includes a character that identifies the format and a number that indicates the displayed decimal places. The format code (F2), for example, indicates a fixed format with two decimal places.

Because the date-and-time formats don't use decimal places, the number in a date or time code reflects the option number on the **D**ate or **T**ime submenu.

Table 5.2 describes each format option available on the /**St**yle **N**umeric Format menu. Figure 5.5 displays numbers formatted with each format available on the **N**umeric Format submenu. Each cell's format code has been added to the right of the example.

Table 5.2 Numeric Formats

Format	Description
Fixed	Displays values with leading zeros and a user-specified number of decimal places
Scientific	Displays values in scientific notation form, such as 1.23E+03 for the number 1,230
Currency	Displays values with a currency symbol and commas to separate thousands; shows negative numbers in parentheses
, (comma)	Displays values with commas to separate thousands; shows negative numbers in parentheses
General	Displays numbers as they are entered
+/–	Transforms values into a horizontal bar graph in which + represents a positive integer, – represents a negative integer, and the decimal point (.) represents zero
Percent	Displays values as percentages
Date	Displays values in user-specified date-and-time formats; you can use five standard date-and-time formats and several international formats
Text	Displays formulas as text rather than results
Hidden	Conceals the display of value and label entries; when the cell is selected, entries still appear on the input line
User Defined	Applies a custom numeric format created with the /**St**yle **D**efine Style command
Reset	Returns the numeric format for this block to the default format (specified with the /**O**ptions **F**ormats Numeric Format command); reveals entries hidden with the **H**idden format

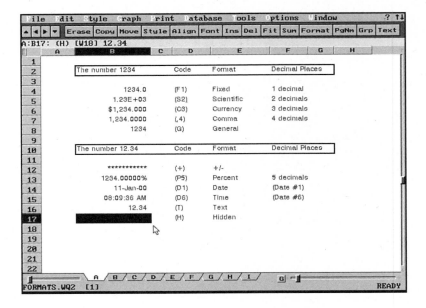

Formatting Values

When you enter a number into a cell, Quattro Pro displays the number using the **G**eneral format, which displays most numbers in the form you entered. In some cases—for example, when a value is longer than the width of its cell—Quattro Pro displays a rounded value.

Quattro Pro always rounds a decimal value that has an equal or greater number of digits than the width of the column in which the value is positioned. The program begins rounding with the last digit in the value. If you enter the decimal value 0.399 into a cell that is 5 characters wide, for example, Quattro Pro displays 0.4. If you enter 0.309 into a cell of the same width, Quattro Pro displays 0.31 (see fig. 5.6).

Quattro Pro always displays a whole value in scientific notation when the number of digits in the value is greater than the character width of the active column less 1 character. If you enter a value that is 7 characters long into an 8-character-wide column, for example, the value is displayed as a whole value. If you enter the whole value 3999999 into a cell 7 characters wide, Quattro Pro displays 4E+06—the scientific notation form for this value. When you enter this same whole value into a column with a width of 6 characters or less, Quattro Pro displays asterisks.

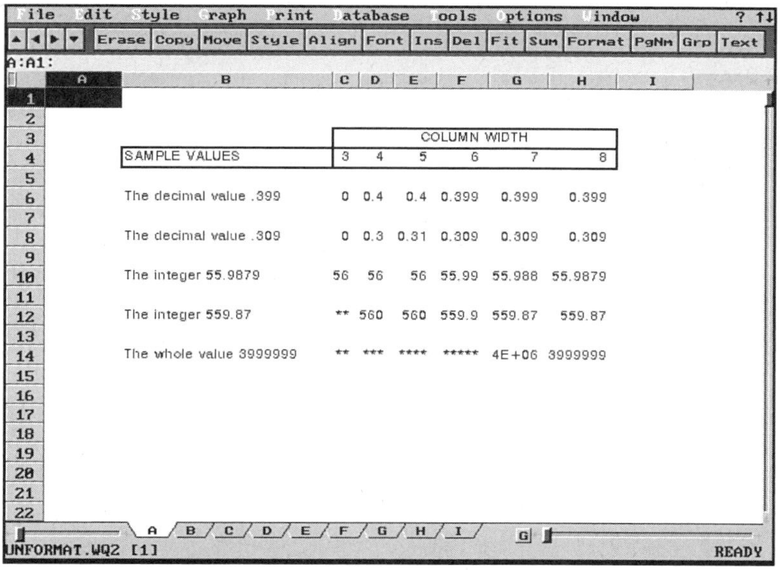

Fig. 5.6

Unformatted values in Quattro Pro.

> **TIP**
>
> When you use text display mode, Quattro Pro's rule for displaying whole values versus scientific notation versus asterisks in a cell is slightly different when you draw lines around a cell with the /**S**tyle **L**ine Drawing command. A drawn line uses up a space equal to one character width. If you draw a line on the left or right edge of a cell, take this extra space into account when determining an appropriate column width.

To format values on a notebook, follow these steps:

1. Preselect a cell block to format.

2. Choose /**S**tyle **N**umeric Format.

3. Choose a format option from the submenu.

4. If prompted, choose the number of decimal places to appear in numbers (from 0 to 15). Only the **F**ixed, **S**cientific, **,** (comma), **Cur**rency, and **P**ercent options display the decimal prompt.

5. Press Enter. Quattro Pro redisplays the numbers in the cell block using the selected format option.

Now that this cell block has a numeric format, you can edit or delete the cell block data without erasing the cell format. When you copy the formatted contents of a cell to another location on the notebook,

Quattro Pro duplicates the cell format in the new location. If you move the formatted contents of a cell, Quattro Pro actually removes the cell format from the source cell and relocates it to the destination cell.

TIP

Press Ctrl+F, the format shortcut key, to choose the /**S**tyle **N**umeric Format command.

Format

You also can click the Format button on the READY mode SpeedBar to display the **N**umeric Format submenu.

The format option you choose may attempt to display data wider than the width of the current cell block. When this situation happens, Quattro Pro fills the cell block with asterisks. To correct this display problem, press Ctrl+W and widen the column until the data reappears.

Hiding Data

The first nine **N**umeric Format options are intended to enhance the display of values, dates, and times. You can use the **H**idden option to remove the display of labels, values, dates, and times from your screen.

NOTE

When you hide cell data, Quattro Pro removes the data from view—but you still can overwrite the contents of a hidden cell. To prevent the accidental erasure of a hidden cell, see "Protecting Important Data" later in this chapter.

Formatting a label with any other **N**umeric Format command has no effect on the label. If you format a label using **C**urrency and two decimal places, for example, Quattro Pro continues to display the label in its original form, even though the input line displays (C2). If you replace the label with a value, the currency format takes effect for the value.

When the selector is in a hidden cell, Quattro Pro displays the cell contents on the input line. To reveal a hidden label, choose /**S**tyle **N**umeric Format **R**eset.

Formatting Dates

To enter a date value onto a Quattro Pro notebook, follow these steps:

1. Press Ctrl+D.

2. Enter a date using the exact form of date format 1, 2, or 3 (see table 5.3). You also can enter a date using formats 4 and 8, 5 and 9, 6 and 10, or 7 and 11 using the /**O**ptions International **D**ate command to choose one pair as the global format.

Table 5.3 Date Command Formats

Format	Type
1. DD-MMM-YY	Day, month, year
2. DD-MMM	Day, month
3. MMM-YY	Month, year
4. MM/DD/YY	Long international #1
5. DD/MM/YY	Long international #2
6. DD.MM.YY	Long international #3
7. YY-MM-DD	Long international #4
8. MM/DD	Short international #1
9. DD/MM	Short international #2
10. DD.MM	Short international #3
11. MM-DD	Short international #4

Another way to enter a date is to use a date @function command and then reformat the cell using the **D**ate command. (Chapter 6, "Using Functions," covers the @DATE, @DATEVALUE, @TODAY, and @NOW commands.)

You also can enter a date as a date serial number and then reformat the cell using the **D**ate command. A *date serial number* is a unique integer that Quattro Pro assigns to historical dates.

You easily can decipher a date serial number when you know how Quattro Pro creates the number. A date serial number equals the number of days between the date you enter and December 30, 1899. The serial number for December 30, 1899, for example, is 0, and the serial number for December 30, 1900, is 365—the number of days between the two dates. Figure 5.7 shows the decimal equivalents for several historical dates.

Fig. 5.7

Date serial numbers.

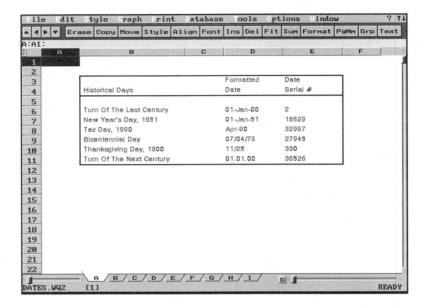

Historical Days	Formatted Date	Date Serial #
Turn Of The Last Century	01-Jan-00	2
New Year's Day, 1951	01-Jan-51	18629
Tax Day, 1990	Apr-90	32967
Bicentennial Day	07/04/76	27945
Thanksgiving Day, 1900	11/25	330
Turn Of The Next Century	01.01.00	36526

NOTE

The date serial numbers for all dates before December 30, 1899, are negative. The date serial number for December 29, 1899, for example, is –1.

To enter and format a date serial number, follow these steps:

1. Enter a valid date serial number in a cell. Valid serial numbers can be any integer in the range from –36463 for March 01, 1800, to 73050 for December 31, 2099.

2. Choose **D**ate from the /**S**tyle **N**umeric Format menu.

3. Choose a format option.

Whichever way you enter a date, Quattro Pro always stores a date in its serial number form so that you can use dates in notebook calculations. When you enter a date serial number into a cell, you can edit the date as you can any other number. To add one day to the serial number 500, for example, change the number to 501.

If you press Ctrl+D and then enter a date using an acceptable date format, Quattro Pro displays the serial number as a date on the notebook. If you press F2 and edit the serial number, the date reverts to a serial number display when you press Enter. The only way to affix a date format to a serial number is to format the date with the /**S**tyle **N**umeric Format **D**ate command.

Formatting Times

To enter a value in a time format, follow these steps:

1. Press Ctrl+D.

2. Enter a time using time format 1 or 2 (see table 5.4). You also can enter a time using the /**O**ptions **I**nternational **T**ime command to choose format pairs 3 and 7, 4 and 8, 5 and 9, or 6 and 10 as the global format.

Table 5.4 Time Command Formats

Format	Type
1. HH:MM:SS AM/PM	Hour, minute, second
2. HH:MM AM/PM	Hour, minute
3. HH:MM:SS	Long international #1
4. HH.MM.SS	Long international #2
5. HH,MM,SS	Long international #3
6. HHh,MMm,SSs	Long international #4
7. HH:MM	Short international #1
8. HH.MM	Short international #2
9. HH,MM	Short international #3
10. HHhMMm	Short international #4

Another way to enter a time is to use a time @function command and then reformat the cell using the /**S**tyle **N**umeric Format **D**ate **T**ime command. (Chapter 6, "Using Functions," covers the @TIME, @TIMEVALUE, and @NOW commands.)

You also can enter a time as a time serial number and then reformat the cell using the **T**ime command. The code that Quattro Pro uses to represent a time is different from the code used for a date. Quattro Pro records time as a percentage of the 24-hour day. Quattro Pro assigns the decimal 0.5 to noon, for example, because 12 p.m. occurs 50 percent of the way through a 24-hour day. Figure 5.8 shows the Quattro Pro decimal equivalents for each hour.

Fig. 5.8

Time serial numbers
assigned by Quattro
Pro.

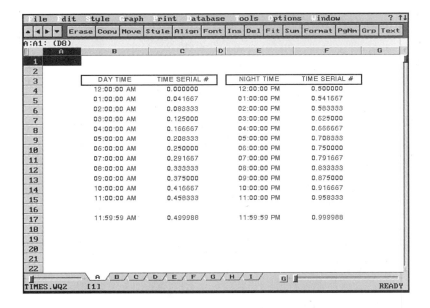

To enter and then format a time serial number, follow these steps:

1. Enter a valid time serial number in a cell.

2. Choose **D**ate and then choose **T**ime from the /**S**tyle **N**umeric Format menu.

3. Choose a format option.

Quattro Pro always stores a time in its serial number form so that you can use times in notebook calculations.

When you enter a time serial number into a cell, you can edit the time like you can any other number. To add 1 minute to the serial number 0.5, for example, add 0.000694 (the decimal value that equals 1 minute divided by 1,440 minutes in a day).

TIP

Quattro Pro accepts 24-hour, or military, clock times. When you use **N**umeric Format, Quattro Pro converts 24-hour times into 12-hour clock time equivalents. For example, 23:00:00 displays as 11:00:00 PM.

If you press Ctrl+D and then enter a time using an acceptable time format, Quattro Pro displays the serial number as a time on the notebook. If you press F2 and edit the serial number, the program reverts to a serial number display when you press Enter to record the editing changes. The only way to affix a time format to a serial number is to format the number with the /**S**tyle **N**umeric Format **D**ate **T**ime command.

Figure 5.9 shows a revised version of the notebook from figure 5.4. This notebook contains all the appropriate numeric formats. A blank column has been added to the left of the data, and columns have been widened where necessary to display all the detail.

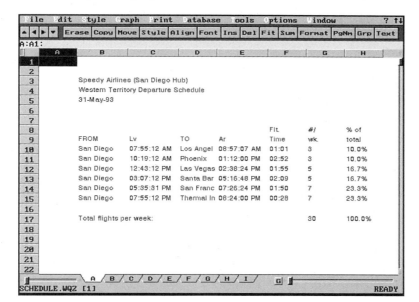

Fig. 5.9

A notebook with numeric formats.

Changing Formats

Quattro Pro offers two ways to change cell formats. First, you can choose /**S**tyle **N**umeric Format **R**eset and cancel all format settings for a cell block that you define. Second, you can reformat a cell by choosing /**S**tyle **N**umeric Format and then selecting a new format option. When you reformat a cell, Quattro Pro replaces the original format with the new format.

When you reformat a cell, Quattro Pro sometimes displays a value that doesn't make sense. When you format the value 50 using the **C**urrency option with two decimal places, for example, Quattro Pro displays

$50.00. If you reformat this value using the **P**ercent option with 2 decimal places, Quattro Pro displays 5000%. You may have to edit the value to create the correct display.

Protecting Important Data

The process of protecting a notebook involves two operations: global notebook protection and individual cell protection. To protect cells from change, the global protection and the individual cell protection settings must be on.

By default, all cells on a Quattro Pro notebook are in protected mode, but the setting for notebook protection is disabled. Use the /**O**ptions **P**rotection command to enable or disable global notebook protection.

Protecting Notebook Cells

Quattro Pro doesn't enable you to edit, replace, or delete entries from protected cells. You also cannot delete a column or row containing a protected cell. You can erase the entire notebook, however, even if the notebook contains protected cells.

To protect a block of cells, follow these steps:

1. Select the block of cells.

2. Choose /**S**tyle **P**rotection.

3. Choose **P**rotect.

Quattro Pro protects the preselected cell block. When you use /**O**ptions **P**rotection **E**nable to turn protection on, Quattro Pro displays PR on the input line for every protected cell that you make active.

Remember that when global notebook protection is disabled using /**O**ptions **P**rotection **D**isable, you can overwrite data on the notebook, regardless of the individual protection status of the notebook cells.

When global notebook protection is enabled, however, Quattro Pro displays an error message if you try to alter the contents of cells explicitly formatted as protected with /**S**tyle **P**rotection **P**rotect. Press Esc to cancel the error message and return to the active notebook.

Unprotecting Notebook Cells

To remove cell protection from a block of cells, follow these steps:

1. Select the block of cells.

2. Choose /**Style** **P**rotection.

3. Choose **U**nprotect.

Quattro Pro removes protection from the preselected cell block. When you use /**Style** **P**rotection to unprotect a cell, Quattro Pro displays U on the input line when you make that cell active.

> Quattro Pro makes locating unprotected cells easy, because the program always displays the contents of unprotected cells in a bright cyan color on a color monitor and in high intensity on a monochrome monitor. You may have to adjust the foreground and background intensity knobs on a monochrome monitor to see this display.

TIP

Password-Protecting Formulas

You can protect important notebook formulas from being altered by assigning a password to the notebook. After you assign a password, the only way you can edit cells containing formulas is by re-entering the password to remove the protection. This feature works independently of the global protection feature that is enabled and disabled with the /**Options** **P**rotection command.

> When you password-protect notebook formulas without enabling global notebook protection, you can change labels or values on the notebook.

NOTE

To assign formula protection to your notebook, follow these steps:

1. Choose /**Options** **P**rotection **F**ormulas **P**rotect.

2. Type a password.

   Remember this password because you will need it to remove formula protection so that you can edit cells containing formulas.

3. Press Enter.

4. When prompted to verify the password, retype it and press Enter. If you type a different password the second time, you see the message Passwords don't match. Press Esc and repeat the entire procedure again.

NOTE

Passwords are case-sensitive. You must re-enter them exactly as you originally entered them. If you enter a password in all lowercase letters, re-enter it the same way.

After you protect formulas in your notebook, any user who tries to edit a formula will receive the message Formula protection is enabled. Formula protection also prevents users from performing other operations that can overwrite the cell, such as **C**opy, **M**ove, or **I**nsert.

To remove formula protection from the notebook, follow these steps:

1. Choose /**O**ptions **P**rotection **F**ormulas **U**nprotect.

2. When prompted, type the password.

Quattro Pro removes the protection. If you close the file without saving it, however, formula protection is reinstated.

FOR RELATED INFORMATION

▶▶ "Password-Protecting Your Files," p. 365.
How to use the /**F**ile Save **A**s command to assign password protection to notebook files.

▶▶ "Using a Database as a Data-Entry Form," p. 653.
How to protect only parts of a Quattro Pro notebook.

Working with Columns and Rows

The middle group of commands on the **S**tyle menu—**C**olumn Width, **R**eset Width, **H**ide Column, and **B**lock Size—are column-adjustment commands. You can use these four commands to change the width of a column or a block of columns and to hide a group of columns on the active notebook. **C**olumn Width widens and narrows the current column; **R**eset Width returns the active column back to the default column width; **H**ide Column removes a selected group of columns from display; and **B**lock Size performs operations on a block of columns and rows.

Setting the Width of a Column

Quattro Pro enables you to set the width of an individual column using the /**St**yle **C**olumn Width command. Valid column widths range from 1 to 254 characters. To widen or narrow the width of a column, follow these steps:

1. Place the selector in a target column.

2. Choose /**St**yle **C**olumn Width.

3. Type the number of the desired width (the default is 9) and then press Enter.

Quattro Pro adjusts the width of the active column to the number of characters you specify. After you change the width of a column, Quattro Pro displays the new width in brackets on the input line. [W12], for example, indicates a column width of 12.

Ctrl+W is the default shortcut for the /**S**tyle **C**olumn Width command.   **TIP**

Setting the Width with the Arrow Keys

Sometimes estimating the appropriate width for a column is difficult. If you are unsure about which width to use, you can use the following adjustment technique:

1. Place the selector in a target column.

2. Choose /**St**yle **C**olumn Width.

3. Press the right-arrow key to widen or the left-arrow key to narrow the target column.

4. Press Enter when you create a visually acceptable width.

Setting the Width with a Mouse

If you have a mouse, you easily can change the width of a column by following these steps:

1. Click the target column's letter at the top of the notebook.

2. Drag the column letter to the right to widen the column or left to narrow the column.

3. Release the mouse button when you attain the ideal width.

 If you click the Fit button on the READY mode SpeedBar, Quattro Pro widens or narrows the active column to accommodate the largest cell entry in that column. Clicking the Fit button duplicates the /**S**tyle **B**lock Size **A**uto Width command. (See "Working with Multiple Columns" later in this chapter for more on the /**S**tyle **B**lock Size command.)

Setting the Width in a Window Pane

The capability to split a notebook into two window panes presents an interesting possibility for column widths, because with the /**S**tyle **C**olumn Width command, you can change column widths independently in either window pane.

If you split a window into two vertical or horizontal panes, for example, you can choose different widths for the same column in each pane. When you close a split window, however, Quattro Pro retains only those changes made to columns in the top (horizontal split) or left (vertical split) pane. (See the section "Viewing the Notebook" in Chapter 3 for instructions on splitting windows.)

TIP

Press F6 to switch between panes in a split window.

Resetting a Column's Width

Use the /**S**tyle **R**eset Width command to reset the width of an adjusted column to its default setting. Follow these steps:

1. Place the selector in the target column.

2. Choose /**S**tyle **R**eset Width.

Quattro Pro resets the width of the active column to nine characters (unless you have changed the default width using /Options Formats Global Width, described in the "Changing the Default Global Settings" section early in this chapter). After you reset the width of a column, Quattro Pro erases from the input line the brackets containing the preceding width.

> You can change the default global column width by choosing /**O**ptions **F**ormats **G**lobal Width and typing a new width value.   **TIP**

Working with Multiple Columns

Use the /**S**tyle **B**lock Size command to set the width of multiple columns. When you choose this command, Quattro Pro displays four choices on the submenu; the first three operate on columns.

Choose **S**et Width to assign a width to multiple columns or **R**eset Width to reset multiple columns to the default width. Use the third command, **A**uto Width, to adjust the width of a block of columns according to the longest entry in each column. The fourth command, **H**eight, controls row height.

Setting the Width of a Block of Columns

Use the **S**et Width command to set the width of multiple columns in a block. Follow these steps:

1. Preselect the columns in the target block.

2. Choose /**S**tyle **B**lock Size **S**et Width.

3. Type any number from 1 to 254 (to represent the width in characters), or use the left- or right-arrow key to indicate the width on-screen.

4. Press Enter.

Quattro Pro adjusts each column included in the block to the specified width.

To reset the width of all columns in a block, follow these steps:

1. Choose /**S**tyle **B**lock Size **R**eset Width. Quattro Pro prompts you for the block to adjust.

2. Specify the block to adjust by highlighting the block or by typing the block address on the input line.

Quattro Pro resets the width of all columns in the block to the default value. Initially, the default column width is 9, but you can change this width using the /**O**ptions **F**ormats **G**lobal Width command.

Automatically Setting the Width of a Block of Columns

Figure 5.10 shows what the notebook in figure 5.9 looks like before widening the column widths from 9 to 12 characters. Notice that asterisks appear in cell B5 and in columns C and E. The asterisks appear because the chosen numeric format creates a display wider than the width of the column. Look at the input line at the top of the notebook to see that cell B5's data is intact.

Fig. 5.10

A notebook before column widths accommodate long numbers.

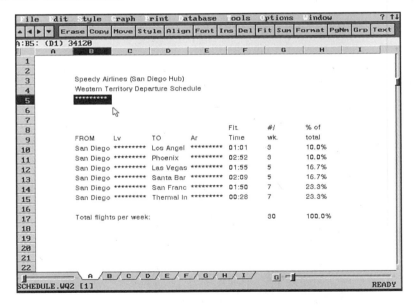

The **A**uto Width command provides yet another way to set your notebook column widths. This command is particularly useful when the column data has a similar width—like a date or time serial number—because the command enables you to create a width quickly that accommodates the common length.

To use the **A**uto Width command to adjust column widths, follow these steps:

1. Preselect cell block B8..H17.

2. Choose /**S**tyle **B**lock Size **A**uto Width.

3. When prompted, press Enter to add an extra space to the longest entry in each column (see fig. 5.11).

You may specify from 0 to 40 extra spaces to add to the longest label or value when you choose this command. Normally, allowing 1 to 3 extra spaces creates enough distance between columns for you to see your data. Figure 5.12 shows the notebook with auto-adjusted columns.

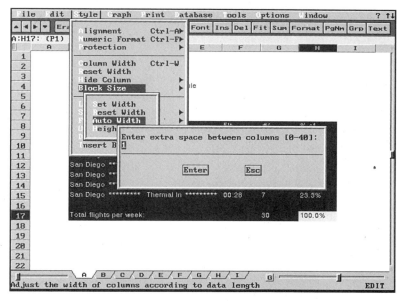

Fig. 5.11

Adding one space to the longest column entry to determine column width.

When looking for the longest entry, Quattro Pro examines the first row and all cells following that row. The program then resets the widths of the columns according to the following formula: length of longest entry in the block + extra characters.

Fig. 5.12

The auto-adjusted
notebook.

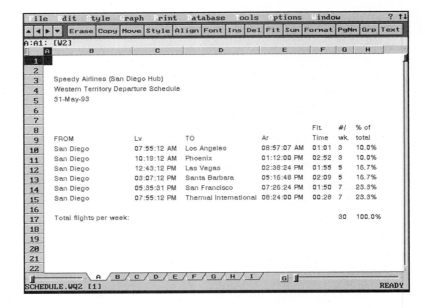

If the longest entry is 10 characters long and you specified 2 extra
spaces, for example, Quattro Pro sets the width of the column to 12.

If your notebook contains an entry that is substantially longer than any
other entry, preselect a cell block that doesn't include this entry. If you
are working with the notebook in figure 5.10, for example, you don't
want to include the 37-character label in cell B4 in the cell block.

If the long entry appears in the middle of the notebook, perform two
auto-adjustment operations: one on the block above and one on the
block below the long entry.

TIP

Sometimes using the **A**uto Width command pushes the right edge of the
active notebook out of view. If this happens, you can fine-tune the widths
of individual columns using /**S**tyle **C**olumn Width until you achieve the
appropriate display. To show the entire notebook page in figure 5.12,
for example, the width of column A was changed to 2.

Hiding a Column

Quattro Pro enables you to hide and reveal columns of data temporarily by using the /Style Hide Column command. This command enables you to prevent unauthorized viewing of proprietary data. When you hide a column, Quattro Pro retains the column data in memory so that you can reveal the column.

Hiding Data in Columns

To hide columns from view, follow these steps:

1. Preselect the target column(s).

2. Choose /Style Hide Column.

3. Choose Hide from the submenu.

4. Press Enter to hide the target column(s).

When Quattro Pro hides columns, your notebook looks as though the target columns are erased and the bordering columns are connected. In other words, Quattro Pro doesn't reletter the column names when you execute this command. Instead, the program joins the bordering columns to the right and left of the hidden columns so that no blank areas are on the notebook.

> The **H**ide Column command creates an interesting screen effect similar to a vertical window split. Figure 5.13 illustrates how hiding columns F through P produces a split window effect without the annoying vertical border from the second pane.

TIP

Now suppose that you create a vertically or horizontally split window with /Window Options and then hide columns in the notebook. Quattro Pro keeps hidden only those columns initially hidden on the top or left pane when you clear the window with /Window Options Clear.

> Quattro Pro doesn't include hidden columns on the printout of a notebook.

TIP

Fig. 5.13

The **H**ide Column command causes a split-window effect.

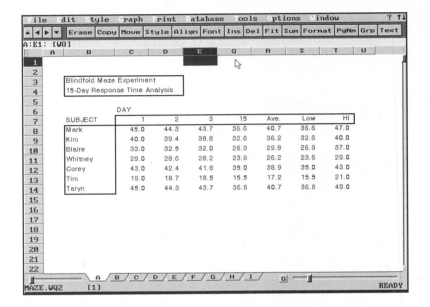

Displaying Hidden Data in Columns

To display hidden columns, follow these steps:

1. Choose /**S**tyle **H**ide Column **E**xpose. Quattro Pro reveals hidden columns with asterisks (*) next to the column letters.

2. Type a cell address or cell block address that includes the columns you want to expose.

3. Press Enter to display the hidden columns.

Quattro Pro removes the asterisks and rehides columns that you choose not to expose when you execute this command.

Using certain menu commands, such as /**E**dit **M**ove and /**E**dit **C**opy, causes Quattro Pro to display temporarily all hidden columns on the active notebook. When you finish executing the command, Quattro Pro hides the columns again.

TIP

If you preselect a cell block that contains hidden columns before executing a **S**tyle menu command, Quattro Pro enhances the cells in the hidden columns. If you preselect cell block C7..T7 in figure 5.13 and then choose /**S**tyle **L**ine Drawing **O**utside, for example, Quattro Pro also draws lines around cell block F7..P7, the area hidden in this figure.

Setting the Height of a Row

You can set the height of an individual row with the /Style Block Size Height command. Quattro Pro rows are measured by point size, unlike columns, which are measured by character widths. In general, Quattro Pro makes the default height of a row slightly taller than the largest point size used on that row. Valid row heights range from a point size of 1 to 240, with a default setting of 15.

When you format a cell using a font with a large point size and then manually shorten the row height of that cell's row, Quattro Pro may truncate data that you enter into the cell. When this happens, you can adjust the height of the row containing truncated data.

To raise or lower the height of a row, follow these steps:

1. Place the selector in a target row.

2. Choose /Style Block Size Height Set Row Height.

3. Type the number of the desired height (the default is 15) and press Enter.

Quattro Pro adjusts the height of the active row to the point size you specify.

Setting the Row Height with the Arrow Keys

Sometimes estimating the appropriate height for a row is difficult. If you are unsure about a height setting, use the following adjustment technique:

1. Place the selector in a target row.

2. Choose /Style Block Size Height Set Row Height.

3. Press the up-arrow key to raise or the down-arrow key to lower the height of the target row.

4. Press Enter when you find an acceptable height.

Setting the Row Height with a Mouse

If you have a mouse, you easily can change the height of a row by doing the following:

1. Click the target row's number at the left edge of the notebook.

2. Drag the row number up to raise the height of the row or down to lower the height of the row.

3. Release the mouse button when you attain the ideal height.

Setting the Row Height in a Window Pane

Changing row height in a split window is like changing it with columns. With the /Style Block Size Height Set Row Height command, you can change row heights independently in either window pane.

If you split a window into two vertical or horizontal panes, for example, you can choose different heights for the same row in each pane. Use the F6 (Window) key to move the selector between panes in the window, and then adjust row heights as described earlier. When you close a split window, however, Quattro Pro retains only those changes made to rows in the top (horizontal split) or left (vertical split) pane.

Resetting a Row's Height

You can use the /Style Block Size Height Reset Row Height command to reset the height of an adjusted row to its default setting. To do so, follow these steps:

1. Place the selector in the target row.

2. Choose /Style Block Size Height Reset Row Height.

Quattro Pro resets the height of the active row to a point size slightly larger than the tallest font in the row.

Although Quattro Pro has no command to change the default global row height, you can change the height by choosing the /Style Define Style Create command, and changing the default font to a larger point size as specified by the NORMAL named style.

Figure 5.14 shows that when you vary the point size of a font—Swiss in this case—Quattro Pro adjusts the row height so that the font fits on that row.

Working with Multiple Rows

You also can use the /Style Block Size Height command to set the height of multiple rows. Choose Set Row Height to assign a height to multiple rows or Reset Row Height to reset multiple rows to the default height.

Setting the Height of a Block of Rows

You can use the Set Row Height command to set the height of multiple rows in a block. To do so, follow these steps:

1. Preselect the rows in the target block.

2. Choose /Style Block Size Height Set Row Height.

3. Type any point size value from 1 to 240, or use the up- or down-arrow key to indicate the height on-screen.

4. Press Enter.

Quattro Pro adjusts each row included in the block to the specified height.

Recall that preselecting a cell block is just one of three ways to tell Quattro Pro about the notebook area that you want to affect. Examples of using the two other methods—highlighting the cell block or typing the cell block address—appear next.

To reset the height of all rows in a block, follow these steps:

1. Choose /**Style B**lock Size **H**eight **R**eset Row Height. Quattro Pro prompts you for the block to adjust.

2. Specify the block to adjust by highlighting the block or by typing the block address on the input line.

Quattro Pro resets the height of all rows in the block to one slightly larger than the largest font in that row.

Automatically Setting the Height of a Block of Rows

In WYSIWYG display mode, Quattro Pro automatically manages notebook row height for you. When you add a font with a large point size to a notebook, for example, Quattro Pro adjusts the height of the current row to accommodate the new font.

Unlike the default column width, the point size of the font on each row determines the default height of a row. As mentioned earlier, Quattro Pro makes the default height of a row slightly taller than the largest point size on that row. If row 2 uses a 14-point font, for example, Quattro Pro sets the default height of that row to at least 14 points. In some cases, Quattro Pro establishes a default row height that is a few points larger than the font point size so that you can see all text on a line.

NOTE

You already know that Quattro Pro's default notebook font (Swiss-SC 12-point) requires a row height with a point size equal to 15. Because the program can use virtually hundreds of fonts—including the SC fonts that arrive with your Quattro Pro package and those available from third-party vendors—no cut-and-dried rule of thumb exists for determining the exact default row height point size that Quattro Pro requires for a particular font.

As with column widths, Quattro Pro saves all custom row heights with the notebook when you choose the /File Save command. A word of caution: If you shrink the height of a row below the default height, Quattro Pro cuts off the top of the text on that row. Use the Set Row Height command to enlarge the row height and reveal the top portion of the cut-off text.

Selecting Presentation-Quality Options

The last group of commands on the Style menu are the presentation-quality commands for adding stylistic enhancements to your note-books. You can draw lines and boxes, add shading to cells, include multiple fonts, and add bullets. You also can assign style attributes directly to fonts, create and save customized notebook styles, and in-sert page breaks to help control notebook printing.

Previewing Enhancements

In WYSIWYG display mode, you can see on a notebook all Style menu enhancements as soon as you add them to a cell. Quattro Pro immediately shows new data alignments, numeric formats, unprotected cells, column widths, hidden columns, drawn lines, and shading effects after you add them to a notebook.

> With the exception of drawn lines and shading effects, all of these Style menu enhancements appear in text display mode as well.

TIP

Notebook enhancements such as custom font typefaces and cell bullets also display immediately in a notebook. If you are in text display mode, you don't have immediate "presentation-quality" display. In this case, Quattro Pro gives you an alternate feature to preview all your notebook enhancements before you print a notebook.

To use Quattro Pro's Screen Preview command, follow these steps:

1. Preselect a cell block on the active notebook that you want to preview.

2. Choose /**P**rint **B**lock. Quattro Pro displays the cell block address at the right margin of the **P**rint menu, next to the **B**lock command.

3. Choose **D**estination and then select the **S**creen Preview option. Quattro Pro returns you to the **P**rint menu.

4. Choose **S**preadsheet Print. Quattro Pro displays your notebook, complete with its presentation-quality settings.

If your computer doesn't have a graphics display system, you cannot use the Screen Previewer. You must print out a notebook to review the look of your presentation-quality settings. (See Chapter 9, "Printing," for a complete discussion of printing in Quattro Pro.)

Drawing Lines and Boxes

You can add lines to a notebook in the following three ways: enter a repeating hyphen into a cell so that the hyphens fill the cell, use the I symbol for vertical lines, or use the commands on Quattro Pro's Line Drawing submenu.

Quattro Pro uses graphic imaging to form the lines and boxes on a notebook. Rather than draw lines in cells, therefore, the program actually adds the graphics image between cells on a notebook.

To use the /**S**tyle Line Drawing menu to draw single, double, or thick lines and boxes around your notebook cell data, follow these steps:

1. Preselect a block of cells.

2. Choose /**S**tyle Line Drawing.

3. Choose a placement option from the Placement submenu that appears when you choose Line Drawing (see table 5.5).

4. Choose a line type from the Line types submenu. (Your choices are **N**one, **S**ingle, **D**ouble, and **T**hick.)

5. Choose **Q**uit to exit the Placement submenu and return to the notebook.

Table 5.5 Line Placement Options

Option	Description
All	Draws a box around the target cell block and adds vertical and horizontal lines between all cells
Outside	Draws a box around the target cell block
Top	Draws a horizontal line on top of the first row in the target cell block
Bottom	Draws a horizontal line below the last row in the target cell block
Left	Draws a vertical line along the left edge of the leftmost column in the target cell block
Right	Draws a vertical line along the right edge of the right-most column of the target cell block
Inside	Draws vertical and horizontal lines between all cells in the target cell block
Horizontal	Draws lines between each row in the target cell block; does nothing if the target cell block contains only one row
Vertical	Draws lines between each column in the block; does nothing if the target cell block contains only one column
Quit	Returns to the notebook without making any changes

Figure 5.15 shows how adding lines to Speedy Airline's report highlights the arrival and departure data.

NOTE

Drawn lines occasionally spill off screen when you add them to a row or column that isn't entirely visible in the notebook area. To create the notebook display shown in figure 5.15, for example, you must reduce the width of columns A and I to 2.

Erasing Lines and Boxes

To remove all lines and boxes from a notebook, follow these steps:

1. Preselect the cell block containing the lines or boxes (the cell block you originally selected as the target cell block).

2. Choose /**S**tyle **L**ine Drawing.

3. Choose the **A**ll placement option.

4. Choose the **N**one type option.

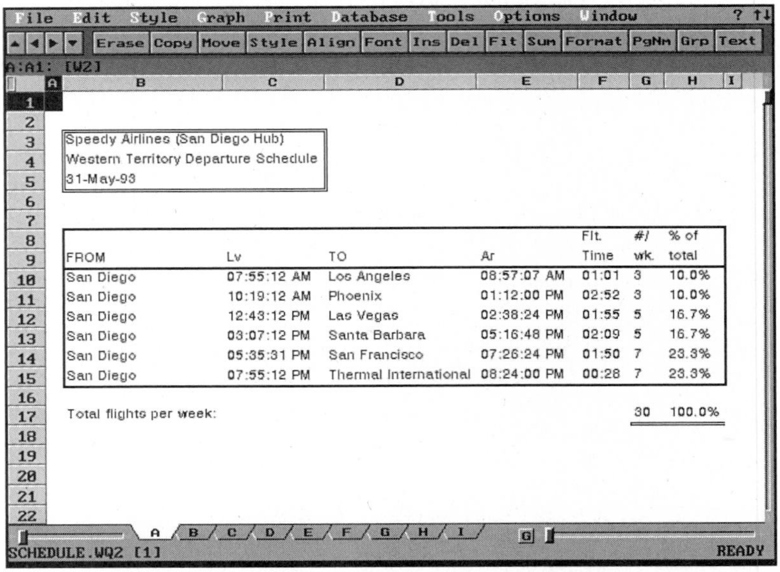

Fig. 5.15

Lines and boxes added
to the Speedy Airlines
report.

TIP

Quattro Pro enables you to partially remove lines from a notebook. To
remove the bottom line from a box, for example, highlight the target cell
block and choose /**S**tyle **L**ine Drawing **B**ottom **N**one. To remove the top
line, choose /**S**tyle **L**ine Drawing **T**op **N**one.

Printing Lines and Boxes

You can print a notebook containing lines and boxes in draft or graphics mode. In draft mode, Quattro Pro uses +, −, and the letter l to print
lines and boxes. In graphics mode, Quattro Pro uses graphics characters to print smooth lines and boxes.

To print in graphics mode, set the /**P**rint **D**estination setting to **G**raphics Printer. (See Chapter 9 for information about printing.)

Shading Cell Data for Effect

Use the /**S**tyle **S**hading command to shade notebook cells. With this command, you can shade in gray or black. The most common applications for cell shading are to indicate a data input area and to point out a block of protected cells.

To shade an area of a notebook, follow these steps:

1. Preselect a block of cells to shade.

2. Choose /**S**tyle **S**hading.

3. Choose a shade option from the **S**hading submenu.

Quattro Pro displays the target cells with shading. When you use the **Gray** shading option, notice that the entire cell is colored gray rather than only the data. On a monochrome screen, black shading appears as boldface.

To print shaded cells, you first must choose the /**P**rint **D**estination **G**raphics **P**rinter command to tell Quattro Pro to print in graphics mode. If you don't choose this command, Quattro Pro doesn't print the shaded cells.

When you shade cells bordered by drawn lines, Quattro Pro sometimes overlaps the lines, but this effect happens only on-screen. When you print the notebook, Quattro Pro properly encloses the shading in the lined cells.

Figure 5.16 shows how adding cell shading to cell B5 and cell blocks C10..C15 and E10..E15 makes important data stand out on a report.

Fig. 5.16

Cell shading added to the Speedy Airlines report.

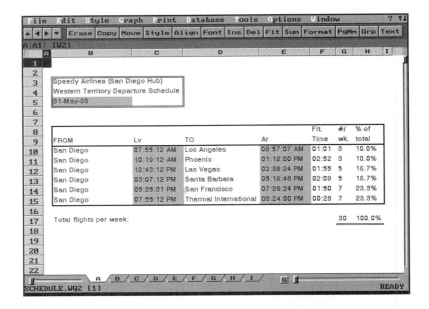

Selecting Fonts

Quattro Pro provides a very efficient method for selecting fonts for your notebooks: You can select fonts and their display attributes *on the fly* (spontaneously) directly from a dialog box.

Use the /**S**tyle **F**ont command to select a font typeface and its display attributes (point size, color, boldface, italics, and underline) and then apply the font to a notebook. Selecting fonts on the fly enables you to experiment with an unlimited number of different fonts and font attributes in WYSIWYG display mode until you find the most appropriate look for a notebook. Figure 5.17 shows examples of the built-in fonts that you can add to your Quattro Pro notebooks.

In WYSIWYG display mode, the /**S**tyle **F**ont command affects the fonts that Quattro Pro uses for printing and for screen display. Quattro Pro also displays a notebook's custom font options when you use the **S**creen Preview command on the **P**rint menu. (See Chapter 9 for complete coverage of the **P**rint menu.)

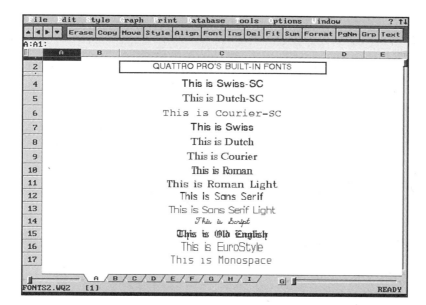

Fig. 5.17

Built-in fonts you can apply to notebooks.

NOTE

Periodically, Quattro Pro pauses to render fonts—for example, when you add a font that wasn't rendered during a recent work session. When Quattro Pro renders fonts, you must wait a few moments until the program is finished before you can continue with the current work session.

If you don't want Quattro Pro to render fonts and interrupt your work sessions, choose /**O**ptions **G**raphics Quality and then **D**raft from the submenu. If you want Quattro Pro to render fonts on an as-needed basis so that you can display them immediately in your notebooks, however, select the **F**inal option from the submenu.

Selecting a Different Font

To assign a new font to a cell block on a notebook, follow these steps:

1. Preselect the target cell block.

2. Choose /**Style** Font.

3. Select the font typeface and display attributes from the options listed on the submenu.

4. Choose **Quit** to apply the new font and return to the notebook.

When you apply fonts in text display mode, you don't see any changes in the notebook. To verify the font you chose for a cell, make that cell active and review the font name next to the **Typeface** option when you choose /Style **F**ont.

NOTE

If you are upgrading from Quattro Pro Version 4.0, notice that the Font**T**able command no longer appears on the **S**tyle menu. This command has been eliminated because selecting fonts on the fly with the /**S**tyle **F**ont command is much more efficient.

`Font`

You also can access the /**S**tyle **F**ont menu by clicking the Font button on the READY mode SpeedBar and then highlighting the block. If you highlight the block before clicking the Font button, you only need to select the font attributes to apply them.

Adding Bullets

Quattro Pro has a special stylistic feature called *bulleting* that enables you to add bullets and boxes to your notebooks. You cannot find this option anywhere on a Quattro Pro menu. To use this option, you must enter a special code into a notebook cell.

To create a bullet, enter the following code into the cell in which you want the bullet to appear:

'\bullet #

In place of the # symbol, use the bullet style number (0-6).

To enter a bullet into a cell by itself, precede the bullet code with a label prefix ('). If you don't, Quattro Pro interprets the first \ as a re-peating label prefix and repeats the entry in the cell. To specify a bullet style, choose one of the numbers listed in fig. 5.18.

When you are in WYSIWYG display mode, Quattro Pro instantly shows the bullet graphic on the notebook. In text display mode, however, you see only the bullet code in the notebook cell. When you print a note-book containing a bullet code, Quattro Pro reveals the bullet character instead of the code.

TIP

Press Alt+F5 to remove a bullet code immediately after you enter the code into a notebook cell.

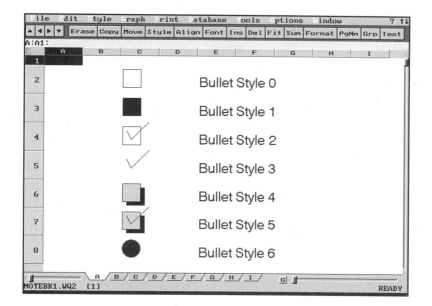

Fig. 5.18

Quattro Pro's bullet styles.

In text display mode, you can review how the bullet character looks on-screen by choosing /**P**rint **B**lock and typing the address of a cell block to print. Next, set the /**P**rint **D**estination command to **S**creen Preview and choose **S**preadsheet Print.

You also can include bullet characters in a Quattro Pro graph using the graph Annotator. See Chapter 11, "Customizing Graphs," for complete coverage of graph annotation.

NOTE

If the bullet code doesn't appear when you print or preview the notebook, widen that column until the code appears.

Figure 5.19 shows the final, presentation-quality version of the Speedy Airlines notebook. Note the addition of custom fonts to the report title and to the data labels in rows 8 and 9. This notebook also contains bullet graphics in column A.

FOR RELATED INFORMATION

▶▶ "Setting Graphics Quality Options," p. 798.
How to use the /**O**ptions **G**raphics Quality **D**raft command to speed up printing for notebooks that contain many fonts.

Fig. 5.19

The final presentation-quality version of the Speedy Airlines notebook.

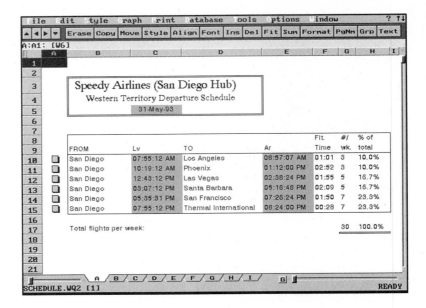

Using Custom Notebook Styles

Quattro Pro offers custom style features to help you easily create top-notch presentations and business reports. As you learned earlier, you can apply font style attributes on the fly using the /Style Font command. If you like the look of a particular combination of font style attributes, you should name that combination as a custom style. You can apply custom styles quickly to other parts of the same notebook or to other notebook files that you open into memory. This process saves you the time of re-creating the font style by reselecting commands.

Custom styles can include other style attributes, though. You can create a custom style that includes drawn lines, a label alignment, cell shading, and numeric formats. You can create up to 120 unique custom styles per notebook. When you must produce several documents with similar style attributes, you will enjoy the easy-to-use, time-saving nature of custom styles.

The /Style Define Style command offers all the options necessary for creating and managing custom style definitions that you can use to format the current notebook. The following table lists these options.

Option	Description
Create	Creates a new style or edits an existing one
Erase	Clears a custom style from a notebook, leaving the character formatting intact (except font and data-entry attributes)
Remove	Deletes the custom style from the notebook; blocks previously assigned this style retain their character formatting (except font and data-entry attributes)
File	Saves and retrieves custom style files

The **D**efine Style options enable you to erase and remove custom styles from the current notebook. One option enables you to create style files that can contain all your favorite custom styles. Style files have a STY file name extension and can be retrieved for use in formatting any notebook open in Quattro Pro's memory.

Creating a Custom Style

To assign a name to a group of style attributes that exist in a cell block in the current notebook, follow these steps:

1. Select the block containing the style attributes to be named.

2. Choose /**S**tyle **D**efine Style **C**reate.

3. When Quattro Pro prompts you to name the style, type a name (up to 15 characters) and then press Enter. Quattro Pro displays a dialog box of style attributes that you can change.

4. Double-check that the currently selected attributes are acceptable.

5. Choose **Q**uit to save the newly named custom style and return to the **S**tyle menu.

Figure 5.20 shows a list of the named custom styles for the sample notebook.

If a particular combination of style attributes you want to use doesn't yet exist, you can create the custom style from the ground up. To do so, choose /**S**tyle **D**efine Style **C**reate. When Quattro Prompts you to name the style, type a name of up to 15 characters long and then press

Enter. On the style attributes submenu, select the attributes you want to appear in the new custom style. Choose **Q**uit to return to the **S**tyle menu, and then press Esc to return to the notebook.

Fig. 5.20

The custom style names for the sample notebook.

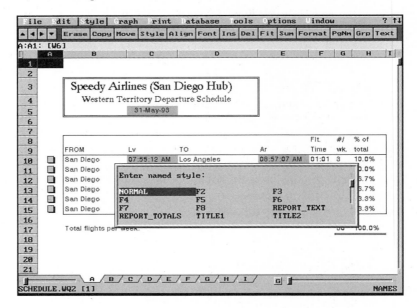

Applying Custom Styles

After you create a custom style, you can apply that style to the current notebook by using the /**S**tyle **U**se Style command. Follow these steps:

1. Select the block you want to apply the style to.

2. Choose /**S**tyle **U**se Style. Quattro Pro displays a box listing all custom styles.

3. Use the arrow keys to highlight the custom style you want to use and then press Enter (or click the custom style).

Quattro Pro assigns the custom style to the block. When the selector is inside a block assigned a named style, the style name appears on the input line.

Style

You also can click the Style button on the READY mode SpeedBar to display a list of custom styles. To apply a style using the Style button, preselect the block you want to apply the style to, click the Style button, and then click the desired custom style.

Creating a Custom Numeric Format

In addition to the numeric formats offered on the /**S**tyle **N**umeric Format menu, Quattro Pro enables you to create custom numeric formats to enhance the way numbers, dates, and times appear on your notebooks. Special codes, comprised of characters or symbols, are used to define Quattro Pro's custom numeric formats. Some code examples follow:

- The following code displays a number to four decimal places:

    N9.0000

    If you select this code, the number 104.8 displays as 104.8000 in your notebook.

- The following code displays a date and time in the form of the day of the week the date falls on, and the time in hours, minutes, and seconds, separated by colons:

    TWeekday, H:M:S

    If you select this code, the date 1/15/92 at 5:25 and 10 seconds displays as Wednesday, 5:25:10.

To create a custom numeric format, follow these steps:

1. Choose /**S**tyle **D**efine Style **C**reate.

2. When prompted, type a name (up to 15 characters) and then press Enter.

3. Choose **N**umeric Format **U**ser Defined.

4. When prompted, enter the format code for the custom numeric format you want to display, using the symbols and syntax described in table 5.6.

5. Customize any other aspects of the style, such as **F**ont, **L**ine Drawing, **S**hading, **A**lignment, and **D**ata Entry by choosing the appropriate option.

6. Choose **Q**uit after you make all your desired changes.

Now, apply the custom numeric style using the /**S**tyle **U**se Style command, just as you would other custom styles.

Table 5.6 lists the special characters used to format codes. If you include any other characters as part of a defined numeric format, Quattro Pro displays them "as is" when you apply the style to a cell or block.

Table 5.6 Numeric Format Symbols

Symbol	Action
Number Format	
N	Tells Quattro Pro the code following N denotes a format for numbers, not dates or time.
0	Displays the digit whether or not the number includes a digit in this position.
9	Displays the digit unless the number doesn't include a digit in this position.
%	Displays the number as a percentage.
, (comma)	Inserts a comma for a thousands separator.
. (period)	Inserts a period for a decimal separator.
E+ or e+	Displays the number in scientific notation, preceding negative and positive exponents with a minus or plus sign, respectively. If the format includes at least one 0 or 9 following this symbol, Quattro Pro displays the number in scientific notation and inserts E or e; if the exponent contains more digits than 9's or 0's following this symbol, the extra digits are displayed.
Date-and-Time Format	
T	Tells Quattro Pro the code following denotes a format for dates and times, not numbers.
d or D	Displays the day of the month as a one- or two-digit number (1-31).
dd or DD	Displays the day of the month as a two-digit number (01-31).

Symbol	Action
wday, Wday, WDAY	Displays the day of the week as a three-character abbreviation all lowercase, lowercase with the first letter capitalized, or all uppercase
weekday, Weekday, WEEKDAY	Displays the day of the week all lowercase, lowercase with the first letter capitalized, or all uppercase
m or M	Displays the month as a one- or two-digit number (1-12 for January through December), if not preceded by h, H, hh, or HH; otherwise, displays the minute as a one- or two-digit number (1-59)
mm or MM	Displays the month as a two-digit number (01-12) if not preceded by h, H, hh, or HH; otherwise, displays the minute as a two-digit number (01-59)
Mo	Displays the month as a one- or two-digit number (1-12)
MMo	Displays the month as a two-digit number (01-12)
mon, Mon, MON	Displays the month as a three-character abbreviation all lowercase, lowercase with the first letter capitalized, or all uppercase
month, Month, MONTH	Displays the name of the month all lowercase, lowercase with the first letter capitalized, or all uppercase
yy or YY	Displays the last two digits of the year (00-99)
yyyy or YYYY	Displays all four digits of the year (0001-2099)
h or H	Displays the hour as a one- or two-digit number; if the format includes ampm or AMPM, the number is between 1-12; if ampm or AMPM isn't included, 24-hour format is used (0-23)
hh or HH	Displays the hour as a two-digit number; if the format includes ampm or AMPM, the number is between 01-12; if ampm or AMPM isn't included, 24-hour format is used (00-23)
Mi	Displays the minute as a one- or two-digit number (1-59)
MMi	Displays the minute as a two-digit number (01-59)
s or S	Displays the second as a one- or two-digit number (1-59)

(continues)

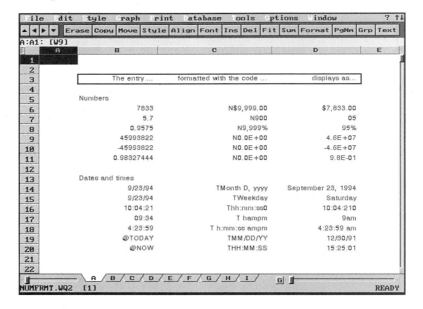

Table 5.6 Continued

Symbol	Action
ss or SS	Displays the second as a two-digit number (01-59)
ampm or AMPM	Displays the time in 12-hour format with characters for morning (AM) or afternoon (PM)
Miscellaneous Format	
\	Displays the next character in the format (to display a backslash, type \\)
*	Fills the column by repeating the character to the right of the asterisk, if the formatted entry is shorter than the column width
" "	Displays the characters inside the quotation marks as part or all the cell contents

Figure 5.21 shows examples of user-defined numeric formats and the codes required to create them.

Fig. 5.21

Custom numeric format styles created for a sample notebook.

Erasing Custom Styles from a Block

When you edit a custom style, Quattro Pro reflects those changes in all notebook blocks that you previously formatted with that custom style. To guard against this occurrence, you can erase a custom style from a notebook block without actually removing the character formatting.

To erase a custom style from a notebook block, follow these steps:

1. Select the block you want to clear the custom style from.

2. Choose /**S**tyle **D**efine Style **E**rase.

Quattro Pro removes the name from the block. The style attributes remain.

Removing Custom Styles from a Notebook

You should delete custom styles that you no longer use to keep the /**S**tyle **U**se Style menu uncluttered. Deleting custom styles doesn't remove styles from blocks that already have been formatted with that style, but the style name no longer displays on the input line when the selector is in a cell formatted with the deleted custom style.

To remove a custom style name from a notebook, follow these steps:

1. Choose /**S**tyle **D**efine Style **R**emove. Quattro Pro prompts you to select the name of the style you want to remove.

2. Highlight the style name.

If the style is used elsewhere in the notebook, Quattro Pro prompts you to confirm its deletion.

3. Choose **Y**es.

Quattro Pro removes the custom style. Any blocks previously assigned that custom style retain their style attributes, but the style name no longer appears in the list of custom styles or on the edit line when the selector is within the block.

Saving Custom Styles in Files

With Quattro Pro, you can save the custom styles you created for your current notebook to a custom style file. You can retrieve and use these files to format other notebooks that you open into Quattro Pro's memory.

To save all custom styles in the current notebook to a file, follow these steps:

1. Choose /**S**tyle **D**efine Style **F**ile **S**ave. Quattro Pro displays a list of existing style sheets and prompts you to enter a style sheet name.

2. Type the name of the style sheet—for example, **STYLE1**—and then press Enter.

Quattro Pro saves the styles to a custom style sheet file with a STY file extension. If you choose /**S**tyle **D**efine Style **F**ile **R**etrieve, STYLE1.STY appears as a custom style sheet. You now can retrieve this custom style sheet for use in formatting any notebook in memory.

Retrieving a Style Sheet to the Active Notebook

To retrieve a file of custom styles, follow these steps:

1. Choose /**S**tyle **D**efine Style **F**ile **R**etrieve. Quattro Pro prompts you to choose a style sheet.

2. Use the arrow keys to highlight the named style you want to retrieve and press Enter, or click the name. Quattro Pro returns to the **D**efine Style submenu.

3. Choose **Q**uit to return to the active notebook.

Now you can apply any of the style sheet's named styles by selecting /**S**tyle **U**se Style, and then selecting the style's name.

Editing a Custom Style

A custom style is an ideal tool for automating the task of formatting notebooks with a specific group of style attributes. When your preferences in notebook style change, Quattro Pro enables you to edit the style attributes for a custom style without having to re-create the style.

To change the attributes of an existing custom style, follow these steps:

1. Choose /**S**tyle **D**efine Style **C**reate. Quattro Pro displays a box listing all custom styles.

2. Use the arrow keys to highlight the custom style you want to edit and then press Enter, or click the custom style. Quattro Pro displays a submenu of style attributes you can change.

3. Edit the desired attributes using the same procedure that you followed for creating a custom style. Each time you change an attribute, Quattro Pro displays the attribute settings dialog box to show your current selections.

4. Choose **Q**uit to return to the **S**tyle menu.

When you edit a style, blocks previously assigned the style change. Changes to custom styles are saved with the notebook.

Editing the Default Style

To customize the style Quattro Pro uses as its default style, follow these steps:

1. Choose /**S**tyle **D**efine Style **C**reate.

2. Choose NORMAL. (Because the option already is highlighted, you need only to press Enter.) Quattro Pro displays a submenu of style attributes you can change.

3. Make any changes.

4. After you finish making changes to the style, highlight **Q**uit and then press Enter.

Quattro Pro returns to the **D**efine Style submenu. Choose **Q**uit to return to the notebook.

NOTE

In WYSIWYG display mode, every change that you make to a font appears on-screen instantly. In text display mode, however, font changes don't appear on-screen, so changing the color of a font produces no visible change on your color display. (Use the **C**olor option only if you own a color printer.)

The printed size of the font also isn't the same as on the notebook. Therefore, you may need to change a column's width to accommodate all the characters you want to print.

Certain Quattro Pro fonts support only some features available from the /**S**tyle **F**ont menu. The Courier font, for example, doesn't support the **B**old option. Although Quattro Pro enables you to specify **B**old on the **F**onts submenu, the program doesn't boldface characters on your printouts.

Using Page Breaks To Control Printing

Quattro Pro inserts soft page breaks in a notebook according to the page length specified by the /**P**rint **L**ayout **M**argins **P**age Length command. If you want to insert hard page breaks to modify further how a notebook is printed, use the /**S**tyle **I**nsert Break command.

Hard page breaks enable you to break one large print block into many smaller pieces. This technique is useful when you want to print a column of names and addresses on mailing labels, for example, or form-fed index cards.

Inserting a Page Break

You use the /**S**tyle **I**nsert Break command to insert a hard page break on a notebook at the selector. To insert a hard page break, follow these steps:

1. Move the selector to the first cell in the row in which you want to begin a new page.

2. Choose /**S**tyle **I**nsert Break.

Quattro Pro inserts a blank row and enters the symbol for a hard page break (¦::) at the specified location. Note that Quattro Pro has no soft page break symbol; the program uses the page length setting to determine normal page breaks.

> **TIP**
>
> To enter a page break manually, type **¦::** in the leftmost column of your print block. The manual page break symbol cannot be part of a left or top heading. Quattro Pro doesn't print data appearing on the same row as a page break.

Deleting a Page Break

To delete a page break when you want to enable Quattro Pro to manage the page break location, follow these steps:

1. Move the selector to the cell that contains the page break.

2. Press Del on the numeric keypad.

Quattro Pro deletes the hard page break but doesn't delete the inserted row.

> **TIP**
>
> Press Alt+F5 immediately after inserting a hard page break to remove it from a notebook.

> **FOR RELATED INFORMATION**
>
> ▶▶ "Controlling Page Breaks," p. 437.
> How to manage page breaks inserted into a notebook so that your documents print properly.

Questions & Answers

This chapter introduces you to Quattro Pro's commands for formatting cells, adjusting columns and rows, and adding presentation-quality enhancements. If you have questions about any topic covered in this chapter, scan this section for solutions to common problems.

Controlling the Display of Your Data

Q: How do you manually edit the alignment of a number or a formula on a notebook?

A: The only way to align values on a Quattro Pro notebook is by using the /**S**tyle **A**lignment command. Because Quattro Pro values don't have alignment prefixes, you cannot edit their alignment while in EDIT mode.

Q: When I enter time serial numbers, why doesn't Quattro Pro display recognizable times?

A: Unless you first press Ctrl+D, Quattro Pro displays date and time serial numbers as integers. To display serial numbers as dates, choose **D**ate or **T**ime from the **N**umeric Format submenu.

Q: When I enter and then format dates, why does Quattro Pro display the wrong date?

A: If you type a date into a cell (using hyphens or slashes) without *first* pressing Ctrl+D, Quattro Pro evaluates the entry as a formula. The date entry 10-09, for example, produces the value 1 when treated as a formula (10 minus 9 equals 1). When you format this cell by using /**S**tyle **N**umeric Format **D**ate, Quattro Pro sees the date serial number 1 and displays the date December 31, 1899.

Q: How do I perform mathematical operations on dates?

A: You can perform mathematical operations on dates and times just as you do on other numbers. Remember, dates and times are stored in cells as serial numbers—not as date labels.

Q: I protected cells on a notebook, but Quattro Pro still enables me to write over the data in the cells. Why?

A: Turn global notebook protection on with the /**O**ptions **P**rotection **E**nable command. With protection enabled, you cannot modify any cells unless they are explicitly unprotected.

Working with Columns and Rows

Q: Why does Quattro Pro display an error message when I try to delete columns and rows on my notebooks?

A: Turn global notebook protection off with the /**O**ptions **P**rotection **D**isable command. Quattro Pro doesn't delete rows and columns when a notebook has protected cells and global protection is enabled.

Q: I used the /**S**tyle **B**lock Size **A**uto Width command to auto-set column widths on a notebook. Now all my columns are too wide. What can I do?

A: Your target cell block probably included a cell with a long label, such as a report title. Choose the same target block and use the **R**eset Width command to return the columns to their default width. Then try the **A**uto Width command again, excluding the cell containing the long label.

Q: Why are some of my notebook rows taller than others?

A: You chose a font point size that is larger than the point size Quattro Pro uses for its default row height (15). If you shrink the row height of a "tall" row, Quattro Pro may truncate the text on that row.

Selecting Presentation-Quality Options

Q: Why did nothing happen when I changed several font definitions on my notebook?

A: Quattro Pro is in text display mode. In text display mode, you can review a notebook cell's font setting in three ways: on-screen using /**P**rint **D**estination **S**creen **P**review, on a printout using /**P**rint **D**estination **G**raphics Printer, or by making a cell active and reviewing the font code on the input line.

Although the first two methods enable you to inspect the look of a font, the third method doesn't. Even so, if you work with a particular font often, reviewing the font code on the input line at least enables you to verify that you used the correct font.

Q: Why don't my custom fonts, shading, and drawn lines look right on my notebook printouts?

A: Choose /**P**rint **D**estination **G**raphics Printer to print custom fonts and shadings. For this option to work, you must have a printer that can print in graphics mode, and /**O**ptions **G**raphics Quality must be set to **F**inal. (See your printer manual to determine whether your printer can print in graphics mode.)

Q: Why don't the font styles on my printouts correspond to the styles I specified in my notebook cells?

A: Make sure that the /**O**ptions **G**raphics Quality command is set to **F**inal. When this command is set to **D**raft, Quattro Pro doesn't use any Bitstream fonts that haven't been rendered.

Q: When I edited the attributes for a custom style I created, Quattro Pro changed the appearance of formatted blocks in my notebook. I really wanted to start with an existing style and add a few new attributes to the style without changing the rest of the notebook. What did I do wrong?

A: You should have disassociated the original custom style from the formatted notebook blocks by using the /**S**tyle **D**efine Style **E**rase command. Then you can edit and apply the custom style to other blocks in the same notebook without affecting any existing character formatting.

Q: I pressed Alt+F5 to remove a custom style I just added to a notebook block, but nothing happened. Why?

A: Like with presentation-quality options that you add to your notebooks one at a time, you cannot reverse custom styles by using Alt+F5. Instead, choose the /**S**tyle **D**efine Style **E**rase command to remove a custom style from a notebook block.

Summary

This chapter shows you how to align, format, and protect your notebook data. You also learned how to widen and narrow columns and how to perform operations on blocks of columns. The chapter concluded with an in-depth review of drawing lines, shading cells, and using and modifying fonts on a notebook.

Having completed this chapter, you should understand the following Quattro Pro concepts:

- Aligning values and labels manually with a **S**tyle menu command

- Selecting meaningful and appropriate numeric format values, labels, dates, and times

- Protecting and unprotecting cell data and enabling and disabling global notebook protection

- Setting, resetting, and auto-setting the width of a column, a row, or a block of columns and rows

- Setting column widths in a window pane

- Hiding and unhiding column data

- Drawing, erasing, and printing lines and boxes

- Using, modifying, and printing shaded cells on a notebook

- Selecting, changing, and customizing notebook fonts to create presentation-quality reports

- Adding bullets to and inserting hard page breaks in a notebook

- Changing default global format settings on the **O**ptions menu to create your own default notebook formats

- Creating custom styles to associate character formatting options so that you easily can apply the styles to notebook blocks

- Creating files that contain custom style names so that you can apply the custom styles to any notebook open in memory

In Chapter 6, you learn how to incorporate Quattro Pro's powerful built-in @function commands into your notebook applications. With these special commands, you can do complex mathematical, statistical, and database operations. These commands also enable you to manipulate data strings on a notebook and extend the notebook's capability to do what-if analyses with logical operators.

Using Functions

In the preceding chapters, you learn how to build notebook applications and how to manage the form and content of your reports by using Quattro Pro's menu commands. You also learn how to create basic formula relationships so that you quickly can add, subtract, multiply, and divide data on a notebook.

So far, you have created formulas primarily using mathematical operators. To add cells A5 and C9 and subtract cell D20, for example, enter **+A5+C9–D20** into a third cell.

But what if you want to sum the contents of a large block of cells, compute an average, display the total number of values used in the calculations, and then display each piece of information in a separate cell? This type of analysis requires Quattro Pro's special built-in formulas, called *@function commands*.

@Function (pronounced "at function") commands perform a variety of special calculations and tasks that are too difficult or cumbersome for you to accomplish using simple mathematical formulas. These commands are the basic building blocks of all advanced notebook applications. You can use these commands to average a group of numbers, to look up data in a block of cells, to create conditional formulas, and to perform calculations that help you determine the worth of an investment.

Other @function commands do tasks that are impossible to accomplish with basic mathematical formulas. Suppose that you want to generate a random number, convert a value to its hexadecimal equivalent, or determine how much system RAM is available for Quattro Pro. You easily can meet these and many other objectives by using Quattro Pro's @function commands.

Quattro Pro has 116 @function commands, divided into eight categories:

- Mathematical
- Statistical
- String
- Miscellaneous
- Logical
- Financial
- Date & Time
- Database

In this chapter, you learn how to use @functions in your own notebooks to solve unique, specific problems. In the first part of this chapter, you review the *structure*—or syntax—of the @function commands. When you understand the command syntax, go directly to the @function category that interests you most. The material in these sections reviews each command and often provides examples of how to use the command in a Quattro Pro notebook.

NOTE ▶

All examples in this chapter show @function results as they would appear in a cell that uses the default width of 9 characters. You may get slightly different results in your notebook if the column width is different or it you formatted the cell with /**S**tyle **N**umeric Format.

Understanding Command Syntax

Each @function command has a three-part syntax: the @ symbol, the function name, and the argument(s). These three parts are described as follows:

Syntax Element	Description
@	Indicates an "at function" command.
Function name	Describes the type of operation to be performed.
Argument(*n*)	Denotes the data to use. An argument can be a value or a cell address. The value *n* defines the order in which Quattro Pro evaluates an argument in an @function operation.

A typical @function command looks like the following:

@AVG(C5..C8)

In this command, the @ character tells Quattro Pro to expect an @function. AVG is the name of the @function that averages numbers, and (C5..C8) is the argument that defines the cell block containing the four numbers to average. Quattro Pro assumes that all cells in the block are on the current page.

If you want to use the @AVG command in a 3-D cell block, the @function would look like the following:

@AVG(A..B:A1..B1)

In this command, Quattro Pro averages the four numbers in the A1..B1 cell block on pages A and B.

> **NOTE**
>
> Any optional argument is enclosed in angle brackets (<>) in the @function syntax. *Don't* type the brackets when using optional arguments in an @function that you are typing into a cell.

Entering @Function Commands

Quattro Pro accepts three types of @function command arguments: numeric values, block values, and string values.

A *numeric value* can be a number, a cell that contains a number, or a reference to another cell that contains a number. Quattro Pro accepts as valid arguments block names and formulas that result in numeric values. You can create many different combinations of arguments, using all these types of numeric numbers.

@AVG(JAN,2500,A25..E30,(@ABS(G50))), for example, is a valid use of the @AVG command as long as the following conditions are true:

- JAN is the name of a block that contains numerical data.

- Block A25..E30 contains numerical data.

- @ABS doesn't return ERR as its result.

A *block value* can be a single cell, any two valid cell coordinates, a 3-D cell block, a reference to data on another page or notebook, a block name, or any combination of these items.

A *string value* can be a string enclosed in quotation marks, a cell that contains a label, a reference to a cell on another page or notebook that contains a label, a block name that contains a label, or another @function command that returns a string value. You can create many different combinations using each type of argument.

@LENGTH(JAN,"Data Set #1",A25..E30,(@PROPER(G50))), for example, is a valid use of the @LENGTH and @PROPER commands as long as the following conditions are true:

- JAN is the name of a block that contains a text string.

- Block A25..E30 contains text string data.

- @PROPER doesn't return ERR as its result.

When you enter @function commands into a notebook, remember the following simple rules:

- Don't enter extra spaces between the @ symbol, the function name, and the argument; Quattro Pro cannot interpret an @function properly with extra spaces.

- You can use upper- or lowercase characters when entering an @function; Quattro Pro always displays the function in uppercase.

- The arguments in an @function must be enclosed in parentheses.

- The number and types of arguments used are different for each @function command.

- You can use an @function command as an argument in another @function command.

Press Alt+F3 to display a list of Quattro Pro's @function commands. To select a command from the list, highlight the command name and press Enter. Quattro Pro displays the function with a left parenthesis on the input line. To complete the operation, enter the appropriate arguments, a right parenthesis, and then press Enter to calculate a result in the active cell.

You also can click the @ button on the EDIT mode SpeedBar to display the list of @function commands. Clicking an @function places it on the edit line at the cursor position. (Remember, you must be in EDIT mode to access the EDIT mode SpeedBar.)

Using Mathematical @Functions

The mathematical @functions fall into two categories: arithmetic and trigonometric. The mathematical @functions duplicate operations commonly found on scientific and financial calculators. By using these commands, you can calculate natural and common logarithms; absolute values; cosine, sine, tangent, and their inverses; square roots and random numbers; and many other types of mathematical functions.

Keep the following guidelines in mind when using mathematical @functions:

■ Express @SIN, @COS, and @TAN angles in radians, not in degrees.

■ The @ASIN, @ACOS, and @ATAN functions return angles in radian measure.

■ To convert degrees to radians, use the @RADIANS function or multiply the degree value by @PI/180.

■ To convert radians to degrees, use the @DEGREES function or multiply the radian value by 180/@PI.

■ The base value of natural logarithms is *e*. The value *e*, as stored in Quattro Pro's memory, is 2.718281828459.

Using Arithmetic Commands in a Notebook

Table 6.1 lists the arithmetic @function commands. The definitions in the following sections include examples of how you can use these commands in your own notebooks.

Table 6.1 Arithmetic Mathematical @Function Commands

@Function	Description
@ABS(x)	Returns the absolute value of x
@EXP(x)	Returns the constant e, raised to the xth power
@INT(x)	Drops the fractional portion of the number x
@LN(x)	Returns the natural logarithm of x
@LOG(x)	Returns the base 10 logarithm of x
@MOD(x,y)	Divides x by y and returns the remainder
@RAND	Supplies a random number between 0 and 1
@ROUND(x,n)	Rounds the value of x to n decimal places
@SQRT(x)	Returns the square root of x

@ABS(x)

@ABS returns the absolute or positive value of x when x is a numerical value.

Examples: @ABS(−20) = 20
@ABS(0) = 0
@ABS(A1) = 0, if A1 contains a label or is blank

@EXP(x)

The @EXP function gives the mathematical constant e, raised to the xth power, where x is a numeric value less than or equal to 709. The @EXP function is the inverse of a natural logarithm function (@LN).

Examples: @EXP(1) = 2.718282
@EXP(0) = 1.00000
@EXP(A1) = 1, if A1 contains a label or is blank
@EXP(800) = ERR

@INT(x)

The @INT function drops the fractional portion of x when x is a numeric value and returns its integer value.

Examples:	@INT(1.9834) = 1
	@INT(0.9921) = 0
	@INT(A1) = 0, if A1 contains a label or is blank

@LN(x)

The @LN function returns the natural logarithm of x when x is a numeric value greater than 0. In any natural logarithm, the mathematical constant e is used as the base. You also can use @LN to return the inverse of @EXP.

Examples:	@LN(1.00000) = 0
	@LN(2.718282) = 1
	@LN(@EXP(10)) = 10
	@LN(−1) = ERR
	@LN(A1) = ERR, if A1 contains a label or is blank

@LOG(x)

@LOG returns the base 10 logarithm of x when x is a numeric value that is greater than 0.

Examples:	@LOG(0) = ERR
	@LOG(1) = 0
	@LOG(10) = 1
	@LOG(A1) = ERR, if A1 contains a label or is blank

@MOD(x,y)

The @MOD function divides the x argument by y and returns any remainder. In this syntax, x must be a numeric value, and y must be a numeric value that isn't equal to 0.

Examples:	@MOD(10,10) = 0
	@MOD(10,3.5) = 3
	@MOD(10,0) = ERR
	@MOD(A1,1) = 0, if A1 contains a label or is blank
	@MOD(3,A1) = ERR, if A1 contains a label or is blank

@RAND

The @RAND function returns a fractional random number between 0 and 1. @RAND is useful when you must create a set of random numbers to use in statistical analysis.

To generate random numbers outside the 0 to 1 range, multiply the @RAND function by the difference between the high and low end of the new range, and then add the new low end number. This formula is expressed as follows:

@RAND * (*high number – low number*) + *low number*

Examples: @RAND*6+1 = returns a random number between 1 and 7

@RAND+7 = returns a random number between 7 and 8

> **NOTE**
>
> Quattro Pro generates a new random number for each existing @RAND function on a page every time you enter data into the page or press F9 to recalculate.

@ROUND(*x,Num*)

The @ROUND function rounds the value of *x* to *Num* decimal places. In this syntax, *x* must be a numeric value, and *Num* must be a numeric value that falls in the range –15 to 15.

Examples: @ROUND(4.53494,3) = 4.535
@ROUND(4.5,1) = 4.5
@ROUND(0.5994,16) = ERR
@ROUND(5.3,A1) = 5, if A1 contains a label or is blank
@ROUND(A1,3) = 0, if A1 contains a label or is blank
@ROUND(13.25,–1) = 10

@SQRT(*x*)

The @SQRT function supplies the square root of *x* when *x* is a numeric value that is greater than or equal to 0. Quattro Pro returns the value 0 when *x* is a label or a reference to a cell containing a label.

Examples: @SQRT(16) = 4
@SQRT(–25) = ERR
@SQRT(A1) = 0, if A1 contains a label or is blank

Using Trigonometric Commands in a Notebook

Table 6.2 lists the trigonometric @function commands. The following definitions include examples of how to use these commands in your own notebooks.

Table 6.2 Trigonometric @Function Commands

@Function	Description
@ACOS(x)	Returns the arc cosine of radian angle x
@ASIN(x)	Returns the arc sine of radian angle x
@ATAN(x)	Returns the arc tangent of radian angle x
@ATAN2(x,y)	Returns the arc tangent of radian angle with coordinates x and y
@COS(x)	Returns the cosine of radian angle x
@DEGREES(x)	Converts x radians to degrees
@PI	Returns the value 3.141593
@RADIANS(x)	Converts x degrees to radians
@SIN(x)	Returns the sine of radian angle x
@TAN(x)	Returns the tangent of radian angle x

@ACOS(x)

@ACOS returns the arc cosine of angle x when x is a numeric value between –1 and 1. The result is a radian angle with x as a cosine.

Examples: @ACOS(–1) = 3.141593
@ACOS(0) = 1.570796
@ACOS(1) = 0
@ACOS(2) = ERR

To convert radians to degrees, use @DEGREES.

    Examples: @DEGREES(3.141593) = 180
                        @DEGREES(1.5707964) = 90
                        @DEGREES(@ACOS(1)) = 0

@ASIN(x)

@ASIN returns the arc sine of angle x when x is a numeric value between –1 and 1. The result is a radian angle whose sine is x.

    Examples: @ASIN(–1) = –1.5708
                        @ASIN(0) = 0
                        @ASIN(1) = 1.570796
                        @ASIN(2) = ERR

To convert radians to degrees, use @DEGREES.

    Examples: @DEGREES(–1.570796) = –90
                        @DEGREES(0) = 0
                        @DEGREES(@ASIN(1)) = 90

@ATAN(x)

@ATAN returns the arc tangent of angle x when x is a numeric value between –1 and 1. The result is a radian angle with the tangent x.

    Examples: @ATAN(–1) = –0.7854
                        @ATAN(0) = 0
                        @ATAN(1) = 0.785398

To convert radians to degrees, use @DEGREES.

    Examples: @DEGREES(–0.785398) = –45
                        @DEGREES(0) = 0
                        @DEGREES(@ATAN(1)) = 45

@ATAN2(x,y)

@ATAN2 returns the arc tangent of an angle with coordinates x and y when x and y are numeric values. The result is a radian angle with the tangent x/y.

Examples: @ATAN2(2,3) = 0.982794
                   @ATAN2(0,3) = 1.570796
                   @ATAN2(0,0) = ERR

To convert radians to degrees, use @DEGREES.

Example: @DEGREES(ATAN2(0,3)) = 90

@COS(x)

@COS returns the cosine of angle x when x is a numeric value entered in radians.

Examples: @COS(–1) = 0.540302
                   @COS(0) = 1
                   @COS(1) = 0.540302

To convert degrees to radians, use @RADIANS.

Example: @COS(@RADIANS(45)) = 0.707107

@DEGREES(x)

@DEGREES converts x radians to degrees when x is a numeric value. To convert x radians to degrees, you also can multiply x by 180/@PI.

Examples: @DEGREES(0.5235987) = 30
                   @DEGREES(1.0471975) = 60
                   @DEGREES(1.5707964) = 90

@PI

@PI returns the value of pi as 3.141593. *Pi* is the ratio of a circle's circumference to its diameter.

@RADIANS(x)

@RADIANS converts x degrees to radians when x is a numeric value. To convert x degrees to radians, you also can multiply x by @PI/180.

Examples: @RADIANS(30) = 0.523599
                   @RADIANS(60) = 1.047198
                   @RADIANS(90) = 1.570796

@SIN(x)

The @SIN function returns the sine of the radian angle x when x is a numeric value entered in radians.

Examples: @SIN(–1) = –0.84147
@SIN(0) = 0
@SIN(1) = 0.841471

To convert degrees into radians, use @RADIANS.

Example: @SIN(@RADIANS(30)) = 0.5

@TAN(x)

The @TAN function returns the tangent of the radian angle x when x is a numeric value entered in radians.

Examples: @TAN(–1) = –1.55741
@TAN(0) = 0
@TAN(1) = 1.557408

To convert degrees into radians, use @RADIANS.

Example: @TAN(@RADIANS(45)) = 1

Using Statistical @Functions

The statistical @function commands calculate common statistical measures using sample and population data sets. Table 6.3 describes the statistical @functions.

Most of the statistical @functions use the *List* argument to define the location of the data set. In this syntax, *List* can be one or more numeric or block values. *List* also can be a 3-D cell block. When you use more than one cell block in an argument, separate the blocks with commas.

Table 6.3 Statistical @Function Commands

@Function	Description
@AVG(*List*)	Calculates the average of the values in *List*
@COUNT(*List*)	Counts the number of non-blank cells in *List*
@MAX(*List*)	Returns the maximum numeric or date value in *List*

@Function	Description
@MIN(*List*)	Returns the minimum numeric value in *List*
@STD(*List*)	Returns the population standard deviation of *List*
@STDS(*List*)	Returns the sample standard deviation of *List*
@SUM(*List*)	Sums all the numeric values in *List*
@SUMPRODUCT (*Block1,Block2*)	Returns the sum and product of *Block1* and *Block2*
@VAR(*List*)	Returns the population variance of *List*
@VARS(*List*)	Returns the sample variance of *List*

Figure 6.1 shows an application that uses the statistical @function commands to analyze automobile production statistics. In this figure, *List* is block C5..C8 for the @AVG formula shown in cell C10. The block corresponding to *List* can change depending on which column contains the @function and which grouping of data from block C5..G8 is to be used in a particular calculation.

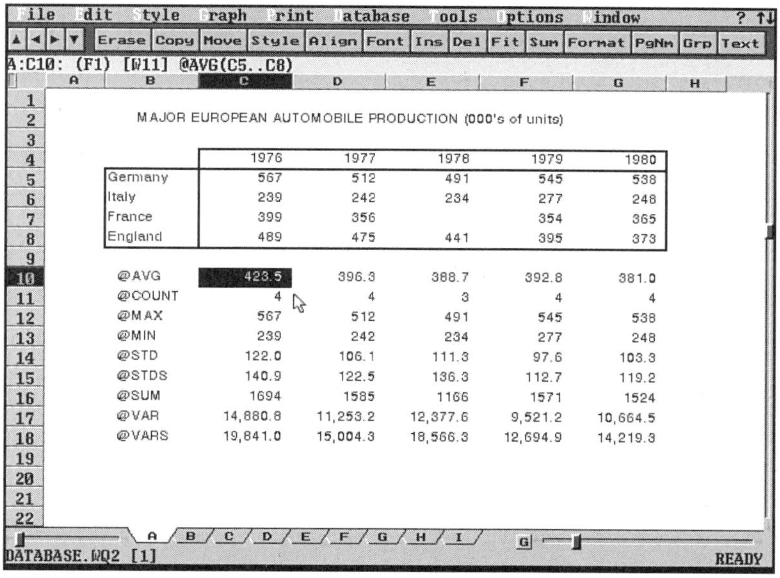

Fig. 6.1

A statistical @function application.

As you read through the following command definitions, refer to figure 6.1 to learn more about how to use a particular command in an application.

@AVG(*List*)

The @AVG function calculates the average of all values in *List*. Quattro Pro ignores blank cells and treats labels as 0 when calculating an average. (Refer to fig. 6.1 for the following examples.)

Examples: @AVG(C5..C8) = 423.5
@AVG(D5..D8) = 396.3

@COUNT(*List*)

The @COUNT function counts the number of non-blank cells in *List*. This function can return the number of cells in *List* that contain data or locate the number of missing entries in a range of cells that always contains a fixed number of entries. (Refer to fig. 6.1 for the following examples.)

Examples: @COUNT(C5..C8) = 4
@COUNT(C5..C8,D5..D8) = 8
@COUNT(E5..E8) = 3

@MAX(*List*)

The @MAX function returns the maximum numeric or date value in *List*. You can use this function to find the latest invoice date in a sales notebook, pick the highest production figure from an analysis report, or locate the final transaction number in an accounting journal. (Refer to fig. 6.1 for the following examples.)

Examples: @MAX(D5..D8) = 512
@MAX(C5..C8,D5..D8) = 567

@MIN(*List*)

The @MIN function gives the minimum numeric or date value in *List*. You can use this function to find the first invoice date in a sales notebook, pick the lowest production figure from an analysis report, or locate the first transaction number in an accounting journal. (Refer to fig. 6.1 for the following examples.)

Examples: @MIN(F5..F8) = 277
@MIN(E5..E8,F5..F8) = 234

@STD(*List*)

The @STD function calculates the standard deviation of the values in
List, when *List* is the population data set. The square of this function—
@STD(*List*)^2—returns the population variance.

Standard deviation tells you how much each value in *List* differs from
the average of all the values in *List*. One use of @STD is to determine the
reliability of the average. The lower the standard deviation, the less
each value in *List* varies from the average.

The @STD function ignores blank cells and treats labels as 0. When *List*
contains only blank cells, @STD returns ERR.

Refer to figure 6.1 for the following examples.

    Examples: @STD(G5..G8) = 103.3
                                  @STD(B9..G9) = ERR

@STDS(*List*)

The @STDS function calculates the standard deviation of the values in
List, when *List* is a sample drawn from the population data set. The
square of this function—@STDS(*List*)^2—is the sample variance.

The @STDS function ignores any blank cells and treats labels as 0.
When *List* contains only blank cells, @STDS returns ERR.

    Example: @STDS(F5..F8) = 112.7 (refer to fig. 6.1)

> **NOTE**
>
> @STDS isn't a 1-2-3 compatible @function command. If you must calculate standard deviation for data appearing on a 1-2-3-compatible worksheet, use the @STD function.

@SUM(*List*)

The @SUM function returns the sum total of all numeric values in *List*.
This @function is used to add up data in cell blocks. (Refer to fig. 6.1 for
the following examples.)

    Examples: @SUM(C5..C8) = 1,694
                                    @SUM(D5..D8) = 1,585
                                    @SUM(C5..C8,D5..D8) = 3,279

@SUMPRODUCT(*Block1,Block2*)

The @SUMPRODUCT function returns the sum and the product of the two block arguments. In this syntax, Quattro Pro multiplies each corresponding row value in *Block1* and *Block2* and then adds the results.

To use this command properly, the two blocks must have the same number of rows and columns. The blocks can be a one-dimensional row or column but must be equal in length. Quattro Pro returns ERR when the two blocks are unequal in length.

Suppose that the following cells contain the data shown:

D10 = 1	E10 = 1
D11 = 2	E11 = 2
D12 = 3	E12 = 3
D13 = 4	E13 = 4

The data in these cells yield the following results:

@SUMPRODUCT(D10..D11,E10..E11) = 5

@SUMPRODUCT(D12..D13,E12..E13) = 25

@SUMPRODUCT(D10..D13,E10..E13) = 30

NOTE

@SUMPRODUCT isn't a 1-2-3 compatible function. Don't use it in a worksheet that requires 1-2-3 compatibility.

@VAR(*List*)

The @VAR function calculates the variance of non-blank, numeric cells in *List*, when *List* represents the population data set. The @VAR function uses the n method (biased), which divides the sum of components by n in determining population variance. In this syntax, Quattro Pro treats text as 0. Take the square root of this function to derive the population standard deviation.

Examples: @VAR(E5..E8) = 12,377.6
@VAR(G5..G8) = 10,664.5

@VARS(*List*)

The @VARS function supplies the variance of non-blank, numeric cells in *List*, when *List* represents a sample drawn from the population data set. The @VARS function uses the $n-1$ method (unbiased), which divides the sum of components by $n-1$ in determining sample variance. In this syntax, Quattro Pro treats text as 0. Take the square root of this function to derive the sample standard deviation.

Examples: @VARS(E5..E8) = 18,566.3
                          @VARS(G5..G8) = 14,219.3

> **NOTE**
>
> @VARS isn't a 1-2-3 compatible function. Don't use it in a worksheet that requires 1-2-3 compatibility.

Using String @Functions

The string @function commands give you the power to manipulate letters and numbers that appear in a label. These commands work only on labels, although they treat a number appearing in a label as though the number is text.

Among other things, these special functions enable you to add and subtract text strings, alter the upper- and lowercase settings for any character in a string, and search through and replace data in labels. Table 6.4 describes the string @functions.

Table 6.4 String @Function Commands

@Function	Description
@CHAR(*Code*)	Returns the ASCII character corresponding to *Code*
@CLEAN("*String*")	Removes all non-printable ASCII characters from *String*
@CODE("*String*")	Changes the first character in *String* to ASCII

(continues)

Table 6.4 Continued

@Function	Description
@EXACT("*String1*", "*String2*")	Compares the value of *String1* to *String2*
@FIND("*SubString*", "*String*",*StartNumber*)	Searches through *String* for *SubString*, starting at the character position specified by *StartNumber*
@HEXTONUM("*String*")	Converts the hexadecimal number in *String* to its equivalent decimal value
@LEFT("*String*",*Num*)	Displays the far-left *Num* characters in *String*
@LENGTH("*String*")	Returns the number of characters in *String*
@LOWER("*String*")	Converts *String* to lowercase characters
@MID("*String*", *StartNumber*,*Num*)	Returns the first *Num* characters in *String*, starting with character number *StartNumber*
@N(*Block*)	Returns the numeric value of the upper left cell in *Block*
@NUMTOHEX(*x*)	Converts *x* to its hexadecimal string value
@PROPER("*String*")	Converts the first letter of every word in *String* to uppercase
@REPEAT("*String*",*Num*)	Returns *Num* copies of *String* as one continuous label
@REPLACE("*String*", *StartNum*,*Num*, "*NewString*")	Replaces *Num* characters in *String* with *NewString*, starting at the character position specified by *StartNum*
@RIGHT("*String*",*Num*)	Displays the last *Num* characters in *String*
@S(*Block*)	Returns the string value of the upper left cell in *Block*
@STRING(*x*,*DecPlaces*)	Converts *x* to a string, rounded to *DecPlaces*
@TRIM("*String*")	Removes extraneous spaces from *String*
@UPPER("*String*")	Returns *String* in uppercase characters
@VALUE("*String*")	Converts *String* into a numeric value

Manipulating strings is like doing mathematical operations on letters. Quattro Pro can manipulate strings because these @functions use special arguments. Table 6.5 describes these string @function arguments.

Table 6.5 String @Function Command Arguments

Argument	Description
Block	A block value
Code	A numeric ASCII value between 1 and 255
DecPlaces	A numeric value between 0 and 15 that represents decimal places
NewString	A string value that represents the characters to insert at position *Num*
Num	A numeric value >= 0
StartNumber	A numeric value >= 0 that denotes the character position at which to begin the search
String	A string value or a hexadecimal number in quotation marks
String1, String2	Valid string values
SubString	A valid string value to search through
x	A numeric value

@CHAR(*Code*)

The @CHAR function displays the ASCII character equivalent of *Code*. The valid code range is 1 to 255. This function is the reverse of the @CODE function.

Examples: @CHAR(0) = ERR
@CHAR(60) = <
@CHAR(65) = A
@CHAR(94) = ^
@CHAR(256) = ERR
@CHAR(A1) = ERR, if A1 contains the code 256 or is blank

NOTE

Any time you use a cell address as an argument in a string function, the contents of the cell must be a string (preceded by one of the four label prefixes). When you use strings and cell addresses as arguments in a string function, remember this important difference: Double quotation marks must enclose a string argument within the formula, but a label prefix must precede a value or label in a referenced cell.

@CLEAN("*String*")

The @CLEAN function erases all non-printable ASCII characters (0-31) encountered in *String*.

> **Examples:**   @CLEAN("HELLO♥") = HELLO, where ♥ is the non-printable character associated with ASCII code 3
>
> @CLEAN("HELLO♂") = HELLO, where ♂ is the non-printable character associated with ASCII code 11

@CODE("*String*")

The @CODE function displays the ASCII code equivalent of the first character it encounters in *String*. This function is the reverse of the @CHAR function.

> **Examples:**   @CODE("<") = 60
> @CODE("A") = 65
> @CODE("^") = 94
> @CODE(A1) = 94, when A1 contains the string ^

@EXACT("*String1*","*String2*")

The @EXACT function compares *String1* to *String2*. When the values are identical, Quattro Pro returns 1; otherwise, it returns 0.

Enclose both compare strings in quotation marks except when the string is a block name. When Quattro Pro compares labels, it ignores numbers and label prefixes.

> **Examples:**   @EXACT("trust","Trust") = 0
> @EXACT("Trust","Trust") = 1
> @EXACT(50,"50") = ERR
> @EXACT(A1,B1) = 1, when A1 contains the string *Trust* and B1 contains the string *Trust*

@FIND("*SubString*","*String*",*StartNumber*)

@FIND searches through *String* for *SubString*. If Quattro Pro finds *SubString*, it returns the character position of the first occurrence of *SubString*.

Quattro Pro begins the @FIND operation at position *StartNumber* in *String*. The first character in *String* is designated as 0, the second as 1, and so on. *StartNumber* cannot be greater than the number of characters in *String*, minus 1.

Use the @FIND function with @REPLACE to perform a search-and-replace operation. When @FIND fails to find at least one occurrence of *SubString*, Quattro Pro returns ERR.

Examples: @FIND("i","girth",0) = 1
@FIND("h","girth",0) = 4
@FIND("G","girth",0) = ERR
@FIND(A1,B1,0) = 4, when A1 contains the string *h* and B1 contains the string *girth*

@HEXTONUM("String")

@HEXTONUM converts the hexadecimal number in *String* to its equivalent decimal value. In this syntax, *String* must be enclosed in quotation marks. This function is the reverse of the @NUMTOHEX function.

Examples: @HEXTONUM("f") = 15
@HEXTONUM("35") = 53
@HEXTONUM(A1) = 53, when A1 contains the string 35

@LEFT("String",Num)

The @LEFT function displays the number (*Num*) of characters specified that it finds in *String*. This function extracts characters from the left side of *String*.

Quattro Pro returns ERR when *String* is a numeric value, a date value, or a blank cell. Quattro Pro returns all of *String* if *Num* is longer than the length of *String*.

Examples: @LEFT("John",2) = Jo
@LEFT("John",10) = John
@LEFT(45,2) = ERR
@LEFT(A1,10) = John, when A1 contains the string *John*

@LENGTH("String")

@LENGTH returns the character length of *String*, including spaces. Use the ampersand (&) to combine strings and cell addresses. Place quotation marks around *String* when it is a text string. Quattro Pro returns ERR if *String* references a blank cell or isn't enclosed with quotation marks.

Examples:
@LENGTH("John") = 4
@LENGTH("Hello"&"Greetings") = 14
@LENGTH(123456) = ERR
@LENGTH(A1) = 4, when A1 contains the string *John*

@LOWER("String")

@LOWER converts *String* to a lowercase character display. Quattro Pro doesn't alter numbers and symbols appearing in *String* but returns ERR when *String* is a blank cell or is a number or date value.

Examples:
@LOWER("STRING") = string
@LOWER("Hello, John.") = hello, john.
@LOWER("94 Carroll Canyon") = 94 carroll canyon
@LOWER(32876) = ERR
@LOWER(A1) = john, when A1 contains the string *JOHN*

@MID("String",StartNumber,Num)

@MID extracts the first *Num* characters in *String*, beginning with character number *StartNumber*. In this syntax, *String* must be a text string enclosed in quotation marks or a reference to a cell containing a text string enclosed with quotation marks. Quattro Pro returns a blank cell when *StartNumber* is greater than the length of *String* and when *Num* is 0.

You cannot enter strings without quotation marks. If you try, the program beeps and displays an error message.

Examples:
@MID("John Donovan",5,7) = Donovan
@MID("Tim Atkins",20,5) = returns a blank cell
@MID("Scott Matthews",6,4) = Matt
@MID(2519,1,2) = ERR

@MID(A1,5,7) = Donovan, when A1 contains the
string *John Donovan*

@N(*Block*)

The @N function returns the numeric value located in the upper left cell
of *Block*. @N returns a 0 if the upper left cell in *Block* contains a label or
is blank.

Examples: @N(A1..A5) = 25, when A1 contains the value
25
@N(A1..A5) = 0, when A1 is blank
@N(A1..A5) = 0, when A1 contains the label
"DATA"

Quattro Pro uses the @N function for compatibility with other electronic spreadsheet programs. Other programs use this function to
avoid ERR values resulting from attempts to do calculations using
labels.

@NUMTOHEX(*x*)

The @NUMTOHEX function returns the hexadecimal equivalent of *x* as a
string value. This function is the reverse of the @HEXTONUM function.

Examples: @NUMTOHEX(106) = 6A
@NUMTOHEX(219) = DB
@NUMTOHEX(A1) = DB, when A1 contains the
value 219
@NUMTOHEX(A1) = 0, when A1 contains a label
or is blank

@PROPER("*String*")

@PROPER modifies *String* so that the first letter of each word in *String* is
uppercase and all other letters are lowercase. Blank spaces, punctuation marks, and numbers signify the end of a word.

Examples: @PROPER("JOHN doNAVAN") = John Donavan
@PROPER("JAMES J. PARKER") = James J. Parker
@PROPER("1990's census") = 1990'S Census
@PROPER(A1) = James J. Parker, when A1
contains the string *JAMES J. PARKER*

@REPEAT(" *String*",*Num*)

The @REPEAT function returns *Num* copies of *String* as a single, continuous label. In this syntax, *Num* is a numeric value that is greater than or equal to 0. When repeating a text string, enclose *String* in double quotation marks.

Examples: @REPEAT("hello!",3) = hello!hello!hello!
@REPEAT("*",20) = ********************
@REPEAT(A1,3) = hi!hi!hi!, when A1 contains
the string *hi!*

@REPLACE(" *String*",*StartNum,Num,*" *NewString*")

The @REPLACE function enables you to replace *Num* characters in *String* with *NewString*, beginning at character *StartNum* in *String*. In this syntax, *Num* is a numeric value greater than or equal to 0 that identifies the number of characters to replace.

Examples: @REPLACE("O'Nickels",2,7,"Grady") = O'Grady
@REPLACE("Jenny L. Peters",6,3,"") = Jenny
Peters
@REPLACE("Inventory Figures",10,0," Control")
= Inventory Control Figures

TIP

When you use this command to insert one string into another, leave a blank space after the opening quotation mark for *NewString*. This space ensures the proper number of spaces between words.

@RIGHT(" *String*",*Num*)

The @RIGHT function displays the last *Num* characters in *String*. Use this function to extract characters from the right side of a label or string.

@RIGHT returns ERR when *String* isn't a valid string. @RIGHT returns a blank cell when *Num* is 0. Quattro Pro returns the entire string when the character length of *Num* is greater than the number of characters in *String*.

Examples: @RIGHT("Jeff Turner",6) = Turner
@RIGHT("Jeff Turner",11) = Jeff Turner
@RIGHT("123",1) = 3
@RIGHT(567,1) = ERR
@RIGHT(A1,1) = 3, when A1 contains the string *123*

@S(*Block*)

@S returns the string value located in the upper left cell of *Block*. Quattro Pro returns a blank cell if *Block* contains a numerical value, a date value, or a blank cell.

Examples: @S(A1..A5) = DATA, when A1 contains the label DATA
@S(A1..A5) = returns a blank cell when A1 is blank
@S(A1..A5) = returns a blank cell when A1 contains the value 25

@STRING(*x,DecPlaces*)

The @STRING function converts *x* to a string rounded to *DecPlaces* decimal places. In this syntax, *x* is a numeric value, and *DecPlaces* must be a numeric value between 0 and 15.

After you convert a number or date to a label with the @STRING function, Quattro Pro doesn't enable you to format the display of the returned value.

Examples: @STRING(14.88,0) = 15
@STRING(78.7,2) = 78.70
@STRING("John",3) = 0.000
@STRING(A1,2) = 78.70, when A1 contains the value 78.7

@TRIM("*String*")

@TRIM removes extraneous spaces from *String*. This function deletes spaces after the last non-space character or before the first non-space character. @TRIM also eliminates extra spaces between words. Quattro Pro returns ERR when *String* is empty or contains a numeric value.

Examples:	@TRIM("extra spaces") = extra spaces
	@TRIM("no extra spaces") = no extra spaces
	@TRIM(456) = ERR
	@TRIM(A1) = ERR, when A1 contains the value 456

@UPPER("*String*")

@UPPER returns *String* in uppercase characters. Quattro Pro doesn't alter numbers and symbols and returns ERR when *String* is a numerical value, a date value, or a blank cell.

Examples:	@UPPER("upper") = UPPER
	@UPPER("Hello there") = HELLO THERE
	@UPPER(1234) = ERR
	@UPPER("94 Carroll Canyon") = 94 CARROLL CANYON
	@UPPER(A1) = UPPER, when A1 contains the string *upper*

@VALUE("*String*")

The @VALUE function converts *String* into a numeric value. *String* may contain arithmetic operators, but Quattro Pro ignores dollar signs, commas, and leading and trailing spaces. If Quattro Pro encounters an embedded space in *String*, this function returns ERR.

Examples:	@VALUE(" 4.58") = 4.58
	@VALUE(" 4.33 ") = 4.33
	@VALUE("10. 25") = ERR
	@VALUE(12/4) = 3
	@VALUE("200,872") = 200872 (comma is omitted)
	@VALUE(A1) = 1528, when A1 contains the string *1528*

Using Miscellaneous @Functions

The miscellaneous @function commands supply you with information about your notebook and the current work session. These commands tell you the number of rows or columns in a block, for example, display the format attributes for a cell, and display the amount of extended or expanded memory now available to Quattro Pro.

When a command's syntax contains *Attribute* as an argument, you can use any attributes listed in table 6.6. *Attribute* must be enclosed in quotation marks or must refer to a cell that contains a valid attribute. (For a listing of possible formats, see tables 6.8, 6.9, and 6.10.)

Table 6.6 Valid Quattro Pro Attribute Codes

Code	Description
"address"	Specifies the address of the upper left cell in *Block*.
"row"	Specifies the row number of the upper left cell in *Block*; the "row" code ranges from 1 to 8192.
"col"	Specifies the column number of the upper left cell in *Block*; the "column" code ranges from 1 to 256.
"sheet"	Specifies the page number on which *Block* now resides; pages numbers 1 through 256 correspond to page names A through IV.
"NotebookName"	Specifies the name of the active notebook up to a maximum of eight characters; the file name extension isn't included with the name, as in ATTR for a notebook named ATTR.WQ2.
"NotebookPath"	Specifies the directory path name a full file name of the active notebook, as in C:\QPRO\ATTR.WQ2.
"TwoDAddress"	Specifies the 2-D address for the cell referenced in the upper left corner of *Block* (for example, $B$10). The page name isn't supplied with the 2-D address even if *Block* exists on a page other than the active one.
"ThreeDAddress"	Specifies the 3-D address for the cell referenced in the upper left corner of *Block*—for example, $C:$B$10.
"FullAddress"	Specifies the notebook name without the file name extension followed by the 3-D address, for the cell referenced in the upper left corner of *Block*, as in [ATTR]$C:$B$10.
"contents"	Specifies the contents of the upper left cell in *Block*.
"type"	Specifies the type of data in the upper left cell in *Block*, as follows: b is a blank cell l is a cell that contains a label v is a cell that contains a formula or number

(continues)

Table 6.6 Continued

Code	Description
"prefix"	Specifies the label-prefix character of the upper left cell in *Block*, as follows: \ is the repeating label prefix " is the right-aligned label prefix ^ is the centered label prefix ' is the left-aligned label prefix
"protect"	Specifies the protection status of the upper left cell in *Block*, as follows: 0 is an unprotected cell 1 is a protected cell
"width"	Specifies the width of the column containing the upper left cell in *Block*; the "width" code ranges from 1 to 254
"rwidth"	Specifies the width of *Block*
"format"	Specifies the current numeric format of the upper left cell in *Block*; table 6.7 shows the valid numeric formats

Table 6.7 Valid Numeric Formats

Code	Description
+ +/−	Bar graph
,n	Commas, where n = 0 to 15 decimal places
Cn	Currency, where n = 0 to 15 decimal places
En	Exponential, where n = 0 to 15 decimal places
Fn	Fixed, where n = 0 to 15 decimal places
G	General
H	Hidden
Pn	Percent, where n = 0 to 15 decimal places
Sn	Scientific, where n = 0 to 15 decimal places
T	Formulas displayed as text

Table 6.8 Valid Date Formats

Code	Description
D1	*dd-mmm-yy*
D2	*dd-mmm*
D3	*mmm-yy*
D4	*mm/dd/yy* *dd/mm/yy* *dd.mm.yy* *yy-mm-dd*
D5	*mm/dd* *dd/mm* *dd.mm* *mm-dd*

You can choose one of four settings for codes D4 and D5 in table 6.8 by choosing the /**O**ptions **I**nternational command. When you choose a new default setting, that setting becomes the default long international date format when you choose /**S**tyle **N**umeric Format **D**ate **1** (Long Intl.) or **2** (Short Intl.).

Table 6.9 Valid Time Formats

Code	Description
D6	*hh:mm:ss am/pm*
D7	*hh:mm am/pm*
D8	*hh:mm:ss* (24-hour) *hh.mm.ss* (24-hour) *hh,mm,ss* (24-hour) *HHhMMmSSs*
D9	*hh:mm* (24-hour) *hh.mm* (24-hour) *hh,mm* *HHhMMm*

You can choose one of four settings for codes D8 and D9 in table 6.9 by choosing the /**O**ptions **I**nternational command. When you choose a new default setting, that setting becomes the default long international time format when you choose /**S**tyle **N**umeric Format **D**ate Time **1** (Long Intl.) or **2** (Short Intl.).

Miscellaneous @function commands also enable you to look up entries in a data table. In a horizontal lookup table, Quattro Pro searches for values beginning in the top row, moving from left to right. In a vertical lookup table, Quattro Pro searches for values beginning in the left column, moving from top to bottom. Table 6.10 describes the miscellaneous @function commands.

Table 6.10 Miscellaneous @Function Commands

@Function	Description
@@(*Cell*)	Returns the contents of *Cell* as an address or cell block when *Cell* is a label
@CELL(*Attribute,Block*)	Returns attributes for a cell in *Block*
@CELLINDEX(*Attribute, Block,Column,Row<,Page>*)	Returns attributes for a cell offset *Column* columns, *Row* rows, and optionally *Page* pages
@CELLPOINTER (*Attribute*)	Returns attributes for the active cell
@CHOOSE(*Number,List*)	Returns the value from *List* located in the *Number* position
@COLS(*Block*)	Returns the number of columns in *Block*
@CURVALUE("*GeneralAction*", "*SpecificAction*")	Describes the most recent menu command execution
@ERR	Returns ERR in a cell
@HLOOKUP(*x,Block,Row*)	Searches for the first value <= *x* and returns the value located *Row* rows below it in *Block*
@INDEX(*Block,Column, Row<,Page>*)	Searches through *Block* and returns the value in a cell offset *Column* columns, *Row* rows, and (optionally) *Page* pages
@MEMAVAIL	Returns the number of available bytes of conventional memory
@MEMEMSAVAIL	Returns the number of available bytes of expanded memory
@NA	Returns the special value NA (not available)
@ROWS(*Block*)	Returns the number of rows in a given block

@Function	Description
@SHEETS(*Block*)	Returns the number of pages in a given 3-D cell block
@VERSION	Supplies the version number of Quattro Pro
@VLOOKUP(*x,Block,Column*)	Searches for the first value <= *x* and returns the value located *Column* columns to the right of it in *Block*

Figure 6.2 shows how to use a table to analyze every possible attribute for three cells using the @CELL command. The attributes for the data appearing in D3, E3, and F3 appear in block D4..F13. (Note that cell F3 contains the label *Star material*, which is formatted as a hidden cell.) As you read the next four command definitions, refer to figure 6.2 to learn more about how to use a particular command in an application.

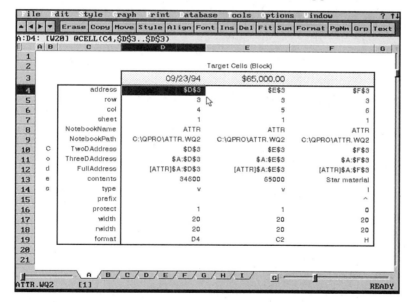

Fig. 6.2

Analyzing attributes in a table.

@@(Cell)

The @@(*Cell*) function provides two ways of referencing a cell—directly or indirectly. If, for example, cell B10 contains the value 150, the function @@("B10") returns the value 150. This type of reference is a direct cell reference. In this syntax, *Cell* must be a single-cell address enclosed in quotation marks or a block name that has been assigned to a single-cell block, also enclosed in quotation marks. (Refer to figure 6.2 for the following five examples.)

Examples: @@("C5") = row
@@("D5") = 3
@@("TEST") = 3, when cell D5 is named TEST
@@(D5) = ERR
@@(TEST) = ERR

Normally, the @@(*Cell*) function returns ERR when the *Cell* argument isn't enclosed in quotation marks. When indirectly referencing a cell, however, don't enclose the *Cell* argument in quotation marks. If, for example, cell B10 contains the label *Z100* and cell Z100 contains the number 150, the function @@(B10) returns the value 150.

NOTE   The following examples *don't* refer to figure 6.2.

Examples: @@(A1) = 5, when cell A1 contains the label *B5* and cell B5 contains the value 5

@@(A1) = Cool, when cell A1 contains the label *TEST* and the name TEST has been assigned to cell B5, and cell B5 contains the label *Cool*

@@(A1) = 0, when cell A1 contains the label *B5* and cell B5 is blank

@@(A1) = ERR, when cell A1 is blank

@CELL(*Attribute,Block*)

The @CELL function evaluates *Block* and returns an attribute code of the upper left cell in a block. In this syntax, *Attribute* must be one of the attribute codes from table 6.6, and *Block* must be a value or label.

You can enter *Attribute* in upper- or lowercase but must enclose it in quotation marks. *Attribute* also can be the address of a cell that contains a value or label.

Examples: @CELL("address",D3) = $D$3
@CELL("format",E3) = C2
@CELL("protect",F3) = 0
@CELL("contents",F3) = Star material
@CELL("NotebookPath",E3) =
C:\QPRO\ATTR.WQ2

@CELL doesn't recalculate automatically. Press F9 to recalculate and display current values.

@CELLINDEX(*Attribute,Block,Column,Row<,Page>*)

The @CELLINDEX function evaluates *Block* and returns an attribute of the cell in the specified column, row, and (optionally) page. In this syntax, *Attribute* must be one of the attribute codes from table 6.6, and *Block* must be a value or label. Refer to figure 6.2 for the following examples.

Examples: @CELLINDEX("type",D4..F19,2,4) = 1
@CELLINDEX("width",D4..F19,0,0) = 20
@CELLINDEX("ThreeDAddress",D4..F19,1,10)
= $A:$E$14

This function works like @CELL but returns the attribute for a cell offset *Column* columns, *Row* rows, and *Page* pages from the first coordinate in *Block* (refer to fig. 6.2).

@CELLINDEX doesn't recalculate automatically. Press F9 to recalculate and display current values.

@CELLPOINTER(*Attribute*)

The @CELLPOINTER function evaluates the active cell (where the selector is located) and returns an *Attribute* code. In this syntax, *Attribute* must be one of the attribute codes from table 6.6.

This function works like @CELL and @CELLINDEX but returns the specified *Attribute* code for the active cell. If you move the selector to a different cell, press F9 to calculate a new result for the @CELLPOINTER function (refer to fig. 6.2).

Examples: @CELLPOINTER("rwidth") = 20, when F12 is the active cell
@CELLPOINTER("contents") = 65000, when E13 is the active cell

@CHOOSE(*Number,List*)

The @CHOOSE function returns the value from *List* located in the *Number* position. In this syntax, *Number* is a numeric value that is less than or equal to the number of items in *List* minus 1, and *List* is equal to a group of numeric or string values separated by commas. Each individual item in *List* must be enclosed by quotation marks.

The value of *Number* determines which *List* value is selected. For example, 0 selects the first value in *List*, 1 the second, 2 the third, and so on. *Number* may be a cell address, an integer, a string, or a mixture of the three. *List* must not exceed 254 characters.

Examples:	@CHOOSE(0,"John","Pat","Craig") = John
	@CHOOSE(1,"John","Pat","Craig") = Pat
	@CHOOSE(2,"John","Pat","Craig") = Craig
	@CHOOSE(5,"John","Pat","Craig") = ERR

@COLS(*Block*)

The @COLS function returns the number of columns in *Block*. In this syntax, *Block* may be a cell block or a block name.

Examples:	@COLS(A1..IV1) = 256
	@COLS(A1..A1) = 1

@CURVALUE("*GeneralAction*","*SpecificAction*")

The @CURVALUE function returns a description of a menu command setting specified by *GeneralAction* and *SpecificAction*. In this syntax, *GeneralAction* is a general menu category such as File, and *SpecificAction* is a specific menu choice such as Save **As**. Quotation marks must enclose both arguments.

Examples:	@CURVALUE("file","save") = C:\QPRO\SALES.WQ2 (the name of the last file saved with the Save **As** command on the **F**ile menu)
	@CURVALUE("file","directory") = C:\QPRO (the name of the current directory setting on the File menu)

@CURVALUE("graph","type") = Stacked Bar (the current **G**raph Type setting on the **G**raph menu)

@ERR

The @ERR function returns the value ERR, which isn't a label but a unique number that Quattro Pro reserves to identify error conditions on a page. Use this function to return ERR in the active cell and in any other cells that reference the active cell. When used with the @IF function, @ERR is useful for calling attention to errors on the active page.

The following @function commands don't return ERR when they reference a cell containing ERR: @COUNT, @DCOUNT, @ISERR, @ISNA, @ISNUMBER, @ISSTRING, and @CELL.

@HLOOKUP(x,Block,Row)

The @HLOOKUP function moves through *Block* horizontally, looking for the last value that is less than or equal to *x*. This function provides you with an effective way to access information stored in a data table.

In this syntax, *x* can be a character string, a number, a cell address, or block name that references a label or value. When *x* is a string, Quattro Pro searches for an exact match. @HLOOKUP returns the highest number in the row that isn't more than *x* when Quattro Pro cannot find an equal number.

Block must be a cell block address that describes the location of the data table. *Block* can describe the whole table or part of the table to restrict the lookup operation.

Row tells Quattro Pro how many rows to look through to find the value that the program returns. The *Row* argument cannot exceed the number of rows in the data table, or Quattro Pro returns ERR. When *Row* is 0, @HLOOKUP returns the *x* value itself.

Quattro Pro searches from left to right through the table rows, looking for a match to *x*. When the program finds an exact match, it stops at that column. When it doesn't find an exact match, the program stops at the column that contains the value closest to but not greater than *x*.

Figure 6.3 shows different ways to look through a data table using the @HLOOKUP command.

Fig. 6.3

A data table search with @HLOOKUP.

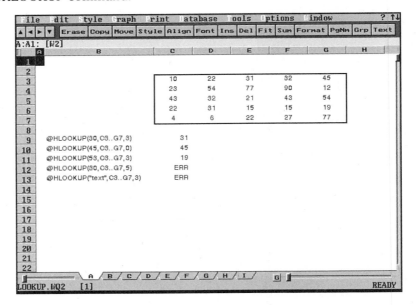

In the first example, Quattro Pro searches through the first row in block C3..G7. When the program locates the last value that is less than or equal to 30 before encountering a value that is greater than 30 (it stops at 22), Quattro Pro displays the cell value three rows down (the value 31).

In the second example, Quattro Pro searches through the first row in block C3..G7. When the program locates the last value that is less than or equal to 45 before encountering a value that is greater than 45 (it stops at 45), Quattro Pro displays the value in the cell 0 rows down (the value 45).

In the third example, Quattro Pro searches through the first row in block C3..G7. When the program locates the last value that is less than or equal to 53 before encountering a value that is greater than 53 (it stops at 45), Quattro Pro displays the cell value three rows down (the value 19).

In the fourth example, Quattro Pro searches through the first row in block C3..G7. When the program locates the last value that is less than or equal to 30 before encountering a value that is greater than 30 (it stops at 22), Quattro Pro tries to display the value in the cell five rows down. Because this cell falls outside the defined *Block*, Quattro Pro displays ERR.

In the fifth example, Quattro Pro searches through the first row in block C3..G7. When the program encounters the illegal definition for the *x* argument ("text"), Quattro Pro displays ERR.

@INDEX(*Block,Column,Row<,Page>*)

The @INDEX function uses the data table specified by *Block*. This function returns a value offset *Column* number of columns, *Row* number of rows, and (optionally) *Page* number of pages.

In this syntax, *Column*, *Row*, and *Page* aren't cell addresses, but offset values. In an @INDEX operation, Quattro Pro starts with the top left cell in *Block*, moves right *Column* number of columns, moves down *Row* number of rows, moves across *Page* number of pages, and then returns the value located in the active cell.

Column, *Row*, and *Page* must be values less than the number of rows, columns, and pages in the block and greater than or equal to zero. If a decimal is specified, Quattro Pro drops the fractional part of the decimal, rounding the value.

Figure 6.4 shows different ways to look through a data table using the @INDEX command.

In the first example, Quattro Pro begins at the first cell in block C3..G7. The program offsets 3 columns (to the 32 value) and 1 row (to the 90 value) and then displays 90.

In the second example, Quattro Pro begins at the first cell in block C3..G7. The program offsets 0 columns (to the 10 value) and 0 rows (to the 10 value) and then displays 10.

In the third example, Quattro Pro begins at the first cell in block C3..G7. The program offsets 4 columns (to the 45 value) and 4 rows (to the 77 value) and then displays 77.

In the fourth example, Quattro Pro begins at the first cell in block C3..G7. The program offsets 4 columns (to the 45 value) and 5 rows. Because this row offset falls outside the area defined in the *Block* argument, Quattro Pro displays ERR.

Fig. 6.4

A data table search with
@INDEX.

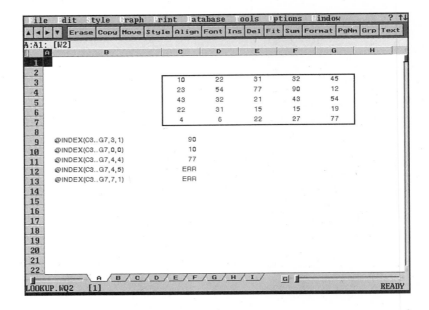

In the fifth example, Quattro Pro begins at the first cell in block C3..G7.
The program offsets 7 columns. Because this column offset falls outside
the area defined in the *Block* argument, Quattro Pro displays ERR.

@MEMAVAIL

@MEMAVAIL displays the number of bytes of conventional memory
now available to Quattro Pro.

> **Example:**   @MEMAVAIL = 46923 (46,923 bytes of
> available memory)

@MEMEMSAVAIL

The @MEMEMSAVAIL function displays the number of bytes of expanded memory (EMS) now available to Quattro Pro. If your system
doesn't contain expanded memory, Quattro Pro returns NA (not available).

> **Example:**   @MEMEMSAVAIL = 28000, if your system
> contains approximately 28K of free EMS

@NA

The @NA function returns the value NA. Like ERR, NA is a unique number and not a label. When your notebook contains formulas that reference a value entered as @NA, Quattro Pro returns NA.

@NA helps prevent the trickle-down effect of displaying erroneous data in a notebook, because Quattro Pro treats NA as a value and not as an ERR.

Figure 6.5, for example, shows the selector in cell F12. The formula in this cell uses data displayed in the range F7..F10. @NA is placed in cell F10 because this expense figure isn't available. Quattro Pro displays NA as the result in all cells with formulas that depend on the data in block F7..F10. Therefore, NA appears in all cells that contain formulas that rely directly on the data, such as the formula in cell F12, or those that rely indirectly on the data, such as other formulas that use the F12 result in their own formula.

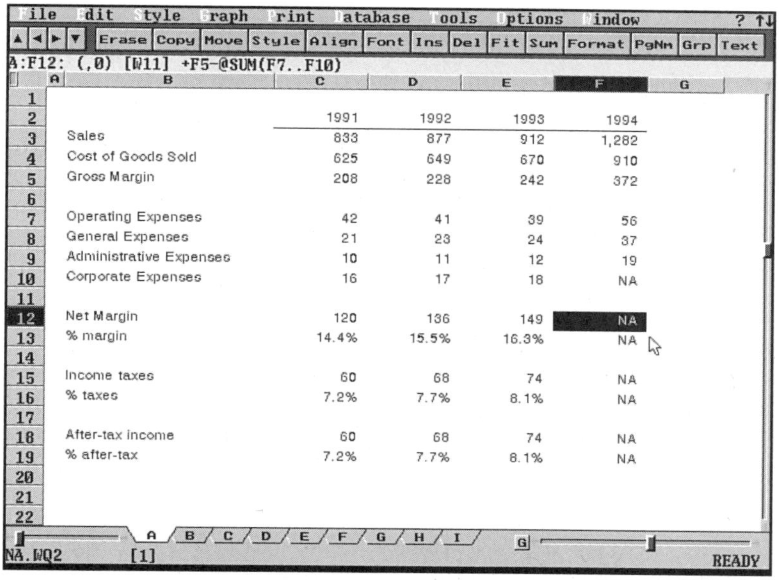

Fig. 6.5

Using @NA to indicate data not yet available.

@ROWS(*Block*)

The @ROWS function returns the number of rows in *Block*. In this syntax, *Block* may be a cell block or a block name.

Examples:	@ROWS(A1..IV1) = 1
	@ROWS(A1..A10) = 10
	@ROWS(ADDRESS) = 50, if ADDRESS = A1..A50

@SHEETS(*Block*)

The @SHEETS function returns the number of pages in a given *Block*. You use this function typically to establish the number of pages in a 3-D cell block. When the block you define exists on single page, Quattro Pro always returns the value 1. In this syntax, *Block* may be a cell block or a block name.

Examples:	@SHEETS(A1..BZ175) = 1
	@SHEETS(A..D:A1..IV1) = 4
	@SHEETS(A..IV:SALES) = 256

@VERSION

The @VERSION function displays Quattro Pro's version number in a user-specified cell.

@VLOOKUP(*x,Block,Column*)

The @VLOOKUP function works like @HLOOKUP, except that it searches through *Block* by columns instead of by rows.

The @VLOOKUP function moves through *Block* vertically, looking for the last value that is less than or equal to *x*. When the search succeeds, Quattro Pro returns the value located *Column* number of columns to the right. This function gives you an effective way to access information stored in a data table.

In this syntax, *x* can be a character string, a number, a cell address, or block name that references a label or value. When *x* is a string, Quattro Pro searches for an exact match and returns ERR if it doesn't find an exact match. When *x* is a number, @VLOOKUP returns the highest number in the column not more than *x* when Quattro Pro cannot find an equal number.

Block must be a cell block address that describes the location of the data table. *Block* can describe the whole table or part of the table to restrict the lookup operation.

Column tells Quattro Pro how many columns to look through to find the value. If the *Column* argument exceeds the number of columns in the data table, Quattro Pro returns ERR. When *Column* is 0, @VLOOKUP returns the *x* value itself.

Quattro Pro searches from top to bottom through the table rows, looking for a match to *x*. When the program finds an exact match, it stops at that row. When Quattro Pro doesn't find an exact match, it stops at the row containing the value closest to but not greater than *x*.

Figure 6.6 shows different ways to look through a data table using the @VLOOKUP command.

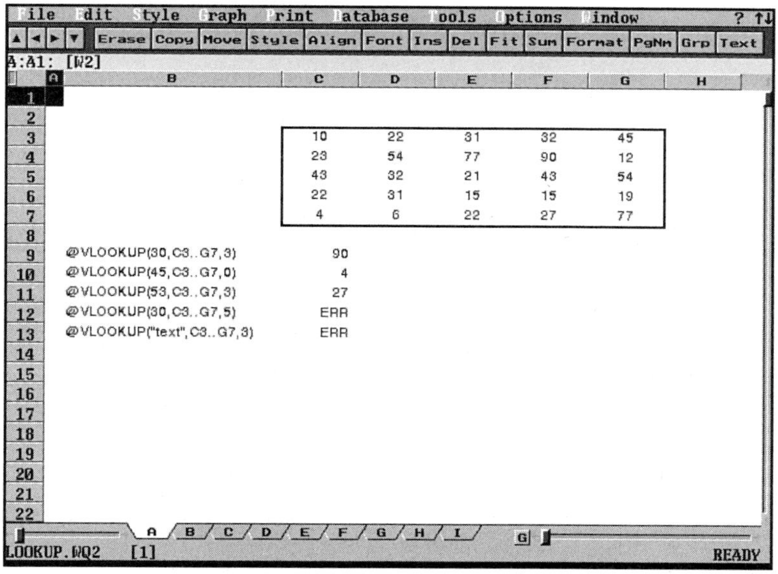

Fig. 6.6

A data table search with @VLOOKUP.

In the first example, Quattro Pro searches through the first column in block C3..G7. When the program locates the last value that is less than or equal to 30 before encountering one that is greater than 30 (it stops at 23), Quattro Pro displays the cell value three columns to the right (the value 90).

In the second example, Quattro Pro searches through the first column in block C3..G7. When the program locates the last value that is less than or equal to 45 before encountering a value that is greater than 45 (it stops at 4), Quattro Pro displays the value in the cell 0 columns to the right (the value 4).

In the third example, Quattro Pro searches through the first column in block C3..G7. When the program locates the last value that is less than or equal to 53 before encountering one that is greater than 53 (it stops at 4), Quattro Pro displays the cell value three columns to the right (the value 27).

In the fourth example, Quattro Pro searches through the first column in block C3..G7. When the program locates the last value that is less than or equal to 30 before encountering a value that is greater than 30 (it stops at 23), Quattro Pro tries to display the value in the cell 5 columns to the right. Because this cell falls outside the defined *Block*, Quattro Pro displays ERR.

In the fifth example, Quattro Pro displays ERR in cell C13 because the *x* argument ("text") doesn't exist in *Block*.

Using Logical @Functions

The logical @function commands, listed in table 6.11, test logical conditions. Depending on the outcome of the tests, these @functions return different values and perform different actions.

Table 6.11 Logical @Function Commands

@Function	Description
@FALSE	Returns the logical value 0
@FILEEXISTS("*Filename*")	Returns the logical value 1 when *Filename* exists
@IF(*Cond,TrueExpr, FalseExpr*)	Evaluates a logical condition
@ISAAF("*Addin.Function*")	Tests whether a custom @function is defined in a loaded add-in
@ISAPP("*Addin*")	Tests whether an add-in is loaded into memory
@ISERR(*x*)	Checks the contents of a cell for errors
@ISNA(*x*)	Tests for the special value NA in a cell

@Function	Description
@ISNUMBER(x)	Determines whether a cell contains a numeric value
@ISSTRING(x)	Determines whether a cell contains a label or text
@TRUE	Returns the logical value 1

Use these functions to control and validate the type of data entered into a cell; for example, you can make sure that cell B3 contains a value and not a label by entering the following function into cell B4:

@IF(@ISNUMBER(B3)=1," ","Needs a number")

This function says that if the data in B3 is a value (1 equals the TRUE condition), then display a blank; otherwise, display the message Needs a number.

One of the most potent applications for logical @functions is the creation of error-trapping formulas. Whenever a formula returns ERR, for example, every other cell that references the original cell also displays ERR. You can prevent this ripple effect by using logical @function commands.

As you read through the following command definitions, refer to the examples to learn more about how to use a particular command in an application.

@FALSE

The @FALSE function displays the logical value 0 when Quattro Pro encounters a false condition. This function commonly is used in @IF formulas to test the validity of numerical calculations and text string comparisons.

Examples: @FALSE = 0
@IF(100=100,50,@FALSE) = 50
@IF(10=60,"Yes",@FALSE) = 0
@IF(A1="September",@TRUE,@FALSE) = 1,
when A1 = September

@FILEEXISTS("Filename")

The @FILEEXISTS function returns the value 1 when Quattro Pro finds *Filename* in the current directory. When *Filename* doesn't exist in the current directory, Quattro Pro returns a 0. In this syntax, *Filename* must include the file extension and must appear in quotation marks.

To search for a file in a different directory, include the directory path as part of the *Filename* argument.

@IF(Cond,TrueExpr,FalseExpr)

The @IF function evaluates *Cond* and returns *TrueExpr* when *Cond* is true, and returns *FalseExpr* when *Cond* is false. In this syntax, *Cond* is a logical expression representing the condition to be tested, and *TrueExpr* and *FalseExpr* are string values enclosed in quotation marks or numbers. *Cond* must be some logical expression that Quattro Pro can evaluate as true or false.

Typically, *Cond* is a formula similar to B5=40, as shown in the following function:

> @IF(B5=40,@TRUE,@FALSE)

You can create compound conditions by adding #AND#, #OR#, or #NOT# between the logical conditions. When you use #AND#, both expressions must be true for the entire condition to be true. When you use #OR#, at least one of the expressions must be true for the entire condition to be true. When you use #NOT#, the single expression must be false for the entire condition to be true.

Examples:
@IF(10>1#AND#25=15,"TRUE","FALSE") = FALSE
@IF(10>1#OR#25=15,"TRUE","FALSE") = TRUE
@IF(#NOT#10>1,"TRUE","FALSE") = FALSE
@IF(#NOT#10<1,"TRUE","FALSE") = TRUE

The @IF function is most effective when you test multiple conditions from within one @IF function command by nesting other conditions. To nest conditions, include a second @IF function command as one of the expressions.

Example:

@IF(A1="Larry",1,@IF(A1="Curly",2,@IF(A1="Moe",3,"No Stooges")))

This expression tells Quattro Pro to return a 1 if A1 contains the label Larry. If A1 doesn't contain the label Larry, Quattro Pro evaluates *FalseExpr*. This expression tells Quattro Pro to return a 2 if A1 contains the label Curly. If it doesn't contain the label Curly, Quattro Pro evaluates the *FalseExpr*. This expression tells Quattro Pro to return a 3 if A1 contains the label Moe. If it doesn't contain the label Moe, Quattro Pro evaluates the *FalseExpr* and displays the label No Stooges.

> **NOTE**
>
> Valid nested @IF expressions cannot exceed 254 characters.

@ISAAF("*Addin.Function*")

@ISAAF tells you whether an @function is defined in an add-in module you have loaded into memory. This function returns the value 1 if *Addin* is loaded and *Function* is defined in the add-in; otherwise, the function returns the value 0. Refer to the documentation that came with your third-party add-in to determine the correct names for arguments *Addin* and *Function*.

Example: @ISAAF("SALES.FINANCE") = 1, when the SALES.QLL add-in is loaded into memory and @FINANCE is defined in that add-in

> **NOTE**
>
> Don't include the @ symbol before the function name that appears as the argument (FINANCE in the example) in an @ISAFF function.

@ISAPP("*Addin*")

@ISAPP tells you whether an add-in module is loaded into memory. This function returns the value 1 if *Addin* is loaded and returns the value 0 if the add-in isn't loaded into memory. Refer to the documentation that came with your third-party add-in to determine the correct name for the argument *Addin*.

Example: @ISAPP("SALES") = 1, when the SALES.QLL add-in is loaded into memory

TIP   Choose /**T**ools **L**ibrary **L**oad to load a third-party add-in into memory.

@ISERR(*x*)

The @ISERR function reviews the active cell for errors. When Quattro Pro finds ERR, it returns 1; otherwise it returns 0.

Use the @ISERR function with the @IF function to prevent the ripple effect of formula errors.

    Example: @IF(@ISERR(A50),@NA,1.05*SALES)

@ISNA(*x*)

@ISNA tests to see whether *x* returns the value NA. When *x* equals NA, Quattro Pro returns a 1; otherwise it returns 0. In this syntax, *x* can be a cell address or an expression.

Quattro Pro doesn't interpret a label entered in the form NA as the special NA value. To create this value on a page, you must use the @NA function.

    Examples: @ISNA("NA") = 0
                      @ISNA(@NA) = 1

@ISNUMBER(*x*)

@ISNUMBER tests to see whether *x* contains a numerical value. When *x* contains a numeric value, ERR, NA, or is a blank cell, Quattro Pro returns a 1; otherwise the program returns 0. In this syntax, *x* can be a cell address or an expression.

    Examples: @ISNUMBER(100) = 1
                      @ISNUMBER("100") = 0
                      @ISNUMBER(4/26/90) = 1
                      @ISNUMBER(@ERR) = 1
                      @ISNUMBER("ERR") = 0

@ISSTRING(x)

@ISSTRING tests to see whether *x* contains a label or a text string. When *x* contains either item, Quattro Pro returns 1. Quattro Pro returns 0 when *x* is a blank cell, a numeric value, or a date value. In this syntax, *x* can be a cell address or an expression.

    Examples: @ISSTRING("STRING") = 1
                            @ISSTRING(12345) = 0
                            @ISSTRING(4/26/85) = 0
                            @ISSTRING("") = 1
                            @ISSTRING(@ERR) = 0

@TRUE

@TRUE returns the logical value 1 when Quattro Pro encounters a true condition. This function commonly is used in @IF formulas.

    Examples: @IF(10=10,@TRUE,@FALSE) = 1
                            @IF(10=9,@TRUE,@FALSE) = 0

Using Financial @Functions

Quattro Pro's financial @functions provide you with powerful, real-world tools to help you manage your personal and business finances. You can use Quattro Pro's financial @function commands to help with capital budgeting, to predict results of various investments, to compute payment schedules, and to evaluate annuities.

@NPV(0.12,B5..B10), for example, tells you the net present value of a series of 6 future incoming cash flows at a 12 percent interest rate. Such information can help you determine the desirability of an investment.

You also can calculate depreciation for assets by using a variety of accepted methods; for example, @SLN(20000,3000,10) tells you that the yearly depreciation expense for a 10-year asset that costs $20,000 and has a $3,000 salvage value is $1,700.00.

You must follow these general rules when using financial @function commands:

- Use positive numbers to enter cash inflows and negative numbers to enter cash outflows. The 1-2-3 compatible @functions described later in this section don't distinguish between positive and negative cash flows.

- You can enter interest rates as a percent (8%) or in decimal form (0.08). Quattro Pro converts percent entries to a decimal format.

- Make sure that the time units within an @function are standard for all arguments, a particularly important concern when using term and interest rate arguments. If you have an annual interest rate of 15% and a term of 36 months, for example, convert the annual interest rate to a monthly rate (15%/12) or express the months argument in terms of years (3).

Table 6.12 lists the financial @function commands.

Table 6.12 Investment Analysis @Function Commands

@Function	Description
@CTERM(*Rate,Fv,Pv*)	1-2-3-compatible form of the @NPER function when the investment is an ordinary annuity
@DDB(*Cost,Salvage,Life,Period*)	Calculates accelerated depreciation
@FV(*Pmt,Rate,Nper*)	1-2-3-compatible form of the @FVAL function
@FVAL(*Rate,Nper,Pmt<,Pv><,Type>*)	Returns the future value of an ordinary annuity
@IPAYMT(*Rate,Per,Nper,Pv<,Fv><,Type>*)	Returns the interest portion of a loan payment
@IRATE(*Nper,Pmt,Pv<,Fv><,Type>*)	Returns the periodic interest rate
@IRR(*Guess,Block*)	Returns an investment's internal rate of return

@Function	Description
@NPER(*Rate,Pmt,Pv<,Fv><,Type>*)	Returns the number of periods
@NPV(*Rate,Block<,Type>*)	Returns the net present value of discounted cash flows
@PAYMT(*Rate,Nper,Pv<,Fv><,Type>*)	Returns the payment amount for a loan
@PMT(*Pv,Rate,Nper*)	1-2-3-compatible form of the @PPAYMT function
@PPAYMT(*Rate,Per,Nper,Pv<,Fv><,Type>*)	Returns the principal portion of a loan payment
@PV(*Pmt,Rate,Nper*)	1-2-3-compatible form of the @PVAL function
@PVAL(*Rate,Nper,Pmt<,Fv><,Type>*)	Returns the present value of an annuity
@RATE(*Fv,Pv,Nper*)	1-2-3-compatible form of the @IRATE function
@SLN(*Cost,Salvage,Life*)	Calculates straight-line depreciation
@SYD(*Cost,Salvage,Life,Period*)	Calculates sum-of-the-years'-digits' depreciation
@TERM(*Pmt,Rate,Fv*)	1-2-3-compatible form of the @NPER function, when the investment is an ordinary annuity

NOTE

Angle brackets shown in table 6.12 indicate an optional argument. *Don't* type the brackets around an optional argument when you include it in a function. If one or both optional arguments are omitted, Quattro Pro assumes that the values for both optional arguments are 0.

Many financial @function commands use the same arguments, but in different order. Table 6.13 defines each argument that Quattro Pro requires for the financial @function commands.

Table 6.13 Financial @Function Command Arguments

Argument	Description
Rate	The fixed interest rate per compounding period
Fv	The value an investment will reach
Pv	The present value of an investment
Cost	The cost of an asset
Salvage	An asset's worth at the end of its useful life
Life	The expected useful life of an asset
Period	The depreciable period of an asset
Pmt	The amount of the period payment
Nper	The number of periods (an integer >= 2)
Type	0 denotes end-of-period payments; 1 denotes beginning-of-period payments
Per	The current payment period in *Nper*
Guess	An estimate of an internal rate of return
Block	A block containing the cash-flow values

Five financial @function commands have two syntax forms so that you can save them on a notebook in a Lotus-compatible format. The Quattro Pro syntax, however, is more precise than its Lotus 1-2-3 equivalent. The compatible @function commands are as follows:

Quattro Pro Syntax	Lotus 1-2-3 Syntax
@FVAL(*Rate,Nper,Pmt<,Pv><,Type>*)	@FV(*Pmt,Rate,Nper*)
@IRATE(*Nper,Pmt,Pv<,Fv><,Type>*)	@RATE(*Fv,Pv,Nper*)
@NPER(*Rate,Pmt,Pv<,Fv><,Type>*)	@CTERM(*Rate,Fv,Pv*) @TERM(*Pmt,Rate,Fv*)
@PAYMT(*Rate,Nper,Pv<,Fv><,Type>*)	@PMT(*Pv,Rate,Nper*)
@PVAL(*Rate,Nper,Pmt<,Fv><,Type>*)	@PV(*Pmt,Rate,Nper*)

@CTERM(*Rate,Fv,Pv*)

The @CTERM function returns the number of time periods necessary for an investment of *Pv* to grow to *Fv*. In this syntax, the investment earns *Rate* interest per compounding period.

This function is based on the following formula (where ln stands for natural logarithm):

$$\frac{\ln(Fv/Pv)}{\ln(1+Rate)}$$

The @CTERM function assumes that the investment is an ordinary annuity. In an ordinary annuity, the cash flows occur at the end of the period. For example, how long would it take a savings account deposit of $5,000 to grow to $10,000, when the annual interest rate is 8, 9, and 10 percent?

@CTERM(.08,10000,5000) = 9.01 (years)

@CTERM(.09,10000,5000) = 8.04 (years)

@CTERM(.10,10000,5000) = 7.27 (years)

@DDB(*Cost,Salvage,Life,Period*)

The @DDB function returns the periodic depreciation expense for an asset, using the double-declining balance method. For this function to work properly, the following conditions must be true:

- *Life* >= *Period* >= 1
- *Life* and *Period* must be integers
- *Cost* >= *Salvage* >= 0

The depreciation value (DDB) and book value are calculated as follows:

- Book Value = *Cost*
- DDB = (2*Book Value)/*Life*
- Book Value = Book Value - DDB

What are the first three annual depreciation expenses, for example, for an asset that costs $100,000, has a salvage value equal to $17,500, and has a useful life of 10 years?

> @DDB(100000,17500,10,1) = 20,000 (see fig. 6.7)
>
> @DDB(100000,17500,10,2) = 16,000
>
> @DDB(100000,17500,10,3) = 12,800

Fig. 6.7

The year 1 depreciation expense under the double-declining balance method.

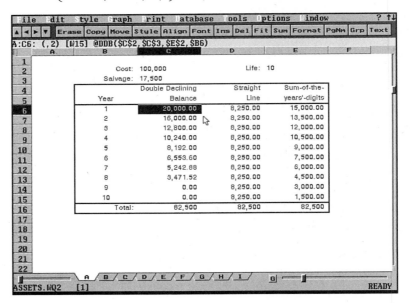

@FV(*Pmt,Rate,Nper*)

The @FV function calculates the future value of an investment when *Pmt* is invested for *Nper* periods at the rate of *Rate* per period. This function is based on the following formula:

$$\frac{(1+Rate)^{Nper}-1}{Pmt*Rate}$$

What is the future value, for example, of making a single $1,000 deposit into three separate savings accounts that earn 8, 9, and 10 percent for periods of 5, 10, and 15 years, respectively?

@FV(1000,.08,5) = $5,866.60

@FV(1000,.09,10) = $15,192.93

@FV(1000,.10,15) = $31,772.48

@FVAL(*Rate,Nper,Pmt<,Pv><,Type>*)

The @FVAL function is a more precise version of the @FV function. In this syntax, the *Pv* and *Type* arguments are optional. Quattro Pro assumes that their values are zero if you omit *Type* or *Pv* and *Type*.

> **NOTE**
>
> This function is incompatible with Lotus 1-2-3. If you must save your notebook in a Lotus-compatible format, use the @FV function. During the conversion process, Quattro Pro will save only the active page. To save multiple pages in a Lotus 1-2-3 file format, you must save each page one at a time. Also remember not to precede cash outflows with a negative sign when you use the @FV function.

What are the future values, for example, of making 5 annual end-of-year deposits versus 5 annual beginning-of-year deposits of $1,000 into a bank account earning 8 percent, whose current balance is $500?

@FVAL(.08,5,–1000,500,1) = $5,601.26

@FVAL(.08,5,–1000,500,0) = $5,131.94

What is the future value of making 15 annual deposits of $1,000 into a money market account that earns 10 percent interest?

@FVAL(.10,15,–1000) = $31,772.48

@IPAYMT(*Rate,Per,Nper,Pv<,Fv><,Type>*)

The @IPAYMT function returns the value of the interest portion of a loan payment. In this syntax, *Fv* and *Type* are optional arguments. Quattro Pro assumes that their values are zero if you omit *Fv* or *Type*.

For example, what is the first year's interest deduction on a 15-year, 9.5 percent mortgage on a $300,000 loan? What is the fifth year's interest deduction?

@IPAYMT(.095/12,1*12,15*12,300000) = –$2,306.34

@IPAYMT(.095/12,5*12,15*12,300000) = –$1,926.15

@IRATE(*Nper,Pmt,Pv<,Fv><,Type>*)

@IRATE returns the periodic interest rate earned (paid) on an investment (loan) equal to *Pv*. Here, *Nper* is the compounding term of the investment (loan); *Pmt* represents the per period interest payment earned (paid); and *Pv* is the current value of the investment.

The @IRATE function is a more precise version of the @RATE function. In this syntax, *Fv* and *Type* are optional. Quattro Pro assumes that their values are zero if you omit *Type* or *Fv* and *Type*.

For this function to work properly, the first and last cash flows must have opposite signs; one must represent a positive cash flow and the other a negative cash flow. If they don't, Quattro Pro assumes that the transaction may not have a meaningful rate, so it returns ERR.

Suppose that you want to finance the purchase of a $20,000 car and have the choice of paying $675.81 per month for three years or $538.54 per month for four years. Which is the better deal for you?

@IRATE(36,–675.81,20000) = 1.10% per month (13.2% per year)

@IRATE(48,–538.54,20000) = 1.10% per month (13.2% per year)

What annual interest rate do you need to earn to accumulate $20,000 at the end of three years if you make three annual deposits of $3,000, and your account balance is $5,000 today?

@IRATE(3,–3000,–5000,20000) = 21.37%

NOTE

This function is incompatible with Lotus 1-2-3. If you must save your notebook in a Lotus-compatible format, use the @RATE function. Remember, don't precede cash outflows with a negative sign when you use the @RATE function. Also, Quattro Pro will save only the active page during the conversion process. To save multiple pages in a Lotus 1-2-3 file format, you must save each page one at a time.

@IRR(*Guess,Block*)

The @IRR function calculates the internal rate of return on an investment. The @IRR function returns the interest rate that causes the net present value of an investment to be 0. Net present value (NPV) is the net worth today of investing a sum and receiving future cash flows. When the NPV of an investment is 0, the investment is considered to be a break-even venture.

When you calculate NPV, you discount future cash flows using an interest rate. This rate is equal to your opportunity interest rate—the maximum rate you can earn by investing elsewhere. In other words, if the best you can do is earn 12.5 percent in a bank account, your opportunity interest rate is 12.5 percent.

To evaluate the worth of potential investments, you must design a table that describes how the cash flows in and out of the investment. Figure 6.8 contains a 10-year cash flow table, which describes the same investment opportunity ($50,000) with differently timed cash flows. In this syntax, *Block* contains the cash flows and *Guess* is a user-supplied estimate of the internal rate of return.

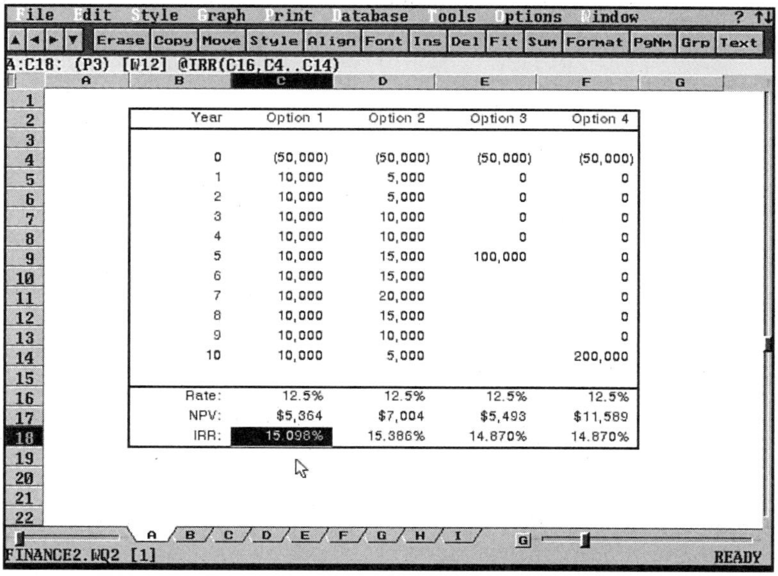

Year	Option 1	Option 2	Option 3	Option 4
0	(50,000)	(50,000)	(50,000)	(50,000)
1	10,000	5,000	0	0
2	10,000	5,000	0	0
3	10,000	10,000	0	0
4	10,000	10,000	0	0
5	10,000	15,000	100,000	0
6	10,000	15,000		0
7	10,000	20,000		0
8	10,000	15,000		0
9	10,000	10,000		0
10	10,000	5,000		200,000
Rate:	12.5%	12.5%	12.5%	12.5%
NPV:	$5,364	$7,004	$5,493	$11,589
IRR:	15.098%	15.386%	14.870%	14.870%

Fig. 6.8

The formula that calculates the internal rate of return for investment option 1.

To use this function properly, you first must create a data table that contains each periodic cash flow. Negative signs must precede cash outflows. (Notice that negative values in fig. 6.8 are formatted to show parentheses rather than a minus sign.) The first cash flow must be negative to indicate that it's the initial investment. The ensuing cash flows can vary from period to period in size and sign.

What is the internal rate of return of investing $50,000 today, using the cash flow streams shown in figure 6.8?

> Option 1: @IRR(.125,C4..C14) = 15.098%
>
> Option 2: @IRR(.125,D4..D14) = 15.386%
>
> Option 3: @IRR(.125,E4..E9) = 14.870%
>
> Option 4: @IRR(.125,F4..F14) = 14.870%

@NPER(*Rate,Pmt,Pv<,Fv><,Type>*)

The @NPER function determines the number of periods it takes for *Pv* to equal *Fv* when investing *Pmt* per period at a rate of *Rate*.

The @NPER function is a more precise version of the @CTERM and @TERM functions. In this syntax, *Fv* and *Type* are optional. Quattro Pro assumes their values are zero if you omit *Type* or *Fv* and *Type*.

NOTE

This function is incompatible with Lotus 1-2-3. If you must save your notebook in a Lotus-compatible format, use @CTERM or @TERM. Remember, don't precede cash outflows with a negative sign when you use the @CTERM or @TERM functions. Also, Quattro Pro will save only the active page. To save multiple pages in a Lotus 1-2-3 file format, you must save each page one at a time.

How long does accumulating $5,000 take if you deposit $1,000 annually into a bank account that pays 10 percent?

> @NPER(.10,–1000,0,5000) = 4.25 (years)

How long does accumulating $5,000 take if you deposit $250 annually into a bank account that pays 10 percent and has a current balance of $2,500?

> @NPER(.10,–250,–2500,5000) = 4.25 (years)

How long does accumulating $1 million take if you deposit $1,000 annually into a bank account that pays 10 percent?

> @NPER(.10,–1000,0,1000000) = 48.42 (years)

@NPV(*Rate,Block<,Type>*)

The @NPV function calculates the net present value of the cash flows in *Block*, discounted at a periodic interest rate of *Rate*.

The @NPV function has one optional argument, *Type*. If the cash flows occur at the beginning of the period, set *Type* to 0. If they occur at the end of the period, enter 1.

The optional argument *Type* isn't 1-2-3 compatible.   **NOTE**

What's the net present value of an investment that requires you to invest $50,000 today and pays back dividends per the cash flow streams shown in figure 6.9?

> Option 1: @NPV(.125,C4..C14,1) = $5,364
>
> Option 2: @NPV(.125,D4..D14,1) = $7,004
>
> Option 3: @NPV(.125,E4..E9,1) = $5,493
>
> Option 4: @NPV(.125,F4..F14,1) = $11,589

Notice in cell E17 in figure 6.9 that the rate argument in that formula is in cell E16. The value in cell E16, 12.5%, is actually the decimal value .125 formatted to display as a percentage.

@PAYMT(*Rate,Nper,Pv<,Fv><,Type>*)

The @PAYMT function returns the fully amortized value of a loan payment. This function is a more precise version of the @PMT function. In this syntax, *Fv* and *Type* are optional arguments. Quattro Pro assumes that their values are zero if you omit *Type* or *Fv* and *Type*.

Fig. 6.9

The formula that calculates the net present value for investment option 3.

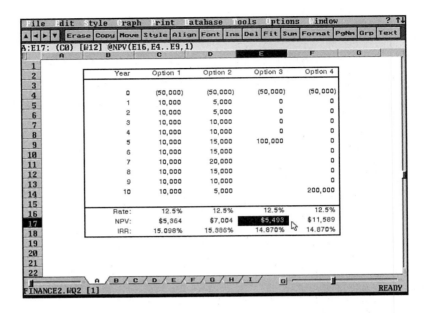

This function is incompatible with Lotus 1-2-3. If you must save your notebook in a Lotus-compatible format, use @PMT. Remember, don't precede cash outflows with a negative sign when you use the @PMT function. Also, Quattro Pro will save only the active page. To save multiple pages in a Lotus 1-2-3 file format, you must save each page one at a time.

How much must you deposit in an account earning 25 percent to accumulate $10,000 in 5 years?

@PAYMT(.25,5,0,10000) = –$1,218.47

What is the monthly payment for a $225,000, 15-year, 12 percent fixed-interest mortgage? What if the loan term is stretched to 30 years?

@PAYMT(.01,180,225000) = –$2,700.38

@PAYMT(.01,360,225000) = –$2,314.38

@PMT(*Pv,Rate,Nper*)

@PMT returns the fully amortized payment when borrowing *Pv* dollars at *Rate* percent per period over *Nper* periods. In this syntax, interest is assumed to be paid at the end of each period.

The @PMT function assumes that the investment is an ordinary annuity. In an ordinary annuity, the cash flows occur at the end of the period.

What is the total annual payment on a $100,000, 30-year, 10 percent fixed-interest mortgage?

> @PMT(100000,.10,30) = $10,607.92

What is the monthly payment for a $225,000, 15-year, 12 percent fixed-interest mortgage? What if the loan term is stretched to 30 years?

> @PMT(225000,.01,180) = $2,700.38
>
> @PMT(225000,.01,360) = $2,314.38

@PPAYMT(*Rate,Per,Nper,Pv<,Fv><,Type>*)

The @PPAYMT function returns the value of the principal portion of a loan payment. In this syntax, *Fv* and *Type* are optional arguments. Quattro Pro assumes their values are zero if you omit *Type* or *Fv* and *Type*.

What's the first year's principal payment on a 15-year, 9.5 percent mortgage on a $300,000 loan? What is the fifth year's principal payment?

> @PPAYMT(.095/12,1*12,15*12,300000) = –$826.33
>
> @PPAYMT(.095/12,5*12,15*12,300000) = –$1,206.52

@PV(*Pmt,Rate,Nper*)

The @PV function calculates the present value of an investment when *Pmt* is received for *Nper* periods and is discounted at *Rate* percent per period.

This function is based on the following formula:

$$\frac{1-(1+Rate)^{-Nper}}{Pmt*Rate}$$

The @PV function assumes that the investment is an ordinary annuity. In an ordinary annuity, the cash flows occur at the end of the period.

What's the most that you can pay today for an investment that provides you $500 per year for 10 years, if you can earn 7.5 percent on your money elsewhere? What if the investment provides you $750 per year? Or $1,000 per year?

@PV(500,.075,10) = $3,432.04

@PV(750,.075,10) = $5,148.06

@PV(1000,.075,10) = $6,864.08

@PVAL(Rate,Nper,Pmt<,Fv><,Type>)

The @PVAL function is a more precise version of the @PV function. In this syntax, the *Fv* and *Type* arguments are optional. Quattro Pro assumes that they are zero if *Type* or both arguments are omitted.

NOTE

> This function is incompatible with Lotus 1-2-3. If you must save your notebook in a Lotus-compatible format, use @PV. Remember, don't precede cash outflows with a negative sign when you use the @PV function. Also, Quattro Pro will save only the active page. To save multiple pages in a Lotus 1-2-3 file format, you must save each page one at a time.

Suppose that the local lottery official offers you 3 alternative annuities, all which pay 10 percent. The first pays you $3,850 per year for 10 years, the second pays you $3,350 for 13 years, and the third pays you the lump sum of $100,000 after 15 years. Which annuity is the best alternative?

@PVAL(.10,10,–3850) = $23,656.58

@PVAL(.10,13,–3350) = $23,796.24

@PVAL(.10,15,0,–100000) = $23,939.20

@RATE(Fv,Pv,Nper)

The @RATE function calculates the interest rate needed for an investment of *Pv* to be worth *Fv* in *Nper* compounding periods. If you enter *Nper* in years, @RATE returns the annual interest rate; if you enter *Nper* in months, it returns the monthly interest rate.

This function is based on the following formula:

$$\left(\frac{Fv}{Pv}\right)^{\frac{1}{Nper}} -1$$

The @RATE function assumes that the investment is an ordinary annuity in which the cash flows occur at the end of the period.

What interest rate must you earn for $100,000 to grow to $1,000,000 in 10 years?

@RATE(1000000,100000,10) = 25.89%

What interest rate must you earn for $1,000 to grow to $2,000 in 5 and 10 years?

@RATE(2000,1000,5) = 14.87%

@RATE(2000,1000,10) = 7.18%

@SLN(*Cost,Salvage,Life*)

The @SLN function returns one year's depreciation expense for an asset, using the straight-line method. This function is based on the following formula:

$$\frac{\textit{Cost–Salvage}}{\textit{Life}}$$

What's the annual depreciation expense for an asset that costs $100,000, has a salvage value equal to $17,500, and has a useful life of 10 years?

@SLN(100000,17500,10) = $8,250 (see fig. 6.10)

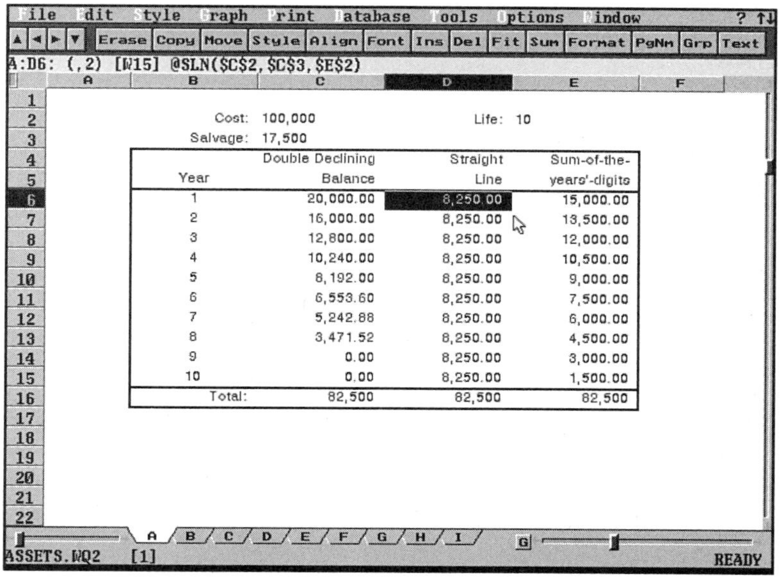

Year	Double Declining Balance	Straight Line	Sum-of-the-years'-digits
1	20,000.00	8,250.00	15,000.00
2	16,000.00	8,250.00	13,500.00
3	12,800.00	8,250.00	12,000.00
4	10,240.00	8,250.00	10,500.00
5	8,192.00	8,250.00	9,000.00
6	6,553.60	8,250.00	7,500.00
7	5,242.88	8,250.00	6,000.00
8	3,471.52	8,250.00	4,500.00
9	0.00	8,250.00	3,000.00
10	0.00	8,250.00	1,500.00
Total:	82,500	82,500	82,500

Fig. 6.10

The formula that calculates the straight-line depreciation expense for year 1.

@SYD(*Cost,Salvage,Life,Period*)

The @SYD function returns the periodic depreciation allowance for an asset, using the accelerated depreciation method. This function offers higher depreciation in the earlier years of the asset's life. This function is based on the following formula:

$$\frac{(Cost-Salvage)*(Life-Period+1)}{Life*(Life+1)/2}$$

For this function to work properly, the following conditions must be true:

   Cost >= *Salvage* >= 0

   Life >= *Period* >= 1

What are the last three annual depreciation expenses for an asset that cost $100,000, has a salvage value equal to $17,500, and has a useful life of 10 years (see fig. 6.11)?

   @SYD(100000,17500,10,8) = $4,500.00

   @SYD(100000,17500,10,9) = $3,000.00

   @SYD(100000,17500,10,10) = $1,500.00

Fig. 6.11

The year 10 sum-of-the-years'-digits depreciation expense.

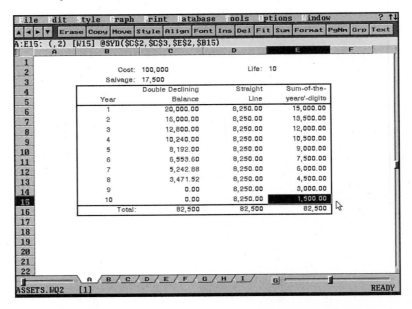

@TERM(*Pmt,Rate,Fv*)

The @TERM function calculates the number of payment periods required to accumulate holdings worth *Fv*. In this syntax, *Pmt* represents regular payments made while accruing interest at the rate of *Rate*. This function is based on the following formula:

$$\frac{\ln(1+Fv/Pmt*Rate)}{\ln(1+Rate)}$$

The @TERM function assumes that the investment is an ordinary annuity in which the cash flows occur at the end of the period.

How long does accumulating $10,000 take if you make annual deposits of $1,000 into a bank account that pays 7.5 percent, 8.5 percent, or 9.5 percent?

> @TERM(1000,.075,10000) = 7.74 (years)
>
> @TERM(1000,.085,10000) = 7.54 (years)
>
> @TERM(1000,.095,10000) = 7.36 (years)

Using Date and Time @Function Commands

Quattro Pro's date and time @functions have many uses. One popular use for these @functions is to determine elapsed time between two date or time entries. This type of operation is often a necessary part of business reporting, time management, project scheduling, and so forth.

Date and time @functions also are useful tools when you build notebook applications. Put the @TODAY function, for example, at the top of your notebook so that Quattro Pro displays the current date in that cell each time you load the notebook.

Many date and time @function commands use the same arguments. Table 6.14 lists the commands. Table 6.15 defines each argument Quattro Pro requires for the date and time @function commands.

Table 6.14 Date and Time @Function Commands

@Function	Description
@DATE(*Yr,Mo,Day*)	Returns the date serial number of a date
@DATEVALUE("*DateString*")	Returns the date serial number that corresponds to *DateString*
@DAY(*DateTimeNumber*)	Converts a date or time serial number into the number associated with that day (1-31)
@HOUR(*DateTimeNumber*)	Returns the hour portion of the argument
@MINUTE(*DateTimeNumber*)	Returns the minute portion of the argument
@MONTH(*DateTimeNumber*)	Returns the month portion of the argument
@NOW	Returns the serial number for the system's current time and date
@SECOND(*DateTimeNumber*)	Returns the second portion of the argument
@TIME(*Hr,Min,Sec*)	Returns the time serial number portion of the argument
@TIMEVALUE("*TimeString*")	Returns the time serial number for the argument
@TODAY	Returns the numeric value of the system's date
@YEAR(*DateTimeNumber*)	Returns the year portion of the argument

Table 6.15 Date and Time @Function Command Arguments

Argument	Description
Yr	A numeric value between 0 and 199 that represents the number of years since 1900
Mo	A numeric value between 1 and 12 that represents the number of months in a year
Day	A numeric value between 1 and 31 that represents the maximum number of days in a month
"*DateString*"	A numeric or string value in any valid date format, enclosed in quotation marks

Argument	Description
DateTimeNumber	Any number under 73050, which represents the date number for December 31, 2099
Hr	A number between 0 and 24, representing the hour
Mi	A number between 0 and 60, representing the minute
Sec	A number between 0 and 60, representing the second
"TimeString"	A numeric or string value in any valid time format, enclosed in quotation marks

As you read through the following command definitions, refer to the examples to learn more about how to use a particular command in an application.

@DATE(*Yr,Mo,Day*)

The @DATE function displays the date serial number specified by year, month, and day. A valid serial number ranges from 0 to 73,050, which represents the number of days between December 31, 1899, and the date referenced in the formula. December 31, 2099, is the highest date available. Quattro Pro returns ERR when it encounters an illegal date.

Examples: @DATE(87,2,29) = ERR (1987 wasn't a leap year)

@DATE(88,1,1) = 32143 (the serial date for January 1, 1988)

@DATEVALUE(*"DateString"*)

The @DATEVALUE function displays the date serial number that corresponds to *DateString*. Quattro Pro displays ERR when *DateString* isn't in a valid date format or isn't enclosed in quotation marks.

The five valid *DateString* formats follow:

- *dd-mmm-yy* ("02-Jan-90")
- *dd-mmm* ("02-Jan")
- *mmm-yy* ("Jan-90")
- The default Long International date format
- The default Short International date format

Examples: @DATEVALUE("02-Jan-90") = 32875

@DATEVALUE("02-Jan") = 32875 (Quattro Pro assumes the current year)

@DATEVALUE("Jan-90") = 32874 (Quattro Pro assumes the first day of the month)

@DAY(*DateTimeNumber*)

The @DAY function converts *DateTimeNumber* into the number associated with that day of the month (1-31). In this syntax, *DateTimeNumber* can be a day or time serial number.

Examples: @DAY(31779) = 2 (1/2/87)

@DAY(73055) = ERR (the number entered was larger than 73050.9999999)

@HOUR(*DateTimeNumber*)

The @HOUR function displays the hour portion of *DateTimeNumber*. In this syntax, *DateTimeNumber* is a numeric value between 1 and 73050.999999 (the combined date and time serial numbers).

The integer portion of the number is disregarded because only the decimal portion of a serial number pertains to time. The result is between 0 (midnight) and 23 (11 p.m.).

Examples: @HOUR(.25) = 6
@HOUR(.5) = 12
@HOUR(.75) = 18

@MINUTE(*DateTimeNumber*)

The @MINUTE function displays the minute part of *DateTimeNumber*. The integer portion of the number is disregarded because only the decimal value in a serial number pertains to time. The result is between 0 and 59.

To extract the minute portion of strings in time format rather than se-rial format, use the @TIME function within the @MINUTE function to translate the time into a serial number.

Examples:	@MINUTE(.3655) = 46
	@MINUTE(@TIME(3,15,22)) = 15

@MONTH(*DateTimeNumber*)

The @MONTH function displays the month portion of *DateTimeNumber*. The only portion used is the integer portion, and the result is between 1 (January) and 12 (December).

To extract the month portion of a string in date format rather than se-rial format, use the @DATEVALUE within the @MONTH function to translate the date into a serial number.

Examples:	@MONTH(69858) = 4
	@MONTH(@DATEVALUE("3/5/88")) = 3

@NOW

The @NOW function displays the serial number corresponding to the current date time of your system's clock. When you perform any func-tion that re-evaluates the notebook, the value generated by @NOW is updated to the current date and time each time you press the F9 (Calc) key.

The decimal portion pertains to time and the integer part of the date or time serial number pertains to the date.

Example:	@NOW = 31905.572338 or 5/8/87 or 1:45 PM
	(the value returned depends on the cell's format)

@SECOND(*DateTimeNumber*)

The @SECOND function displays the second part of *DateTimeNumber*. The integer portion of the number is disregarded because only the decimal portion of a serial number pertains to time. The result is be-tween 0 and 59.

Use the @TIMEVALUE within the @SECOND function to translate the time into a serial number to extract the second portion of a string that's in time format instead of serial format.

Examples: @SECOND(.3655445) = 23
@SECOND(@TIMEVALUE ("10:08:45 am")) = 45

@TIME(*Hr,Min,Sec*)

The @TIME function displays the date or time serial number that is represented by *Hr,Min,Sec*. Each argument must be within the given range, and any fractional portions are omitted.

Examples: @TIME(3,0,0) = 0.125 (3:00 a.m.)
@TIME(18,15,59) = 0.76109953704
(6:15:59 p.m.)

@TIMEVALUE("*TimeString*")

The @TIMEVALUE function displays the serial time value that corresponds to the value in *TimeString*. ERR results if the value in *TimeString* isn't in the correct format or isn't enclosed in quotation marks.

The four valid *TimeString* formats are as follows:

- *hh*:*mm*:*ss* AM/PM (03:45:30 PM)
- *hh*:*mm* AM/PM (03:45 PM)
- The default Long International time format
- The default Short International time format

Examples: @TIMEVALUE("03:30:15 AM") =0.1460069444
@TIMEVALUE("18:15:59") = 0.76109953704

@TODAY

The @TODAY function enters the numeric value of the system's date. This function is equal to the @INT(@NOW) expression.

Examples: @NOW = 33047.8687 (for June 23, 1990, at
08:50:57 p.m.)
@TODAY = 33047 (for June 23, 1990)
@INT(@NOW) = 33047 (for June 23, 1990)

@YEAR(*DateTimeNumber*)

The @YEAR function gives the year portion of the *DateTimeNumber*.
The result is between 0 (1900) and 199 (2099). You can display the actual year by adding 1900 to the result of @YEAR. To extract the year
portion of a string in date format, use @DATEVALUE within the @YEAR
function to convert the string into a serial number.

Examples: @YEAR(22222) = 60 (1960)
@YEAR(@DATEVALUE("12-Oct-54")) = 54

Using Database @Function Commands

The database @function commands perform the same operations as the
statistical @function commands. Here, though, the @functions operate
on a specific field entry in the database instead of a block defined as
List.

Table 6.16 lists the functions. The database @function commands have
in common the arguments shown in table 6.17.

Table 6.16 Database @Function Commands

@Function	Description
@DAVG(*Block,Column,Criteria*)	Calculates the average of selected field entries in a database
@DCOUNT(*Block,Column,Criteria*)	Counts the number of selected field entries in a database
@DMAX(*Block,Column,Criteria*)	Returns the maximum value in a database

(continues)

Table 6.16 Continued

@Function	Description
@DMIN(*Block,Column,Criteria*)	Returns the minimum value in a database
@DSTD(*Block,Column,Criteria*)	Returns the population standard deviation
@DSTDS(*Block,Column,Criteria*)	Returns the sample standard deviation
@DSUM(*Block,Column,Criteria*)	Returns the total of selected field entries in a database
@DVAR(*Block,Column,Criteria*)	Returns the population variance
@DVARS(*Block,Column,Criteria*)	Returns the sample variance

Table 6.17 Database @Function Command Arguments

Argument	Description
Block	The cell block containing the database, including field names.
Column	The number of the column containing the field you want to evaluate. The first column in *Block* is 0, the second is 1, and so on.
Criteria	A cell block containing search criteria. You can specify all or part of the database as *Block*, but you must include the field names for each field including *Block*. *Criteria* is defined as the coordinates of a block containing a criteria table; a criteria table specifies the search information.

As you read through the following command definitions, refer to the examples in the statistical @function section to learn more about how to use a particular command in an application.

@DAVG(*Block,Column,Criteria*)

The @DAVG function averages selected field entries in a database. Only those entries in column number *Column* whose records meet the criteria specified in *Criteria* are included.

The field specified in the criteria and the field being averaged don't have to be the same. The field averaged is contained within the column you specified as *Column*.

@DCOUNT(*Block,Column,Criteria*)

The @DCOUNT function counts selected field entries in a database. Only those entries in column number *Column* whose records meet the criteria specified in block *Criteria* are included.

The field specified and the field being counted don't have to be the same. The field counted is contained within the column you specified as *Column*.

@DMAX(*Block,Column,Criteria*)

The @DMAX function finds the maximum value of selected field entries in a database. Only those entries in column number *Column* whose records meet the criteria specified in block *Criteria* are included.

The field specified in your criteria and the field whose maximum values you are finding don't have to be the same. The field for which you are finding the maximum values is that contained within the column you specified as *Column*.

@DMIN(*Block,Column,Criteria*)

The @DMIN function finds the minimum value of selected field entries in a database. Only those entries in column number *Column* whose records meet the criteria specified in block *Criteria* are included.

The field specified in your criteria and the field for which you are finding the minimum value don't have to be the same. The field for which you are finding the minimum value is that contained within the column specified as *Criteria*.

@DSTD(*Block,Column,Criteria*)

The @DSTD function finds the population standard deviation for selected field entries in a database.

Only those entries in column number *Column* whose records meet the criteria specified in block *Criteria* are included in @DSTD.

The field specified in your criteria and the field for which the standard deviation is being found don't have to be the same. The field for which you are finding the standard deviation is the field contained within the column you specified as *Column*.

@DSTDS(*Block,Column,Criteria*)

The @DSTDS function finds the sample standard deviation for the selected field in a database. @DSTDS computes the standard deviation of the population data.

NOTE

> This function is incompatible with Lotus 1-2-3. Use @DSTD if your notebook requires 1-2-3 compatibility. Also, Quattro Pro will save only the active page. To save multiple pages in a Lotus 1-2-3 file format, you must save each page one at a time.

@DSUM(*Block,Column,Criteria*)

The @DSUM function adds up the selected entries in a database. Only those entries whose records meet the criteria specified in block *Criteria* are included in the column number *Column*.

The field specified in the criteria and the field whose sum is being found don't have to be the same. The field contained within the column you specified as *Column* is the field whose sum you are finding.

@DVAR(*Block,Column,Criteria*)

The @DVAR function calculates the population variance for the selected field in a database and computes the variance of the sample data.

Only those entries in column number *Column* whose records meet the criteria specified in block *Criteria* are included in @DVAR.

The field specified in the criteria and the field for which the variance is being calculated don't have to be the same. The field counted is contained within the column you specified as *Column*.

@DVARS(*Block,Column,Criteria*)

The @DVARS function calculates the sample variance for the selected field entries in a database and computes the variance of the population data.

NOTE

Questions & Answers

This chapter introduced you to @function commands. If you have any questions concerning particular situations that aren't addressed in the examples given, look through this section.

Q: Remembering the syntax for @function commands to use them on my notebooks is difficult. Is a quick and easy way to get this information available?

A: Press Alt+F3 to display a list of Quattro Pro's @function commands, and then press F1 to display the Function Index window, a context-sensitive help window. Highlight the command that you want to use and press Enter. Quattro Pro displays a definition and the appropriate syntax for the highlighted @function command.

Q: When I use @AVG to calculate the average for a block of values, Quattro Pro returns an answer that I know is incorrect. What should I do?

A: Whenever an @function returns a result that you believe is incorrect, immediately examine the cell block containing the values used as arguments. In the case of the @AVG command, check to make sure that the cell block address you typed is valid, that addresses include page letters if the block is three-dimensional, that all the cells in the block contain values and not strings, and that the cells aren't blank. Remember, Quattro Pro counts blank cells as 0 when it calculates some @functions like @AVG.

Q: When I refer back to @functions at a later date, I have difficulty recalling the names and types of the arguments just by looking at them. I find that I must refer back to the original cell address on the notebook to figure out what value the argument represents. Can I use an easier way to recall an argument's origin?

A: Quattro Pro offers two ways to help you remember the origin of an argument used in an @function. First, assign a block name to an argument using the /Edit Names Create command. You can use cell block names instead of cell addresses in formulas and @function commands. (See the section titled "Naming a Block" in Chapter 4, "Manipulating Data," for more information.)

Second, attach a comment to the @function command as you enter it into a cell. Comments serve to jog your memory about the purpose and origin of the arguments used in an @function. To attach the comment *Computes 1994 total sales* to @SUM(B10..B15), for example, type the following:

@SUM(B10..B15);Computes 1994 total sales

The length of such an entry (@function command plus the comment) cannot exceed 254 characters.

Q: I notice that several @function commands have two forms that seem to perform the same calculation. When do I use one and not the other?

A: Several @function commands have two forms: a Quattro Pro version and a 1-2-3 compatible version. If you don't require 1-2-3 compatibility for your Quattro Pro notebooks, you should use the Quattro Pro version of an @function command. The Quattro Pro versions are always more precise than their 1-2-3 counterparts. Several financial @functions, for example, fall into this category: @FVAL and @FV, @IRATE and RATE, @NPER and CTERM, @PAYMT and @PMT, and @PVAL and @PV.

Note that the Quattro Pro versions of these @function commands require additional arguments, which are what enable the Quattro Pro versions of the @function commands to return more precise results.

If you require 1-2-3 worksheet compatibility, don't use the Quattro Pro form of any @function command that has a 1-2-3 form. If you do, the @functions return incorrect results when retrieved into 1-2-3.

Q: The financial @function that I entered is displaying a negative value when it should be displaying a positive value. What's wrong?

A: A negative value indicates that you are paying out money, such as when you make an investment. A positive value indicates that you are receiving cash, such as when you earn interest in a bank account. To ensure that the @function result displays the correct sign, make sure to use the correct signs for the arguments appearing in the @function command.

Q: With respect to using the financial @function commands, how do I know whether an argument should be positive or negative?

A: Use a positive number to indicate an inflow of cash, such as when you receive an interest payment, withdraw money from a bank account, or cash out an investment. Use a negative number to indicate an outflow of cash, such as when you make a loan payment, deposit a sum in a bank, or invest in an annuity. If the value contained in the original cell is negative and you want to supply a cell address as the argument, don't enter a negative argument (such as –C3).

Q: The result returned by a financial @function command is dramatically different than what I expected. What should I look for?

A: When a financial @function command returns a result that is much larger or smaller than you anticipated, the time periods used to express the arguments may be mismatched. For example,

> @FVAL(.12,3,–1000)

returns $3,374.44—the value after 3 years of investing $1,000 in a bank account that earns 12% annually. If you instead enter

> @FVAL(.12,36,–1000)

Quattro Pro returns the value $484,463.12. Here, the second argument is entered accidentally in months (36) instead of in years (3). Always make sure to match the time periods (all months, all years, and so on) for the arguments you enter into a financial @function.

Summary

Chapter 6 showed you how to use all Quattro Pro @function commands. Having completed this chapter, you should understand the following Quattro Pro concepts:

- Using the correct syntax for an @function command

- Selecting and entering an @function command on a page

- Using arithmetic and trigonometric @functions

- Using statistical @functions to return data about sample and population data sets

- Using string @functions to perform mathematical operations on text and string labels

- Using miscellaneous @functions to monitor notebook formulas and available system memory

- Using logical @functions to create test conditions that return values

- Using financial @functions to evaluate investments, amortize loans, and depreciate assets

- Using database @functions to perform statistical analyses of data appearing in a database

Chapter 7 examines methods for analyzing @functions and other types of formulas. The chapter features two commands: the /Tools Solve For command and the /Tools Audit command. The Solve For command enables you to solve formulas backwards, and the Audit command monitors and troubleshoots notebooks that rely on accurate formulas.

Analyzing Notebooks

In Chapter 3, "Entering and Editing Data," you learned how to enter numbers, formulas, and @function commands into a notebook. You also learned how to correct obvious errors in formulas.

In Chapter 6, "Using Functions," you learned all about using @function commands in your notebooks. That chapter's topics ranged from basic mathematical operations to methods for using logical and string functions to tips about how to turn notebooks into statistical, scientific, and financial analysis tools.

Chapter 7 shows you how to analyze @functions and other notebook formulas using two commands found on the Tools menu. The Solve For command enables you to solve formulas backwards. You supply the answer, and Solve For locates the variables that produce that answer. With the Audit command, you can monitor and troubleshoot notebook applications that depend on accurate formulas.

In this chapter you learn how to use the Solve For and Audit commands to do the following activities:

- Solve the @SLN function backwards to locate an asset life that produces a certain straight-line depreciation expense

- Verify the accuracy of an investment return by solving the @IRR and @NPV functions backwards

- Solve the @IPAYMT function backwards to locate a principal value that produces a certain annual interest expense

- Simultaneously run what-if analyses and Solve For operations

- Identify formula dependencies and locate circular, blank, label, and ERR references in notebook formulas

- Monitor external formula links to other notebook files

Using the Solve For Command

With the Solve For command, you can solve formulas backwards. You pick the answer and then tell Quattro Pro to adjust your formula so that it produces that answer. This technique for analyzing notebook data is efficient because it eliminates the need for trial-by-error number crunching and enables you to concentrate on the more important details of the analysis at hand.

One of the most powerful uses for the Solve For command is in notebooks that use @functions. In a mortgage application, for example, the @PAYMT function determines the payment for a loan when the principal, rate, and term of the loan are known.

Suppose, however, that you also want to know the interest rate that produces a payment amount that is $250 less a month. Alternatively, suppose that you want to determine the loan term that produces a payment amount that is $500 less a month. You can use the @RATE and @TERM commands to locate these answers, but that method means entering two additional @functions and the appropriate arguments onto the page.

With the Solve For command, you can find answers to these types of questions all from one menu, with no additional notebook entries required.

Reviewing the Solve For Submenu

When you choose /Tools Solve For, Quattro Pro displays the Solve For submenu. The six commands on this submenu, listed in table 7.1, define each element in the formula that Quattro Pro is to solve.

NOTE

The order in which you choose the **S**olve For options and identify values isn't important as long as you supply a value or cell address for each before you choose **G**o.

Table 7.1 The Solve For Submenu Commands

Command	Description
Formula Cell	Prompts you to identify the cell location of the mathematical formula you want to solve
Target Value	Prompts you for the value of the answer you seek
Variable Cell	Prompts you to identify the location of the cell that Quattro Pro varies in an attempt to reach the **Target Value**
Parameters	Defines rules for Quattro Pro to follow when executing a **S**olve For operation
Go	Executes a **S**olve For operation
Reset	Clears all **S**olve For submenu settings and returns them to their default values

Understanding the Rules for Using Solve For

Before executing your first **S**olve For operation, you must know some rules about what will and will not work when recording the settings on the **S**olve For submenu:

- The **F**ormula Cell must contain a formula or a cell address that references a formula. The **F**ormula Cell cannot contain string values or text formulas.

- The **T**arget Value must be a value, a formula, or a cell address that references a value or formula. Any value that includes positive and negative numbers of up to eight significant digits is considered valid for this type of entry. The **T**arget Value doesn't change if the referenced cell's contents change.

- The **Variable Cell** is one that already is included in the **Formula Cell** calculation and now contains an answer. Examples of invalid cells are protected cells or cells that contain formulas, dates, times, or text.

- On the **Parameters** submenu, choose **Max** Iterations to define the number of attempts Quattro Pro should make to solve the formula. By default, Quattro Pro makes 5 attempts to solve a formula; the program can make up to 99 attempts.

- On the **Parameters** submenu, choose **Accuracy** to specify the accuracy for the computed **Target Value**. Enter a fractional number between 0 and 1. This feature enables you to control **Solve** For's solutions up to 8 decimal places, resulting in answers that are within a certain number of decimal places of your **Target Value**. By default, Quattro Pro computes to an accuracy of 0.0005.

NOTE

The /**S**olve For **P**arameters **A**ccuracy setting for files created with Quattro Pro Version 3.0 is converted to the Version 5.0 default setting.

- You can perform a **Solve** For operation on data found on the same notebook page or on a 3-D cell block that spans several pages.

In the next few sections you work with real-life examples that demonstrate the power of the **Solve** For command. Keep in mind that you can apply these same techniques to your own notebooks, even if they contain different formulas or @functions.

Solving for a Depreciation Expense

Figure 7.1 shows a notebook that contains a typical Quattro Pro calculation using the @SLN command. In this example, you supply three numerical variables: Cost, Salvage, and Life. The formula in cell C7 is @SLN(C4,C5,C6). Quattro Pro computes the straight-line depreciation expense at $8,500 per year for a 10-year asset that originally cost $100,000 and is expected to be worth $15,000 at disposal.

Suppose, however, that you require at least $12,500 in write-offs on this asset each year. Because the Cost and Salvage values generally are assumed to be constant, you must vary the Life variable until the formula returns the value $12,500.

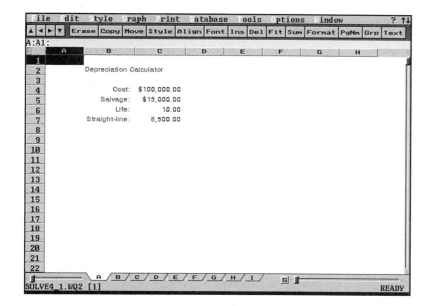

Fig. 7.1

A notebook containing a formula to be solved.

To solve this formula backwards, follow these steps:

1. Choose /**T**ools **S**olve For. Quattro Pro displays the **S**olve For submenu.

2. Choose **F**ormula Cell, type **C7**, and then press Enter to record the location of the cell containing the formula.

> Quattro Pro stores your entry as A:C7..C7 to reflect the name of the active page; you don't have to type it.

NOTE

3. Choose **T**arget Value, type **12500** (no commas), and press Enter to record the value of the answer you seek.

4. Choose **V**ariable Cell, type **C6**, and press Enter to record the location of the cell that you want Quattro Pro to vary. Quattro Pro stores your entry as A:C6..C6 to reflect the name of the active page; you don't have to type it.

5. Choose **G**o to execute the **S**olve For command and solve the formula.

6. Choose **Q**uit to return to the active notebook.

Figure 7.2 shows the **S**olve For submenu settings necessary to perform the operation. Figure 7.3 shows the outcome of this **S**olve For operation.

Fig. 7.2

Using the **S**olve For command to solve an @SLN command backwards.

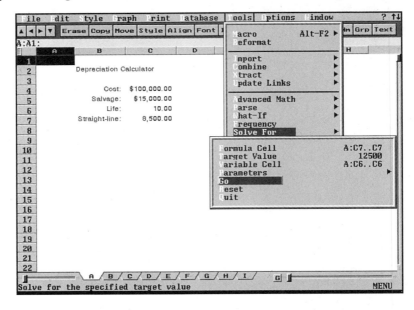

Fig. 7.3

When yearly depreciation is $12,500.00, Life equals 6.80.

As you see in figure 7.3, Quattro Pro adjusts the value in C6, the variable cell, to 6.80 years. Quattro Pro recalculates the @SLN command with this value, producing a yearly depreciation expense of $12,500.00—the exact target answer you seek. The value in C6 (6.8000000001287) isn't a whole number because the variables used in this calculation don't divide evenly into each other.

> **TIP**
>
> Return to the current notebook and press Alt+F5, the Undo key, to reverse a **S**olve For operation and return the contents of the active notebook to their original form.

Solving for an Investment Return

Figure 7.4 shows another way to use the **S**olve For command for investment calculations. This notebook shows 10 years of cash-flow data for an investment. The formulas in this figure are as follows:

C17: @NPV(C16,C4..C14,1)

C18: @IRR(0.10,C4..C14)

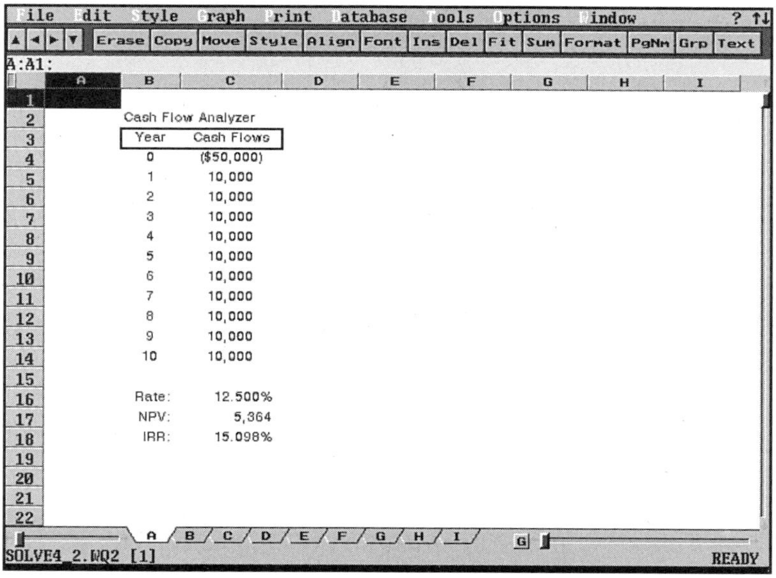

Fig. 7.4

Using the **S**olve For command to verify investment calculations.

Suppose that your investment counselor indicates that this investment offers a 15.098 percent internal rate of return (IRR). Given that your banker offers only a 12.5 percent return on similar investments, the first investment appears more profitable. When you calculate the net present value of this cash-flow stream, as shown in cell C17, you discover that the investment's NPV is $5,364—so far so good.

To verify that your investment counselor's IRR calculation is correct, recall the relationship between IRR and NPV. The IRR provides the rate of return that causes an investment's NPV to equal 0.

Use the **S**olve For command to verify the IRR calculations by following these steps:

1. Choose /**T**ools **S**olve For. Quattro Pro displays the **S**olve For submenu.

2. Choose **F**ormula Cell, type **C17**, and press Enter to record the location of the cell containing the formula.

3. Choose **T**arget Value, enter **0**, and press Enter to record the value of the answer you seek.

4. Choose **V**ariable Cell, type **C16**, and press Enter to record the location of the cell that you want Quattro Pro to vary.

5. Choose **G**o to execute the **S**olve For command and solve the formula.

6. Choose **Q**uit to return to the active notebook.

Figure 7.5 shows the **S**olve For submenu settings necessary to accomplish the objective. Figure 7.6 shows the outcome of this **S**olve For operation. As you can see, your investment counselor's calculation is exactly correct.

Solving for a Mortgage Interest Payment

Figure 7.7 shows yet another application for the **S**olve For command. The @IPAYMT command shown in cell C9 uses four arguments to compute the total interest paid in the first year of a home loan: Interest Rate, Current Year, Total Years, and Principal.

Suppose that your goal is to structure the terms of your home mortgage so that the first year's total interest payment equals $30,000.

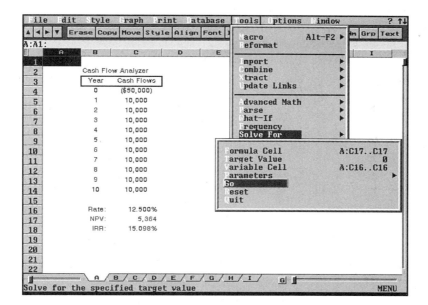

Fig. 7.5

Using the **S**olve For command to solve an @NPV command backwards.

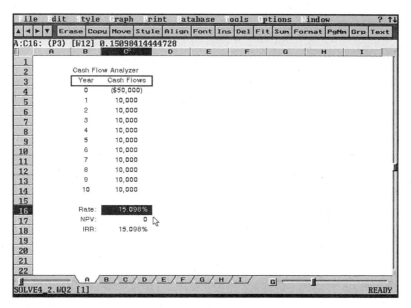

Fig. 7.6

When Net Present Value (NPV) equals 0, Rate equals 15.098 percent.

Fig. 7.7

Using the **S**olve For command to solve an @IPAYMT command backwards.

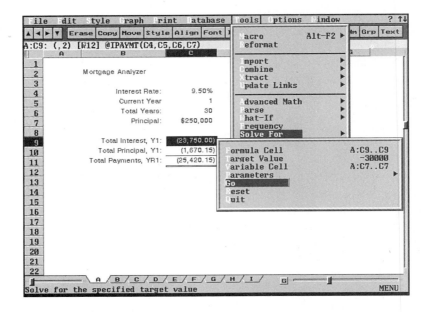

You must pay special attention to **S**olve For submenu definitions when using complex formulas and @functions. The @IPAYMT formula shown in figure 7.7, for example, uses four arguments to compute the value $250,000. At first glance, you may think that any of these arguments can work as the **V**ariable Cell. Only the Interest Rate and Principal arguments work, however. If you define Current Year or Total Years as the **V**ariable Cell, Quattro Pro displays the error message `Solve For is not converging on a solution`.

> **NOTE**   Quattro Pro may fail to execute a **S**olve For operation for several reasons. The most likely reason is that you defined an invalid parameter.

In the example, you shouldn't define the Total Years value as the **V**ariable Cell because large fluctuations of this value affect the interest payment only minimally. You shouldn't define the Current Year value as the **V**ariable Cell because this argument specifies the year for which the @IPAYMT command calculates the total interest paid. In most cases, you pay the highest amount of interest in year 1 (the current definition in cell C5). Because year 1 is the exact year for which you are running the analysis, cell C5 (the Current Year value) also isn't a candidate as the **V**ariable Cell.

When you define the **T**arget Value, make sure that it has the same positive or negative sign as the formula's initial result. Notice, for example, that the **T**arget Value field shown in the **S**olve For submenu in figure 7.7 is negative. Quattro Pro's @IPAYMT command always returns a negative value to show how much interest you pay out of pocket.

NOTE

As a rule, if a formula is expected to return a negative number, you must make the **T**arget Value a negative number.

Figure 7.8 shows the outcome of this **S**olve For operation. The **S**olve For submenu settings indicate that Total Interest, Y1 (in cell C9) is specified as the **F**ormula Cell, and Principal (cell C7) is specified as the **V**ariable Cell.

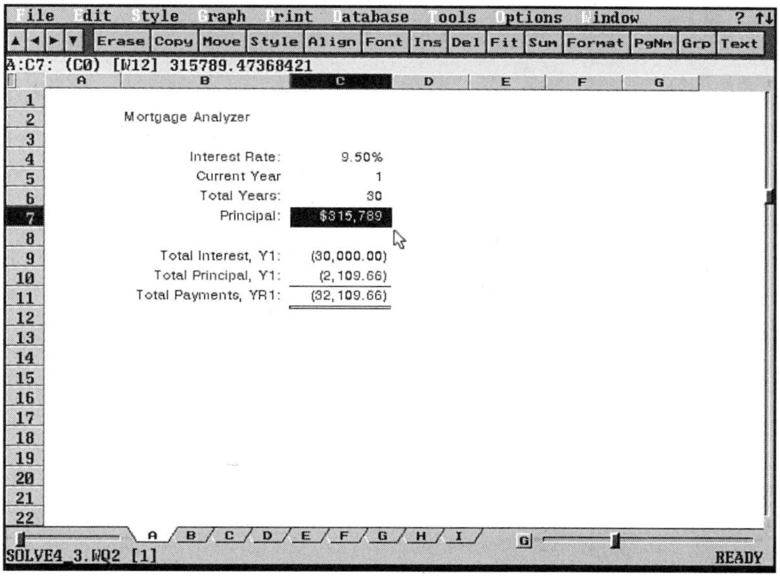

Fig. 7.8

When Total Interest equals ($30,000), Principal equals $315,789.

Now, after pressing Alt+F5 to undo the change to the principal, rerun this calculation by specifying cell C4, the Interest Rate value, as the **V**ariable Cell. Quattro Pro returns an Interest Rate value equal to 12 percent.

Reflect on the significance of the solutions that Quattro Pro returns for these two Solve For operations. Remember, in this example your goal is to structure the terms of a home mortgage so that the first year's total interest payment equals $30,000. Which would you rather do: borrow $315,789 at 9.5 percent or borrow $250,000 at 12.0 percent? Of course, the answer you pick depends on how much money you need to borrow, because the total interest paid on both loans is exactly the same.

Solving for a What-If Analysis

The Solve For command also can perform what-if analyses with more sophisticated notebook applications, such as the one shown in figure 7.9. This notebook calculates royalties and total earnings for a moderately successful yet undeniably ambitious rock star.

Fig. 7.9

Use the **S**olve For command to perform a what-if analysis.

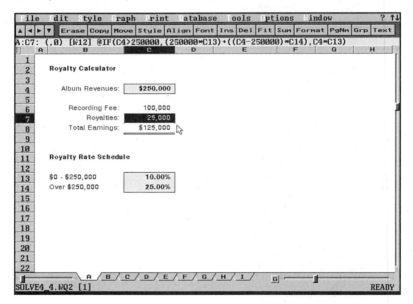

The value in cell C4, 250,000, represents the total revenues to date for album revenues. The value in cell C6, 100,000, represents a flat fee paid to the rock star for recording an album. The highlighted formula in cell C7 uses the @IF command to evaluate the total royalties to be paid to the rock star according to the royalty rate schedule shown in block C13..C14.

The formula in cell C7 is as follows:

@IF(C4>250000,(250000*C13)+((C4–250000)*C14),C4*C13)

This formula states that if album revenues are greater than $250,000 (C4>250000), multiply the first $250,000 by the initial royalty rate listed in cell C13 (250000*C13). For every revenue dollar over $250,000 the formula adds an additional royalty per the royalty rate listed in cell C14 ((C4–250000)*C14). If album revenues don't exceed $250,000, Quattro Pro uses the second condition listed in the formula, C4*C13, which multiplies current album revenues by the initial royalty rate of 10 percent.

Based on this formula and current album revenues, the rock star has earned $125,000 to date ($100,000 plus 10 percent of $250,000).

Suppose now that the rock star is curious about how to increase his Total Earnings figure to $200,000. One way to increase that figure is to determine the level of album revenues necessary to increase Total Earnings to $200,000, given that the Recording Fee is a one-time payment. The notebook in figure 7.10 shows the **S**olve For submenu settings necessary to perform this what-if analysis.

In this operation, Quattro Pro evaluates the Royalties formula in cell C7 and varies the value of Album Revenues in cell C4 until the Royalties value equals 100,000. At this level of Royalties, Total Earnings equals $200,000 (see fig. 7.11).

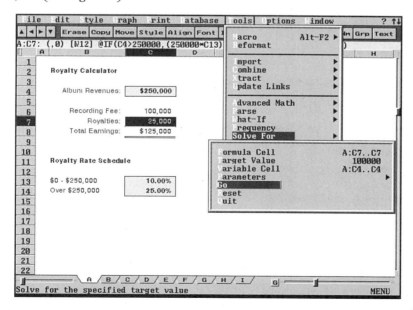

Fig. 7.10

Changing the Album Revenues value to increase Total Earnings.

Fig. 7.11

When Royalties equal
$100,000 and Total
Earnings equal
$200,000, Album
Revenues equal
$550,000.

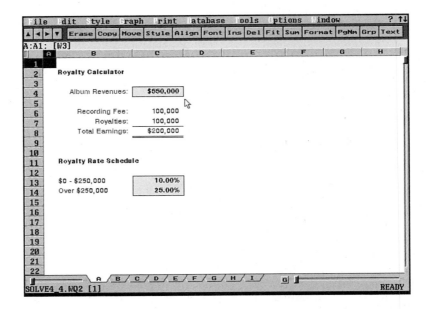

An equally efficient way to accomplish the same objective is to choose
the Total Earnings value in cell C8 as the **F**ormula Cell and change the
Target Value figure to 200000. This approach works because cell C8
also contains a formula, +C6+C7, which Quattro Pro can evaluate to
determine the relationship between Album Revenues, the Recording
Fee, the Royalties, and Total Earnings. Figure 7.12 shows the **S**olve For
submenu settings required for this analysis and the final results after
choosing **G**o.

Because the rock star probably cannot influence album revenues after
the record is cut (his mug is just a bit too gloomy for a rock video), he
may approach this problem from a different direction. Suppose that he
wants to determine the initial Royalty Rate necessary to increase Total
Earnings to $200,000. Figure 7.13 shows the **S**olve For submenu settings
required for this analysis and the final results after choosing **G**o.

Reflect on the significance of the solutions that Quattro Pro returns
for these **S**olve For operations. Remember, the rock star's goal is to
increase his Total Earnings figure to $200,000. Which strategy, then,
appears more likely: increasing album revenues to $550,000 or renego-
tiating the recording contract for a higher initial royalty rate?

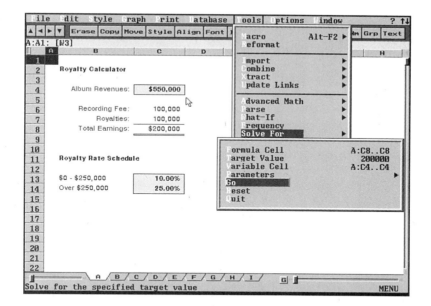

Fig. 7.12

Using the Total Earnings formula as the Formula Cell.

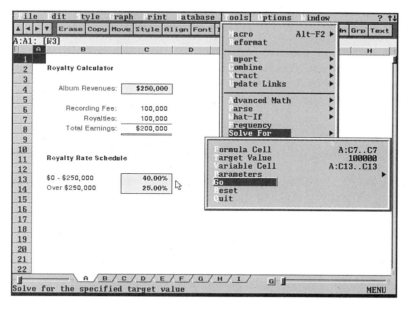

Fig. 7.13

When Total Earnings equal $200,000, the initial Royalty Rate equals 40 percent.

FOR RELATED INFORMATION

◄◄ "Using Financial @Functions," p. 295.
Descriptions of the commands used in the examples showing the uses
for the **S**olve For command.

◄◄ "Using Logical @Functions," p. 290.
A complete description of the @IF command, used in the final example demonstrating the uses for the **S**olve For command.

Using the Audit Command

The /**T**ools Au**d**it command enables you to analyze notebook formulas
and provides you with useful information for the ongoing development
and maintenance of your notebook applications. If you are responsible
for periodically updating notebook applications, or if someone wants
you to evaluate a complex notebook that you have never seen before,
you can use Quattro Pro's auditing tools to make your job easier.

The options on the Au**d**it submenu can depict graphically specific details about formula relationships in a notebook—information such as
cell dependencies, circular references, and the presence of ERR values.
The Au**d**it command performs detailed analyses of all formulas in a
notebook, one cell at a time.

Reviewing the Audit Submenu

When you choose /**T**ools Au**d**it, Quattro Pro displays the Au**d**it
submenu. The first six commands on this submenu (listed in table 7.2)
direct Quattro Pro to perform formula audits, and the last command
records the output location for an audit report.

Table 7.2 The Audit Submenu Commands

Command	Description
Dependency	Depicts a tree diagram of cells that are dependent on others for data
Circular	Depicts a tree diagram of cells that contain circular references

Command	Description
Label References	Displays addresses of cells that contain formulas referring to labels
ERR	Displays addresses of cells that contain formulas returning ERR as a result
Blank References	Displays addresses of cells that contain formulas referring to blank cells
External Links	Displays addresses of cells that contain formulas linking to other notebooks
Destination	Determines whether Quattro Pro sends an audit report to the printer or to the screen

Auditing Notebook Formulas

You use the following steps to generate any of the audit options available on the Audit submenu. (Remember, you use the Destination command only to identify where to send the audit report.)

To generate an audit report, follow these steps:

1. Choose /**T**ools Au**d**it. Quattro Pro displays the Au**d**it submenu.

2. If you want to direct the audit report to a printer rather than the screen, choose Destination **P**rinter.

3. Choose one of the six audit report options listed on the submenu. To generate an audit report of ERR values in the current notebook, for example, choose the **E**RR option.

4. When Quattro Pro prompts you for a notebook block to audit, type a valid block address and press Enter.

Quattro Pro immediately begins evaluating formulas in the specified block in the current notebook and then displays the audit report (or sends the report to the printer if you chose that as the destination). After you finish reviewing a displayed audit report, press Esc to return to the current notebook with the Au**d**it submenu displayed.

The next few sections describe each type of audit report available on the Au**d**it submenu and the circumstances under which you may want to view a particular type of report. The sample application audited in these sections appears in figure 7.14. Except for the values in cell D7

($81,148) and in ranges D12..F12 (the Management Fees) and D16..F16 (the Janitorial/Landscaping costs), every cell in range D7..I21 contains a formula, making this notebook an ideal one for testing Quattro Pro's auditing capabilities.

Fig. 7.14

The Brandenburg Property Partnership application to be audited.

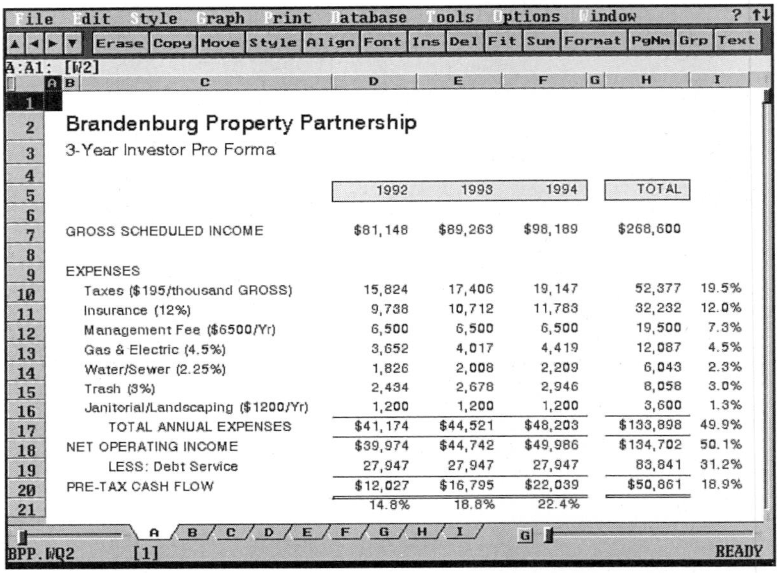
File Edit Style Graph Print Database Tools Options Window

Erase Copy Move Style Align Font Ins Del Fit Sum Format PgNm Grp Text

A:A1: [W2]

	B / C	D	E	F	G	H	I
1							
2	Brandenburg Property Partnership						
3	3-Year Investor Pro Forma						
4							
5		1992	1993	1994		TOTAL	
6							
7	GROSS SCHEDULED INCOME	$81,148	$89,263	$98,189		$268,600	
8							
9	EXPENSES						
10	Taxes ($195/thousand GROSS)	15,824	17,406	19,147		52,377	19.5%
11	Insurance (12%)	9,738	10,712	11,783		32,232	12.0%
12	Management Fee ($6500/Yr)	6,500	6,500	6,500		19,500	7.3%
13	Gas & Electric (4.5%)	3,652	4,017	4,419		12,087	4.5%
14	Water/Sewer (2.25%)	1,826	2,008	2,209		6,043	2.3%
15	Trash (3%)	2,434	2,678	2,946		8,058	3.0%
16	Janitorial/Landscaping ($1200/Yr)	1,200	1,200	1,200		3,600	1.3%
17	TOTAL ANNUAL EXPENSES	$41,174	$44,521	$48,203		$133,898	49.9%
18	NET OPERATING INCOME	$39,974	$44,742	$49,986		$134,702	50.1%
19	LESS: Debt Service	27,947	27,947	27,947		83,841	31.2%
20	PRE-TAX CASH FLOW	$12,027	$16,795	$22,039		$50,861	18.9%
21		14.8%	18.8%	22.4%			

A B C D E F G H I G

BPP.WQ2 [1] READY

TIP

The Au**d**it command works as well on 3-D cell blocks as it does cell blocks located on a single page.

Performing a Dependency Audit

A *dependency audit* graphically shows in a tree diagram the cell relationships for the current notebook. You can use this type of report to learn about notebook applications with which you are unfamiliar. Then you don't have to search through a notebook cell by cell to learn how the application works.

TIP

Printing out a dependency report before performing what-if analyses with a notebook is useful. That way, you can be sure of which values to change to test your theories.

To generate a dependency audit report, follow these steps:

1. Choose /**T**ools Au**d**it. Quattro Pro displays the Au**d**it submenu.

2. Choose **D**ependency.

3. When Quattro Pro prompts you for a notebook block to audit, type the block address—**D7..I21** for the example—and press Enter.

Quattro Pro immediately displays on the audit screen a graphical tree diagram depicting the dependency relationships for cells in the notebook. Figure 7.15 shows the dependency audit report for the Brandenburg Property Partnership application.

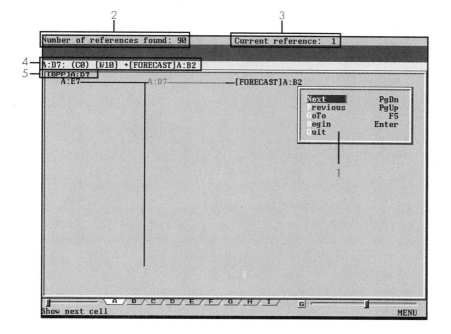

Fig. 7.15

A dependency report on the audit screen.

The audit screen displays different types of information about the current audit operation. All the following elements apply to each report type:

- A menu activated by pressing the forward slash key (/) displays the following commands: **N**ext, **P**revious, **G**oTo, **B**egin (for the dependency and circular reports only), and **Q**uit (item 1 in fig. 7.15).

- The `Number of references found` prompt at the top of the screen (item 2 in fig. 7.15) displays the number of cell references located in a notebook for the current audit. In figure 7.15, the number of references is 90.

- The `Current reference` prompt (item 3 in fig. 7.15) displays a number that represents the position number in the audit block for the currently highlighted cell—in the example, cell number 1.

- The *input line* (item 4 in fig. 7.15) shows the cell address of the audited cell, all formatting information, and the contents of the cell.

- Just below the input line, the *audited cell* appears after the *audited file name* (item 5 in fig. 7.15). These references are the cell and notebook file whose dependencies now are depicted on the audit screen. In figure 7.15, `A:D7` is the audited cell and `[BPP]` is the audited notebook file.

TIP

If an audited cell contains a formula link to a cell on another page or notebook, Quattro Pro displays the linking reference directly to the right of the audited cell in the tree diagram. See Chapter 8, "Managing Files and Windows," for more information about file linking.

Table 7.3 contains a list of the menu commands and keys that you can use to maneuver around an audit screen. As you can see, each key corresponds to one of the commands listed in the audit screen menu, shown at the top of the audit screen in figure 7.15.

Table 7.3 The Audit Screen Menu Commands and Keys

Command and Key	Function
/Next (Page Down)	Displays the next cell in the audit block
/Previous (Page Up)	Displays the previous cell in the audit block and makes that cell the audited cell
/GoTo (F5)	Exits the audit screen and returns to the current notebook at the location of the last audited cell
/Begin (Enter)	Audits the cell that now is highlighted on the audit screen
/Quit (Esc)	Returns to the current notebook with the Audit submenu still active

On the audit screen, all dependencies fall to the left of the audited cell. Press the left-arrow key to move through the tree diagram of cell dependencies. In the sample notebook, for example, pressing the left-arrow key four times moves you to cell I10, the last cell on that branch that depends on the audited cell (see fig. 7.16).

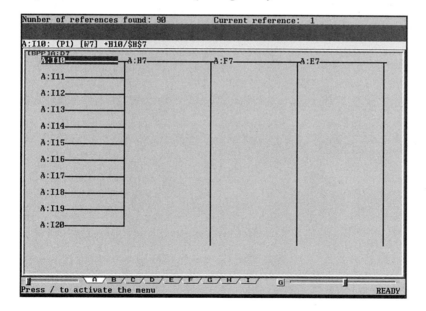

Fig. 7.16

The last cell on a branch for the audited cell.

If the first cell displayed on an audit screen has no dependents, pressing the arrow keys has no movement effect. In the example, choose /**N**ext or press Page Down until a cell with branches appears. Then, press the arrow keys to trace the pathway of that cell's dependent cells.

No matter where you move the highlight, the audit screen displays information about the audited cell until you select another cell by choosing /**N**ext or /**B**egin. To audit another cell that's displayed in a tree diagram, highlight the cell and choose /**B**egin, or choose /**N**ext to audit the next cell in the audited block. To audit cell I10 in the sample notebook, for example, highlight the cell and choose /**B**egin (see fig. 7.17).

Fig. 7.17

Selecting a different cell to audit.

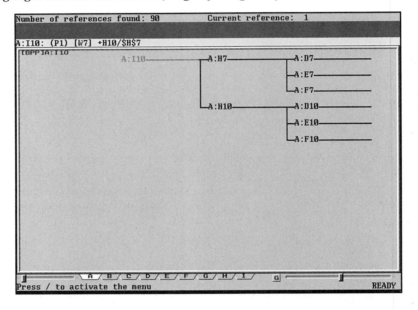

TIP

When you audit a cell that resides in the left half of the audit screen, Quattro Pro displays a tree diagram that is oriented from left to right rather than from right to left, as seen in previous figures.

Performing a Circular Audit

A *circular audit* graphically shows in a tree diagram all circular cells located in the current notebook. A circular cell contains a formula that refers to itself, such as the formula @SUM(B5..B6) entered into cell B5.

Although Quattro Pro provides other means for locating circular cells (/**O**ptions **R**ecalculation and /**W**indow **O**ptions **M**ap View), this approach is the most efficient because it displays all other cells affected by the circular cell.

To generate a circular audit report, follow these steps:

1. Choose /**T**ools Au**d**it. Quattro Pro displays the Au**d**it submenu.

2. Choose **C**ircular.

Quattro Pro immediately displays a graphical tree diagram depicting the circular relationships for cells in the notebook. Figure 7.18 shows the circular audit report for the Brandenburg Property Partnership application (a circular reference was created intentionally for this example).

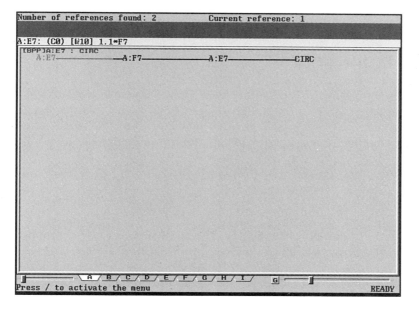

Fig. 7.18

Reviewing a circular report on the audit screen.

When a notebook contains more than one circular cell, Quattro Pro highlights the first cell it encounters when it displays the audit screen. In figure 7.18, Quattro Pro is highlighting cell E7. Because the formula in cell E7 contains a reference to cell F7, which in turn refers back to cell E7, Quattro Pro draws a branch between both cells. The CIRC indicator at the end of the branch identifies this relationship as a circular relationship.

You may have noticed that the circular cell audit screen looks much like the dependency audit screen. In fact, not only do they look alike, you can use many of the same keys and commands listed earlier in table 7.3 to maneuver around the circular audit screen. (Note that the /**B**egin command operates only from a dependency audit screen.)

TIP

Choose /**G**oTo from a circular audit screen to return to the notebook at the exact cell location where the first circular cell was encountered. There, you can correct the cell referencing error quickly by changing the formula so that it doesn't refer to the cell in which it resides.

When no circular cells are found in the current notebook, Quattro Pro displays the message No circular references found. Press Esc to return to the Au**d**it submenu.

Performing a Label Reference Audit

A *label reference audit* displays information about cells containing formulas that refer to labels rather than values. Because Quattro Pro treats labels as zeros when they appear in formulas, math calculations return incorrect answers. This auditing tool, therefore, is useful for verifying that your notebook formula results are correct.

To generate a label reference audit report, follow these steps:

1. Choose /**T**ools Au**d**it.

2. From the Au**d**it submenu, choose **L**abel References.

Quattro Pro immediately displays the audit screen with information about the first notebook formula encountered that refers to a label. Figure 7.19 shows the label reference audit report for the Brandenburg Property Partnership application.

NOTE

On the label reference audit screen, you can use the same menu selections and shortcuts you use on other audit screens.

The information on the label reference audit screen helps you locate what may be incorrect entries in your notebooks. When a notebook contains more than one formula that refers to a label, press Page Down or choose /**N**ext to review the next occurrence.

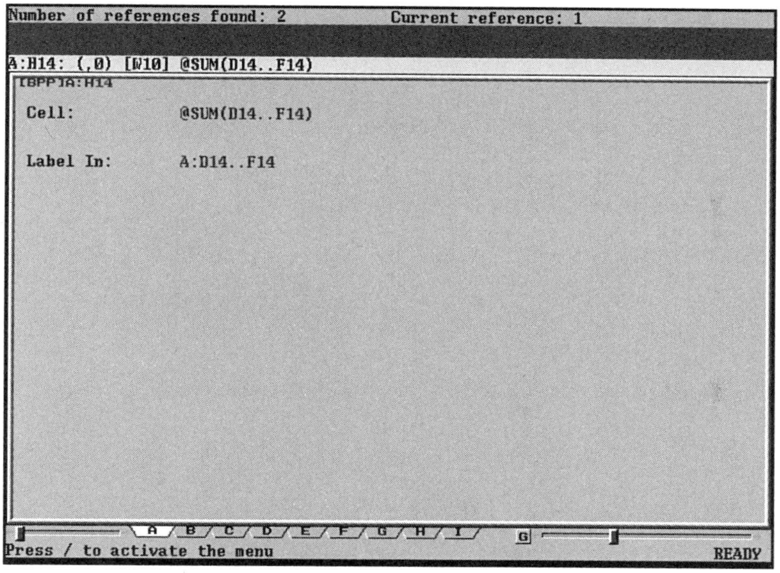

```
Number of references found: 2              Current reference: 1
A:H14: (,0) [W10] @SUM(D14..F14)
 [BPPJA:H14
     Cell:          @SUM(D14..F14)

     Label In:      A:D14..F14









    A / B / C / D / E / F / G / H / I        G
Press / to activate the menu                          READY
```

Fig. 7.19

Reviewing a label reference report on the audit screen.

In the sample notebook, note that the audited cell, cell H14, contains the formula @SUM(D14..F14). This message tells you that the range address in the formula is incorrect or that a label rather than a value is included somewhere in range D14..F14.

The easiest way to determine the cause of the problem is to choose /**G**oTo and return to the notebook. Quattro Pro places the selector in the audited cell, cell H14 (see fig. 7.20). A quick glance at the data on row 14 reveals that the entry in cell F14 appears to be a label rather than a value.

When no label references are included in the current notebook, Quattro Pro displays the message No such references found. Press Esc to return to the Au**d**it submenu.

Performing an ERR Audit

An *ERR audit* displays information about cell formulas that return the value ERR as their result. Complex notebooks containing many formulas often pass their results along as input to other formulas. When one cell returns ERR, all cells that rely on that cell's data return ERR—this phenomenon is known as the *ERR trickle-down effect*. The ERR audit tool is useful for locating and correcting ERR values that appear in your notebooks.

Fig. 7.20

Returning to the note-
book to search for the
cause of a label
referencing problem.

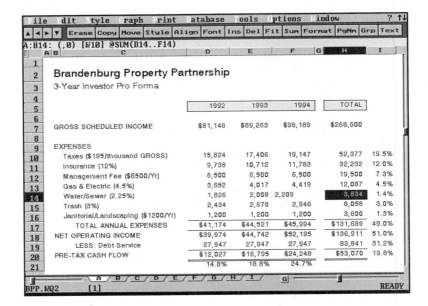

To generate an ERR audit report, follow these steps:

1. Choose /**T**ools Au**d**it.

2. From the Au**d**it submenu, choose **ERR**.

Quattro Pro displays the audit screen with information about the first
notebook formula encountered that returns the value ERR. Figure 7.21
shows the ERR audit report for the Brandenburg Property Partnership
application.

When a notebook contains more than one formula that returns ERR,
press Page Down or choose /**N**ext to review the next occurrence.

In the sample notebook, note that the audited cell (F10) contains the
formula 195*(F7/0). Any formula that tries to divide by 0 returns ERR as
its result.

The easiest way to correct any ERR problems is to choose /**G**oTo and
return to the notebook. Quattro Pro places the selector in the audited
cell—cell F10 in the example. Correct the formula, and Quattro Pro
replaces all ERR values with the correct results.

When no ERR values are found in the current notebook, Quattro Pro
displays the message No such references found. Press Esc to return to
the Au**d**it submenu.

Performing a Blank Reference Audit

A *blank reference audit* displays information about cells containing formulas that refer to blank cells. Because Quattro Pro treats blanks as zeros when they appear in formulas, some math calculations return incorrect answers. This auditing tool therefore is useful for verifying that your notebook formula results are correct.

To generate a blank reference audit report, follow these steps:

1. Choose /**T**ools Au**d**it. Quattro Pro displays the Au**d**it submenu.

2. Choose **B**lank References.

Quattro Pro immediately displays the audit screen with information about the first notebook formula encountered that refers to blank cells.

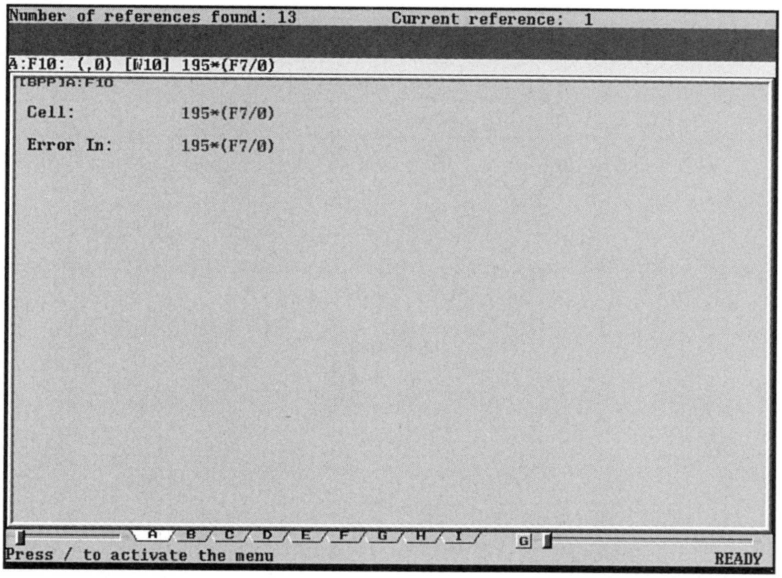

Fig. 7.21

An **ERR** report on the audit screen.

The information on the blank reference audit screen helps you locate what may be missing entries in your notebooks. When a notebook contains more than one formula that refers to a blank cell, press Page Down or choose /**N**ext to review the next occurrence.

When no blank references are found in the current notebook, Quattro Pro displays the message No such references found. Press Esc to return to the Au**d**it submenu.

Performing an External Links Audit

An *external links audit* displays information about cells containing formulas that link to other notebooks. Choose /**T**ools Au**d**it **E**xternal Links to search through a notebook for linking formulas before moving or erasing documents.

After you choose External Links, Quattro Pro displays the audit screen with information about the first notebook formula encountered that links to another notebook. Figure 7.22 shows the external links audit for the Brandenburg Property Partnership application.

In the sample notebook, Quattro Pro locates a single linking formula in cell D7, the audited cell. This formula links to cell B2 in a notebook named FORECAST. If you ever need to delete FORECAST from your hard disk, change the linking reference in cell D7 in the current notebook to a value before doing so. Otherwise, the next time you retrieve the BPP.WQ2 notebook, cell D7 and all other cells that depend on the value in cell D7 will display NA.

Fig. 7.22

An external links report on the audit screen.

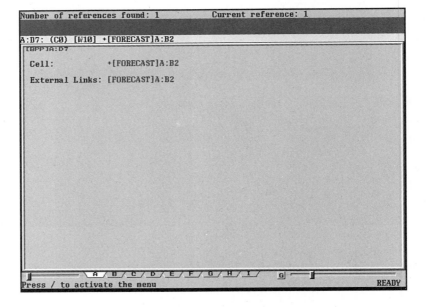

```
Number of references found: 1            Current reference: 1

A:D7: (C0) [W10] +[FORECAST]A:B2
[BPP]A:D7

   Cell:             +[FORECAST]A:B2

   External Links: [FORECAST]A:B2
```

```
    \ A / B / C / D / E / F / G / H / I /    G
Press / to activate the menu                              READY
```

When a notebook contains more than one linking formula, press Page Down or choose /**N**ext to review the next occurrence.

> **TIP**
>
> Quattro Pro finds all linking formulas in a notebook, regardless of whether the notebooks to which the audited notebook is linked are open in memory at the time.

When no linking formulas are found in the current notebook, Quattro Pro displays the message No such references found. Press Esc to return to the Au**d**it submenu.

> **FOR RELATED INFORMATION**
>
> ◄◄ "Using Logical @Functions," p. 290.
>   A complete description of the @IF command.
> ►► "Creating Linking Formulas," p. 401.
>   How to create a formula that links information found in two different notebooks.

Questions & Answers

This chapter introduces you to two of the analytical tools found on the **T**ools menu: **S**olve For and Au**d**it. If you have questions concerning particular situations that the examples in this chapter don't address, look through this section.

Solving Formulas

Q: I want to run multiple **S**olve For operations in a row, but I must exit the **S**olve For submenu each time I want to review data in the notebook that the menus are blocking. What can I do?

A: Press F6, the Window key, to toggle the display of the **S**olve For submenu so that you can view data in the notebook. Press F6 again to display the menus when you are ready to execute the next operation.

Q: Quattro Pro cannot locate an answer to a problem I defined—the program keeps displaying the message No feasible solution is attainable. I'm certain that the problem variables are realistic, so what went wrong?

A: Possibly Quattro Pro isn't trying to solve the problem enough times, or perhaps the required **A**ccuracy setting is unrealistic.

Choose /**T**ools **S**olve For **P**arameters **M**ax Iterations and choose 99, the maximum number allowed. Also check the **A**ccuracy setting on the **P**arameters submenu; you may have chosen an unrealistic setting (such as 0.0000000000001).

Q: I tried to use the **S**olve For command on criteria appearing in a database notebook, but Quattro Pro keeps displaying the error message Invalid value in Variable Cell. My formula appears to be valid, so what else can be wrong?

A: Even though Quattro Pro accepts formulas for use in certain notebook operations, the formulas may not be appropriate for use in **S**olve For operations. The formula +MONTH is an example of a valid criteria formula that you can use in database operations. You cannot define such a value, however, as the **V**ariable Cell in a **S**olve For operation. Just remember not to use formulas with the **S**olve For command that return dates, times, or strings.

Auditing Formulas

Q: The current audit report has located so many references that I am having a difficult time getting an overall picture of the notebook I am reviewing. Does Quattro Pro offer an easier way to do this process?

A: Choose /**W**indow **O**ptions **M**ap View to display general audit information for the current notebook. In map view, Quattro Pro uses special characters to represent labels, formulas, circular references, and other types of notebook entries. See Chapter 8, "Managing Files and Windows," for more information.

Q: I am having difficulty auditing a different cell in the current audit report. Each time I highlight the new cell, the audited cell reference displays the address of the cell Quattro Pro originally audited. What should I be doing?

A: Highlighting a cell appearing in an audit report doesn't cause Quattro Pro to audit that cell. To change the audited cell from within an audit screen, highlight the target cell and choose /**B**egin.

Q: How do I display the graphic tree diagram in a blank or label reference audit?

A: The audit screen that Quattro Pro displays for dependency and circular audits is different from the one it displays for ERR, blank, label reference, and external link audits. The main difference is that the audit screens for the latter group of audits don't display in a graphic tree diagram.

Summary

In this chapter, you learned how to analyze your data using two commands found on the **T**ools menu. These two commands, **S**olve For and Au**d**it, enable you to turn a Quattro Pro notebook into an efficient environment for analyzing information.

Having completed this chapter's material, you should understand the following concepts:

- Solving a formula backwards

- Auditing notebook formulas for dependencies

- Auditing notebook formulas for circular references

- Auditing notebook formulas for blank and label references

- Auditing notebook formulas for ERR results

- Auditing notebook formulas for links to other notebooks

- Printing an Au**d**it report to the screen or to a printer

In Chapter 8, you learn how to use one of Quattro Pro's most notable features: multiple notebook operations. With these techniques, you learn how to link data on notebooks and pass information between applications. Chapter 8 also introduces you to the File Manager— Quattro Pro's built-in file-management utility. With the File Manager, you never again need to exit Quattro Pro to copy, move, or erase files.

Managing Files and Windows

This chapter shows you how to create and use files, workspaces, and windows; oversee file operations with the File Manager; link multiple notebooks with special formulas; and combine and extract notebook data. You can perform these operations using the commands from the File, Window, and Tools menus.

In the first section of this chapter, you learn how to create, preserve, and recover notebook files by choosing commands from the File menu. This section continues by explaining how to create a workspace file and save Quattro Pro notebooks in file formats that other programs can read.

The next section explains how to use the File Manager, with which you can perform DOS-like file management operations without leaving Quattro Pro. You can copy, move, rename, and erase files from the File Manager, for example, and display a directory-tree graphic showing the organization of files on your hard disk drive.

Next, you learn about managing Quattro Pro windows. You learn how to display, move, resize, pick, and split windows. This section also shows you how to create special display effects for windows.

The chapter continues by introducing you to linked notebooks. By creating linked formulas, you can pass data between notebook applications. Linked notebooks can improve your productivity and Quattro Pro's speed of execution.

The final section of this chapter introduces advanced file operations. By using commands found on the Tools menu, you learn how to import, combine, and extract data from multiple notebook files.

Reviewing the File Menu Commands

You can use the 13 File menu commands to create, retrieve, and save files, and to manage the directories in which your files are stored (see fig. 8.1). The File menu consists of three types of commands: file access commands, file management commands, and miscellaneous file commands.

Fig. 8.1

The **F**ile menu commands.

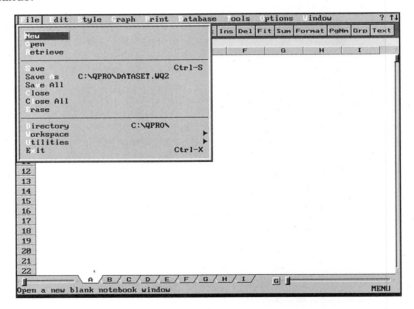

The file access commands control the flow of file data from your hard disk drive into Quattro Pro's operating environment. With these commands, you can create a notebook file, load a saved file into its own window, and retrieve a previously saved file.

The file management commands move file data from Quattro Pro's operating environment onto your hard disk drive. These commands save, rename, close, and erase notebook files.

The miscellaneous commands perform operations such as setting the current directory, creating a workspace file, entering the DOS shell, and accessing file utilities.

Table 8.1 describes each **File** menu command.

Table 8.1 File Menu Commands

Command	Description
New	Loads a new, blank notebook into its own window
Open	Loads a previously saved notebook file into its own window
Retrieve	Loads a previously saved notebook file into the current window, closing the current notebook
Save	Saves the current notebook with a previously entered file name; prompts you to supply a file name if one hasn't been specified
Save As	Prompts you for a file name and location; then saves the current notebook using that name
Save All	Saves all currently open notebooks using a previously entered file name; prompts you to supply a file name if one hasn't been specified
Close	Closes the notebook in the current window
Close All	Closes all notebooks in all open windows
Erase	Erases the current notebook from RAM (but not from your hard disk or floppy disk) and displays a new, blank notebook
Directory	Designates the default directory path name for storing files on the hard disk drive
Workspace	Saves the names of all open notebooks to a workspace file name or restores previously saved workspaces
Utilities	Exits to DOS, activates the File Manager window, sets the SQZ! file compression options, or consolidates 2-D spreadsheets into a notebook
Exit	Ends a work session by closing all open windows, exits Quattro Pro, and returns system control to DOS

In figure 8.1, the active notebook, DATASET.WQ2, is stored in the current directory named QPRO. Your screen always will show the active notebook (unless the notebook is NOTEBK1.WQ2, the default notebook) and the current directory name for your computer.

After creating your own library of notebook files, you can use the File menu to develop workspace applications that juggle several notebooks at one time. You can use workspace applications to save non-linked notebooks as one unit, save a File Manager window with a group of notebooks, and help preserve the screen position and sequential order of a group of notebooks.

Working with Files

This section reviews the processes that every user goes through in a Quattro Pro work session. Before reading the section, however, keep in mind a few basic terms.

Notebook describes the physical area containing pages, rows, and columns into which you enter data. After you finish entering data, assign a unique file name to the notebook so that you easily can locate and recall the notebook the next time you want to use that data.

Page is the term used to describe a unique work area of a notebook. Each notebook has 256 unique pages.

Quattro Pro enables you to open and view up to 32 windows at a time. A *window* is the area in which Quattro Pro displays the current notebook. Each time you open a new notebook, Quattro Pro assigns the notebook a window number from 1 to 32 and displays the number in brackets on the status line to the right of the notebook name.

Workspace describes a group of related notebook files open in Quattro Pro's memory at the same time. When you restore a workspace file name, Quattro Pro loads each notebook in the workspace into RAM.

Creating, Opening, and Retrieving Files

Each time you access Quattro Pro from your PC, the program displays a new, blank notebook named NOTEBK1.WQ2 in the current window, unless you specify another file to be loaded automatically. With this notebook, you can enter data, ignore the blank notebook and open a saved notebook, or close the blank notebook by retrieving a saved notebook.

The top three commands on the File menu give you access to new and saved notebook files. To display another new, blank notebook, choose /File New. You can load up to 32 notebooks into Quattro Pro's memory.

To load a previously saved notebook into the current window without affecting other notebooks open in memory, choose /File Open. Quattro Pro displays the file list box, which lists the names of notebook files saved in the current directory.

While this list box is on-screen, you can execute several keystrokes to display more information about your files. Table 8.2 describes the effect of the keystrokes you can use while the file list box is on-screen. If you press the plus key (+) on the numeric keypad and then press F3, for example, you can create a fully enlarged view of the file list box (see fig. 8.2).

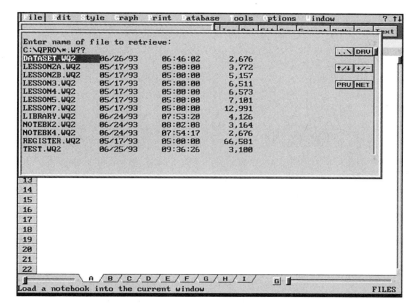

Fig. 8.2

The file list box, fully enlarged.

Table 8.2 Keys Affecting File List and File Name Prompt Boxes

Key	Description
Backspace	Displays a list of all files in the parent directory
Ctrl+Backspace	Removes the default prompt and file list
Enter	Accepts the file name highlighted on the list
Esc	Erases data on the line, one directory path name at a time
F2	Enters Search mode so that you can enter the first letter of the file for which you are searching
F3	Expands the file list so that it fills the screen; press again to reduce the file list to its normal size
+	Displays the file size and the last date altered for the files in the file list
−	Removes the file size and the last date altered from the file list display
Space bar	Highlights the next file name in the list

You also can use the six buttons on the right side of the file list box to display details about files, directory paths, and disk drives on your PC. With one click, you can view a list of all available drives, directories, files opened in the current Quattro Pro work session, and more.

TIP

If you don't have a mouse, you can access these buttons by pressing the slash (/) key, using the arrow keys to move between buttons, and pressing Enter to choose a button. To switch from the buttons back to the file list, press Esc.

The following table describes each button in the file list box.

Button	Action
..\	Lists the files in the parent directory
DRV	Lists all available drives
↑/↓	Expands or contracts the file name prompt box
+/−	Reveals and hides the date-and-time stamp for each file
PRV	Lists all files previously opened during your current Quattro Pro work session so that you can open a file from that list
NET	Shows network drive mappings, if any exist

To load a notebook into Quattro Pro's memory, highlight the file name in the file list box or in the list of previously opened files and then press Enter. Press the plus key (+) and F3 to enlarge the file list box to its full size (refer to fig. 8.2).

To load a saved notebook into the current window, choose /File **Re**trieve. Like the **O**pen command, this command displays a file name box. Highlight a file name and press Enter to retrieve that notebook.

> If you have an unsaved notebook in the current window when you issue this command, Quattro Pro asks whether you want to lose your changes. Choose **N**o to return to the notebook so that you can save the file, or **Y**es to erase the notebook from memory.

NOTE

The major difference between /File **O**pen and /File **R**etrieve is that Quattro Pro closes the current notebook when you retrieve a saved notebook file. After you choose /File **O**pen, Quattro Pro loads the notebook file on top of all existing open notebooks.

You use the **O**pen command most when you link notebooks with formulas. The **O**pen command enables you to open and work simultaneously with several Quattro Pro notebooks.

Saving, Closing, and Erasing Files

The six commands in the middle of the **File** menu enable you to save notebook files permanently, close previously saved files without saving changes, and erase the current notebook from Quattro Pro's memory.

After you finish entering data, choose /File **S**ave. Quattro Pro prompts you to enter a name. If the exact path name where you want to save the notebook appears next to the prompt, type a file name in the prompt box and then press Enter to store the name permanently. To change the path name that appears at the prompt—for example, to save the notebook in a different directory—press Esc to remove the current directory name from the prompt. Continue pressing Esc until only the directory where you want to save the notebook remains, type a file name in the prompt box, and then press Enter to store the name permanently.

When you choose /File **S**ave in the future with the same notebook, Quattro Pro displays a File already exists prompt if the file has been saved before and you opened or retrieved it. The program remembers the notebook's name and asks you to specify whether you want to cancel the operation, replace the stored notebook file with the current notebook, or create a backup of the notebook file. This last command also transfers a copy of the file onto your hard disk drive with the file extension BAK.

TIP

> Press Ctrl+S, the Ctrl+*key* shortcut for the **S**ave command, to save a Quattro Pro notebook file.

After a notebook is saved to a file, you can recall the notebook by using the **O**pen or **R**etrieve command on the **F**ile menu.

To give the current notebook a new file name, choose /**F**ile Save **A**s. When prompted, type a new file name and press Enter to copy the notebook. You don't necessarily duplicate the file; you can save a notebook with changes to a new name and leave the original intact. After you press Enter to save the notebook, Quattro Pro displays the new file name and window number on the status line.

To save all notebooks open in memory, choose /**F**ile Save All. Quattro Pro first prompts you to save the active notebook. If you previously saved the active notebook, Quattro Pro asks you to specify whether you want to replace the stored notebook file with the current notebook, create a backup of the notebook file, or cancel the operation. Quattro Pro activates the next notebook open in memory and repeats this save operation. This process continues until the program saves all notebooks open in memory.

To close a notebook and remove its window from the screen, choose /**F**ile **C**lose. To perform this operation for all open notebook windows, use /**F**ile Close All.

TIP

> To close a notebook quickly, click the close box to the left of the column letters, just above the row numbers. Quattro Pro treats a notebook closed in this manner like one closed by choosing /**F**ile **C**lose. When you click the close box, Quattro Pro prompts you to save changes before closing the notebook.

You occasionally may want to erase a notebook from Quattro Pro's memory without deleting the file from your hard disk drive. Choose /**F**ile Erase. Quattro Pro asks whether you really want to erase the notebook. Choose **N**o to cancel the operation or **Y**es to blank the screen. If you have made changes to the file and want to save those changes, you must save the changes before erasing the file from the workspace.

> **NOTE**
>
> The difference between the /**F**ile **C**lose and the /**F**ile **E**rase commands is subtle. When you close a notebook, Quattro Pro closes the notebook file and its window. This command is useful for freeing up additional memory when multiple notebooks are open in RAM.
>
> When you erase a notebook, Quattro Pro discards changes made to the current notebook since the last save operation, closes the current notebook, and leaves a new, blank notebook in its place. If the current notebook is unnamed, Quattro Pro discards the entire notebook. During a work session, you can use this command to erase the notebook and start over.

Password-Protecting Your Files

Quattro Pro offers you the option of password-protecting your files to prevent unauthorized viewing of confidential data. You can retrieve password-protected files only when you have the correct access code. Because Quattro Pro passwords are case-sensitive, you must supply the access code in the exact form (upper- and lowercase) in which you created the code.

To password-protect a Quattro Pro file named NPV.WQ2, type the file name followed by a space and the letter **P**. Follow these steps:

1. Make NPV.WQ2 the active notebook.

2. Choose /**F**ile Save **As**.

3. When prompted, type **npv p** and press Enter to invoke the password-protection facility.

4. Type a password consisting of up to 15 characters. (Quattro Pro doesn't display the characters as you type.)

5. Press Enter to assign the password to the NPV notebook.

6. When prompted, re-enter the password to verify it (see fig. 8.3). If you type the password incorrectly, Quattro Pro displays an error message. In this case, press Esc and return to step 3 to continue.

7. Press Enter to store the password.

Fig. 8.3

The password entry box.

Password entry box

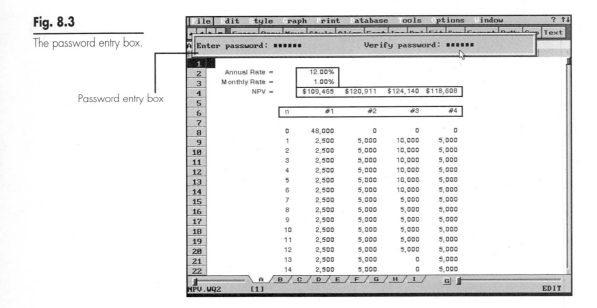

CAUTION

After you assign a password to a file, you cannot access the file except by entering the correct sequence of characters in the correct case. Quattro Pro has no facility for recovering a forgotten password. When a password is lost, so is the file.

You can rename or remove a notebook password, but only when the notebook is active. When a password-protected notebook is active, the /**F**ile Save **As** file prompt box displays [Password Protected] next to the file name.

To remove password protection from the NPV notebook, follow these steps:

1. Choose /**F**ile **R**etrieve.

2. Type **npv** and press Enter.

3. When prompted, type the password and press Enter to retrieve the file.

4. Choose /**F**ile Save **As**.

5. When Quattro Pro displays the file prompt box, press the Backspace key once to delete [Password Protected] from the line.

6. Press Enter and choose **R**eplace to save NPV without a password.

To rename the password assigned to the NPV notebook, follow these steps:

1. Choose /**F**ile **R**etrieve.

2. Type **npv** and press Enter.

3. When prompted, type the password and press Enter to retrieve the file.

4. Choose /**F**ile Save **A**s.

5. When Quattro Pro displays the file prompt box, press the Backspace key once to delete [Password Protected] from the line.

6. Enter **P** after the file name (insert a space between the file name and the P) and then press Enter to invoke the password-protection facility.

7. Type a new password.

8. Press Enter to assign the new password to the NPV notebook.

9. When prompted, re-enter the password to verify it.

Setting the Directory Path Name

The current directory setting determines where Quattro Pro looks just for files on your hard disk drive. The current setting appears at the right margin of the **F**ile menu next to the **D**irectory command.

Choose /**F**ile **D**irectory to create a current directory setting. When prompted, type a path name and press Enter to record the setting. When you choose this command and change the name of the current directory, the new setting remains in effect only for the current work session.

TIP

After you choose /**F**ile **D**irectory, you also can press F2 to enter EDIT mode and then use the arrow, Backspace, and Delete keys to insert and delete information in the directory name prompt box. This way, you quickly can change the current directory setting—for example, adding a subdirectory name to the current directory setting—without having to retype the drive letter and directory path.

You can change a **Directory** command setting permanently so that Quattro Pro recognizes the directory as the default directory each time you begin a new work session. Choose /**Options S**tartup **D**irectory and specify a new directory name. See Chapter 16, "Customizing Quattro Pro," for complete coverage of Quattro Pro's start-up options.

Creating a Workspace File

The /**File W**orkspace command is a notebook file-organization tool. Whenever you design applications that use more than one open note-book at a time, consider creating a workspace to group the associated notebooks under one file name. Grouping the notebooks makes reloading the files you are using together much easier.

To save five notebooks now open in Quattro Pro's memory to a workspace file named SALES.WSP, for example, follow these steps:

1. Choose /**File W**orkspace **S**ave.

2. When prompted, type **sales** and press Enter to record the new workspace file name.

In the workspace file, Quattro Pro stores the name, the window number, and the position number for all open notebooks (maximum of 32). This command doesn't save changes made to individual notebooks. After you finish with the current work session, you must save and re-place each file before exiting Quattro Pro.

To reload the SALES.WSP workspace file, follow these steps:

1. Choose /**File W**orkspace **R**estore.

2. When prompted, highlight SALES.WSP on the list and press Enter. Quattro Pro loads all five notebooks into memory in their original order.

To dismantle a workspace, just delete the WSP file. Quattro Pro doesn't alter any of the notebooks in a deleted workspace. To move a notebook from one workspace to another, open the notebook and then the work-space, and resave the workspace by choosing /**File W**orkspace **S**ave.

Translating Files

Quattro Pro can save notebook files in non-Quattro Pro file formats that several popular spreadsheet and database programs can retrieve. Table 8.3 presents a complete list of the file formats to which Quattro Pro can write. These file formats fall into four major categories: spreadsheet files, database files, compressed files, and graphics files.

Table 8.3 File Formats Quattro Pro Can Read and Write

File Extension	Program Name
Spreadsheet File Formats	
DIF	VisiCalc
SLK	Multiplan Version 1 or 2
WKS	Lotus 1-2-3 Release 1A
WK1	Lotus 1-2-3 Releases 2.x
WK3	Lotus 1-2-3 Releases 3.x
FMT	Impress
FM3	Lotus 1-2-3 Release 3.x Wysiwyg
ALL	Allways
WRK	Symphony Version 1.2
WR1	Symphony Version 2.0
WKQ	Quattro
WQ1	Quattro Pro Versions 1.0 to 4.0
WB1	Quattro Pro for Windows (import only)
WKP	Surpass
Database File Formats	
DB	Paradox
DB2	dBASE II
DBF	dBASE III, III Plus, and IV
DB4	dBASE 4
RXD	Reflex Version 1
R2D	Reflex Version 2

(continues)

Table 8.3 Continued

File Extension	Program Name
Compressed File Formats (SQZ!)	
WK$	Lotus 1-2-3 Release 1A
WK!	Lotus 1-2-3 Release 2.01
WR$	Symphony Version 1.2
WR!	Symphony Version 2.0
WKZ	Quattro (earlier versions)
WQ!	Quattro Pro Versions 1.0 to 4.0
Graphics File Formats	
CHT	Harvard Graphics Version 2.x
HG3	Harvard Graphics Version 3.x

To save a Quattro Pro notebook in one of the file formats listed in table 8.3, append the appropriate extension to the file name. Choose /**F**ile Save **A**s, for example, and then press F2 to enter EDIT mode. Press the Backspace key three times to erase the WQ2 extension, type the appropriate extension from table 8.3, and then press Enter to save the notebook in the new file format.

TIP

This operation is one of only two Quattro Pro operations that require you to supply a file extension (the other is SQZ!). In all other cases, the program appends the extension specified with the /**O**ptions **S**tartup **F**ile Extension command. With no extension specified, Quattro Pro appends WQ2, the default file extension.

NOTE

Allways, Impress, and Lotus 1-2-3 Release 3.x Wysiwyg files shouldn't be loaded directly. These files simply store the formatting information for various Lotus 1-2-3 worksheet files.

Using dBASE File Formats

Translating Quattro Pro notebooks into dBASE file formats requires a slightly different approach. Although their file formats are different, dBASE II and III use the same file extension (DBF). To differentiate between the versions, Quattro Pro assigns a temporary extension (DB2) to notebook files that you translate for use with dBASE II. Before you retrieve a translated file into dBASE II, rename the file so that the extension is DBF.

To save a Quattro Pro notebook named DATA.WQ2 in a dBASE II file format, for example, follow these steps:

1. Make DATA.WQ2 the active notebook.

2. Choose /**File** Save **As**.

3. When prompted, type **data.db2** and press Enter.

4. When prompted, choose the **View** Structure option to examine the database structure information (Field name, Type, Width, and Decimals) before saving the file as a database file.

5. Choose **Write** to create the dBASE II file.

6. Press Ctrl+X to return to DOS. Type **ren data.db2 data.dbf** and press Enter to rename the file.

7. Load dBASE II and retrieve the file named DATA.DBF.

> **TIP**
>
> The **V**iew Structure and **W**rite options also are available for other database translations.

Using Lotus 1-2-3 2.x File Formats

Quattro Pro is fully compatible with Lotus 1-2-3 Release 2.x files. This enhancement is significant because 1-2-3 Release 2.x has file-linking capabilities similar to those available with Quattro Pro. When you retrieve a 1-2-3 Release 2.x worksheet, Quattro Pro converts all 1-2-3 file-linking references into Quattro Pro's own linking syntax.

If you import a 1-2-3 worksheet containing a formula link such as +<<C:\123\DATASET.WK1>>A1, for example, Quattro Pro converts the formula link to +[C:\123\DATASET.WK1]A1.

NOTE

Quattro Pro doesn't fully translate a 1-2-3 Release 2.x worksheet that contains links to more than 62 unique worksheets. After importing the data for the 62nd link, Quattro Pro stops reading data from the worksheet. To import the remaining worksheet data, you must return to 1-2-3 and modify the worksheet so that all links beyond the 62nd link are converted to their results.

When you retrieve a 1-2-3 Release 2.2 or 2.3 file into Quattro Pro, you can save the file to one of three file formats: Quattro Pro, 1-2-3 Release 2.01, or 1-2-3 Release 2.2.

To save the file as a Quattro Pro notebook, choose /File Save **As**. When Quattro Pro displays the file name prompt box, press F2, erase the default extension, and then add the WQ2 extension to the file name.

To save the file as a 1-2-3 worksheet, choose /File **S**ave. After Quattro Pro displays the file name prompt box, press Enter to accept the default file name (with the WK1 extension) and choose **R**eplace to replace the file. If the file wasn't retrieved from the Lotus format, choose /File Save **As** and then change the extension to WK1. Quattro Pro displays a new prompt box telling you that the program encountered a formula with a link translated to a value (see fig. 8.4).

Fig. 8.4

Saving a 1-2-3 Release 2.2 file that contains a formula link.

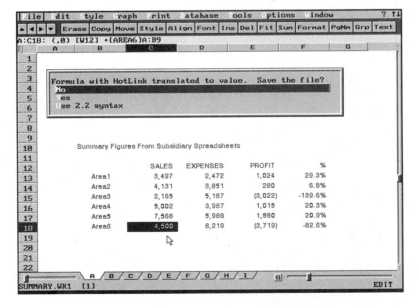

Choose **No** to cancel the save operation and erase the notebook from your hard drive, **Yes** to convert all links to their end results for use with 1-2-3 Release 2.01 (Release 2.01 doesn't support linking), or **Use 2.2 Syntax** to keep all formula links intact for use with 1-2-3 Release 2.2.

> **TIP**
>
> 1-2-3 Releases 2.2 and 2.3 use the same linking syntax and the WK1 file extension. To save a 1-2-3 Release 2.3 worksheet and keep all formula links intact, treat the worksheet as though it is a Release 2.2 worksheet. Choose **/F**ile Save **A**s, press Enter, and choose the **U**se 2.2 Syntax option shown in figure 8.4.

If you choose **No** or press Esc in response to the prompt, Quattro Pro erases the original notebook from your hard disk drive and displays a warning message informing you of this action. If you want to keep a copy of the file, make sure that you save the file before ending the current work session. Otherwise, you lose the file permanently.

Using Lotus 1-2-3 3.x File Formats

Quattro Pro Version 5.0 is fully compatible with Lotus 1-2-3 Release 3.x files. You can import and export 1-2-3 Release 3.x files by specifying the WK3 extension when you open, retrieve, or save files. If the WK3 file contains no features unique to 1-2-3 Release 3.x, Quattro Pro opens and converts the file as though the file were a 1-2-3 Release 2.x file. If features in the worksheet are specific to Release 3.x, however, Quattro Pro makes some changes during conversion.

If the 3.x file contains multiple worksheets, Quattro Pro asks you whether you want the sheets saved as separate files. You can save up to 32 separate files. If the 1-2-3 file contains more than 32 sheets, you must break down the file in 1-2-3 before bringing the file into Quattro Pro.

Multiple 1-2-3 worksheets saved as separate files are named based on the original file name. To name 1-2-3 worksheets, Quattro Pro uses the first six characters of the file name and then adds a letter, sequenced from A to Z and then AA to IV. The file named DIV.WK3, for example, which contains three worksheets, converts into Quattro Pro as DIVA.WQ2, DIVB.WQ2, and DIVC.WQ2.

3-D cell references in 3.x files containing multiple worksheets convert to linked references in Quattro Pro. If the formula +A:B25*1.15 is in DIV.WK3, for example, the reference changes to +[DIVA.WK3]B25*1.15 in Quattro Pro.

When converting 3.x files to Quattro Pro, labels longer than 254 characters are truncated, and formulas longer than 254 characters are read but are truncated on the edit line. 1-2-3 @functions that don't exist in Quattro Pro convert to labels. @SHEETS, for example, converts to '@SHEETS. Similarly, references to 3-D blocks convert to labels. @SUM(A:A1..C:D25), for example, becomes '@SUM(A:A1..C:D25). References to external files convert to labels. Macro references, 3-D or otherwise, aren't converted. Any WK3 graph feature not supported in Quattro Pro is lost.

Except for the first range, all multiple ranges in files with the WK3 extension are ignored. (This process applies only to 1-2-3 database and statistical @functions, and to the 1-2-3 **/P**rint **R**ange and **/D**ata **Q**uery **I**nput commands.)

Due to differences in the way Quattro Pro and Lotus 1-2-3 store numbers, extremely large numbers (larger than 10^{308}) convert to ERR and extremely small numbers (smaller than 10^{-308}) convert to 0. 1-2-3 formula annotations are ignored. Numeric formatting of blank cells aren't identical to the original cells after conversion.

After a WK3 file is converted, Quattro Pro displays a message box showing how many labels have been truncated and how many 3-D blocks have been changed to labels. Press Esc to remove the message. To export a Quattro Pro file back to 1-2-3 Release 3.x format, save the file with the WK3 file extension.

Using Other File Formats

Quattro Pro 5.0 also is compatible to several additional file formats, including Allways, Impress, and Harvard Graphics files. As with all import and export operations, you must specify the correct file extension.

Allways Files

If you have worksheets created with 1-2-3 Release 2.01 or 2.2 and designed with Allways, you can load these files directly into Quattro Pro. If Quattro Pro finds a file with the ALL extension and with the same name as the 1-2-3 file you're loading, the program asks whether you want to load the Allways file at the same time. If you answer yes, translation is automatic. Quattro Pro retrieves the WK1 file, reads the ALL file, and then applies the Allways formatting to the worksheet.

Quattro Pro doesn't import AFS, ALS, or ENC files. To import multiple saved formats or font sets, create a separate WK1 file for each saved format with a corresponding ALL file.

Quattro Pro doesn't support Allways inserted graphs. In Allways, you must store graphs in separate PIC files; in Quattro Pro, you can store named graphs right in the notebook.

Quattro Pro imports format options such as font selection, line style, shading, boldface, underline, and font colors. Allways display (screen) colors don't import.

> **NOTE**
>
> Quattro Pro converts up to 255 different combinations of font, color, boldface, underline, and italic. Any additional combinations convert to Normal style in Quattro Pro.

Some layout options import, including margins, titles, borders (top and left), and line weight; others don't, such as page size, borders on the bottom, and grid on printing. Labels aligned with spillover to the left, usually found in centered labels, also don't import.

Quattro Pro imports the print range option but not the printer type, orientation, print settings, and port bin print options.

For worksheet options, column width (rounded up to whole character widths) and row heights do import, but page breaks, column page breaks, and display zoom options don't.

Wysiwyg and Impress Files

Quattro Pro 5.0 can import 1-2-3 files created with 1-2-3's Wysiwyg or Impress add-in programs. When you retrieve a WK1, WKS, or WK3 file that has a corresponding FMT or FM3 file, Quattro Pro loads the 1-2-3 file and then asks whether you want to load the WYSIWYG/Impress file. choose **Yes** to retrieve the file with its formatting or **No** to retrieve the file without any Wysiwyg or Impress formatting.

ENC files created by Impress or Wysiwyg aren't imported. When you retrieve a WK1 or WKS file, only the worksheet file is loaded. You cannot load a FM3 or FMT file directly.

Quattro Pro retrieves and applies various graph formats. Not all graph formats are retained, however. Blank graphs and inserted graphs based on PIC or CGM files don't convert to Quattro Pro.

Quattro Pro retrieves many Impress formatting features, including assigned fonts, lines, shading, boldface, underline, italics, and font colors. Custom styles convert to /**S**tyle **U**se Style, but descriptions aren't preserved. Quattro Pro doesn't retain line shadow settings and colors or formatting embedded in text.

Quattro Pro converts text alignment settings, except for label alignment with left-side spillover. The **D**isplay command settings, however—including **C**olors, **M**ode, **F**ont-Directory, **R**ows, and **O**ptions—don't convert. As for worksheet settings, row height and page break options convert, but column width and column page breaks don't.

Quattro Pro imports the following print settings: range, configuration/orientation, settings, layout/compression (which converts to /**P**rint **P**rint-To-Fit and /**P**rint **L**ayout **P**ercent Scaling), layout margins, and layout titles. Quattro Pro cannot import the grid on printing, frame, and settings options, nor can it import print configuration commands or page size and borders on bottom print layout settings.

Harvard Graphics Files

To export a Quattro Pro file as a Harvard Graphics file, save the file with the CHT extension. To export into the Version 3.x format, use the HG3 extension.

Quattro Pro and Harvard Graphics have inherent differences that should cause you to exercise caution. First, Harvard Graphics doesn't support multiple graphs in one file. When you export a Quattro Pro graph to a Harvard Graphics file, only the current graph exports; named graphs aren't transferred. Second, Harvard Graphics files can hold only graph information. Any non-graph data in the Quattro Pro file, such as notebook formatting and macros, isn't transferred.

Quattro Pro converts a Harvard Graphics graph to the most similar Quattro Pro graph type. Occasionally, Quattro Pro cannot convert the graph, so the file opens as empty. Quattro Pro converts all Harvard Graphics graphs except organization charts, multiple pie graphs (only the first pie is imported), and multiple graphs (combinations of graph types).

Some Harvard Graphics fill patterns and graph options don't have an exact match in Quattro Pro. In these cases, Quattro Pro applies the closest match available. Data series in Harvard Graphics appear as values in the notebook in Quattro Pro.

After opening or retrieving the Harvard Graphics file, press F10 to see the graph. You can edit the graph in the Annotator like you can with any Quattro Pro graph.

Setting the SQZ! File Compression Options

Quattro Pro has a built-in file compression utility that helps you conserve storage space on your hard disk drive. Use this facility when copying large spreadsheet files onto a floppy disk and before transmitting files over a modem line.

> **NOTE**
>
> This utility can compress spreadsheets created in Quattro Version 1.0, and Quattro Pro Versions 1.0 through 4.0. This feature *cannot* compress notebooks created in Quattro Pro 5.0, but it can compress Lotus 1-2-3 2.x worksheet files.

Before you squeeze a Quattro Pro file, you need to specify options that control how much data Quattro Pro eliminates from a file before squeezing the spreadsheet. To change these settings, choose /**F**ile Utilities **S**QZ! (see fig. 8.5). After you make your changes, choose /**O**ptions Update to save the options as the defaults.

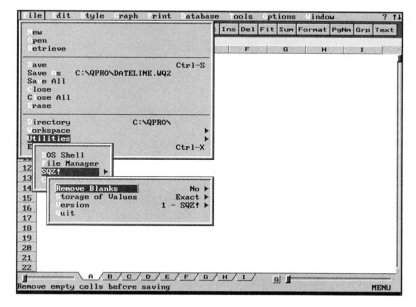

Fig. 8.5

The **S**QZ! submenu options.

One way Quattro Pro can conserve space is to remove all the blank cells from a spreadsheet. To remove the blank cells, choose the **R**emove Blanks option and choose **Y**es.

Another way to conserve storage space is to have Quattro Pro remove spreadsheet values that result from formula calculations. Quattro Pro retains the formulas themselves but removes the cell results. After you retrieve the file, Quattro Pro recalculates all the formulas before displaying the spreadsheet. To invoke this setting, choose the **St**orage of Values option and then choose **R**emove. You also can choose **A**pproximate so that Quattro Pro saves formula values using 7 (instead of 15) significant digits. The **E**xact option stores exact formula values up to 15 significant digits.

The third **S**QZ! submenu option enables you to choose the SQZ! version to use. If you don't intend to use your compressed files in Symphony, choose the **S**QZ! Plus option. In any case, Quattro Pro expands the compressed file the next time you retrieve the file.

After you specify the SQZ! settings, you can compress a file by appending the appropriate extension after typing a name at the file name prompt (refer to table 8.3). To compress a file named DATELINE.WQ1, for example, follow these steps:

1. Make DATELINE the active spreadsheet.

2. Choose /**F**ile Save **A**s.

3. When prompted, type **dateline.wq!** and press Enter to compress the file.

TIP

To compress files created in Quattro Version 1.0 (Quattro Pro's predecessor), you must specify the WKZ file extension. To compress Lotus 1-2-3 worksheet files, specify the WK! file extension.

To decompress a file, choose /**F**ile **R**etrieve, type the name of the file to retrieve, and press Enter. Quattro Pro automatically expands the file to its original appearance.

Using the DOS Shell

The /**F**ile **U**tilities **D**OS Shell command enables you to execute DOS commands without first having to exit Quattro Pro. The DOS shell has two levels: partial and full.

The partial DOS shell enables you to execute a single DOS command (such as DIR), review the results of the command execution, and then return to Quattro Pro. Figure 8.6 shows the partial DOS shell, which you can call up by choosing /**File** **U**tilities **D**OS Shell.

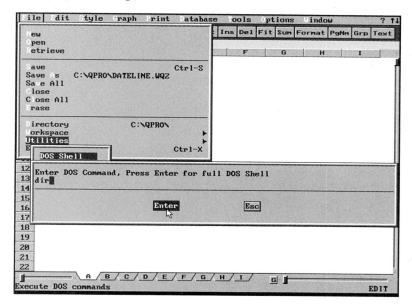

Fig. 8.6

The DOS DIR command in the partial DOS shell.

To review a list of files in the current directory, for example, type **dir** and press Enter. Quattro Pro returns to the DOS environment and displays a list of files for the current directory. As soon as the DOS file listing finishes scrolling across your screen, Quattro Pro immediately returns you to the active notebook.

TIP

The file list may scroll by quickly, so be prepared to press Ctrl+S to pause the scrolling. Press any key to resume the scrolling.

The full DOS shell returns temporarily to DOS command level, where you may execute as many DOS commands as you want. To use the full DOS shell, choose /**File** **U**tilities **D**OS Shell and press Enter. Quattro Pro disappears from the screen and displays the DOS command prompt. To return to Quattro Pro, type **exit** at the DOS command prompt and then press Enter.

While in the DOS shell, you can execute any valid DOS command. You probably shouldn't delete Quattro Pro program files or load other application programs into memory from the shell because doing so may cause memory allocation problems that may lock up your PC. If this problem occurs, press Ctrl+Alt+Delete to reboot your computer and clear its memory.

Using the File Manager

The File Manager enables you to link Quattro Pro directly to the DOS command environment. The File Manager can perform many useful file management activities without requiring that you first exit Quattro Pro or use the DOS Shell feature.

Use the File Manager to list, move, copy, rename, and delete files, using the same wild-card designations that you use in DOS. This tool also can sort files by name, extension, size, and DOS order; show the time stamp on files; and display a tree graphic that shows the structure of the directory paths on the current disk.

Reviewing the File Manager Window

To display the File Manager in the current window, choose /File Utilities **F**ile Manager. After you load this utility into the active window, File Manager fills the screen. Repeat this command to open a second File Manager window. To close the active File Manager, choose /File **C**lose—the same command that closes a notebook.

The File Manager window is divided into three sections: the control pane, the file pane, and the tree pane (see fig. 8.7). At the bottom of the window is the directory status line, which shows statistics about the listed directory, such as the number of files, the total bytes used, and the number of bytes of free storage space.

> **TIP**
>
> Quattro Pro initially doesn't show tree pane information in the File Manager window.

All file management operations that you perform with this tool are accomplished from inside one of the three panes. By default, Quattro Pro makes the control pane active each time you load the File Manager. (The three panes are discussed in more detail in the following sections.)

Control pane

Tree pane (see fig. 8.8)

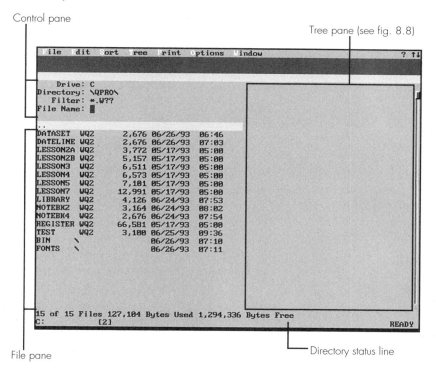

Fig. 8.7

The default File Manager window.

File pane

Directory status line

Notice also in figure 8.7 that the File Manager has its own set of menus across the top of the screen. You activate these menus and choose the menu commands as though a notebook is in the active window. Table 8.4 reviews the purpose and function of each menu.

Table 8.4 File Manager Menus

Menu Name	Description of Commands
File	Creates, opens, and closes windows (including a File Manager window); reads existing directories and creates directories; accesses DOS; exits Quattro Pro
Edit	Copies, moves, erases, pastes, duplicates, and renames files
Sort	Sorts files using DOS wild-card characters
Tree	Opens, resizes, and closes the tree pane
Print	Prints a list of files in a directory
Options	Sets File Manager display options and standard notebook options
Window	Resizes, reorganizes, and picks active windows

Table 8.5 lists all the keystrokes you can use to navigate through the File Manager window.

Table 8.5 File Manager Window Keys

Key	Key Name	Description
Shift+F5	Pick Window	Displays a list of all windows open in memory; also works by pressing Alt+0
F6	Pane	Activates the next pane in the File Manager window; also works by pressing Tab
Shift+F6	Next Window	Activates the next open File Manager window; activates a notebook if no window is open
Alt+F6	Zoom Window	Enlarges and shrinks the active File Manager window if you are in text display mode
Alt+#		Pressing Alt plus a window number causes Quattro Pro to make that window active

Using the Control Pane

The *control pane* displays the current drive letter, the current directory path name, the filter prompt, and the File Name prompt. While in the control pane, you can change any of these settings to create a different type of directory display.

To display, for example, all files with a WQ2 extension in a directory called FINANCE, follow these steps:

1. Press the up-arrow key twice to highlight the current directory path name, or click it to highlight it.

2. Press Esc to erase the entry.

3. Type **\finance** and press Enter to record the new directory path name. Quattro Pro moves the cursor back to the File Name prompt.

4. Press the down-arrow key to move to the filter prompt setting.

5. Press Backspace twice to erase the question marks.

6. Type **wq2** and press Enter to store the new filter setting.

Quattro Pro displays all files in the FINANCE directory that have a WQ2 file extension.

To create a negative filter, place the filter setting inside square brackets. Quattro Pro searches for all files that don't meet the bracketed condition. The filter setting [*.WQ2], for example, searches for all files that *don't* have a WQ2 file extension.

The File Name prompt is blank each time you load the File Manager. You can make any notebook file active by typing a file name in this field. After you type the first letter of a file name, Quattro Pro moves the cursor to the first file in the current directory that begins with that letter. This search-and-highlight procedure continues as long as you continue to enter additional letters.

Table 8.6 lists all the keys that affect data displayed in the control pane.

Table 8.6 Control Pane Navigation Keys

Key	Key Name	Description
F2	Rename	Duplicates the action of choosing /**E**dit **R**ename while at the File Name prompt
F5	GoTo	Searches through every directory on the active drive for the file specified at the File Name prompt and then displays it in the file pane
Esc		Erases the current setting at a control pane prompt
Enter		Moves the cursor to the blank File Name prompt, displays the subdirectory indicated next to the prompt settings in the file list pane, or opens the highlighted file into a notebook window
Delete		Deletes the character at the cursor position
Home		Moves the cursor to the beginning of the prompt entry
End		Moves the cursor to the end of the prompt entry

Using the File Pane

The *file pane* shows the file names and directory path names that meet the conditions specified on the control pane. The file pane lists the full name, byte size, and the date last altered for each file.

TIP

To move to the file pane from the control pane, press F6 or Tab.

Use the /**O**ptions **F**ile List command to specify a **F**ull View or a **W**ide View of the data displayed in the file pane.

Table 8.7 lists the keystrokes that you can use when the file pane is active. You also can press any arrow key to move around the file pane.

Table 8.7 File Pane Navigation Keys

Key	Key Name	Description
F2	Rename	Duplicates the action of choosing the /**E**dit **R**ename command
Shift+F7	Select	Selects and deselects a highlighted file name
Alt+F7	All Select	Selects all the file names in the displayed list or deselects those already selected with Shift+F7
Shift+F8	Move	Transfers selected files to the paste buffer
Delete		Deletes all highlighted or selected files
F9	Calc	Duplicates the action of choosing the /**F**ile **R**ead Dir command, which refreshes the list of files in the file pane
Shift+F9	Copy	Copies selected files into the paste buffer
Shift+F10	Paste	Moves all files from the paste buffer to the current directory
Esc		Cancels file selections and moves the cursor to the File Name prompt in the control pane
Enter		Opens the file indicated next to the prompt settings into its own notebook window, or displays a list of files in the file pane for the directory or subdirectory whose name appears next to the prompt settings
Home		Moves the highlight bar to the parent directory (. .)
End		Moves the highlight bar to the end of the file list
Page Up		Moves the file list display up one screen
Page Down		Moves the file list display down one screen

Using the Tree Pane

Choose / **Tree O**pen to display the tree pane in the right side of the File Manager window. A tree pane initially displays the root directory drive letter, several application directory names, and two levels of application subdirectory names.

Use the / **Tree R**esize command to reveal additional subdirectory names in the tree pane. This command enables you to specify a value (from 10 to 100) that represents the percent of the File Manager window that the tree pane occupies. Figure 8.8, for example, shows a tree pane that occupies 40 percent of the File Manager window.

Fig. 8.8

A tree pane in the File Manager window.

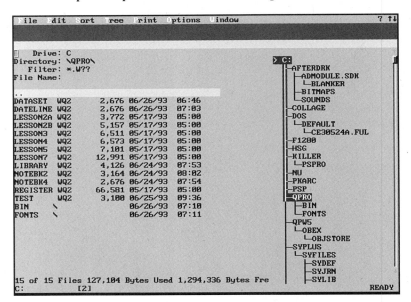

In the tree pane, Quattro Pro highlights the application directory name that matches the directory path name appearing in the control pane. The files stored in the highlighted directory appear in the file pane. To display new files in the file pane again, press Tab until the tree pane is active and then highlight a different directory name. Quattro Pro immediately displays that directory's files in the file pane.

The tree pane lists all directories and subdirectories on your hard disk in alphabetical order. This way, you quickly can scan the contents of any directory by highlighting its name in the tree pane and then reviewing the files in the file pane. To perform file operations such as erasing or copying, you first must move back into the file pane.

To learn how to navigate through a tree pane, review the keys defined in table 8.8.

Table 8.8 Tree Pane Navigation Keys

Key	Key Name	Description
Esc		Moves the cursor out of the tree pane and into the control pane, next to the File Name prompt
F9	Calc	Duplicates the action of choosing the /**File R**ead Dir command, which refreshes the display of files in the file pane
Page Up		Scrolls the active directory highlight up the tree pane
Page Down		Scrolls the active directory highlight down the tree pane

To remove a tree pane from the active window, choose / **Tree C**lose.

Manipulating Files with the File Manager

Many of the menu commands in the File Manager are the same commands you use to manipulate data in notebook files. A few other commands also perform operations not available with notebooks. These special commands are covered in the following sections.

Performing Multiple File Operations

The one characteristic shared by all the **E**dit menu commands in the File Manager is that each can perform an operation simultaneously on many files. You can copy, move, and erase all files in the current directory.

These maneuvers are possible due to the inclusion of two special menu commands: **S**elect File and **A**ll Select. After you select a file, Quattro Pro displays the file name in reverse intensity or in a different color and places a check mark at the end of the cursor so that you can see clearly that the file is selected. By using the / **E**dit **A**ll Select command, you can select all the files displayed in the file pane. Quattro Pro doesn't highlight the names of subdirectories (see fig. 8.9).

Fig. 8.9

Selecting all files in the file pane.

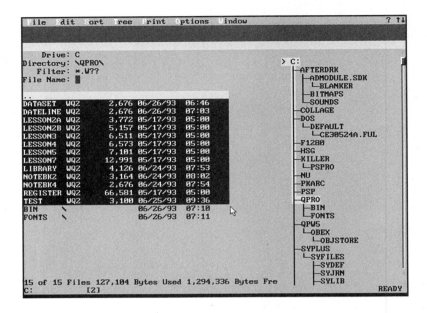

| File | Edit | Sort | Tree | Print | Options | Window | ? ↑↓ |

```
    Drive: C
Directory: \QPRO\                                    > C:
   Filter: *.W??                                     ├AFTERDRK
File Name: █                                         │ ├ADMODULE.SDK
                                                     │ │ └BLANKER
..                                                   │ ├BITMAPS
DATASET   WQ2    2,676 06/26/93   06:46              │ └SOUNDS
DATELINE  WQ2    2,676 06/26/93   07:03              ├COLLAGE
LESSON2A  WQ2    3,772 05/17/93   05:00              ├DOS
LESSON2B  WQ2    5,157 05/17/93   05:00              │ └DEFAULT
LESSON3   WQ2    6,511 05/17/93   05:00              │   └CE30524A.FUL
LESSON4   WQ2    6,573 05/17/93   05:00              ├F1280
LESSON5   WQ2    7,101 05/17/93   05:00              ├HSG
LESSON7   WQ2   12,991 05/17/93   05:00              ├KILLER
LIBRARY   WQ2    4,126 06/24/93   07:53              │ └PSPRO
NOTEBK2   WQ2    3,164 06/24/93   08:02              ├NU
NOTEBK4   WQ2    2,676 06/24/93   07:54              ├PKARC
REGISTER  WQ2   66,581 05/17/93   05:00              ├PSP
TEST      WQ2    3,100 06/25/93   09:36              ├QPRO
BIN       \             06/26/93   07:10             │ ├BIN
FONTS     \             06/26/93   07:11             │ └FONTS
                                                     ├QPW5
                                                     │ └OBEX
                                                     │   └OBJSTORE
                                                     ├SYPLUS
                                                     │ └SYFILES
                                                     │   ├SYDEF
15 of 15 Files 127,104 Bytes Used 1,294,336 Bytes Fre│   ├SYJRN
C:          [2]                                      │   ├SYLIB     READY
```

TIP

To select a single file in the File Manager in preparation for a copy, move, or erase operation, highlight the desired file and press Shift+F7.

After you select the files, you can perform any File Manager command on that block of files—a feature not available in other electronic spreadsheet programs.

The following steps show, for example, how to erase all selected files from a hard disk:

1. Choose /**E**dit **A**ll Select or press Alt+F7 to highlight the names of all files displayed for the current directory.

2. Choose /**E**dit **E**rase. Quattro Pro displays the prompt, Are you sure you want to delete the marked files?

3. Choose **Y**es to begin erasing the selected files or **N**o to cancel the operation and return to the File Manager window.

Printing File Manager Data

The **P**rint menu in the File Manager is an abbreviated version of the **P**rint menu accessible when a notebook is active. By using the commands on this menu, you can print lists of files in the displayed directory, a copy of the entire directory tree, or both (see fig. 8.10).

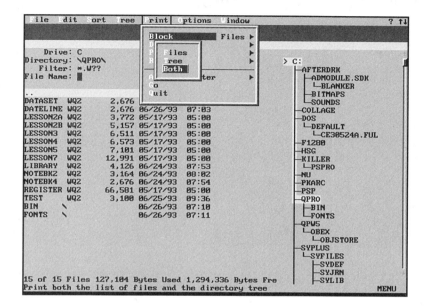

Fig. 8.10

Printing a report that includes files and the directory tree.

Working with Notebook Windows

You can have up to 32 notebook windows open in Quattro Pro's memory at one time, but you can work in only one window at a time—the active window.

Even if you never create an application that uses 32 windows, you eventually may need at least 2, 3, or 4 windows open at the same time. As a result, you must understand how to manage multiple windows, using the options in the **W**indow menu.

By using the **W**indow menu commands, you can zoom in and out, tile and stack, and move and size windows open in Quattro Pro's memory. You also can create special displays for your notebooks by using the commands on the **O**ptions submenu (see fig. 8.11).

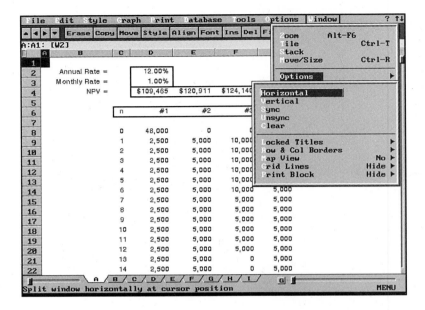

The **O**ptions submenu consists of display options that enable you to
work with large notebooks. You can split the active window into two
panes, for example, or create a condensed map view of an entire notebook. (The section "Creating Special Display Effects" later in this chapter provides more information about splitting windows and creating
condensed map views.)

Whenever you are unsure about the number of files open in memory,
choose /**W**indow **P**ick. Quattro Pro displays a complete list of all open
windows and their file names. You also can press Alt+0 (zero) or
Shift+F5, the Pick Window key, to produce the same display.

To move from window to window, press Shift+F6, the Next Window key.
If you already know the number of the window to which you want to
move, press Alt and the window number to activate that window.

Organizing Windows On-Screen

Quattro Pro offers several alternatives for managing a window or for
displaying all open windows. The following three sections teach you
how to execute the **W**indow menu commands that organize windows
on-screen.

> The following **W**indow menu commands have no effect when Quattro Pro is in WYSIWYG display mode: **Z**oom, **S**tack, and **M**ove/Size. These commands are active when Quattro Pro is in text or extended text display mode. (To zoom a notebook while in WYSIWYG display mode, use the /**O**ptions **W**YSIWYG Zoom % command, described in Chapter 16.)

NOTE

Enlarging and Shrinking Windows

In text display mode, when you want the active window to fill your screen, choose /**W**indow **Z**oom or press Alt+F6, the Zoom key. Choosing this command twice in succession causes the active window to return to its original size.

Mouse users can perform this operation quickly by clicking the zoom icon located in the upper right corner of the screen (the two opposing arrows in the top right corner, above the SpeedBar).

> You cannot enlarge or shrink a window in WYSIWYG display mode.

NOTE

Tiling and Stacking Windows

Another useful way to display multiple windows involves processes called tiling and stacking. (Refer to figs. 8.19 and 8.20 later in this chapter for examples of notebook tiling.)

Tiling reduces each window to a size that enables Quattro Pro to display the windows side by side. To tile all windows open in memory, choose /**W**indow **T**ile or press Ctrl+T, the Ctrl+*key* shortcut for this command.

Stacking shuffles the open windows into sequential order by window number and displays the windows in layers. In a stacked window display, the top of each window is revealed so that you can see the file name and window number. To stack all windows open in memory, choose /**W**indow **S**tack.

All Quattro Pro display modes support tiling, although only text and extended text display modes support notebook window stacking.

Moving and Sizing Windows

The /**Window M**ove/Size command enables you to fine-tune the size and position of a notebook in the active window. You can use this technique when tiling and stacking don't create the display effect that you want. To change the size and position of a notebook in a window, choose /**Window M**ove/Size or press Ctrl+R.

> **NOTE** You cannot move or size a window that is in WYSIWYG display mode.

Quattro Pro highlights the outside edges of the notebook and displays MOVE in a box at the upper left corner of the notebook. Initially, you cannot move the notebook because it already fills the display. You first must resize the notebook.

To resize the notebook by using your keyboard (mouse steps are covered later), follow these steps:

1. Press the Scroll Lock key until MOVE changes to SIZE.

2. Hold down the Shift key and press the arrow keys until the notebook is the correct size (see fig. 8.12).

3. Press Enter to store the new notebook size.

Quattro Pro draws the resized notebook in the current window (see fig. 8.13).

Fig. 8.12

Resizing a notebook in the current window.

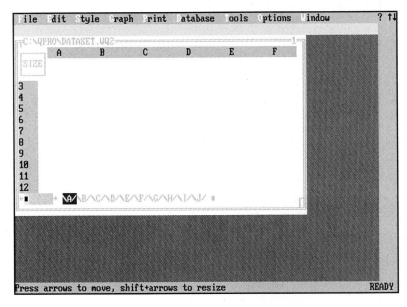

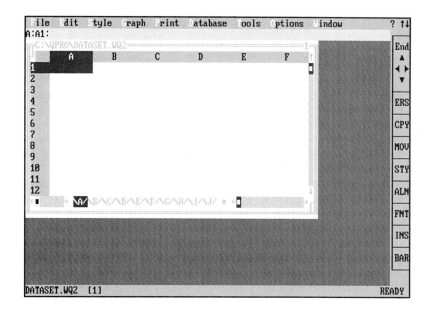

Fig. 8.13

The resized notebook in the current window.

When a notebook is smaller than the current window, you can move the notebook around the screen display. To move a notebook, follow these steps:

1. Choose /Window Move/Size. Quattro Pro highlights all four notebook borders.

2. Press the arrow keys to move the notebook to another part of the current window.

3. Press Enter to store the new notebook location. Quattro Pro redraws the notebook at that location.

If you have a mouse, you quickly can move and size a notebook. The next sequence of steps describes the most efficient way to do both:

1. Put the mouse rectangle on the resize box located at the bottom right corner of the notebook and then hold down your mouse button. Quattro Pro highlights the notebook borders and displays SIZE in the upper left corner.

2. Drag the box to resize the notebook.

3. Release the mouse button to retain a size. Quattro Pro draws the resized notebook.

4. To move a resized notebook, put the mouse pointer on any border and then drag the entire notebook elsewhere in the current window (see fig. 8.14). The word MOVE appears in the upper left corner.

5. Release the mouse button. Quattro Pro redraws the notebook at that location.

Fig. 8.14

Moving the current window.

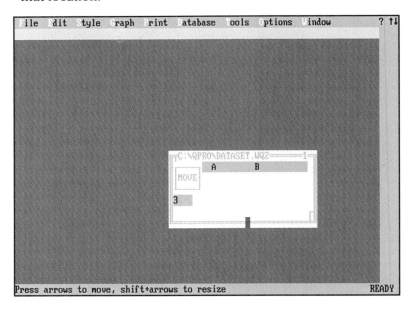

Press Alt+F6 to enlarge or shrink the active notebook in the current window.

Creating Special Display Effects

The /Window Options menu gives you access to commands that can create special window display effects. These effects are by no means strictly cosmetic. Each effect can help you locate, organize, and manipulate notebook data. These options work in text and WYSIWYG display modes.

Splitting Windows into Panes

Choose the /**W**indow **O**ptions **H**orizontal command to split a window into two horizontal panes at the position of the selector, as long as the selector isn't in row 1 or 8192 (see fig. 8.15). This effect is useful when a notebook has more row data than column data. The **H**orizontal command also helps you enter cell formulas that reference data in distant parts of the active notebook.

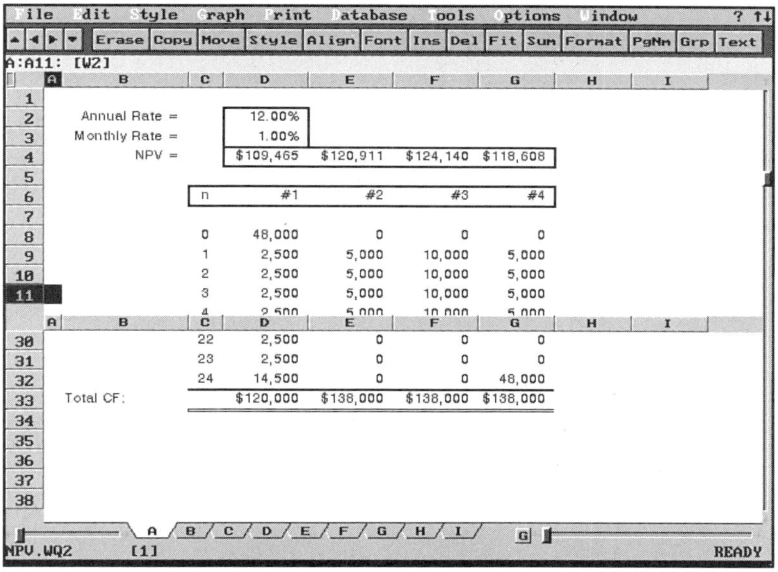

Fig. 8.15

A notebook window split into two horizontal panes.

Choose /**W**indow **O**ptions **V**ertical to split a window into two vertical panes at the position of the selector, as long as the selector isn't in column A or IV. You can use this effect when a notebook has more column data than row data. The **V**ertical command, like its counterpart, helps in the process of entering formulas into a notebook.

To move between panes in a split window, press F6, the Pane key, or click the desired pane. To reset a split window to one pane, choose /**W**indow **O**ptions **C**lear.

Unsynchronizing Window Panes

By default, split window panes are synchronized so that any selector movement in one pane is duplicated in the second. To scroll window panes independently of each other, you must unsynchronize the panes

by choosing /**W**indow **O**ptions **U**nsync, which enables you to scroll
around one pane without affecting the other. To return the panes to
synchronized scrolling, choose /**W**indow **O**ptions **S**ync.

Clearing Split Window Pane Settings

Choose /**W**indow **O**ptions **C**lear to return split windows to a single
window display. When you issue this command, Quattro Pro retains
the column width, locked title, and hidden column settings for only
the top or left pane. Any changes made to the right or lower pane are
discarded.

Locking Titles

Title locking is a useful display tool for a notebook that contains numerous rows or columns of data. By anchoring a row (or column) of labels,
you can scroll through the data under or to the right without moving
the titles and column headings out of the notebook area (see fig. 8.16).
Quattro Pro shades the cell block containing locked title data so that
you can identify clearly where the locking begins.

Fig. 8.16

Notebook titles locked
to restrict cursor move-
ment to the data-entry
area.

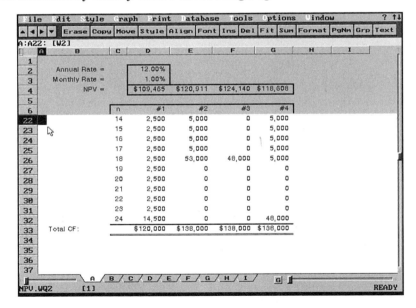

When in WYSIWYG display mode, to alter the color used to shade locked titles and locked titles text, use the /**O**ptions **C**olors **S**preadsheet **W**YSIWYG Colors Titles **B**ackground command. If you are in text display mode, use /**O**ptions **C**olors **S**preadsheet **T**itles to change the color.

To lock notebook titles, place the selector in the row below or the column to the right of the titles you want to lock. Then choose /**W**indow **O**ptions **L**ocked Titles. Quattro Pro displays a submenu offering four options: **H**orizontal, **V**ertical, **B**oth, and **C**lear. Quattro Pro locks titles above or to the left of the selector, depending on which locked title option you choose.

When locked titles are in effect, Quattro Pro doesn't enable you to move the selector into the locked title area with the usual arrow-key techniques. Only by using F5 (Goto) and specifying a cell or block can you go to a cell in the locked titles area.

Removing Row and Column Borders

In some notebook applications, removing the row and column borders can make a notebook look more like a report. If you create an application that prompts a user to enter figures into a data-entry form, for example, displaying the row and column borders isn't critical. Someone unfamiliar with the look of a notebook may find the borders distracting. By eliminating the borders from your screen, you also can view more of the notebook area at one time.

To remove column and row borders from your display, choose /**W**indow **O**ptions **R**ow & Col Borders. When prompted, choose the **H**ide option. Quattro Pro redraws the screen without row and column borders (see fig. 8.17). To display the row and column borders again, choose /**W**indow **O**ptions **R**ow & Col Borders again and then choose the **D**isplay option.

The row and columns border setting is page dependent; when you choose /**F**ile **S**ave, Quattro Pro saves this display setting only for the active page with the current notebook.

Fig. 8.17

Removing row and column borders.

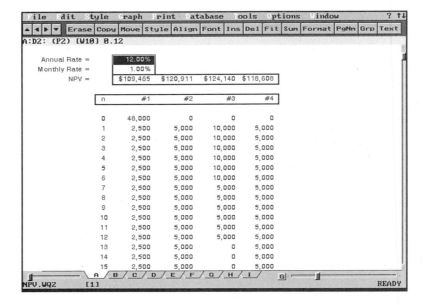

Creating a Map View

The /**W**indow **O**ptions **M**ap View command creates a unique on-screen effect that can be described as a "bird's-eye view" of a notebook (see fig. 8.18). In this mode, Quattro Pro compresses the column widths to one character space and then assigns and displays one character code that identifies the kind of data in each cell. The following table lists these character codes.

Code	Type of Cell Data
l	Label
n	Number
+	Formula
–	Linked formula
c	Circular cell formula

NOTE

While in Map mode, inserted graphs are virtually indistinguishable because the notebook column widths are reduced to a single character (refer to the graph in the middle of the notebook shown in fig. 8.18).

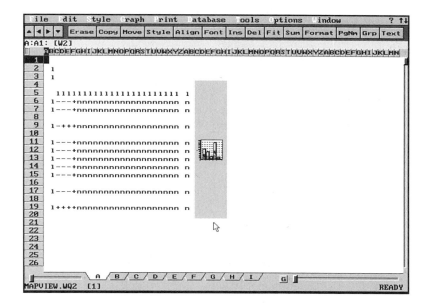

Fig. 8.18

A bird's-eye view of a notebook.

You can use the /Edit Search & Replace command to locate data quickly on a notebook displayed in Map mode. Rather than specify a label or number for which to search, you can use any code listed in the preceding table. You can use the Search & Replace command, for example, to locate the presence of a circular formula by specifying **c** as the text for which to search.

Displaying Notebook Grid Lines

The /**W**indow **O**ptions **G**rid Lines command controls the display of grid lines on individual notebooks. By default, grid lines are turned off for any new notebook you create in Quattro Pro. To add grid lines to a notebook, use the **D**isplay option. To turn off notebook grid lines so that you can see style enhancements such as drawn lines and shaded cells better, choose the **H**ide option.

> A grid lines setting is page dependent. When you choose /**F**ile **S**ave, Quattro Pro saves this display setting only with the active page within the current notebook.

NOTE

Linking Notebooks

Linked notebooks simplify complex relationships, help you design more flexible applications, access information from a database, and enable Quattro Pro to be more memory-efficient. Like a group of related notebooks that you save to a workspace file, linked notebooks have something in common: they share data. Specifically, you can pass information between linked notebooks using live formula references.

An ordinary formula references data in cells on the current notebook and displays the result in another cell on the same notebook. A live formula references data in cells on supporting notebooks open in Quattro Pro's memory and displays the result in a cell on a primary notebook, also open in memory. When you change data on a supporting notebook, Quattro Pro updates the data displayed on the primary notebook, as long as all the notebooks are open in memory at the same time.

Linked notebooks introduce a new set of possibilities for creating Quattro Pro applications. You can break down a large database notebook into several smaller ones that are easier to access and update, for example. You also can create a small bookkeeping application that stores ledger transactions on supporting notebooks and transfers the end-of-period balances, using live formula references, to a group of primary financial statement notebooks.

After you learn how to create the links that tie notebooks together, you can begin to envision your own uses for this type of application.

TIP

Although the following sections are devoted to illustrating techniques for sharing data between reports with linking formulas, keep in mind that the formula linking technique works equally well for sharing data between pages within the same notebook. Page A, for instance, could be considered the primary document with pages B, C, D, and so on acting as the supporting documents. With a few exceptions, the technique for consolidating information stored on pages within the same notebook is essentially the same as the notebook file-linking technique described throughout the following sections.

Creating Linking Formulas

You can use several techniques to create linking formulas. You can type the formula directly on the input line; create three-dimensional consolidation formulas to link notebooks with common structures; and, if you have a mouse, use the familiar clicking method to create formulas as you go.

Before examining the process of building live formulas, review the linked notebook application shown in figure 8.19. The active notebook in the upper left corner of figure 8.19, PARENT.WQ2, is the primary document in a linked notebook application. The data that eventually appears on this notebook comes from SUBSID_1.WQ2, SUBSID_2.WQ2, and SUBSID_3.WQ2 income statement notebooks for each of Auntie Deborah's three subsidiaries.

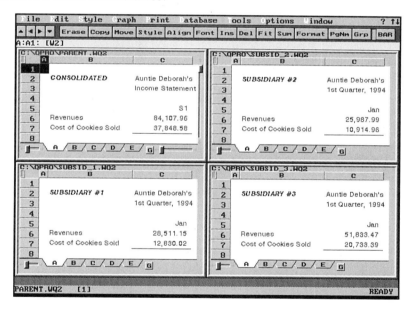

Fig. 8.19

A linking application that uses one primary and three supporting notebooks.

Figure 8.19 shows that in linked notebook applications, you must design and create two or more notebooks. In the sample application, the structure of each notebook—except for a few label descriptions—is the same.

You can use one of three procedures to create formulas that link notebooks.

Typing a Linking Formula

A *linking formula* is a basic Quattro Pro formula that contains a reference to an external notebook file name. In figure 8.20, the formula appearing in cell C6 on PARENT.WQ2 is created by doing the following:

1. Open all the notebooks to be linked into Quattro Pro's memory (in this case, just PARENT.WQ2 and SUBSID_1.WQ2).

TIP

One easy way to make sure that you have open only those notebook files that you want to link is to use the workspace feature.

2. Make cell C6 on PARENT.WQ2 active.

3. Type +[subsid_1]f6 on the input line.

4. Press Enter to record the linking formula.

Quattro Pro evaluates cell F6 on SUBSID_1.WQ2 and displays the value 84,107.96 in the active cell on PARENT.WQ2.

Fig. 8.20

Creating the initial linking formula.

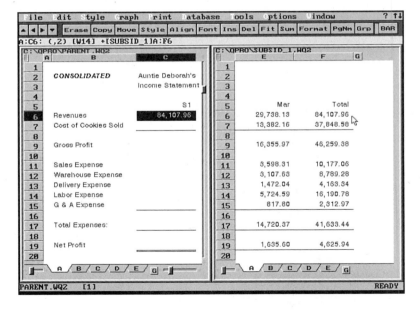

Every linking formula contains three elements: a plus sign (+), a bracketed file name, and an external cell (or block) reference from the file named in the brackets.

The + tells Quattro Pro that you are entering a formula. If you omit this important symbol, the program thinks you are entering a label.

When Quattro Pro encounters a file name in brackets, the program recognizes that it must look at another notebook file open in memory. The description SUBSID_1 tells Quattro Pro the name of a specific supporting notebook.

The third element in this syntax is the cell or block reference. Quattro Pro uses this reference to link to a specific cell address or block address on the notebook file indicated in the brackets. In the example, the cell reference is F6—a cell address on SUBSID_1.

The syntax of this formula indicates that the primary and supporting notebooks reside in the same directory on the same disk drive. If the notebooks aren't in the same directory, the formula may look something like the following:

    +[A:\REPORT\SUBSID_1.WQ2]F6

This syntax says that the supporting notebook is stored in a directory called \REPORT on a disk in drive A.

Although you may link notebooks in different directories on different drives, you always should create and save the notebooks in the same directory on the same disk drive. When you then create linking formulas, you don't have to wonder whether you entered the correct drive name and path name, and you don't have to place a disk into a disk drive every time you want to work with the application. This strategy also keeps the length of your linking formulas to an absolute minimum—an important point when you create longer, more complex formulas.

TIP

If the formula link is to another page in the same notebook, simply omit the file name and use the page name (without the brackets) followed by a colon and then the cell (or block) reference. To create a formula link to cell F6 on page C and place that formula in cell A5 on page A, for instance, make cell A5 on page A active; then type **+c:f6**.

Creating 3-D Consolidation Formulas

Creating linking applications that use supporting notebooks with exactly the same structure has a great advantage: you have an additional formula-entry alternative at your disposal. This method, called *3-D formula consolidation*, uses wild-card designations in a linking formula to create live references to the same location on all notebooks open in Quattro Pro's memory.

NOTE

> Creating 3-D consolidation formulas is different than the 2-D spreadsheet consolidation procedure described later in the section "Consolidating 2-D Linked Files into a Single Notebook." 3-D consolidation formulas simplify the process of creating linking formulas in your notebooks. To consolidate a 2-D spreadsheet linking application into a single Version 5.0 notebook, you use the /**F**ile **U**tilities **C**onsolidate command. Don't confuse these two similarly named techniques.

Substituting the familiar wild-card code * (asterisk) in place of a file name in a linking formula causes Quattro Pro to look at all open notebooks. To do more than look, you must include an @function command that performs a mathematical operation.

Every 3-D consolidation formula contains three elements: an @function command, a bracketed 3-D link code, and an external cell (or block) reference.

NOTE

> This method references all notebooks open in Quattro Pro's memory. Before you begin, remember to close every notebook file that will not be a part of the linking application.

The @function command indicates a mathematical operation for Quattro Pro to perform. To average all the values appearing in the same cell on three supporting notebooks, for example, use the @AVG function.

A properly constructed 3-D link code is critical to the success of this operation. The link code tells Quattro Pro which notebooks the program should look at when performing the mathematical operation indicated by the @function command. If you want Quattro Pro to perform a mathematical operation using data on all the supporting notebooks open in memory, for example, use the [*] link code. To look only at those notebooks with file names that begin with the letter S, for example, enter **[S*]** as the code.

The third element in this syntax is the cell or block reference. Quattro Pro examines the value residing in this cell on each notebook open in memory, according to the 3-D link code specification. To look at block A5..A10 on all open notebooks, for example, type **a5..a10** as the reference.

Suppose that you re-enter the linking formula shown earlier in figure 8.20 as @SUM([*]F6). This formula tells Quattro Pro to sum the F6 values from all open supporting notebooks and display the total in the active cell on the primary notebook.

The formula displays total subsidiary revenues for the first quarter of 1992—a useful figure for this application, but one that doesn't belong in this particular cell. The viability of a consolidation formula depends mostly on its proper placement on a notebook. In this example, the consolidation formula makes more sense appearing in a column that displays data for all subsidiaries.

With a little bit of forethought, you can streamline the process of building a linking application by duplicating your notebook structures and then building formulas using 3-D consolidation. Be careful, however, to consolidate similar information in the correct location on the primary notebook.

Creating Linking Formulas by Pointing and Clicking

Look at the formula displayed in cell C6 on PARENT.WQ2 in figure 8.20 earlier in this chapter. The final method for building linking formulas is achieved when your screen looks like the one pictured in this figure.

To enter the same linking formula using a mouse, follow these steps:

1. Tile two notebook windows so that the windows appear side by side—in this example, PARENT.WQ2 and SUBSID_1.WQ2.

2. Click the primary notebook to make that notebook active. Choose a cell as the destination cell and then click that cell to make it active. For this example, click cell C6 on PARENT.WQ2.

3. Press the + key to enter VALUE mode.

4. Click the supporting notebook to make that notebook active. Then click the cell containing the value you want to use as the external reference. For this example, click cell F6 on SUBSID_1.WQ2.

The cell reference—complete with the external file name—has been copied onto the input line.

5. Click [Enter] on the input line to record the linking formula.

Quattro Pro evaluates cell F6 on SUBSID_1.WQ2 and again displays the value 84,107.96 in the active cell on PARENT.WQ2.

You can use this technique in a way that doesn't require you to tile windows. With the primary notebook displayed in a full-screen format, enter VALUE mode, press Alt+0, choose a window from the displayed menu, click the target cell, and then click [Enter] to record the linking formula. If you already know the number of the window, press Alt plus the window number to move directly there.

Moving and Copying Linking Formulas

Now that you are familiar with each method for creating and entering linking formulas, you can return to the sample application and complete PARENT.WQ2. After you create a linking formula, you can copy the formula to other cells on the primary notebook. Quattro Pro adjusts the copied formulas so that the file name stays the same (SUBSID_1), but adjusts the cell references so that they link to the correct cells on the supporting notebook (see fig. 8.21).

Fig. 8.21

Subsidiary 1's data linked to the primary document.

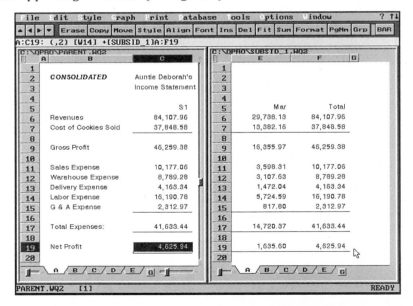

To duplicate the linking formula in cell C6, for example, make that cell active in the primary document and then follow these steps:

1. Choose /**E**dit **C**opy and press Enter to select C6 as the source block, or click the cell with your mouse.

2. Make cell C7 active, press Enter to select cell C7 as the destination block, press the period key to anchor the cell and then highlight other destination cells, or click cell C7 with your mouse.

Quattro Pro copies the formula into cell C7. Continue copying the linking formula into the appropriate cells until you fill in all subsidiary data in the primary notebook or the block you specify. After you finish, you have one final task: sum the values in each column to derive the parent company's totals. You can enter @SUM functions that total the subsidiary data or use the 3-D consolidation technique to create additional linking formulas.

Review the notebook shown in figure 8.22. The formula displayed on the input line results when the 3-D consolidation formula @SUM([*]F6) is entered into cell F6 on PARENT.WQ2. Quattro Pro converts the consolidation formulas into results so that you later can edit the individual external references.

You can copy this formula into the remaining cells in column F to complete the linking application.

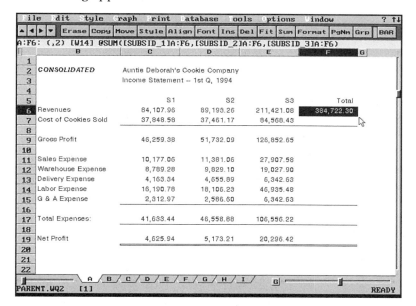

Fig. 8.22

A 3-D consolidation formula that sums values entered on the supporting notebooks.

When you apply **C**opy and **M**ove operations to linking formulas, Quattro Pro treats relative and absolute references the same as other formulas. If you move a linking formula into the notebook that the formula references, however, Quattro Pro cancels and erases the link from the formula.

Opening and Updating Linked Notebooks

After you create the primary and supporting notebooks, you should save the notebooks to disk. You normally create a workspace file for multiple notebooks, which is helpful when you want to save and later load all the associated notebooks. Loading linked notebook applications, however, requires special handling.

Loading a Linked Notebook Application

If you choose /**F**ile **R**etrieve to load the sample application, specify PARENT.WQ2 as the notebook to retrieve. When you retrieve a primary file in a linked notebook application, Quattro Pro displays the Link options menu shown in figure 8.23.

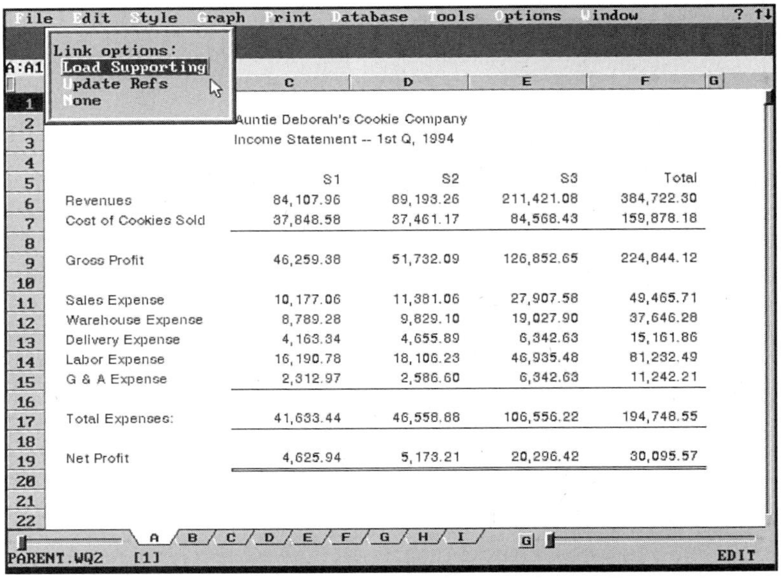

Fig. 8.23

Three options for retrieving a linked notebook application.

To load each supporting notebook, choose the **L**oad Supporting option. The **U**pdate Refs option causes Quattro Pro to update the linked formula results on the primary notebook using data from the unopened supporting notebooks.

If you don't want to update the linking references on the primary notebook, choose the **N**one option. This option causes Quattro Pro to display NA (not available) values in each cell on the primary notebook that has a linking reference to an unopened supporting document (see fig. 8.24).

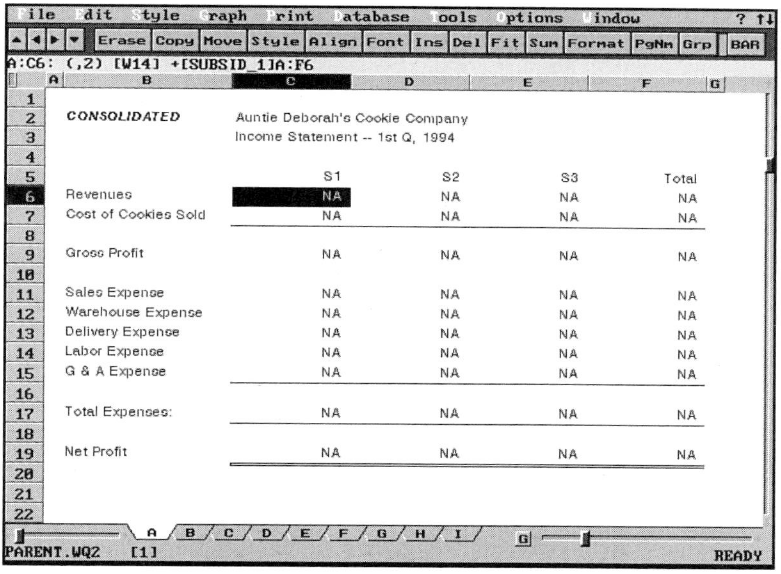

Fig. 8.24

NA values displayed in the primary notebook.

This display of NA values enables you to review the structure of a primary document in a large linking application without first having to load each supporting document.

Updating the Notebook Links

Choose / **T**ools **U**pdate Links to display four options that enable you to control the interaction between primary and supporting documents in a linked notebook application.

Choose the **O**pen option to open individual supporting notebooks without reloading the entire linked application. When prompted, highlight the names of the notebooks you want to open and then press Enter to load those notebooks (see fig. 8.25).

Fig. 8.25

Loading unopened
supporting notebooks
into Quattro Pro.

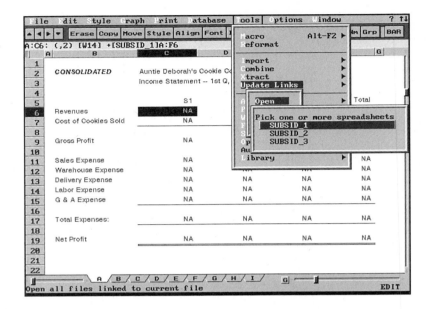

When no supporting notebooks are open in Quattro Pro's memory, choose the **R**efresh option to recalculate results for the linking formulas on a primary notebook without opening that notebook. When prompted, highlight the names of the supporting notebooks that contain cell values referenced by linking formulas on the primary notebook. Press Enter to refresh the linking formula results on the primary notebook.

Choose the **C**hange option to unlink a supporting notebook from the primary notebook and relink it to a new notebook (see fig. 8.26).

Choose the **D**elete option to erase links between the primary notebook and one or more supporting notebooks. This technique is useful when you want to disassociate old or outdated supporting notebooks from the primary notebook.

Consolidating 2-D Linked Files into a Single Notebook

You can consolidate into a single Version 5.0 notebook any multifile linking applications created in earlier versions of Quattro Pro. One reason for doing so is that you may find the multipage structure of the

Version 5.0 notebook better suited to your report development needs. Another reason is that you can reduce the number of files associated with an application (if you use the example files shown in the discussion so far, the number of files would shrink from 4 to 1). Also, after all the data is in a single notebook, you can take advantage of Quattro Pro's Group mode to format or modify all pages at once.

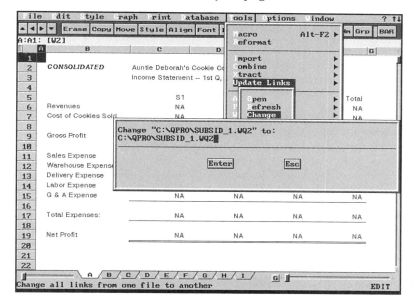

Fig. 8.26

Quattro Pro prompts for the name of the notebook to which you want to relink.

NOTE

Don't confuse this technique with the 3-D consolidation formulas discussed earlier, in the section "Creating 3-D Consolidation Formulas." 3-D consolidation formulas simplify the process of creating linking formulas in your notebooks.

To consolidate linked files into a single notebook, follow these steps:

1. Choose the /**File** Utilities **C**onsolidate command.

2. Select the name of the primary notebook in your linking application.

Quattro Pro first opens a single window, where it displays the primary notebook. One by one, each supporting file is loaded into its own page in the same notebook window. Quattro Pro names the pages in the new notebook using the file name from each supporting file. Finally, all linked formulas from the various linked files are converted into 3-D references (see fig. 8.27).

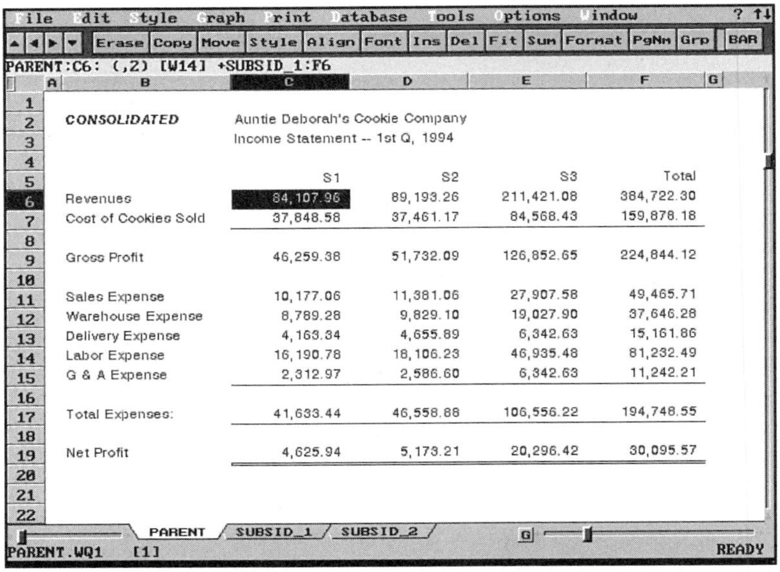

Fig. 8.27

A Version 4.0 linked file application consolidated into a single Version 5.0 notebook.

> **TIP**
>
> This procedure is designed specifically for consolidating multiple WQ1 notebook files into a single WQ2 file. You cannot consolidate multiple WQ2 files into a single WQ2 file. If you want to do so, you must use the /**E**dit **C**opy command to copy information from the various pages in the supporting notebooks into pages within the primary notebook file.

After your files are consolidated, you must perform one more step. Choose /**F**ile Save **As** and change the name of the new notebook (PARENT.WQ1 in the figure) to one that uses the WQ2 file extension.

> **CAUTION**
>
> If you forget to supply WQ2 as the file extension for the consolidated notebook, Quattro Pro will save only the first page (page A) of the notebook and convert the file to a WQ1 format.

Using Advanced File Tools

The first three commands in the middle of the **Tools** menu provide you with the means to import, combine, and extract notebook data. These commands can operate on notebook data and data from other programs. By continuing with the sample application (for Auntie Deborah's Cookie Company), you learn how to use each command to manipulate files in special ways.

Importing a File

The **Import** command enables you to load data from text files into a Quattro Pro notebook. This operation is recommended for users who want to access data stored in file formats that Quattro Pro can't translate. Importing text from a word processing file and financial data stored in a file used by an accounting software program, for example, is common.

When you translate a file, Quattro Pro generally does a good job of preserving the layout and formatting from the source file. When you have a file that Quattro Pro cannot translate directly, however, your only option is to import data directly from the file. When you import data this way, Quattro Pro usually can't reproduce the layout and formatting from the source file; only the raw words and numbers appear.

The **Import** command can access data stored in three common file formats: ASCII text, comma delimited, and comma and quotation mark delimited. When you import data, Quattro Pro reads the foreign file format and copies the data into one column on the current notebook.

To import text into a Quattro Pro notebook, follow these steps:

1. Place the selector into the cell in which you want Quattro Pro to begin copying the imported data.

2. Choose / **Tools Import** and then choose **ASCII Text File, Comma &** " " **Delimited File,** or **Only Commas** from the displayed list.

3. When prompted, type the name of the file to import and then press Enter to begin importing text from that file.

Review the data after Quattro Pro finishes importing the text. Depending on the source file format, Quattro Pro may have copied the imported data into one column without breaking up long labels. This situation occurs, for example, when you import data from an ASCII text file that doesn't delineate separate items that are grouped together on the same row. The item Franklin Tracy E., for example, may end up as FranklinTracyE. To break up the long labels, you can use the /**Tools Parse** command. (See Chapter 14, "Analyzing and Manipulating Data," for comprehensive coverage of this command.)

Generally, Quattro Pro copies comma- and quote-delimited files into separate columns on the notebook, based on the delimiters.

Combining Two Files

The **Combine** command enables you to copy, add, and subtract data on two notebooks. You can use this command for applications that aren't formula linked yet require a certain level of data association.

In most cases, linked formulas are easier to work with and provide you a greater degree of flexibility when designing and building notebook applications. Sometimes, however, that is simply impossible. You may not, for instance, have ready access to all the files that are part of the application. The files may be scattered throughout the 12 divisions in your company, for example, or you may be responsible for compiling notebook data from several different managers, each of whom creates their own layout for the report.

Return to the sample application introduced earlier in the discussion on linking notebooks. Start by assuming that the four notebooks are no longer linked by formulas. PARENT.WQ2 also contains no values. By using the **Combine** command, you can create the same end result achieved with linked formulas.

TIP

Combined files don't update each other automatically as linked files do. To refresh the values in combined files, you must choose the command again and then recombine the data.

Before issuing this command, you must gather data about the notebooks whose data you want to combine. First, jot down the exact block coordinates of the data from the source notebooks. Second, review the destination notebook and then select an area to which you want to combine data.

> **CAUTION**
>
> Before executing the command, note that Quattro Pro overwrites existing cell data (including protected cells) on the destination notebook, unless you are performing an **A**dd or **S**ubtract combine operation. See "Adding and Subtracting Data" later in this chapter for complete details.

Copying Data

To combine data from PARENT.WQ2 and SUBSID_1.WQ2, follow these steps:

1. Retrieve PARENT.WQ2 and place the selector in cell E6.

2. Choose /**T**ools **C**ombine **C**opy.

3. When prompted, choose the **B**lock option to copy only a block of data.

4. When prompted, type **c6..c19** and press Enter to record the source block.

5. After Quattro Pro displays the file list box, highlight SUBSID_1.WQ2 and press Enter.

Quattro Pro begins copying block C6..C19 from SUBSID_1.WQ2 to PARENT.WQ2, beginning at the location of the selector (cell E6). After you choose the **C**ombine **C**opy command, Quattro Pro reproduces the data exactly as the data appears in the source block, including cell formatting and presentation-quality display settings.

Exercise extreme caution when using the /**T**ools **C**ombine **C**opy command to copy formulas. Quattro Pro may not display the answer you expect. Suppose that you copy the Total column data of column F from SUBSID_1.WQ2 to PARENT.WQ2. At first glance, this technique appears to be a good way to reproduce sales totals for Subsidiary 1 on PARENT.WQ2. If you had taken this approach, however, you would have created a circular reference.

Recall that in column F on SUBSID_1.WQ2, each formula sums data appearing in columns C, D, and E. When copied to PARENT.WQ2, these formulas now sum data appearing in columns C, D, and E on PARENT.WQ2. A circular formula results because the original copy destination on PARENT.WQ2 (column E) is included in the formula.

Be careful. Solving one problem sometimes reveals another. Suppose that you shift the copy destination to column F on PARENT.WQ2. This action eliminates the circular reference but exposes another problem. On PARENT.WQ2, a formula that sums data in columns C, D, and E returns a value of 0 because these columns are empty.

TIP

To copy formula results from one notebook to another, convert formulas to their results using the /**E**dit **V**alues command. Then, return to the notebook containing the formulas and press Alt+F5 to reverse the /**E**dit **V**alues operation. Quattro Pro displays the formulas again in their original form.

Adding and Subtracting Data

To add data from SUBSID_2.WQ2 to PARENT.WQ2, follow these steps:

1. Retrieve PARENT.WQ2 and place the selector in cell E6.

2. Choose /**T**ools **C**ombine **A**dd.

3. When prompted, choose the **B**lock option to add only a block of data.

4. When prompted, type **c6..c19** and press Enter to record the source block.

5. After Quattro Pro displays the file list box, highlight SUBSID_2.WQ2 again and press Enter.

Quattro Pro adds the values from the source block to the corresponding values on the active notebook, beginning at the location of the selector. When you **A**dd data, Quattro Pro doesn't alter any cell formatting or presentation-quality display settings in the target block, whereas **C**opy brings the formatting in along with the data.

Repeat the **A**dd operation again, except add the results from cell block C6..C19 on SUBSID_3.WQ2 to PARENT.WQ2. Your notebook now contains the same values that appear in column C on PARENT.WQ2 in the linked notebook application (refer to fig. 8.22).

The **S**ubtract option on the **C**ombine submenu works like the **A**dd option, except that the **S**ubtract option subtracts the source-block values from the destination block values.

> **NOTE**
>
> Labels and formulas are unaffected by adding and subtracting, but dates are affected.

Extracting Part of a File

The /**T**ools **X**tract command copies and saves part of a notebook in a new notebook file. This command is useful for breaking large notebook applications into several smaller, more manageable notebooks.

When Quattro Pro performs an extraction operation, the program retains all block names, graph names, and format settings that applied to the source block before extraction. You also can extract **F**ormulas or **V**alues from the source notebook. Choosing the /**T**ools **X**tract **V**alues option is like choosing the /**E**dit **V**alues command.

To extract data from one notebook and add the data to another, follow these steps:

1. Choose /**T**ools **X**tract.

2. Choose **F**ormulas or **V**alues.

3. When prompted, type a file name for the notebook that will receive the extracted data.

4. When prompted, type the coordinates of the source block and press Enter to extract the data.

Questions & Answers

This chapter shows you how to create, use, and manage files, workspaces, and windows. If you have questions concerning situations not addressed in the examples given, look through this section.

Managing Files

Q: After I loaded two notebooks into Quattro Pro, I pressed Alt+0 to reveal the open window list, but only one file name was displayed. What happened to my second notebook?

A: You chose /**File R**etrieve to open the second document when you should have used /**File O**pen. The latter command overlays the current notebook window with a saved notebook, but the former command loads a saved notebook into the current window, erasing the current notebook from memory.

Q: Why doesn't Quattro Pro save my /**File D**irectory command setting for new work sessions?

A: You can save the settings, but not with the **Directory** command. Choose /**Options S**tartup **D**irectory to choose a new default directory setting. Also choose /**Options U**pdate to save the new setting. Quattro Pro writes the new default directory name on the **File** menu next to the **Directory** command.

Q: Why don't my presentation-quality settings appear when I retrieve notebook files saved in non-Quattro Pro file formats?

A: The file formats for many of the programs to which Quattro Pro can read and write don't support features such as line drawing, font selections, inserted graphs, and formula links. These features are Quattro Pro-specific and should be added only to notebook files with the WQ2 extension.

If you try to save them in a format that doesn't support them, you get the error message `Desktop settings are removed. Save the file?` You have the option to save the file without the unsupported features.

Q: When I save a Quattro Pro notebook in a Lotus 1-2-3-compatible format, why don't the notebook's graphs display in color?

A: Quattro Pro doesn't store graph color information when you create 1-2-3-compatible worksheets from your Quattro Pro notebooks. If you retrieve the 1-2-3-compatible worksheet into Quattro Pro, however, the graph colors return to their default settings.

Q: I don't remember the password for a notebook. How can I display a list of the current passwords?

A: You can't. Quattro Pro doesn't let you access a password-protected file without the password. If you have forgotten the password, you must rebuild the notebook.

Q: How do I rename a notebook file without returning to DOS?

A: Choose /**F**ile Save **A**s and type a new file name when prompted. This method copies the original notebook. You also can highlight a name in the file pane of the File Manager window and choose /**E**dit **R**ename or press F2. Quattro Pro prompts you for a new name. This method doesn't duplicate the file.

Displaying Windows

Q: Why can't Quattro Pro sometimes split a notebook window into two panes?

A: Quattro Pro cannot execute the **V**ertical or **H**orizontal commands on the **W**indow menu in the following cases:

- When the selector is in row 1 or 8192, you cannot split a window into two horizontal panes.

- When the selector is in column A or IV, you cannot split a window into two vertical panes.

- When a notebook window already is split into two panes, you cannot select another split setting.

To change the split pane style, choose /**W**indow **O**ptions **C**lear before you select a new split pane setting.

Q: I cannot seem to scroll my split window panes together. Am I doing something wrong?

A: You have chosen /**W**indow **O**ptions **U**nsync. Choose /**W**indow **O**ptions **S**ync to return the inactive pane to the location of the active pane.

Linking Notebooks

Q: When I try to enter a linking formula, Quattro Pro beeps and displays an error message that says a drive isn't ready. Then, the program displays NA in the cell. What's going on?

A: You created and tried to enter a linking formula containing a drive letter before the file name reference. The drive you specified doesn't contain a disk now. Quattro Pro tries to read the drive for several seconds and then records the formula anyway; because the file name reference isn't valid, however, the program displays the NA value in the cell.

If you intend to include the drive letter, place the disk in the drive and then re-enter the formula. This time, Quattro Pro finds the value and displays the correct formula result. If you don't intend to use the drive letter, delete the letter from the formula. In both cases, the NA value disappears.

Q: Why does Quattro Pro sometimes not display the link options prompt after I load a linking application?

A: Quattro Pro displays the link options prompt whenever you open a notebook containing references to unopened notebooks. When you load the primary notebook before the supporting notebooks, Quattro Pro always displays the link options prompt. When you load supporting document(s) first and then load the primary document, Quattro Pro doesn't need to display this prompt.

Q: I loaded the primary notebook in a linking application, and Quattro Pro displayed a prompt box asking me to change a linking reference to a different file name. Why?

A: You deleted or renamed a notebook file referenced by a primary notebook in a linking application.

Press Esc until you cancel this prompt box, and Quattro Pro continues to load the rest of the linking application. When the application is completely loaded, Quattro Pro shows NA values in the cells that reference the unknown document. If you have renamed the notebook, change the name back so that Quattro Pro displays the correct values. If you accidentally deleted the notebook, you must edit the linking formulas and remove the references to this file name.

Q: I created a circular formula when I combined data from two notebooks in a linking application. What happened?

A: Don't use the /**Tools Combine** command to copy blocks containing formulas. If you use this command, you run the risk of creating circular formulas. Instead, choose /**Tools Xtract Values** so that Quattro Pro copies the formula results instead of the formulas.

Summary

Chapter 8 demonstrates some basic file management skills and advanced file tools that you can use to link notebooks. This chapter reviews the **F**ile, **T**ools, and **W**indow menu commands and introduces you to the File Manager.

Having completed this chapter, you should understand the following Quattro Pro concepts:

■ Creating, opening, and retrieving files

■ Saving, closing, and erasing files

■ Translating notebooks to and from non-Quattro Pro file formats

■ Password-protecting your files

■ Using the File Manager to perform multiple file operations

■ Enlarging, shrinking, tiling, stacking, moving, and sizing windows

■ Splitting windows into panes

■ Turning notebook grid lines on and off

■ Creating linking formulas by pointing and clicking

■ Moving and copying linking formulas

■ Importing and combining files

Chapter 9 introduces you to techniques for printing your Quattro Pro documents and offers comprehensive coverage of the **P**rint menu commands. You learn how to print draft-quality and final-quality copies of documents and a large notebook block so that it fits on a single page. You also learn about previewing the printed look of a document in the Screen Preview environment.

Printing and Graphing

Printing

Quattro Pro provides you with the tools to format and print notebook reports and graphs in several ways. You can print an unformatted snapshot of your screen's display, a specific block of notebook values, or a presentation-quality version of a notebook report. In this chapter, you learn the many printing techniques available in Quattro Pro's **P**rint menu.

In the first section, you look at each step in the process of printing a small notebook report. You also learn a technique for generating a rough-draft screen preview of your notebook data—a useful prelude to creating the final version of every printed report.

Next, you see how to access, understand, and set all the options that control the appearance of a printed notebook report. Specifically, you learn how to set layout options—such as footers, margins, and page orientation—that enable you to print larger notebook reports successfully.

The chapter continues by explaining the two format styles that Quattro Pro can use in printing out a notebook report.

Then you learn ways to prepare for a printing session. You learn how to align paper, issue form feeds, and skip lines to control the movement of paper in your printer.

Next, you learn why and how to choose various destinations for your printed output. You can print to a printer, to a file, or to your screen.

This chapter continues by reviewing the procedures for printing a graph. As with a notebook report, you can reproduce a graph on paper, print a graph to a file, and preview the finished form of a graph on-screen. An additional graph-printing option enables you to print to a file that you can use to produce 35mm slides.

The final section of this chapter looks at Quattro Pro's powerful print job management features: the Borland Print Spooler and the Print Manager. The Print Spooler enables you to continue working with the current notebook while jobs are being printed, and the Print Manager displays vital information about the print jobs waiting in the printing queue.

Reviewing the Print Menu

You can use the 11 **P**rint menu commands to define a print block or a heading block, create a custom layout, control the movement of paper in a printer, and generate printouts of notebook reports and graphs (see fig. 9.1). Quattro Pro displays the current system settings for certain commands in the right margin of the **P**rint menu.

Fig. 9.1

The **P**rint menu commands.

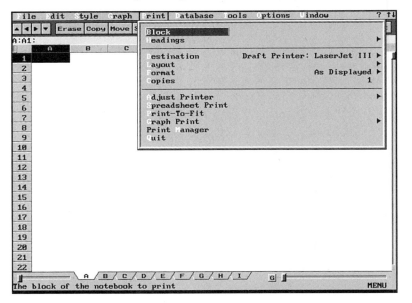

The **P**rint menu consists of three types of commands: block definition, printer control, and report formatting.

The block definition commands tell Quattro Pro which block to print and which block to use as a heading at the top of each printed page.

The **D**estination command—a printer-control command located in the middle section of the **P**rint menu—enables you to choose whether Quattro Pro prints a report to a printer, to a file, or to the screen. (The name of the default printer appears next to the **D**estination command when **D**estination is set to Draft **P**rinter, **G**raphics Printer, or **S**creen Preview, but not to Text **F**ile or **B**inary File.)

The remaining commands in this section of the menu are report formatting commands. They enable you to set print margins, set the page length, and alter the print orientation of a report. You can choose to print notebook cell data as the data appears on-screen or in a report that lists each cell and its contents. You also can tell Quattro Pro to print multiple copies of any notebook, page, or graph.

The commands at the bottom section of the **P**rint menu control the printer. The first command enables you to advance the paper in the printer one line or one page at a time and then to align the printer to the top of the form. The second command tells Quattro Pro to print a notebook, using the print settings in the **L**ayout submenu. The third command tells Quattro Pro to print a notebook so that the notebook fits onto your printer paper, regardless of the settings in the **L**ayout submenu. The fourth command is for printing graphs. The fifth command opens a Print Manager window so that you can view the status of your print jobs.

NOTE

The important thing to remember about printing with Quattro Pro is that the program offers two different printing modes: draft and final quality. In draft mode, Quattro Pro sends only characters to your printer. Your printer controls items such as line spacing, font, character size, and characters per inch. When you print to a graphics printer in final quality mode, Quattro Pro sends characters and report-formatting instructions to your printer. These report-formatting instructions include the choices you made on the **S**tyle menu (such as shaded cells and drawn lines).

Printing Small Notebook Reports

Before learning how to use each print option, you should review two ways of obtaining a basic printout of a notebook report.

First, you can obtain a draft-quality printout of a notebook by using the **B**lock, **A**djust Printer, and **S**preadsheet Print commands. This simple printing method, which doesn't require you to alter any of Quattro Pro's default print settings, works well for producing a working draft of a notebook that is no more than 80 characters wide. Follow these steps:

NOTE

Before trying this operation, be sure that your printer is on-line.

1. Choose /**F**ile **R**etrieve and retrieve a notebook report.

2. Choose /**P**rint **B**lock.

3. When prompted, type the block coordinates of the area you want to print. The area can be a block on a single page in the notebook or a 3-D block that spans several notebook pages.

4. Turn the printer on, position the paper at the top of a page, and choose **A**djust Printer **A**lign to set Quattro Pro's line and page counters to the top of the form.

5. Choose **S**preadsheet Print. Quattro Pro begins to print the data.

6. Choose **A**djust Printer **F**orm Feed to advance the last page of the printout to the top of the form so that the printer is ready for the next printout.

TIP

Press Ctrl+Break to abort a print operation and return to the active page. If you use the Borland Print Spooler to manage your print jobs, however, this key sequence will not halt a print operation. See "Printing in the Background" later in this chapter for details about disabling the print spooler so that Ctrl+Break works.

Second, you can print part of an on-screen page by performing a *screen dump*. A screen dump sends to the printer an unformatted "snapshot" of the displayed data. This quick-print method is convenient for producing rough-draft versions of your printouts. Printing a rough draft enables you to verify the cell formats, the accuracy of data, and the spelling of labels and report headings before you print the final draft.

To perform a screen-dump operation, Quattro Pro must be in text display mode; otherwise, the program prints a page full of unrecognizable graphic symbols.

Follow these steps to produce screen-dump output:

1. Choose /**O**ptions **D**isplay Mode **A**:80x25.

2. Choose **Q**uit to quit the **O**ptions menu and return to the active page.

3. Press Shift+Print Screen. (If this keystroke doesn't work, try pressing only the Print Screen key.) Quattro Pro begins printing text.

NOTE

Because the output from a screen-dump operation is "rough" in appearance (even in text mode), Quattro Pro offers ways to produce higher-quality versions of your printouts. Creating better printouts that display fonts, drawn lines, and shaded cells is fairly simple. Later, this chapter covers Quattro Pro's layout options and the procedures for generating higher-quality notebook and graph printouts.

FOR RELATED INFORMATION

▶▶ "Setting Display Mode Options," p. 788.
How to specify several display mode settings beneficial for viewing large spreadsheet reports on-screen before printing them.

Printing Large Notebook Reports

The real benefit of using an electronic spreadsheet program is that you can create complex reports made up of hundreds of rows and columns of data. When you print large reports, Quattro Pro occasionally wraps the text so that the text fits within the margins specified by the default print settings.

Text wrapping typically occurs when you define a right margin that is much wider than the width of your printer or try to print more characters across a page than your printer can accommodate. (Some dot-matrix printers, for example, can print only 80 characters across a page.) If you try to print a report that contains 30 columns of data, each of which is 15 characters wide, the printed report needs to be at least 450 characters wide.

When your notebook report is wider than the width of a page, Quattro Pro prints as many columns as will fit on the page and then prints the remaining columns on a new page (see fig. 9.2).

Fortunately, you have several alternatives for printing such a large notebook so that it reproduces in more readable form.

If you have access to a wide-carriage printer, you can print your report on wider paper, but your printouts still will be restricted to a width of approximately 132 standard characters. You also can use wider paper, change the default margins, and print in compressed mode, giving you a report width of up to 250 characters.

An alternative way of dealing with text wrapping involves using a heading row or heading column at the top edge or left edge of each printed page. This technique doesn't control text wrapping, but helps make the text more presentable in a printed report.

You can create many different report styles by changing Quattro Pro's default print settings. The /**P**rint **H**eadings command, for example, enables you to print column and row headings on each page. When you choose /**P**rint **H**eadings, Quattro Pro displays a submenu in which you specify whether to print a **L**eft Heading or a **T**op Heading. A left heading appears along the left border of each page, and a top heading prints at the top of each page.

To specify a block to be printed as a heading, follow these steps:

1. Choose /**P**rint **H**eadings.

2. Choose **L**eft Heading or **T**op Heading.

3. Type the coordinates of a block (on the active page) that contains the heading you want to use.

Make sure that you exclude the heading block from the print block. If you specify a column or row of labels as a heading and then include the same column or row as part of the print block, Quattro Pro prints the heading twice on the first page—once as data and once as a heading.

```
Business Decisions Consulting, Inc.
6-Month Cash Flow Report
                              +-------------------------------------
                              |  Jan      Feb      Mar      Apr
                              +-------------------------------------
                                 (a)      (a)      (a)      (a)

INFLOWS
   C.Ed. Software              8,629      846    4,476    3,559
   Definite Solutions, Inc.   8,187    8,430    8,596    6,051
   S.D. County School District 1,259    8,005    1,915    5,058
   Miscellaneous Consulting    4,000    8,809    5,380    5,381
                              -------------------------------------

   Total Cash Inflows        22,075   26,090   20,367   20,049
   Cumulative Inflows        22,075   48,165   68,532   88,581

OUTFLOWS
   Rent                       2,500    2,500    2,500    2,500
   Utilities                    425      415      395      387
   Supplies                   1,745    1,299      366      244
   Salaries                  10,000   10,000   10,000   10,000
   Debt Service               2,500    2,500    2,500    2,500
   Subcontractor Payments         0        0        0        0
   Taxes and Legal                0        0      575        0
   Other Expenses             1,273    2,633    1,225    1,274
                              -------------------------------------

   Total Cash Outflows       18,443   19,347   17,561   16,905
   Cumulative Outflows       18,443   37,790   55,351   72,256

NET CASH FLOW                 3,632    6,743    2,806    3,144
CUMULATIVE CF                 3,632   10,375   13,181   16,325

Beginning Cash:               1,199    4,831   11,574   14,380
     Ending Cash:             4,831   11,574   14,380   17,524
                              -------------------------------------
```

```
-------------------+
   May      Jun |
-------------------+
   (a)      (pf)

 2,997        0
   540    6,220
 7,467    9,731
 6,519    9,902
-------------------

17,523   25,853
106,104  131,957


 2,500    2,500
   490      425
 1,443      750
10,000   10,000
 2,500    2,500
     0    1,000
     0      575
 1,419    1,225
-------------------

18,352   18,975
90,608  109,583

  (829)   6,878
15,496   22,374

17,524   16,695
16,695   23,573
-------------------
```

Fig. 9.2

The notebook report from Business Decisions Consulting, Inc.

Printing Multiple-Page Notebook Reports

Not all reports exist on a single notebook page. When you are working with a multipage notebook report, you can create a 3-D print block that spans several consecutive notebook pages. This technique enables you to print information from many pages at one time, rather than print one page at a time. To use this capability, you must have your information organized in the same cell block on each page in the notebook. This technique is ideally suited for printing notebook page groups.

Follow these steps to print a 3-D block:

1. Choose /**P**rint **B**lock.

2. When you are prompted, use the arrow keys to select the block coordinates of the area you want to print on the first page.

3. Press Ctrl+Page Down to include the same block on the next page.

4. Continue pressing Ctrl+Page Down until the same block is selected for each consecutive page you want to print.

5. Press Enter.

To use the mouse to select a 3-D print block quickly, choose the /**P**rint **B**lock command, select the first print block, hold down the Shift key, click the tab for the last page to be included in the printout, and then press Enter. When a 3-D cell block is selected, the block coordinates appear in the **P**rint menu next to the **B**lock command. For example, the coordinates A..C:A5..H25 define the same cell block—A5..H25—on pages A, B, and C.

Quattro Pro prints the 3-D cell block from each page separately. In the preceding example, Quattro Pro would create a three-page printout: one for page A, one for page B, and one for page C. You can change this method of printing multipage notebook reports by using the **N**otebook Page Skip command. For more details, see "Controlling Multipage Printouts" later in this chapter.

Choosing Layout Options

Initially, Quattro Pro uses default print settings to produce printouts. Quattro Pro assumes, for example, that you are using standard 8 1/2-by-11-inch printer paper, printing each page in portrait orientation, and inserting margins around the entire printed document. You can change the default settings for an individual notebook or for all future notebooks.

The /**Print** **L**ayout menu commands create report headers and footers; print reports without page breaks, footers, or headers; enable you to change the default margins, dimensions, and print orientation; and send special setup strings to your printer.

Quattro Pro stores the **L**ayout submenu settings with the current notebook. If you open a new file or exit Quattro Pro and then return to the **L**ayout submenu, each command displays its original default setting.

To save custom settings as the new defaults, choose the /**Print** **L**ayout **U**pdate command. To reinstate the preceding set of default settings, choose /**Print** **L**ayout **R**eset.

Using the Print Layout Dialog Box

By default, Quattro Pro displays the /**Print** **L**ayout menu as a dialog box (see fig. 9.3). By using this dialog box, you quickly can scan and set all print layout options—such as header and footer text, margins, and orientation—from one screen. The dialog box eliminates the need to move through layers of submenus to choose and verify print layout settings.

In the Print Layout Options dialog box, Quattro Pro displays an asterisk next to the current setting or displays a value for each option. To change a setting, type the highlighted letter in the option name; then press the arrow keys to move the asterisk to the new setting or type a new value. Press Enter. If you have a mouse, click the option you want to use so that Quattro Pro moves the asterisk there. After you finish setting options, choose **Q**uit to return to the **P**rint menu.

Fig. 9.3

The Print Layout Options dialog box.

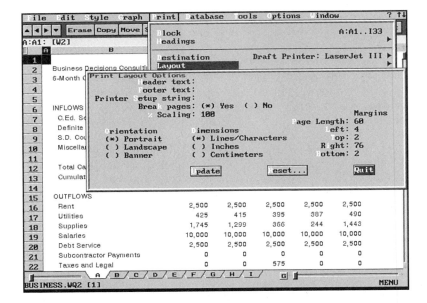

To change the **%** Scaling setting to 80%, for example, press %. When prompted, type **80** and press Enter to store the new scaling setting. To change the Margins **T**op setting to 1 line, type **T**, type **1**, and then press Enter to store the new top margin setting. Choose **Q**uit to accept the current settings and return to the **P**rint menu. Choose **U**pdate to save all current settings as the new default, and choose **R**eset to return all settings to their original default setting.

> **NOTE**
>
> By default, Quattro Pro Version 5.0 displays dialog boxes rather than menus at start-up. If you are upgrading from a previous version of Quattro Pro and prefer to display the menus instead of the dialog boxes, choose /**O**ptions **S**tartup **U**se Dialogs **N**o. Subsequently, each time you choose /**P**rint **L**ayout, you see the menu to which you are accustomed.

The following table reveals discrepancies that exist between commands appearing on the /**P**rint Layout menu and those appearing in the Print Layout Options dialog box.

Menu Command	Dialog Box Option
Break Pages	Brea**k** Pages
Notebook Page Skip	(not available)
Percent scaling	**%** Scaling

The rest of this chapter features menus rather than dialog boxes. If you prefer to use dialog boxes, you can continue to follow the step-by-step instructions provided.

Reviewing the Layout Submenu Settings

Quattro Pro offers a convenient way to review all current **Layout** submenu settings. Choose /**Print Layout Values** to display the settings screen shown in figure 9.4. The settings screen summarizes the current layout settings and current printer destination.

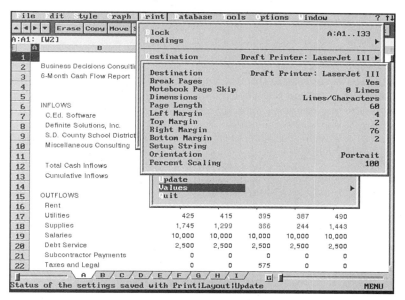

Fig. 9.4

The current page layout settings.

The screen shown in figure 9.4 is available only for review purposes. You cannot change print settings on this screen. The /**Print Layout Values** command also isn't available when you use dialog boxes instead of menus (refer to the preceding section).

Adding Headers and Footers

Headers and footers are lines of text (up to 254 characters long) that may be added to the top or bottom of each page in a notebook print-out.

NOTE

A header (/**P**rint **L**ayout **H**eader) is different from a heading (/**P**rint **H**eadings). A *header* is text that you type into a dialog box; a *heading* is a block of labels already in the body of a page.

Use headers and footers to append text to a printout. The advantage of using headers and footers is that you need to enter them only once for Quattro Pro to reproduce them on every page. If the header or footer data changes, you need to change the header or footer definition only once to update the text for all printed pages.

Commonly used header types include dates, file names, and titles. Commonly used footer types include comments, file names, and data legends. To add a footer to the sample notebook report pictured earlier in figure 9.2, for example, follow these steps:

1. Choose /**P**rint **L**ayout **F**ooter.

2. At the prompt, type the text of the footer with any alignment prefixes. To add text to the printout to help a reader discern between actual data and *pro forma* (forecast) data, for example, type

  |**(a) = actual; (pf) = pro forma**

and press Enter to record the footer text (see fig. 9.5).

The vertical bar (|) centers the footer text (everything to the right of the vertical bar) on the bottom of each page in the printout. Quattro Pro displays this new setting in the right margin of the **L**ayout submenu, next to the **F**ooter command.

Fig. 9.5

Adding a footer to a notebook report.

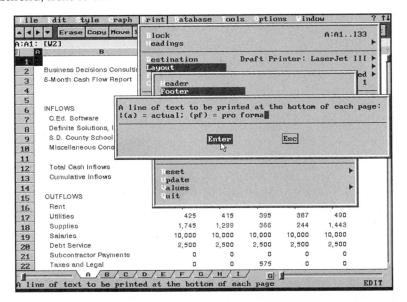

You can use the vertical-bar character (|) to justify headers and footers on a page. You also can use the pound (#) and at (@) characters to display information on the page. When you include one of these characters as part of the text entry, the following actions take place:

Character	Action
#	Displays the current page number
@	Displays the current date
		Justifies text (right or center)

Actually, the header and footer | symbol is like a Tab key that has two justification settings: center and right. In a Quattro Pro printout, text is left-justified automatically. When you precede text with a | symbol, Quattro Pro centers the text on the page. When you precede text with two | symbols, Quattro Pro right-justifies the text. For example, the header text

@|Inventory Analysis Report|Page #

may result in the following header information:

04/19/94   Inventory Analysis Report   Page 5

Quattro Pro formats header and footer text with the font attributes specified with the Normal style. To change these font attributes, choose the /**S**tyle **D**efine Style **N**ormal **F**ont command, which is discussed in "Using Custom Notebook Styles" in Chapter 5.

Controlling Page Breaks

Quattro Pro observes hard and soft page breaks. You insert hard page breaks by using the /**S**tyle **I**nsert Break command or by typing the text |:: in a cell. Soft page breaks occur automatically between pages.

By default, soft page breaks occur every 56 rows. This row count assumes that your notebook uses the default margin settings covered in the later section "Setting Margins." When you change the default margin settings, you alter the number of rows that Quattro Pro prints.

You can suppress the automatic placement of soft page breaks—a technique that results in data being printed in one continuous block. Quattro Pro continues to observe hard page breaks, however.

To suppress soft page breaks, follow these steps:

1. Choose /**P**rint **L**ayout **B**reak Pages.

2. Choose **N**o from the displayed submenu.

NOTE ▶ When you set **B**reak Pages to **N**o, headers and footers also don't print.

To undo this command so that Quattro Pro continues inserting soft page breaks, choose the **B**reak Pages command again and choose **Y**es.

Controlling Multipage Printouts

Quattro Pro normally prints a 3-D print block as though the cell block on each page were selected and then printed individually. A 3-D print block that spans four pages, for example, would generate a printout at least four pages long. You can change this method of printing a multipage notebook report with the /**P**rint **L**ayout **N**otebook Page Skip command.

The default setting for the **N**otebook Page Skip command, **F**orm Feed, instructs Quattro Pro to eject each page before printing the next page in the 3-D print block. To separate the print blocks by a specific number of lines, choose the **S**kip Lines option instead. Quattro Pro prompts you for the number of lines to insert between pages. One line corresponds to a sixth of an inch, and 6 lines equal an inch. To separate each page of the 3-D print block by 2 inches, for example, choose the **S**kip Lines option and type **12** as the setting.

Notice that regardless of which **N**otebook Page Skip option you choose, Quattro Pro continues to observe the automatic placement of soft page breaks every 56 notebook rows. To further fine-tune the positioning of information in a printout, you should coordinate the other **L**ayout command options with the **N**otebook Page Skip command.

Scaling a Notebook Printout

Quattro Pro enables you to scale the printed size of notebook text without first requiring you to adjust font point sizes (see Chapter 5,

"Formatting Data"). The /**P**rint **L**ayout **P**ercent Scaling command is a tool you can use to scale notebook printouts. By default, Quattro Pro scales all printouts at 100 percent. To shrink text in a printout, choose a scaling factor of 1 percent to 99 percent. To magnify text, choose a scaling factor of 101 percent to 1,000 percent.

> **NOTE**
>
> Scaling percentages greater than 200 enlarge a printout so much that in most cases, Quattro Pro must print the notebook on two or more sheets of paper.

The **P**ercent Scaling command operates only when the print destination is a graphics printer. Choose /**P**rint **D**estination **G**raphics Printer before you try to print a scaled notebook. Quattro Pro ignores the scaling percentage setting when you use the /**P**rint **P**rint-To-Fit command to generate a printout. Use the **S**preadsheet Print command to print a scaled notebook.

You can use the Screen Preview tool to preview a scaled notebook before printing it. In the Screen Preview environment, you can verify that you have selected an appropriate scaling-percentage setting. See the later section "Previewing a Printout On-Screen" for more details.

Setting Margins

The **M**argins submenu commands enable you to set margins and alter the number of lines that Quattro Pro prints on a page. By default, Quattro Pro places 1/2-inch margins on the top, bottom, left, and right sides of a document and prints 66 lines per page.

To change any of these settings, choose one of the commands described in the following sections.

To change the right margin of the sample notebook, for example, perform the following steps:

1. Choose /**P**rint **L**ayout **M**argins.

2. Choose **R**ight.

3. Type **511** and press Enter to record the new right margin setting (see fig. 9.6). You would want to choose a right margin setting of this size if you're printing in compressed mode (at about 30 characters per inch) on wide paper.

Quattro Pro displays the new setting in the right margin of the **M**argins submenu, next to the command.

Fig. 9.6

Changing the right margin of a notebook report.

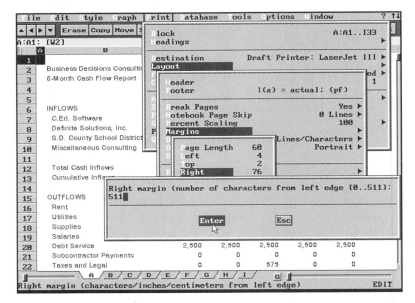

Page Length

The **P**age Length command determines how many lines are to be printed on each page. The default setting—66 lines—is the standard for most printers. Laser-printer owners should try a setting of about 60 lines per page. If your pages don't seem to break in the correct places in your printouts, adjust the **P**age Length command until you achieve the effect that you want.

When you calculate page length, a good rule of thumb is that length should equal the lines-per-inch value times the number of printable inches per page. Most dot-matrix printers print 6 lines per inch on a standard 8 1/2-by-11-inch page; therefore, page length equals 6x11, or 66 lines. The maximum page-length setting for Quattro Pro is 100.

Left Margin

The **L**eft margin command determines how much space is left between the left edge of the paper and the first column of data. The default setting is 4 characters, or approximately 1/2 inch. Choose **L**eft and enter a new setting to change the left margin. The maximum left margin setting for Quattro Pro is 254.

Be careful that you don't choose a left margin setting that is to the right of the right margin setting—for example, left margin equal to 80 and right margin equal to 30. In such a case, Quattro Pro cannot print your notebook and displays an error message requesting that you change the margin settings.

Top Margin

The **T**op margin command determines how much space is left between the top edge of the paper and the first row of data. The default setting is 2 rows, or approximately 1/3 inch. To change the default, choose **T**op and enter a new setting. The maximum setting is 32, or about 5 1/3 inches.

> Quattro Pro reserves three lines at the top and bottom of a page for headers and footers, whether or not the document has headers and footers, when **B**reak Pages is set to **Y**es. The top and bottom margin settings are in addition to these three lines.

NOTE

Right Margin

The **R**ight margin command determines the space to leave between the left edge of the paper and the beginning of the right margin. The default setting is 76 characters, leaving approximately 1/2 inch at the right margin. To change the default, choose **R**ight and enter a new setting. The maximum setting is 511.

Bottom Margin

The **B**ottom margin command determines the number of blank lines to leave at the bottom of each page. The default setting is 2 rows, or approximately 1/3 inch. To change the default, choose **B**ottom and enter a new setting. The maximum setting is 32, or 5 1/3 inches.

Defining Dimensions

By default, Quattro Pro specifies the page length and margin settings in terms of characters. The default size of a character is 1/10 inch horizontally and 1/6 inch vertically. Rather than specify the margins and page length in terms of characters, you may want to use inches or centimeters. Choose /**P**rint **L**ayout **D**imensions and choose the measurement system you prefer.

The measurement system that Quattro Pro uses is important because the layout settings control where text appears on a printout. Using the Inches measurement system, for example, shows **L**ayout submenu command settings in terms of inches or fractions of inches. The top and bottom margins may be 0.5 inches, the page-length setting may be 8.5 inches, and so on.

Settings that affect the top-to-bottom orientation of a printout—page length and top and bottom margins—generally are expressed in terms of lines. On the other hand, settings that shift printouts left or right on the paper—left and right margins—are expressed in terms of characters.

TIP

> Defining margins in terms of lines and characters is easiest when **D**estination is set to Draft **P**rinter. In inches, defining margins is easiest when **D**estination is set to **G**raphics Printer.

Choosing a Print Orientation

By default, Quattro Pro prints a notebook in portrait (vertical) orientation. By choosing the **O**rientation command, you can print a report in landscape (horizontal) or banner orientation.

To print a notebook in landscape orientation, follow these steps:

1. Choose /**P**rint **L**ayout **O**rientation.

2. Choose **L**andscape.

The **D**estination command must be set to **G**raphics Printer, or Quattro Pro cannot print a notebook with landscape orientation.

A third orientation option enables you to print sideways across several sheets of continuous-feed paper. The **B**anner option performs landscape printing, minus the usual page breaks. Rather than eject the first page before printing the second page, Quattro Pro prints a continuous stream of text. Banner-style printing requires continuous-feed paper, so laser-printer owners cannot use this orientation style.

Except for the right margin setting, Quattro Pro applies all header and margin settings in banner printing. Quattro Pro ignores the right margin setting because a banner's right margin is determined by the size of your print block. Quattro Pro prints sideways from left to right until the entire print block is printed.

> When you save a notebook, Quattro Pro automatically saves the **O**rientation setting. If you later want to print the notebook, your original orientation setting is intact.

TIP

Using Setup Strings

All printers require codes to create non-standard printing effects such as underlining, compressed and enhanced printing, and character strikethrough. Many manufacturers enable you to choose various printing modes directly from your printer's control panel. If you cannot achieve a certain printing effect from your panel, Quattro Pro enables you to send the control codes directly to your printer by means of the **S**etup String command.

Because each manufacturer uses a different set of printer codes, you need to refer to your printer manual for a list of the available printing effects and their corresponding codes. When you enter a printer code, you must supply the code in keyboard terms (the ASCII code equivalent) before entering the code as a setup string.

To print the sample notebook in compressed mode, for example, follow these steps:

1. Choose /**P**rint **L**ayout **S**etup String.

2. When you are prompted, type the appropriate setup string and press Enter. For this example, type **\027(s16.66H** (the compressed printing code for an HP LaserJet) and then press Enter to accept the setup string (see fig. 9.7).

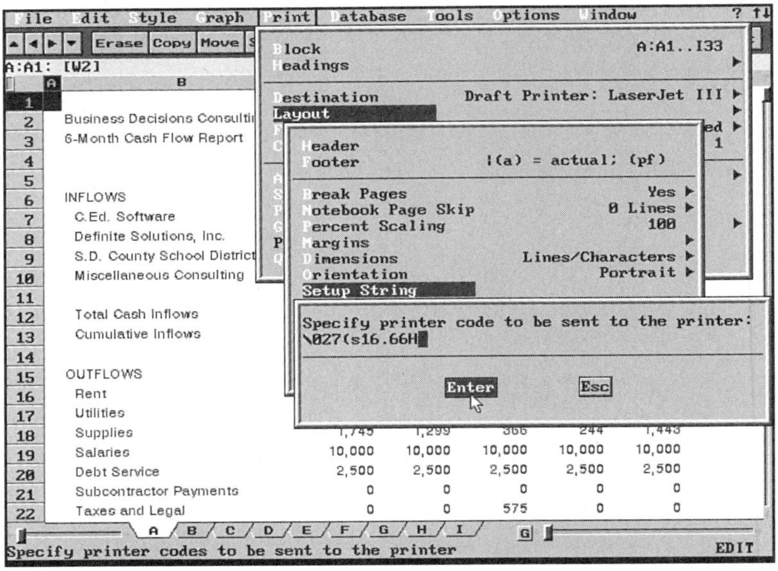

Fig. 9.7

Adding a setup string to a notebook report.

<table>
<tr><td colspan="11">File Edit Style Graph Print Database Tools Options Window   ? ↑↓</td></tr>
</table>

TIP

You also can send a compressed print instruction to Quattro Pro when the /**P**rint **D**estination command is set to **G**raphics Printer. Choose the /**S**tyle **F**ont command, select the block you want to compress, choose the **P**oint Size option, and then choose a 6- or 8-point font.

Setup strings are printer-dependent. The \015 compressed mode printing string, for example, works for most IBM dot-matrix and Epson-compatible printers, and for some OKIDATA printers. Other printers use different setup strings for compressed-mode printing. If you own an OKIDATA Microline, for example, you must enter **\029**; for the Toshiba P1350, enter **\027\091**. Check your printer manual for the specific codes when you want to enter setup strings into your notebooks.

Quattro Pro displays the new setting in the right margin of the Layout submenu, next to the command.

You can combine two or more printing effects by typing multiple setup strings one after another. Valid setup strings may contain up to 39 characters; you cannot enter spaces between strings.

The **S**etup String command causes the printer to apply the printer codes to the entire printed notebook. To create two printing effects for different parts of the same notebook, you can embed extra printer codes in a notebook.

To embed a setup string in a notebook, type two vertical-bar characters (| |) and then the setup string in a blank cell just above the area where you want to create the second printing effect. This cell must be in the first column of the print block. If the code appears in any other column in the print block, Quattro Pro will ignore it.

To embed the IBM setup string that cancels compressed-mode printing on a dot-matrix printer and to print the rest of a document in draft mode, follow these steps:

1. Select a blank cell directly above where you want to begin printing in draft mode, and make that cell active.

2. Type | |\018.

3. Press Enter to embed the setup string.

Cells that follow this code now reflect this print setting.

Updating and Resetting the Layout Options

If you find that you use the same custom print settings for all your printouts, you can store the values permanently by choosing the /**P**rint Layout **U**pdate command.

To restore a notebook's saved defaults, choose the /**P**rint Layout **R**eset command (see fig. 9.8). Quattro Pro displays a menu of four choices. Choose **A**ll to reset all **P**rint menu settings, **P**rint Block to reset only the current print-block settings, **H**eadings to reset print headings, or **L**ayout to reset all settings stored in the **L**ayout submenu.

Fig. 9.8

The **R**eset command resets some or all print-layout settings.

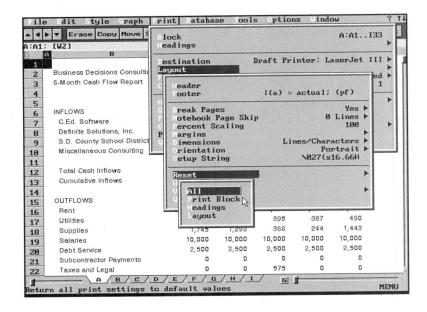

FOR RELATED INFORMATION

▶▶ "Converting ASCII Codes into Printer Setup Strings," p. 868.
How to create printer setup strings using information found in the software codes section of your printer manual.

▶▶ "Setting Display Mode Options," p. 788.
How to use extended text mode display settings, which enable you to see more columns and rows than you normally see in a notebook.

▶▶ "Choosing Printers," p. 767.
How to configure Quattro Pro to work with your printer, including choosing layout options on the **P**rint menu, configuring a second printer, and choosing a different resolution setting.

Using Other Print Commands

In the following sections, you learn how to use various other **P**rint menu commands to control the appearance of your printouts. These commands are useful for fine-tuning a print operation when changing the options in the /**P**rint **L**ayout menu doesn't seem to address a situation.

In the next few sections, you learn how to change the display format that Quattro Pro normally uses to print a selected print block, how to print multiple copies of a document, how to adjust paper in your printer before printing, and how to force Quattro Pro to print a wide document on paper of a certain size without incurring the text-wrapping effect described earlier in the section "Printing Large Notebook Reports."

Choosing the Display Format

After you choose the /**P**rint **F**ormat command, Quattro Pro displays the Format submenu. The **C**ell-Formulas format displays the address, the numeric format, the column-width settings, and the contents of each cell in the print block. This display format provides you a quick way to ensure that data was entered into cells correctly. Figure 9.9 shows the result of using this format to print block B1..D13 in the sample notebook. Notice that each printed line looks like what you would see on the input line if you had put the selector on the cell.

```
A:B2:  [W29] 'Business Decisions Consulting, Inc.
A:B3:  [W29] '6-Month Cash Flow Report
A:C4:  [W9] "Jan
A:D4:  [W9] "Feb
A:C5:  [W9] "(a)
A:D5:  [W9] "(a)
A:B6:  [W29] 'INFLOWS
A:B7:  [W29] '  C.Ed. Software
A:C7:  (,0) [W9] 8629
A:D7:  (,0) [W9] 846
A:B8:  [W29] '  Definite Solutions, Inc.
A:C8:  (,0) [W9] 8187
A:D8:  (,0) [W9] 8430
A:B9:  [W29] '  S.D. County School District
A:C9:  (,0) [W9] 1259
A:D9:  (,0) [W9] 8005
A:B10: [W29] '  Miscellaneous Consulting
A:C10: (,0) [W9] 4000
A:D10: (,0) [W9] 8809
A:B12: [W29] '  Total Cash Inflows
A:C12: (,0) [W9] @SUM(C7..C10)
A:D12: (,0) [W9] @SUM(D7..D10)
A:B13: [W29] '  Cumulative Inflows
A:C13: (,0) [W9] +C12
A:D13: (,0) [W9] +C13+D12
```

Fig. 9.9

A notebook printed in **C**ell-Formulas format.

The printout shown in figure 9.9 doesn't list many of the cells that are part of the print block—for example, cells B1, B4, B5, and B11—because when you use **C**ell-Formulas format, Quattro Pro prints only cells that contain data. When you print a notebook in **C**ell-Formulas format, Quattro Pro also ignores formatting specifications such as page breaks, headers, and margins.

Specifying the Number of Copies

The /**P**rint **C**opies command enables you to specify how many copies of a particular notebook to print. Valid numbers of copies range from 1 (the default) through 1,000. If you choose a large number of copies, be sure that you have enough paper on hand to complete the operation.

Adjusting the Printer

The **A**djust Printer submenu commands help you position paper in your printer. This submenu offers three commands: **S**kip Line moves the paper forward one line, **F**orm Feed advances the paper to the top of the next page, and **A**lign tells Quattro Pro that the paper in your printer is positioned at the top of the page.

TIP

Before sending data to a printer, make sure that your printer is on-line and supplied with paper.

You always must align the paper in your printer before printing, whether you use a dot-matrix or a laser printer. To tell Quattro Pro that the paper is aligned and ready for printing, choose /**P**rint **A**djust Printer **A**lign and then press Enter (see fig. 9.10).

When you execute the **A**lign command, nothing changes on-screen. The only way to check whether you correctly issued the command is to view a printout. When you see large blank areas in the middle of a printout where there should be a continuous block of text, Quattro Pro is using the wrong top-of-page location. To fix this problem, reset the paper to the top of the page and issue the **A**lign command before printing again.

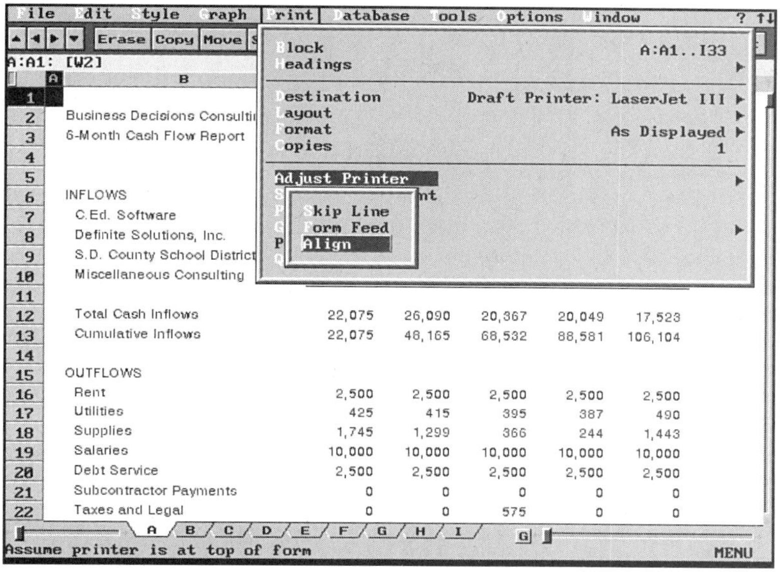

Fig. 9.10

The **A**djust Printer submenu.

Whenever the Form Feed light on your laser printer is lit, a single page is waiting to be printed. You can eject the page manually by taking your printer off-line and then pressing the Form Feed button, or you can use the /**P**rint **A**djust Printer **F**orm Feed command to eject the final page in a printout (or the first page, when you are printing only one page).

If you own a daisywheel printer, you also can use the commands in the **A**djust Printer submenu to prepare your printer for printing. Choose the **S**kip Line and **F**orm Feed commands to move your paper so that the print head is placed at the top of a page. Then use the **A**lign command to notify Quattro Pro that the paper is set to the top of the form in your printer.

Printing a Notebook that Fits

The /**P**rint **P**rint-To-Fit command is useful when your print block is too large to fit on a single page. When you choose **P**rint-To-Fit, Quattro Pro automatically adjusts the point size of the fonts so that the printout fits on a single page. If the print block is so large that it cannot fit on a single page, Quattro Pro prints the block on as few pages as possible.

The shrinking of font point sizes takes place behind the scenes; you don't see notebook data shrinking on-screen. This command operates in WYSIWYG and text (or extended text) display modes, but **Gr**aphics Printer must be the print destination.

You cannot use the /**P**rint **L**ayout **P**ercent Scaling command with the /**P**rint **P**rint-To-Fit command. When you use the **P**rint-To-Fit command, Quattro Pro ignores the setting for the **P**ercent Scaling command.

FOR RELATED **INFORMATION**

▶▶ "Choosing Printers," p. 767.
How to configure Quattro Pro to work with your printer.

Choosing a Print Destination

The commands on the /**P**rint **D**estination menu enable you to specify where Quattro Pro sends a printout. You have two draft-mode and three final-quality destination options, as shown in figure 9.11.

Fig. 9.11

The **D**estination submenu.

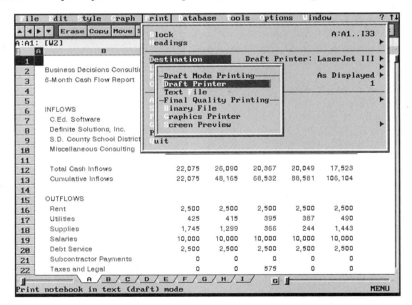

The first, most obvious destination choice is to print a document on a printer. The Draft **P**rinter option is the default destination setting. Choosing this command sends an unformatted, basic printout to your default printer. You also can choose the options described in the following sections.

Printing to a Text File

If you want to import Quattro Pro notebook data into other programs for additional processing, you can print a notebook to a text file. A text file stores only the notebook data and print format settings but doesn't retain presentation-quality options created with the **S**tyle menu commands.

You can import a text file into any program that can read DOS text-file formats because this file format contains only ASCII characters. Most word processing, electronic spreadsheet, and database programs read ASCII text-file formats.

By loading a Quattro Pro text file into a word processing program, you can include notebook data in your reports. To tap the power of a dedicated database program, load a text file into the program and use your notebook data to create a database. (To save a Quattro Pro notebook in a format used by other programs, see "Translating Files" in Chapter 8.)

> **NOTE**
>
> If your default printer is a PostScript-type printer, you must choose **B**inary File as the print destination. See the next section, "Printing to a Binary File," for more details.

To print to a text file, perform the following steps:

1. Choose /**P**rint **D**estination Text **F**ile.

2. At the prompt, type a file name consisting of up to eight characters and press Enter. (Quattro Pro automatically adds a PRN extension to your file name.)

3. Change the print layout and format settings the way you want.

4. Choose **S**preadsheet Print. Quattro Pro writes the data to the file you specified.

5. Choose **Q**uit to quit the **P**rint menu and close the text file.

Quattro Pro doesn't close the text file until you specify another text file, choose a new print destination, or choose **Q**uit to exit the **P**rint menu. As long as you continue to execute commands on the **P**rint menu, Quattro Pro continues to append data to the open text file. To print a second block and include it in the same text file, for example, specify the block and again choose **S**preadsheet Print.

When you quit the **P**rint menu, Quattro Pro closes the text file and adds a PRN extension to the file name.

TIP

> When you create a text file, be sure to use the **A**lign command before and the **F**orm Feed command after printing the document, just as though you are printing the notebook on paper. Your document reproduces correctly when you print the text file on a printer.

To eliminate soft page breaks from the file, set /**P**rint **L**ayout **B**reak Pages to **N**o. The file then will appear as a single, unformatted ASCII text block.

To print a text file on a printer, follow these steps:

1. Choose /**F**ile E**x**it to exit Quattro Pro.

2. Type **copy *filename*.PRN prn** at the DOS prompt.

3. Press Enter to begin printing the data on your printer.

If you remembered to issue a **F**orm Feed command when you created the file, your printer is now reset to the top of the form.

Printing to a Binary File

When you print notebook data to a binary file, unlike with the text file, Quattro Pro records all the presentation-quality settings created with the **S**tyle menu commands.

You can load a binary graphics file into any program that can convert the file into its own graphics file format. A conversion facility that comes with the software usually accomplishes this conversion.

WordPerfect, for example, enables you to create and embed WPG graphics files in your word processing documents. The program also has a facility that converts a binary graphics file to a WPG graphics file. When you print your document in WordPerfect, the program reproduces a near-presentation-quality version of your graph in the word processing document.

To print a notebook to a disk file in binary form, follow these steps:

1. Choose /**P**rint **D**estination **B**inary File.

2. At the prompt, type a file name of up to eight characters and press Enter. (Quattro Pro automatically adds a PRN extension to the file name.)

3. Return to the **P**rint menu to change the print layout and format settings.

4. Choose **S**preadsheet Print. Quattro Pro writes the data to the file you specified.

5. Choose **Q**uit to return to the **P**rint menu and close the text file.

Like with a text file, Quattro Pro doesn't close a binary file until you specify another text file, choose a new print destination, or quit the **P**rint menu. Quattro Pro then closes the file and adds a PRN extension to the file name.

> **NOTE**
> The only way to tell the difference between a text file and a binary file created from the same notebook is that the binary file is much larger than the text file.

To print a binary file on a printer, follow these steps:

1. Choose /**F**ile **E**xit to exit Quattro Pro.

2. Type **copy** *filename***.PRN /b lpt1** at the DOS prompt.

> **NOTE**
> This command sequence sends the binary file to the LPT1 printer port. If your printer is connected to a different port, type that port address in place of LPT1, or use PRN as the destination when you aren't sure of the port designation for your printer.

3. Press Enter to begin printing the data on your printer.

Printing to a Graphics Printer

Graphics Printer is one of three final-version printing options available in the /Print Destination menu. Actually, you can achieve two different results with this command, depending on the current /Options Graphics Quality command setting.

When /Options Graphics Quality is set to Draft, the Graphics Printer command in the Destination submenu produces draft-graphics-quality printouts. This style of printout contains all the presentation-quality graphics that you expect, such as drawn lines, shaded cells, and custom fonts. This printout is considered to be draft-quality because if Quattro Pro encounters a Bitstream font that hasn't been rendered, the program substitutes a Hershey font rather than pause to render the font.

When /Options Graphics Quality is set to Final, the Graphics Printer command on the Destination submenu produces final-graphics-quality printouts. Like the draft-graphics-quality printouts, this style contains presentation-quality graphics. If Quattro Pro encounters a Bitstream font that hasn't been rendered, however, the program pauses to render the font before printing the final graphics version.

NOTE

Quattro Pro must render a Bitstream font only once. You then can use the font immediately in other notebooks; Quattro Pro doesn't stop to render the font again.

To produce a final draft version of a report that contains presentation-quality settings, choose the Graphics Printer option from the Destination submenu.

Previewing a Printout On-Screen

Before you print a notebook, you can use Quattro Pro's Screen Preview feature to see how the notebook will look on a printed page. To use this feature, choose Screen Preview from the /Print Destination menu and then choose Spreadsheet Print. With Screen Preview as a destination, Quattro Pro displays the notebook in the form the notebook will take when printed (as though Destination were set to Graphics Printer), including all the special print settings and presentation-quality options (see fig. 9.12).

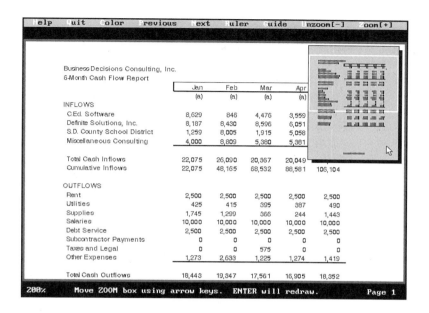

Fig. 9.12

The Screen Previewer.

The Screen Previewer displays a group of commands at the top of the screen, as listed in table 9.1.

Table 9.1 Screen Previewer Command Options

Command	Description
Help	Invokes a context-sensitive help window
Quit	Quits to the active notebook
Color	Toggles between a black-and-white and color screen
Previous	Displays the preceding page of the print job
Next	Displays the next page of the print job
Ruler	Overlays a 1-inch grid on-screen
Guide	Displays a miniature page in the upper right corner of the screen in a zoomed view (refer to fig. 9.12); press the arrow keys to move the box around the miniature page and then press Enter once to relocate the screen to that portion of the notebook
Unzoom[–]	Shrinks the display, moving down one zoom level
Zoom[+]	Enlarges the display by 100, 200, or 400 percent

Use any of the following methods to choose a Screen Previewer command:

■ Press the boldface letter key in a command name.

■ Click the command with the mouse.

■ Press / to activate the command bar, use the arrow keys to highlight the desired command, and then press Enter.

While you are viewing a notebook report in the Screen Previewer, you can use the keys listed in table 9.2 to navigate through the report.

Table 9.2 Screen Previewer Navigation Keys

Key	Description
Esc	Exits the Screen Previewer
Arrow keys	Scrolls a zoomed display in four directions
Page Up	Moves to the preceding page
Page Down	Moves to the next page
Home	Displays the top of a zoomed page
End	Displays the bottom of a zoomed page
Del	Removes the page guide when a page is zoomed
F1	Displays Screen Previewer help
Ins	Redisplays the page guide for a zoomed display

In text-display mode, you must preview notebook printouts to see presentation-quality settings such as drawn lines, shaded cells, and custom fonts.

Previewing a notebook often reveals incorrect fonts, missing text, and so on. These mistakes occur because, in text-display mode, Quattro Pro uses graphics characters to display some on-screen presentation-quality settings. When you draw lines in a notebook, for example, Quattro Pro inserts extra spaces between rows and columns.

You sometimes don't know what effect the presentation-quality settings have until you preview your notebook. When you insert a font with a large point size into a cell, for example, Quattro Pro doesn't display the font. Instead, the program assigns a font code to the cell; the code tells Quattro Pro which font to use for printing.

You must return to the notebook and increase column widths to accommodate larger fonts and lopped-off text, or you must enlarge the print-block setting in the **Print** menu so that all drawn lines appear in the printout.

> WYSIWYG display mode is the most direct method of previewing the presentation-quality version of a notebook or graph. Switch to WYSIWYG display mode by choosing /**O**ptions **D**isplay Mode **B**: WYSIWYG. Quattro Pro shows you exactly how your notebook will look when printed.

TIP

Previewing Print Blocks

When you are in WYSIWYG display mode, you can tell Quattro Pro to display your print block and page breaks with dotted lines. You then can continue to edit the document and resize the print block accordingly before printing. Data that you add to the document falls outside the print block when the print block is full.

This preview feature also enables you to see whether your page breaks are in the correct places. If not, you can insert page breaks manually.

To display print blocks, follow these steps:

1. Set the /**Print Destination** command to **Binary File, Graphics Printer,** or **Screen Preview.**

2. Make sure that your screen display is in WYSIWYG display mode.

3. Choose /**Window Options Print Block Display.**

The print-block and page-break lines remain visible until you choose /**Window Options Print Block Hide** or choose a print destination other than **Graphics Printer, Screen Preview,** or **Binary File.** Quattro Pro saves the current print-block setting with a notebook.

Printing Graphs

To print a Quattro Pro graph, your printer must support a graphics character set. As a rule, most dot-matrix and all laser, inkjet, and thermal wax transfer printers can print graphics images. Daisywheel printers cannot print Quattro Pro graphs because these printers are designed to produce text-only printouts.

When you choose the **G**raph Print command, Quattro Pro displays the **G**raph Print submenu (see fig. 9.13). The commands on this submenu are similar to those that you use to control the printing of notebook reports, except that these commands control the printing of graphs.

Fig. 9.13

The **G**raph Print submenu.

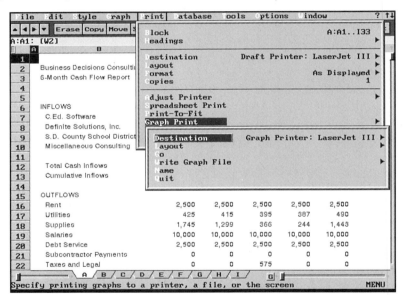

The basic procedure for printing a graph follows:

1. Choose /**F**ile **R**etrieve and retrieve a notebook file.

2. Choose /**P**rint **G**raph Print **N**ame and select a graph to print.

3. Change the layout options on the **L**ayout submenu as desired.

4. Choose **A**djust Printer **A**lign from the **P**rint menu to align your printer to the top of the form.

5. Choose **G**raph Print **G**o.

After you execute the command, Quattro Pro begins printing the current graph.

Choosing a Destination

Three options appear on the /**P**rint **G**raph Print **D**estination menu: Binary **F**ile, **G**raph Printer, and **S**creen Preview. The default setting is **G**raph Printer.

If you choose Binary **F**ile, Quattro Pro prints the graph to a disk file. You print a graph to a file by using the procedure for saving a notebook in binary file format.

The **S**creen Preview option tells Quattro Pro to display the graph so that you can preview the graph's final printed form. The preview feature works exactly the same for a graph as for a notebook (see fig. 9.14). See "Previewing a Printout On-Screen" earlier in this chapter for details on the **S**creen Preview option.

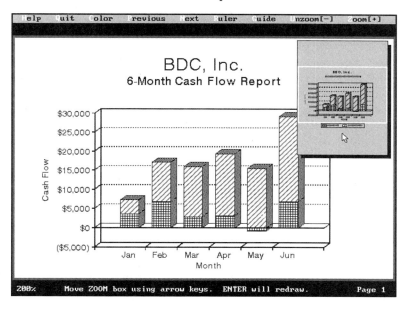

Fig. 9.14

Previewing a graph before printing.

Creating the Layout of the Graph

Choose **Layout** to access commands that enable you to alter the margins, size, page orientation, and aspect ratio of the printed graph (see fig. 9.15). These options are described in the following sections.

Fig. 9.15

The /**P**rint **G**raph Print **L**ayout menu.

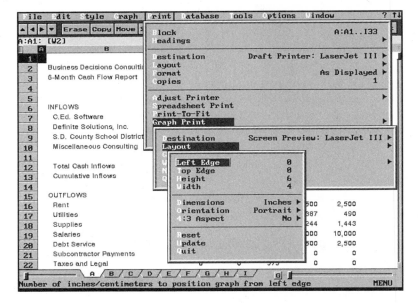

Setting the Graph Margins

By altering the margin settings in the Layout submenu, you can create a graph of virtually any size. These settings consist of the **Left Edge**, **Top Edge**, **Height**, and **Width** options.

The **Left Edge** option defines the distance between the left edge of the paper and the location where Quattro Pro prints a graph. The **Top Edge** option defines the distance between the top edge of the paper and the location where Quattro Pro prints a graph. The **Height** and **Width** options determine the height and width of the graph.

The **Dimensions** option specifies whether the edge and size settings are measured in inches or centimeters. This command is similar to the /**Print Layout Dimensions** command. The default setting for this command is **Inches**.

Positioning and Scaling the Graph

You can use the **O**rientation option to change the orientation of the graph on a printed page. Just as you can with a notebook, you can print a graph in **P**ortrait or **L**andscape orientation.

The **4**:3 Aspect option determines whether Quattro Pro uses the default margin settings or prints a graph with your preferred settings. By default, this option is set to **Y**es. In the default condition, every Quattro Pro graph has a size ratio of 4 to 3. If you want Quattro Pro to print a graph to your own margin specifications, choose **N**o; Quattro Pro scales a graph to fit precisely within the area you defined.

> In Chapter 10, "Creating Graphs," you learn how to insert a graph into a notebook. When you want to insert a graph so that the graph fills any notebook block that you highlight, set the **4**:3 Aspect option to **N**o.

TIP

Figure 9.15 shows the **L**ayout submenu with four custom command settings. The **L**eft Edge, **T**op Edge, **H**eight, and **W**idth commands are set to 0, 0, 6, and 4, respectively. To enable these commands to go into effect for printing, the **4**:3 Aspect command is set to **N**o.

> When all the margin settings are 0, Quattro Pro sizes the graph automatically. Because changing any setting disables automatic sizing, try to set parameters for all the settings if you want to change one setting. If you set a top edge of 2 inches and leave the other settings at 0, for example, Quattro Pro may do strange things when it prints the graph.

NOTE

Sometimes when you alter the shape of a graph, Quattro Pro pauses to render additional fonts. This hesitation occurs whenever the **L**ayout submenu command settings are far enough from the default conditions that Quattro Pro requires different font sizes.

Updating and Resetting the Layout Options

Choose the /**P**rint **G**raph Print **L**ayout **U**pdate option to replace the default graph-layout settings with new settings. To restore the last saved set of defaults, choose the **R**eset option.

Depending on the speed of your personal computer, Quattro Pro may need some time preparing a graph image for printing. If you need to halt the printing process, press Ctrl+Break. Quattro Pro returns to the active page.

Creating a Special Graph File

You can load a Quattro Pro graph into any graphics-image editing program that can read EPS or PIC file formats. You can load EPS files into desktop-publishing programs such as Ventura Publisher and Page-Maker and into word processing programs such as Borland's Sprint, WordPerfect, and Freelance. Some programs (such as WordPerfect) have built-in conversion utilities that enable you to convert EPS or PIC files into formats that can be loaded and modified from within the program.

When you choose the /**P**rint **G**raph Print **W**rite Graph File command, Quattro Pro displays the submenu shown in figure 9.16.

Fig. 9.16

The **W**rite Graph File submenu.

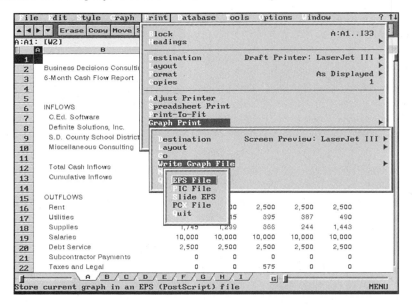

Choose **E**PS File to convert a graph to an encapsulated PostScript file format. (To print an EPS file, you must have a PostScript printer.) Choose **P**IC to convert a graph to a file format that Lotus 1-2-3 can access.

The **S**lide EPS command, like the **E**PS File command, creates an encapsulated PostScript file. Both commands convert Quattro Pro's Bitstream fonts into the closest PostScript font. The difference is that the **S**lide EPS command creates a file that contains the exact specifications needed to create 35mm slides. With such a file, any graphics-production company can reproduce your graph's color combinations, screen orientation, and height-to-width ratio in 35mm slide form.

The PC**X** File command creates a file in PC Paintbrush format, the most widely used graphics file format. You can edit PCX files in a graphics editor program such as PC Paintbrush or Microsoft Paintbrush. After you load a PCX graph file into a graphics editor program, use the program tools to modify the graph. You cannot, however, modify a PCX graph file—or any graph file, for that matter—and then bring the file back into Quattro Pro. Likewise, any changes that you make in a PCX graph file with a graphics editor program don't affect the original Quattro Pro graph. To see these changes, retrieve the original Quattro Pro notebook and press F10 to display the graph again.

> **TIP**
>
> Although you can create 35mm slides from PCX and EPS graph files, the final display resolution of the file types varies. The crispness of an image produced from a PCX graph file depends on your screen's resolution. Alternatively, because EPS graph-file resolution is output-device-dependent, devices that support higher resolution settings than your screen display can produce higher-resolution output from an EPS graph file.

FOR RELATED INFORMATION

▶▶ "Creating a Basic Graph," p. 495.
The quickest way to create a Quattro Pro graph.

Managing Multiple Print Jobs

With Quattro Pro's Print Spooler feature, you can continue to work with your notebooks after sending multiple print jobs to the printer. The Borland Print Spooler program (BPS.COM) collects print jobs, temporarily saves them to your hard disk drive, and then releases control of Quattro Pro to you. This process is known as *background printing*. While you continue to work with the current notebook, the Print Spooler sends print data to the printer "in the background."

The Quattro Pro Print Manager enables you to keep track of and manipulate multiple print jobs. You can view each job's status and delete or suspend selected print jobs.

Printing in the Background

To print jobs in the background with Quattro Pro, you must do two things: load the BPS.COM program into your PC's memory before loading Quattro Pro and then activate background printing with the /Options **H**ardware **P**rinters **B**ackground command.

NOTE

Always load the BPS.COM program first, *before* you load other TSR programs into memory. Also, if you include BPS.COM in your AUTOEXEC.BAT file so that it automatically loads into memory each time you start your computer, don't load the program into high memory with the LH command.

To load the BPS.COM program into your PC's memory, start at the DOS command prompt before you load Quattro Pro. Then follow these steps:

1. Type **bps** and press Enter.

2. Press **Q** to load Quattro Pro and press Enter.

TIP

You can load the Borland Print Spooler program with command-line options that define how the program will operate with your PC. If you prefer, after you type **bps** you can include the following options on the command line:

S*n*   Sets the transfer speed rate at which information is sent to the printer, where *n* is a number between 0 and 9 (0 is the slowest). The default setting is 3.

C*n*   Sets the asynchronous communication handshake, where *n* is one of the following: 0 = none; 1 = Xon/Xoff; 2 = DTR then CTS/DSR (the default); and 3 = CTS only.

After loading BPS.COM, make sure that the /Options **H**ardware **P**rinters **B**ackground command is set to **Y**es (the default setting). This command tells Quattro Pro that if BPS.COM is loaded into memory, Quattro Pro should send all print jobs to the Borland Print Spooler. Now when you print in Quattro Pro, the Print Spooler, not Quattro Pro, manages the print jobs.

The Borland Print Spooler program stores print jobs in temporary files, creating and saving these files to your hard disk. Large, complex print jobs necessarily require large temporary files and can use a significant amount of disk space. If you have a limited amount of space available on your hard disk drive, you may want to free additional space—at least 1M is a good rule—before trying to print large jobs in the background.

The Borland Print Spooler program remains in your PC's memory until you unload the program or turn off your PC. To remove the Print Spooler from memory without turning off your PC, follow these steps:

1. Choose /File Exit to exit Quattro Pro.

2. At the DOS command prompt, type **bps u** and press Enter.

If you unload the Print Spooler or turn off your PC while print jobs are in the queue, and then reload the Print Spooler and load Quattro Pro, the Print Spooler resumes its processing of any print jobs left in the queue. If you don't want print jobs from former sessions to print, delete all files with an SPL file extension from your hard disk before you load Quattro Pro.

> **CAUTION**
>
> The Print Spooler doesn't replace—and may conflict with—a network print spooler. If you choose to use the Print Spooler on a network, load the program before you load the network shell. If you encounter problems, use the network spooler or the Borland Print Spooler—not both. (See Appendix B for more information on using Quattro Pro on a network.)

Monitoring Multiple Print Jobs

After you send multiple print jobs to the Print Spooler, you can view their status by choosing /Print Print **M**anager. In the Print Manager window that appears, you can view, delete, suspend, and resume print jobs. When the Print Spooler isn't loaded, Quattro Pro displays the message No queue selected in the Print Manager window.

NOTE

If the default printer's device is a network queue, the Print Manager window displays a NetWare print queue. This Print Manager window contains slightly different information from the BPS queue window. You will see, for example, information about the print banner, a description of the program from which you printed (such as Quattro Pro), and a print job number.

The Print Manager window includes six information columns that track the progress of all print jobs residing in the print queue (see fig. 9.17). These columns include the following:

- *Seq.* Displays the sequence in which your print jobs are printing.

- *File Name.* Displays the temporary file name that Quattro Pro has assigned to each print job in the queue. These names resemble QPPRN1.SPL, QPPRN2.SPL, and so on.

- *Status.* Displays messages about the status of the current print job. The message Active indicates that the print job now is printing; Ready indicates that the print job is ready to print and is waiting its turn in the queue; and Held indicates that the print job has been suspended.

- *Port.* Shows the location to which you are printing, as determined by the /**O**ptions **H**ardware **P**rinters **1**st (or **2**nd) Printer **D**evice setting.

- *File Size.* Displays the size (in bytes) of each temporary print-job file.

- *Copies.* Shows the number of copies that will be printed for each print job, as determined by the /**P**rint **C**opies setting.

TIP

To change how often Quattro Pro updates the information in the Print Manager window, choose /**O**ptions **N**etwork **R**efresh Interval and enter a lower or higher refresh-interval setting. The default setting is 30 (seconds).

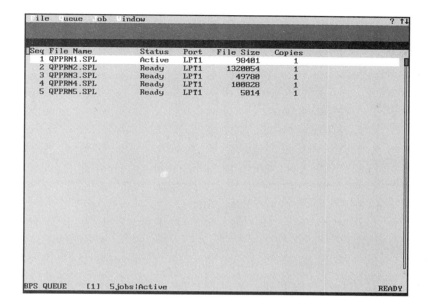

Fig. 9.17

The Print Manager window, with five print jobs in the print queue.

Changing the Status of Print Jobs

When you are working in the Print Manager window, Quattro Pro displays a unique menu bar. You access the commands from this menu bar as you do any Quattro Pro command and use them to control the progress of a selected print job in the print queue. Table 9.3 lists the commands in the Print Manager menu bar.

> **TIP**
>
> To select a print job, highlight it by using your arrow keys, click it, or press Shift+F7 (the Select key) or Alt+F7 (the Select All key). In figure 9.17, print job number 1 is the selected print job.

Table 9.3 Print Manager Menu Bar Commands

Command	Function
/File Close	Closes the Print Manager window
/File Close All	Closes all open windows
/Queue Background	Enables you to view the BPS (DOS) queue

(continues)

Table 9.3 Continued

Command	Function
/Queue Network	Enables you to choose a network print queue to display in the window
/Job Delete	Deletes a print job from the queue
/Job Hold	Holds a print job in the queue and keeps the job from printing
/Job Release	Releases a print job that has been held in the queue to resume printing

NOTE

The commands in the **W**indow menu in the Print Manager window are the same as those available in a notebook window.

Figure 9.18 shows the menu that appears when you are about to delete a print job from the print queue. Choose **Yes** to delete the selected print job or **No** to cancel the current operation and return to the Print Manager window.

Fig. 9.18

Deleting a print job from the Print Manager print queue.

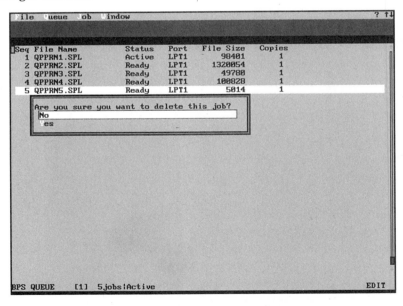

▶▶ "Adding Users to the Network," p. 856.
How to prepare a new workstation to operate Quattro Pro—
specifically, how to prepare a workstation so that it can print to
a network printer.

▶▶ "What's Different about Using Quattro Pro on a Network," p. 858.
Issues that everyone using Quattro Pro on a network should know
about. Also, a quick reference table of Quattro Pro's network features.

FOR RELATED INFORMATION

Questions & Answers

This chapter introduces the **P**rint menu commands. If you have questions about situations that aren't addressed in the preceding examples, look through this section.

Printing the Notebook

Q: I want to generate a simple printout of a notebook. I specified a print block and selected the **S**preadsheet Print command, but nothing happened. Why?

A: Make sure that your printer is on and in on-line mode.

Also, Quattro Pro may not be able to write to your printer because your printer may be configured incorrectly. Choose /**O**ptions **H**ardware **P**rinters and then reconfigure the **D**efault Printer settings to match your printer's definition.

Q: I am trying to print on legal-size paper. Why isn't my **P**age Length definition creating the exact length I need?

A: Use the /**P**rint **L**ayout **D**imensions command to tell Quattro Pro to use **I**nch measurements. Then specify your page length as 14 inches. Finally, set /**O**ptions **H**ardware **P**rinters **1**st Printer to a legal-mode setting.

Q: Why do the drawn lines in my notebook appear as dots and dashes instead of solid lines?

A: Before you can create a printout that reflects all the presentation-quality options defined in a notebook, specify the **G**raphics Printer options in the **/P**rint **D**estination menu.

Q: Quattro Pro is placing in the middle of my printouts gaps that don't exist in the notebook I am printing. Why?

A: You forgot to issue the **A**djust Printer **A**lign command before printing. When the paper in your printer isn't aligned properly, Quattro Pro cannot recognize where the top of the form is, and the program prints gaps in the printout.

Q: When I tried to print a binary file on my printer, why didn't the printer reproduce the presentation-quality settings I saved with the file?

A: Two situations are possible.

First, make sure that you saved the file by choosing the **B**inary File command from the **D**estination submenu—not the Text **F**ile command. In both cases, Quattro Pro adds a PRN extension to a print file. The only way to tell the difference between a text file and a binary file created from the same notebook is that the binary file is much larger than the text file.

Second, when you print a binary file, you must use the following syntax: COPY *filename*.PRN /B LPT1. (Don't forget to add the PRN extension to the file-name argument.) To print a binary file named DATA.PRN, for example, type **copy data.prn /b lpt1** as the command. To print a text file with the same name, type **copy data.prn prn** as the command.

Q: Why isn't Quattro Pro printing the fonts that I specified in my notebook?

A: Make sure that the **/O**ptions **G**raphics Quality command is set to Final. If this command is set to **D**raft, Quattro Pro doesn't print any Bitstream fonts that aren't rendered already.

Printing a Graph

Q: I am trying to print a graph. When I choose /**P**rint **S**preadsheet Print, my printer hangs up. Why?

A: This procedure isn't correct for printing a graph. You must use the **G**raph Print command to print graphs and the **S**preadsheet Print command to print notebooks.

Q: I printed a graph using landscape orientation. Why are my margin alignments completely wrong?

A: When you print a graph horizontally, the orientation of the margin commands changes—for example, **H**eight becomes **W**idth, and **W**idth becomes **H**eight. Return to the **G**raph Print **L**ayout submenu and switch the definitions for the margin settings.

Q: Why did Quattro Pro cut off the left and right portion of the title text when I printed my graph?

A: Be very careful about choosing new margin, height, and width settings. When you enter a large left margin (say, 6) and choose a large **W**idth setting, Quattro Pro may not have enough space to print an entire report title. In this case, you can alter the margin and aspect settings, shorten the title by selecting the /**G**raph **T**ext command, or do a combination of both.

Summary

This chapter discussed many different methods for printing notebooks and graphs in rough-draft and final-draft form. Having completed this chapter, you now should be able to complete these procedures:

- Print a screen dump of notebook data
- Generate draft-form, cell-listing-form, and final-form printouts of a notebook
- Add headings, headers, and footers to a printout
- Scale a printout so that it fits on one page
- Adjust the margins and page length of a printout
- Print in portrait and landscape orientation
- Add special printing effects with setup strings
- Scale a printout so that it fits onto one page
- Control the movement of paper in your printer
- Print a notebook to text- and binary-file formats
- Use the Screen Previewer feature to examine notebooks and graphs before printing them
- Cause a notebook to print to fit

■ Print a graph on a printer or to a file

■ Adjust the margins and aspect settings to alter the shape of a printed graph

■ Write a graph to PIC and EPS file formats

■ Load the Borland Print Spooler program

■ Open a Print Manager window and track the progress of jobs in the print queue

Chapter 10 introduces the topic of creating graphs in Quattro Pro. You learn the **G**raph menu commands, examine each major component in a graph, and then proceed with a hands-on exercise that teaches two methods for creating a basic graph. The chapter concludes with a preview of some of Quattro Pro's graph enhancing commands, a topic covered in depth in Chapter 11.

Creating Graphs

In previous chapters, you learned how to enter, edit, view, and print notebook data. You also learned how to improve the style of your notebooks and manage multiple documents. Creating versatile, stylish-looking reports is important, yet sometimes getting an overall picture of the data by looking at numbers on a notebook is difficult. In this chapter, you learn how to create, manage, and display Quattro Pro graphs as alternatives and complements to notebooks.

A Quattro Pro graph offers several advantages over a numerical report. Graphs call attention to variations in data. Graphs summarize data, enabling you to consider several different relationships at the same time. Most importantly, graphs disclose trends and pinpoint problem areas that otherwise may go unnoticed on a notebook.

The first section of this chapter reviews the **G**raph menu commands and the system hardware that you need to display Quattro Pro graphs. The next section defines the utility and anatomy of a graph. You learn Quattro Pro's graph terminology, survey each element that makes up a graph, and study the 12 graph styles that Quattro Pro can display.

The sample graphs shown in the first section use realistic applications. After reviewing these sample graphs, you should understand better how to match your data with the most appropriate graph style.

The chapter continues by demonstrating two ways to create a basic Quattro Pro graph: from the ground up and by using the **F**ast Graph command. This command enables you to preview your notebook data as a plain, unformatted graph—an important feature when you have 12 distinct styles from which to choose.

Next, you learn how to enhance the appearance of the basic graph by adding titles, legends, and customized fonts.

The final section in this chapter shows you how to manage graph files. When you save graph settings with a notebook, a change on the notebook is reflected on the graph. Finally, you learn two techniques for displaying your graphs: you can put them in a slide show, and you can insert them as "live graphs" in the notebook from which the graph was created.

NOTE

The rules and techniques for printing Quattro Pro graphs appear in the last section of Chapter 9, "Printing."

Reviewing the Graph Menu

The **G**raph menu consists of three types of commands: graph-building commands, graph customizing commands, and graph management commands (see fig. 10.1). This chapter covers all the graph-building commands (except **A**nnotate) and all the graph management commands. Chapter 11, "Customizing Graphs," offers complete coverage of the graph customizing commands and Quattro Pro's graph annotation tool. Chapter 12, "Analyzing Graphs," introduces you to analytical graphing.

You use the graph-building commands at the top of the **G**raph menu to choose a graph style, to record the location of the data to be graphed, and to add text to the basic graph.

You use the graph customizing commands in the middle of the **G**raph menu to customize an individual data series, to change the x- and y-axis scaling, and to format the background of the whole graph. (Graph customizing commands are covered in Chapter 11, "Customizing Graphs.")

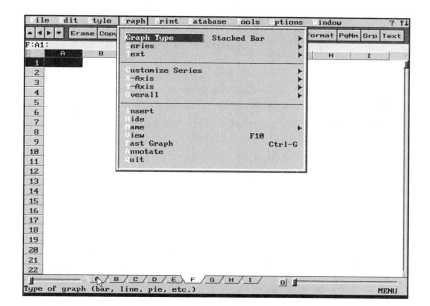

Fig. 10.1

The **G**raph menu commands.

Graph management commands, located at the bottom of the **G**raph menu, perform operations on a graph after the graph is created. With graph management commands, you can insert a graph onto a notebook, assign a graph name to a particular graph, or view a graph on-screen.

The final menu command, **A**nnotate, calls up a Quattro Pro editing tool for adding finishing touches to your graphs. Chapter 11 covers the **A**nnotate command.

Table 10.1 explains the functions of the **G**raph menu commands. Like most other Quattro Pro commands, **G**raph menu commands are intuitive. To use a particular type of graph, for example, choose **G**raph Type; to add text to a graph, choose **T**ext; and to insert a graph into a notebook, choose **I**nsert.

TIP

After you create the basic graph, press F10 to display the graph. As you add features to a graph, you can re-examine the new graph settings by pressing F10 at any time or by choosing /**G**raph **V**iew.

Table 10.1 Graph Menu Commands

Command	Description
Graph Type	Chooses one of 12 graph types
Series	Specifies the notebook cell blocks to graph and performs analytical graphing operations
Text	Adds titles and a legend to a graph and changes the attributes of the text
Customize Series	Customizes the display of a data series
X-Axis	Adjusts the display and scaling of the x-axis
Y-Axis	Adjusts the display and scaling of the y-axis
Overall	Adds lines, patterns, colors, and 3-D effects to parts of a graph
Insert	Inserts a copy of a graph onto a notebook
Hide	Removes a copy of a graph from a notebook
Name	Creates, uses, and deletes named graphs
View	Displays a graph using the current graph settings
Fast Graph	Produces a rudimentary graph using a cell block
Annotate	Activates the Annotator (discussed in Chapter 11, "Customizing Graphs")

Reviewing Hardware Requirements

Quattro Pro enables anyone to create a graph, but to view a graph, your system must have the correct display hardware. Your screen and the display adapter card must be capable of displaying graphics. If your system doesn't have a graphics display adapter, you cannot view a graph on-screen.

If you are using an older PC or XT system, you may not have a graphics display adapter. Although you cannot view graphs on-screen, you still can print them on a graphics printer.

Fortunately, most of today's PCs come equipped with at least a mono-chrome graphics display adapter. (See Appendix A, "Installing and Con-figuring Quattro Pro," for a complete list of the display adapters that Quattro Pro supports.) To view Quattro Pro graphs, you must have one of the following types of display adapter systems or compatibles:

- Hercules monochrome graphics card (MGA or MCGA)

- Color Graphics Adapter (CGA)

- Enhanced Graphics Adapter (EGA)

- Video Graphics Array (VGA)

The monochrome and CGA graphics cards show Quattro Pro graphs in black and white, whereas the EGA and VGA cards show graphs in color. EGA and VGA adapter systems display graphics with a much sharper resolution than the monochrome or CGA systems.

TIP

Choose /**O**ptions **H**ardware **S**creen **R**esolution and pick the highest resolution that your display adapter supports. See "Choosing a New Screen" in Chapter 16 for complete coverage of the **O**ptions menu commands that affect the display of graphs.

If your PC doesn't have any of the preceding graphics systems, you can see your graphs if you have the correct printer or plotter. To view a graph, print the graph to the printer specified by the /**O**ptions **H**ard-ware **P**rinters **D**efault Printer command. If you use a dot-matrix or laser printer, your graph printouts will contain various shades of gray.

FOR RELATED INFORMATION

▶▶ "Setting Up the Ideal System Configuration," p. 820.
How to create an ideal computer environment for Quattro Pro, including the various graphics display standards.

Understanding Graphs

To explain how graphs can provide a clearer medium for analyzing your notebook data, the following sections cover the benefits of graph-ing, the anatomy of a graph, and the types of graphs that Quattro Pro offers.

Utility of Graphs

Graphs help you arrive at conclusions about notebook data. Graphs also point out problem areas with a clarity often not available with even the most comprehensive notebook reports. Figure 10.2 shows a Quarterly Revenue Analysis report for a hypothetical firm, Christensen Advertising.

Fig. 10.2

The Christensen Advertising notebook report.

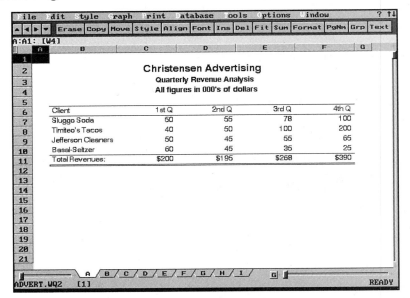

The notebook in figure 10.2 shows that Christensen's revenues nearly doubled over the course of the year (from $200,000 to $390,000). The report also shows that the firm's growth in revenues dipped between the first and second quarters (from $200,000 to $195,000).

Now look at the same report displayed as a stacked-bar graph (see fig. 10.3). Graphs sometimes display data trends that you didn't anticipate.

Take another look at figure 10.3 and see whether you can spot a third, less obvious trend. Notice that during the first and second quarters, revenues were divided pretty evenly among all four clients. In the third and fourth quarters, however, revenues from Basal-Seltzer declined, and revenues from Timiteo's Tacos skyrocketed.

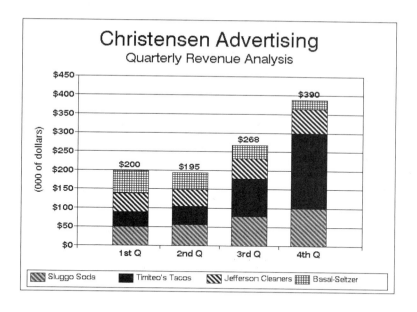

Fig. 10.3

A stacked-bar graph created from Christensen's report.

The stacked-bar graph indicates that something is awry with the Basal-Seltzer account. Did Basal-Seltzer spend less with Christensen and more with other advertisers? Is Basal-Seltzer having fiscal difficulties? Should management now pay special attention to the Timiteo's Tacos account? These are the types of questions an analyst would consider when reviewing this graph.

Graphs can convey in a picture what sometimes is hard to articulate. Imagine the difficulty of evaluating revenue growth trends on a report if Christensen had 100 clients instead of only four.

Anatomy of Graphs

Just as a medical student learns about human anatomy, so must a Quattro Pro user learn about the elements that make up a graph. In this section, you learn about the purpose and function of each part of a Quattro Pro graph, and the terminology that defines each part.

Line graphs show how data changes over time. In this type of graph, the *x-axis* (horizontal axis) represents time, whereas the *y-axis* (vertical axis) represents a data category. When you locate an intersection between the two axes, you have a *data point*.

Most graphs have several data points, each one representing a different intersection between the x- and y-axis. A collection of x-axis data points forms a *data series*, as does a collection of y-axis data points. On a notebook, a data series appears in a cell block. Cell blocks can be vertical, as in block D5..D10, or horizontal, as in block D5..H5. They even can span several pages, as in the 3-D cell block A..C:D5..H5. You tell Quattro Pro which data to display on a graph by specifying the cell block.

Quattro Pro also can use notebook labels when displaying a graph. A block of notebook labels, for example, can appear on a graph to signify a time period (January, February, March, and so on), to identify the parts of a group (Client A, Client B, or Client C), or to display as a title. The range of data points associated with an axis form a *scale*.

Graphs also are used to show the relationship between two or more categories of data; one category is expressed as a function of another. *Function* implies that one of the categories is a dependent variable and the other is an independent variable; the value of one category depends on the value of the second. Business owners, for example, express profit as a function of revenue. When revenue increases, profit also is expected to increase. Profit is the dependent variable, and revenue is the independent variable.

Some research psychologists might graph intelligence as a function of age because of the idea that as people get older, they accumulate more knowledge. In this case, the dependent variable, intelligence, depends on the independent variable, age.

Family physicians plot approximate weight as a function of height to monitor a child's growth. Again, as children get taller (independent variable), they are expected to gain weight (dependent variable).

How do you know when a data category is an independent or a dependent variable? Common sense dictates this relationship most of the time. Consider the family physician example—children don't get taller just because they gain some weight.

Now consider the graph pictured in figure 10.4. This graph expresses the height-weight relationship. The range of height values appears on the x-axis and the range of weight values on the y-axis. Together, the x-axis data points form a data series, as do all the y-axis data points.

Tick marks—the hyphens that cross the axes beside each weight and height—are used to mark off regular intervals in the scale of those axes. Notice that the x-axis is scaled at intervals of 1/2 foot, and the y-axis scale is marked off in intervals of 20 pounds.

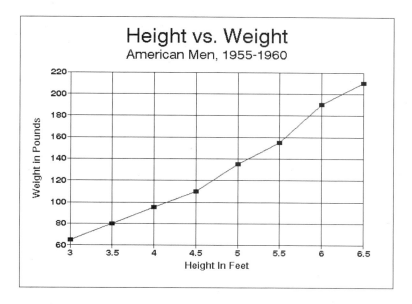

Fig. 10.4

A graph showing the relationship between height and weight for American males.

Each pair of values on a notebook report corresponds to exactly one data point on a graph. In this example, therefore, each height on the x-axis corresponds to a weight on the y-axis. Together, these paired values can be found on the original notebook report.

Quattro Pro can express data relationships using 12 styles of graphs. Many of these graphs share the same anatomy as the examples just described.

Basic Graphs

The first step in the process of creating a basic graph is choosing a graph style for your data. When you choose /**G**raph **G**raph Type in WYSIWYG mode, Quattro Pro displays a Graph Type options box (see fig. 10.5). In text mode, Quattro Pro displays a list of the 12 graph type names.

You often can use two or three graph styles to show the same data. You also can show data on a bar graph, for example, on a rotated bar graph or on a line graph. To change the graph type after you create a graph, again choose the /**G**raph **G**raph Type command and pick a new style.

Fig. 10.5

Choose a graph style from the **G**raph Type submenu.

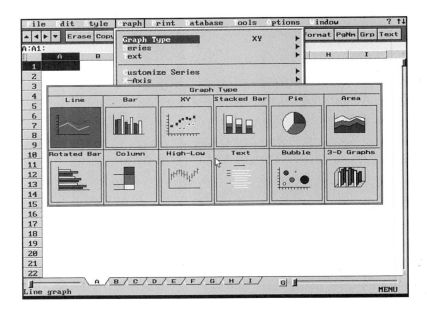

At other times, the data is so specific that it makes sense only when viewed using a particular graph style. The high-low (open-close) graph type, for example, plots a range of prices for a firm's stock. This type of data makes little sense displayed in a pie or column graph.

Take a look at all 12 graph styles. As you examine each style, pay close attention to the types of data that work well with each graph type.

Line Graphs

The line graph—one of the most recognized graph types—provides a useful way to track trends over time and to use current data to predict irregularities. Business and scientific communities use line graphs to show a progression of values over a period of time. A line graph is good, for example, for summarizing monthly sales data from an annual report or for plotting the results of an IQ test taken over an 80-year period. In either case, because time is the independent variable, time is plotted on the x-axis.

Figure 10.6 shows that citizens from country A have higher tested IQs than citizens from countries B and C. This graph reveals a second, more telling trend. Regardless of a country's percentile ranking versus the world, the tested IQs for all three countries declined as their citizens grew older.

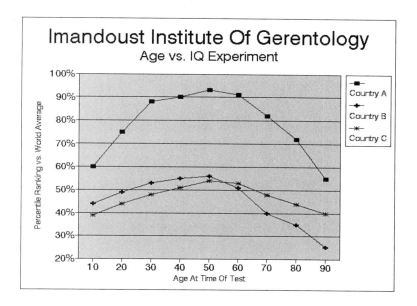

Fig. 10.6

A line graph showing IQ test results over an 80-year period.

Bar Graphs

The bar graph is useful for comparing the values of different items at set periods in time. The primary advantage of a bar graph is that it clearly shows differences in the magnitude of the data: the higher the bar, the bigger or larger the value.

In figure 10.7, the bar graph is used to summarize the results of a six-month crop production report for two products: dates and nuts.

On the bar graph, you easily can spot the peak seasons for dates and nuts by examining the different bar heights. According to this report, date production peaks in February, and nut production peaks in April. Because those months are the peak for harvesting, the months immediately following the peak months have the lowest production.

XY Graphs

The XY graph, also called a *scatter graph*, is different from the graphs discussed so far. This graph type is used commonly in social science research to relate the value of one economic variable to another.

Fig. 10.7

A bar graph showing a six-month crop production report.

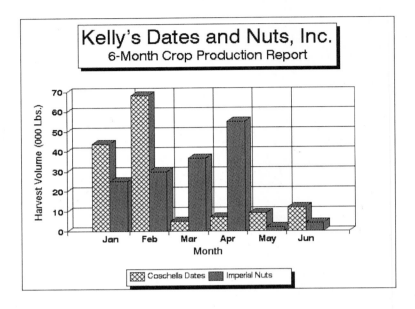

At first glance, an XY graph resembles a line graph. The x-axis and y-axis, however, are scaled with numeric data. In most of the graphs you have seen so far, the x-axis has represented a point in time—for example, a month or a quarter. Generally, XY graphs directly relate one set of data to one or more other sets of data without regard to time.

An XY graph, for example, is useful for showing the relationship between production volume, revenues, and costs for a manufacturing firm. The XY graph shown in figure 10.8 plots a range of production volumes on the x-axis. The x-axis measurement isn't time, but production quantity. The associated costs and revenues at each production level appear on the y-axis. The bottom line is that on an XY graph, the x-axis must display numeric data—not labels or text.

Stacked-Bar Graphs

Stacked-bar graphs are useful for looking at broader performance statistics (total sales) and for evaluating individual performance statistics (territory sales). The stacked-bar graph in figure 10.9 shows total sales per quarter and breaks down sales by territory for each quarter. At first glance, stacked-bar graphs resemble bar graphs.

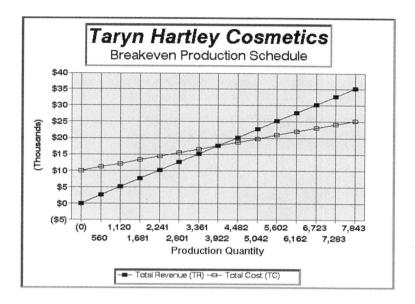

Fig. 10.8

An XY graph showing total revenue, total cost, and production quantity.

To create a stacked-bar graph, Quattro Pro first sums the value of each item in a data set. The program then plots the total value at a specific period in time, showing the contribution that each item makes to the total. The area graph and the pie graph share this latter characteristic.

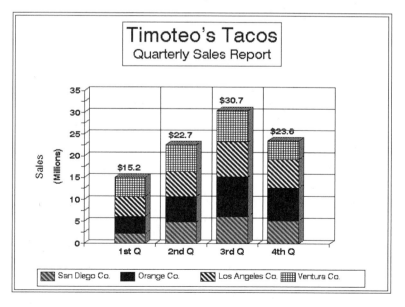

Fig. 10.9

A stacked-bar graph showing total quarterly sales by territory.

Pie Graphs

The pie graph shows the contribution of individual values to a whole. The individual values are called *slices*, and the whole value is called the *pie*. Figure 10.10 shows the percentage of total expenses allocated to each category in a sample household budget.

Fig. 10.10

A pie graph showing allocated expenses in a household budget.

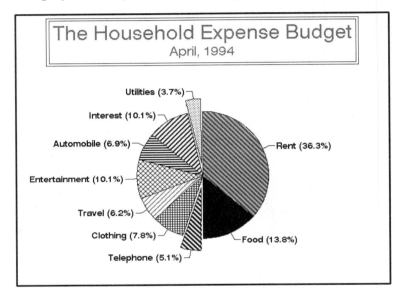

The two smallest pieces of this pie are set slightly out of the pie. This technique, called *exploding*, draws attention to key figures in the graph. Exploding also helps improve the display of pie graph slices that are too small to fit easily in the graph.

Area Graphs

The area graph combines the line graph and bar graph. This graph type emphasizes changes in magnitude (like a bar graph) at a point in time and reveals trends over time (like a line graph). When plotting two or more data series, Quattro Pro stacks each data series on top of the other to convey a sense of "total area" for the graph. Figure 10.11, for example, is a graphic representation of Kelly's 12-month crop production report. A 6-month version of this report appeared in figure 10.7.

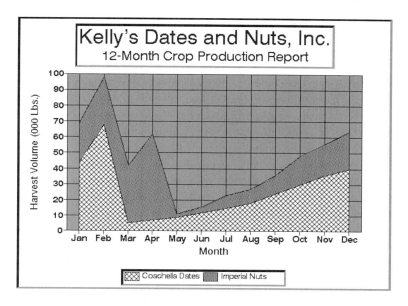

Fig. 10.11

An area graph showing a 12-month crop production report.

This report shows Kelly's total harvest volume for each month and the contribution made individually by dates and nuts. By looking at the entire graph, you also see how Kelly's total date and nut production volume fluctuates during the year.

Rotated Bar Graphs

The rotated bar graph basically is a bar graph turned on its side. Here, the x-axis and y-axis are reversed so that the graph bars extend horizontally. Using a rotated bar graph instead of a bar graph, or vice versa, is solely an aesthetic decision. Typically, you use rotated bar graphs to show the results of a competitive event such as a sales competition, a leg race, or a typing test. Often, this graph type is used to express data already displayed on a bar graph. Figure 10.12 shows the rotated bar graph form of the data displayed in figure 10.9.

Column Graphs

The column graph, like the pie graph, shows the contribution of individual values to a whole. The individual values in a column graph also are called *slices*. Quattro Pro stacks the slices one on top of another to form the column. The column graph provides plenty of room for label descriptions next to each slice.

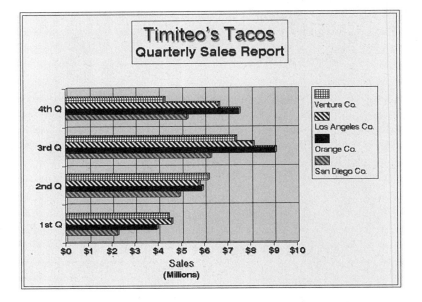

The column graph shown in figure 10.13 displays a typical college student's expense budget. The height of the bar is the expected annual expense, and the sections within the bar indicate the portion of the annual expense allocated to tuition, books, rent, and so on.

High-Low (Open-Close) Graphs

The high-low (open-close) graph is a data-specific graph. To use this graph properly, you need the high and low price of a stock at some point in time. You also may include the opening and closing prices to provide a complete assessment of a stock's performance (see fig. 10.14).

Although this kind of graph generally is used to plot stock performance data, you can use a high-low graph to plot high, low, open, and close prices for other commodities, such as gold, silver, or pork bellies. You also can plot any item in which you may want to track high and low numbers only, such as temperatures, prices of homes, or interest rates.

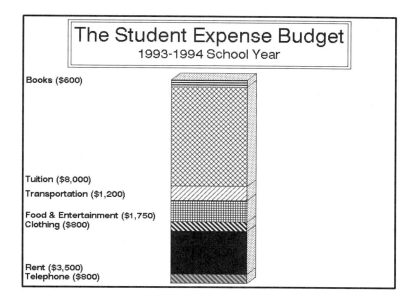

Fig. 10.13

A column graph showing allocated expenses in a student budget.

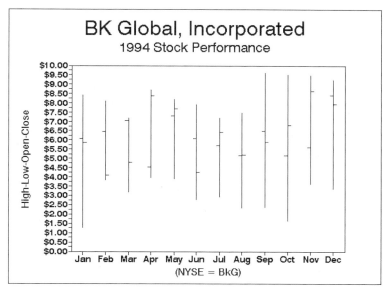

Fig. 10.14

A high-low (open-close) graph showing the one-year performance for BK Global stock.

The top of the vertical bar on this graph represents the high price, whereas the bottom of the bar represents the low price of the stock during each month. The small vertical bar facing right indicates the opening price, and the bar facing left shows the closing price.

Text Graphs

A text graph is radically different from any graph covered so far. This type of graph has no x-axis, no y-axis, and no data series. Instead, a text graph consists of only text and special graphics available with the Annotator tool (covered in Chapter 11).

A popular use for the text graph is to draw an organizational chart showing the hierarchy of management in a firm. Another use for a text graph is to display two or three simple, enlarged words. Then, using Quattro Pro's "slide-show" capability, you can flash text graphs that say "Sales Up!" or "Increased Profits!" during a presentation.

Bubble Graphs

With a bubble graph, you can float bubbles of different sizes in an XY graph. As with an XY graph, the x- and y-axes in a bubble graph are scaled with numeric data. To determine how big the bubbles will be in relation to one another, you enter an additional data series that numbers the bubble sizes from smallest to largest.

A bubble graph is an excellent graph to use for comparing and relating data points. The bubble graph enables you to compare data not only by position on the graph, as in an XY graph, but also by the relative size of each data point bubble (see fig. 10.15).

Fig. 10.15

A bubble graph showing water and air temperature readings for San Diego Harbor.

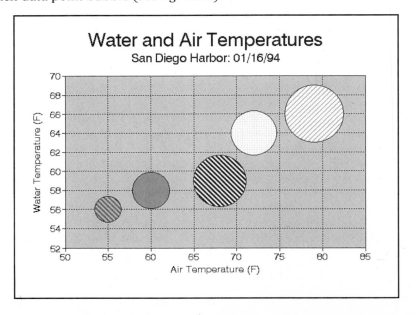

In a bubble graph, the largest bubble need not always reflect the data point with the highest value. For instance, you may be pitching a proposal to downsize the corporation's regional sales offices. In this case, you may want to use the largest bubble for the office carrying the lowest sales profits to draw attention to it as a poor performer and as a place to begin cutbacks.

3-D Graphs

The 3-D graph displays notebook data on a three-dimensional grid formed by the x-axis, the y-axis, and the z-axis. The *z-axis* begins at the *graph origin* (the intersection of the x-axis and y-axis) and projects outward, away from the viewer's perspective (see fig. 10.16). In this case, the more data series that appear on the graph, the longer the z-axis.

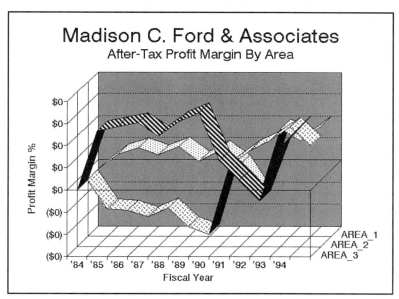

Fig. 10.16

A 3-D ribbon graph showing 10 years of after-tax margin data.

Three-dimensional graphs offer several advantages over two-dimensional graphs: they more easily accommodate large numbers of data series, are ideal for summarizing data from several graphs in a slide show, and simply are more visually appealing.

In 3-D graphs, the data series appear in front of each other as opposed to under, above, or on top of each other as with the two-dimensional variety. When designing a 3-D graph, keep in mind that Quattro Pro places the first data series in the back of the graph, the second data series in front of that one, and so on. If at all possible, try to arrange your notebook data so that the larger numbers are graphed before the smaller numbers. This strategy ensures that the bigger data series is graphed behind the smaller data series.

3-D graphs consist of four types: ribbon, bar, step, and area, as discussed in the following sections.

3-D Ribbon Graph

The 3-D ribbon graph is similar to the two-dimensional line graph. Like the regular line graph, the 3-D ribbon graph is useful for showing a progression of values over time (refer to fig. 10.16).

To create a combination 3-D ribbon and line graph, choose /**G**raph **O**verall **T**hree-D **N**o. Doing so forces the ribbons to display as lines but doesn't remove the z-axis from the graph. As a result, Quattro Pro displays two-dimensional lines floating in a three-dimensional grid. This type of graph is useful as a transition graph in a slide show that depicts both types of graphs.

3-D Bar Graph

The 3-D bar graph is similar to the two-dimensional bar graph. Like the regular bar graph, the 3-D bar graph is useful for comparing the values of different items at set periods in time (see fig. 10.17).

The 3-D bar graph works best with sets of steadily increasing or decreasing numbers. If the numbers fluctuate, Quattro Pro may conceal the smaller bars (smaller values) behind the larger bars (larger values).

To create a combination graph, choose /**G**raph **O**verall **T**hree-D **N**o. Doing so forces the bars to display as flat bars but doesn't remove the z-axis from the graph. As a result, Quattro Pro displays two-dimensional bars floating in a three-dimensional grid.

3-D Step Graph

The 3-D step graph resembles a 3-D bar graph. In a 3-D step graph, the bars for each data series are connected, forming a series of steps (see fig. 10.18).

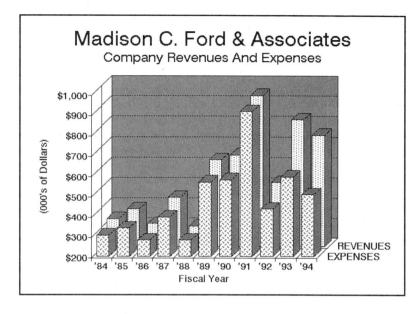

Fig. 10.17

A 3-D bar graph showing 10 years of revenue and expense data.

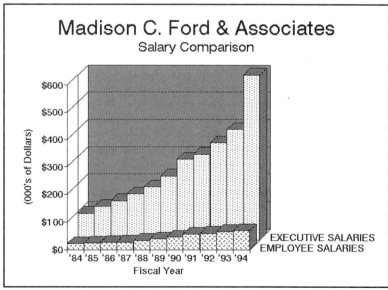

Fig. 10.18

A 3-D step graph showing 10 years of salary data.

In a 3-D step graph, you should graph the larger numbers before the smaller numbers to keep the larger steps from concealing the smaller steps.

To create a combination 3-D step and bar graph, choose /**G**raph **O**verall **T**hree-D **N**o. Doing so forces the steps to display as flat bars but doesn't remove the z-axis from the graph. As a result, Quattro Pro displays two-dimensional bars floating in a three-dimensional grid.

3-D Area Graph

The 3-D area graph is a two-dimensional line graph with the area under the lines filled in. Like the regular line graph, the 3-D area graph helps you track trends by displaying a progression of values over a period of time (see fig. 10.19).

Fig. 10.19

A 3-D area graph showing 10 years of income tax data.

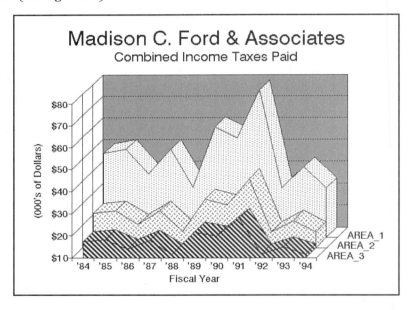

NOTE ▶

The 3-D area graph differs from the two-dimensional area graph. A regular area graph stacks the data series areas on top of one another to review the cumulative effect of a trend. The 3-D area graph, however, displays the data series areas in front of one another, which clearly highlights differences in magnitude—a good way to analyze individual trends and the aggregate contribution to an overall trend.

To create a combination graph, choose /**G**raph **O**verall **T**hree-D **N**o. Doing so forces the areas to display flat but doesn't remove the z-axis from the graph. As a result, Quattro Pro displays two-dimensional areas floating in a three-dimensional grid.

Creating a Basic Graph

With Quattro Pro, you can create a basic graph in two ways: from the ground up or by using the **Fast** Graph command. Although both methods achieve roughly the same result, the **Fast** Graph command is much easier to use.

When you execute the **Fast** Graph command, Quattro Pro evaluates a selected block of data on the active notebook and builds a graph from that block. Building a graph from the ground up is covered in "Building a Customized Graph" later in this chapter.

Preselecting a Block

Building Quattro Pro graphs with the **Fast** Graph command is easy when you know how to preselect a block to graph. This preselecting technique is discussed in Chapter 4, "Manipulating Data."

The following rules describe how Quattro Pro evaluates a preselected block when the block has more rows than columns:

- Each column is considered a single series.

- Labels appearing in the first column are designated as the x-axis labels.

- Labels appearing in the first row are designated as the graph legend labels.

- When the preselected block doesn't contain labels in the first column or row, Quattro Pro creates a graph without labels or legends.

- When graphing a 3-D cell block, each series forms by associating the same column of data from each page in the 3-D cell block. Suppose that the data you are graphing resides in cell block A..C:A1..C4. Assuming that this block contains row and column labels, then the first series contains the data found in A..C:B2..B4, the second series contains the data found in A..C:C2..C4, and the x-axis labels are derived from the data found in block A..C:A2..A4. The labels used to display the graph legend come from cells B1 and C1 on page A, the first page in this 3-D cell block.

The following rules describe how Quattro Pro evaluates a preselected block when the block has more columns than rows:

- Each row is considered a single series.

- Labels appearing in the first row are designated as the x-axis labels.

- Labels appearing in the first column are designated as the graph legend labels.

- When the preselected block doesn't contain labels in the first column or row, Quattro Pro creates a graph without labels or legends.

- When graphing a 3-D cell block, each series forms by associating the same row of data from each page in the 3-D cell block. Suppose that the data you are graphing resides in A..C:A1..D3. Assuming that this block contains row and column labels, then the first series contains the data found in block A..C:B2..D2, the second series contains the data found in block A..C:B3..D3, and the x-axis labels are derived from the data found in block A..C:B1..D1. The labels used to display the graph legend come from cells A2 and A3 on page A, the first page in this 3-D cell block.

Creating a Fast Graph

When you preselect a block of data on the active notebook and then choose /**G**raph **F**ast Graph, Quattro Pro draws a bare-bones graph on-screen. A bare-bones graph shows only the basic graph elements: a scaled x-axis, a scaled y-axis, and the graphed data. When the pre-selected block contains labels in the first row and column, the graph also shows a legend and axes labels.

By default, Quattro Pro creates a stacked-bar graph when you choose **F**ast Graph.

Before you choose the **F**ast Graph command, make sure that the pre-selected block doesn't contain any blank rows or columns, because Quattro Pro will show the rows or columns as gaps within the graph.

TIP

To remove blank areas from a graph, return to the active notebook and delete all blank rows and columns from the selected data block. Next, select the data block again and then choose /**G**raph **F**ast Graph. Quattro Pro displays the same graph without the gaps.

The preselected data block shown in figure 10.20 (B5..E9) is ready to be fast-graphed. To create a bare-bones stacked-bar graph (the default graph type), follow these steps:

1. Highlight cell block B5..E9 on the active notebook.

2. Choose /**G**raph **F**ast Graph (or press Ctrl+G, the Ctrl+*key* shortcut for this command).

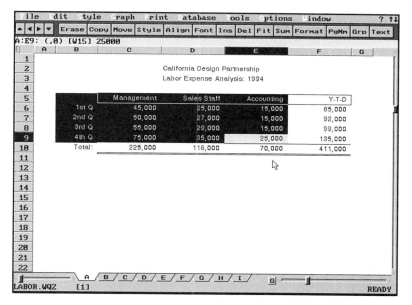

Fig. 10.20

A preselected cell block on a notebook.

NOTE

If you choose **F**ast Graph before preselecting a block, Quattro Pro returns you to the notebook and asks you to enter the block address containing the data you want to fast graph.

After you choose the **Fast Graph** command, Quattro Pro builds a graph on-screen (see fig. 10.21). Notice that because the selected block (B5..E9) had more rows than columns, the labels in the first column are x-axis labels (see the preceding rules). To return to the active notebook, press any key except the slash (/); the / activates the Annotator.

Fig. 10.21

A bare-bones stacked-bar graph created from the preselected data block.

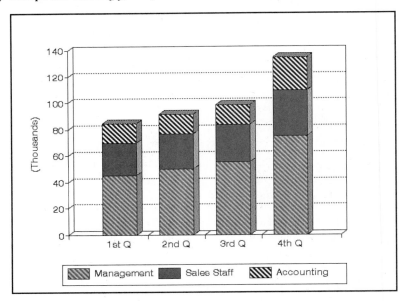

A review of the four-step process that Quattro Pro used to create the fast graph follows:

1. If the selected block has more rows than columns, Quattro Pro follows the first set of rules outlined in the preceding section and uses the second set of rules when the selected block has more columns than rows.

2. Quattro Pro creates x-axis labels using the labels appearing in the first column of the block (B6..B9).

3. Quattro Pro creates a legend using the labels appearing in the first row of the block (C5..E5).

4. Quattro Pro uses the remaining row data (C6..E9) to create four unique series.

Because fast graphs are so easy to create, they are natural what-if analysis tools. After you make a fast graph, choose **Q**uit from the **G**raph menu to return to the active notebook. Now modify any of the values in your graph block. When the data is edited to your satisfaction, press F10 to view the updated graph.

This approach to building graphs requires minimal effort on your part. The major drawback of using this method is that the **F**ast Graph command interprets only one block of data. When evaluating that block, Quattro Pro builds a graph based on one of only two possible conditions: whether the number of columns is greater than the number of rows, or whether the number of rows is greater than the number of columns. But what if the number of rows equals the number of columns? Or what if you want to use data from different locations on the same notebook?

The **F**ast Graph command cannot meet all possible graph-building needs. In fact, this command doesn't offer the flexibility that custom graph building provides. See Chapter 11, "Customizing Graphs," for more details.

Building a Customized Graph

The /**G**raph **S**eries menu commands enable you to choose up to six data series to graph. The primary advantage of using **S**eries submenu commands instead of the **F**ast Graph command is that you can choose the data series that appears on the graph.

> **TIP**
>
> You can edit the **S**eries submenu settings that were created with **F**ast Graph by reselecting each series option and specifying a different cell block.

In Quattro Pro, a valid series can be numbers in adjacent rows or columns, numbers from different parts of the same active notebook, or numbers from two or more consecutive pages. You even can use linked cells in your series—Quattro Pro uses the results of formulas and links the graph.

When you choose /**Graph S**eries, Quattro Pro displays the **S**eries submenu. The commands on this submenu are listed as follows:

Command	Description
1st-6th Series	Defines up to six data series for Quattro Pro to graph
X-Axis Series	Defines a block containing labels to be used for the x-axis labels or values for an XY or bubble graph
Group	Defines a block of data to be graphed
Analyze	Accesses analytical graphing tools (see Chapter 12, "Analyzing Graphs," for complete coverage of this command)

TIP

On an XY graph, the **X**-Axis Series command defines a data series rather than a block containing labels (as with all other graph types). With XY and bubble graphs, the x-axis must contain data.

When you choose the **G**roup command, Quattro Pro asks you to specify how to create a series from the block of data by **C**olumns or **R**ows. If you choose the **C**olumns option, Quattro Pro assigns each column of values to a series; choosing the **R**ows option assigns each row of values to a series. The benefit of using the **G**roup command is that you can avoid specifying each individual series.

Now use the data from the notebook pictured earlier in figure 10.20 to create a basic graph by specifying the data series, one at a time.

Specifying Individual Series

You can specify individual data series one at a time and achieve the same result as with the Fast Graph command. When you build a graph in this manner, you can choose data series from anywhere on the active notebook. You even can link a graph to data in other notebooks open in Quattro Pro's memory or stored on disk. Also, the **S**eries command is invaluable when you want to go back and append additional data series to an existing graph, even one that you created using Fast Graph.

To build a graph by specifying each individual data series, follow these steps:

1. Choose 1st Series from the **Series** submenu.

2. Type or highlight the range containing the first series—**C6..C9**, for example—and then press Enter to record the first series. Repeat this step for the second and third series.

3. Choose **X**-Axis Series from the **Series** submenu.

4. Type or highlight the range containing the labels—**B6..B9**, for example—and press Enter to record the x-axis labels.

5. Choose **Quit** to return to the **Graph** menu.

6. Choose View to examine the graph.

Your displayed graph now should look like figure 10.21, which was created earlier using **Fast Graph**.

> When defining series for XY and bubble graphs, remember that your x-axis must display numeric data, not labels or text. Choose **S**eries **X**-Axis Series and enter the coordinates of your x-axis series. Then, choose **1**st Series to enter the y-axis. For bubble graphs, you also must use a **2**nd Series that defines the relative size of the bubbles.

TIP

Specifying a Group Series

The **Group** command works like the **Fast Graph** command, except that you can choose how the data series are retrieved from the notebook, by **Columns** or **Rows**. The **Fast Graph** command doesn't give you this option because the command retrieves the data series according to the dimensions of the preselected data block and the two rules outlined earlier.

To build a graph by specifying a group data series, follow these steps:

1. Choose /**Graph Series Group**.

2. Choose **Columns** from the **Group** submenu.

3. Type or highlight the range containing the data series—**C5..E9**, for example—and press Enter to record the data series.

4. Choose **X**-Axis Series from the **Series** submenu.

5. Type the range containing the labels—**B6..B9**, for example—and press Enter to record the x-axis labels.

6. Choose **Q**uit to return to the **G**raph menu.

7. Choose **V**iew to examine the graph.

Except for the legend, your displayed graph should look like figure 10.21.

FOR RELATED INFORMATION

◄◄ "Working with Cell References and Blocks," p. 111.
How to work with blocks of data in a Quattro Pro notebook. Block selection techniques are an important part of building graphs in Quattro Pro.

►► "Customizing a Graph Data Series," p. 534.
Techniques you can use to enhance the appearance of your graph's data series, such as changing colors, selecting fill patterns, choosing markers and lines, and exploding pie slices.

Enhancing the Appearance of a Basic Graph

So far, you have learned how to build a basic, unadorned graph. Although some of the graphs you create with **Fast Graph** show axis labels or a legend, they often lack a finished quality common to most professional reports. In this section, you learn how to use the **Text** command to turn a basic graph into a presentation-quality visual report.

The **Text** submenu commands add titles to a graph, append descriptive labels to the x-axis and y-axis, insert a legend, and control all the fonts appearing on the graph. When you choose the **Text** command, the **Text** submenu appears. Table 10.2 lists the **Text** submenu commands.

Table 10.2 Text Submenu Commands

Command	Description
1st Line	Adds a main title above the graph
2nd Line	Adds a secondary title to a graph below the main title
X-Title	Adds a descriptive label below the x-axis
Y-Title	Adds a rotated vertical label to the left of the y-axis
Secondary Y-Axis	Adds a rotated vertical label to the right of the y-axis
Legends	Inserts and positions a graph legend
Font	Controls the typeface, point size, color, and style of the fonts appearing on the graph

Adding Titles

Use the first five commands on the **Text** submenu to add titles to a basic graph. Titles add definition and lend clarity. The main title, for example, generally defines the name of a company or a report. The secondary title clarifies the main title by specifying a relevant time period (*Fiscal Year 1994*), the name of a department (*Sales & Marketing Division*), or the abbreviation style used for numbers appearing in the graph (*All Values in Thousands of Dollars*).

You can create other titles to describe specific parts of the graph, such as the x- and y-axis data. *Legends* are a type of title that describe the data series appearing on a graph. You can create the graph shown in figure 10.22, for example, by using the commands on the **Text** submenu. The graph shown in figure 10.22 conveys more information to the viewer than does the original fast graph shown earlier in figure 10.21.

To add a main title to the top of a graph, follow these steps:

1. Choose **1st Line** from the **Text** submenu.
2. Type the title when prompted.
3. Press Enter to record the title.
4. Press F10 or choose **View** from the **Graph** menu to see the new graph title.

You can perform the same operation for the remaining title commands because the commands work the same.

To remove a title from the graph, choose the command again, press Esc, and then press Enter to record a blank space in place of the old title.

Figure 10.23 shows the **Text** submenu after all the titles shown in figure 10.22 are entered. Figure 10.23 shows the two ways in which Quattro Pro can recognize title data. When you enter a graph title through the **Text** submenu, Quattro Pro reproduces your keyboard entry at the right margin of the submenu. The **X**-Title and **Y**-Title entries, for example, reflect the text titles *Fiscal Year Quarter* and *Dollars*.

Fig. 10.22

Titles added to the basic graph.

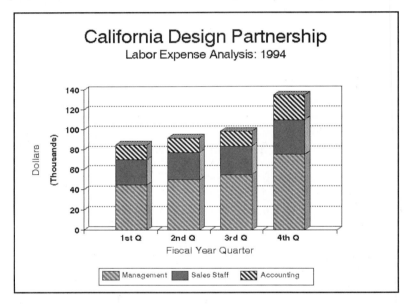

Look at the title entries recorded with the **1**st Line and **2**nd Line commands. These entries are a combination of a backslash and a cell address. To use a label appearing on the active notebook as a graph title, enter a backslash followed by the label's cell address, or type the text to appear for that title.

TIP

You also can enter bullet characters as part of a graph title by preceding the title text with a backslash character followed by the bullet code. See the section "Adding Bullets" in Chapter 5 for a review of the valid bullet codes.

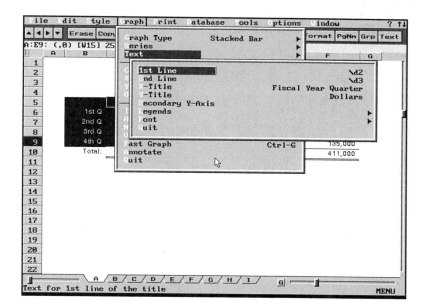

Fig. 10.23

The title entries on the
Text submenu.

Adding Legends

The **Legends** command adds a legend to a graph. A *legend* is a coding
system that defines the individual parts that make up a data series on
a graph. The legend shown at the bottom in figure 10.22 shows which
section of each stacked bar represents management, sales staff, and
accounting labor expense.

To add and position a legend on a graph, follow these steps:

1. Choose **Legends** from the /**G**raph **T**ext menu.

2. Choose **1**st Series, type the text, and press Enter to record the
first legend series.

Repeat this step for each remaining legend series.

3. Choose **P**osition and choose a legend position from the **P**osition
submenu. Quattro Pro displays three choices: **B**ottom, **R**ight, and
None.

Figure 10.24 shows the **P**osition submenu for the **L**egends command.

Fig. 10.24

The entries that define
each series in the
legend.

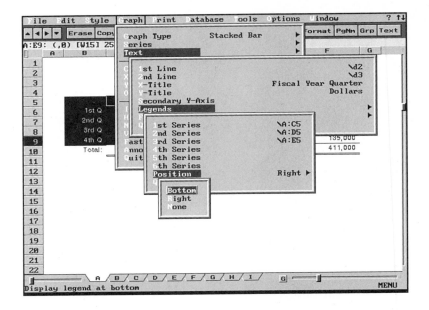

Like the title entries, the legend series entries can be a combination of
a backslash and a cell address. To use a label appearing on the active
notebook as legend text, enter a backslash and then the label's cell
address, or type the text to appear in the legend box.

Changing the Font

With the /**Graph Text Font** command, you can change the typeface,
point size, style, and color of each text element on a graph. This command is powerful because with **Font**, you can alter the appearance of
text on a graph like a typesetter can manipulate the appearance of a
resume or a restaurant menu. To change the font used to display a
legend's text, for example, choose /**Graph Text Font Legends** and then
alter each available font characteristic.

NOTE

When you use /**G**raph **T**ext **F**ont **D**ata & Tick Labels to change the point
size of labels, all markers and symbols automatically are scaled to the
new size you selected.

When you choose /**G**raph **T**ext **F**ont, the Font submenu appears. The commands found on this submenu are listed as follows:

Command	Description
1st Line	Changes the font display of the main title
2nd Line	Changes the font display of the secondary title
X-Title	Changes the font display of the x-axis title
Y-Title	Changes the font display of the y-axis title
Legends	Changes the font display of the legend text
Data & Tick Labels	Changes the font display of the tick labels, scaling data, and 3-D graph legends

Changing the Typeface

Quattro Pro's default typeface is Swiss-SC. To change the typeface used to display the main title on a graph, for example, follow these steps:

1. Choose /**G**raph **T**ext **F**ont **1**st Line **T**ypeface.

2. Choose a new typeface from the submenu by pressing the down arrow key, highlighting a typeface, and then pressing Enter, or by clicking the typeface name (see fig. 10.25).

3. Press F10 to review the new typeface on the graph.

If you choose a typeface that Quattro Pro hasn't rendered, the program displays a Now building font message. After a font is rendered, Quattro Pro doesn't need to render the font again.

If you have a laser printer, Quattro Pro displays additional fonts at the bottom of the **F**ont submenu. These extra fonts are printer-specific fonts. If you install an HP LaserJet, for example, Quattro Pro displays fonts that work with LaserJet printers. Likewise, if you install a PostScript printer, Quattro Pro displays PostScript-specific fonts.

TIP

Fig. 10.25

The **T**ypeface submenu
selections.

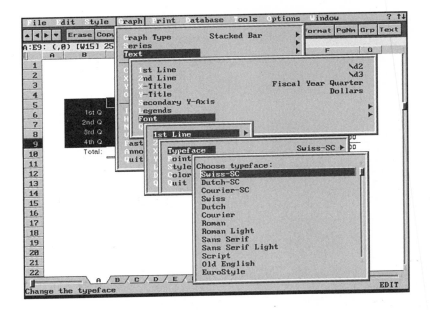

Changing the Point Size

Quattro Pro has different default point sizes for each text element on a
graph. For example, the **1**st Line title appears in 36-point type, the **2**nd
Line title appears in 24-point type, and all other text appears in 18-point
type. Point size measures the height of letters; thus, the larger the point
size, the larger the letters.

To change the point size used to display the secondary title on a graph,
for example, follow these steps:

1. Choose /**G**raph Text Font **2**nd Line.

2. Choose **P**oint Size.

3. Choose a new point size from the submenu by clicking it or by
pressing the down-arrow key, highlighting a point size, and then
pressing Enter (see fig. 10.26).

4. Press F10 to review the new point size on the graph.

NOTE

Because some LaserJet typefaces have fixed point sizes, you may not be able to change point sizes by using the **P**oint Size submenu commands. Check your printer manual. For these fonts you must choose the appropriate point size in the **T**ypeface submenu as well. You may see, for example, a typeface with the name 10-point Courier PC8 or 8-point LinePrinter Roman8. If you try to change the point size on a typeface with a fixed point size, you get the message `Non-scalable font selected.` `Choose size with the Typeface menu.`

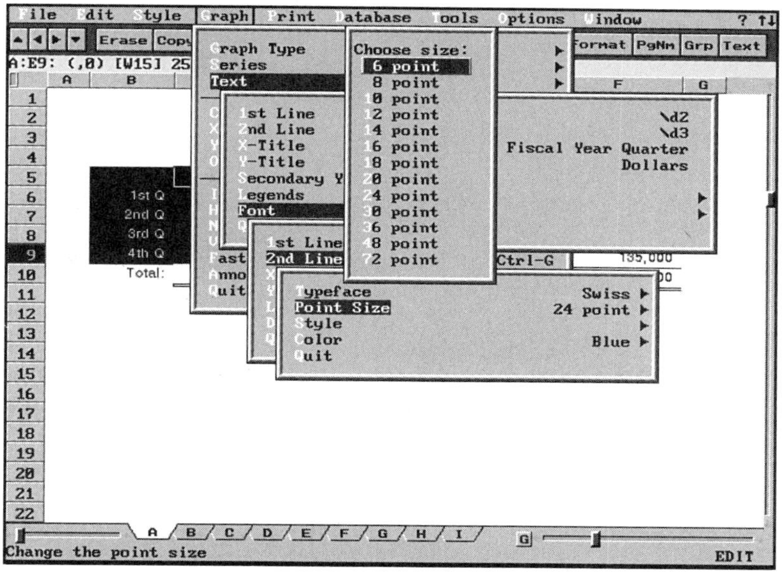

Fig. 10.26

The **P**oint Size submenu selections.

Changing the Style

Quattro Pro has five font styles: regular (default), bold, italic, underlined, and drop shadow. To change the font style used to display the text in a legend, for example, follow these steps:

1. Choose /**G**raph **T**ext **F**ont **L**egends.

2. Choose **S**tyle.

3. Choose a new font style from the submenu (see fig. 10.27).

4. Press F10 to view the new font style on the graph.

Fig. 10.27

The **S**tyle submenu selections.

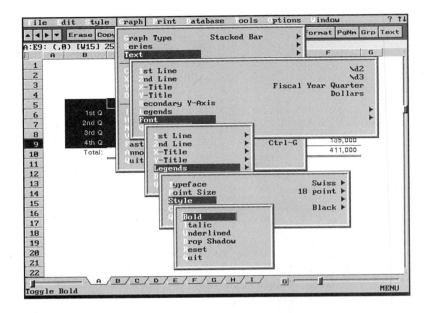

NOTE

Because LaserJet typefaces have fixed styles as well as fixed point sizes, you cannot change styles using the **F**ont submenu commands. Also, not all typefaces support all the listed styles. If a style is unavailable, Quattro Pro uses the default (regular) style. To return a text element to its original font style display, choose **R**eset from the **S**tyle submenu.

Changing the Colors

Quattro Pro enables you to change the colors used to display text on a graph with the **C**olor command. If you don't own a color monitor, you still can use this command to control the color-coding scheme transmitted to color printers and plotters.

To change the colors used to display the data and tick labels, for example, follow these steps:

1. Choose /**G**raph **T**ext **F**ont **D**ata & Tick Labels.

2. Choose **C**olor.

3. Choose a new color from the color palette (see fig. 10.28). In text display mode, Quattro Pro displays a list of the color names instead of the palette.

TIP

Use the arrow keys to move around the color palette. If you have a mouse, click a color to select it; then press Enter to choose a color.

4. Press F10 to view the new font color on the graph.

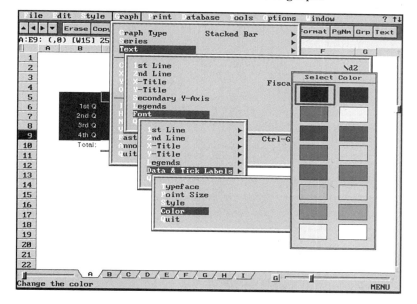

Fig. 10.28

The **C**olor submenu selections.

FOR RELATED **INFORMATION**

◄◄ "Selecting Fonts," p. 228.
How to determine the appearance of type in a notebook, including choosing new fonts, picking different point sizes, selecting various font styles, and using color.

►► "Customizing the X-Axis and Y-Axis," p. 551.
Techniques you can use to enhance the appearance of your graph's axes, such as adjusting the axes scales, adding tick marks for clarity, and alternating the display of ticks.

Managing Graph Files

Managing graph files is an important part of every graph-building work session. When you build a graph, you must store that graph's settings with the active notebook, or you lose the graph if you leave the current notebook without saving the current changes. A graph's settings include the data series definitions, the title text, the legend, the font definitions, and so on—everything that makes the graph more than just a blank screen.

Fortunately, every time you save a notebook, Quattro Pro also saves the current graph settings with the notebook. The next time you retrieve the notebook, you can press F10, and Quattro Pro will display the graph. This mechanism, however, works with only one graph per notebook and doesn't actually name the graph.

Eventually, you may want to build more than one graph from a notebook. Then you need to use the /**Graph N**ame menu commands to help manage your graph files. Table 10.3 defines the **N**ame submenu commands.

Table 10.3 Name Submenu Commands

Command	Description
Display	Displays a graph that has been saved with a name
Create	Names a graph and saves it with a notebook
Autosave Edits	Automatically saves edits to a graph when you switch to another graph
Erase	Erases a saved graph name from a notebook
Reset	Erases all saved graph names from the current notebook
Slide	Displays a named graph for a user-specified number of seconds or when any key is pressed
Graph Copy	Copies a graph from one notebook to another

Naming and Saving a Graph

You must name a graph only when you want to create a second graph from the same notebook. Save every graph under a unique name to ensure that you don't accidentally overwrite one graph's settings with another.

To name a graph and assign that graph's settings to the active notebook, follow these steps:

1. Choose /**G**raph **N**ame **C**reate. Quattro Pro displays a list of graph names, if any exist.

2. If you are creating a graph, enter a name for the graph when prompted. (You can use up to 15 characters.) If you are saving an existing graph, highlight the name on the list.

> Quattro Pro will not warn you if you are overwriting an existing graph. **◄ CAUTION**

3. Press Enter to assign the graph name to the current notebook.

Autosaving Edited Graphs

When you create two or more graphs from data on the same notebook, use the /**G**raph **N**ame **A**utosave Edits command to guard against overwriting one graph's settings with another graph's settings. This command has two settings: **Y**es (auto-save is on) and the default value, **N**o (auto-save is off).

With auto-save on, Quattro Pro saves the current graph's settings as soon as you make another graph's settings current. If the first graph has no name, Quattro Pro prompts you to name the graph before it makes the second graph current.

When **A**utosave Edits is set to **N**o, be careful if you are working with multiple graphs. Always remember to save the current graph's settings with the /**G**raph **N**ame **C**reate command before you make another graph current with the /**G**raph **N**ame **D**isplay command.

Displaying a Saved Graph

When you create two or more graphs from the same notebook data, you need a way to choose which group of settings to display when you press F10.

To display a graph assigned to the active notebook, follow these steps:

1. Choose /**G**raph **N**ame **D**isplay. Quattro Pro displays a list of graph names, if any exist.

2. Highlight a graph name on the list.

3. Press Enter to retrieve the graph settings assigned to that name.

NOTE

Before you execute the **D**isplay command, be sure that you have saved the current graph settings because Quattro Pro discards the current settings and shows those of the graph you specified in step 3.

When you execute /**G**raph **N**ame **D**isplay, Quattro Pro displays the graph. Press Enter to return to the active notebook.

Erasing a Saved Graph

To erase a graph name from the active notebook, follow these steps:

1. Choose /**G**raph **N**ame **E**rase. Quattro Pro displays a list of graph names, if any exist.

2. Highlight a graph name on the list.

3. Press Enter to erase the graph settings assigned to that name.

Resetting the Current Graph Settings

When you have 10 or 20 names to choose from, finding a particular graph can become tedious. Deleting the entire list of names and then saving the current settings under a new name often is easier.

To erase all the saved graph names assigned to the active notebook, follow these steps:

1. Choose /**G**raph **N**ame **R**eset. Quattro Pro displays a dialog box asking whether you want to delete all named graphs.

2. Choose **Y**es to erase all graph names or **N**o to cancel the operation.

Copying a Saved Graph

Quattro Pro enables you to copy saved graphs to other notebooks open in Quattro Pro's memory. This feature is particularly helpful when you want to use one notebook's saved graph in another notebook's slide show (covered later in the section "Creating a Slide Show").

Before you try to copy a graph to another notebook, follow these steps:

1. Assign a unique name to the active graph with the /**G**raph **N**ame **C**reate command.

> **CAUTION**
>
> Make sure that the name you choose doesn't exist for a graph in the destination notebook. If you choose a duplicate name, Quattro Pro will overwrite that name (and graph settings) when you complete the operation, and the overwritten graph settings will be lost.

2. Open the destination notebook into Quattro Pro's memory with the /**F**ile **O**pen command.

3. Press Alt+0 to display a list of the open windows. Highlight the name of the source notebook—the one with the graph—and then press Enter to make that notebook active.

To copy the saved graph from the source notebook to the destination notebook, follow these steps:

1. Choose /**G**raph **N**ame **G**raph Copy. Quattro Pro displays the names list.

2. Highlight the name of the graph you want to copy and press Enter.

Quattro Pro prompts you to point to the destination notebook.

3. Press Alt+0 to display a list of the open windows. Highlight the name of the source notebook and press Enter to make that notebook active.

> **TIP**
>
> You also can press Shift+F6, the Next Window key, to activate other windows open in Quattro Pro's memory.

4. Press Enter or click anywhere on the destination notebook to copy the graph.

Keep the following facts in mind as you prepare to copy a graph from one notebook to another:

- Copying a graph creates formula links between the source notebook and the copied graph on the destination notebook. If you change the numbers (on the source notebook) on which the graph is based, Quattro Pro redraws the graph on the destination notebook.

- Copying text graphs doesn't create formula links.

- When you name the graph that is to be copied, be sure that the name doesn't already exist on the destination notebook. If it does, the copied graph permanently replaces the existing graph settings on the destination notebook.

FOR RELATED INFORMATION

◀◀ "Working with Files," p. 360.
The ins and outs of managing notebook files. Because each graph you create is an integral part of a notebook, you must be familiar with saving, retrieving, and file-replacing techniques.

◀◀ "Translating Files," p. 369.
How to import graphs from programs such as 1-2-3 and Harvard Graphics.

Displaying a Graph

You already have learned two methods for displaying a graph: pressing F10 or choosing /**Graph View**. Three other techniques for viewing graphs go beyond displaying them. You can zoom and pan a graph on-screen, create a slide show, and insert the graph into the notebook.

Using Graph Zoom and Pan

If you have a mouse, you can use Quattro Pro's Graph Zoom and Pan feature to enlarge portions of a graph series and to scroll left and right to examine areas of the graph in detail, one section at a time.

To use Zoom and Pan while viewing a graph, press the left and right mouse buttons at the same time. The Zoom and Pan palette appears in the upper-left corner of the screen, and a position bar appears at the top of the graph. As you move around your graph, the position bar reflects your actions.

When you zoom, the position bar shrinks to indicate that a smaller percentage of the graph is displaying. When you pan, the position bar moves with you to indicate how far left or right you have scrolled. This feature reminds you where you are in the graph and is especially helpful when displaying a small, detailed section of a graph. Table 10.4 describes the functions of the buttons on the Graph Zoom and Pan palette.

Table 10.4 The Graph Zoom and Pan Palette

Button	Function
++	Zooms in on the left-most portion of the graph; each time you click this button, you see less of the graph, but in greater detail
--	Zooms out to show a larger percentage of the graph in less detail
==	Displays 100% of the graph
<<	Pans left, after you engage the zoom and display a smaller percentage of the graph; click repeatedly to pan to the left-most portion of the graph
>>	Pans right, after you engage the zoom and display a smaller percentage of the graph; click repeatedly to pan to the right-most portion of the graph

Click the right mouse button to clear the Zoom and Pan palette but continue to display the graph.

Creating a Slide Show

This chapter has shown you techniques to create presentation-quality graphics for use in important business meetings or at sales presentations. Quattro Pro's Slide command can help you prepare for these meetings by creating an on-screen slide show of named graphs. By using the procedures outlined in Chapter 9, you can create special files that a slide production company can convert into 35mm slides for slide-show presentations.

To use the slide show tool, you first must create a data table on the active notebook that lists the name of the graph and the length of time you want the graph on-screen (see fig. 10.29).

Fig. 10.29

Slide show instructions
entered into a notebook.

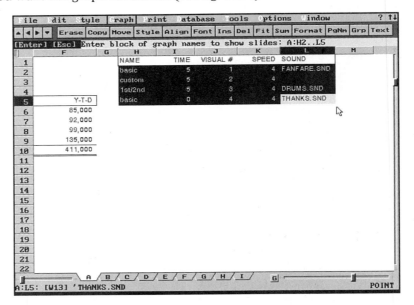

The first column of data shown in figure 10.29 tells Quattro Pro to display four named graphs in a slide show. Notice that an integer follows each graph name in a second column to the right. The integer tells Quattro Pro the number of seconds to pause between each slide. To continue displaying a slide until you press a key, enter 0 (zero) next to the graph name. The third, fourth, and fifth columns contain special-effect data. (See the following section for complete details.)

To create this slide show, follow these steps:

1. Enter the data table (refer to fig. 10.29).

2. Preselect the range containing the data table.

3. Choose /**G**raph **N**ame **S**lide.

TIP

If you omit the column of data containing the slide display intervals, Quattro Pro assumes a value of 0 for each slide. To scroll forward through the slide show, you have to press a key after Quattro Pro shows each slide. Press the Backspace key or the right mouse button to scroll backward through the slide show.

When you execute /**G**raph **N**ame **S**lide, Quattro Pro begins the slide show. If a graph name doesn't exist, Quattro Pro skips that slide and moves down the list.

TIP

If you construct large slide shows that cause the program to become sluggish, you can tell Quattro Pro to store the slide show in expanded memory (if available). To use this technique, choose /**O**ptions **O**ther **E**xpanded Memory. When prompted, choose **S**preadsheet Data or **B**oth.

Enhancing a Slide Show

You can enhance any Quattro Pro slide show with visual transitions and sound effects. These special effects can turn a predictable, ordinary slide show into a professional presentation that appeals to nearly all the senses.

Adding Visual Transitions

Visual transitions are special commands for creating slide-to-slide transitions like those a film editor creates between scenes in a movie. By default, Quattro Pro cuts from slide to slide, showing the next slide immediately after it removes the current slide from your screen. With visual transitions, you control the style of this transition. You can wipe from slide to slide, for example, scroll up or down, or even dissolve (fade out) the current slide until the next slide appears.

Quattro Pro has 24 visual transitional effects, appropriately numbered 1 to 24. To use a transition, add the visual effect number to the third column in the slide show next to the column containing the slide pause times. In the fourth column, enter a number (for seconds) to specify the duration of the effect. During a slide show, Quattro Pro looks into columns 3 and 4 for visual effect numbers and duration numbers. If none are found for any single slide, Quattro Pro immediately cuts to the next slide after the time interval for that slide concludes.

TIP

The best way to review all the visual transition effects in one sitting is to create a 24-graph slide show, and apply one visual effect to each graph in the show. Highlight the **S**lide command on the **N**ame submenu and press F1 for help, choose Slide, and then choose visual and sound effects to learn more about the individual transition effects.

Adding Sound Effects

To add *sound effects* to a slide show, create a fifth column in the slide show block. In this column, enter the name of a special digitized sound file. Sound effects can play through your computer's internal speaker (the default) or through an added sound card. If you install a sound card, Quattro Pro detects and uses it automatically. You can use any sound card compatible with Sound Blaster, including Sound Blaster Pro and AdLib. Additional sounds are available from RealSound, Inc.

Quattro Pro includes three sound effect files: FANFARE.SND (trumpets), DRUMS.SND (snare drum and cymbal), and THANKS.SND (voice saying "Thank you"). The ProView Power Pack that arrives with Quattro Pro includes other sound effect files.

TIP

If you have trouble with the sound effect files, try unloading all non-essential TSR (terminate-and-stay-resident) programs from your computer's memory. If you are logged onto a network, try logging out and then running Quattro Pro again. Alternatively, if you are running Quattro Pro under Microsoft Windows in 386 Enhanced mode, try switching to real mode (in Windows 3.0) or Standard mode (in Windows 3.1).

Inserting a Graph onto a Notebook

The Insert command offers another way to view a graph. By using this command, you can insert up to eight graphs onto a notebook so that you can view simultaneously the graph and the data that created the graph (see fig. 10.30).

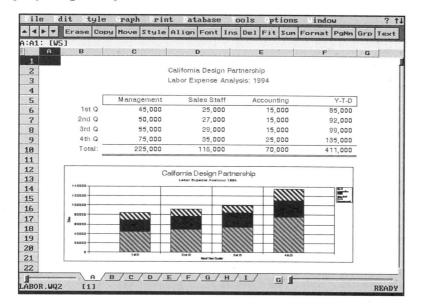

Fig. 10.30

A notebook containing an inserted graph.

To view an inserted graph on a notebook, you must have an EGA or VGA graphics adapter system. You also must invoke Quattro Pro's WYSIWYG display mode. When you insert a graph while in text display mode, Quattro Pro displays a blank, highlighted cell block. (With any display mode you use, you can print a notebook containing an inserted graph as long as you include the graph in the print range and choose /**Print D**estination **G**raphics Printer.)

To insert this graph onto the notebook, follow these steps:

1. Choose /**O**ptions **D**isplay Mode **B**:WYSIWYG.

2. Preselect the target insert range—for example, B12..F21.

NOTE

The target range cannot be larger than 32 rows and 12 columns, no matter how small or large the rows and columns are.

3. Choose /**G**raph **I**nsert.

4. Highlight a graph name from the displayed names list.

5. Press Enter to insert the graph onto the notebook.

When you insert a graph onto a notebook, Quattro Pro floats the graph image in the target block that you specify. If this block is a cell, the inserted image is unreadable. In this situation, you have two choices:

■ You can place the selector in the target block and press F10 so that the graph fills your entire screen. This method is only a temporary fix, however, because when you press Enter and return to the active notebook, the inserted graph still appears in the cell.

■ A better method for solving this problem is to select a larger target block and then choose /**G**raph **I**nsert again.

To remove the inserted graph from the notebook, follow these steps:

1. Preselect any single cell in the range—for example, B12.

2. Choose /**G**raph **H**ide.

3. Highlight the graph's name on the displayed names list.

4. Press Enter to remove the inserted graph.

Questions & Answers

This chapter introduces you to the **G**raph menu commands. If you have questions concerning situations not addressed in the examples given, look through this section.

Creating a Graph

Q: When I press F10, why don't my graphs appear on-screen?

A: Remember that to display Quattro Pro graphs, you must have a graphics adapter system, and to display a graph inserted on a notebook, you must set the /**O**ptions **D**isplay Mode command to **B**:WYSIWYG. Some graphics cards, such as the Hercules card, don't support the **B**:WYSIWYG display mode. You still can view a graph, just not one inserted onto a notebook.

If you don't have at least a monographics display adapter system, you still can create and print graphs, but you can't view them.

Q: Why can't I show a fast graph on my screen?

A: Assuming that you have the correct display adapter system, make sure that you have selected a valid block of data to fast graph. Quattro Pro doesn't make this selection for you.

The easiest way to create a fast graph is to preselect (highlight) a block of data on the active notebook and then press Ctrl+G.

Q: Why doesn't my bubble graph show bubbles when I press F10 to display it?

A: Unlike XY graphs, bubble graphs require a second data series that describes the relative sizes of the bubbles. To define the relative sizes of five bubbles, for example, place the numbers 1 through 5 in a column or row next to the notebook data being used as the first series data. Next, choose /Graph Series 2nd Series and define this data as the second series. Now press F10 to see your bubbles on the graph.

Enhancing the Appearance of a Basic Graph

Q: I created special fonts for a graph. Why aren't they showing when I press F10 to display the graph?

A: Some Bitstream font typefaces don't support bold and italic styles. Try choosing a different font typeface/style combination. Some fonts listed on the Typeface submenu also are printer fonts—that is, they may look different on-screen than they do on the printed page because Quattro Pro substitutes the closest screen font when you format a graph with a printer font.

Q: How do I stop Quattro Pro from rendering so many fonts when I want to preview a graph?

A: Choose /Options Graphics Quality Draft to turn font-rendering off. Quattro Pro substitutes Hershey fonts for every Bitstream font that isn't rendered already. While the on-screen difference between these two font styles isn't dramatic, the differences on a graph printout are.

If you want to use Bitstream fonts for printing graphs, choose /Options Graphics Quality Final before printing a graph. Quattro Pro then renders the necessary fonts for the printout.

Displaying Graphs

Q: Why do my pie graphs look like cigars?

A: Choose /**O**ptions **H**ardware **S**creen **A**spect Ratio and press the arrow keys until the object on-screen becomes a perfect circle.

Q: I have a color graphics display system. Why does Quattro Pro show my graphs in black and white?

A: When your system has an EGA or VGA color graphics display, Quattro Pro can display graphs in black and white to give you an idea of how the graphs will appear in printed form. To do this, choose /**G**raph **O**verall **C**olor/B&W and choose **N**o.

If you have a color graphics adapter (CGA) card or a monochrome display, Quattro Pro can display graphs only in black and white.

Q: Why does the slide show I created display only some of the graphs I entered into the data table?

A: The slide show works only for graph names assigned to the active notebook. If you included the names of graphs from other notebooks, Quattro Pro ignores them and continues reading down the column.

Be sure that the graph names match those created for the active notebook. To check, choose /**G**raph **N**ame **D**isplay. Quattro Pro then shows a list of the valid graph names for the active notebook.

You accidentally may have deleted all the named graphs from the active notebook by using the /**G**raph **N**ame **R**eset command. If so, you have to re-create and save each graph again.

Q: Why is the graph I inserted onto a notebook too small to see?

A: To increase the size of the inserted graph, select a larger target block and choose /**G**raph **I**nsert again.

Q: Why doesn't the graph I inserted onto a notebook fill the target block that I preselected before executing the /**G**raph **I**nsert command?

A: Choose /**P**rint **G**raph Print **L**ayout 4:3 Aspect and choose **N**o. This command forces an inserted graph to fill the entire target cell block on the notebook.

Q: I added sound effects to a slide show, but I hear nothing when I run the show. What's going on?

A: First, verify the correct spelling of the sound effect file. Next, check to make sure that you entered the file name into the fifth column in the slide-show data block. Then, verify that the name entered into the first column (the graph to which you are attaching the sound effect) is a valid graph name. Finally, be sure that the sound effect file exists and is in your /QPRO directory, or at least in a directory whose name appears in the PATH statement of your AUTOEXEC.BAT file.

Q: The sound effects that I added to a slide show are barely audible when I run the show. Is there anything I can do to amplify the sound?

A: If you're using Quattro Pro on a portable or laptop computer, you may have difficulty hearing sound effects because these systems tend to have small, low-volume output speakers. In this case, you can use a public-address (PA) system to amplify the sound effects as needed.

Terminate-and-stay-resident (TSR) programs, network shell drivers, and Microsoft Windows may impede, distort, or otherwise interfere with the sound reproduction quality from your computer. If at all possible, remove these programs from memory before running the slide show.

Summary

In this chapter, you learned how to build and enhance the basic Quattro Pro graph and how to manage graph files. You also learned techniques for displaying a graph and inserting the graph into a notebook.

Having completed this chapter, you should understand the following Quattro Pro concepts:

- ■ Understanding the anatomy and utility of a basic graph
- ■ Choosing appropriate graph types for different data
- ■ Creating a fast graph from a preselected block of data
- ■ Creating a basic graph from the ground up

- Choosing individual or group series from which to create graphs
- Adding titles, legends, and customized fonts to a graph
- Creating, displaying, and erasing graph names
- Zooming and panning a graph on-screen
- Producing a slide show using graph names assigned to the active notebook
- Using visual transition effects and digitized sound files to enhance a slide show
- Inserting a graph onto a notebook
- Removing an inserted graph from a notebook
- Copying graphs from one notebook to another

Chapter 11 continues the discussion of building Quattro Pro graphs. In Chapter 11, you learn how to use the graph customizing commands, located in the middle of the **G**raph menu, and how to use Quattro Pro's graph editing tool to produce finished-quality, presentation-ready graphs.

Customizing Graphs

In Chapter 10, you learn how to create and enhance the basic Quattro Pro graph. A basic graph is suitable for applications in which viewers can draw their own conclusions about the graph data. Basic graphs convey general ideas and impressions about notebook data.

To leave a viewer with more than a general feeling, use the four commands located in the middle of the **G**raph menu to add impact to the graph. By using the **C**ustomize Series command, for example, you can customize the fill pattern in a bar graph, select unique marker symbols for a line graph, create unique color schemes for a pie graph, and turn basic graphs into three-dimensional displays. If you have trouble choosing between two graph types for a data set, you also can create a combination graph that uses both.

You also can customize each element connected to the graph axes. If you don't like the default axis scale, design one that meets your own specifications.

Figure 11.1 shows an example of a fully customized graph created by using only a few of the available customizing tools. You aren't obligated to use every customizing command on your graphs. The best way to learn which commands go well together is to experiment with your graphs. This chapter provides the information you need to do so.

Fig. 11.1

The finished form of a customized graph.

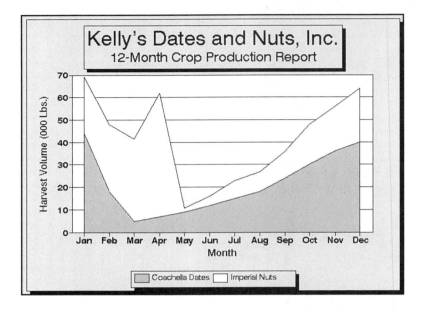

In this chapter's first section, you learn how to customize individual data series by changing colors, adding patterns, thickening lines, and using marker symbols. You also learn how to affect your data by changing bar widths and appending labels to each point in a data series.

The next section covers the process of creating combination graphs and teaches you how to plot a second y-axis. You also learn the differences in customizing pie and column graphs and the other Quattro Pro graph types.

The chapter continues with a presentation of the rules for customizing a graph's x-axis and y-axis. You learn how to scale an axis manually, format the values associated with tick marks, and switch between normal and logarithmic display mode.

In the next section, you learn how to customize the overall appearance of a graph by displaying grid lines, designing special foreground and background color combinations, adding boxes around titles and legends, and displaying a graph in 3-D.

This chapter concludes with an overview of Quattro Pro's built-in Graph Annotator tool.

Using the Graph Customize Dialog Box

Quattro Pro enables you to display the /Graph Customize Series menu as a dialog box (see fig. 11.2). By using this dialog box, you quickly can scan and set graph customizing options such as colors, line styles, bar width, interior labels, and marker symbols. The Graph Customize dialog box eliminates the need to move up and down the layers of submenus on the /Graph Customize Series menu to choose and verify graph customizing options.

NOTE

By default, Quattro Pro 5.0 displays dialog boxes instead of menus at start-up. If you are upgrading from a previous version of Quattro Pro and prefer to display menus instead of dialog boxes, choose /Options Startup Use Dialogs No. Subsequently, each time you choose /Graph Customize Series, you see the menus to which you are accustomed.

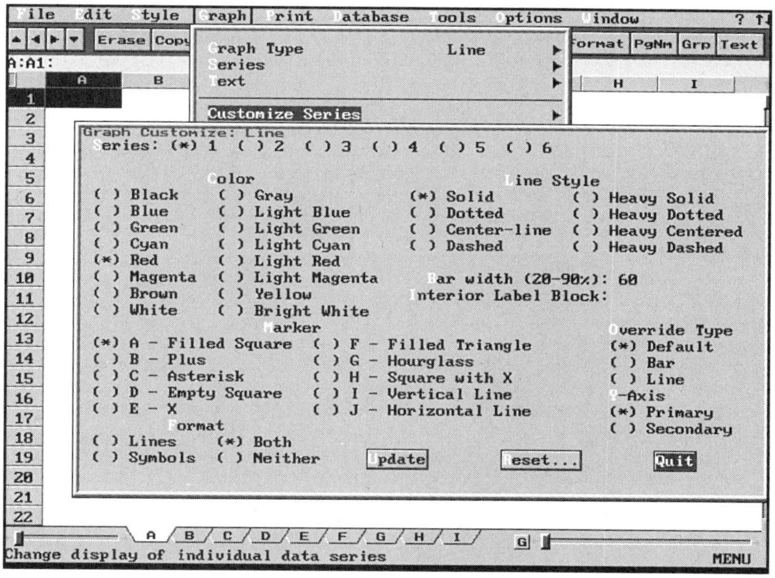

Fig. 11.2

The Graph Customize dialog box for line graphs.

Notice that the graph data series appears along the top edge of the dialog box. You must select a series number before you can set the options for that series. For example, press S to select **S**eries; then press the right arrow to activate the second series and press Enter, or click 2. Then you can set all options for this series.

Quattro Pro puts an asterisk next to the current setting, or value, for each option in the Graph Customize dialog box. To change a setting, type the highlighted letter in the option name, press the arrow keys to move the asterisk to the new setting, or type a new value; then press Enter. To move between option categories, such as **S**eries to **C**olor, press Tab. Alternatively, click the option setting you want to use, and Quattro Pro immediately moves the asterisk there.

After you finish setting options for a series, select another series or choose **Q**uit to save all current settings and return to the **G**raph menu, **U**pdate to save all current settings as the new default, or **R**eset to return all settings to their original default setting.

After you set the options for all series, you can view them by selecting the series number. This feature is helpful when coordinating fill patterns or line styles and markers for multiple graph series.

NOTE

The options in the Graph Customize dialog box vary depending on the graph type selected with the /**G**raph **G**raph Type command (see fig. 11.3).

Fig. 11.3

The Graph Customize dialog box for bubble graphs.

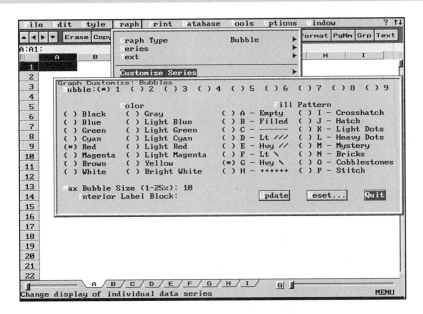

For complete coverage of the other dialog boxes available on the **G**raph menu, see the sections titled "Using the X-Axis and Y-Axis Dialog Boxes" and "Using the Graph Overall Dialog Box" later in this chapter.

The following table reveals discrepancies that exist between commands appearing on the /**G**raph **C**ustomize Series submenu and those appearing in the Graph Customize dialog box.

Menu Commands	Dialog Box Options
Markers & Lines	**M**arker and Line Style
Pies Patterns and **B**ubbles Patterns	**F**ill Pattern

The rest of this chapter features menus instead of dialog boxes. If you prefer to use dialog boxes, you will have no trouble following the step-by-step menu instructions.

FOR RELATED INFORMATION

▶▶ "Using Dialog Boxes," p. 795.
How to enable and disable the display of dialog boxes during a Quattro Pro work session.

Reviewing the Customize Series Submenu Commands

The 11 commands on the /**G**raph **C**ustomize Series menu enable you to fine-tune the appearance of a basic graph by customizing its individual parts (see fig. 11.4). Each command works on a specific part of a graph. To change the colors used to display a particular series, for example, choose the **C**olors command. To change the design of the patterns that fill the bars on a bar graph, use the **F**ill Patterns command.

Certain commands on the **C**ustomize Series submenu require that you choose colors, fill patterns, line styles, and marker symbols. When you operate in text display mode, Quattro Pro displays a submenu of word choices. The **C**olors submenu, for example, contains the names of each available color (see fig. 11.5). To make a selection, press the boldfaced letter key appearing in the option name, use the arrow keys to move to a selection and press Enter, or click the name.

Fig. 11.4

The **C**ustomize Series submenu.

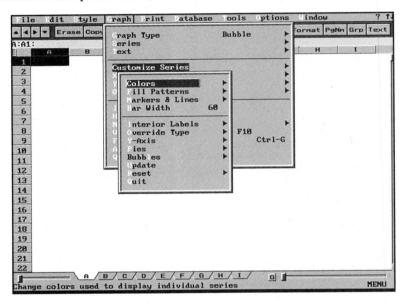

If you have a graphics screen display system and operate in WYSIWYG display mode, Quattro Pro displays "graphic" menus, such as a palette or a gallery. The **C**olors command displays a coloring palette in WYSIWYG display mode (see fig. 11.6). To make a selection, highlight the option and press Enter (or click the option) to record the new setting.

All figures and instructions in this chapter assume that you are operating in WYSIWYG display mode. To see whether your system can support graphics display mode, choose /**O**ptions **D**isplay Mode. If the selection **B**: WYSIWYG appears, choose that option.

If you are using a monochrome screen display, Quattro Pro displays all data series in black. When you choose any other color on the palette, Quattro Pro displays that data series in white.

TIP

Press + (the Expand key) to display the current settings for any **C**ustomize Series command if the current settings don't display when you choose a particular command.

If you are using the same customizing commands repeatedly, consider choosing /**G**raph **C**ustomize **S**eries **U**pdate to store those settings as the new default settings for use in other notebooks.

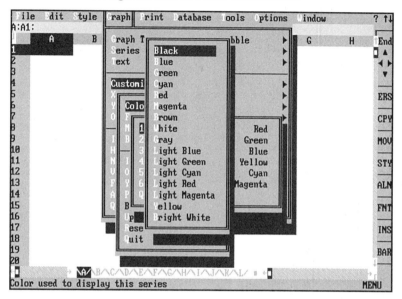

Fig. 11.5

Color names on the **C**olors **1**st Series submenu.

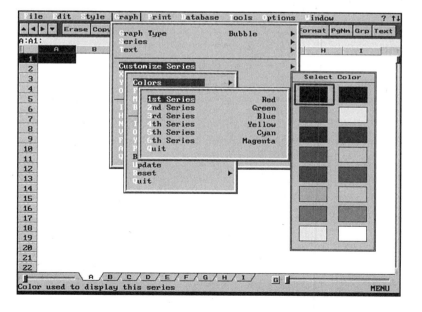

Fig. 11.6

The **C**olors **1**st Series coloring palette.

FOR RELATED **INFORMATION**

▶▶ "Setting Display Mode Options," p. 788.
How to use the /**O**ptions **D**isplay Mode command, which provides
you access to Quattro Pro's various display mode settings.

▶▶ "Using an Autoload File," p. 791.
How to use command-line switches to tell Quattro Pro to start each
new work session using a specific display setting.

Customizing a Graph Data Series

When the default settings Quattro Pro uses to display a basic graph
don't enhance your work, you can use any or all the following commands to give your graphs "that extra something."

Take the time to learn how to use the customizing commands. After
you are comfortable with their purpose and use, experiment with them
on your own graphs. You eventually may find a use for each command
during your graph-building sessions.

A word of caution, however: You easily can go overboard when customizing a graph. With the hundreds of commands at your disposal, you
may try to use too many of them on the same graph. Keep in mind that
the purpose of customizing a graph is to enhance the graph data, not
obscure it with unnecessary frills.

TIP

When you customize a graph, save the graph often with the /**G**raph
Name **C**reate command to ensure that you preserve the most immediate
changes should your PC unexpectedly fail or lose power. When customizing several graphs during the same work session, use the /**G**raph
Name **A**utosave Edits command to gain similar protection. (See
"Autosaving Edited Graphs" in Chapter 10 for detailed information on
using the **A**utosave Edits command.)

Changing Colors

The **C**olors command stores the color settings for each data series on a graph. By default, Quattro Pro assigns a different color to each series so that you can distinguish one from the other. On a line graph in which the data series often parallel and intersect each other, for example, colored lines can help you follow the progression of a particular series.

To change the color assignment of a data series, follow these steps:

1. Choose /**G**raph **C**ustomize Series **C**olors. Quattro Pro displays a submenu listing six data series and their current color assignments.

2. Choose the number of the series you want to change. Quattro Pro displays the coloring palette.

3. Highlight a color on the palette and then press Enter to record the new color assignment for that series.

Quattro Pro returns to the **C**olors submenu, where you can choose a new series to change.

4. After you finish making your changes, choose **Q**uit to return to the **C**ustomize Series submenu.

Changing Fill Patterns

The **F**ill Patterns command stores the pattern settings for each data series on a bar graph. Fill patterns help you distinguish one data series from the next, particularly when you are printing a graph on a black-and-white printer. Without fill patterns to distinguish between each data series, a viewer has to match the height of each bar to a value on the notebook.

To change the fill pattern assignment for a data series, follow these steps:

1. Choose /**G**raph **C**ustomize Series **F**ill Patterns. Quattro Pro displays a submenu listing six data series and their current fill pattern assignments.

2. Choose the number of the series you want to change. Quattro Pro displays the Select Pattern gallery (see fig. 11.7).

Fig. 11.7

Fig. 11.7

Selecting a fill pattern
from the gallery.

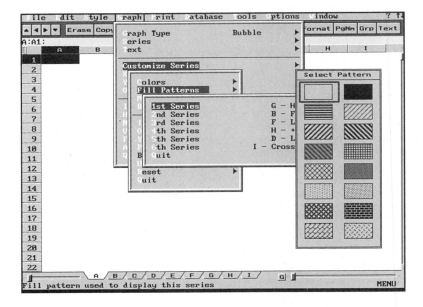

3. Highlight a pattern in the gallery and press Enter to record the
new fill pattern assignment for that series.

Quattro Pro returns to the **F**ill Patterns submenu, where you can
choose a new series to change.

4. After you finish making your changes, choose **Q**uit to return to the
Customize Series submenu.

The **F**ill Patterns command affects only bar and area graphs. (To
change fill patterns for pie and bubble graphs, you use the **P**ies and
Bubbles options on the **C**ustomize Series submenu.) Altering the fill
pattern assignments for data series that appear on a line graph or XY
graph has no visible effect on the display of that graph. Figure 11.8
shows a graph that has custom fill patterns.

Changing Markers and Lines

The **M**arkers & Lines command stores the marker symbol and line style
settings for each data series on line and XY graphs. This command also
enables you to create your own display combinations for markers and
lines.

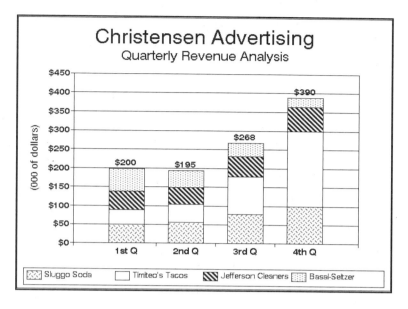

Fig. 11.8

Creating a custom look with fill patterns.

Marker symbols indicate the location of each data point in a series. Without markers, line graphs lose much of their impact because they can describe only an overall trend rather than a series of intermediate trends. In cases in which showing an overall trend is the objective of the graph, however, you can eliminate the display of markers from a line graph.

To change the line style setting for a data series, follow these steps:

1. Choose /**G**raph **C**ustomize **S**eries **M**arkers & Lines **L**ine Styles. Quattro Pro displays a submenu listing six data series and their current line style assignments.

2. Choose the number of the series you want to change. Quattro Pro displays the Select Line gallery (see fig. 11.9).

3. Highlight a line style and press Enter to record the new line style assignment for that series.

Quattro Pro returns to the **L**ine Styles submenu, where you can choose a new series to change.

4. After you finish making your changes, choose **Q**uit to return to the **M**arkers & Lines submenu.

Fig. 11.9

Selecting a new line
style from the gallery.

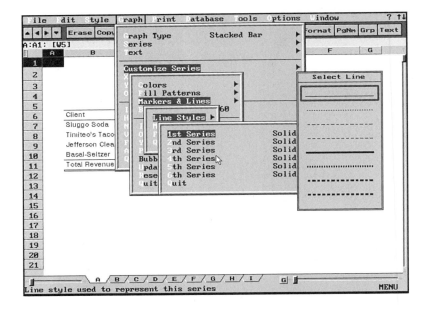

To change the marker symbol setting for a data series, follow these
steps:

1. Choose /**G**raph **C**ustomize Series **M**arkers & Lines **M**arkers.
   Quattro Pro displays a submenu listing six data series and their
   current symbol assignments.

2. Choose the number of the series you want to change. Quattro Pro
   displays the marker symbol gallery (see fig. 11.10).

3. Highlight a symbol in the gallery and press Enter to record the
   new symbol assignment for that data series.

   Quattro Pro returns to the **M**arkers submenu, where you can
   choose a new series to change.

4. After you finish with your changes, choose **Q**uit to return to the
   Markers & Lines submenu.

When you want to create a custom display format for markers and
lines, follow these steps:

1. Choose /**G**raph **C**ustomize Series **M**arkers & Lines **F**ormats.
   Quattro Pro displays a submenu listing six individual data series
   command choices and one for the entire graph called **G**raph.

2. Choose the number of the series you want to change or choose **G**raph to change all six data series. Quattro Pro displays a second submenu listing four choices: **L**ines, **S**ymbols, **B**oth, and **N**either.

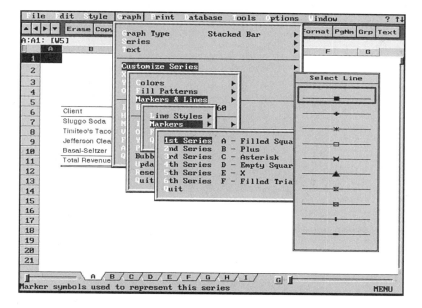

Fig. 11.10

Selecting a new marker symbol from the gallery.

3. Press a letter to choose a display combination.

Quattro Pro returns to the **F**ormats submenu, where you can choose a new series to change.

4. After you finish with your changes, choose **Q**uit to return to the **M**arkers & Lines submenu.

5. Choose **Q**uit again to return to the **C**ustomize Series submenu.

Figure 11.11 shows a line graph that has customized line styles and marker symbols.

Changing the Width of Bars

The **B**ar Width command stores a value that Quattro Pro uses to determine the width of bars on a bar graph. By default, Quattro Pro creates bar widths that occupy 60 percent of the x-axis (bar) or y-axis (rotated bar) area. You can change this setting to any value in the range between 20 and 90 percent. The lower the value, the thinner the bar; the higher the value, the thicker the bar.

Fig. 11.11

A line graph enhanced
with customized line
styles and marker
symbols.

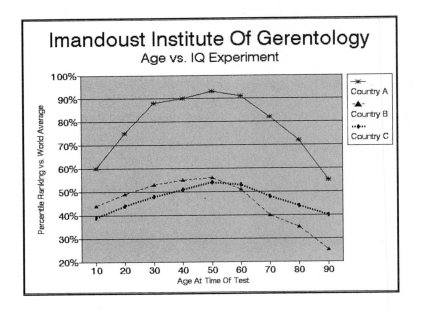

To change the width value that Quattro Pro uses to build bars, follow
these steps:

1. Choose /**Graph C**ustomize Series **B**ar Width. Quattro Pro displays
a dialog box listing the default width setting of 60 percent.

2. Type a number between 20 and 90 and press Enter to record that
value.

When you execute this command, Quattro Pro stores the new bar width
setting at the right margin of the **C**ustomize Series submenu, next to the
Bar Width command.

Press F10 to view the new bar width on the current graph.

Adding Interior Labels

The **I**nterior Labels command places a value or a label from the active
notebook directly onto a particular data series on a graph. You can use
this command to point out the exact magnitude of a data series when
the axis scaling is too vague to permit accurate visual inspection. You
also can add an interior label to a data series to function as an interior
legend.

The **I**nterior Labels command has display restrictions dependent on the type of graph. This command has no effect on area, pie, and column graphs, for example. Interior labels always appear above a data series on a bar graph and to the right of a data series on a rotated bar graph. On a stacked-bar graph, Quattro Pro can display interior labels for only the last, or top, data series. On a bubble graph, Quattro Pro always positions interior labels in relation to the center of the bubble.

> To learn how to create and add custom annotations to any type of graph, see "Annotating Graphs" later in this chapter.

TIP

To add interior labels to a data series, follow these steps:

1. Choose /**G**raph **C**ustomize Series **I**nterior Labels. Quattro Pro displays a submenu listing the six data series.

2. Choose the number of the series to which you want to add a label. Quattro Pro returns to the active notebook.

3. Enter the cell address of a value or label to use.

4. Press Enter to record the address. Quattro Pro displays a second submenu listing six placement choices.

5. Choose a placement choice from the submenu. Quattro Pro returns to the **I**nterior Labels submenu, where you can choose a new series to change.

6. After you finish with your changes, choose **Q**uit to return to the **C**ustomize Series submenu.

Figure 11.12 shows a graph that has been customized by widening the bars and adding interior labels.

Creating Combination Graphs

If you have difficulty deciding which graph type to use for a particular set of data, consider the following novel approach to graph-building in Quattro Pro: the combination graph. This type of graph displays two graph types simultaneously on one graph.

Figure 11.13 shows a combination line and bar graph. This graph plots key financial data used in a firm's employee profit-sharing program. A line graph plots the firm's profits, and a bar graph plots the revenue dollars.

Fig. 11.12

A basic bar graph enhanced with wider bars and interior labels.

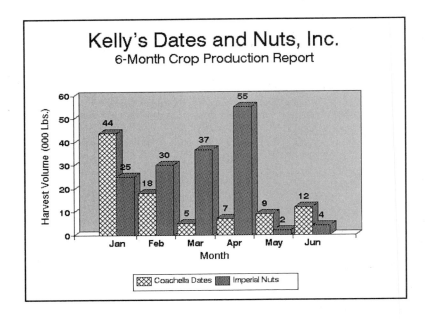

Fig. 11.13

A combination line and bar graph

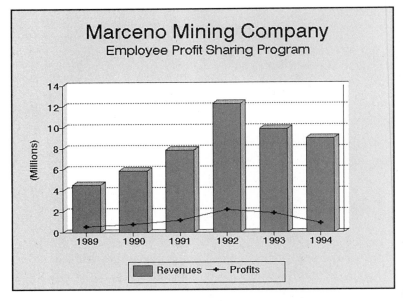

To create this effect, use the **O**verride Type command on the **C**ustomize Series submenu. Follow these steps:

1. Choose /**G**raph **C**ustomize Series **O**verride Type. Quattro Pro displays a submenu listing six data series.

2. Choose the number of the series you want to change.

3. When prompted, choose **D**efault, **B**ar, or **L**ine. Quattro Pro returns to the **O**verride Type submenu.

4. Choose **Q**uit to return to the **C**ustomize Series submenu.

5. Press F10 to review the combined graph on-screen.

If you choose not to override all the data series, Quattro Pro continues to use the default settings prescribed by the original **G**raph Type command selection.

Some graph types make little or no sense when united on a combination graph. Consider the difficulty you would have deciphering data appearing on a combination pie and line graph. As a result, Quattro Pro doesn't enable you to override area, stacked-bar, pie, column, bubble, and 3-D area graphs.

To return the current graph to its original look, choose **D**efault for each altered series on the **O**verride Type submenu.

Plotting a Second Y-Axis

The **Y**-Axis command creates a second y-axis on the current graph. This technique is useful particularly for displaying data set values that have dramatically different magnitudes or use completely different systems of measurement.

Suppose that your manager has told you to create a bar graph depicting a subsidiary firm's total yearly postage expense versus the parent company's total revenues. Because the difference in the magnitudes of these two data sets is dramatic, consider creating the dual y-axis bar graph shown in figure 11.14.

Note that the word *Thousands* appears by the second y-axis to indicate that values have been scaled by a multiple of 1,000. This notation helps you spot the bars that relate to this axis' scale—namely, the Revenues bars (the Postage Expense values aren't likely to run into the hundreds of thousands of dollars).

To create a graph with a second y-axis, follow these steps:

1. Choose /**G**raph **C**ustomize Series **Y**-Axis. Quattro Pro displays a submenu listing six data series.

2. Choose the number of the series you want to plot on the second y-axis.

Fig. 11.14

A bar graph with two
y-axes.

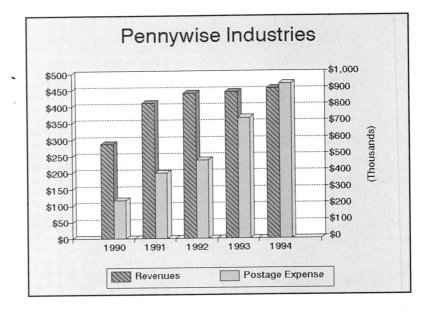

3. When prompted, choose **S**econdary Y-Axis. Quattro Pro returns you to the **Y**-Axis submenu.

4. Choose **Q**uit to return to the **C**ustomize Series submenu.

5. Press F10 to review the graph with two y-axes.

You can move a data series to another axis by selecting that data series and then choosing **P**rimary Y-Axis or **S**econdary Y-Axis. You can continue adding data series to the secondary y-axis. Every time you add data series, Quattro Pro rescales the secondary y-axis to reflect the absolute-upper and absolute-lower range of values contained in both data series.

Now consider the graph shown in figure 11.15. This graph is derived from the graph shown in figure 11.13. In figure 11.13, the profits and revenues data series are measured in terms of dollars. The profit-sharing data series in figure 11.15 is expressed as a percentage of total revenues.

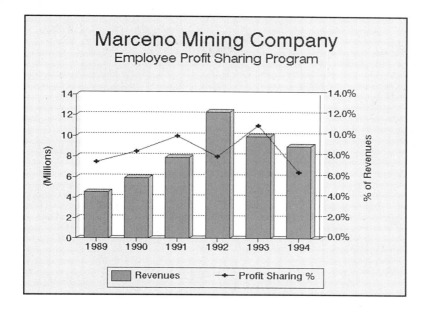

Fig. 11.15

A graph that uses data series with different systems of measurement.

Customizing Pie Graphs and Column Graphs

Pie graphs and column graphs are so different from other Quattro Pro graph types that these graphs merit their own submenu of customizing commands. To access this submenu, choose /**G**raph **C**ustomize Series **P**ies. Quattro Pro displays the submenu shown in figure 11.16.

The following sections focus on customizing pie graphs, but the options also apply to column graphs. The only option discussed in the following sections that works exclusively for pie graphs is the **E**xplode option. For more information on column graphs, see Chapter 10, "Creating Graphs."

Changing the Label Format

Quattro Pro has four format options for labeling the slices of a pie graph and column graph: **V**alue, **%** (percent), **$** (dollar), and **N**one. By default, Quattro Pro displays the pie and column graphs using percent labels.

Fig. 11.16

The **P**ies submenu
commands.

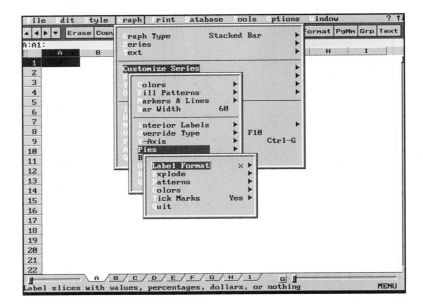

To change the label format, follow these steps:

1. Choose /**G**raph **C**ustomize Series **P**ies **L**abel Format.

2. Choose a label option from the displayed submenu. Quattro Pro returns to the **P**ies submenu, where you can choose a new item to change.

3. Press F10 to review the graph with the new label format.

The **L**abel Format command affects only the six data series elements on the **S**eries submenu; the command doesn't affect any data series selected with the /**G**raph **X**-Axis command.

Exploding a Piece of the Pie

What pie graph is complete without at least one piece appearing removed (*exploded*) from the rest of the pie? Quattro Pro includes this feature, which is recurrent in all data graphing programs. To explode an element in a pie graph, follow these steps:

1. Choose /**G**raph **C**ustomize Series **P**ies **E**xplode. Quattro Pro displays nine data series.

2. Choose the series you want to explode.

3. When prompted, choose **Explode**. Quattro Pro returns to the **Explode** submenu, where you can choose a new pie slice to explode.

4. Choose **Quit** to return to the **Pies** submenu.

5. Press F10 to view the pie graph with an exploded slice.

Figure 11.17 shows a pie graph of a household budget report. The Entertainment category is exploded from the pie, and the percent symbol is added to the labels for effect.

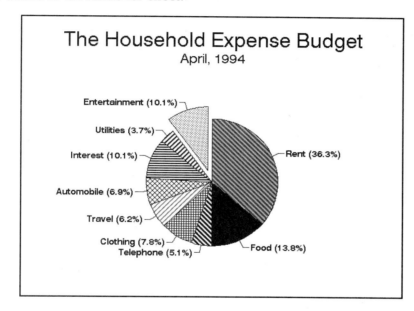

Fig. 11.17

A pie graph with an exploded pie slice, drawing attention to a data series.

If you want to unexplode a piece of the pie, choose the data series and then choose the **Don't Explode** option. If your data exceeds nine data series, the 10th will explode or not explode as the first slice option is specified.

Changing Fill Patterns in Pie Graphs

The **Patterns** command on the **Pies** submenu stores the pattern settings for up to 9 slices of pie. Although 16 patterns are available on the fill patterns gallery, you can use only 9 at a time. When your data set exceeds 9 data series, Quattro Pro repeats the fill patterns beginning with slice 10. (In other words, slice 10 and slice 1 share the same pattern setting, slice 11 and slice 2 share the same pattern setting, and so on.)

Fill patterns help you distinguish one pie slice from another. Without fill patterns or labels, a viewer has difficulty distinguishing between the data series values.

To change the fill pattern assignment for a data series, follow these steps:

1. Choose /**Graph** **C**ustomize Series **P**ies **P**atterns. Quattro Pro displays nine pie slice series and their current fill pattern assignments.

2. Choose the series you want to change. Quattro Pro displays the Select Pattern gallery.

3. Highlight a pattern in the gallery and press Enter to record the new fill pattern assignment for the selected series.

   Quattro Pro returns to the **P**atterns submenu, where you can choose a new series to change.

4. After you finish with your changes, choose **Q**uit to return to the **P**ies submenu.

5. Press F10 to view the new fill patterns in the graph.

Changing Colors in Pie Graphs

The **Colors** command stores the color settings for each pie slice or column section on a graph. By default, Quattro Pro assigns a different color to each series so that you can distinguish one from the other. When your data set exceeds 9 data series, Quattro Pro repeats the colors again, starting with slice 10. (In other words, slice 10 and slice 1 share the same color setting, slice 11 and slice 2 share another color setting, and so on.)

To change the color assignment of a data series, follow these steps:

1. Choose **Colors** from the **P**ies submenu. Quattro Pro displays nine pie slice series and their current color assignments.

2. Choose the series you want to change. Quattro Pro displays the coloring palette.

3. Highlight a color on the palette and press Enter to record the new color assignment for the selected pie slice series.

   Quattro Pro returns to the **Colors** submenu, where you can choose a new pie slice series to change.

4. After you finish with your changes, choose **Quit** to return to the **Pies** submenu.

5. Press F10 to view the new color selections on the graph.

Removing Tick Marks from Pie Graphs

A *tick mark* is the little line drawn from a data series label to the slice of the pie. Each time you create a column graph or pie graph, Quattro Pro draws tick marks.

To remove the tick marks from a pie graph, follow these steps:

1. Choose /**Graph Customize Series Pies Tick Marks**. Quattro Pro displays an options menu.

2. Choose **No** to remove the tick marks or **Yes** to return the tick marks to the graph.

Customizing Bubble Graphs

You customize bubbles in your bubble graph as you do slices in a pie graph. Fill patterns and colors are customized with the **Patterns** and **Colors** commands on the /**Graph Customize Series Bubbles** menu. Like a pie graph, when a bubble graph has more than nine bubbles, Quattro Pro repeats the patterns and colors beginning with the tenth bubble.

Customizing the Colors and Fill Patterns in Bubble Graphs

To customize the fill patterns on a bubble graph, follow these steps:

1. Choose /**Graph Customize Series Bubbles Patterns**.

2. Choose the bubble you want to change.

3. Choose the fill pattern.

Repeat these steps for all bubbles in which you want to change fill patterns.

To customize the color of each bubble, follow these steps:

1. Choose /**Graph Customize Series Bubbles Colors**.

2. Choose the bubble you want to change.

3. Choose the color.

Repeat these steps for all bubbles whose colors you want to change.

Changing Bubble Sizes

Use the /**G**raph **C**ustomize Series Bubbles **M**ax Bubble Size command to establish the radius of the largest bubble on a bubble graph. The radius is the distance from the center of the bubble to any point on the exterior of the bubble.

You can enter any number between 1 and 25 (see fig. 11.18). The default is 10. Quattro Pro views this number as a percentage of the x-axis. Therefore, if you enter 25%, the largest bubble will be one quarter the length of the x-axis; if you enter 10%, the largest bubble will occupy 10% of the x-axis, and so on. All other bubbles in the graph are sized relative to the largest bubble.

Fig. 11.18

Changing the maximum bubble size for a bubble graph.

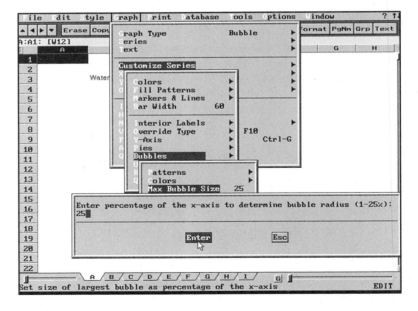

Updating and Resetting Default Settings

If you use many of the same custom graph settings for all your graphs, consider storing the values permanently by choosing the /**Graph C**ustomize Series **U**pdate command.

To erase the current graph settings and begin building a new set, choose /**Graph C**ustomize Series **R**eset **G**raph. To reset an individual series, choose the series name rather than **Graph**.

FOR RELATED INFORMATION

◄◄ "Creating a Fast Graph," p. 496.
"Building a Customized Graph," p. 499.
The two methods for building a Quattro Pro graph. Refer to these sections for guidance about working with notebook block selections that you intend to use as graph data series.

◄◄ "Enhancing the Appearance of a Basic Graph," p. 502.
How to perform basic graph customization, including adding legends and titles, changing fonts, selecting colors, and more.

Customizing the X-Axis and Y-Axis

You also can enhance the basic graph by altering the scale and format of a graph axis with the /**Graph X**-Axis and /**Graph Y**-Axis commands. When you create a graph, Quattro Pro scales it by looking at the range of values in each data series, recording the highest and lowest values, and then creating an axis value range encompassing these values.

A Quattro Pro graph can have up to four axes: an x-axis, a y-axis, a secondary y-axis, and a z-axis (which is reserved for 3-D graphs). Because the commands for adjusting the scales and formats of these axes are nearly identical, you generally can see how to adjust any axis by reviewing the /**Graph Y**-Axis command. When necessary, though, differences in the procedures or commands for adjusting an axis are pointed out in this chapter.

552

Using the X-Axis and Y-Axis Dialog Boxes

Quattro Pro enables you to display the /**Graph X**-Axis and **Y**-Axis menus as dialog boxes. Figure 11.19 shows the dialog box that replaces the **X**-Axis submenu. This dialog box is nearly identical to the **Y**-Axis dialog box (look for a mention of the differences later in this section).

By using these dialog boxes, you quickly can scan and set graph axis customizing options such as the axis scale, the low and high axis values, and the number of minor tick marks on an axis. The X-Axis and Y-Axis dialog boxes eliminate the need to move up and down the layers of submenus on the **X**-Axis and **Y**-Axis menus to choose and verify graph axis settings.

Fig. 11.19

The X-Axis options dialog box.

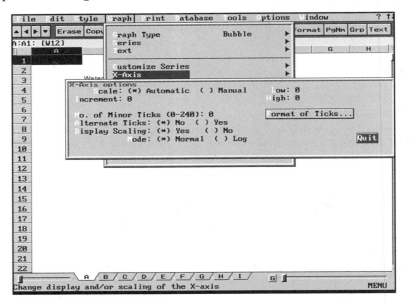

Quattro Pro displays an asterisk next to the current setting or a value for each option in the X-Axis and Y-Axis dialog boxes. To change a setting, type the highlighted letter in the option name, press the arrow keys to move the asterisk to the new setting, or type a new value; then press Enter. To move between option categories, such as **S**cale and **I**ncrement, press Tab. Alternatively, click the option that you want to use, and Quattro Pro immediately moves the asterisk there. Choose the **F**ormat of Ticks button to apply a numeric format to the values displayed along the current axis.

After you set options for an axis, choose **Q**uit to return to the **G**raph menu.

By default, Quattro Pro displays dialog boxes rather than menus at start-up. If you are upgrading from a previous version of Quattro Pro and prefer to display the menus instead of the dialog boxes, choose /**O**p-tions **S**tartup **U**se Dialogs **N**o. Subsequently, each time you choose /**G**raph **X**-Axis or /**G**raph **Y**-Axis, you see the menu to which you are accustomed.

For complete coverage of the other dialog boxes that are available on the **G**raph menu, see the sections "Using the Graph Customize Dialog Box" and "Using the Graph Overall Dialog Box" elsewhere in this chapter.

The rest of this chapter features menus instead of dialog boxes. If you choose to use the dialog boxes rather than the menus to make changes to your graphs, you can skim over the following sections to get an idea of what the settings in the X-Axis and Y-Axis dialog box do. (The following sections use the **Y**-Axis submenu as an example; the **X**-Axis submenu has the same options available, with two exceptions, discussed later.)

Adjusting the Scale of an Axis

Quattro Pro develops the scale of an axis by using the highest and lowest values in the selected data series. By changing the scale of an axis, you can enlarge a graph so that Quattro Pro compresses each data series to fit within a specified percentage of the graph area. You also can zoom in on a graph. Quattro Pro expands each data series so that portions of each data series may not appear on the graph.

Choose /**G**raph **Y**-Axis and review the **Y**-Axis submenu commands. Use the **S**cale, **L**ow, **H**igh, and **I**ncrement commands to change the scale of the y- or x-axis on a graph. You can adjust the scale of the y-axis for the graph shown in figure 11.20, for example.

Manually Scaling an Axis

The default setting for axis scaling is **A**utomatic. When you create a graph, Quattro Pro uses values from the data series to determine the scale.

Fig. 11.20

The scale for a graph using data series values from the notebook.

To adjust the scale of the y-axis on a graph, follow these steps:

1. Choose /**Graph Y**-Axis **S**cale. Quattro Pro displays two **S**cale options.

2. Choose **M**anual. Quattro Pro returns to the **Y**-Axis submenu.

When the **S**cale command is set to **M**anual, Quattro Pro uses the values stored in the **L**ow and **H**igh prompt boxes to determine how to scale an axis. To enter high and low scaling values, follow these steps:

1. Choose **L**ow from the **Y**-Axis submenu. Quattro Pro displays the **L**ow prompt box.

2. Type a number that you want to represent the smallest value on the y-axis. This number should be equal to or less than the smallest number in the data series. To zoom in, choose a number greater than the smallest number in the data series.

3. Press Enter to record that number. Quattro Pro returns to the **Y**-Axis submenu.

4. Choose **H**igh from the **Y**-Axis submenu. Quattro Pro displays the **H**igh prompt box.

5. Type a number that you want to represent the largest value on the y-axis. This number should be equal to or greater than the largest number in the data series. To zoom in, choose a number less than the largest number in the data series.

6. Press Enter to record that number. Quattro Pro returns to the **Y**-Axis submenu.

Choosing a Scale Increment

Quattro Pro positions numbers on an axis by using the **I**ncrement command setting's value. To scale an axis in increments of a thousand, for example, enter **1000** as the increment.

To set an increment value, follow these steps:

1. Choose **I**ncrement from the **Y**-Axis submenu. Quattro Pro displays the Increment dialog box. An increment of 0 enables Quattro Pro to increment automatically.

2. Type the number you want to use as the incremental axis scaling value.

3. Press Enter. Quattro Pro returns to the **Y**-Axis submenu.

Figure 11.21 shows the **Y**-Axis submenu after customizing values are entered.

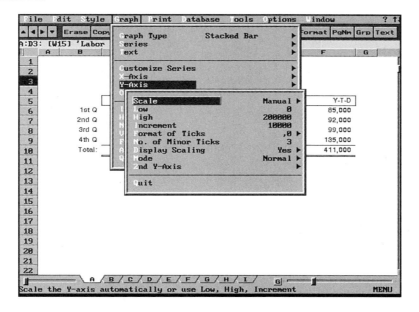

Fig. 11.21

The new scale settings stored at the right margin of the **Y**-Axis submenu.

You can press F10 to view the newly scaled graph on-screen. If the scaling is unacceptable, press Enter to return to the **Y**-Axis submenu and adjust each value accordingly. Figure 11.22 shows the new form of the graph in figure 11.20 after Quattro Pro has redrawn the graph using the new axis scaling settings.

Fig. 11.22

An alternative display for the sample graph after manually setting the scaling values.

Adjusting Axis Ticks

Axis ticks help you match an axis label to its data point on a graph. Ticks also delineate regular scale intervals on an axis. In Quattro Pro, you can adjust the format and display of ticks on an axis.

Formatting Ticks

The Format of Ticks command enables you to choose a numeric display format for each value that corresponds to a tick on a graph axis. The numeric format menu that Quattro Pro displays when you choose this command is the same as the menu displayed when you choose /**Style** Numeric Format.

To format the ticks on the y-axis, follow these steps:

1. Choose /**Graph Y**-Axis Format of Ticks.

2. When Quattro Pro displays the Format of Ticks submenu, highlight a format and press Enter to record the new format for the selected series.

3. Enter the number of decimal places, if required.

4. Press Enter. Quattro Pro returns to the **Y-Axis** submenu.

TIP

To format the ticks on the x-axis of an XY graph, choose **/G**raph **X**-Axis **F**ormat of Ticks.

Adding Minor Ticks

When you add labels to a graph axis, Quattro Pro sometimes displays labels that overlap each other, because the width (or height) of the graph isn't sufficient to accommodate the total combined width (or height) of the labels. The **No.** of Minor Ticks command can correct the problem of overlapping labels by replacing labels with tick marks. This command works on all graph types except pie and column graphs.

To skip labels on the y-axis, follow these steps:

1. Choose **/G**raph **Y**-Axis **N**o. of Minor Ticks.

2. When prompted, type a number of minor ticks to appear between each labeled tick.

3. Press Enter. Quattro Pro returns to the **Y-Axis** submenu.

The default value for this command, which displays all graph labels, is 0. If you enter a number larger than the number of labels in the graph, only tick marks (and no labels) will appear.

Figure 11.22 shows the graph presented in figure 11.20 with tick marks replacing some of the y-axis labels.

Alternating the Display of Ticks

Setting the number of minor ticks is one way to correct the problem of overlapping labels on either axis. Another way to solve this problem specifically for the x-axis is to use the **Alternate Ticks** command.

This command is available only on the **X-Axis** submenu; you cannot alternate ticks for the y-axis. When you choose this command, Quattro Pro reproduces every other tick label slightly below the x-axis labels so that long labels display in full.

To alternate tick labels on the x-axis, follow these steps:

1. Choose **/G**raph **X**-Axis **Alternate Ticks**.

2. When prompted, choose **Yes** to alternate the labels. Quattro Pro returns to the **X-Axis** submenu.

The default setting for this command, which displays all graph labels next to each other on the x-axis, is **No**.

Changing the Display of an Axis Scale

One final technique for adjusting the display of graph scales involves two commands on the **X-Axis** and **Y-Axis** submenus. The **D**isplay Scaling command determines whether Quattro Pro truncates long values on an axis and then appends a scale label. The **M**ode command enables you to toggle the display of your graph between normal and logarithmic modes.

Adding and Removing Scaling Labels

When Quattro Pro encounters a data series that contains large numbers, the program reduces the numbers by a factor of 1,000 or 10,000 to save space on the graph area. Quattro Pro then appends a label by the axis, indicating that the numbers have been reduced.

By reducing the number 10,000,000 to 1,000, for example, Quattro Pro frees up space equal to 5 character widths—space that you can use for displaying the graph.

If you don't want Quattro Pro to scale large numerical data, follow these steps:

1. Choose /**G**raph **Y**-Axis **D**isplay Scaling.

2. When prompted, choose **No**. Quattro Pro returns to the **Y**-Axis submenu.

3. Press F10 to view the new form of your graph.

If you decide that your graph looks better with scaled data, choose /**G**raph **Y**-Axis again and then choose **Yes** on the **D**isplay Scaling submenu.

Displaying Data on a Logarithmic Scale

A logarithmically scaled graph is different from the graphs covered so far in this chapter. In normal scale mode, each data series value corresponds to a value on the graph. On a logarithmically scaled graph, each major axis division represents 10 times the value of the preceding division. You can use this scaling mode when the values in your data series have substantially different magnitudes.

Graphing zeros and negative numbers on a logarithmic scale is impossible. If you try to do so, Quattro Pro beeps and displays an error message. To scale a graph in logarithmic mode, use the following steps, which include an extra step that the other scale customizing commands don't use:

1. If the lowest value on the axis to be scaled is zero or negative, rescale the axis using the **Low** command and reset the value to 1.

2. Choose /**G**raph **Y**-Axis **M**ode. Quattro Pro displays the **M**ode submenu.

3. Choose **L**og. Quattro Pro returns to the **Y**-Axis submenu.

4. Press F10 to view the newly scaled graph. To return to a normal scale mode, choose the command again and choose **N**ormal from the **M**ode submenu.

Customizing the Secondary Y-Axis

The final command on the **Y**-Axis submenu is **2**nd Y-Axis. The menu that Quattro Pro displays after you choose /**G**raph **Y**-Axis **2**nd Y-Axis closely resembles the one shown in figure 11.21. The **2**nd Y-Axis command enables you to alter the display of any graph's second y-axis, such as the one shown earlier in figure 11.15.

FOR RELATED **INFORMATION**

▶▶ "Using Linear Fit Analysis," p. 613.
"Using Exponential Fit Analysis," p. 617.
How to analyze graph data. These two methods use techniques that temporarily adjust the x- and y-axis values in pursuit of trends and patterns in the data.

Customizing the Overall Graph

Consider the graph shown in figure 11.23. After you alter the individual parts of the graph, you can evaluate the overall look of the graph. Is the coloring OK? Have other customizing operations caused the graph titles and legend to lose their impact?

By using the **O**verall submenu commands, you can enhance each part of this graph's overall display. You can add grid lines, draw outlines around the report titles, lighten the background colors, and even change the graph to a three-dimensional display.

Fig. 11.23

A properly scaled graph ready for the finishing touches.

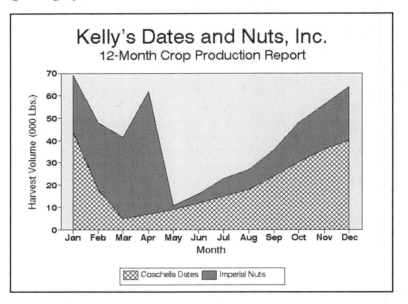

Using the Graph Overall Dialog Box

Quattro Pro enables you to display the /**G**raph **O**verall menu as a dialog box. Figure 11.24 shows the dialog box that replaces the **O**verall submenu. By using this dialog box, you quickly can scan and set overall graph customizing options such as outlines around titles, the legend, and the graph; the grid line style; and the colors displayed in the graph. The Graph Overall dialog box eliminates the need to move up and down the layers of submenus on the **O**verall menu to choose and verify the overall graph settings.

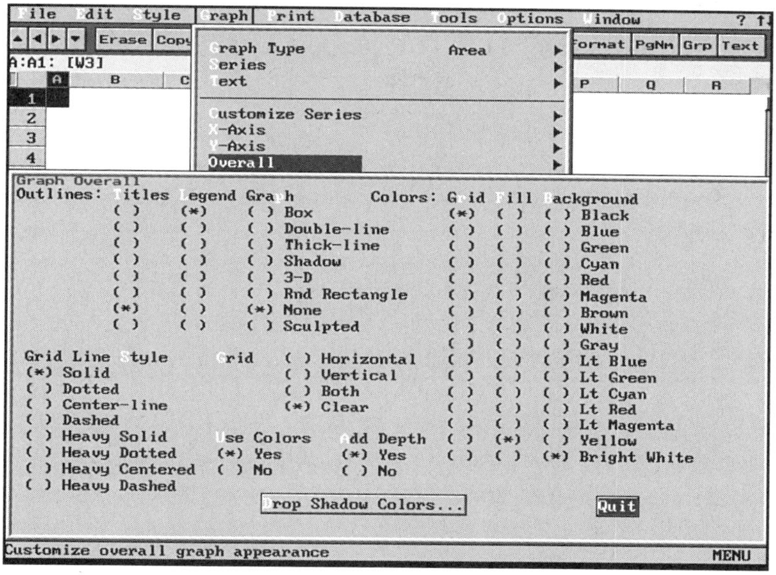

Fig. 11.24

The Graph Overall
dialog box.

Quattro Pro displays an asterisk next to the current setting, or a value
for each option in the Graph Overall dialog box. To change a setting,
type the highlighted letter in the option name and then press the arrow
keys to move the asterisk to the new setting or type a new value; then
press Enter. To move between option categories, such as Titles and
Legend, press Tab. Alternatively, click the option setting you want to
use, and Quattro Pro immediately moves the asterisk there.

Choose the Drop Shadow Colors button to display a menu on which
you can select the color pairings used to display drop shadows on a
graph. After you set options for the graph, choose Quit to return to the
Graph menu.

> By default, Quattro Pro displays dialog boxes rather than menus at start-
> up. If you are upgrading from a previous version of Quattro Pro and
> prefer to display the menus instead of the dialog boxes, choose /Op-
> tions Startup Use Dialogs No. Subsequently, each time you choose
> /Graph Overall, you see the menu to which you are accustomed.

NOTE

For complete coverage of the other dialog boxes available on the Graph
menu, see the sections titled "Using the Graph Customize Dialog Box"
and "Using the X-Axis and Y-Axis Dialog Boxes" earlier in this chapter.

The following table shows discrepancies that exist between commands on the /**G**raph **O**verall menu and those appearing in the Graph Overall dialog box.

Menu Command	Dialog Box
Grid **G**rid Color	Grid
Grid **L**ine Style	Grid Line **S**tyle
Outlines **G**raph	Graph
Three-D	**A**dd Depth
Color/B&W	**U**se Colors

If you choose to use the dialog boxes rather than the menus to make changes to your graphs, you can skim over the following sections to get an idea of what the dialog box options do.

Using Grid Lines on a Graph

Quattro Pro enables you to draw grid lines behind the data appearing in the graph area. Grid lines are like an on-screen ruler, enabling you to match data series points to corresponding axis values easily. You can see examples of grid lines in many of the graphs pictured in this chapter.

Adding Grid Lines

To add grid lines to a graph, follow these steps:

1. Choose /**G**raph **O**verall **G**rid. Quattro Pro displays the **G**rid submenu.

2. Choose **H**orizontal, **V**ertical, or **B**oth.

3. Press F10 to view the grid lines on the current graph.

To remove grid lines from a graph, choose **C**lear on the **G**rid submenu.

Changing the Grid Color

The **G**rid Color command determines the color used to display the lines surrounding the following items: the main title, legend, bars on a bar graph, pie and column slices, areas, and overall graph. To change the color of the grid lines, follow these steps:

1. Choose /Graph Overall Grid Grid Color. Quattro Pro displays the coloring palette.

2. Highlight a color on the palette and press Enter to record the new color assignment for the selected series. Quattro Pro returns to the Grid submenu.

3. Choose Quit twice to return to the notebook.

Changing the Line Style

You can change the line style used to display grid lines. To do so, follow these steps:

1. Choose /Graph Overall Grid Line Style. Quattro Pro displays a submenu of line styles.

2. Pick a new line style. Quattro Pro returns to the Grid submenu.

3. Choose Quit twice to return to the notebook.

Changing the Fill Color

You also can determine the color that Quattro Pro uses to display the graph area (the area behind the grid lines). When you change the colors used to display grid lines, you probably should change the graph area color setting. White grid lines, for example, are invisible on a graph whose fill color also is white.

To change the default color selection, follow these steps:

1. Choose /Graph Overall Grid Fill Color. Quattro Pro displays the coloring palette.

2. Choose a new color from the palette. Quattro Pro returns to the Grid submenu.

3. Choose Quit twice to return to the notebook.

Adjusting Outlines

When you create a graph, Quattro Pro draws a box around the legend but doesn't draw a box for any other part of the graph. To draw a box around other parts of the graph, use the Outlines command.

To draw boxes on a graph, follow these steps:

1. Choose /**Graph O**verall **O**utlines. Quattro Pro displays the Outlines submenu.

2. Choose **Titles**, **Legend**, or **Graph**. Quattro Pro displays a submenu of outline styles.

3. Choose an outline from the submenu. Quattro Pro immediately returns to the **O**utlines submenu.

Quattro Pro offers eight outline styles, including the **N**one style that removes a drawn box from the graph for the selected item. These outline styles appear on the outline styles submenu shown in figure 11.25.

Fig. 11.25

The eight outline styles available.

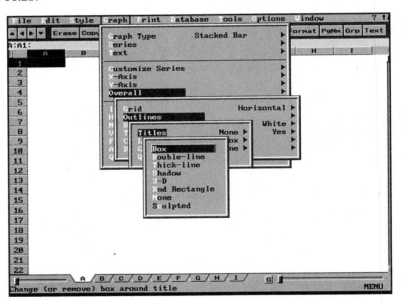

Changing the Background Color

You can change the portion of your screen outside the graph area (the area not affected by the /**Graph O**verall **G**rid **F**ill **C**olor command). Like other color commands, when you begin to change one or more colors, you usually end up changing all the colors to maintain proper consistency.

To change the color outside the graph area, follow these steps:

1. Choose /**G**raph **O**verall **B**ackground Color. Quattro Pro displays the coloring palette.

2. Highlight a new color on the palette and then press Enter to record the new color setting. Quattro Pro returns to the **G**raph menu.

3. Press F10 to view the new custom color setting.

Displaying a Graph in 3-D

Quattro Pro's capability to turn a flat graph into a three-dimensional display is one of the most impressive customizing tools on the **O**verall submenu. Quattro Pro displays most graphs in this mode.

To turn a two-dimensional graph into a three-dimensional display, follow these steps:

1. Choose /**G**raph **O**verall **T**hree-D.

2. When prompted, choose **Y**es.

3. Press F10 to view the new dimensional display setting.

To revert to the original two-dimensional display, choose the command again and choose **N**o.

Toggling On-Screen Color

The **C**olor/B&W command on the **O**verall submenu toggles the current graph between color and black and white. To use this command, choose /**G**raph **O**verall **C**olor/B&W and then choose an option from the menu.

Changing Drop Shadow Colors

In Chapter 10, "Creating Graphs," you learned that the /**G**raph **T**ext **F**ont 1st Line **S**tyle menu offers several options for customizing the appearance of graph text. The **D**rop Shadow Color option adds background highlighting to title, legend, and axes text. Quattro Pro creates drop shadows by pairing dark colors with light colors. You can fully customize these color pairs. To change drop shadow color pairings, choose /**G**raph **O**verall **D**rop Shadow Color.

FOR RELATED **INFORMATION**

▶▶ "Creating Special Display Effects," p. 394.
How to turn grid lines on and off in the notebook. In the notebook environment, grid lines help you develop a report or notebook; similarly, graph grid lines help you view and understand graph data.

▶▶ "Using Quattro Pro's Coloring Palette," p. 774.
How to change colors for the various parts of the screen. Use these options with the /**G**raph **O**verall settings to achieve the right color mix for the background and drop shadows in your graphs.

Annotating Graphs

By using the **C**ustomize Series submenu commands, you easily can turn a basic graph into a finished product. When your graph is missing that extra something, use Quattro Pro's Graph Annotator tool to finish the job.

The Graph Annotator is the final link in the graph-building process. This built-in graphics editor enables you to add descriptive text, boxes, lines, arrows, and other geometric shapes to your graphs.

Using the mouse is the easiest way to annotate a graph, although you can annotate graphs from the keyboard. Without a mouse, however, you cannot use the graph buttons. (For more details about graph buttons, see "Managing Graphs with Graph Buttons" later in this chapter.)

To access this tool, choose /**G**raph **A**nnotate. Quattro Pro loads the current graph into the Annotator environment. To load a different graph, choose **Q**uit to quit the annotator and return to the **G**raph menu. Then choose /**G**raph **N**ame **D**isplay, highlight the name of the graph you want to load, and press Enter to display the graph. After the graph appears, press the forward slash key (/). Quattro Pro loads the graph into the annotator environment.

NOTE

To use the Graph Annotator, your graphics display system must meet the specifications outlined in Chapter 10.

Reviewing the Annotator Screen

A quick look at the Annotator screen reveals that this tool has many of the same features as stand-alone graphics editor programs (see fig. 11.26). In fact, finding a tool of this caliber in an electronic spreadsheet program is surprising.

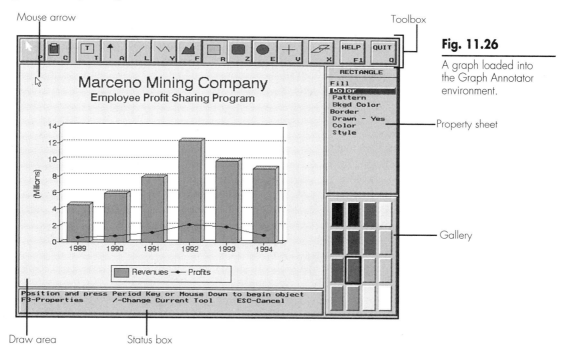

Fig. 11.26

A graph loaded into the Graph Annotator environment.

The Annotator screen contains various icons, boxed areas, letters, and a few commands that you should find familiar.

NOTE

A graphics editor is essentially a mouse-driven tool, but you can execute all the Graph Annotator commands directly from your keyboard.

Draw Area

Quattro Pro displays a graph in the *draw area*. In the draw area, you position, move, resize, delete, draw geometric elements, and paste clip art into the current graph.

Toolbox

The *toolbox* is the long, rectangular row of symbols at the top of the screen. These icons describe actions that you can perform on a graph. You can add text boxes, draw arrows and lines, add geometric elements, link data series, invoke a help window, and quit the Annotator from this feature. See table 11.1 for descriptions of the various buttons available from the toolbox.

If you have a mouse, click any icon to activate that tool. Otherwise, press / to activate the toolbox; then press the capital letter in the bottom right corner of the icon or scroll through the toolbox by pressing the left- or right-arrow key.

Table 11.1 Graphics Design Elements in the Toolbox

Icon	Description
White arrow (/P)	Enters edit mode and enables you to change existing elements
Clipboard (/C)	Displays a list of commands in the property sheet to cut and paste existing elements
Boxed T (/T)	Adds boxed text
Arrow (/A)	Draws a line with an arrowhead at the end
Line (/L)	Draws a straight line anchored at each end
Polyline (/Y)	Draws a line anchored in two or more places, up to 1,000 points
Polygon (/F)	Draws a multisided figure with up to 1,000 points; same as Polyline, except that its two ends are connected
Rectangle (/R)	Draws a rectangle with any dimensions
Rounded rectangle (/Z)	Draws a rounded rectangle with any dimensions

Icon	Description
Ellipse (/E)	Draws a circle or oval using dimensions you specify
Vertical/horizontal line (/V)	Draws vertical and horizontal lines
Link icon (/X)	Links one or more elements to a specific point on a graph so that the elements move when the graph series change in size
Help (/H)	Displays a help window specific to the Annotator and its features
Quit (/Q)	Quits the Annotator and displays a full-screen version of the graph

Property Sheet

The property sheet lists the command options available with each toolbox element. When you choose the rectangle tool, for example, the property sheet lists six command options: for the Fill category, Color, Pattern, and Bkgd Color; for the Border category, Drawn, Color, and Style (refer to fig. 11.26).

To activate the property sheet from elsewhere in the Annotator, press F3. Quattro Pro displays the command options for the active element.

Gallery

In the gallery, Quattro Pro displays special tools used with commands from the property sheet. When the rectangle tool is activated, for example, choose Color from the property sheet to see the coloring palette in this area.

Status Box

The status box displays instructions, points out keyboard shortcuts, and describes menu commands when the commands are activated.

Learning Keyboard Assignments

Table 11.2 lists the Annotator-specific keys that you use to operate the feature.

Table 11.2 Graph Annotator Keys

Key	Description
F2	Enters EDIT mode when a text element is activated
F3	Activates the property sheet of the active element
F7	Resizes a group of selected elements
Shift+F7	Selects multiple elements in the draw area when used with the Tab key, with each Tab adding an additional element to the group without deselecting the current selection
F10	Redraws the Annotator screen in full
Tab	Selects the next element in the draw area
Shift+Tab	Selects the preceding element in the draw area
Shift (used with mouse)	Selects multiple elements in the draw area; puts the mouse in a curve draw mode when drawing a polygon or polyline
Delete	Erases a selected element or a group of selected elements
Period (.)	Anchors the selected element, alternating among the four corners as you press the period so that you can resize it
Home, End, Page Up, Page Down	Move the corners of the active area diagonally
Arrow keys	Move or resize elements
Ctrl+Enter	Starts a new line when you are entering text or when you are in EDIT mode
Backspace	Deletes one character at a time to the left when you are in EDIT mode; connects a line with the line above it if you are at the beginning of the line
/	Activates the toolbox
Esc	Exits a menu selection and cancels an operation from the draw area

Key	Description
Enter	Accepts the results of an Annotation operation in the draw area
Alt	When used with a mouse, selects multiple elements when in proportional resizing mode

You also may use the mouse and arrow keys to move and resize a selected element or group of elements.

Annotating a Graph

When you understand how to operate the Graph Annotator, this tool is quite fun to use. To use the Annotator, follow these steps:

1. Load a graph into the Graph Annotator. (See the earlier section "Annotating Graphs" for complete details.)

2. Highlight an icon in the toolbox.

3. Position the pointer at the part of the graph you want to annotate.

4. Press Enter to move the pointer into the draw area, or click in the draw area.

5. Annotate symbols and text to the graph.

6. Type /Q to quit the Annotator and to display the full-screen version of the graph.

7. Press any key except the / to return to the active notebook.

8. Save the newly annotated graph with the /**Graph N**ame **C**reate command.

Figure 11.27 shows the results of annotating boxed text to a graph using these steps.

Selecting a Design Element

Selecting a design element is like selecting a cell on a notebook. When a notebook cell is active, the cell is highlighted; when a design element is selected, Quattro Pro places *handles* (small squares) around the element (see fig. 11.28).

Fig. 11.27

Boxed text added to a graph.

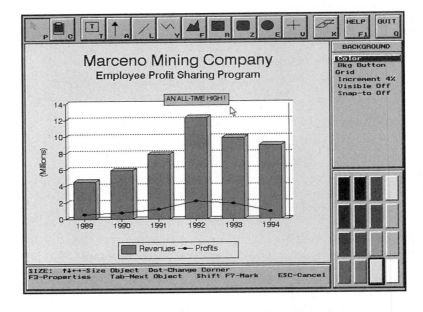

Fig. 11.28

A selected design element with handles.

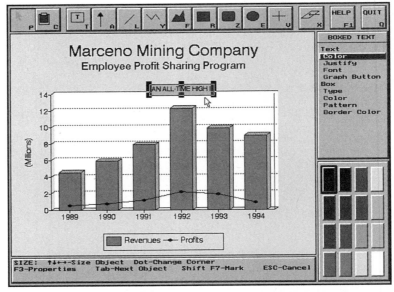

Before you can perform operations on a design element, you must select that element. To select a design element using the keyboard, follow these steps:

1. Press Esc and move to the draw area.

2. Type /**P** to activate the arrow pointer.

3. Press Tab and Shift+Tab to relocate the arrow pointer to the target design element.

4. Press Shift+F7 to retain the current design element selection and continue selecting additional elements.

With a mouse, the process of selecting design elements is more direct: Just click the design element. To select multiple elements, hold down the Shift key and click each element you want to select and add to the group.

Moving a Design Element

Moving a design element is like moving data from one cell to another. In the Annotator, you move a design element to reposition it on the graph.

To move a design element using the keyboard, follow these steps:

1. Press Esc and move to the draw area.

2. Select the design element you want to move.

3. Press the arrow keys to relocate the element elsewhere on the graph.

4. Press Enter to anchor the design element to the new location.

5. Press Esc to deselect the design element.

To move a design element with a mouse, first select the design element. Click inside the element's box anywhere except on the handles, drag the box to a new location on the graph, and release the button when you want to anchor the element. In figure 11.29, the boxed text is being moved to the left side of the graph.

Resizing a Design Element

Quattro Pro enables you to resize any element created in the Annotator environment. This capability gives you complete flexibility when you annotate a Quattro Pro graph. If you can change the typeface of a notebook font, why not the size of a graph element?

To resize an element using the keyboard, follow these steps:

1. Press Esc and move to the draw area.

2. Select the design element you want to resize.

3. Press the period key (.) to enter resize mode.

4. Continue pressing the period key until you highlight the corner of the element you want to resize (see fig. 11.30).

Fig. 11.29

Dragging a design element to a new location on the graph.

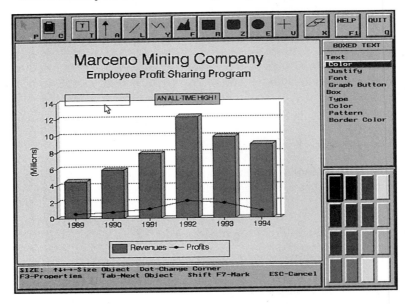

Fig. 11.30

A handle displayed in the corner of the element being resized.

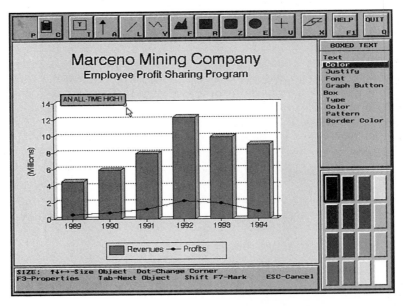

5. Press the arrow keys to resize the element or Home, End, Page Up, or Page Down to resize it diagonally.

Rather than perform steps 4 and 5, you can drag any edge of the selected element in the direction that you want to resize.

TIP

6. Press Enter to retain the new size. Press Esc twice to deselect the element and not change the size.

To resize an element with the mouse, begin by selecting the element. Click any box appearing on the outline of the selected element and drag until the desired size is attained. Release the mouse button to retain the new size.

Editing a Text Design Element

To edit any text design element that originated in the Annotator environment, follow these steps:

1. Press Esc and move to the draw area.

2. Select a text design element to edit.

3. Press F2 to enter EDIT mode.

4. Edit a design element's text using the same keys and procedures you use for editing notebook cells.

5. When you finish editing the text, press Enter to reaffix the modified design element to the graph.

You also can perform Clipboard operations on a selected design element. To delete a group of selected elements, position the arrow pointer over the element and press Del.

NOTE

Setting Design Element Properties

Each design element has a unique set of cosmetic properties that determines how Quattro Pro displays the element. If you annotate boxed text to a graph, for example, you can return later and change its color, justification, box style, text font, border color, and fill pattern. You also can set all the design element properties beforehand; later, when you annotate that element to a graph, the preset properties are in effect.

To preset the properties for a design element, follow these steps:

1. Select a design element icon from the toolbox.

2. Press F3 to display that element's property commands in the property sheet.

3. Press the boldfaced letter key in the command name to select the command.

4. Choose the desired property from the options displayed in the gallery area. Quattro Pro returns you to the property sheet.

5. Continue editing properties as desired.

6. Press Esc to return to the draw area.

The new properties will be in effect for the next time you select that element. In figure 11.31, several boxed text properties have been altered.

Fig. 11.31

Altered design element properties add clarity and impact to a graph.

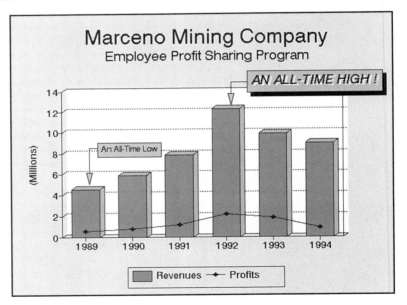

The new font is in an italic typeface with a drop shadow, and the box now appears with a shaded background. Finally, an arrow is added to connect the boxed text to a data series on the graph.

Using the Clipboard

When you activate the Clipboard toolbox button, Quattro Pro displays nine commands in the property sheet area. Use these commands to manage your annotation elements.

These commands, listed in table 11.3, enable you to cut, copy, paste, and delete selected elements in the draw area. You also can create and paste clip art to and from other graphs by using these commands. In fact, Quattro Pro comes with its own library of clip art that you can import into the Annotator for use with your graph files.

Table 11.3 The Clipboard Commands

Command	Description
Cut	Moves a selected object into the Clipboard and then removes the object from the current graph
Copy	Copies an object from the current graph into the Clipboard
Paste	Pastes an object from the Clipboard into the current graph
Delete	Deletes selected objects from the current graph
To Top	Moves the selected object(s) to the foreground of the current graph
To Bottom	Moves the selected object(s) to the background of the current graph
Cut To	Copies the selected object(s) into a file and then removes the object(s) from the current graph
Copy To	Copies the selected object(s) into a file
Paste From	Copies objects from a named file into the current graph

Quattro Pro comes with a library of clip art files for use with your Quattro Pro graphs or with applications that can read the CLP file format. The following is an example of how to import a Quattro Pro clip art file into the current graph:

1. Activate the Clipboard icon by typing /C.

2. Select the **P**aste From command. Quattro Pro displays a file name prompt box.

3. Type the path and name of the clip art file you want to paste into the current graph, and then press Enter.

Quattro Pro pastes the clip art image into the graph displaying in the Annotator. Selection handles appear around the clip art so that you can resize or move the object to incorporate it into the design layout for the graph. When the clip art image is properly sized and positioned, press Esc once to deselect the object.

TIP

Quattro Pro can import clip art in the Computer Graphics Metafile (CGM) file format. To import a CGM file, follow the same rules to import Quattro Pro's CLP clip art.

If you want to export modified clip art to use in a different graphics editor program, such as PC Paintbrush, follow these steps:

1. Activate the Clipboard icon by typing /**C**.

2. Choose **C**opy To to create a copy of the modified clip art file.

3. When prompted, type a file name and specify the CLP file-name extension. Press Enter to record the new clip art file name.

The following example shows how to combine two Clipboard operations. Follow these steps to copy an object from the current graph into a second graph:

1. Select an object in the draw area.

2. Activate the Clipboard icon by typing /**C**.

3. Choose **C**opy to copy the selected object.

4. Choose Quit (type /**Q**) to quit the Annotator. Quattro Pro returns you to the current graph (or to the active notebook if no graph is displayed).

5. Select /**G**raph **N**ame **D**isplay to display a different graph.

6. Press / to load the displayed graph into the Annotator.

7. Activate the Clipboard icon by typing /**C**.

8. Choose **P**aste From to copy the element from the Clipboard into the draw area.

Use these sample operations as a guideline for choosing and executing Clipboard operations. In most cases, the sequence of steps is the same. Fortunately, you quickly can learn the Clipboard commands because their functions are fairly obvious from their names.

Linking an Element to a Graph Data Series

The Graph Annotator redraws itself periodically as you move in and out of the draw area. When redrawing happens, Quattro Pro retains the integrity of the selected elements with which you are working.

If later you recall an annotated graph into the Annotator, the graph looks the same, as long as you haven't modified any of the original graph settings. One way to guard against the possibility of ruining your annotation work, if you choose to alter a graph's settings, is to link an annotation element to a graph data series.

This technique maintains the original organization of the annotated graph as long as the original data series definition stays intact. When you do change series settings and remove the data point that you linked to, Quattro Pro moves the linked annotation element with the data series.

To link an annotation element to a data series on the current graph, follow these steps:

1. Select the element in the draw area.

2. Type /X to choose the Link command.

3. When prompted, choose the number of the data series you want to link.

4. When prompted, type in the link index number (the relative position of the data series point to the whole data series).

5. Press Enter to create the link.

The link between the data series and the selected element remains intact until you reset a data series by choosing the /Graph Customize Series Reset command or change the series to include fewer elements than the link index number.

Managing Graphs with Graph Buttons

Quattro Pro offers additional graph management capabilities with special-action buttons called graph buttons. A *graph button* is boxed text that you place onto a graph. To distinguish a graph button from other boxed text, use the **G**raph Button command that appears in the property sheet area when you activate the Boxed T icon (type **/T**). This command enables you to assign special actions to the boxed text.

After you assign an action to boxed text, it becomes a graph button. When you click a graph button, Quattro Pro executes the action assigned to the button. Clicking a graph button may, for example, display another graph, execute a macro, or even start a slide show. You decide what action the graph button takes.

NOTE

You must use a mouse if you want to execute a graph button on a graph. No keyboard method exists for executing a graph button. Even without a mouse, however, you can create and add graph buttons to a graph. This option is useful if you later want to test the graph buttons on a PC that has a mouse.

Figure 11.32 shows one way to use graph buttons. The six graph buttons (labeled 1989 through 1994) on the Marceno Mining Company graph perform six separate tasks. When you click graph button 1989, for example, Quattro Pro displays a graph containing detailed financial information for 1989. The boxed text containing the label Detail? is just that—boxed text. No special operation is assigned to this element, so the boxed text serves as an introductory heading for the six graph buttons below it.

To use graph buttons, you need to know the following rules:

- You must use the **G**raph Button command (accessed through the Boxed T icon) to activate a graph button.

- A graph button is "live" only when the graph displays in full-screen mode. To display the graph full screen, press F10 or choose **/G**raph **V**iew.

- You must have a mouse to use a graph button. When you display a graph that contains graph buttons, Quattro Pro also displays the mouse arrow pointer.

- Graph buttons appearing on graphs in a slide show can branch only to other graphs. Quattro Pro ignores macros assigned to graph buttons if you try to run them during a slide show.

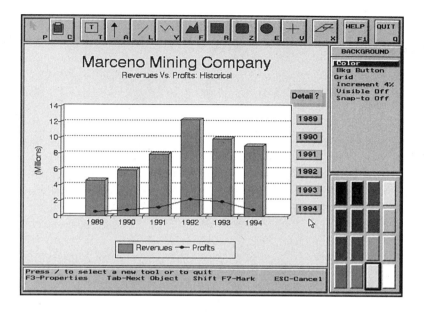

Fig. 11.32

A graph with graph buttons used to branch to other graphs.

Creating and Activating a Graph Button

Before you can use a graph button, you must draw and then activate the button with the **Graph Button** command.

A graph button does nothing until you execute the **Graph Button** command. If you draw boxed text elements on a graph and then forget to activate them, the elements don't work when you click them.

To create and activate a graph button, follow these steps:

1. Load a graph into the Graph Annotator environment.

2. Draw a boxed text element on the graph. Include a word or two in the boxed text that describes the action you want the graph button to take.

3. Move and resize the boxed text so that you easily can see it. The text shouldn't interfere with data shown on the graph.

4. Highlight the boxed text element.

5. Choose the **Graph Button** command from the property area. Quattro prompts you to supply a name.

6. If you want the button to branch to another graph, type the name of a graph that's saved with the active notebook and then press Enter (see fig. 11.33).

Fig. 11.33

Entering the name of a
graph to activate the
graph button.

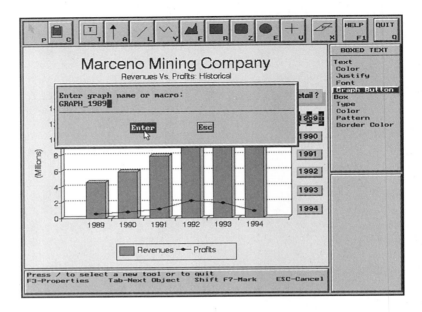

If you want the button to execute an existing macro, type the
name of the macro. If you want the button to execute a macro
command, type any string of macro command(s) of up to 80 characters. Then press Enter.

7. Choose Quit (type **/Q**) to leave the Graph Annotator. Quattro Pro
displays a full-screen version of the active graph.

8. Press Enter or Esc to return to the active notebook.

9. Choose **/Graph Name Create** and save the current graph settings,
including the new graph button settings, unless **Autosave Edits** is
set to **Yes.**

Graph buttons aren't active when the graph is in the Graph Annotator
environment or when the graph is inserted onto a notebook. To activate a graph button, you must display the graph so that it fills your
screen entirely (see fig. 11.34). When you click a button on a fully displayed graph, Quattro Pro performs an action, such as displaying another graph or returning to the original graph.

Renaming and Deactivating a Graph Button

You can redefine a graph button's action by assigning a new graph or
macro name to that button. Follow these steps:

1. Reload the graph into the Graph Annotator environment.

2. Highlight the graph button you want to edit and then choose the **G**raph Button command located in the property sheet area. Quattro Pro displays a dialog box with the current name.

3. Press Backspace until you delete the name entirely.

4. Type a new name and press Enter to rename the graph button.

To deactivate a graph button, follow these steps:

1. Reload the graph into the Graph Annotator environment.

2. Highlight the graph button you want to edit and then choose **G**raph Button. Quattro Pro displays a dialog box with the current name assignment.

3. Press Backspace until you delete the name entirely.

4. Press Enter to deactivate the graph button.

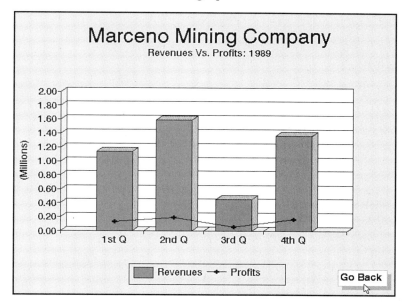

Fig. 11.34

A full-screen graph with a graph button.

Turning a Graph Background into a Graph Button

By default, clicking a graph background while in full-screen display removes the graph from your screen and returns to the notebook. With respect to graph buttons, this feature can be a nuisance. Suppose that in an attempt to execute a graph button, you inadvertently click just outside the boxed text area. Doing so causes Quattro Pro to cancel the graph and return to the notebook. Because you didn't intend this result, you must display the graph again and start over.

You can eliminate this nuisance with the **B**kgd Button command. This command enables you to assign a special operation to the background of a graph as though it were a graph button. To access this command, type **/P** or click the Edit icon (the button with the white arrow on it). The **B**kgd Button command appears in the property sheet area. Now assign a special operation to the background of a graph so that clicking that area doesn't remove the graph from your screen. The logical operation to assign is one that tells Quattro Pro to display the current graph every time you click the graph background. Do so by typing the name of the current graph.

After you have the background set up to serve as a button, you can exit back to the notebook by pressing any key but the forward slash key (/).

NOTE

When you click the background of a graph that has been defined as a graph button, the mouse pointer disappears from the screen. The pointer disappears regardless of the operation you assign to the graph background. Slide the mouse in any direction to display the pointer again.

Annotating and Managing Multiple Graph Elements

The Graph Annotator has several commands that enable you to annotate and manage multiple graph elements more easily. The first set of commands simplifies the process of aligning elements as you add them to a graph. These commands appear on the Background menu of the property sheet area when you activate the Edit icon. The second set of commands performs operations on groups of elements you have annotated to a graph. These commands appear on the Group menu of the property sheet area whenever you select more than one element.

Adding Multiple Elements to a Graph

A rudimentary but frequently used method for aligning elements on a graph involves moving and resizing the elements after they are annotated. This method relies on your visual inspection skills and usually requires you to spend extra time fine-tuning the placement of the element to get it just right.

The Annotator alignment grid is very useful when you have specific placement objectives for multiple elements that you are annotating to a graph. The Annotator alignment grid also enables you to align elements automatically as you annotate them to a graph.

To display the alignment grid, follow these steps:

1. Load a graph into the Graph Annotator environment.

2. Type **/P** to activate the Edit icon or click the Edit icon in the toolbox.

3. If you are using a keyboard, press F3 to move to the property sheet, highlight the **Visible** command, and press Enter. With a mouse, click **Visible** in the property sheet area.

Quattro Pro displays the alignment grid at the top of the graph now displayed in the Annotator. To show that the grid is active, Quattro Pro displays the word On next to the **Visible** command in the property sheet area.

Use the Increment command to fine-tune further the element placement process. This command alters the distance between the dots in the alignment grid. You can achieve very small placement differences between multiple elements on a graph, for example, by increasing the density of the dots in the alignment grid. This method is similar to using a measurement system based on millimeters rather than centimeters.

To alter the density of the dots appearing in the alignment grid, follow these steps:

1. Load a graph into the Graph Annotator environment.

2. Type **/P** to activate the Edit icon or click the Edit icon in the toolbox.

3. If you are using a keyboard, press F3 to move to the property sheet, highlight the **Increment** command, and press Enter. When using a mouse, click **Increment** in the property sheet area.

Quattro Pro prompts you to enter an increment setting in the range from 1 to 25. A setting of 1 produces the highest density of dots, whereas a setting of 25 produces the lowest density. The percentage refers to percent of an edge, with an edge consisting of 100 dots; therefore, 4% is 25 dots by 25 dots, 25% is 4 dots by 4 dots, 1% is 100 dots by 100 dots, and so on.

4. Type a number and press Enter.

Quattro Pro immediately redraws the alignment grid to reflect the new **I**ncrement command setting.

When the alignment grid is on, you can use the **S**nap-to command to align elements while you annotate them to a graph. When the **S**nap-to command is set to On, each object you add to a graph moves to the nearest grid line. To align multiple elements, place the elements near the same grid line as you annotate them to a graph. This command can save you valuable time when building a graph because it eliminates the need to inspect and fine-tune object placements after you annotate them to a graph.

Follow these steps to align elements while you annotate them to a graph:

1. Load a graph into the Graph Annotator environment.

2. Type **/P** to activate the Edit icon, or click the Edit icon in the toolbox.

3. If you are using a keyboard, press F3 to move to the property sheet, highlight the **S**nap-to command, and press Enter. With a mouse, click **S**nap-to in the property sheet area. The word On appears next to the **S**nap-to command in the property sheet area.

NOTE

With **S**nap-to set to On, the alignment grid aligns elements annotated to a graph whether the **V**isible command is set to On or Off.

Performing Operations on Groups of Elements

After you annotate several elements to a graph, you may want to modify the alignments of those elements. Again, the rudimentary method for doing so involves a great deal of moving and resizing. Quattro Pro, fortunately, provides you with a much more efficient way to change the alignments of a group of elements.

By using the **A**lign command, you can realign a group of selected elements simultaneously. The alignment choices for this command are as follows: **L**eft Sides, **R**ight Sides, **V**ert (vertical) Centers, **T**ops, **B**ottoms, and **H**oriz (horizontal) Centers.

The following steps show how to modify the alignment for a group of selected elements:

1. Load a graph into the Graph Annotator environment.

2. By using the element selection procedure described earlier in the section "Selecting a Design Element," select a group of elements that you want to align. Quattro Pro displays the Group menu commands in the property sheet area.

3. If you are using a keyboard, press F3 to move to the property sheet, highlight the **A**lign command, and press Enter. With a mouse, click **A**lign in the property sheet area.

4. Choose an alignment option from the menu that Quattro Pro displays. Quattro Pro immediately realigns the group of selected elements.

> **TIP**
>
> You can modify other characteristics for a group of selected elements by using the remaining commands on the **G**roup menu. You can change simultaneously the fill **C**olor, the fill **P**attern, or the **B**kgd (background) Color, for example, for a group of selected elements.

Questions & Answers

This chapter introduces you to Quattro Pro's graph customizing commands. If you have questions concerning particular situations that aren't addressed in the examples given, look through this section.

Q: When I press F10, why don't my graphs appear on-screen?

A: Remember, to display Quattro Pro graphs, you must have a graphics adapter system, and to display a graph inserted on a notebook, the /**O**ptions **D**isplay Mode command must be set to **B**: WYSIWYG.

Q: Why do most of my color selections for the data series appear white?

A: You probably have a monochrome display system. With this type of system, you should change color selections with care. Remember that any color selection other than black always appears white when you display the graph.

Q: Why doesn't Quattro Pro show the fill pattern selections I make for my pie graphs and column graphs?

A: You used the /**Graph C**ustomize Series **F**ill Patterns command to choose the new fill pattern. Instead, choose the /**Graph C**ustomize Series **P**ies **P**atterns command.

Q: Why is Quattro Pro showing the same marker symbol for all the text appearing in a legend box?

A: You selected the same marker symbol for every data series through the /**Graph C**ustomize Series **M**arkers & Lines **M**arkers command. Choose this command again and specify a different marker symbol for each data series. Quattro Pro updates the displayed symbol in the legend box.

Q: I can't see any marker symbol assignments on the **M**arkers submenu. Where are they?

A: Press the Expand key (+) on your numeric keypad to display a full view of the **M**arkers submenu (or any menu for that matter) marker assignments.

Q: Quattro Pro keeps displaying a line graph when I want to display an area graph. How can this happen?

A: If you began by creating a combination graph, you must reset any overridden data series before selecting a new graph type. Choose /**Graph C**ustomize Series **O**verride Type **D**efault and reset all applicable data series.

Q: Does a quick way exist to erase a graph and begin all over again?

A: Yes. Choose /**Graph C**ustomize Series **R**eset Graph. Quattro Pro erases the current graph and returns to the default graph settings. Change the default settings to the current settings by choosing /**Graph C**ustomize Series **U**pdate.

Q: I cannot seem to adjust the x-axis scale on a line graph. What's going on?

A: Quattro Pro enables x-axis scale adjustments only to XY graphs. To get around this restriction, you can add extra data series on your notebook that define the upper and lower limits of the scale you want to create. Be sure to choose the /**Graph S**eries command again and define the new series so that Quattro Pro shows the series on a graph. If you don't want these numbers to show, choose /**G**raph **C**ustomize **S**eries **M**arkers & Lines **F**ormats, choose the series option you want to change, and then choose **N**either.

Q: I can't seem to alter the numeric format of the x-axis values on an area graph by using the /**G**raph **X**-Axis **F**ormat of Ticks command. What's going on?

A: Quattro Pro enables x-axis numeric format adjustments only to XY graphs. To get around this restriction, return to the active notebook, choose /**S**tyle **N**umeric Format, and format the cell data you want to alter. When you display the graph again, it reflects the new numeric formats.

Q: I thought that Quattro Pro displays most 2-D graphs in 3-D form. Why aren't any of my graphs displaying in 3-D?

A: The 2-D graphs you create may make three-dimensional display impossible for Quattro Pro, even when /**G**raph **O**verall **T**hree-D is set to **Y**es. When a bar graph has numerous bars or when a pie graph has many slices, for example, the program may be incapable of displaying in three dimensions. To correct this situation, you can reduce the number of displayed data points in each series until the graph does display in 3-D, or change **B**ar Width to 90%.

If you saved a set of graph defaults where the **T**hree-D option is set to **N**o, Quattro Pro doesn't display graphs this way. To change this situation, choose /**G**raph **O**verall **T**hree-D **Y**es, and then choose /**G**raph **C**ustomize **S**eries **U**pdate.

Alternatively, choose /**G**raph **G**raph Type **3**-D and choose one of the four new three-dimensional graphs styles available on this submenu.

Q: Why does Quattro Pro superimpose a text graph on my current graph?

A: Anything you do in the Graph Annotator environment affects the current graph. To create a text graph by itself, save the current graph setting with the /**G**raph **N**ame **C**reate command and then reset the current graph settings. Choose /**G**raph **C**ustomize **S**eries **R**eset **G**raph.

Summary

In this chapter, you learned how to turn a finished graph into a presentation-quality visual aid by using the commands found in the middle section of Quattro Pro's **G**raph menu. You also learned how to use the Graph Annotator tool, Quattro Pro's special built-in graphics editor facility.

Having completed this chapter, you should understand the following Quattro Pro concepts:

- Changing colors, fill patterns, markers and lines, and bar widths for individual data series

- Appending labels to individual points in a data series

- Creating combination bar and line graphs

- Plotting two y-axes on one graph

- Plotting two or more data series that use different systems of measurement

- Changing label formats, colors, fill patterns, and tick marks on pie and column graphs

- Changing colors, fill patterns, and bubble sizes on bubble graphs

- Updating and resetting the default **C**ustomize Series submenu command settings for use with other notebooks

- Manually adjusting the default axis scale

- Adjusting, formatting, adding, and deleting axis tick marks

- Displaying a graph on a logarithmic scale

- Using grid lines, outlines, background colors, and special display settings to enhance the overall appearance of a graph

- Using the Graph Annotator to append boxed text, arrows, lines, and geometric figures to a graph

- Pasting clip art to and from the Annotator tool for use on graphs

- Using and managing graph buttons

Chapter 12 concludes the discussion of Quattro Pro graphs by introducing you to a feature known as *analytical graphing*. In that chapter,
you learn how to use the commands on the /**G**raph **S**eries **A**nalyze
menu to combine a large data set into a smaller data set—making it
easier to graph and interpret the data—without changing any information in your notebook. The chapter also shows you how to analyze
graphs using moving averages, linear fit lines, and exponential fit lines.

Analyzing Graphs

In this chapter, you learn another method for analyzing notebook data that also involves graphs. This technique, called *analytical graphing*, is much different than the graphing techniques described in Chapters 10 and 11.

Analytical graphing enables you to graph the same data in several different ways without modifying the notebook itself. With analytical graphing, you can display custom groupings of data, moving averages, "best fit" linear lines, and more. You perform all these operations by using the commands on the /**G**raph **S**eries **A**nalyze menu.

In the first section of this chapter, you learn about the commands on the **A**nalyze submenu. This material provides you with all the specifics you need to apply analytical graphing techniques to your own notebook data.

The second section explains an analytical graphing technique called *aggregation*, or the grouping of data. Aggregation helps convey general impressions about large sets of data. You may want to graph average quarterly stock performance by using a notebook that contains only daily totals, for example.

The next section introduces an analytical graphing technique based on the concept of moving averages. A *moving average graph* smooths widely fluctuating values by displaying progressive averages. When computer chip production totals vary widely, for example, a moving average graph may help shed light on an overall production trend.

The chapter continues by showing how to use a third analytical graphing tool called *linear regression*. This tool enables you to graph a line that is representative of—or "best fits"—the data you are evaluating. Statisticians, economists, and forecasters use linear regression to predict future events (such as next year's sales) based on historical data.

The final analytical graphing technique is called *exponential graphing*. Like the linear fit line, data displayed in an exponential fit line often reveal general trends when trends exist. The exponential fit line, however, actually looks like a decreasing or increasing curve.

Defining Analytical Graphing

By now you realize that although designing and building complex, involved notebook applications can be challenging and even fun, the real fruits of your labor should come in the form of healthier decision-making, improved reporting, and increased productivity. After all, you use Quattro Pro to aid you in the task of managing and presenting your data.

In other words, how you organize your notebook data affects your ability to access and use that information efficiently. A notebook that organizes total daily expense figures is overkill when management wants to analyze average weekly expenses. To correct the situation, should you start all over and build a new notebook application?

Figure 12.1 shows a typical notebook. In this application, the historical annual sales figures in column C are used in the formulas that appear in columns D through F. These formulas produce other values that are used to create a sales forecast for future years. The content of this notebook isn't as important as is the notion that to evaluate sales information in terms of trends and historical performance, you must create formulas to manipulate the raw data.

If browsing through the numbers in this notebook isn't sufficient to convey an impression about what's in store for J. Testa Clothiers in the future, the next step may be to display all the information in a graph (see fig. 12.2).

J. Testa Clothiers

Sales History: 1983 - 1994

Year	Sales ($000)	3-year moving ave.	5-year moving ave.	Growth in sales
1983	125			
1984	200	161.7		60.0%
1985	160	203.3	207.0	-20.0%
1986	250	236.7	232.0	56.3%
1987	300	266.7	257.0	20.0%
1988	250	291.7	285.0	-16.7%
1989	325	291.7	315.0	30.0%
1990	300	341.7	325.0	-7.7%
1991	400	350.0	350.0	33.3%
1992	350	375.0		-12.5%
1993	375			7.1%
1994	To be forecast			

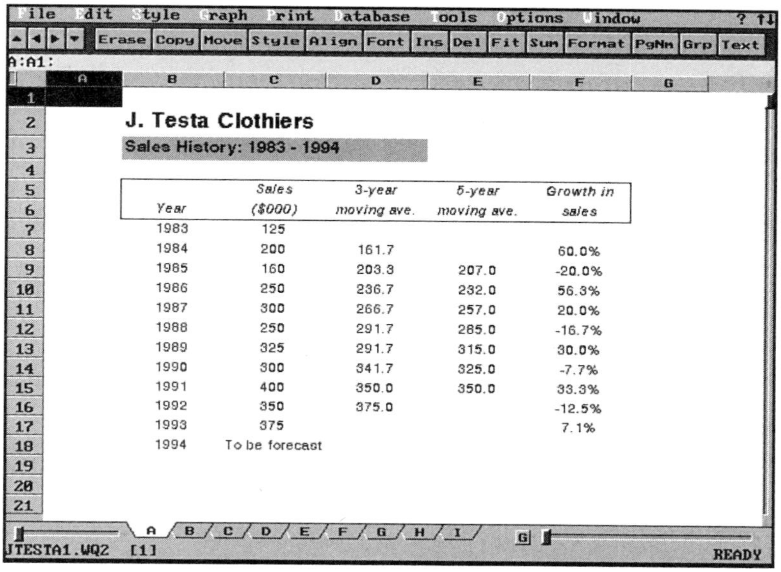

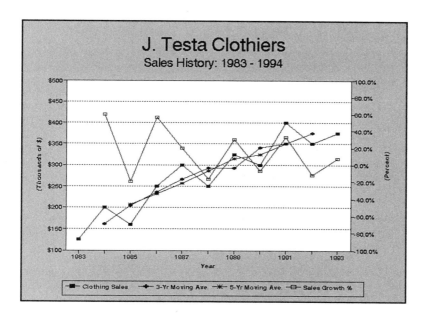

Fig. 12.1

The J. Testa Sales History notebook application.

Fig. 12.2

The J. Testa Clothiers Sales History graph.

TIP

You can use the graph customizing commands described in Chapter 11, "Customizing Graphs," to add a legend and custom axis formatting to the graph.

Instead of one, you now have two documents in hand, and the task of evaluating your information suddenly becomes twice as challenging. To streamline such efforts, Quattro Pro offers a powerful data evaluation tool called *analytical graphing*. In analytical graphing, you make menu selections (rather than build new notebooks) when you want to evaluate your data in a different light.

To use this tool, you start with a notebook containing data and access the commands on the /Graph Series Analyze menu.

Reviewing the Analyze Submenu Commands

You use the commands on the **Analyze** submenu to select a data series—including x-axis data that displays on an XY graph—for analysis. You must select at least one data series to do analytical graphing. To perform the same type of analysis for every data series defined on the /**Graph Series** menu, choose the **All** option.

Each **Analyze** submenu command is described as follows:

Command	Description
nth Series	Selects one of six series for analysis
X-Axis Series	Selects the x-axis data series for analysis
All	Selects all data series, including the x-axis data series, for analysis

You have complete freedom to choose which series you want to analyze. Quattro Pro enables you to analyze any data series, as long as the series has been defined on the /**Graph Series** menu. You can analyze the first and third series, for example; the first, second, and fourth series; the sixth series by itself; and so on.

Selecting the Analysis Option

Selecting a series for analysis always leads to the same submenu, on which you identify the type of analysis you want to perform on the selected series. When you choose **1**st Series, for instance, you see the same menu of choices as you do when you choose **2**nd Series, **3**rd Series, and so on.

Table 12.1 describes the purpose of each analysis option on the **Ana**-lyze **n**th Series submenu.

Table 12.1 Analyze nth Series Submenu Commands

Command	Description
Aggregation	Identifies the series time period, selects the aggregation time period, and chooses a method for transforming the data
Moving Average	Identifies a number of data points to average and chooses whether to create a weighted average
Linear Fit	Displays data on a "best fit" linear regression line
Exponential Fit	Displays data on an increasing or decreasing exponential curve
Reset	Clears the **A**nalyze submenu settings in preparation for a new analysis
Table	Displays analytical graphing data in a table in the notebook

> **TIP**
>
> To perform three different types of analysis on the same data series and to display the results of each analysis on the same graph, choose **/G**raph **S**eries **1**st Series through **3**rd Series and identify the same notebook range each time. On the **A**nalyze submenu, select a different analysis type for each data series to be analyzed.

The next few sections define the rules and outline the procedures for using the four analytical graphing tools: aggregation, moving average, linear fit, and exponential fit. In the following sections, examples are provided to explain the use of each tool and to help you envision uses for analytical graphing in your own daily notebook activities.

You also learn how to use the **R**eset and **T**able options to clear menu settings and copy the results of an analysis into the current notebook.

NOTE

> The examples throughout this chapter offer sufficient coverage of each analytical graphing tool to enable you to use all or most of the features available on each menu. You can consult an economics, mathematics, or sales forecasting text for more comprehensive presentations of the proofs and axioms on which these tools are based.

Using Aggregation Analysis

By using aggregation, you can group (or *transform*) two or more data points and plot them as a single point on a graph. The plotted point can represent the sum, average, standard deviation, minimum, or maximum of the data.

Plotting aggregated data is useful for making large, unwieldy data sets more manageable to work with. Displaying aggregated data on a graph also can reveal relationships that may not be obvious just by looking at the numbers in your notebook.

Reviewing the Aggregation Options

The options on the **Aggregation** submenu (listed in the following table) enable you to define the scope of a data transformation. All you need to know is the time frame represented in a data series, the time frame you want to see in the aggregated data, and the method for transforming the data.

Command	Description
Series Period	Defines the current time period of a data series
Aggregation Period	Selects the aggregation time period for a data series
Function	Selects the method for transforming the data series

The **S**eries Period option tells Quattro Pro about the time frame represented in a data series. When identifying a series period for your data, you have five choices: **D**ays (the default), **W**eeks, **M**onths, **Q**uarters, and **Y**ears. If your data series contains daily values, for example, choose **Days** on this submenu. If the data series contains yearly data, and for your purposes a year represents 360 days, choose **Years**.

Quattro Pro treats data identified with the **Weeks**, **Months**, **Quarters**, and **Years** settings as being equal to 7, 30, 90, and 360 days, respectively. Even though certain months have 31 days and a year consists of 365 days, this method for defining time periods has a negligible effect on the results from an analysis.

The **Aggregation Period** option tells Quattro Pro the time frame to use when grouping a data series. You always must choose an aggregation period that is larger than the series period. If you specify an aggregation period that is smaller than the series period, Quattro Pro displays the error message `Series period interval must be smaller than aggregation period interval` when you try to view the graph.

When identifying the aggregation period for your data, you have five choices: **Weeks** (the default), **Months**, **Quarters**, **Years**, and **Arbitrary**. If you want to aggregate weekly data into quarterly data, for example, choose the **Quarters** option.

> No daily aggregation period exists because daily is the smallest available series period. In other words, aggregating daily figures into daily figures doesn't make sense.

NOTE

You use the **Arbitrary** setting to identify aggregation periods that aren't available on this submenu. When you select this option, Quattro Pro prompts you for an aggregation period value. Enter any value between 2 and 1000 that represents the number of days you want to use. If your data is organized by days and you choose an arbitrary aggregation setting of 3, for instance, Quattro Pro aggregates the data into groups of three days.

Although this rule may not make much sense to you now, it may become clearer to you after you learn how Quattro Pro transforms aggregated data. This process is discussed in the next section, "Performing a Basic Aggregation Analysis," in which you learn how to perform a typical aggregation analysis.

The **Function** option tells Quattro Pro how to transform the data when the program aggregates the data. Quattro Pro offers six methods for transforming data values, each of which is based on one of the six following @function commands:

- The **SUM** setting uses the @SUM function to total the values appearing in a data series.

- The **AVG** setting uses the @AVG function to average the values appearing in a data series.

- The **STD** setting uses the @STD function to calculate a population standard deviation for the values appearing in a data series.

- The **STDS** setting uses the @STDS function to calculate a sample standard deviation for the values appearing in a data series.

- The **MIN** setting uses the @MIN function to locate the minimum value for the values appearing in a data series.

- The **MAX** setting uses the @MAX function to locate the maximum value for the values appearing in a data series.

Think of data aggregation as an expedient method for regrouping notebook data without actually having to re-enter numbers or create new formulas manually. During analytical graphing, Quattro Pro makes no changes to the raw data, so you can be sure that nothing has changed when you return to the notebook.

Performing a Basic Aggregation Analysis

The notebook shown in figure 12.3 contains monthly sales data for J. Testa Clothiers. Suppose that you want to evaluate the average quarterly sales performance for 1993. By using this notebook, you can enter formulas to average 3 months' worth of data at a time. Then you can display the information in a line graph.

By using aggregation analysis, you can accomplish both objectives simultaneously in much less time. To perform this basic aggregation analysis using the data shown in figure 12.3, follow these steps:

1. Choose /**G**raph **G**raph Type and choose the **L**ine graph type.

2. Choose **S**eries **1**st Series. When prompted for the range to graph, type **C7..C18** and press Enter.

3. Choose **X**-Axis Series. When prompted for the x-axis range, type **B7..B18** and press Enter.

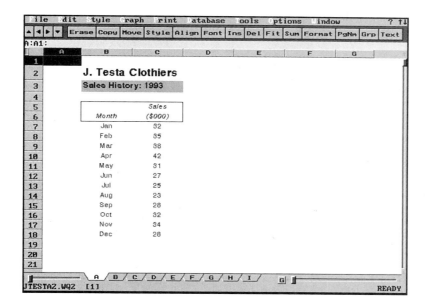

Fig. 12.3

The J. Testa Clothiers
monthly sales report.

4. Choose Analyze 1st Series Aggregation.

5. To identify the time period represented in the 1st Series values, choose Series Period and then choose the Months option.

6. To identify the time period you want to use for the aggregated data, choose Aggregation Period and then choose the Quarters option.

7. To select a method for transforming the data, choose Function and then choose the AVG option.

8. Press F10 to view the graph.

9. Press Enter and choose Quit four times to return to the notebook.

Remember to use /**G**raph **N**ame **C**reate to save the current graph settings in case you want to view or print the graph later.

TIP

Figure 12.4 shows all the menu settings required to perform this basic aggregation analysis. Note that the series selection on the Series submenu corresponds to the series selection on the Analyze submenu (both are 1st Series). On the Aggregation submenu, the Series Period selection appropriately is smaller than the **A**ggregation Period selection.

Fig. 12.4

The menu settings required for a basic aggregation analysis.

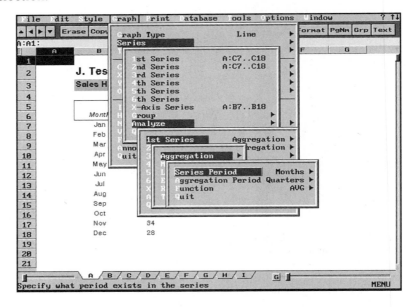

Figure 12.5 shows the final version of the graph that this analysis creates. The line graph type works well with aggregated data because the graph clearly shows a progression over time and reveals trends. You can use the graph customizing commands described in Chapter 11, "Customizing Graphs," to prepare fully formatted, presentation-quality graphs similar to the one shown in this figure.

Quattro Pro displays the correct x-axis labels for aggregated data as long as you first define an **X**-Axis Series range on the **S**eries submenu. In this graph, for instance, Quattro Pro knows to display every third label from the range B7..B18 shown in figure 12.3 because the aggregation period selected is **Q**uarters.

NOTE

Quattro Pro doesn't aggregate numerical x-axis data on a line graph, even if you choose /**G**raph **S**eries **A**nalyze **X**-Axis Series **A**ggregation. Instead, the program treats the numbers as x-axis labels and displays the labels on the graph. To aggregate numerical data appearing on an x-axis, you first must display the data on an XY graph (choose /**G**raph **G**raph Type **X**Y).

To aggregate x-axis series data appearing on an XY graph, choose
/**Graph S**eries **A**nalyze **X**-Axis Series Aggregation. Then, follow the pro-
cedure outlined for defining the **S**eries Period, **A**ggregation Period, and
Function settings.

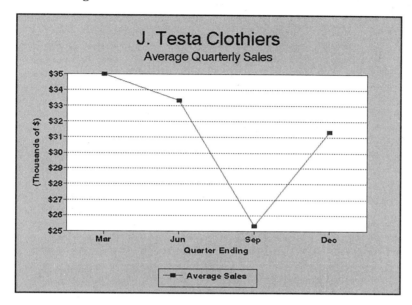

Fig. 12.5

The Average Quarterly
Sales graph for J. Testa
Clothiers.

Performing Aggregation Analysis with Multiple Series

You easily can enhance any analytical graphing operation by viewing
the same data series on one graph and then choosing different aggregation methods. Examining total quarterly sales figures with the average
quarterly sales figures from the preceding example may be interesting,
for instance.

> You can use the /**G**raph **S**eries and /**G**raph **S**eries **A**nalyze menu set-
> tings from the preceding exercise for the next exercise.

NOTE

To add the same data series to the existing graph using a different
aggregation method, follow these steps:

1. Choose /**G**raph **S**eries **2**nd Series. When prompted for the range to graph, type **C7..C18** and press Enter.

Because you are analyzing the same data series with a different aggregation method, be sure to specify the same range for the **1**st Series and **2**nd Series settings.

2. Choose **A**nalyze **2**nd Series **A**ggregation.

3. To identify the time period represented in the 2nd Series values, choose **S**eries Period and then choose the **M**onths option.

4. To identify the time period you want to use for the aggregated data, choose **A**ggregation Period and then choose the **Q**uarters option.

5. To select a new method for transforming the data, choose **F**unction and then choose the SUM option.

6. Press F10 to view the graph.

7. Press Enter and choose **Q**uit four times to return to the notebook.

Figure 12.6 shows all the menu settings required to perform this multiple series aggregation analysis. Note that the series selection on the **S**eries submenu corresponds to the series selection on the **A**nalyze submenu (both show **1**st Series and **2**nd Series). On the **A**ggregation submenu, however, the **F**unction option for the 2nd Series displays the SUM setting.

Figure 12.7 shows the final version of the graph that this analysis creates. A legend has been added to the line graph to distinguish Average Sales data from Total Sales data. The graph title aptly reflects the addition of a new aggregated data grouping.

Quattro Pro continues to display the correct x-axis labels for this aggregated data because the **A**ggregation Period setting is the same: **Q**uarters. Trying to graph multiple series with different periods of aggregation can result in inaccurate plot points on the graph, even though the values of the transformed data always are correct in relation to the values appearing on the y-axis. Using the same **A**ggregation Period setting is better, therefore, when you evaluate multiple data series in a graph.

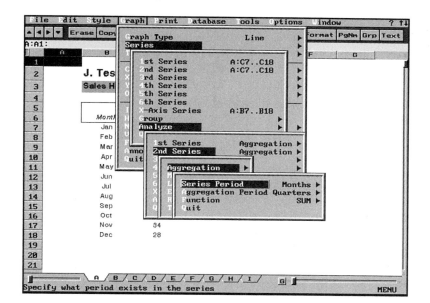

Fig. 12.6

The menu settings for a multiple series aggregation analysis.

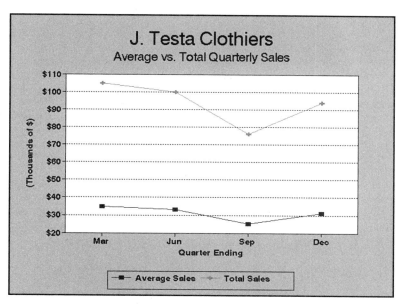

Fig. 12.7

The Average versus Total Quarterly Sales graph for J. Testa Clothiers.

Quattro Pro also ignores the last aggregate grouping of data if the sum of the number of items in your notebook isn't a multiple of the aggregation period. If you choose the **Months** setting for your aggregation period and your notebook contains 302 entries, for example, Quattro Pro plots 10 groups of 30 data points and ignores the remaining 2 data points.

Creating a Table of Aggregation Values

The **T**able command on the /**G**raph **S**eries **A**nalyze **n**th Series menu copies analytical graphing information into a notebook range that you specify. Use this command to retain permanent records of the values that Quattro Pro calculates for each series analyzed during an aggregation analysis. You can use these numbers in reports and as input for other analytical commands such as those available on the **T**ools menu.

Use the following steps to copy the aggregation values produced for the first series into the current notebook:

1. Choose /**G**raph **S**eries **A**nalyze **1**st Series **T**able.

2. When Quattro Pro prompts you for a target table block, type the address of a cell that is well away from the notebook area in which the raw data resides.

You can supply an entire range address or just the first cell in the range as the target block. When you specify a single cell, Quattro Pro copies the data downward into the column specified. The single cell you specify can exist on another page. To specify a target table block on page D beginning in cell F10, for example, type **D:F10** as the block.

3. Press Enter to copy the data.

4. Choose **Q**uit three times to return to the notebook.

When determining where to place the table, remember that Quattro Pro requires a single column and as many rows as necessary to accommodate the aggregated data. If you are aggregating 900 values by **M**onths, for example, then you need 30 rows for the table (900/30).

TIP

Use the /**G**raph **C**ustomize Series **I**nterior Labels command to label graph points with the values that Quattro Pro copies into a table. For more details, see the section titled "Adding Interior Labels" in Chapter 11, "Customizing Graphs."

Resetting the Graph Series Analyze Settings

To reset the /Graph Series Analyze menu settings so that you can perform a completely new analytical graphing task, choose /Graph Series Analyze All Reset. To reset the settings for a single series—for example, the 2nd Series—on the Analyze submenu, choose 2nd Series Reset.

> **TIP**
>
> To reset all **G**raph menu settings, including those on the **A**nalyze submenu, choose /**G**raph **C**ustomize Series **R**eset **G**raph.

Using Moving Average Analysis

Moving average analysis helps you identify general trends in your data by *smoothing*, or averaging, the data set values. This type of analytical graphing also is known as *time-series analysis*.

With moving average analysis, you are more interested in conveying overall impressions about a data set than in providing precise information about individual values. Although comparing unemployment rates for Boston and San Diego may be interesting, for example, national unemployment figures give a more telling indication of the state of the nation.

The mechanics of moving average analysis are simple to grasp. Suppose that you want to create a three-period moving average for the following five numbers:

6 2 4 9 104

To start, Quattro Pro plots the value 6. Next, the program averages the first 2 values and plots that value (4). Then, it averages the first 3 values and plots that value (4). For the fourth plot value, Quattro Pro drops the first value and calculates the average for the second, third, and fourth values (5). For the fifth and final value, Quattro Pro drops the second value and calculates the average for the last three (39)—a much lower value than the actual value of 104.

Moving average analysis smooths fluctuating data values because earlier values temper later values, thus providing you with a global impression of the direction that a data set is taking. In the preceding example,
you can see how the average values 6, 4, 4, 5, and 39 seem less wild
than 6, 2, 4, 9, and 104.

Reviewing the Moving Average Options

The options on the **M**oving Average submenu enable you to define the
scope of a data transformation. All you need to know is the number of
data points you want to average and whether you want Quattro Pro to
calculate a weighted moving average. The options are as follows:

- *Period.* Specifies the number of points to average. This option
  defines the number of data values that Quattro Pro uses when
  calculating the moving average. High period values produce
  smoother curves but may mask the trends you are trying to
  disclose.

- *Weighted.* Selects whether to use a weighted moving average. This
  option enables Quattro Pro numerically to place greater emphasis, or *weight*, on more recent data values and less weight on older
  values. This option helps compensate for abnormally low or high
  values appearing in the latter part of a data set. By default, this
  option is set to **No**. If you want to use weighted moving average
  analysis, set this option to **Yes**.

Performing a Basic Moving Average Analysis

In this section, you learn the steps to follow to perform a typical moving average analysis. Before beginning this procedure, however, choose
/**Graph** Customize Series **R**eset Graph to reset all graph settings. Then
follow these general steps to calculate a moving average for a single
data series and to display that average on a line graph:

1. Choose /**Graph** Graph Type **L**ine.

2. Choose **S**eries 1st Series. When prompted, type a valid range for
   the current notebook and then press Enter.

3. Choose **X**-Axis. When prompted, type the range that contains the labels you want to display on the x-axis and then press Enter.

4. Choose **A**nalyze **1**st Series **M**oving Average.

5. Choose **P**eriod, type a period value, and press Enter.

6. Press F10 to view the graph.

7. Press Enter and then choose **Q**uit four times to return to the **G**raph submenu.

Moving average analysis is most revealing when you include different period scenarios for the same data series. The next section examines how to use this approach on your own data.

Performing Moving Average Analysis with Multiple Series

You easily can enhance any moving average analysis by viewing the same data series on one graph with different period intervals. If you suspect that daily sales totals are higher during the weekend than during the week and also are typically higher toward the middle and end of the month, for example, putting 7- and 14-day moving averages together on the same graph may reveal this trend.

The notebook in figure 12.8 contains daily sales data for J. Testa Clothiers. Suppose that you want to create 7- and 14-day moving averages and display them on a line graph. By using moving average analysis, you can create both moving averages simultaneously in a short period of time.

To perform a moving average analysis with the data shown in figure 12.8, follow these steps:

1. Choose /**G**raph **G**raph Type and choose the **L**ine graph type.

2. Choose **S**eries **1**st Series. When prompted for the range to graph, type **C6..C36** and press Enter.

3. Choose **2**nd Series. When prompted for the range to graph, type **C6..C36** and press Enter.

Fig. 12.8

The J. Testa Clothiers
daily sales report.

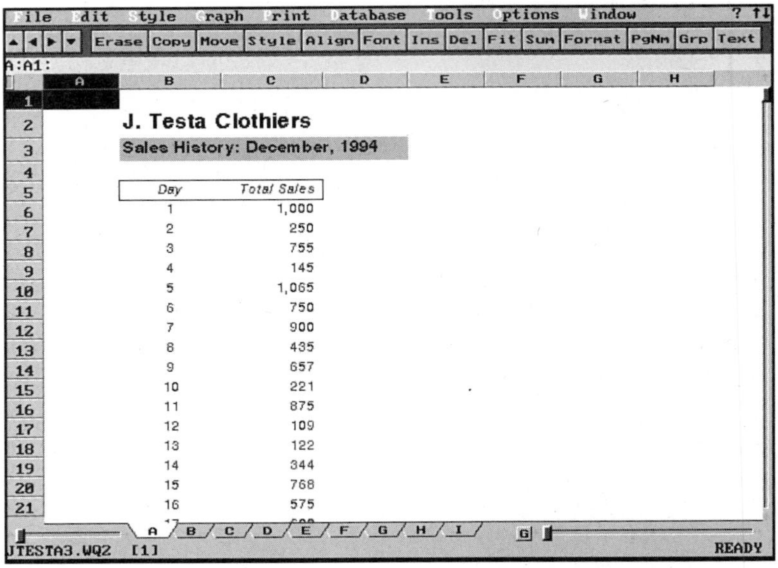

NOTE

Because you are analyzing the same data series with a different moving average period, be sure to specify the same range for the **1**st Series and **2**nd Series settings.

4. Choose **X**-Axis Series. When prompted for the x-axis range, type **B6..B36** and press Enter.

5. Choose Analyze **1**st Series **M**oving Average.

6. To identify the time period for which you want to calculate the first moving average, choose **P**eriod, press 7, and then press Enter.

7. Choose **Q**uit to return to the **A**nalyze submenu.

8. Choose **2**nd Series **M**oving Average.

9. To identify the time period for which you want to calculate the second moving average, choose **P**eriod, type **14**, and then press Enter.

10. Press F10 to view the graph.

11. Press Enter and choose **Q**uit four times to return to the notebook.

Remember to use /**G**raph **N**ame **C**reate to save the current graph settings in case you want to view or print the graph later.

Figure 12.9 shows all the menu settings required to perform this moving average analysis. The final dialog box in this figure shows how to specify the number of periods to use for the second moving average (in this case, a 14-day period). Note that the series selections on the **S**eries submenu correspond to the series selections on the **A**nalyze submenu (both show **1**st Series and **2**nd Series).

Figure 12.10 shows the final version of the graph that this analysis creates. The line graph type works well with moving average data because the graph clearly shows a progression over time and reveals trends.

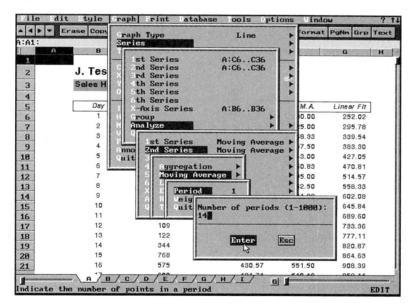

Fig. 12.9

The menu settings for a multiple series moving average analysis.

Quattro Pro displays the correct x-axis labels for moving average data as long as you first define an **X**-Axis Series range on the **S**eries submenu. In this graph, Quattro Pro displays every other label because the /**G**raph **X**-Axis **N**o. of Minor Ticks command is set to 1 (the default is 0). See "Adding Minor Ticks" in Chapter 11 for more details.

Fig. 12.10

The 7-day and 14-day moving average graph for J. Testa Clothiers.

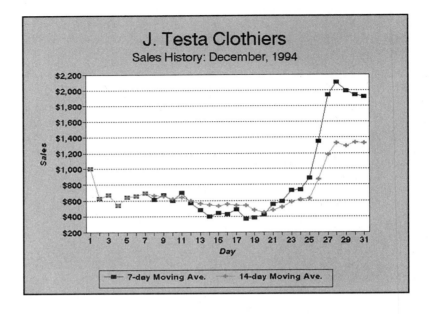

Creating a Table of Moving Average Values

The **Table** command on the **/Graph Series Analyze n**th Series menu copies analytical graphing information into a notebook range that you specify. Use this command to retain permanent records of the values that Quattro Pro calculates for each series analyzed during a moving average analysis. You can use these numbers in reports and as input for other analytical commands, such as those available on the **Tools** menu.

Use the following steps to copy the moving average values produced for the first series into the current notebook:

1. Choose **/Graph Series Analyze 1**st Series **Table**.

2. After Quattro Pro prompts you for a target table block, type the address of a cell that is well away from the notebook area in which the raw data resides.

   You can supply an entire range address or just the first cell in the range as the target block. When you specify a single cell, Quattro Pro copies the data downward into the column specified.

The single cell you specify also can exist on another page. To specify a target table block on page D beginning in cell F10, for example, type **D:F10** as the block.

3. Press Enter to copy the data.

4. Choose **Q**uit three times to return to the notebook.

When determining where to place the table, remember that Quattro Pro requires a single column and as many rows as necessary to accommodate the moving average data. If you are calculating a moving average for 60 values, for example, you need 60 rows for the table.

> Use the /**G**raph **C**ustomize Series **I**nterior Labels command to label graph points with the moving average values that Quattro Pro copies into a table. For more details, see the section "Adding Interior Labels" in Chapter 11.

TIP

Using Linear Fit Analysis

When you choose the /**G**raph **S**eries **A**nalyze **n**th Series **L**inear Fit command, Quattro Pro uses simple linear regression to generate a line that "best fits" the data you selected. You can use this type of analytical graphing to show a general trend among fluctuating points. Grasping regression information in graph form also is easier than in a table full of numbers.

Linear fit analysis requires no special advance understanding. You just identify the series for which you want to fit a linear line and choose **L**inear Fit from the **A**nalyze **n**th Series submenu.

Performing a Basic Linear Fit Analysis

By using the same daily sales totals notebook from figure 12.8 in the preceding section, you can create a linear fit line for J. Testa Clothiers and add the line to the moving averages graph.

To create a linear fit line, use the following steps:

NOTE

The following exercise assumes that you already have created a moving average analysis for the first two data series.

1. Choose /**G**raph **S**eries **3**rd Series. When prompted, type **C6..C36** and then press Enter.

2. Choose **A**nalyze **3**rd Series **L**inear Fit.

3. Press F10 to view the graph.

4. Press Enter and choose **Q**uit three times to return to the notebook.

TIP

The **L**inear Fit command calculates and plots linear regression information in the notebook, even if your data has no obvious general trend.

Figure 12.11 shows all the menu settings required to perform this linear fit analysis. Note that the first two series are set for moving average analysis and the third series is set for linear fit analysis. Although displaying a linear fit in a graph by itself works fine, the linear fit leaves a greater impression when displayed next to the moving average lines from the previous example. Figure 12.12 shows the final version of the graph that this analysis creates.

Fig. 12.11

The menu settings for a linear fit analysis.

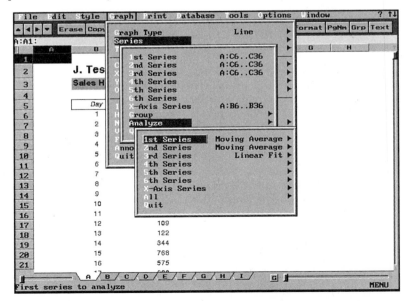

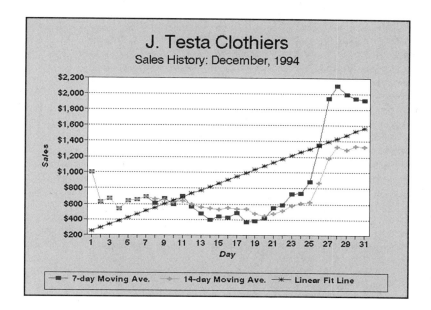

Fig. 12.12

The linear fit line on the moving average graph for J. Testa Clothiers.

Creating a Table of Linear Fit Regression Values

The Table command on the /**Graph S**eries **A**nalyze **n**th Series menu copies analytical graphing information into a notebook range that you specify. Use this command to retain permanent records of the values that Quattro Pro calculates for each series analyzed during a linear fit operation. You can use these numbers in reports and as input for other analytical commands, such as those available on the **Tools** menu.

Follow these steps to copy the linear fit and moving average values produced for the first three series into the current notebook:

1. Choose /**Graph S**eries **A**nalyze **1**st Series **T**able.

2. Type **E6** when Quattro Pro prompts you for a target table block.

3. Press Enter to copy the data.

4. Choose **2**nd Series **T**able.

5. Type **F6** when Quattro Pro prompts you for a target table block.

6. Press Enter to copy the data.

7. Choose **3**rd Series **T**able.

8. Type **G6** when Quattro Pro prompts you for a target table block.
9. Press Enter to copy the data.
10. Choose **Q**uit three times to return to the notebook.

You can supply an entire range address or just the first cell in the range as the target block. When you specify a single cell, Quattro Pro copies the data downward into the column specified.

When determining where to place the table, remember that Quattro Pro requires a single column and as many rows as necessary to accommodate the linear fit data. If you are calculating a linear fit line for 25 values, for example, you need 25 rows for the table.

TIP

Use the /**G**raph **C**ustomize Series **I**nterior Labels command to label graph points with the linear fit values that Quattro Pro copies into a table. For more details, see "Adding Interior Labels" in Chapter 11.

Figure 12.13 shows the results of copying the linear fit and moving average values into the daily sales totals notebook. Column headings and lines have been added to the table to provide division and clarity.

Now, choose /**G**raph **C**ustomize Series **R**eset **G**raph to reset all settings in preparation for the final analytical graphing example.

Fig. 12.13

A table of values in the J. Testa Clothiers notebook.

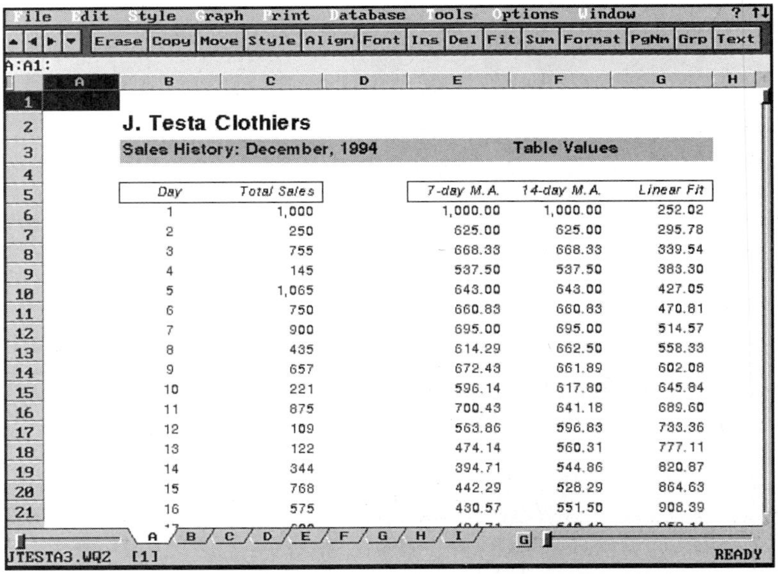

J. Testa Clothiers

Sales History: December, 1994 — Table Values

Day	Total Sales	7-day M.A.	14-day M.A.	Linear Fit
1	1,000	1,000.00	1,000.00	252.02
2	250	625.00	625.00	295.78
3	755	668.33	668.33	339.54
4	145	537.50	537.50	383.30
5	1,065	643.00	643.00	427.05
6	750	660.83	660.83	470.81
7	900	695.00	695.00	514.57
8	435	614.29	662.50	558.33
9	657	672.43	661.89	602.08
10	221	596.14	617.80	645.84
11	875	700.43	641.18	689.60
12	109	563.86	596.83	733.36
13	122	474.14	560.31	777.11
14	344	394.71	544.86	820.87
15	768	442.29	528.29	864.63
16	575	430.57	551.50	908.39

Using Exponential Fit Analysis

Exponential Fit generates a curve to fit data that increases or decreases exponentially. For this feature to work, all values in the series must be nonzero and must have the same sign (positive or negative).

> **NOTE**
> For the purposes of exponential fit graphing, Quattro Pro treats all blank cells in a data series as zeros.

Fitting exponential data with a curve is as simple and direct as creating a linear fit line. Select the series containing the data to be graphed and then choose /**G**raph **S**eries **A**nalyze **n**th Series Exponential Fit.

Performing a Basic Exponential Fit Analysis

By using the same daily sales totals notebook from the preceding section, you can create an exponential fit line for J. Testa Clothiers and add the line to a line graph that displays the actual daily sales figures.

To create an exponential fit line, follow these steps:

1. Choose /**G**raph **G**raph Type and then choose the **L**ine graph type.

2. Choose **S**eries **1**st Series. When prompted for the range to graph, type **C6..C36** and press Enter.

3. Choose **2**nd Series. When prompted for the range to graph, type **C6..C36** and press Enter.

> **NOTE**
> Because you are analyzing the same data series using the exponential fit technique, be sure to specify the same range for the **1**st Series and **2**nd Series settings.

4. Choose **X**-Axis Series. When prompted for the x-axis range, type **B6..B36** and press Enter.

5. Choose **A**nalyze **2**nd Series Exponential Fit.

6. Press F10 to view the graph.

7. Press Enter and choose **Q**uit four times to return to the notebook.

Figure 12.14 shows all the menu settings required to perform this exponential fit analysis. Note that the first series has no analytical graphing setting and the second series is set for exponential fit analysis. The exponential fit line, like the linear fit line, leaves much more of an impression when displayed next to the data from which it was created.

Fig. 12.14

The menu settings for an exponential fit analysis.

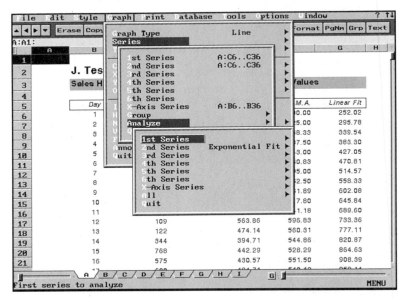

Figure 12.15 shows the final version of the graph that this analysis creates.

Creating a Table of Exponential Fit Regression Values

The **T**able command on the /**G**raph **S**eries **A**nalyze **n**th Series menu copies analytical graphing information into a notebook range that you specify. Use this command to retain permanent records of the values that Quattro Pro calculates for each series analyzed during an exponential fit operation. You can use these numbers in reports and as input for other analytical commands, such as those available on the **T**ools menu.

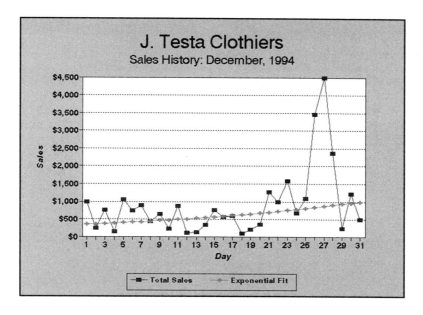

Fig. 12.15

The exponential fit line on the line graph for J. Testa Clothiers.

Use the following steps to copy the exponential fit values for the first data series into the current notebook:

1. Choose /**G**raph **S**eries **A**nalyze **1**st Series **T**able.

2. After Quattro Pro prompts you for a target table block, type the address of a cell that is well away from the notebook area in which the raw data resides.

You can supply an entire range address or just the first cell in the range as the target block. When you specify a single cell, Quattro Pro copies the data downward into the column specified.

The single cell you specify also can exist on another page. To specify a target table block on page D beginning in cell F10, for example, type **D:F10** as the block.

3. Press Enter to copy the data.

4. Choose **Q**uit three times to return to the notebook.

When you determine where to place the table, remember that Quattro Pro requires a single column and as many rows as necessary to accommodate the exponential fit data. If you are calculating an exponential fit line for 25 values, for example, you need 25 rows for the table.

TIP

Use the /**G**raph **C**ustomize Series **I**nterior Labels command to label graph points with the exponential fit values that Quattro Pro copies into a table. See "Adding Interior Labels" in Chapter 11 for more details.

Questions & Answers

This chapter introduces you to the four analytical tools found on the /**G**raph **S**eries **A**nalyze menu. If you have questions concerning particular situations that aren't addressed in the examples given, look through this section.

Using Aggregation

Q: My notebook contains daily data, and I want to evaluate the semi-monthly totals without having to create new formulas and reorganize the data. Will one of the aggregation options enable me to do this?

A: Yes. Choose /**G**raph **S**eries **A**nalyze and select the data series you want to analyze. On the **n**th Series submenu, choose **A**ggregation. Next, set the **S**eries Period option to **D**ays and the **A**ggregation Period option to **A**rbitrary; then, type **15** and press Enter. Finally, choose the SUM setting on the **F**unction submenu. Press F10 to view the graph.

Q: I added a second data series to a moving average graph, but the data doesn't appear on the graph. What's wrong?

A: Check the settings on the /**G**raph **X**-Axis and **Y**-Axis menus. If **S**cale is set to **M**anual and the **L**ow and **H**igh values fall outside the range of values for the data series you added, Quattro Pro doesn't display the new series on the graph. To correct this problem, set **S**cale to **A**utomatic. If you still want to adjust the scale of either axis manually, be sure to choose **L**ow and **H**igh values that include all values appearing in the data series.

Q: Quattro Pro displays the message Not enough data points to aggregate when I press F10 to display an aggregation graph. What did I do wrong?

A: Your graph series number doesn't match the series number se-lected for analysis. After you define a data series on the /**Graph Series** menu, you must select the matching option on the **A**nalyze submenu before you can aggregate data. To analyze the **3**rd Series for a graph, for example, define the range on the **Series** submenu and then choose the **3**rd Series option on the **A**nalyze submenu.

Using Moving Averages

Q: I cannot read the x-axis labels on my moving average graph be-cause the labels are grouped too closely together. Should I define a lower **Period** value to correct this problem?

A: No. Although decreasing the **Period** setting decreases the number of points that appear on a graph, it also eliminates information that may be necessary for the analysis at hand. Instead, to correct the display of x-axis labels that are bunched together, choose /**Graph X-**Axis **No.** of Minor Ticks and enter **1** to display every other label, or **2** to display every second label.

Q: The moving average analysis I just performed hasn't smoothed out my data values as much as I anticipated. The older points in my data set appear to greatly influence the outcome of the analy-sis. Is there anything I can do?

A: By using the weighted average moving analysis method, you can cause Quattro Pro to place greater emphasis on more recent data points and less emphasis on older data points. To use this method, choose **W**eighted on the **M**oving Average submenu, choose **Y**es, and then redisplay your graph.

Summary

In this chapter, you learned how to scrutinize your notebook data closely by using the four analytical graphing commands found on the /**Graph Series A**nalyze menu. You also learned how to add results tables to the current notebook and how to reset the **A**nalyze submenu settings for future analytical graphing operations. These six commands enable you to turn the Quattro Pro graphing environment into an effi-cient mechanism for analyzing notebook information.

Having completed this chapter, you should understand the following concepts:

- Selecting the **A**nalyze submenu option best suited to your analytical graphing needs
- Performing aggregation analyses by using single and multiple data series
- Performing a moving average analysis by using multiple data series
- Creating a linear line that "best fits" a series of data points
- Creating an exponential line to reflect a trend in erratic data
- Displaying the results of an analytical graphing operation in a notebook table
- Resetting the settings on the **A**nalyze submenu in preparation for a new analytical graphing operation

In Chapter 13, you learn how to manage your data by using the commands found on the **D**atabase menu. These commands enable you to turn a Quattro Pro notebook into an efficient environment for storing and accessing database information.

Advanced Spreadsheet Features

PART

III

OUTLINE

Managing Your Data

In addition to serving as an electronic spreadsheet program, Quattro Pro can function as a flat-file database manager. This chapter focuses on this process and shows you how to use the commands on the **D**atabase menu to sort, extract, and delete records—operations basic to every good database software product.

The chapter begins by showing you how to turn a notebook into a database. The discussion defines each part of a typical database, reviews the data management commands, and shows you how to prepare your data for processing into reports and documents.

The next section discusses different techniques you can use to sort database records, guidelines for maintaining the integrity of your database records, and instructions for returning an altered database to its original order. This section concludes with a brief review of how to modify Quattro Pro's default sort rules to meet special needs.

The chapter continues by discussing how to search a database and locate records that meet user-specified criteria. You learn how to locate, extract, and delete records—some of the most useful database operations.

The last section describes how to use a notebook as a data-entry form and explains how to control record accuracy by restricting the types of permissible entries.

Turning a Notebook into a Database

The Quattro Pro database is a powerful information management and report creation tool. With this tool, you can manipulate large amounts of information that you can present in many different ways. Like a notebook, a database helps you organize names and numbers that appear on reports.

To reorganize a notebook report, you usually must execute several involved /**E**dit **C**opy and /**E**dit **M**ove operations. With a database, you can segregate information on a notebook into sets of related data and then instantly reorganize the data to create different reports.

You can use a database to store all kinds of information. A phone book, for example, is a database that stores a set of related information: a name, an address, and a phone number. The uses for a database are limited only by your imagination. You can build a database to catalog your favorite video tapes, to devise a business check register, or to create a statistical report for major-league baseball players.

Often, the structure of an individual database is portable to other applications. If you create a database to catalog your video tapes, for example, you can use the same database structure to catalog your cassettes, CDs, and albums.

You easily can turn a notebook into a database. Figure 13.1 shows the shell of a database that will be used to store performance statistics for the top 10 National League batters. The *database shell* is the framework of the database—the field names row and the database area where the records reside. The border has been added around each area with the /**S**tyle **L**ine Drawing command to show clearly the different parts of this database.

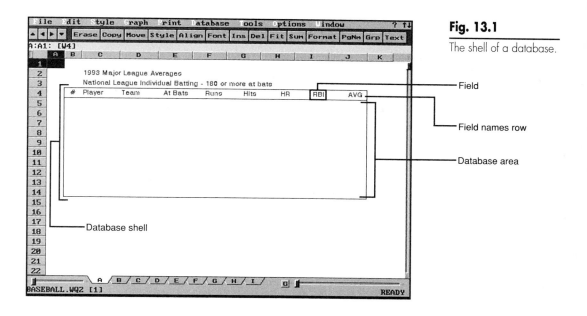

Fig. 13.1

The shell of a database.

- Field
- Field names row
- Database area
- Database shell

TIP

Drawing lines around the database shell is helpful when you build criteria tables and output blocks below the database shell.

Follow these steps to create a database shell like the one shown in figure 13.1:

1. Envision the database application. Do you want to manage employee names, business phone numbers, contact lists, or baseball statistics? Begin by entering a report title at the top of a new, blank notebook that describes the envisioned application.

2. Create field names and enter them on the row below the database title.

   Because each field name corresponds to an element in a database record, such as a phone number, the names should be descriptive of the field data. Create short, single-word names because many database operations enable you to use cell block names.

3. Set the column widths in the database with the /**S**tyle **C**olumn Width command. Draw lines around the shell and the database area with the /**S**tyle **L**ine Drawing command.

A database, like a notebook report, uses label headings to define the type of information stored in a column or row. Each row in a database is a *record*, and each column is a *field*. The *database area* is the part of the notebook in which you store your records.

The baseball database has nine field names that appear on row 4: #, Player, Team, At Bats, Runs, Hits, HR (home runs), RBI (runs batted in), and AVG (batting average). These fields identify the individual performance statistics collected for a group of baseball players.

The shell pictured earlier in figure 13.1 shows the commonly accepted way of creating the shell of a database. As with all good notebook reports, you should create a database that looks like the document or report from which the database was created. To create a database using the names, addresses, and phone numbers of business associates, for example, design one that looks like a page out of your phone book.

When you build a database, follow these guidelines:

■ The database area must be rectangular. Quattro Pro doesn't perform **D**atabase menu operations on unconnected blocks of data.

■ Each column should contain only one type of data: numeric, alphabetic, or date and time serial numbers. (Don't mix dates with labels or labels with numbers.)

■ Don't place an empty row (or column) between the field name row and the first record in the database.

■ A Quattro Pro database can contain a maximum of 8,191 entries per notebook page (8,192 total rows, but one row contains field names).

Reviewing the Database Menu

Use the first four **D**atabase menu commands to sort, search through, control movement, and enter data into a database. Use the fifth command, **P**aradox Access, to switch between Quattro Pro's and Paradox's operating environments so that you can access and share file data between these two programs. Paradox is a powerful database management program available from Borland International, maker of Quattro Pro.

The following table describes the commands available on the **D**atabase menu:

Command	Description
Sort	Changes the order of database records
Query	Searches through a database
Restrict Input	Restricts movement of the selector to unprotected cells
Data Entry	Specifies the data type permitted in a block of cells
Paradox Access	Switches to the Paradox operating environment

Except for the **R**estrict Input command, selecting a **D**atabase menu command displays a submenu. The following sections show how to use each command to build your own database applications.

Entering Data

To enter data into a database, apply the same techniques you use when you enter data into a notebook. Like a notebook, a database can contain several types of data: labels, numbers, and even formulas. Cell J5 in figure 13.2, for example, contains a formula that computes the batting average by dividing the number of Hits by the number of At Bats.

Fig. 13.2

The first record entered into the baseball database.

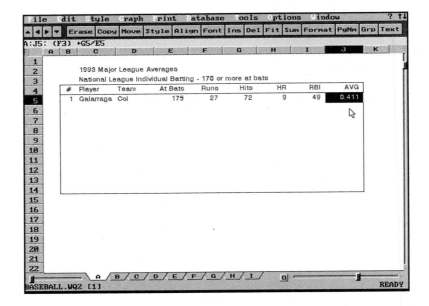

As you enter data into a database, remember the following three simple rules:

- Each category of data should have its own field. If you design a phone book database, for example, create one field for a person's first name and one for the last name. Entering the first and last names into one field offers you no flexibility when creating reports from sorted data.

  When you have two or more people with the same last name, you need to distinguish between them. You can place each person's first name, middle initial, or title into a field of its own.

- Don't enter different types of data into the same field. If you create a field for dates, for example, enter only dates into that field. When you enter a mixture of dates, labels, and numbers into a field, sorting and analyzing database reports becomes more difficult.

- Be careful about entering formulas into the database area. As long as the formulas are record-dependent, you can sort the formulas safely without generating bad data. A record-dependent formula references only values existing on that record's row (see the formula displayed on the input line for cell J5 in fig. 13.2).

In a sort operation, the order of the records is shifted around. If you create field-dependent formulas that rely on the location of one record in relation to another, shifting records can cause formulas to return different data, depending on the order of the records in the database.

After you finish entering data into a database, you are ready to manipulate the data to use in a report. Figure 13.3 shows entries in the baseball database.

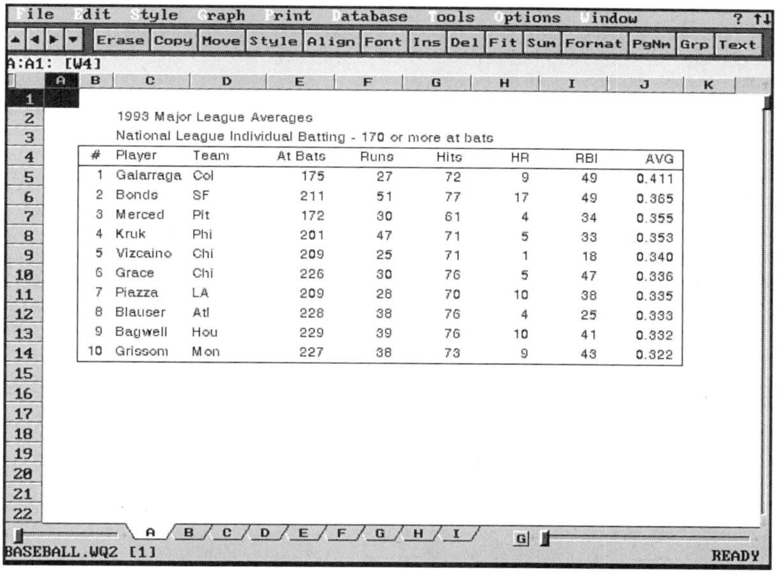

#	Player	Team	At Bats	Runs	Hits	HR	RBI	AVG
1	Galarraga	Col	175	27	72	9	49	0.411
2	Bonds	SF	211	51	77	17	49	0.365
3	Merced	Pit	172	30	61	4	34	0.355
4	Kruk	Phi	201	47	71	5	33	0.353
5	Vizcaino	Chi	209	25	71	1	18	0.340
6	Grace	Chi	226	30	76	5	47	0.336
7	Piazza	LA	209	28	70	10	38	0.335
8	Blauser	Atl	228	38	76	4	25	0.333
9	Bagwell	Hou	229	39	76	10	41	0.332
10	Grissom	Mon	227	38	73	9	43	0.322

Fig. 13.3

The baseball database, complete with 10 records.

Sorting a Database

The **S**ort command, a powerful **D**atabase menu tool, enables you to produce different combinations of the same data set without changing the value of any record in the database. You always should maintain the integrity of a database, because a database's integrity is integral to creating meaningful reports from one data set.

If you sort two fields out of sequence, you destroy the integrity of a database. If, for example, you sort block B5..C14 in figure 13.3 according to last name (Player) in ascending order, the rest of the database (D5..J14) will not sort accordingly. How useful is a database if a person's first name doesn't match the last?

With nine available sort fields, you can create many different reports. You can create a report that lists the players sorted by team. Because the triple-crown honor is awarded to a player who finishes the season with the highest batting average, the greatest number of RBIs, and the most home runs, for example, you also can sort the database three times to locate the best candidates for that honor.

You tell Quattro Pro how to sort your database by specifying sort criteria. You can sort a database alphabetically or numerically, in ascending or descending order.

The fields used to sort the records are called *sort field keys*, or *sort keys*. You can specify up to five sort keys per operation. Quattro Pro sorts a database according to each sort key's priority: the 1st Key has first priority, the 2nd Key has second priority, and so on.

Sort key priorities enable Quattro Pro to perform mini-sort operations. If five records with the same field value are specified by the 1st Key, for example, Quattro Pro re-sorts those records according to the 2nd Key. If two records remain with the same field value specified by the 2nd Key, Quattro Pro re-sorts the two records according to the 3rd Key.

Sorting a database is typically a three-step process: you define the block to be sorted, specify the sort key criteria, and then choose /**D**atabase **S**ort **G**o to begin the sort operation. To reset the sort criteria in preparation for a new operation, choose /**D**atabase **S**ort **R**eset.

Using One Sort Key

Suppose that you want to sort the baseball database alphabetically and in ascending order (A, B, C, and so on) by each player's name. To specify the Player field as the first sort key, follow these steps:

1. Highlight the block you want to sort—for example, B5..J14.

TIP

Omit the field names row from the database block definition; otherwise, Quattro Pro sorts that row of labels into your database. If you don't omit the field names and Quattro Pro performs the sort, press Alt+F5 to undo the sort operation.

2. Choose /**D**atabase **S**ort to display the **S**ort submenu.

3. Choose **B**lock. Quattro Pro records the highlighted block as the sort block.

4. Choose **1st Key**, select any cell in the column you want to use as the first sort key, and press Enter. For this example, select cell C5 by using the mouse or by typing the cell address.

> You can enter any cell address or block that exists in the sort key column. The addresses C1, C5..C14, and C392, for example, all designate column C as the sort key column.
>
> **TIP**

5. When prompted, type **A** to choose ascending order and press Enter.

6. Choose **Go**.

Quattro Pro rearranges the records according to your sort criteria.

Figure 13.4 shows the result of this sort operation and the settings on the **S**ort submenu. Notice that Quattro Pro displays the sort block and sort key definition at the right margin of the **S**ort submenu, next to the **B**lock and **1**st Key commands.

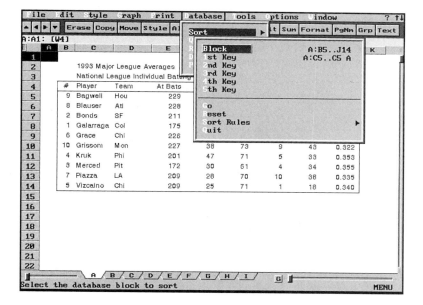

Fig. 13.4

The results of sorting the baseball database alphabetically by Player.

Using Multiple Sort Keys

You also can sort databases using two sort keys instead of one. You may want to organize the database alphabetically by Team in ascending order, for example; you also may want to sort members of the same team by the number of At Bats from highest to lowest. You must specify the Team field as the **1**st Key and the At Bats field as the **2**nd Key.

You always can substitute block names in place of cell addresses—a particularly useful technique for **D**atabase menu operations. To name a database area, select the block you want to name, choose /**E**dit **N**ames **C**reate, type a name, and then press Enter.

By naming the database area DATABASE, for example, you can type that name in place of the block address B5..J14. Likewise, when you name the fields using the names on row 4, you can enter each name in place of a cell address when defining the sort keys. (See Chapter 4, "Manipulating Data," for more information about naming a cell block.)

To define the criteria for this sort operation, follow these steps:

1. Choose /**D**atabase **S**ort to display the **S**ort submenu.

2. Choose **B**lock, type the coordinates or block name, and press Enter.

TIP

After you specify a block or sort key address, Quattro Pro keeps the definition active as long as you are working with the same notebook. When you later create names for your database, Quattro Pro replaces cell blocks and sort key addresses with their new names.

3. Choose **1**st Key, type the key coordinates or name (the block name for this example would be **Team**) and then press Enter.

4. When prompted, choose the sort order—**A** for ascending order, for this example—and press Enter.

5. Choose **2**nd Key, type the second key coordinates or name—**At Bats** for the example—and press Enter.

6. When prompted, choose the sort order and press Enter. For the example, choose **D** (for descending order) and press Enter.

7. Choose **G**o.

Quattro Pro rearranges the records according to your sort criteria (see fig. 13.5).

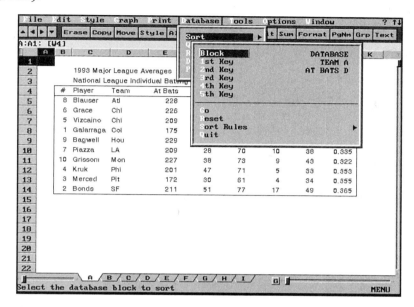

Fig. 13.5

The results of sorting alphabetically by Team and numerically by At Bats.

Figure 13.5 displays the result of this sort operation. Notice that Quattro Pro now displays each sort criterion definition at the right margin of the **S**ort submenu, next to each command.

Experiment with this procedure by altering each sort key definition until you achieve the report style you want.

Returning the Database to Its Original Order

After you sort a database using several different sort keys, you sometimes need to return the database to its original order. Before you face this situation, consider the following three strategies for managing your database operations:

■ Make a backup copy of the database file. When you need to recover the original database, choose /**File R**etrieve, type the name of the backup file, and press Enter to recover the original database.

■ Copy the database records (the database area) to another part of the active notebook. To guarantee the integrity of this data, don't perform any **D**atabase menu operations on the copied data.

■ The most direct method is best understood by looking at the baseball database. Notice that the first field, #, identifies the numerical order of entry for each record. This technique, when used with all your databases, ensures that you always can return a sorted database to its original order. Choose # as the **1**st Key and choose **A** to sort the database in ascending order.

Fine-Tuning a Sort Operation

By default, Quattro Pro sorts data in the following order when ascending order is chosen on a sort key menu:

1st	Blank cells
2nd	Labels starting with numbers (sorted in numerical order)
3rd	Labels beginning with letters and special characters (sorted in ASCII order)
4th	Values (sorted in numerical order)

When descending order (**D**) is chosen on a key menu, Quattro Pro sorts data in the opposite order (from 4th to 1st).

Figure 13.6 shows the three **S**ort Rules submenu options: **N**umbers Before Labels, **S**ort Rows/Columns, and **L**abel Order. The default settings appear at the right margin of the submenu, next to each command.

To change the default sorting order, choose /**D**atabase **S**ort **S**ort Rules **N**umbers Before Labels. When prompted, choose **Y**es to sort numbers before labels.

To change how Quattro Pro sorts labels, choose /**D**atabase **S**ort **S**ort Rules **L**abel Order, and choose **A**SCII (the default) or **D**ictionary. The dictionary method disregards case in sorting labels, so the word *plaque* appears before *Plenty*. The ASCII sort method considers case in sorting labels so that uppercase labels appear before lowercase labels—for example, *Plenty* before *plaque*, *Revere* before *plaque*, and so on. Labels beginning with special characters appear at the end.

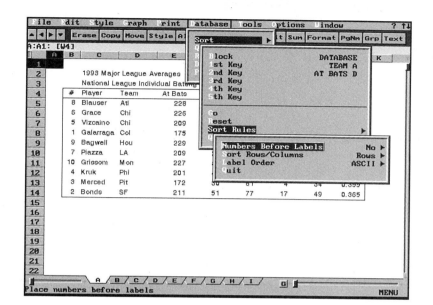

Fig. 13.6

The options on the **S**ort Rules submenu.

TIP

After you change the sort rules, choose **/O**ptions **U**pdate to record those settings for future sort operations.

One command on the **S**ort Rules submenu hasn't been covered yet—**S**ort Rows/Columns. The next section explains how to use this command.

Sorting Columns

Quattro Pro enables you to sort data by columns and by rows. Sorting a database by columns is particularly helpful when you want to reorganize the order in which fields appear in a database, or when the field names appear in unique rows and the records are contained in unique columns. To sort a database by columns, choose **/D**atabase **S**ort **S**ort Rules **S**ort Rows/Columns **C**olumns before initiating the sort operation.

Figure 13.7 shows the baseball database after the database has been sorted by columns. In this sort operation, block B4..J14 has been specified as the sort **B**lock, cell B4 has been specified as the **1**st Key, the sort order is **A** (for ascending), and the **S**ort Rows/Columns command has been set to **C**olumns.

TIP

When you sort a database by column, you must include the field names row in the sort range when your database looks like the one pictured in figure 13.7. Including this row ensures that each column label remains paired with the data below the label after the sort operation. Don't include the field names in the sort block if the names are contained in unique rows; otherwise, Quattro Pro sorts the field names into the database area when you sort the database by column.

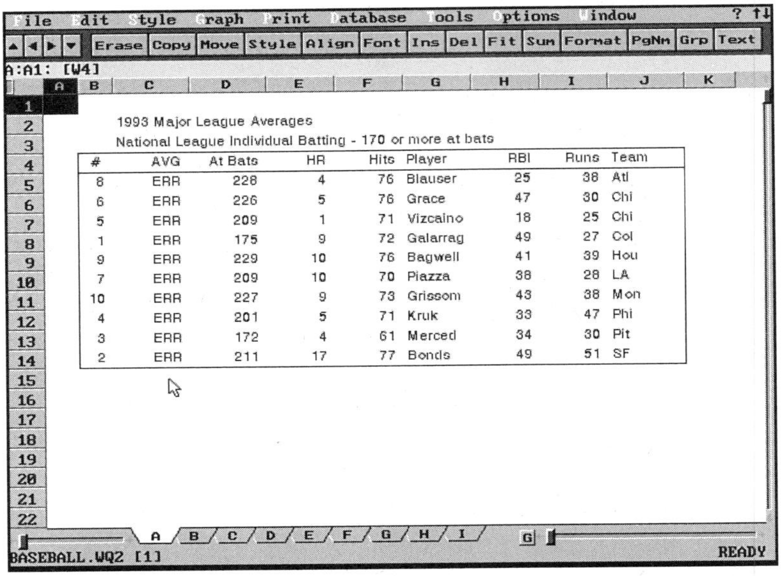

1993 Major League Averages

National League Individual Batting - 170 or more at bats

#	AVG	At Bats	HR	Hits	Player	RBI	Runs	Team
8	ERR	228	4	76	Blauser	25	38	Atl
6	ERR	226	5	76	Grace	47	30	Chi
5	ERR	209	1	71	Vizcaino	18	25	Chi
1	ERR	175	9	72	Galarrag	49	27	Col
9	ERR	229	10	76	Bagwell	41	39	Hou
7	ERR	209	10	70	Piazza	38	28	LA
10	ERR	227	9	73	Grissom	43	38	Mon
4	ERR	201	5	71	Kruk	33	47	Phi
3	ERR	172	4	61	Merced	34	30	Pit
2	ERR	211	17	77	Bonds	49	51	SF

Fig. 13.7

Sorting the baseball database alphabetically, using the sort-by-column rule.

TIP

When you apply the sort-by-column rule to a database that contains record-dependent formulas (such as those in column C of fig. 13.7), Quattro Pro displays ERR values. To guard against this possibility, convert all record-dependent formulas to their values with /**E**dit **V**alues before initiating a sort-by-column operation.

FOR RELATED INFORMATION

◄◄ "Transposing Data in a Cell Block," p. 175.
How to switch the row and column arrangement of data in a cell block—a technique useful for reorganizing the layout of your databases.

Searching a Database

You use the commands found on the /**D**atabase **Q**uery menu to search a database, locate records that meet specific conditions, and then copy the records elsewhere on the same notebook.

The records appearing in the baseball database, for example, come from a larger database containing statistics for all National League baseball players. To create the example database, you can search for the 10 players with the highest batting averages. You can extract the 10 lowest batting averages, the 10 highest averages with at least 120 hits, or all players whose last name begins with the letter Z.

Figure 13.8 shows a database containing inventory data for a sports car rental agency. In figure 13.8, the database shell is block B4..H10, and the database area is block B5..H10. Notice that the database area is a subset of the database shell.

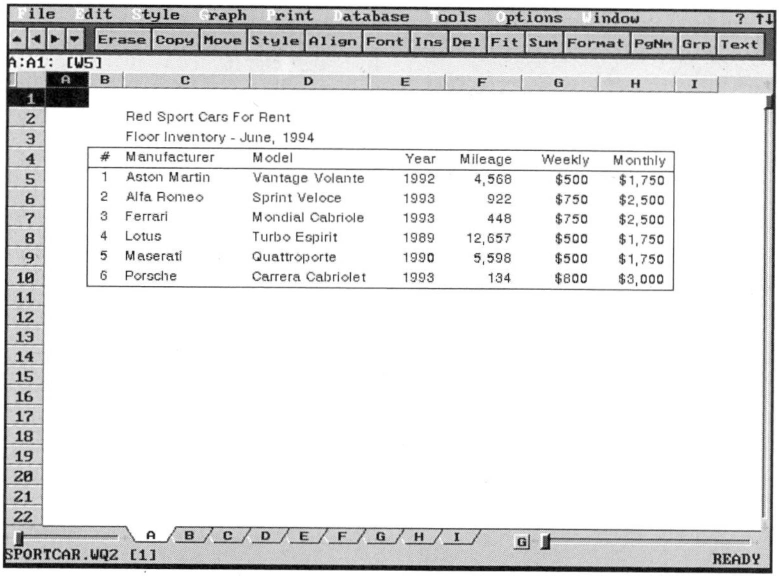

Fig. 13.8

The Red Sports Car rental agency database.

Remember, the database shell is the framework of the database: the field names row, the drawn lines (if any), and the database area where the records reside.

Defining the Search Block

The first step in every search operation is to define the search block. In most cases, the search block includes an entire database. Other valid search blocks include a portion of a database or even a database that resides on another notebook in Quattro Pro's memory. Quattro Pro even can search databases not in memory, but stored on disk. Just supply the familiar linking syntax described in Chapter 8, "Managing Files and Windows."

NOTE ▶ The queried block must be a 2-D cell block. Quattro Pro ignores every page after the first page if you try to search a 3-D cell block.

You must follow one rule when you define a search block: the block must include the database field names that you want to search. Except for a few special cases, however, the search block and the database shell have the same coordinates. This rule is the opposite of the rule applying to sort operations. In sort operations, you omit the field names when naming or defining the database area so that Quattro Pro will not sort the field names into your database.

In a search operation, Quattro Pro doesn't shift the order of the records because the program only looks at the records. When you define the search criteria, you must specify which field names the criteria apply to. After Quattro Pro knows what to search for, you need to indicate where in the search block to begin searching.

TIP ▶ Choose /**E**dit **N**ames **C**reate and assign a unique name to the database shell. In this example, the name SHELL is assigned to block B4..H10.

To specify the search block, follow these steps:

1. Choose /**D**atabase **Q**uery **B**lock.

2. Type the name of the search block (**SHELL** in this example) or type the block coordinates and press Enter.

Whether you choose to name your database shell or to supply block coordinates, be sure to include the field names row in the search block. If you don't, Quattro Pro doesn't search through your database correctly.

Assigning Names to the Field Names Row

You can assign names to the field names for the search operation by choosing /**D**atabase **Q**uery **A**ssign Names. When you execute this command, Quattro Pro names the first entry in the first row below each field, using its field name label. In figure 13.8, for example, the name # is assigned to cell B5, Manufacturer to cell C5, Model to cell D5, and so on. This procedure enables Quattro Pro to begin the search operation at record #1 in the sports car database.

> To execute a **Q**uery submenu operation properly, Quattro Pro requires that your field names be no longer than 15 characters.

TIP

Assigning names to the field names row is optional but makes the process of creating and entering search criteria much easier. A name is easier to remember than a cell address.

Quattro Pro assigns the labels in the field names row to each field in the first record of the database. Quattro Pro knows which is the field names row and which is the first record in the database because when you specified the search block, you included the field names row as part of that block.

Defining the Search Criteria

The next step in the search process is to define the search criteria. You first must choose an area of the notebook in which you can place the search conditions. In figure 13.9, a criteria table is entered into block B12..H13.

A *criteria table* contains field names and the criteria definitions that specify what to look for in a search block. A valid criteria table must include the name of at least one field and a condition (or conditions) to be met.

Fig. 13.9

A criteria table added to the sports car database.

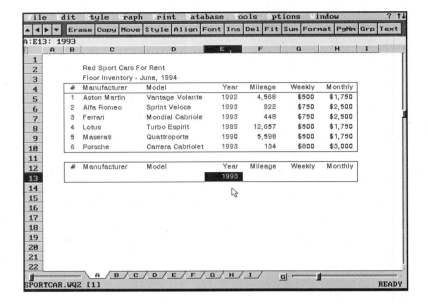

The first line of the criteria table in figure 13.9 is a duplicate of row 4 from the database shell. Although you need to include only one field name, this criteria table format enables you to define criteria selectively for one, some, or all the field names so that you can create an array of search conditions.

TIP

> Use the /**E**dit **C**opy command to copy the field names to the criteria tables, because names must match exactly.

Although the Year field in this criteria table contains only one definition, you easily can define additional criteria for the Year field. Enter the extra criteria definitions in the cells under the first one (for example, in cells E14, E15, and so on).

The following rules explain how Quattro Pro evaluates the search conditions appearing in a criteria table:

■ When you enter more than one criterion definition on a row, Quattro Pro searches for records that satisfy all the search conditions. This operation is called an *AND search*.

■ When fields have multiple criteria definitions, Quattro Pro searches for records that satisfy either condition. This operation is called an *OR search*.

> **NOTE**
>
> When a field in a criteria table has no definition, Quattro Pro ignores that field during a search operation.

The single criterion in figure 13.9 tells Quattro Pro to search for all records whose Year field contains the value 1993.

To set up the criteria table, follow these steps:

1. Highlight block B4..H4.

2. Choose /**E**dit **C**opy.

3. Make cell B12 the active cell.

> **NOTE**
>
> You can put the criteria table anywhere outside the database shell in the notebook—you can even store it on another page in the same notebook—although choosing an area just outside the database shell usually is most convenient.

4. Press Enter to copy the field name labels to the criteria table. (Use the /**S**tyle **L**ine Drawing command to create the border that appears in fig. 13.9.)

5. Make cell E13 the active cell. Type **1993** and press Enter to record the criterion definition.

Now, choose /**E**dit **N**ames **C**reate and assign a unique name to the criteria table. In this example, the name CRITERIA is assigned to block B12..H13.

To define the criteria table, follow these steps:

1. Choose /**D**atabase **Q**uery **C**riteria Table.

2. Type **criteria** and press Enter to record the coordinates of the criteria table.

In step 2, you also can enter the block coordinates of the criterion definition, E12..E13. Either approach returns the same result.

Creating Search Formulas

The criterion definition in figure 13.9 is rather simple. To create more complex definitions, include formulas in your search criteria. You can search the rental car database for all cars whose model year is greater than or equal to 1992 (+YEAR>=1992), for example, or locate those cars whose monthly rental rate is less than four times the value of the weekly rate (+MONTHLY<+WEEKLY*4).

TIP

> If you previously executed the /**D**atabase **Q**uery **A**ssign Names command, use those names instead of cell addresses in your criteria formulas.

Criteria formulas must contain a cell reference or a field name, an operator, and a value. You can use any of the following mathematical and logical operators in a search formula:

Operator	Meaning
=	Equal
<	Less than
<=	Less than or equal
>	Greater than
>=	Greater than or equal
<>	Not equal
#AND#	AND logical operator
#NOT#	NOT logical operator
#OR#	OR logical operator

When you enter a formula as a search criterion, Quattro Pro displays a 1 or a 0 in the cell. A 0 value indicates that the first cell in that particular field of the database returned a FALSE value; a 1 indicates a TRUE value. These displayed values don't affect the search in any way, nor is the value displayed in the formula cell affected by any other cell in the database but the first. If you prefer to display a particular cell formula in text form, make that cell active, and choose /**S**tyle **N**umeric Format **T**ext.

> When creating the search formulas, press F3 to bring up a list of field names you can select rather than type those names.   **TIP**

Using Wild Cards

You also can use wild cards in your criteria table to delineate the conditions of a label search. Quattro Pro uses the following three wild cards:

- A question mark (?) replaces one character in a search label. When the search label is *p?t*, for example, Quattro Pro locates the labels *pat*, *pet*, *pit*, *pot*, and *put*, but not *spot* or *pate*.

- An asterisk (*) replaces any number of characters in a label. When the search label is *tre**, for example, Quattro Pro locates the labels *tree*, *tread*, and *treaty*, but not *retread* or *street*.

- The tilde (~) searches for all labels except those matching the label designation. When the search label is *~T**, for example, Quattro Pro finds all labels that don't begin with T. Quattro Pro can locate the labels *Fox*, *box*, and *CREATE*, but not *tiny* or *TRE-MENDOUS*.

> If you leave the criteria definitions blank in the criteria block, Quattro Pro locates every record in the database.   **NOTE**

Performing the Search

After you define the search block and the criteria table, Quattro Pro stores these definitions at the right margin of the **Q**uery submenu, next to each command (see fig. 13.10). You now are ready to perform a search operation.

Fig. 13.10

The query block and criteria table definitions recorded on the Query submenu.

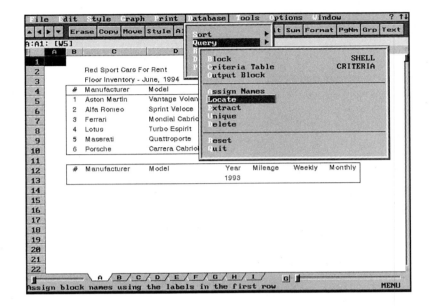

Locating Records

To begin a search-and-locate operation, choose /**D**atabase **Q**uery **Lo**cate. Figure 13.11 shows how Quattro Pro highlights the first field of the first record in the search block whose Year field contains the value 1993.

In the sports car database, the first match that Quattro Pro locates is record #2. To move to the next matching record (record #3), press the down-arrow key; to move to previous matches, press the up-arrow key. Press Home to move to the first matching record in the list and press End to move to the last matching record.

Occasionally, you may want to edit the contents of a highlighted record. Press the right- or left-arrow key until the selector is in the field you want to edit, and then press F2 to enter EDIT mode. Make your changes on the input line and then press Enter to accept the new field data.

Figure 13.12 shows how to use a formula to narrow a search operation. The criterion formula in cell F13, +MILEAGE<400, adds an additional

restriction that tells Quattro Pro to locate the records for all cars built
in 1993 that have mileage under 400 miles. Only one record, #6, meets
this condition (see fig. 13.13).

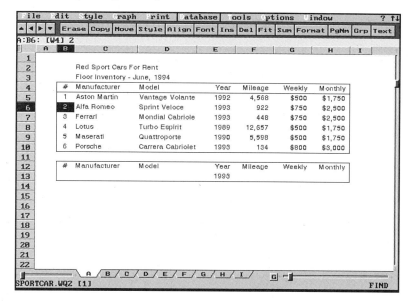

Fig. 13.11

Locating the first record
in the database meeting
the search criterion.

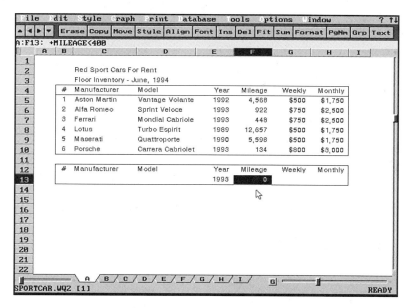

Fig. 13.12

Using a formula to
narrow the search
operation.

Fig. 13.13

Highlighted record #6, the only match in the database.

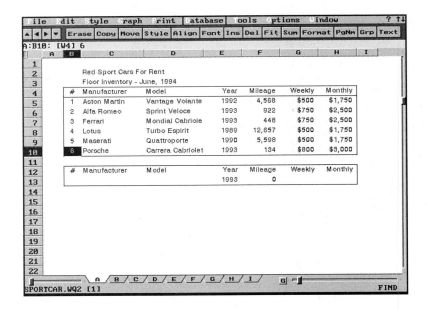

Deleting Records

When you choose /**Database Query D**elete, Quattro Pro removes from the database all records that satisfy the defined criteria. Before deleting these records, Quattro Pro asks you to confirm your selection. Choose **D**elete to delete the records or **C**ancel to abort the operation.

After Quattro Pro deletes all matching records from a database, all other records move up to fill the vacated spaces. If you accidentally delete records that you want to keep, press Alt+F5, the Undo key, to bring the records back.

Setting Up an Output Block

The **E**xtract and **U**nique search commands on the /**Database Q**uery menu find records that satisfy the criteria and then move the records to a different part of the notebook for further processing. Before you use either search command, however, you must define an output block so that Quattro Pro knows where to store the extracted data.

These two commands are useful for extracting data from databases in several locations: notebooks open in memory, notebooks on disk, and other databases.

In figure 13.14, block B20..H20 contains an output block. When Quattro Pro locates records meeting the conditions specified in the criteria table, Quattro Pro copies the records to the output block beginning at the first line below the field names row.

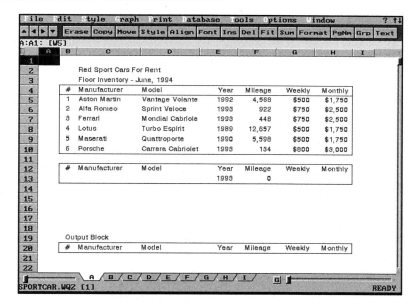

Fig. 13.14

An output block below the database and the criteria table.

To create this output block, follow these steps:

1. Highlight block B4..H4.

2. Choose /**E**dit **C**opy.

3. Make cell B20 the active cell.

4. Press Enter to copy the field name labels to the output block.

To define the output block, perform the following steps:

1. Highlight block B20..H20.

2. Choose /**E**dit **N**ames **C**reate.

3. Type **output** and press Enter to record this name.

4. Choose /Database **Q**uery **O**utput Block.

5. Type **output** and press Enter to record the name of the output block.

An output block, like a criteria table, doesn't need to contain every field name from the database—only the ones that now are being searched. You should create an output block as you would create a criteria table, however, to ensure the greatest flexibility when you perform search operations.

Extracting Records

When you choose /**D**atabase **Q**uery **E**xtract, Quattro Pro copies all the matching records into the output block. Only the fields whose names appear on the first line of the output block are included in the copied records.

If you specify only the field names row when defining the output block, Quattro Pro uses as much space as necessary to copy the matching records. If you specify a limited number of rows below the field names row, Quattro Pro uses that space until that space is filled. When Quattro Pro runs out of space to copy to, the program displays a warning message explaining that all records cannot be extracted into the existing output block.

This problem is fairly easy to correct. First, erase all the records in the output block. Next, redefine the size of the output block. Finally, restart the search operation.

Using the same criteria from the search-and-locate operation from the earlier section "Performing the Search," figure 13.15 shows the result of an extract operation. Rather than highlight a matched record, Quattro Pro extracts a copy of the record and places the copy in the first row below the field names row in the output block.

Identifying Unique Records

When you choose /**D**atabase **Q**uery **U**nique, Quattro Pro copies all unique records that meet the specified criteria into the output block. Unique works like **E**xtract, except that **U**nique doesn't copy duplicate records into the output block.

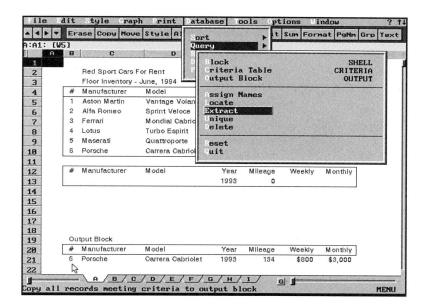

Fig. 13.15

A matching record extracted and copied to the output block.

Consider the revised sports car database shown in figure 13.16. Notice that record #5 appears twice in this version of the database. The larger the database, the greater the chances that you will encounter duplicated records.

The criteria table specifies all records whose # field equals 5 and whose Manufacturer field contains the label Maserati. In this situation, the Unique command copies the unique records that meet these conditions.

Notice that the output block in figure 13.17 contains only one record. Because only two records met the search conditions in the criteria table, and these records are duplicates (all fields are exactly the same), Quattro Pro copies only one record into the output block.

Now look at the split window shown in figure 13.18. The results displayed in this output table were achieved by not specifying any criteria in the criteria table.

Not specifying any criteria forces Quattro Pro to copy all unique records from the database into the output table. This technique is a clever way to update a database when you suspect that duplicate records exist.

Fig. 13.16

Criteria entered to
extract a list of unique
records from the
database.

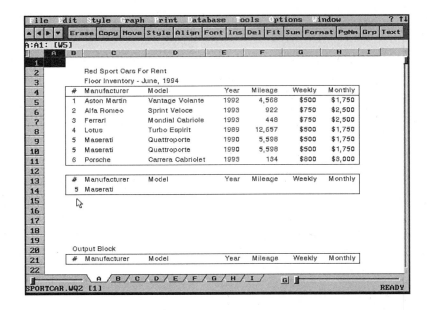

Fig. 13.17

All unique matching
records copied from the
database into the output
block.

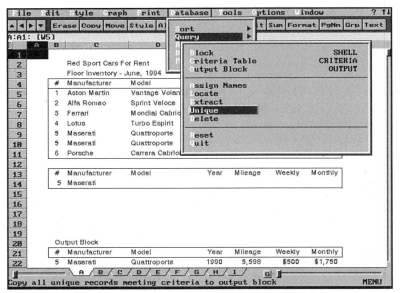

TIP

The information in the output block can be copied back into the database shell without affecting the block name (SHELL) by using the /**E**dit C**o**py Special **C**ontents command. Just be sure to include one blank row for each duplicate record when you choose the source block to copy.

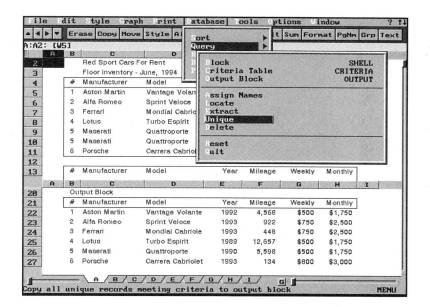

Fig. 13.18

The results of not specifying criteria.

FOR RELATED INFORMATION

◀◀ "Entering Formulas," p. 98.
The rules for entering formulas similar to criteria formulas into a notebook.

◀◀ "Searching for and Replacing Data," p. 176.
How to search through an entire notebook for a label or value, and replace it with another label or value. This approach can be more flexible than the /**D**atabase **Q**uery command.

Using a Database as a Data-Entry Form

The /**D**atabase **R**estrict Input command enables you to set up your notebook as a data-entry form. After executing this command, Quattro Pro limits movement of the selector only to unprotected cells.

To set up the sports car database for data entry, follow these steps:

1. Choose /**S**tyle **P**rotection **U**nprotect.

2. When prompted for a block to unprotect, type a block that excludes the field names row or type the block name (**database** in this example) and press Enter.

3. Choose /**D**atabase **R**estrict Input.

4. Type the block to restrict—**database**—and press Enter.

Quattro Pro immediately restricts movement of the selector to the database area for the sports car database.

When you execute /**D**atabase **R**estrict Input, however, Quattro Pro reframes the database in the window by positioning the first unprotected field in the database at the upper left portion of your screen. To prevent Quattro Pro from reframing your database, perform the following steps before selecting /**D**atabase **R**estrict Input:

1. Place the selector in the first unprotected field in the database (cell B5).

2. Choose /**W**indow **O**ptions **L**ocked Titles.

3. When prompted, choose **B**oth.

4. Choose /**D**atabase **R**estrict Input.

When you perform these steps to lock the titles, your screen looks like the one shown in figure 13.19. On this screen, you cannot move your selector to any location above or to the left of the first cell (cell B5) in DATABASE or below or to the right of the active cell (cell H11). Quattro Pro shades locked titles to delineate cell blocks A1..A8192 and B1..IV4 from the rest of the notebook. Now when you execute the **R**estrict Input command, Quattro Pro doesn't move your database.

While your database is in restricted entry mode, you can use the mouse or the arrow keys to move about the database. To disable restricted access, press Enter or Esc (except in EDIT mode).

FOR RELATED INFORMATION

◀◀ "Protecting Important Data," p. 208.
How to protect and unprotect cell data in your notebooks.

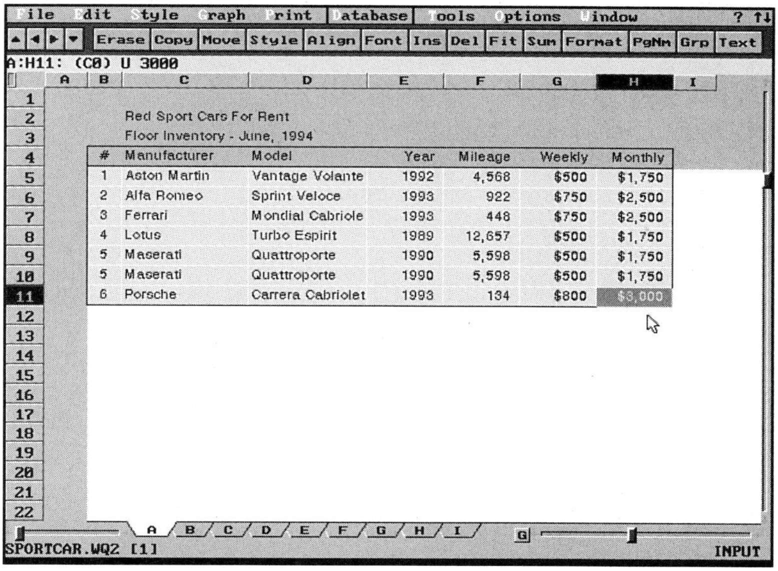

Fig. 13.19

Locked titles in a notebook.

Controlling Data Entry

The /**D**atabase **D**ata Entry command controls the type of data that Quattro Pro accepts into a cell or a block. Use this command to increase the accuracy of data-entry activities. Suppose that a field (column) of data in a database is designated only for dates. By restricting the cells in this column to date-only entries, you can prevent data-entry errors.

To restrict the type of data acceptable in an entry, follow these steps:

1. Choose /**D**atabase **D**ata Entry.

2. When prompted, choose **L**abels Only to restrict all input to labels or choose **D**ates Only to restrict input to dates.

Choose /**D**atabase **D**ata Entry **G**eneral to enable a cell to accept any type of data.

Using Paradox Access

Users of Quattro Pro can read and write Paradox files that have a DB file extension. With this feature, you can load data from a Paradox database file into a Quattro Pro notebook. Quattro Pro Versions 2.0 and later also offer **P**aradox Access, a **D**atabase menu command that enables you to run Quattro Pro from within Paradox Versions 3.5 and later.

Quattro Pro's /**D**atabase **P**aradox Access command switches you into Paradox's operating environment. While in Paradox, you can switch back to Quattro Pro by pressing Ctrl+F10. This program-linking feature places the power of both program environments at your fingertips. You can use Quattro Pro's graph presentation and publishing capabilities to enhance your Paradox data, or use Paradox's sophisticated data management tools to manipulate Quattro Pro notebook data.

Reviewing the Requirements for Using Paradox Access

Paradox and Quattro Pro have different minimum hardware needs. Quattro Pro usually uses expanded memory, whereas Paradox mostly uses extended memory. Although Quattro Pro can load and run on a PC with only 512K of RAM, Paradox's memory needs are somewhat greater. To use the **P**aradox Access command, you must have at least the following software and hardware:

- Quattro Pro (Version 2.0 or later)
- Paradox Version 3.5 or later
- 2M of extended RAM
- An 80286 PC

To achieve peak performance from the Quattro Pro-Paradox link, Borland recommends that you buy a separate product called Paradox SQL Link. This product enables you to access data stored on file servers running SQL (Structured Query Language). Many mainframes, minicomputers, and OS/2 servers support SQL software. Check with your systems administrator to verify that the file server supports Borland's Paradox SQL Link.

Preparing To Use Paradox Access

Before you use the **Paradox** Access command, you must alter the contents of the CONFIG.SYS and AUTOEXEC.BAT files that reside in your root directory. You also must make changes to PXACCESS.BAT or PX4ACCES.BAT, two files that were copied into the /QPRO directory when you first installed Quattro Pro.

> **NOTE**
>
> PXACCESS.BAT is a batch file that prepares Paradox Version 3.5 for a program link and then loads Paradox into system memory. PX4ACCES.BAT is a batch file that prepares Paradox Version 4 for a program link and then loads Paradox into system memory.

Use the following procedure to prepare your computer for a Quattro Pro-Paradox link:

1. Set FILES=40 in your CONFIG.SYS file.

2. Add a line containing the word SHARE to your AUTOEXEC.BAT file. This terminate-and-stay-resident (TSR) program enables Quattro Pro and Paradox to share and lock files.

3. Verify that your AUTOEXEC.BAT file contains Quattro Pro and Paradox in the PATH statement.

4. Verify that Quattro Pro and Paradox are installed and reside in separate directories.

5. Verify that your Paradox working directory and private directory are different. If they aren't different, enter Paradox's Custom Configuration Program and use the **D**efaults **S**et Directory command to change the location of the working directory.

6. Verify that the PXACCESS.BAT or PX4ACCES.BAT file contains the correct memory allocation arguments.

> **TIP**
>
> The last four of these steps are taken care of automatically during installation. Verifying these changes, however, is a good idea.

PXACCESS.BAT and PX4ACCES.BAT contain two commands that serve to prepare your system's memory for the eventual program link. The DOS SHARE command appears on the first line in both files, in case you forget to execute PXACCESS.BAT or PX4ACCES.BAT before establishing a program link. Executing the SHARE command twice causes no harm because DOS ignores the second attempt.

In PXACCESS.BAT, the second command line contains the following statement:

PARADOX –qpro –leaveK 512 –emK 0

In PX4ACCES.BAT, the second and third command lines contain the following statements:

SET DPMIMEM=MAXMEM 2048
PARADOX –qpro –emk 0

The function of each argument appearing on these command lines is defined as follows:

Argument	Function
PARADOX	Loads Paradox into your computer's memory
–qpro	Establishes the Quattro Pro-Paradox link, enables Paradox to work in a multiuser environment, and allocates a minimum of 384K of conventional memory to Quattro Pro
–leaveK 512	Allocates the first 512K of memory to Quattro Pro
–emK 0	Allocates all expanded memory to Quattro Pro so that Paradox doesn't use the memory
set dpmimem= maxmem 2048	Limits the amount of extended memory available to Paradox through the DPMI Loader to a maximum of 2,048K; without this command line, the DPMI Loader reserves all available memory for Paradox

You may need to edit PXACCESS.BAT or PX4ACCES.BAT, depending on the type and amount of memory you have in your system. Consider the following scenarios:

■ Your 80386 computer has 4M of expanded memory and uses the Quarterdeck QEMM-386 expanded memory manager. Edit the second line of PXACCESS.BAT as follows:

PARADOX –qpro –leaveK 3000 –emK 0

Always set the –leaveK argument equal to 1M less than total system memory.

■ Your 80286 computer has an AST RAMpage! expanded memory card with 4M of memory. Edit the second line of PXACCESS.BAT as follows:

    PARADOX –qpro –leaveK 0 –emK 0

■ Your 80286 computer has 4M of memory, which is configured as extended. Edit the second line of your PXACCESS.BAT file as follows:

    PARADOX –qpro –leaveK 2000 –emK 0

Set the –leaveK argument so that it's greater than 512 but less than the total amount of extended memory. Increase this setting if you have difficulty loading large Quattro Pro notebooks.

■ Your 80286 computer has 1M of extended memory. Your PXACCESS.BAT file uses the DOS SHARE file allocation table (FAT) distribution and requires the following changes on the second line:

    PARADOX –qpro –leaveK 512 –emK 0 –share –prot

Finally, set /Options Other Expanded Memory to Both to ensure that memory is allocated in the most efficient manner.

> When you establish a program link, Quattro Pro disables the /x start-up parameter (if you supply the parameter), which enables Quattro Pro to use 512K of extended memory.

TIP

After you edit the CONFIG.SYS, AUTOEXEC.BAT, and PXACCESS.BAT (or PX4ACCES.BAT) files, Quattro Pro and Paradox operate properly each time you load them into your system's memory.

Running Paradox Access

You can initiate the link between Quattro Pro and Paradox from within Paradox and from within Quattro Pro.

Initiating a Program Link from Paradox

The best method for initiating a Quattro Pro-Paradox link is to execute the PXACCESS.BAT or PX4ACCES.BAT file from DOS. Both files initiate file locking and file sharing, properly allocate memory to Quattro Pro and Paradox, and then load Paradox into system memory. Follow these steps:

1. If you are in Quattro Pro, choose /**F**ile **E**xit to return to DOS.

2. At the DOS command prompt, type **pxaccess** (or **px4acces**) and press Enter to load Paradox into your computer's memory.

3. After you are inside Paradox, press Ctrl+F10 to switch to Quattro Pro.

You can load a Quattro Pro file the first time you switch to Quattro Pro from Paradox during a work session (as described in step 3). This feature helps you manage shared file data between these two programs because initially, you always pass the data to the same Quattro Pro notebook.

TIP

If you aren't operating on a network and you get the error message **Cannot lock file for reading**, set the /**O**ptions **O**ther **P**aradox **N**etwork Type command to **O**ther. Choose /**O**ptions **U**pdate to save this setting.

To specify the notebook that Quattro Pro should load, type the file name in brackets and place the file name after the –qpro argument in the second command line in the PXACCESS.BAT file (or the third line in PX4ACCES.BAT). The syntax for using this feature is as follows:

PARADOX –qpro [*filename macroname /options*]

NOTE

This procedure works only once during each work session. If you switch back to Paradox and then return to Quattro Pro at a later time, Quattro Pro autoloads the notebook file specified with the /**D**atabase **P**aradox Access **L**oad File command.

In this syntax, the optional *filename* argument represents a notebook file that you want to load, including the full path. Quattro Pro workspace names and Paradox DB file names are valid substitutes for the optional *filename* argument in the syntax in the example.

If you want to load a Quattro Pro notebook file named PXDATA.WQ2 the first time you switch from Paradox to Quattro Pro during a work session, for example, use the following syntax:

PARADOX –qpro [C:\QPRO\PXDATA.WQ2]

The optional *macroname* argument enables you to specify an autoload macro. If you want Quattro Pro to execute a macro named FORMAT that formats the autoloaded notebook, for example, use the following syntax:

PARADOX –qpro [C:\QPRO\PXDATA.WQ2 FORMAT]

The optional *options* argument enables you to use any of Quattro Pro's start-up parameters. (See the section "Using an Autoload File" in Chapter 16 for more information on these parameters.) To autoload the notebook named PXDATA.WQ2, for example, execute the macro named FORMAT, and initially load Quattro Pro with its monochrome display palette, supply the following statement in the PXACCESS.BAT (or PX4ACCES.BAT) file:

PARADOX –qpro [C:\QPRO\PXDATA.WQ2 FORMAT /IM]

Remember, Quattro Pro disables the /x parameter and instead uses the –leaveK and –emK commands in the PXACCESS.BAT file and the –emK command by itself in PX4ACCES.BAT to manage system memory. See Chapter 16, "Customizing Quattro Pro," for a complete list of Quattro Pro's other start-up parameters.

Initiating a Program Link from Quattro Pro

To initiate a Quattro Pro-Paradox link from Quattro Pro, follow these steps:

1. Load Quattro Pro into your system's memory.

2. Choose /**D**atabase **P**aradox Access. Quattro Pro displays the **P**aradox Access submenu. Choose **G**o to switch to Paradox.

The commands on the **P**aradox Access submenu enable you to control the operation and configuration of Paradox.

The **G**o command switches you from Quattro Pro to Paradox. This command is operable as long as you started the current work session by executing the PXACCESS.BAT or PX4ACCES.BAT file. The **G**o command now is active.

Use the **L**oad File command to specify the name of a file for Quattro Pro to load each time you switch back to Quattro Pro from Paradox. Remember, if you also specify a file-name argument to the –qpro command in PXACCESS.BAT or PX4ACCES.BAT, Quattro Pro loads that file the first time you switch from Paradox to Quattro Pro during the current work session. Every time thereafter, Quattro Pro loads the file specified by the **Load File** command.

The **Autoload** command enables and disables the **Load File** command. If **Autoload** is set to **No**, Quattro Pro doesn't load the file specified by the **Load File** command. If you set /**D**atabase **Paradox Access Autoload** to **Yes**, Quattro Pro ignores the /**O**ptions **Startup Autoload File** command setting.

Questions & Answers

This chapter introduces you to the **Database** menu commands. If you have questions concerning particular situations that aren't addressed in the examples given, look through this section.

Sorting a Database

Q: I want to sort my database so that all clients from Oklahoma (having OK in the STATE field) are at the top of my database. Am I confined to ascending and descending orders?

A: Yes. Sort is confined to a few sorting orders. What you need to do is a search. If you really want to place all OK records on the top rows of your database, use /**D**atabase **Query Extract** and then /**D**atabase **Query D**elete. Finally, copy the extracted records to the top lines of your database.

Q: On the **S**ort submenu, can I specify **1**st Key as an ascending sort, with **2**nd Key as a descending sort?

A: Yes. Quattro Pro prompts you for sort direction after each key. The specified sort rules apply equally to all sort keys and operations, however.

Q: I am unable to decipher the results of a sort operation. Apparently my records have shifted by column but not by row. What should I check for?

A: When database records appear to have been sorted incorrectly, first try pressing Alt+F5 to undo the operation. (If the Undo feature is disabled, refer to Chapter 15's section on "Restoring Parts of the Transcript" to learn how to undo the operation.)

Next, choose /**D**atabase **S**ort **S**ort Rules and review the current setting for the **S**ort Rows/Columns command. If it's set to **C**olumns (or **R**ows) when you want to sort by rows (or columns), choose the opposite setting and try the sort operation again.

Searching a Database

Q: When I enter a formula in my criteria table, I get the warning message Invalid cell or block address. What's wrong?

A: Quattro Pro doesn't recognize the field name you have used. First, make sure that the spelling matches the spelling used in the search block. Second, make sure that you have used the /**D**atabase **Q**uery **A**ssign Names command following any changes you made to the field names. Third, supply the cell address in the formula.

Q: Can I possibly search for (and extract) all records in which any one field is zero?

A: Certainly. Set up a criteria table specifying that records in which field1=0, field2=0, and so on be selected.

Accessing Paradox

Q: When I press Ctrl+F10 to switch from Paradox to Quattro Pro, I get a warning message that says Can't Load Quattro Pro. What's wrong?

A: The QPRO program directory isn't included in the PATH statement found in the AUTOEXEC.BAT file. Edit the contents of the AUTOEXEC.BAT file to include QPRO in your PATH statement; then, rerun PXACCESS.BAT or PX4ACCES.BAT.

Q: When I press Ctrl+F10 to switch from Paradox to Quattro Pro, the program beeps at me. Now what's wrong?

A: You didn't load Paradox with PXACCESS.BAT or PX4ACCES.BAT. Exit Paradox, type **pxaccess** (or **px4acces**) at the DOS command prompt, press Enter to load Paradox, and configure your system for a Quattro Pro-Paradox link.

Q: Quattro Pro didn't autoload the file that I typed next to the –qpro argument in the PXACCESS.BAT (or PX4ACCES.BAT) file. Why did this happen?

A: You forgot to place the file name in brackets, so Quattro Pro ignored your entry. You must place all –qpro arguments inside square brackets.

Q: I just switched to Paradox from Quattro Pro but forgot to save my notebook. Did I lose all my data?

A: No. You need not choose /File Save before switching to Paradox. When you return from the Paradox to the Quattro Pro environment, your notebook appears just as you left it when you first switched. When you try to leave Paradox before saving an altered Quattro Pro notebook, you are prompted to save the changes before quitting the program.

Q: I am having difficulty loading a Quattro Pro notebook. Does this have something to do with the Paradox Access command?

A: In a way, yes. When you load Quattro Pro from within Paradox, presumably by executing PXACCESS.BAT (or PX4ACCES.BAT), your memory is allocated differently than if you load Quattro Pro by itself. If your system has zero expanded memory available to Quattro Pro, for example, you likely can load only smaller notebooks. If Quattro Pro fails to load a notebook in its entirety, increase the –leaveK setting in PXACCESS.BAT (or PX4ACCES.BAT) to free up more expanded memory.

Summary

In this chapter, you learned how to manipulate your data by using the commands found on the **D**atabase menu. These commands enable you to turn a Quattro Pro notebook into an efficient environment for storing and accessing database information.

Having completed this chapter's material, you should understand the following concepts:

■ Creating a database shell on a notebook

■ Entering data into a database

■ Sorting records using field names as sort keys

- Sorting records by rows and by columns

- Searching a database for records that meet specific criteria definitions

- Using a notebook as a data-entry form

- Using the **Paradox** Access command to link Quattro Pro to Paradox

Chapter 14 introduces you to the commands on the **Tools** menu that enable you to perform advanced data analysis. In Quattro Pro, advanced data analysis works on the principles of regression, data parsing, sensitivity analysis, and optimization modeling. The techniques described in this chapter can help you find answers to complex questions about data you have in your notebooks.

Analyzing and Manipulating Data

Even the most complete and meticulously kept notebook application can be ineffective if it doesn't yield simple and interpretable answers to specific questions. In a sales forecast application, for example, what is the effect on revenues of a 10 percent increase in advertising expenditures? In Southern California, what is the relationship between the average annual price of gasoline and the number of gallons consumed? How does a 7 percent decline in the cost of goods sold and a simultaneous 4 percent increase in consumer demand affect a sporting goods store's gross profit?

This chapter starts by introducing you to the **Tools** menu commands that can produce answers to these types of questions, using data that you store in your notebook applications.

Then you learn how to do *regression analysis*, a technique in which you develop formulas to predict future results based on current and historical data. You then learn how to work with mathematical matrices—specifically, how to invert and multiply matrices.

Next, you learn how to reorganize data imported from other software. This technique is called *parsing*, which means breaking apart long lines of data into smaller, more manageable lines. Parsing is useful for preparing your data for further analysis in Quattro Pro.

The next section demonstrates how to perform *sensitivity analysis*, a technique that shows in one notebook many different outcomes to the same formula or problem. You also learn how to create a frequency distribution to group similar elements from a large set of data.

The chapter then covers the use of the Optimizer. This powerful tool enables you to identify optimal solutions to complex problems that contain many interrelated variables.

Finally, you learn how to load add-in @functions into Quattro Pro for use in your notebooks.

NOTE

The examples in this chapter offer sufficient coverage of each command to enable you to use all or most of the features available for each tool. You can consult a statistics textbook for more comprehensive presentations of the mathematical proofs and axioms on which these tools are based.

Reviewing the Tools Menu

You can use the commands at the bottom of the **Tools** menu, shown in figure 14.1, to answer complex questions you have about data in your notebooks. With these commands, you can perform analyses that go well beyond the simple "what-is-the-average-of-these-three-numbers?" type of questions that you have learned to answer by using arithmetic formulas and @functions.

The **A**dvanced Math tools use information from a notebook to perform regression analysis and matrix operations. The **P**arse command breaks long labels from an imported data set and places the individual parts into separate cells. The **W**hat-If command performs one-way and two-way sensitivity analysis. The **F**requency command creates frequency distributions. The **O**ptimizer command enables you to define and solve complex problems that encompass multiple variables and constraints. Finally, the Library command enables you to load custom add-in @functions into Quattro Pro for use with your notebooks.

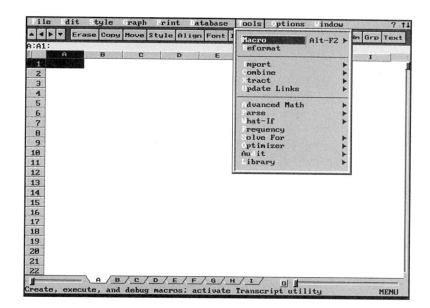

Fig. 14.1

The mathematical tools on the **T**ools menu.

NOTE

See Chapter 7, "Analyzing Notebooks," to learn how to monitor the construction of notebook formulas by using the Au**d**it command and how to solve formulas backwards by using the **S**olve For command.

Using Advanced Math Tools

When you choose **A**dvanced Math from the **T**ools menu, you access a submenu that offers three powerful statistical tools for analyzing different types of data. The **A**dvanced Math commands are as follows:

Command	Description
Regression	Performs single-variable and multivariable data set regressions
Invert	Creates an inverted matrix from a matrix
Multiply	Multiplies one matrix by a second matrix

Performing Regression Analysis

Regression analysis attempts to devise an equation in which an independent variable predicts the value of a dependent variable. You can use more than one independent variable. Regression analysis, in fact, is one of the most effective methods for determining a linear relationship between a set of independent variables and a single dependent variable.

Suppose that you want to determine the relationship between the average yearly price of gasoline and the quantity that you buy. The hypothesis is that your consumption, C(y), depends on the price, P(x), of gasoline. Because only one independent variable—P(x)— exists, this problem is a single-variable regression analysis.

The table in figure 14.2 contains data about average gasoline prices and consumption in gallons for a 10-year period. Notice also that the **R**egression submenu displays the definitions for each variable (independent and dependent), the output block, and a y-axis intercept. You must enter these definitions before executing the **R**egression command.

Fig. 14.2

A data table of yearly gasoline consumption and average yearly price per gallon.

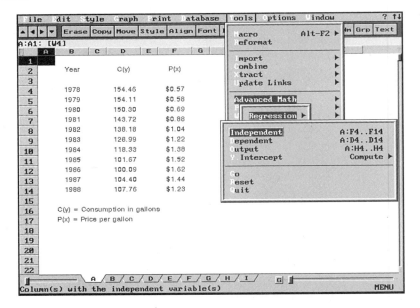

To do a regression analysis, perform the following steps:

1. Choose /**T**ools **A**dvanced Math **R**egression.

2. From the **R**egression submenu, choose **I**ndependent, type the range that includes the independent variables—**F4..F14** in the example—and press Enter.

TIP

To include other independent variables, enter additional data into the columns to the right of the first independent variable. Then include these columns in the block you enter in step 2.

3. Choose **D**ependent, type the range that includes the dependent variables—**D4..D14** in the example—and press Enter.

4. Choose **O**utput, type the cell that should be the upper left corner of the range to which you want to output the analysis—**H4** in the example—and press Enter.

5. Choose **Y** Intercept and then **C**ompute (the default setting).

TIP

Use the **Y** Intercept **C**ompute setting for most basic regression problems. To force the y-axis intercept value to 0, choose **Y** Intercept **Z**ero.

6. Choose **G**o to calculate the regression.

The **R**egression command appraises each pair of points supplied in your data table, which in turn enables you to derive an equation that minimizes each pair's distance from a "best fit" line. Quattro Pro calculates a formula constant and the coefficients for each independent value and then displays the results in a regression table (see block H4..K12 in fig. 14.3). Use the values in the regression table to create the equation with which you can predict a new dependent value based on a new independent value. (This equation appears in block B19..F19 in fig. 14.3.)

The constant and the X coefficient are the key components of the equation. Each independent variable that you specify in your data table always has one constant and one coefficient. Use the following syntax to build a linear predictive formula from the data in this table:

Dependent Variable = Constant +
    (1st X coefficient * 1st independent variable) +
    (2nd X coefficient * 2nd independent variable) +
    . . . + (*n*th X coefficient * *n*th independent variable)

Fig. 14.3

A regression analysis table copied into the output block.

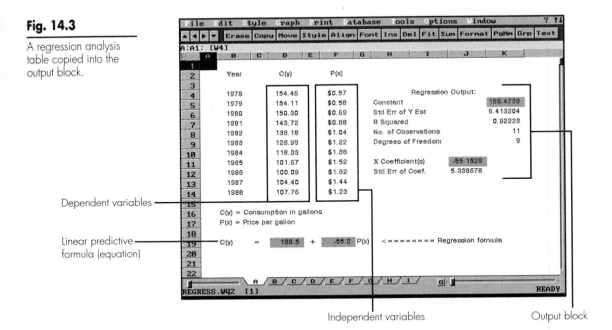

Dependent variables

Linear predictive formula (equation)

Independent variables

Output block

Because the consumption versus price example contains only one independent variable, only one X coefficient exists.

The linear predictive formula appears at the bottom of figure 14.3. To create this formula, the value +K5 was placed in cell D19, and the value +J11 was placed in cell F19. This formula updates itself each time you rerun the regression with new data as long as you don't change the location of the output table. If you add independent variables to your data table, you must create additional cell references in the formula appearing on row 19 to accommodate the new X coefficients.

You can use this formula to test your theories about the relationship between the price of gasoline and the quantity of gasoline bought by consumers. Suppose that a sudden oil crisis pushed the price of gasoline up to $3.00 per gallon. By substituting the value 3 into the linear predictive formula,

$$C(y) - 188.5 = -55.2(3.00)$$

you can predict that average annual consumption will go to 22.9 gallons. Continue substituting values in for the P(x) variable to test other theories you may have.

Inverting and Multiplying Matrices

By using matrices, you can solve multivariable linear equations simultaneously. A *matrix* is a rectangular array of numbers that describes the coefficients for variables in a group of linear equations. If you have to solve linear equations using matrices, use Quattro Pro's Invert and Multiply commands to calculate the answers quickly.

Consider the matrices shown in figure 14.4. Each time you create an inverted matrix, you must go through the four-step process outlined in this figure. The values you are required to supply for this example are shaded.

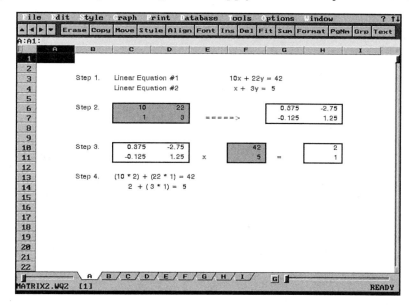

Fig. 14.4

Inverting a matrix to solve two linear equations simultaneously.

Suppose that you want to solve simultaneously the two linear equations pictured on rows 3 and 4 of figure 14.4. You can solve the equations by using the Invert and Multiply commands.

To invert a matrix, follow these steps:

1. By using the coefficients from each linear equation, create an input matrix and enter the matrix into a notebook. The sample input matrix appears in cells C6..D7.

2. Choose /**T**ools Advanced Math **I**nvert.

3. Type the range address for the input matrix—**C6..D7** in the example—and press Enter.

NOTE

You can invert only a square matrix—that is, a cell block that has an equal number of rows and columns. Also, when you multiply two matrices, the number of columns in the first matrix must equal the number of rows in the second matrix. Otherwise, Quattro Pro doesn't perform this operation.

4. Type the number of the upper left cell of the block in which you want to place the inverted matrix—**G6** in the example—and press Enter.

5. Use the /**E**dit **C**opy command to copy the inverted matrix from G6..H7 to block C10..D11 to make working with this data easier in the next few steps.

To multiply matrices, perform the following steps:

1. Create a matrix by using the constants from the original equations, and enter the matrix into the same notebook. The sample constant matrix appears in cells F10..F11 of the notebook shown in figure 14.4.

2. Choose /**T**ools **A**dvanced Math **M**ultiply.

3. Type the range address of the first matrix to multiply—**C10..D11** in the example—and press Enter.

4. Type the range address of the second matrix to multiply— **F10..F11** in the example—and press Enter.

5. Type the upper left cell of the block in which you want to place the solution matrix—**H10** in the example—and press Enter.

The solution matrix provides the two values that solve both linear equations. To prove that these values are correct, review step 4 in figure 14.4.

Another example is shown in figure 14.5. Matrix #1 contains the number of units produced for three products: X, Y, and Z. Matrix #2 contains the units of material (M) and labor (L) required to build a unit of X, Y, and Z. To produce one unit of X, for example, you need four units of material and one unit of labor.

To determine the total number of units of material and labor required to produce 20 units of X, 30 units of Y, and 50 units of Z, multiply matrix #1 by matrix #2. As you can see from the bottom of figure 14.5, you need 420 units of material and 230 units of labor.

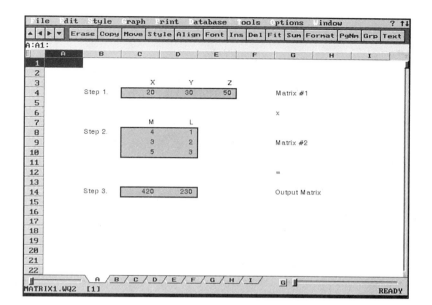

Fig. 14.5

Matrix multiplication used to determine input requirements for a production run.

FOR RELATED INFORMATION

◀◀ "Using Moving Average Analysis," p. 607.
   "Using Linear Fit Analysis," p. 613.
   "Using Exponential Fit Analysis," p. 617.
   How to perform regression-style analyses with graph data.

Using the Parse Command

The **Parse** command on the **Tools** menu is used to break long labels into two or more smaller labels. Although this capability may not sound interesting or useful, consider the **Parse** command in the more familiar context of database management.

In Chapter 8, you learn how to import outside data files into the Quattro Pro notebook environment. When Quattro Pro imports a file, the program often places all the data into one column. This placement really isn't a problem; although the original formatting is lost, the imported file usually retains its general organization (see fig. 14.6).

This database appears to have three individual fields: NAME, SS#, and RATE/HR. In fact, each record is contained in a cell within column B. Look at the input line at the top of the notebook and review record #1.

Fig. 14.6

An imported database in which each record appears in a cell in column B.

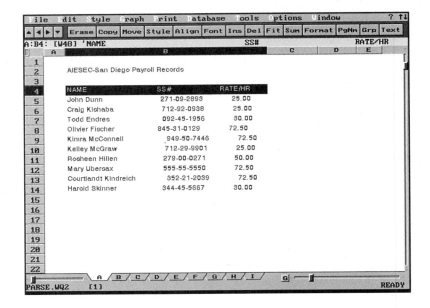

In WYSIWYG display mode, data from an imported file may appear to lose its column justification. In figure 14.6, for example, the SS# and RATE/HR data don't appear justified the same way as the NAME data. This display quirk has more to do with the default font selection in Quattro Pro than with the organization of the data.

 To check this situation, click the Text button on the SpeedBar (or choose /**O**ptions **D**isplay Mode **A**:80x25) and review the same notebook in text display mode (see fig. 14.7).

TIP

Although the RATE/HR data appears to have shifted into column C in figure 14.7, it really hasn't—the data in column B is overlapping into C.

BAR Click the BAR button, and then click the WYS button to return to WYSIWYG display mode. With the **P**arse command, you can re-create this database's original field structure without having to re-enter any records or manually justify the data.

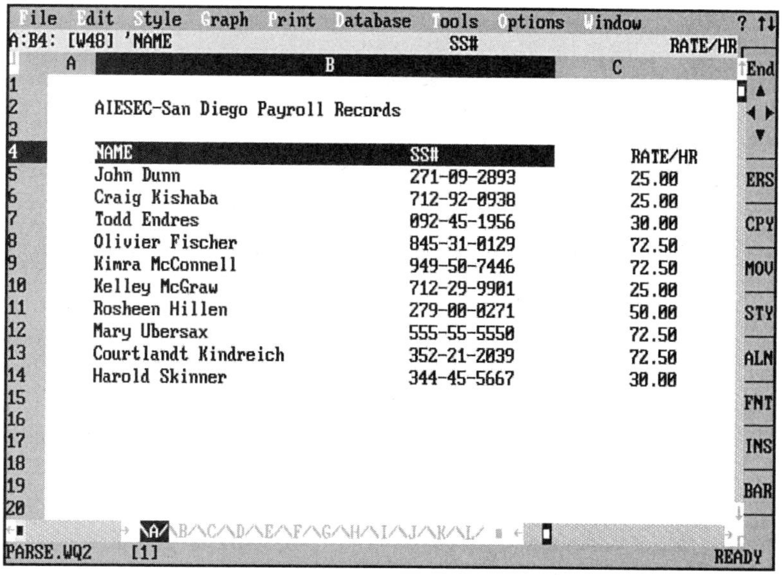

Fig. 14.7

Viewing the imported file data in text display mode.

Executing a Parse Operation

A parse operation involves the following four steps:

1. Create a format line.

2. Define the input block.

3. Define the output block.

4. Choose **Go** to parse the data.

You can use the **Parse** command to reformat the database shown in figure 14.6 by following these steps:

1. Place the cell selector in cell B4, the upper left corner of the block of imported data.

2. Choose **/Tools Parse Create**. Quattro Pro enters a format line in the row directly above the field names row (see fig. 14.8). The format line is Quattro Pro's "best guess" as to how the data should be divided.

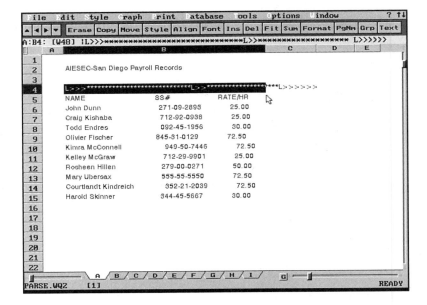

3. Choose **Input**, type **B4..B15**, and then press Enter to record the
   input block.

NOTE

The input block always must include the format line as the first row.

4. Choose **Output**, type **B28**, and then press Enter to record the output block (see fig. 14.9).

5. Choose **Go** to parse the database.

If you have defined the input and output blocks correctly, the results of
the operation should look like figure 14.10. Quattro Pro creates three
columns of data, one for each field name that the program recognized.

Performing Multiple Parse Operations

Quattro Pro has no rule restricting how many times you can parse a set
of data. In the preceding example, you also may want to parse the data
in column B to separate the last name data from the first name data.
You should parse data as long as parsing is easier than re-entering all
the records into a database.

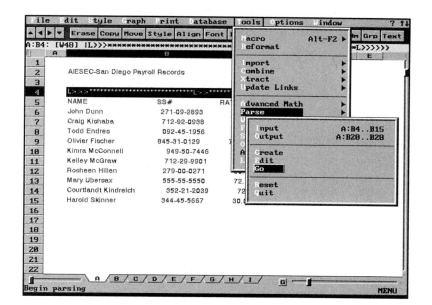

Fig. 14.9

Each element's definition on the right side of the **P**arse submenu.

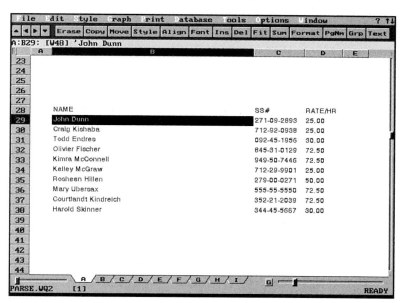

Fig. 14.10

The database restored to its original field name organization.

Fortunately, you seldom need to parse a set of data more than a few times, because the **E**dit command on the /**Tools P**arse menu enables you to create custom format lines. When the "best guess" format line created by the **C**reate command doesn't permit Quattro Pro to adequately parse your data, press Alt+F5 to reverse the most recent parse operations, and then choose **E**dit and create a custom format line, using any of the characters shown in table 14.1.

Table 14.1 Format Line Symbols

Symbol	Description
|	Denotes the beginning of a format line
V	Precedes a value cell entry
L	Precedes a label cell entry
T	Precedes a time value entry
D	Precedes a date value entry
>	Indicates a continuing entry
*	Indicates blank spaces that Quattro Pro can fill in with longer entries
S	Tells Quattro Pro to skip (delete) the character in this position

Performing Advanced Parse Operations

Chapter 13 advises you to create a unique field for each category of information in a database. The logic of creating separate fields for the two parts of a name—one field for the first name and one for the last—was discussed. When a field in your database fails to conform to this logic—such as in the NAME field of the sample database in the preceding section—the **P**arse command is limited.

Although the **P**arse command can create a format line and reorganize long labels into individual columns, the command generally cannot break apart two labels contained within one field.

To understand why, you first must understand how the **P**arse command functions. On the format line shown earlier in figure 14.9, each L symbol tells Quattro Pro exactly where one field ends and another field begins. The data in each field is left-justified and far enough from the data in neighboring fields that Quattro Pro has no problem distinguishing between the fields.

Now take another look at the two elements in the NAME field. The last names aren't left-justified, because the first names have different lengths. Quattro Pro doesn't know where to place the L symbols to distinguish between the two names.

You can use the **P**arse command to break apart multiple labels within a field but only when each label is left-justified and far enough from other labels in that field that Quattro Pro can distinguish between the labels.

With a little imagination and experimentation, however, you can side-step these constraints by combining the capabilities of the **P**arse command with those of the **E**dit menu's **S**earch & Replace command. (See Chapter 4 for complete coverage of the **S**earch & Replace command.)

In the example, you need to place enough distance between the first and last names in the NAME field to enable Quattro Pro to distinguish between the names. Because the longest first name in the NAME field is 10 characters long (Courtlandt), you must left-justify all the last names somewhere past character position number 11.

To allow enough space between first and last names, perform the following steps:

1. Highlight block B29..B38.

2. Choose /**E**dit **C**opy, type **B51**, and press Enter to copy the NAME field data to block B51..B60.

3. Choose /**E**dit **S**earch & Replace.

4. Choose **B**lock, type **B51..B60**, and then press Enter to record the location of the object block.

5. Choose **S**earch String, press the space bar once to enter a blank space, and press Enter.

6. Choose **R**eplace String, press the space bar 15 times to enter 15 blank spaces, and then press Enter. (You want Quattro Pro to replace each single space with 15 spaces.)

7. Choose **N**ext to begin the search-and-replace operation.

After you complete step 7, Quattro Pro displays the screen shown in figure 14.11. The first blank space that Quattro Pro locates is between John and Dunn in the first record. To check this result, look at the input line at the top of the notebook.

Fig. 14.11

A match to the search condition is located.

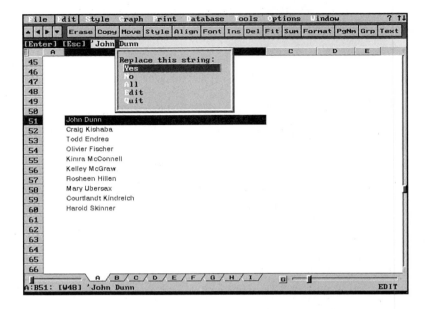

Now, choose the **A**ll option to search and replace each record in the database.

Next, use the /**Tools P**arse **C**reate command to create a "best guess" format line. Quattro Pro stores the format line on row 51. Then use the **E**dit command to add 10 > (greater than) symbols to the end of the format line on row 51 just to be sure that Quattro Pro correctly includes all the characters in each person's last name as part of the continuing entry. (See table 14.2 earlier in this chapter for an explanation of the format line symbols.)

Finally, parse the data appearing in block B51..B61 and store the results beginning in cell B52. The results of this parse operation are shown in figure 14.12.

Notice that the data in column C appears jagged. To use the **S**earch & Replace command to left-justify the last name labels in column C, perform the following steps:

1. Choose /**E**dit **S**earch & Replace **O**ptions **R**eset to reset the search-and-replace conditions.

2. Choose **B**lock, type **C52..C61**, and then press Enter to record the location of the object block.

3. Choose **S**earch String, press the space bar once to enter a blank space, and then press Enter.

4. Choose **N**ext to begin the search operation.

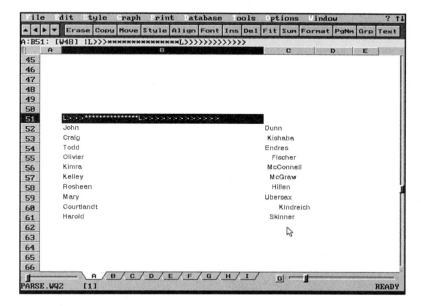

Fig. 14.12

The modified format line produces this parse result.

You didn't enter a replacement string this time. By entering nothing as the **R**eplace String condition, you tell Quattro Pro to search for blank spaces and replace them with nothing—essentially deleting the blank spaces.

After finding the first search match, Quattro Pro displays the screen shown in figure 14.13. The first blank space that Quattro Pro locates is before Kishaba in the second record. To check this result, look at the input line at the top of the notebook.

Now, choose the **A**ll option to search and replace each record in the database. Quattro Pro displays the results (see fig. 14.14).

To complete this exercise, enter the label **FIRST NAME** above the first name data in cell B51 (to overwrite the format line from the parse operation). Next, enter the label **LAST NAME** above the last name data in cell C51. Now you can incorporate the newly parsed data back into the original database shown in figure 14.10. Be sure to insert a blank column between columns B and C to make room for the LAST NAME data.

Fig. 14.13

Quattro Pro finds a match in column C to the search condition.

Fig. 14.14

The left-justified last names.

FOR RELATED INFORMATION

◄◄ "Searching for and Replacing Data," p. 176.
How to use the **S**earch & Replace command, including the various options you can set to clarify how Quattro Pro searches through a notebook.

Using the What-If Function

The **Tools** menu's **What-If** command enables you to create one-way and two-way sensitivity tables. A *sensitivity table* contains a range of column values and row formulas that define the parameters of a problem. When executed, the **What-If** command returns one answer for each row and column intersection.

By using sensitivity analysis, you can review in one table a wide range of solutions for virtually any what-if questions you may encounter.

Performing a One-Way Sensitivity Analysis

A one-way sensitivity analysis table substitutes values into a variable appearing in one or more formulas. You set up a column of substitution values and then create a formula in which to substitute the values.

Suppose that you want to analyze how various sales and costs affect the gross profits for a business. In this business, sales range from $10,000 to $24,000 per month, and costs fluctuate between 55 and 75 percent of sales. The following formula relates sales to costs to gross profit:

Gross Profit = Sales – Cost of Goods Sold

In this example, you want to create a sensitivity table that describes all possible gross profit values that can occur within a given range of sales values and cost percentages.

The first step is to enter the range of sales values into a column. The next step is to enter the formulas that calculate the gross profit values into a row. You enter five formulas, one for each likely cost percentage. You may want to change the format of this row to Text so that you can see the formulas (see fig. 14.15).

Fig. 14.15

Creating a one-way sensitivity table.

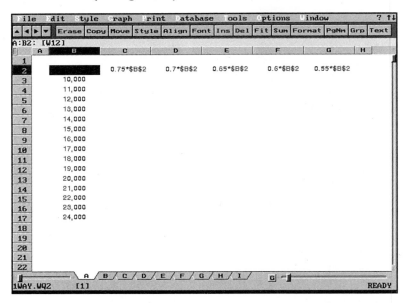

TIP

The formulas you create must contain a cell reference to a single, blank cell in the notebook where Quattro Pro can perform calculations for the one-way sensitivity analysis. Technically called the *input cell*, think of this cell as a temporary scratch pad that Quattro Pro uses and then clears each time it prepares for the next calculation.

In figure 14.15, the formulas on row 2 indicate that cell B2 is designated as the "scratch pad" cell. When you are selecting a blank cell on your notebook, be sure to pick one that falls anywhere outside the block bounded by your row and column data (in the example, cell block C3..G17).

After you enter all the appropriate values and formulas, you are ready to create the one-way sensitivity table by performing the following steps:

1. Choose /**Tools W**hat-If **1** Variable.

2. When prompted, type the data table block—**B2..G17** for the example—and press Enter.

3. When prompted, type the input cell—**B2** for the example—and press Enter.

In the example, Quattro Pro substitutes each sales value into cell B2, multiplies the substituted value by the percentage specified in each formula on row 2, and then places an answer in each intersection cell (see fig. 14.16).

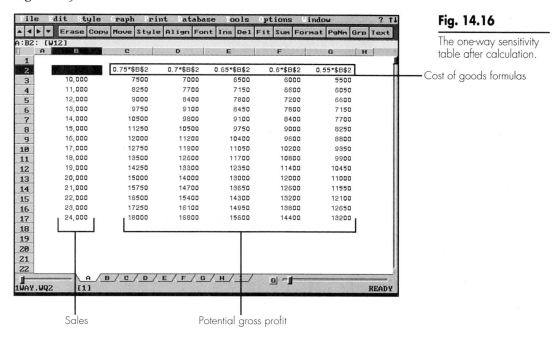

Fig. 14.16

The one-way sensitivity table after calculation.

Cost of goods formulas

Sales

Potential gross profit

Performing a Two-Way Sensitivity Analysis

A two-way sensitivity analysis uses a data table in a slightly different manner: You substitute two sets of values into a formula.

Consider a retail business that sells a particular product for $28 to $38, depending on the cost charged by the wholesale supplier. The following formula relates retail price to wholesale cost and the percent of profit on a sale:

Percent Profit = (Retail Price – Wholesale Cost) / Retail Price

To determine the percent of profit that the business is earning, you can construct a two-way sensitivity table that analyzes various price/cost combinations and computes the corresponding profit percentage.

The first step is to enter the range of retail prices and wholesale costs into a row and a column (see fig. 14.17). The next step is to enter a formula (in cell B5 in this example) that calculates the percent of profit. The formula, (A6–A5)/A6, references two input cells that fall outside the sensitivity table—cells A5 and A6. You may enter the formula into any cell on the notebook as long as it doesn't fall inside the block bounded by your row and column data (cell block C6..H19) and doesn't use either of the two input cells.

Fig. 14.17

Create a two-way sensitivity table.

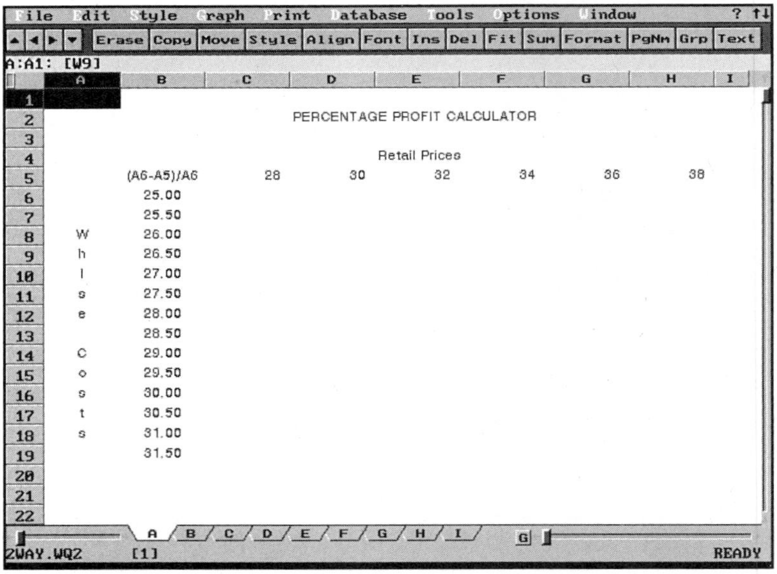

After you enter all the appropriate values and the formula, you are ready to create the two-way sensitivity table. Follow these steps:

1. Choose /Tools **What-If 2** Variables.

2. When prompted, type the data table block—**B5..H19** for the example—and press Enter.

NOTE

Make sure that the data table block encompasses only the area bounded by the row of values and column of values used in the analysis. Don't include the addresses for the blank input cells (A5 and A6), or you will get meaningless data. If this happens, press Esc until all the menus are put away, and then press Alt+F5 to restore the original data. Now perform the steps again, this time supplying the correct cell addresses at each prompt.

3. When prompted, type the input cell for the values in B6..B19 (Whlse Costs)—**A5** for the example—and press Enter.
4. When prompted, type the input cell for the values in C5..H5 (Retail Prices)—**A6** for the example—and press Enter.

Quattro Pro substitutes each pair of retail and wholesale prices into the input cells, performs the operation indicated by the formula in cell B5, and then places an answer in each intersection cell (see fig. 14.18).

NOTE

In figure 14.18, the calculated values are formatted to display in the percent format with one decimal place.

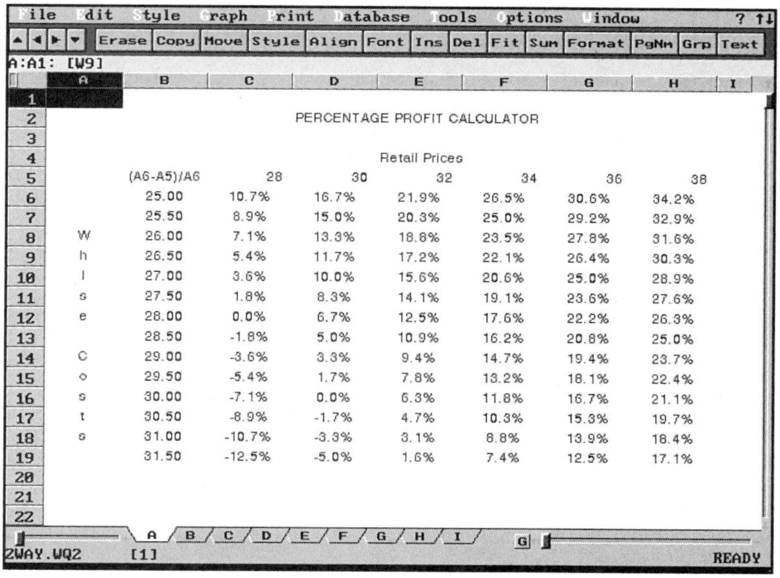

	A	B	C	D	E	F	G	H
5		(A6-A5)/A6	28	30	32	34	36	38
6		25.00	10.7%	16.7%	21.9%	26.5%	30.6%	34.2%
7		25.50	8.9%	15.0%	20.3%	25.0%	29.2%	32.9%
8	W	26.00	7.1%	13.3%	18.8%	23.5%	27.8%	31.6%
9	h	26.50	5.4%	11.7%	17.2%	22.1%	26.4%	30.3%
10	l	27.00	3.6%	10.0%	15.6%	20.6%	25.0%	28.9%
11	s	27.50	1.8%	8.3%	14.1%	19.1%	23.6%	27.6%
12	e	28.00	0.0%	6.7%	12.5%	17.6%	22.2%	26.3%
13		28.50	-1.8%	5.0%	10.9%	16.2%	20.8%	25.0%
14	C	29.00	-3.6%	3.3%	9.4%	14.7%	19.4%	23.7%
15	o	29.50	-5.4%	1.7%	7.8%	13.2%	18.1%	22.4%
16	s	30.00	-7.1%	0.0%	6.3%	11.8%	16.7%	21.1%
17	t	30.50	-8.9%	-1.7%	4.7%	10.3%	15.3%	19.7%
18	s	31.00	-10.7%	-3.3%	3.1%	8.8%	13.9%	18.4%
19		31.50	-12.5%	-5.0%	1.6%	7.4%	12.5%	17.1%

Fig. 14.18

The two-way sensitivity table after calculation.

FOR RELATED **INFORMATION**

◄◄ "Using Logical @Functions," p. 290.
How to use the @IF command, which you can use to create formulas that perform what-if-type analyses.

Creating Frequency Distributions

The **Frequency** command on the **Tools** menu counts the number of values that fall within specified ranges, groups the values into bins, and then produces a frequency distribution table using the bin data. A *frequency distribution table* provides a summary grouping of large data sets, enabling you to get a better picture of their distribution. After you create a table, you can display those values effectively in an XY graph.

Consider a commissioned study that analyzes the distribution of population among cities on Prince Edward Island (see fig. 14.19). The name of each city appears in one column, the population in another, and the bin block definition in a third.

Fig. 14.19

Organize data to be used in frequency distribution analysis.

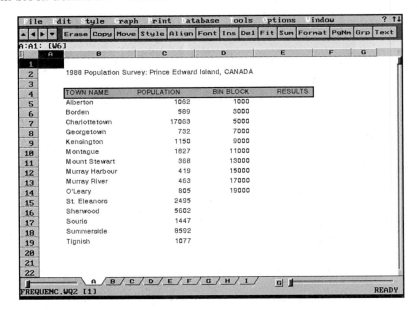

To set up a frequency distribution table that counts the number of cities whose population falls into each bin block, follow these steps:

1. Enter the names of each city into column B and enter each city's population into column C.

2. Define a bin block grouping that specifies the boundaries of the bins into which you want to put values. Generally, working with whole bin numbers that increment by a fixed amount is easiest.

> **NOTE**
>
> Bin block numbers must appear in ascending order on the notebook but don't necessarily require the same interval size.

3. Choose /**Tools Frequency**.

4. When prompted, type **C5..C19** and press Enter to define the values to include in the frequency analysis.

5. When prompted, type **D5..D14** to define the bin block.

6. Press Enter. Quattro Pro automatically copies the results in the column to the right of the bin block, overwriting any data stored there.

After you execute step 6, Quattro Pro copies the results of the frequency analysis into a block beginning at cell E5 (see fig. 14.20). Quattro Pro includes an extra result in cell E15 at the bottom of the results column. This result is 0 as long as Quattro Pro doesn't locate a value in the frequency table that's greater than the largest defined bin number.

> **TIP**
>
> Frequency distribution analyses lend themselves to XY graphing (see Chapter 10, "Creating Graphs," for more information). Figure 14.21 shows a graph constructed with the values appearing in the BIN BLOCK and RESULTS columns.
>
> This graph, often called a *histogram*, was created by defining the BIN BLOCK column data as the x-axis and the RESULTS data as the y-axis. Because the final value in the RESULTS column is 0, this cell isn't included in the x-axis series definition.

Fig. 14.20

A completed frequency distribution analysis.

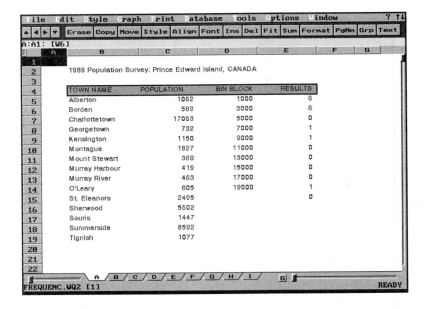

Fig. 14.21

An XY graph showing the distribution of the population on Prince Edward Island.

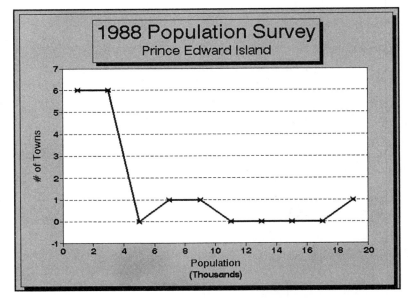

Using the Optimizer

Quattro Pro's **O**ptimizer command, another command on the **T**ools menu, enables you to find the optimal solution to a problem that has more than one variable. Multivariable problems also are known as *non-linear problems*; in many cases, non-linear problems have more than one solution. When a problem has more than one solution, you can define a set of constraints for the problem so that Quattro Pro can locate the "best fit" answer.

The **O**ptimizer solves problems by using a linear programming technique called *optimization analysis*—a tool commonly used in business management and social science research. You may use optimization analysis in any discipline, however, to juggle multiple considerations—for example, pollution levels versus job hazards versus company profits.

> The /**T**ools **O**ptimizer command replaces the /**T**ools **A**dvanced Math **O**ptimization command in Quattro Pro Versions 1.0, 2.0, and 3.0. Macros from Versions 3.0 or earlier that use the /**T**ools **A**dvanced Math **O**ptimization command should execute correctly in Version 5.0 if they contain menu-equivalent commands rather than keystrokes. See Chapter 15, "Creating Macros," for details about these two styles of macros.

NOTE

For complete details about optimization modeling and linear programming, consult a statistics text. To gather ideas about how you can use optimization in your own field, review the journal studies and papers published by professionals in the discipline. In this discussion, you learn how to prepare an optimization model with known financial data for Magnus Manufacturing, a fictitious company that manufactures and sells sporting goods equipment.

Using the **O**ptimizer to solve a problem involves the following four general steps:

1. Define the solution that you seek.

2. Identify the problem variables that the **O**ptimizer can change in an attempt to reach the solution.

3. Define the problem constraints that the **O**ptimizer must accommodate before a solution can be considered "optimal."

4. Execute the model.

You can use the 10 commands on the /**T**ools **O**ptimizer menu to define the cell address for the solution, identify the cells containing variables that can be changed, define the problem constraints, set options that fine-tune an **O**ptimizer operation, start solving the current problem, and review reports about the current solution. Other commands on this submenu restore a previous **O**ptimizer solution, load a predefined model, and reset the submenu to the default settings.

Table 14.2 describes the purpose of each **O**ptimizer submenu command.

Table 14.2 Optimizer Submenu Commands

Command	Description
Solution Cell	Defines the cell containing a value to be maximized, minimized, or equaled (optional)
Variable Cell(s)	Defines the cells containing the variables to be adjusted; must not be protected, cannot contain labels, formulas, dates, or text
Constraints	Defines the cells containing the problem constraints
Options	Offers commands for fine-tuning an **O**ptimizer operation
Answer Report	Displays in the notebook a report containing information about the solution cell, variable cell(s), and constraint cell(s)
Detail Report	Displays in the notebook a report containing the values of the solution cell and variable cell(s) at each iteration in the **O**ptimizer operation
Go	Executes an **O**ptimizer operation
Restore	Reinstates the value of all variable cells before the most recent Optimizer operation; press F9 if /**O**ptions **R**ecalculation **M**ode is set to **M**anual
Model	Saves multiple scenarios for a problem with the current notebook
Reset	Clears all **O**ptimizer settings

Setting Up the Optimizer

Figure 14.22 shows the 1994 production forecast for Magnus Manufacturing's water sporting goods line. This forecast provides information about each variable that influences management's decision to manufacture a particular amount of each product in the line.

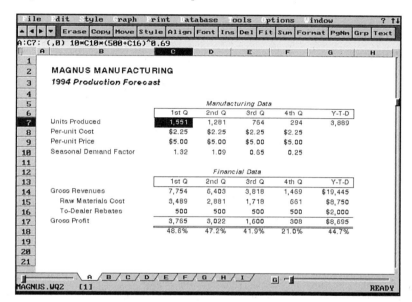

Fig. 14.22

The Magnus Manufacturing 1994 Production Forecast notebook.

The highlighted cell (C7) in figure 14.22 reveals the formula that the Magnus marketing staff has devised to forecast the number of units to produce for the first quarter. This formula—10*C10*(500+C16)^0.69— and the others like it in row 7 relate two key components of the Magnus Manufacturing production forecast: the Seasonal Demand Factor values and the To-Dealer Rebates values.

The Seasonal Demand Factor values in row 10 reflect management's estimate of how consumers will demand their products during each quarter of the year. Because the production department requires at least a month or two lead time to manufacture and ship the water sporting products, management anticipates that the greatest demand for their products will occur in the two quarters preceding the warmest months of the year (Quarter 1 and Quarter 2). The values 1.32 (C10) and 1.09 (D10) reflect management's expectation that demand will be 132% and 109% of average yearly demand during these two quarters.

The To-Dealer Rebates values in row 16 reflect management's long-standing policy of offering rebates to their wholesale sporting goods dealers to influence the level of orders placed.

In general, this formula says that more rebates equate to more gross revenues, but that at some point, each additional rebate dollar offered will produce less than a dollar in additional sales. This formula is based on an economic principle known as *diminishing marginal returns*.

Solving a Basic Optimizer Problem

In this example, management wants to know the level of To-Dealer Rebates required to push first quarter sales up to $10,000. Use the following steps:

1. Choose /**T**ools **O**ptimizer. Quattro Pro displays the **O**ptimizer submenu.

2. Choose **S**olution Cell. Quattro Pro displays the **S**olution Cell submenu.

3. Choose the **C**ell option to specify the cell with the value for which you want to solve. When prompted, type a valid cell address and press Enter. In the example, to solve for cell C14, the Gross Revenues value for the 1st Q, type **C14** and press Enter.

4. Choose the **M**ax,Min,Equal option to specify the target value you want to reach. You have the following four options:

Option	Description
Maximize	Maximizes the resulting value for the formula in the solution cell
Minimize	Minimizes the resulting value for the formula in the solution cell
Equal	Attains a specific value for the formula in the solution cell
None	Searches for a value without considering the solution cell

In the example, to attain a Gross Revenues value of $10,000, choose **E**qual. When prompted, type **10000** and press Enter (see fig. 14.23).

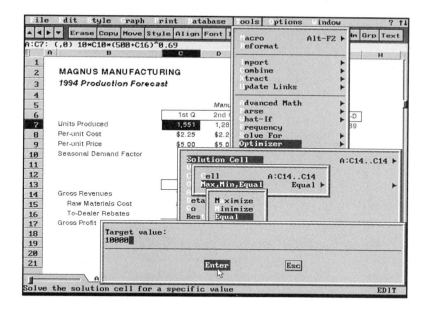

Fig. 14.23

The specified target value for the **O**ptimizer to attain.

5. Choose **V**ariable Cell(s) to specify the cell whose variables Quattro Pro can change to reach an optimal solution. To vary the To-Dealer Rebates value in the example, type **C16** when prompted. Then press Enter.

6. Choose **G**o to begin the search for the optimal solution. After Quattro Pro locates a solution, the **O**ptimizer submenu reappears. Press Esc twice to return to the notebook so that you can review the results.

Figure 14.24 shows the results of solving this basic **O**ptimizer model. Quattro Pro locates the target Gross Revenues value of $10,000 by increasing the To-Dealer Rebates value to 946, which has the corresponding effect of raising Units Produced to 2,000.

But what if Magnus Manufacturing has limits to the number of units it can produce in a year? In the last example, the Y-T-D Units Produced figure rose to 4,338. Suppose that production capacity is 4,000 units, invalidating the solution to the previous problem because the production capacity is unattainable.

In the next example, you learn how to define constraints to solve for more specific goals by using the **O**ptimizer. Choose /**T**ools **O**ptimizer **R**estore to reverse the changes made to your notebook during the most recent **O**ptimizer operation.

Fig. 14.24

The results of solving for a basic **O**ptimizer problem.

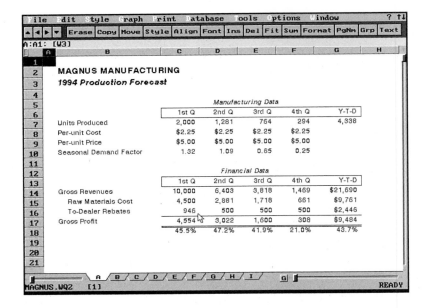

Using Constraints and Defining Multiple Variables

In this example, management wants to know the level of To-Dealer Rebates required to maximize the Y-T-D Gross Revenues value. Given a yearly production capacity of 4,000 units and a budget allocation of $2,000 for To-Dealer Rebates, they want to identify the optimal production schedule. To accomplish this result, they must select a range of variable cells and then identify two constraints for this problem. Expressed in terms that Quattro Pro can understand, these constraints are as follows:

- Y-T-D Units Produced must be less than or equal to 4000; G7<=4000

- Y-T-D To-Dealer Rebates must be less than or equal to $2,000; G16<=2000

Also, so that Quattro Pro can vary the To-Dealer Rebates values for all four quarters, specify cell block C16..F16 for the **V**ariable Cell(s) option.

Use the following steps to solve this problem:

1. Choose /Tools Optimizer. Quattro Pro displays the Optimizer submenu.

2. Choose Solution Cell. Quattro Pro displays the Solution Cell submenu.

3. Choose the Cell option to specify the cell with the value for which you want to solve. When prompted, type a valid cell address and press Enter. To solve for the Y-T-D Gross Revenues value in the example, type **G14** and press Enter.

4. Choose the Max,Min,Equal option to specify the target value you want to reach. To maximize the Y-T-D Gross Revenues value in the example, select the Maximize option.

5. Choose Variable Cell(s) to specify the cells with the variables Quattro Pro can change to reach an optimal solution. In the example, so that Quattro Pro can vary all four To-Dealer Rebates values on row 16, when prompted, type **C16..F16** and then press Enter.

6. Choose Constraints to specify the limits you want to place on the variables' use in the problem. At the <Add New Constraint> prompt, press Enter and construct the constraint expression(s).

   In the example, to constrain the Y-T-D Units Produced and Y-T-D To-Dealer Rebates values, at the <Add New Constraint> prompt press Enter. When prompted for the constraint cell, type **G7** and press Enter. From the Relation submenu, press Enter to choose the default relation operator, <=. When prompted for the constraint value, type **4000** and press Enter. Repeat this process and construct a second constraint that specifies that G16<=2000. The syntax for these two constraints appears on the Constraints submenu shown in figure 14.25.

7. Choose Go to begin the search for the optimal solution.

Figure 14.26 shows the results of solving this more complex Optimizer model. As you can see, Quattro Pro has reallocated the To-Dealer Rebates budget differently among the four quarters. A higher rebate is offered in the first quarter simply because that is when the greatest demand for Magnus Manufacturing's products occur. In this solution, Magnus Manufacturing attains its production capacity of 4,000 units (G7), at which Gross Revenues will be maximized at $20,000 (G14).

Fig. 14.25

Two constraints on the **C**onstraints submenu.

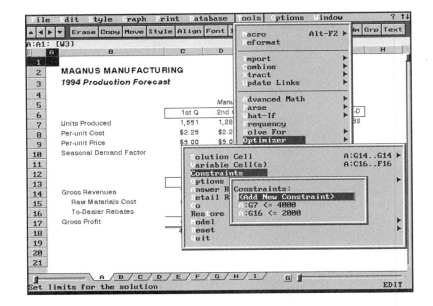

Fig. 14.26

The results of solving for a more complex **O**ptimizer model.

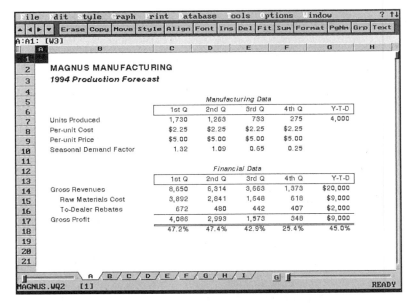

Setting the Optimizer Options

The options on the /**Tools O**ptimizer **O**ptions menu enable you to fine-tune an Optimizer model by adjusting the calculation rules that Quattro Pro uses when searching for solutions to a model. In almost all cases, the default settings on the **O**ptions submenu are sufficient to enable Quattro Pro to locate an acceptable solution. If Quattro Pro cannot find a solution to one of your problems, experiment with the various settings on the **O**ptions submenu, which are defined in table 14.3.

Table 14.3 Options Submenu Commands

Option	Description
Max Time	Specifies a time limit (in seconds) for Quattro Pro to try to find a best solution. Enter a value between 1 and 1000; the default is 100.
Max **I**terations	Specifies the number of times that Quattro Pro will try to find a best solution to the problem. Enter a value between 1 and 1000; the default is 100.
Precision	Describes the precision you want to observe in the answer that Quattro Pro finds. Enter a value between 0 and 1; the default is 0.0005.
Linear or Nonlinear	Sets this option to match the problem type: **L**inear or **N**onlinear (the default).
Show Iteration Results	Tells Quattro Pro whether to pause between iterations so that you can review the current solution. The default setting is **N**o.
Estimates	Selects one of two approaches for obtaining initial estimates of basic variables in each iteration: **Q**uadratic or **T**angent (the default).
Derivatives	Selects one of two differencing methods for estimates of partial derivatives: **C**entral or **F**orward (the default).
Search	Selects the method for computing the search direction: **C**onjugate or **N**ewton (the default)
Tolerance	Specifies a percentage that the Optimizer should come close to the best solution rather than find it. This setting is helpful if the calculation is taking a long time. Enter the percentage as a decimal value—for example, use the value 0.10 to tell Optimizer to come within 10 percent of the best solution.

(continues)

Table 14.3 Continued

Option	Description
Auto Scale	Selects whether Quattro Pro automatically scales models in which the variables vary from the target value by a large amount. Choose **Yes** or **No** (the default).

Producing Optimizer Reports

In optimization modeling, you rarely will locate an acceptable solution to a problem on the first try. In many cases, successful optimization modeling involves identifying different groups of variables in a notebook application to locate acceptable solutions. So that you don't have to create several copies of the same notebook to test your different assumptions and theories, Quattro Pro offers two reports that display the results of the current **O**ptimizer session.

Choose the /**Tools O**ptimizer **A**nswer Report command after completing an optimization session to produce a report that lists the solution cell and variable cells with their original and final values and variable dual values (see fig. 14.27). The Answer Report prints to a block that you specify and contains information about the constraints you identified.

Fig. 14.27

An answer report, starting in cell J2 of the same notebook.

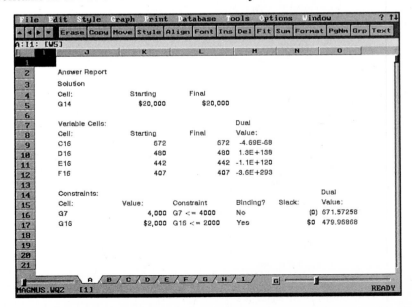

Choose the /**T**ools **O**ptimizer **D**etail Report command to produce a report that lists, at each iteration, the variable cells and the solution cell.

Using Other Optimizer Commands

Choose the /**T**ools **O**ptimizer Re**st**ore command to recover the previous variable cell values in the notebook. If /**O**ptions **R**ecalculation **M**ode is set to **M**anual, you must press F9 after choosing Re**st**ore to recalculate and display the previous values.

Choose the /**T**ools **O**ptimizer **M**odel command to load and save multiple problem definitions containing the **S**olution Cell, **V**ariable Cell(s), and **C**onstraints settings.

Choose the /**T**ools **O**ptimizer **R**eset command to clear Optimizer settings individually. Choose the **A**ll option to clear all settings on the **O**ptimizer submenu.

Loading Add-In @Functions

You can load third-party add-in @functions into Quattro Pro with the /**T**ools Library command. Then you can use the add-in @function with any notebooks you have in memory. All add-in @functions have a QLL file extension.

To load a third-party add-in @function, use the following steps:

1. Choose /**T**ools Library **L**oad.

2. Choose a file with a QLL extension from the file-name prompt box.

3. Press Enter to load the add-in @function into memory.

You must use a special syntax to access an add-in @function after you load the @function into memory. This syntax consists of the @ sign, the module name, a period, the function name, and the arguments entered inside parentheses:

@modulename.function_name(arguments)

The documentation that comes with your add-in @function provides you with the appropriate module name and complete instructions for using the add-in @function in a Quattro Pro notebook.

After you finish using an add-in @function, you should remove it from memory. Follow these steps:

1. Choose /**Tools L**ibrary **U**nload.

2. Highlight the name of the module you want to unload.

3. Press Enter to remove the add-in @function from memory.

TIP

To test for the presence of an add-in @function in memory, use @ISAAF and @ISAPP. See Chapter 6, "Using Functions," for more information about using these two @functions.

Questions & Answers

This chapter introduces you to the analytical tools found on the **Tools** menu. If you have questions concerning particular situations that aren't addressed in the examples given, look through this section.

Using Advanced Math Tools

Q: When I tried to invert a matrix in my notebook, Quattro Pro displayed the error message Not a square matrix. The matrix looks square to me—what could have happened?

A: To invert a matrix, Quattro Pro requires that matrix to contain the same number of rows as columns. Even though your matrix may look square (the currently defined column widths and row heights within your matrix can create the illusion that the data is in a square), it cannot be if you see this error message. Re-create the matrix so that the number of columns equals the number of rows.

Q: I changed several values in the column I defined as the **I**ndependent variable, but Quattro Pro didn't reflect these changes in the results of my regression table. Have I accidentally deleted formulas or done something wrong?

A: No. Quattro Pro doesn't update the results in a regression table automatically if you change the values of your independent or dependent variables. To update the values in your regression table, choose /**Tools A**dvanced Math **R**egression **G**o to rerun the analysis.

Parsing Data

Q: The database information I imported into my Quattro Pro notebook didn't appear to be properly aligned, so I manually deleted and inserted spaces in each record to justify the data. When I parsed the data, though, Quattro Pro occasionally lopped off letters from the front of the field entries. What did I do wrong?

A: When you import database information into a Quattro Pro notebook while in WYSIWYG display mode, your data may not appear justified. This display quirk has to do with your default font selection and often creates the impression that your data isn't justified. To see if your imported data is properly justified, switch to text display mode with /**O**ptions **D**isplay Mode **A**: Text (80x25). If your data appears properly justified in text display mode, continue with your parsing operation.

When you manually delete and insert spaces into imported database records while in WYSIWYG display mode, Quattro Pro will create an incorrect format line when you choose /**T**ools **P**arse **C**reate command. With an incorrect format line, Quattro Pro may lop characters off the front of field entries when you parse the data. Characters get lopped off because Quattro Pro is using incorrect format line information as the basis for deciding where one database field ends and another begins. The best way to proceed if this situation occurs is to import the database records again and then create a new format line by using /**T**ools **P**arse **C**reate.

If working with data that "appears" unjustified annoys you, switch to text display mode when parsing database information.

Using Sensitivity Analysis

Q: I want to perform a two-way sensitivity analysis using the **W**hat-If command. I made my column and row of values, entered my formulas, and calculated the table. Unfortunately, each cell in the table was filled with a copy of my formula. Why?

A: You most likely changed the formula cell to display as text by inserting an apostrophe label prefix at the front of the formula so that you could see the formula. When you create the table, however, Quattro Pro must be capable of deciphering the formula in the cell. Change the cell contents back to a formula by removing the label prefix from the front of the formula.

Using the Optimizer

Q: Each time I tried to define a Solution Cell value for my model, Quattro Pro displays the error message `Solution cell is not a formula`. What am I doing wrong?

A: The Solution Cell definition must be a reference to a cell that contains a formula. Quattro Pro must be able to adjust the formula variables in a solution cell formula for the Optimizer to work.

Q: Each time I choose Go to solve an Optimizer problem, Quattro Pro displays the error message `Objective function changing too slowly` or `No feasible solution can be found`. What can I do to correct this situation?

A: First, check your starting values and ask yourself whether they are realistic. If your values aren't realistic to you, adjust the starting values and choose Go again.

Second, consider constructing constraints for values in your model. If you know, for example, that total production cannot exceed 50,000 units, construct a constraint that tells Quattro Pro so.

Third, try adjusting settings on the Options submenu. For example, try solving the model at a higher Max Iterations value.

Q: When I selected the Restore command to recover the previous variables in my notebook model, nothing happened. How can I recover my original notebook values?

A: First, check to see whether the /Options Recalculation Mode command is set to Manual. If it is, you will see the CALC indicator displaying on the status line. In this case, press F9, and Quattro Pro immediately displays the original values in your notebook.

If the CALC indicator isn't displaying on the status line, you will have to discard the current notebook and retrieve the last saved copy of the notebook to recover the original values.

Q: I want to delete a constraint from my notebook model, but the /Tools Optimizer Reset Constraints command deletes all constraints from the current notebook. What can I do?

A: Choose the /Tools Optimizer Constraints command. On the Constraints submenu, highlight the constraint you want to delete, and then press Delete. Quattro Pro deletes the constraint without affecting other constraints defined for the current notebook.

Summary

In this chapter, you learned how to manipulate and analyze your data by using the commands found on the **Tools** menu. The commands on this menu enable you to turn a Quattro Pro notebook into an efficient environment for storing, accessing, and analyzing database information.

Having completed this chapter's material, you should understand the following concepts:

- Performing regression analysis by using one or more independent variables

- Multiplying and inverting matrices

- Parsing long labels into smaller parts and placing each part into a separate column

- Using the **P**arse and **S**earch & Replace commands together to meet special data-reorganization needs

- Creating one-way and two-way sensitivity tables

- Producing a frequency distribution and graphing the results

- Performing optimization modeling

- Loading and unloading add-in @functions

Chapter 15 introduces you to Quattro Pro macros—mini-programs that you create to reproduce often-used menu commands and to automate repetitive notebook tasks. Chapter 15 provides you with all the fundamental basics that you will need to envision, create, name, test, debug, and then safely execute macros. The chapter also covers Quattro Pro's **T**ranscript command, a tool you use to review a history of all notebook activities that have taken place during the current work session.

Creating Macros

In this chapter, you learn about Quattro Pro's macro programming facility, which you access from the **Tools** menu. A *macro* is a productivity tool that enables users to store commonly used keystrokes and command selections in a file for future use. When a macro is executed, Quattro Pro reproduces exactly each keystroke action and menu command.

You can accomplish a wide variety of tasks with macros. Macros can automate tedious and repetitive actions that you perform during your work sessions. Macros also can be self-running mini-programs that solicit data input from a user and then manipulate and display the data on a report. You even can create macros to generate reports and graphs from your notebook data.

In the first section of this chapter, you learn about creating a basic macro program. The commands on the /**Tools Macro** menu are defined, and then you review a step-by-step process for envisioning, planning, and writing a Quattro Pro macro.

The next section shows you how to create a macro automatically by using the macro recorder. You learn how to paste a recorded macro into a notebook, edit the macro instructions, and then replay the macro.

The chapter continues by showing you how to assign a name to a macro and how to create an autoload macro that executes each time you load a new, blank notebook into Quattro Pro.

Managing notebook macros is the topic of the next section. You learn how to document and create a macro library. This section concludes with a presentation of guidelines for editing and executing a macro and deleting an out-of-date macro.

The rest of this chapter is devoted to advanced macro topics. You learn how to enter macro instructions manually into an autorecorded macro, which is created with the /**T**ools **M**acro **R**ecord command. You are introduced to Quattro Pro's powerful macro debugger, a tool that enables you to locate and correct problems that cause macro execution errors.

This chapter concludes with an overview of the **Transcript** facility. By using this tool, you can reproduce a command history of your work session efforts and monitor and protect these same efforts from power outages and system crashes.

Learning about Macros

A macro program (macro for short) is a collection of special instructions that Quattro Pro can execute. To create a macro, you enter each instruction into a column of cells on the active notebook. When you execute a macro program—much like you execute any other program—Quattro Pro evaluates each cell and then performs the specific action called for by each instruction.

The actions performed by a macro depend entirely on you because you can make a macro duplicate any command action possible on a Quattro Pro menu. You can write a simple macro, for example, that alters the width of a column. You also can write a more involved macro that completely formats a new, blank notebook and then prompts a user to enter data.

A Quattro Pro macro also contains instructions that mimic keystrokes, cursor movements, and other keyboard actions that you perform as you choose menu commands. Many Quattro Pro commands require you to supply block coordinates, type values, or press other keys as part of that command's execution, for example. In a macro program, you store all these keystrokes so that Quattro Pro performs each cell instruction exactly.

Quattro Pro macros also can include macro commands, which perform functions that menu commands cannot accomplish. You can use a macro command to request input from a user during the execution of a macro, for example, much as Quattro Pro requires you to supply data before executing a menu command. Other macro commands meet specific programming objectives, such as looping, branching, and passing program control to macro subroutines.

Reviewing the Macro Menu

You can use the 10 commands found on the /**Tools Macro** menu to create, execute, debug, and delete macros (see fig. 15.1). This Quattro Pro feature has been assigned an Alt+*key* sequence that displays the **Macro** menu from anywhere on the active notebook. To display the **Macro** menu, press Alt+F2.

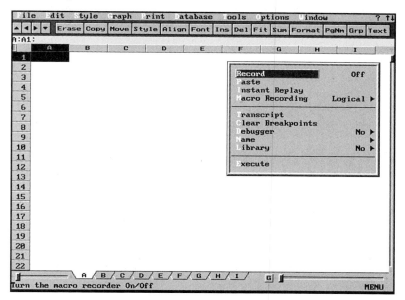

Fig. 15.1

The **M**acro menu commands.

The commands in the top third of this menu are macro-creation commands. By using these commands, you can record and store keystrokes into Quattro Pro's memory, paste a stored macro into a block on a notebook, replay a macro that is stored in memory, and toggle the setting that controls how Quattro Pro interprets your keystrokes.

The commands in the middle part of the **Macro** menu are macro debugging commands. By using these commands, you can display a command history of recent Quattro Pro work sessions, debug your macro programs, and name and create libraries of macro programs for use in future work sessions.

The bottom menu division contains one command. By choosing the Execute command, you can specify the macro you want to run.

Table 15.1 briefly defines each command on the **Macro** menu.

Table 15.1 Macro Menu Commands

Command	Description
Record	Toggles Quattro Pro's macro recorder on and off
Paste	Copies the last recorded macro into a notebook block that you specify
Instant Replay	Replays the last recorded macro
Macro Recording	Toggles between **Keystroke** and **Logical** macro recording modes
Transcript	Displays a command history of all recently executed keystrokes and menu command selections
Clear Breakpoints	Removes debugging breakpoints from a macro
Debugger	Toggles the Macro Debugger on and off
Name	Assigns a name to a macro
Library	Designates a notebook as a macro library
Execute	Executes a macro specified by name

Creating a Basic Macro Program

The process of creating a basic macro program involves at least three steps:

1. Program the macro.

2. Paste and name the macro (optional).

3. Execute the macro.

4. Debug the macro (when a macro doesn't execute as planned).

5. Execute the macro (to test a debugged macro).

First, create the macro program. You must have a clear idea of the tasks you want the program to perform. Even though some people have the uncanny knack of programming as they go, for the rest of us, proper planning and development are essential to achieving success.

Naming a macro is no more complicated than—and very similar to—naming a notebook block. You can create a library of commonly used macros that you can execute quickly on every notebook in a new application.

When programmed, the macro is ready to be executed. If for some reason the macro fails to perform correctly, or if Quattro Pro encounters a macro program error, you need to debug the macro. *Debugging* is the process of testing, editing, and retesting the integrity of your macro program. To help you locate and correct errors, Quattro Pro offers many debugging tools. These tools help you transform even the most bug-infested program into a fully functional, streamlined, and efficient macro tool.

Using the Macro Recorder

The most frightening prospect about programming is the idea that you must learn a new, cryptic way of expressing yourself. Quattro Pro, however, offers you the capability to autorecord macro programs so that you don't have to become a multilingual programming genius.

Suppose that you want to create a macro that enters and aligns label headings in a new, blank notebook. The notebook is used to record high and low automobile repair quotes at an insurance company (see fig. 15.2).

Fig. 15.2

Report headings for an
automobile repair quote
notebook.

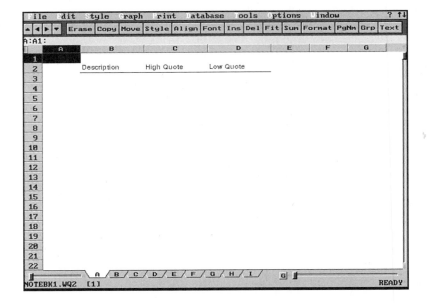

Fig. 15.2

Report headings for an
automobile repair quote
notebook.

To record a macro that reproduces these report headings, follow these
steps:

1. Choose /**T**ools **M**acro **R**ecord. The REC mode indicator appears on
the status line.

You also can press Alt+F2 R to execute the **R**ecord command.

2. Type the headings on row 2, put a single line under row 2, turn off
notebook grid lines (if they are displaying), and then alter the
column widths as desired.

Quattro Pro cannot recognize your mouse clicks when recording a
macro. Use only your keyboard when recording a macro.

3. Choose /**T**ools **M**acro **R**ecord again to turn off the recorder and
return to the active notebook.

You can paste this recorded macro into a block on a notebook to store
the instructions permanently. In future work sessions, retrieve the
notebook, execute the macro, and watch as Quattro Pro reproduces the
headings for this report.

Pasting the Recorded Macro into a Notebook

When you record a macro, Quattro Pro retains the instructions in its memory until you choose **R**ecord and record a new macro. To save a macro so that you can recall and execute the macro later, choose the **P**aste option on the **M**acro menu. This command names and pastes the last recorded macro into a block on the active notebook that you specify.

You can continue pasting the same recorded macro into other notebooks open in memory until the next time you record a macro with the **R**ecord command or until you end the current work session. After you record a new macro or end the current work session, Quattro Pro erases the old macro from memory.

To paste the recorded macro onto the active notebook and to assign a unique name to the macro, follow these steps:

1. Choose /**T**ools **M**acro **P**aste. Quattro Pro prompts you for a macro name to create/modify (see fig. 15.3).

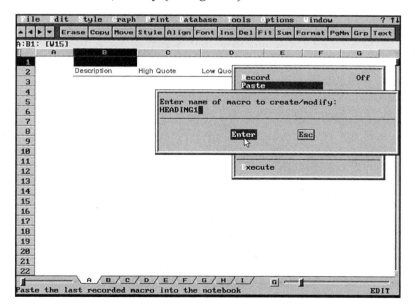

Fig. 15.3

Pasting a recorded macro into a block on the active notebook.

2. Type the name of the macro—**HEADING1** for the example—and press Enter to assign that name to the recorded macro.

3. When prompted for the block to paste to, type **B4** and press Enter to paste the macro.

Quattro Pro can paste recorded macros into a block on the active notebook page, on another page in the same notebook, or into another notebook open in memory. To paste a recorded macro to another notebook, supply the appropriate linking syntax (covered in Chapter 8, "Managing Files and Windows").

By typing **+[PROGRAM]A1**, for example, you can paste the macro onto a notebook named PROGRAM.WQ2, beginning in cell A1. In this syntax, PROGRAM is the name of a notebook (the WQ2 extension is assumed). The brackets tell Quattro Pro that you are performing an operation on a notebook other than the active one. A1 signifies the cell in PROGRAM.WQ2 into which Quattro Pro should copy the macro.

You also can specify that Quattro Pro paste to a block address rather than to a single cell address. Specifying a block address prevents Quattro Pro from overwriting data on the notebook.

When you specify a single-cell address, Quattro Pro pastes the macro beginning in that cell and continues pasting down the column until the entire macro is copied. Quattro Pro overwrites any data inside the paste destination.

Interpreting the Macro

Quattro Pro records macro instructions in one of two formats: keystroke-equivalent or menu-equivalent (see fig. 15.4).

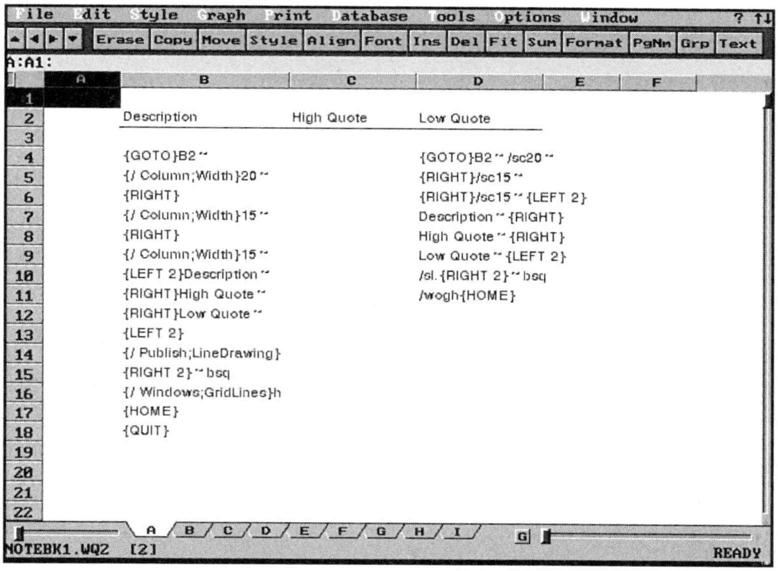

Fig. 15.4

Macro on left uses menu-equivalent instructions; macro on right uses keystroke-equivalents.

The two macros shown in figure 15.4 perform the exact same operation. The macro on the right, however, contains keystroke-equivalent instructions; the macro on the left contains menu-equivalent instructions.

A *keystroke-equivalent instruction* records each menu and command execution that you make in a keystroke-by-keystroke fashion. Such instructions contain the forward slash, followed by each boldfaced letter key that you press to execute a menu command. Keystroke-equivalents often conclude with a tilde (~) to signify that Enter was pressed. Sometimes they conclude with a macro command that mimics the action of pressing a selector-movement key, such as {HOME}.

The first row in the macro shown on the right of figure 15.4, for example, contains two instructions. The first of these instructions, {GOTO}B2~, is a keyboard macro. A *keyboard macro* reproduces the action of pressing a special Quattro Pro key. This instruction indicates that F5, the GoTo key, was pressed, the cell address B2 was typed, and Enter was pressed to move the selector to cell B2.

The second instruction is /sc20~, a keystroke-equivalent instruction indicating that the /**S**tyle **C**olumn Width command was selected, the number 20 was typed, and Enter was pressed to store the column width selection.

Menu-equivalent instructions look different than keystroke-equivalent instructions. These kind of instructions are embedded inside a pair of braces and consist of a forward slash, a space, and two descriptive words separated by a semicolon. When a menu-equivalent instruction requires additional information to perform its operation, that instruction generally concludes with the tilde character.

The instruction in cell B5 of the macro shown on the left of figure 15.4 is {/ Column;Width}20~, which also shows that the /**S**tyle **C**olumn Width command was selected, the number 20 was typed, and Enter was pressed.

Menu-equivalent instructions are easier to read than keystroke-equivalent instructions because, rather than single letters, they contain whole-word descriptions.

You can choose a menu command in two ways: by pressing the bold-faced letter key, or by highlighting the command and then pressing Enter. Quattro Pro records the same macro instructions when you press boldface letter keys as when you highlight a command and press Enter.

NOTE

When the Caps Lock key is on, Quattro Pro records keystroke-equivalent instructions in uppercase instead of lowercase. This method doesn't affect the performance of the macro.

Switching the Macro Recording Mode

By default, the **M**acro Recording command is set to **L**ogical, which instructs Quattro Pro to record macro instructions as menu-equivalents. The **L**ogical setting also tells Quattro Pro to disregard unintentional, extraneous keystrokes, such as selector movements between menu selections.

Quattro Pro macros that contain keystroke-equivalents specific to the Quattro Pro menu tree may not work with other menu trees that you've created. Custom menu trees typically have their own menu names and command names and therefore have different boldfaced letter keys. In the Quattro Pro menu tree, for example, you choose the /**E**dit **C**opy command by typing /**EC**. If you create a 1-2-3-compatible menu tree, you would type /**C** to choose the **C**opy command.

> To ensure complete compatibility between your Quattro Pro macros and your custom menu trees, set **M**acro Recording to **L**ogical. To create a Quattro Pro macro under a 1-2-3-compatible menu tree that you have created and then execute the macro in Lotus 1-2-3, however, you must set this command to **K**eystroke.
>
> **TIP**

To change the default recording setting, follow these steps:

1. Choose the /**T**ools **M**acro **M**acro Recording command.

2. When prompted, choose **K**eystroke.

Viewing an Instant Replay

Use the /**T**ools **M**acro **I**nstant Replay command to execute the last recorded macro in Quattro Pro's memory. This command is useful for testing a macro before pasting the macro into a block on a notebook.

> You also can press Alt+F2 I to execute the **I**nstant Replay command.
>
> **TIP**

Quattro Pro preserves the last recorded macro in memory as long as you are on the same active notebook and haven't recorded another macro. You can choose the Instant Replay command several times in succession as long as these two conditions hold.

Naming a Macro

To save a macro program for future use, you must paste the macro to the active notebook and then save that notebook in a file. When you use the **P**aste command, Quattro Pro requires you to name the macro. To name a macro that you type into a notebook or to assign a new name to a previously named macro, you must use the **N**ame command.

Using the Name Command

Naming a macro is like creating a block name. You can choose the /**E**dit **N**ames **C**reate command to name a macro when you aren't on the

Macro menu. Make sure that you don't assign an existing block name to a macro or vice versa. If you do, the block or the macro loses its name definition.

You can create autoexecute names that turn macros into instant macros. An *instant macro* has a special name that consists of the backslash (\) and a single letter—for example, \h. The backslash represents the action of pressing the Alt key.

You can execute an instant macro directly from your keyboard without having to choose **Instant Replay** or **Execute**. Press Alt and the letter name, and Quattro Pro invokes that macro.

To assign the name \h to the sample macro program, for example, follow these steps:

1. Place the selector in cell B4.

2. Choose the **/Tools Macro Name** command.

3. When prompted, type **\h** and press Enter twice to assign that name to the macro starting in cell B4 (see fig. 15.5).

Fig. 15.5

Assigning a name to an instant macro.

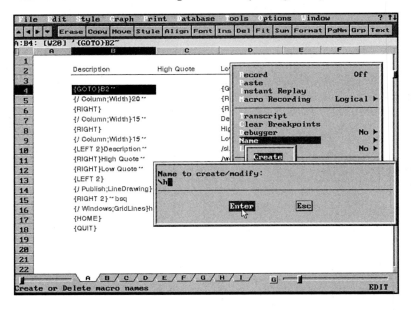

You can assign more than one unique name to a macro. The first name can describe the macro's purpose—HEADING1, for example—and the second name can be an autoexecute name that enables the name to be an instant macro—\h, for example.

TIP

Press F3 from the input line to display the block names choice list. This list shows all block and macro name assignments for the active notebook.

FOR RELATED INFORMATION

◄◄ "Creating Names," p. 161.
How to assign names to cells and blocks in a notebook. This technique is the same as assigning an Alt+key name to a macro.

Creating an Autoload Macro

In Chapter 16, "Customizing Quattro Pro," you learn how to specify an autoload macro name by choosing the /**O**ptions **S**tartup **S**tartup Macro command. By default, the setting for this command is \0.

Each time you load a notebook, Quattro Pro checks for a macro named \0, unless you choose /**O**ptions **S**tartup **S**tartup Macro and type a new name. If the macro exists, Quattro Pro executes it. The autoload macro feature is useful if you consistently perform the same formatting commands before entering data into a new notebook.

Always begin a \0 macro with the {ESC} command. (Press Esc if you are recording the macro, or type the command in the first cell.) This step ensures that your autoload macros work with linked notebooks. (Remember that when you initially load a linked notebook, Quattro Pro displays the Link options menu. Pressing Esc cancels this menu and enables Quattro Pro to continue executing the autoload macro.)

When you use linked notebooks and define an autoload macro in this manner, be sure to update links when the macro finishes executing. Choose /**T**ools **U**pdate **L**inks and choose **O**pen or **R**efresh. Remember, the **O**pen option loads all linked notebooks into Quattro Pro's memory; the **R**efresh option updates only linked references appearing in the active notebook.

TIP

You also can create and delete autoload macro names by choosing the /**T**ools **M**acro **N**ame command and choosing **C**reate or **D**elete.

FOR RELATED INFORMATION

▶▶ "Choosing a Start-Up Macro," p. 793.
How to designate a macro for Quattro Pro to execute each time
you retrieve a notebook into memory.

Managing Quattro Pro Macros

You can store macros on the active notebook, on a different page in the
same notebook, or create a special notebook called a *macro library* to
hold the macros. A macro library enables you to choose and execute a
macro from another notebook open in Quattro Pro's memory. The only
condition is that you also must have the macro library open in
memory.

Another aspect of macro management concerns documentation. A
properly documented macro can be a blessing in disguise. By including
the name and adding brief comments to a macro, you guarantee that
the user can understand what you are trying to accomplish with the
code.

Storing Macros on a Notebook

The execution of a macro isn't affected by its location on the active
notebook. A macro stored in column IV executes as quickly as a macro
stored in column A.

Consider a few points before storing your macros, however. Depending
on the instructions contained within a macro, its location on a notebook relative to the notebook data is significant. As a rule, you should
store macros close to your notebook data, but not so close that the
macro accidentally overwrites itself.

TIP

One way to ensure that a macro doesn't accidentally overwrite itself is to
protect the cells that contain the macro commands (use the /**S**tyle
Protection **P**rotect command). Remember, you also must invoke global
notebook protection with /**O**ptions **P**rotection **E**nable before the macro
commands are truly protected.

Close proximity enables you to move quickly to the macro when you need to review its instructions. Also, the macro should be below and to the right of your data so that inserted or deleted rows and columns don't alter the macro.

Storing Macros on Their Own Page

Another strategy for managing macros is to store them in their own page within a notebook. This placement is ideal if you create macros to perform specific tasks on reports that you group into a single notebook. Using this approach to managing your Quattro Pro macros also has several other advantages:

■ You can store macros in the first few columns (A, B, and C) of the blank macro page because the macro commands are the only entries that will be made into that page. This way, you easily and quickly can switch between your report pages and the macro page. In fact, changing the name of your macro page to something like MACRO with the /**E**dit **P**age **N**ame command is a good idea.

■ You minimize the risk of accidentally overwriting the macro commands should you execute a macro while the macro page is active. Because macros generally are created to format or modify data located elsewhere in a notebook, your macros should begin with the {PREVPAGE} or {NEXTPAGE} commands. These commands activate the previous page or the next page in the active notebook before doing anything else specified in the macro.

Alternatively, you can use the {GOTO} command to send the selector directly to a specific cell on a specific page. The command {GOTO}A:B1~, for instance, activates cell B1 on page A before executing the second command in the macro.

■ You can perform periodic maintenance on your notebook reports without fear of affecting any macro that may exist on the same page. The pages that contain your notebook reports and those that contain the macros can be formatted independently or otherwise modified.

Documenting Macros

You should document your macros so that others can understand what you are trying to accomplish. Documentation also helps you evaluate your program logic during debugging (described later). When you return to a macro that you created long ago, you can refresh your own memory. You may forget the purpose and logic behind a macro after you create 20 or 30 macros.

Macro documentation serves two specific needs: it displays the macro name (and autoexecute name, if one exists) and briefly describes the purpose of each instruction.

Figure 15.6 shows a typical macro library. The macro pictured here is the menu-equivalent version of the macro discussed earlier in this chapter.

Fig. 15.6

Documenting a macro program in a library.

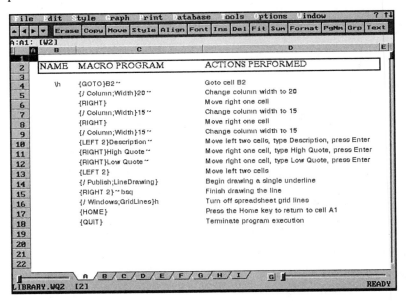

When Quattro Pro executes a macro, the program starts in the first cell and moves down the column until the program encounters the last instruction. By placing macro names in their own column, you can take advantage of Quattro Pro's quick-naming facility.

TIP

Choose the /**E**dit **N**ames **L**abels **R**ight command to assign quickly all names appearing in column B to the macros appearing in column C.

Placing the documentation comments in the column immediately to the right of the macro accomplishes two things. First, this location ensures that the comment labels aren't assigned accidentally as names. Second, this placement prevents Quattro Pro from trying to execute the labels as macro instructions.

Creating Macro Libraries

When you create a macro library, make sure that you follow the instructions outlined for documenting and stopping a macro. So that Quattro Pro doesn't execute a string of macros in the library, also be sure to leave a blank cell between macros and enter {QUIT} as the last macro command (see fig. 15.7). {QUIT} signifies the end of a macro program. This command causes Quattro Pro to stop reading cells and returns control of the keyboard to the user.

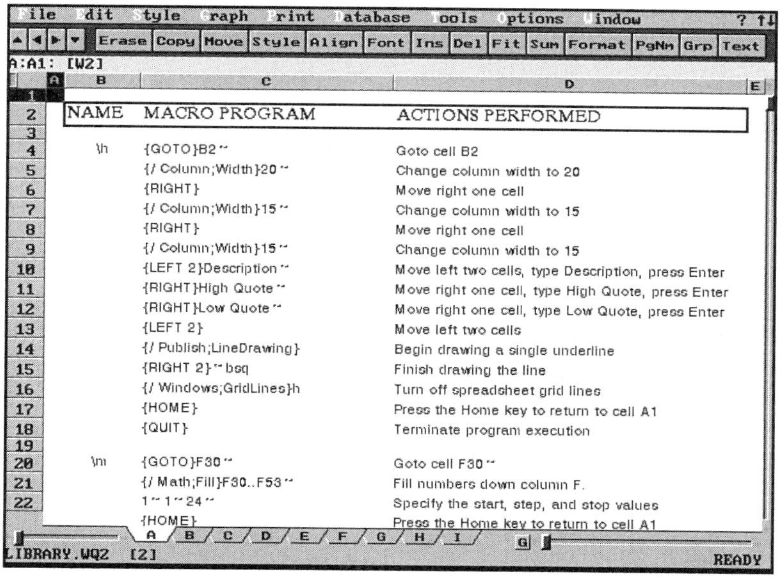

Fig. 15.7

The first two macros in the LIBRARY.WQ2 notebook.

The following advantages of storing macros in a macro library far outweigh those of storing macros on individual notebooks:

- When Quattro Pro cannot locate a macro that you want to execute on the active notebook, the program searches through the macro libraries loaded in memory.

- You can eliminate any possibility of a macro's overwriting itself on the active notebook.

- You conserve notebook file sizes by not having to paste macros repeatedly onto new notebooks.

- A macro library is a permanent reference source, whereas notebooks often outlive their usefulness.

To create the macro library pictured in figure 15.7, follow these steps:

1. Choose /**File New** to open a new notebook into memory.

2. Copy any existing macros into the macro library or type macros directly into the new notebook.

3. Choose the /**Tools Macro Library** command.

4. When prompted, choose **Yes**.

5. Choose /**File Save**, type **LIBRARY**, and press Enter to save the macro library.

You can create as many macro libraries as you want. You can create separate macro libraries for business and personal notebook applications, for example. To execute a macro stored in a library, press Alt+*key* or choose /**Tools Macro Execute**. (The specific use of this command is discussed in the next section, "Executing a Macro.")

The rules that apply to one macro library apply to all. You may create as many unique macro names as you want, but you are limited to 26 Alt+*key* macro names per library. Also be careful about opening two or more macro libraries at the same time. If macro libraries contain duplicate macro names, you cannot predict which macro will execute, if at all.

The instructions in a macro executed from a macro library affect only the active notebook, unless you specify otherwise. An instruction that tells Quattro Pro to choose /**Style Line Drawing** and draw a **S**ingle line around block A20..E25, for example, does so on the active notebook, not on the macro library notebook.

CAUTION

Be careful not to execute library macros when the macro library notebook is active. If you do, Quattro Pro executes the macro on the library notebook. When the executed macro calls for Quattro Pro to delete rows and columns or write labels and values into cells, the macro overwrites itself. Keep backups of your macro library files in case you accidentally overwrite a macro.

An exception to the rule exists about executing a macro on the library in which it resides. Consider a macro that issues the same /Style Line Drawing Single command after a looping subroutine is executed five times. Storing the loop execution value in a cell may seem useful. Because this value pertains specifically to the operation of the macro, however, the value should be recorded in the library near the macro so that the subroutine can refer to it. In this case, the macro actually executes a command on itself before executing a command on the active notebook.

Executing a Macro

To execute a macro that doesn't have an Alt+*key* name, follow these steps:

1. Choose the /**T**ools **M**acro **E**xecute command.

TIP

You also can press Alt+F2 E to execute the /**T**ools **M**acro **E**xecute command.

2. When prompted, type the name of the macro you want to execute.

Quattro Pro executes the macro program. During execution, the word MACRO appears on the status line at the bottom of the notebook.

If you don't know the name of the macro you want to execute, press F3. Quattro Pro displays the block names list. Highlight the name on the list and press Enter to execute the macro.

To execute the insurance heading macro stored on the CLAIMS.WQ2 notebook after you load Quattro Pro into your PC, type **Q CLAIMS \H** and press Enter at the DOS command prompt. Quattro Pro loads into your PC, retrieves the file named CLAIMS.WQ2, and then executes the \h macro. If the macro contains an error, Quattro Pro beeps and displays an error message. If the macro doesn't exist on CLAIMS.WQ2, Quattro Pro ignores the command.

To halt the execution of a macro, press Ctrl+Break and then press Esc to return to READY mode.

TIP

You can use the {BREAKOFF} macro command to disable the effect of pressing Ctrl+Break to disrupt macro execution. When {BREAKOFF} is included in a macro you are trying to stop, Quattro Pro ignores the action of pressing Ctrl+Break. Place the {BREAKOFF} command at the beginning of a macro so that the command is active as soon as the macro begins executing. This technique is useful for preventing macro users from accessing and altering your macro instructions.

Editing a Macro

You have two options for editing a macro: manually or with the Macro Debugger. To edit a macro manually, apply the same editing tools you use with notebook cells. Tables 15.2 through 15.4, in the section "Entering a Macro Manually" later in this chapter, list each of the key-equivalent commands that you can use when writing or editing macros. For details about debugging a macro, see the section "Debugging a Macro" later in this chapter.

Deleting Macros and Macro Names

Deleting macros and macro names is another aspect of macro program management. By deleting out-of-date macros and macro names, you accomplish three things. First, you conserve notebook space. Second, you reduce the number of names displayed on the block names list. Third, by eliminating instant macros, you free up a letter of the alphabet that you can use to create another, more useful instant macro.

Quattro Pro has two commands that meet this macro management objective. Choose /**E**dit **N**ames **D**elete or /**T**ools **M**acro **N**ame **D**elete to display the block names list. Choose a macro name from the list, or type a name, and press Enter to delete the macro name.

This command deletes only the macro name. To delete the macro from the notebook, choose the /**E**dit **E**rase Block command and type the block coordinates for the macro.

NOTE

Deleting a macro and deleting a macro name are two different procedures. If you delete a name but not the macro, you still can use the macro by renaming it. If you delete a macro but not the name, and then try to execute the macro, Quattro Pro does what it always does when encountering a blank cell—the program stops the execution.

FOR RELATED INFORMATION

◀◀ "Managing Pages," p. 181.
How to work with notebook pages in Quattro Pro, including naming a page and moving a page.

◀◀ "Translating Files," p. 369.
How to translate Lotus 1-2-3 worksheets for use in Quattro Pro.

▶▶ "Using an Autoload File," p. 791.
How to designate a notebook file for Quattro Pro to retrieve each time you start the program on your computer.

Using Advanced Macro Techniques

You now know how to record, paste, name, execute, and delete a basic macro. The remaining material in this chapter is devoted to reviewing macro programming techniques that help you manage longer, more sophisticated macros.

In the next sections, you learn how to type macros directly into a notebook, link and debug macros, and enter macro commands directly onto the input line for inclusion in your programs.

Entering a Macro Manually

Consider the following approaches to creating a macro:

- You can use the macro recorder exclusively.

- You can create the macro from scratch by typing each instruction into a column of cells on the active notebook.

- You can use the macro recorder first and then append additional instructions into the macro.

As an advanced macro user, you use the macro recorder for some tasks and enter instructions manually to do other tasks. This approach gives you the best of both worlds. First, you can rely on the macro recorder to duplicate commonly used menu commands. Second, you have the option of applying advanced programming logic to create loops, branches, and subroutines.

Entering a macro manually is no different than entering any other data manually. With a macro, however, you must be careful about the accuracy of your data entry; a single missing brace, disoriented bracket, or misspelled command can cause the macro to crash. When a macro crashes, it stops before executing all its commands, yielding minor or serious consequences.

If the macro that crashes performs notebook operations such as copying data, aligning labels, and formatting numbers, the consequences of a crash are minor. At worst, Quattro Pro abandons the operation, leaving an unfinished or unformatted notebook on-screen. If your macro contains instructions that perform external file operations such as opening a file on disk, writing data to the file, and saving the file, a macro crash may cause irreparable damage to the file.

When a macro crashes, Quattro Pro displays an error message that indicates the cell address at which the execution error occurred. You have only one option: press Esc and return to the active notebook.

To enter instructions manually into a macro after using the macro recorder, follow these steps:

1. Envision the macro application. This planning stage helps you divide tasks into two groups: tasks that can be accomplished with the recorder and tasks that must be entered manually.

2. Sketch out the structure of the macro on paper. For more complex applications, you may want to use the /**Graph A**nnotate command to create a flow chart.

3. Choose /**Tools M**acro **R**ecord and create the part of the macro that will contain menu command selections.

4. Use /**Edit P**aste to paste the macro to a new, blank notebook.

5. Move the selector to a blank area on the macro in which you want to enter instructions manually.

6. Press ' (the apostrophe label-prefix character) to enter LABEL mode, type an instruction, and press Enter to record that instruction.

7. Continue entering instructions until you finish. Then, follow normal procedures for naming and executing the macro.

You must enter macros into cells as labels, particularly if you are writing a keystroke-equivalent macro. If you try to enter the instruction /**FS** into a cell without using a label-prefix character, you find the task impossible. When you type the forward slash character (/), Quattro Pro enters MENU mode.

To include keyboard key-equivalent commands in your macros, use the special key-equivalent commands shown in table 15.2. To include function-key actions in your macros, use the special key-equivalent commands shown in table 15.3. To toggle status keys in your macros, use the special key-equivalent commands shown in table 15.4. You can enter these commands in upper- or lowercase letters.

You also can repeat the action of pressing most of the status keys by specifying a repeat number with the code. To move the selector down 5 pages from its current position, for example, type {**PGDN 5**}, or type {**PGDN B10**} if cell B10 contains the value 5.

Table 15.2 Keyboard Key-Equivalent Commands

Keyboard Key	Key-Equivalent Command
←	{LEFT} or {L}
→	{RIGHT} or {R}
↑	{UP} or {U}
↓	{DOWN} or {D}
Backspace	{BACKSPACE} or {BS}
Ctrl+←	{BIGLEFT}
Ctrl+→	{BIGRIGHT}
Ctrl+I	{DELEOL}
Ctrl+Backspace	{CLEAR}
Ctrl+Backspace (with grouped pages)	{DELETEDOWN}
Ctrl+Break	{BREAK}
Ctrl+D	{DATE}
Ctrl+Enter	{DRILLDOWN}
Ctrl+End	{LASTPAGE}
Ctrl+Home	{FIRSTPAGE}
Ctrl+Page Down	{NEXTPAGE}
Ctrl+Page Up	{PREVPAGE}
Ctrl+Shift+End	{MARKLASTPAGE}
Ctrl+Shift+Home	{MARKFIRSTPAGE}
Ctrl+Shift+Page Down	{MARKNEXTPAGE}
Ctrl+Shift+Page Up	{MARKPREVPAGE}
Delete	{DEL} or {DELETE}
End	{END}
Enter	{CR} or ~
Esc	{ESC} or {ESCAPE}
Home	{HOME}

Keyboard Key	Key-Equivalent Command
Page Up	{PGUP}
Page Down	{PGDN}
Shift+Tab	{BACKTAB}
Tab	{TAB}

Table 15.3 Function Key-Equivalent Commands

Function Key	Key-Equivalent Command
F2	{EDIT}
Shift+F2	{STEP}
F3	{NAME}
Alt+F3	{FUNCTIONS}
Shift+F3	{MACROS}
F4	{ABS}
F5	{GOTO}
Alt+F5	{UNDO}
Ctrl+F5	{TOGGLEGROUPMODE}
Shift+F5	{CHOOSE}
F6	{WINDOW}
Alt+F6	{ZOOM}
Shift+F6	{NEXTWIN}
F7	{QUERY}
Alt+F7	{MARKALL}
Shift+F7	{MARK}
F8	{TABLE}
Shift+F8	{MOVE}
F9	{CALC}

(continues)

Table 15.3 Continued

Function Key	Key-Equivalent Command
F9 (in a File Manager window)	{READDIR}
Shift+F9	{COPY}
F10	{GRAPH}
Shift+F10	{PASTE}

Table 15.4 Status Key-Equivalent Commands

Status Key	Key-Equivalent Command
Caps Lock off	{CAPOFF}
Caps Lock on	{CAPON}
Toggle Insert	{INS} or {INSERT}, on or off
Insert off	{INSOFF}
Insert on	{INSON}
Forward slash (/)	{MENU}
Num Lock off	{NUMOFF}
Num Lock on	{NUMON}
Scroll Lock off	{SCROLLOFF}
Scroll Lock on	{SCROLLON}

Entering Menu-Equivalent Instructions

The easiest and most accurate way to enter a menu-equivalent instruction into a macro is by pressing Shift+F3, the Macro List key. When you press this key, Quattro Pro displays a menu of seven macro command categories. This menu conveniently organizes the hundreds of available macro commands by categories that describe the various purposes of the macro commands. The **K**eyboard category, for example, contains all the macro commands that relate to the function keys, the arrow keys, and the status keys.

To add a menu-equivalent instruction manually to a macro, follow these steps:

1. Press Shift+F3, the Macro List key, to display the seven macro command categories.

2. Highlight a category name and press Enter. Quattro Pro displays another list of subcategories, or a list of all commands in that category.

3. To enter a command onto the input line, highlight the command and press Enter.

4. To store the command in the active cell, press Enter again.

You also can click the Macro button on the EDIT mode SpeedBar to reach the list of menu-equivalent macro categories. From there, choose a main topic to reach a menu of specific actions; then click a menu-equivalent instruction to place it on the input line.

Consider the Expenses macro shown in figure 15.8. This macro writes three expense values onto the notebook and then sums their values. The menu-equivalent command in cell F12, for example, is entered by choosing / Commands from the menu displayed in the figure.

The first six items on the menu are the names of the six macro command categories. The last item, / Commands, enables you to enter menu-equivalent commands.

Using Linking in Macros

Linking enables you to execute a macro in a different notebook, use data from another file, or pass data back and forth between notebook applications. The linking syntax in macro programs is exactly the same as for notebooks (see Chapter 8, "Managing Files and Windows").

Fig. 15.8

Menu-equivalent
instructions directly from
the Macro List menu.

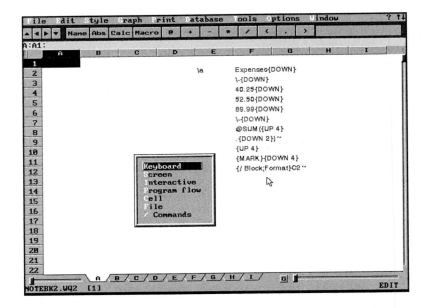

To link a macro to cell F15 on a notebook named SALES that is stored in
a directory named \ACCOUNTING on a disk in drive B, for example,
type the following syntax into the cell on the macro notebook where
you want to display the linked data:

[B:\ACCOUNTING\SALES]F15

In this syntax, B: is the drive name, \ACCOUNTING is the path name,
and \SALES is the file name. (Quattro Pro assumes that the extension
is WQ2.)

The square brackets surrounding the formula tell Quattro Pro that you
are linking to another notebook. F15 indicates the cell in SALES.WQ2 to
which Quattro Pro will link.

If you want to branch directly from a macro library to a cell on the active notebook (in which, for example, another macro exists), use the
standard linking syntax. To branch a macro to cell B10 on the active
notebook, for example, type the following syntax:

{BRANCH []B10}

The closed brackets in this syntax tell Quattro Pro to branch to the active notebook. If the brackets are left out, Quattro Pro branches to cell B10 on the macro library notebook.

FOR RELATED **INFORMATION**

◄◄ "Creating Linking Formulas," p. 401.
   How to create formulas that link data between pages and notebooks.

Debugging a Macro

Quattro Pro's Macro Debugger helps you isolate problems that cause macro execution errors. To use this tool, you execute a macro while Quattro Pro is in DEBUG mode. In DEBUG mode, Quattro Pro executes each macro command one step at a time, pausing until you press any key to tell the program to continue.

You also can insert breakpoints and trace cells into a macro. Quattro Pro suspends execution when the program reaches a *breakpoint* (a cell that you define). Quattro Pro also suspends execution when a program *trace cell* (which contains a logical formula) returns a TRUE value. You also can edit the contents of a macro instruction while Quattro Pro is in DEBUG mode.

To enter DEBUG mode and then execute a macro, follow these steps:

1. Press Shift+F2 to place Quattro Pro in DEBUG mode.

2. Position the selector where you want it to be when the macro executes.

3. Choose the /**Tools M**acro **E**xecute command to invoke the macro you want to debug, or press Alt plus the instant macro letter.

> You also can press Alt+F2 E to execute the macro.   **TIP**

Fig. 15.9

The Debug window
displayed when you
execute a macro in
DEBUG mode.

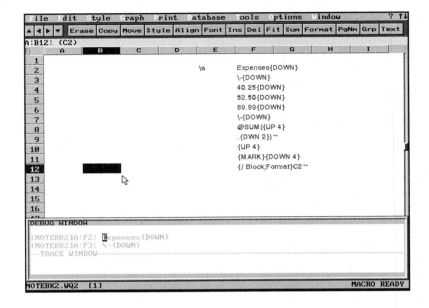

When the macro is executed, Quattro Pro displays the Debug window in the bottom half of your screen and positions the first cell of the macro program in the middle of the Debug window (see fig. 15.9).

The active cell in this figure is B12, so Quattro Pro begins executing the macro in that cell. Quattro Pro highlights the first letter in the first word in the first macro instruction appearing in the Debug window so that you can monitor the progress of the macro execution character by character. When you press the space bar, Quattro Pro does two things: highlights the next character in the instruction displayed in the Debug window and types the character on the input line at the top of the screen.

While in DEBUG mode, Quattro Pro stops when the program encounters an execution error. You can trace macro errors to many things: a missing tilde, an illegal block name, or even an incorrectly spelled macro instruction.

Figure 15.10 shows how Quattro Pro reacts to locating a macro error. The displayed error message gives a specific reference to the notebook name and the cell address in which the error was encountered. A review of the macro in this figure indicates that the arrow-key instruction in cell F9 is misspelled.

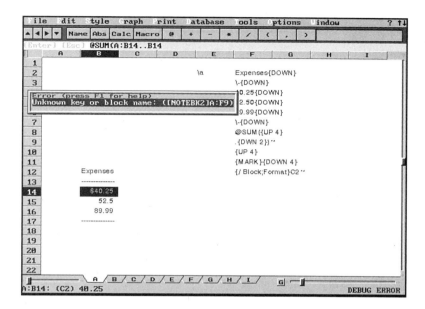

Fig. 15.10

An error encountered
during the execution of a
macro in DEBUG mode.

To fine-tune a debug operation further, Quattro Pro provides you with
an additional set of debugging commands. These commands are located on the Macro Debugger Commands menu, which you can display
by pressing the forward slash key (/) while the Debug window is active.
From this menu, you can fine-tune a DEBUG mode operation by specifying several conditions. You can insert and reset standard and conditional breakpoints, choose trace cells to monitor, and abort DEBUG
mode (see table 15.5). You also can edit individual cells in the macro.

Table 15.5 Macro Debugger Commands Menu

Command	Description
Breakpoints	Specifies macro execution breakpoints
Conditional	Specifies logical conditions for evaluating breakpoints
Trace Cells	Tracks values in up to four cells during DEBUG mode
Abort	Halts macro execution and exits DEBUG mode
Edit a Cell	Enters EDIT mode from within DEBUG mode
Reset	Removes all breakpoint definitions
Quit	Exits DEBUG mode and executes the macro at full speed

Defining Standard Breakpoints

Executing a long macro in DEBUG mode can be time-consuming. By inserting breakpoints in a macro, you can specify which parts of the macro to debug step-by-step and which parts to execute at full speed.

When Quattro Pro encounters a breakpoint, the program pauses execution. Press the space bar to continue in DEBUG mode, or press Enter to resume macro execution until Quattro Pro encounters the next breakpoint. You can define up to four standard breakpoints per notebook.

To see how breakpoints work, insert two into the sample Expenses macro by performing the following steps:

1. Press / (the forward slash key) from within the Debug window. Quattro Pro displays the Macro Debugger Commands menu (see fig. 15.11).

2. Press Enter to choose the **B**reakpoints option.

Fig. 15.11

The **B**reakpoints option on the Macro Debugger Commands menu.

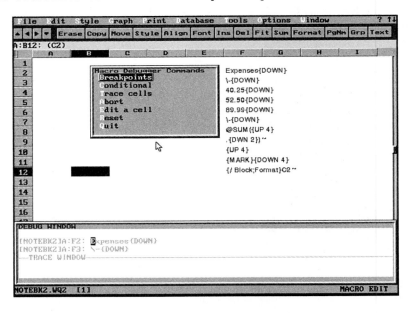

3. When prompted, choose 1 to insert the **1**st breakpoint.

4. When prompted, choose **B**lock, type **F9**, and press Enter to record the first breakpoint. Choose Q to **Q**uit the **1**st breakpoint menu.

5. Choose 2 to insert the **2**nd breakpoint.

6. When prompted, choose **B**lock, type **F12**, and press Enter to record the second breakpoint. Choose Q to **Q**uit the **2**nd breakpoint menu.

7. Choose **Q**uit twice to return to the Debug window.

Defining Conditional Breakpoints

You also may define up to four *conditional breakpoints*. This type of breakpoint causes Quattro Pro to pause the execution of a macro when the value TRUE is returned by a cell condition that you define.

Conditional breakpoints are different from standard breakpoints. When you define a cell as a conditional breakpoint, you also must place some type of logical expression in the cell—for example, B25>=500. This logical expression forces Quattro Pro to wait until the value in B25 becomes greater than or equal to 500 before the program pauses the execution of the macro.

To define a conditional breakpoint, follow these steps:

1. Press / (the forward slash key) from within the Debug window.

2. Choose the **C**onditional option.

3. When prompted, choose the number of the conditional breakpoint you want to define.

4. When prompted, type the address of the cell containing the condition.

5. Set additional conditional breakpoints, if you want.

6. Choose **Q**uit to return to the Debug window.

Defining Trace Cells

Trace cells are cells in a macro that contain values. You can trace the progress of calculations that affect the values in these cells. Advanced macro programs, for example, often use counters to keep track of values that the macro uses during execution. A *counter* is a formula that you enter into a cell that, for example, can store the number of passes a macro makes in a looping operation. Advanced macro programs also store results from macro-generated calculations in results cells.

In either case, in a DEBUG mode operation, you can monitor the values stored in these cells to determine whether the execution error is somehow related. You may specify up to four trace cells per notebook to monitor the values. During a debug operation, Quattro Pro displays the contents of the trace cells in the Trace window at the bottom of the Debug window.

A trace cell can be a useful addition to the sample macro. Remember, the sample macro sums up three expense amounts and places the value in a results cell. By defining the results cell as the trace cell, you can monitor whether the macro program is performing this operation correctly.

To define a trace cell, follow these steps:

1. Press / (the forward slash key) from within the Debug window.

2. Choose the **Trace Cells** option.

3. When prompted, choose 1 to insert the **1st Trace Cell**.

4. When prompted, type **A7** and press Enter to define the trace cell.

5. Choose **Q**uit twice to return to the Debug window.

Editing a Cell in DEBUG Mode

When you locate the problem with a macro, use the **E**dit a Cell command on the Macro Debugger Commands menu to edit the instruction in the problem cell. To review the use of this command, correct the spelling error uncovered in cell F9 during an earlier DEBUG mode operation.

To correct the spelling error in cell F9, follow these steps:

1. Press / (the forward slash key) from within the Debug window.

2. Choose the Edit a Cell option.

3. When prompted, type **F9** and press Enter to enter EDIT mode so that you can edit the instruction.

   Quattro Pro displays the contents of cell F9 on the input line.

4. Correct the misspelling and press Enter to record the correct spelling.

   Quattro Pro displays the Debug window and the Macro Debugger Commands menu.

5. Choose **Q**uit to return to the Debug window.

Figure 15.12 shows the newly edited version of the Expenses macro. In this version of the DEBUG mode operation, Quattro Pro executes the macro commands on the selector location, which was in cell A1 initially.

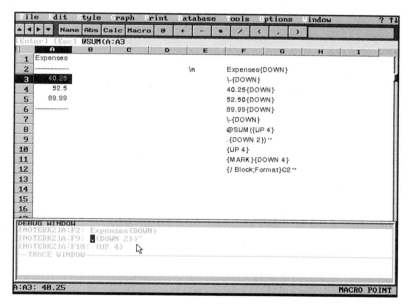

Fig. 15.12

Edit a macro instruction while in DEBUG mode.

The edited instruction from cell F9 now appears in the Debug window when Quattro Pro encounters the first breakpoint. Press Enter to continue executing the macro.

Quattro Pro halts again when the program reaches cell F12, the next breakpoint. Because this breakpoint occurs after the macro already has summed the three expense values, Quattro Pro displays the trace cell result in the Trace window on the Debug window (see fig. 15.13).

Fig. 15.13

A value displayed in the Trace window.

Resetting Breakpoints and Trace Cells

Choose the **R**eset option on the Macro Debugger Commands menu to remove all breakpoints and trace cells set for the notebook.

To reset all breakpoints and trace cells from within the notebook instead of from the Debug window, choose the /**Tools** **M**acro **C**lear Breakpoints command.

Exiting DEBUG Mode

When a macro is finished executing in DEBUG mode, Quattro Pro removes the Debug window from your screen but leaves the DEBUG mode indicator on the status line at the bottom of the screen.

You can exit DEBUG mode in the following ways:

■ Press Shift+F2, the Debug key (which toggles the DEBUG mode on and off).

■ Press Alt+F2, choose **D**ebugger, and then choose **N**o.

To stop the execution of a macro before Quattro Pro finishes debugging it, press the forward slash key (/) and choose the **A**bort option from the Macro Debugger Commands menu. Press Esc to return to the active notebook. If Quattro Pro is in the middle of executing a menu command when you abort the execution, you may have to press Esc several times to return to the active notebook.

> **TIP**
>
> When the Debug window is active, press Esc to return to the active note-book so that you can view the current effects of the macro. Press Esc again to redisplay the Debug window.

Using the Transcript Facility

Quattro Pro's Transcript facility is truly a "behind-the-scenes" tool. Each time you access Quattro Pro, the Transcript facility records each keystroke you make and every menu command you choose. Transcript recording is virtually undetectable; you cannot tell that the Transcript facility is working during your Quattro Pro work sessions.

The Transcript feature enables you to undo notebook mistakes, protect valuable work against power failure and system crashes, audit the changes you make to a notebook, and even create working macros out of pasted transcripts.

This utility stores keystrokes and menu command selections in a transcript. Quattro Pro writes the transcript data periodically to a file called QUATTRO.LOG, which resides in the directory into which Quattro Pro was installed originally. Even during this updating operation, you barely can detect that the Transcript feature is working behind the scenes.

To restore lost work or to reverse mistakes made on the active notebook, play back the transcript. To print a copy of your transcript, copy the transcript to a notebook and use the **P**rint menu commands.

Reviewing a Command History

To review the current entries in the transcript log, choose /**Tools Macro Transcript.** Quattro Pro displays the Transcript window (see fig. 15.14).

Fig. 15.14

The Transcript window.

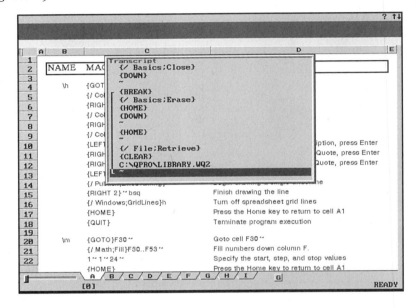

The Transcript window reveals each keystroke and command selection that you have taken during recent work sessions. The last keystroke or command that you execute before invoking the Transcript window appears highlighted at the bottom of the window. In figure 15.14, a tilde (~) is highlighted at the bottom of the Transcript window, indicating that the Enter key was pressed just before executing the **Transcript** command.

Notice the long open square bracket at the left margin of the Transcript window. The commands appearing to the right of this line haven't been written into the QUATTRO.LOG file but still reside in Quattro Pro's memory. These commands represent all the keystroke and menu command selections you have made since the last transcript checkpoint.

Quattro Pro creates a checkpoint each time you choose /File **S**ave, /File **R**etrieve, or /File **E**rase, and saves the transcript to the log file. This action starts a new vertical line in the Transcript window to indicate where Quattro Pro will record new keyboard actions until the next log update.

The commands in the transcript are the same as the commands appearing in macros. If you paste commands from the transcript to the active notebook, you can execute the commands just as you execute a macro. And like a macro, the commands in the transcript can appear as menu-equivalent or keystroke-equivalent commands. Use the /**T**ools **M**acro **M**acro Recording options to create the display format that you prefer.

Use the arrow keys to scroll through the command lines in the transcript. If any command appears to extend beyond the width of the Transcript window, highlight the command so that Quattro Pro displays the entire command on the input line at the top of your screen.

Manipulating a Command History

The Transcript menu contains the commands that enable you to manipulate the data stored in the transcript. To access this menu, follow these steps:

1. Choose /**T**ools **M**acro **T**ranscript to activate the Transcript window.

2. Press / (the forward slash) to display the Transcript menu (see fig. 15.15).

Table 15.6 defines the commands on the Transcript menu.

Table 15.6 Transcript Menu Commands

Command	Description
Undo Last Command	Restores the last recorded command
Restore To Here	Restores the command history from the last checkpoint to the end of the line highlighted in the Transcript window
Playback Block	Plays back a marked block of commands
Copy Block	Pastes a block of commands into a block on the active notebook

(continues)

Table 15.6 Continued

Command	Description
Begin Block	Marks the beginning of a transcript block that will be replayed with the **P**layback Block command
End Block	Marks the end of a transcript block that will be replayed with the **P**layback Block command
Max History Length	Sets the maximum number of transcript characters
Single Step	Replays commands one keystroke at a time
Failure Protection	Sets the maximum number of keystrokes before Quattro Pro writes the transcript to disk

Fig. 15.15

The Transcript menu.

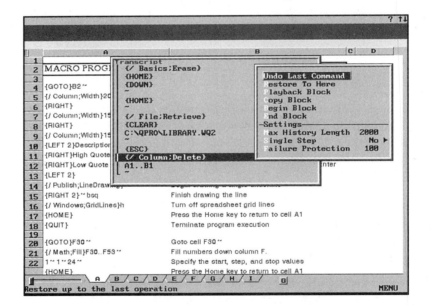

Undoing the Last Command

Suppose that you choose the /**Edit D**elete **C**olumns command and you delete columns A and B on the LIBRARY.WQ2 notebook. Suddenly, you realize that you deleted the wrong columns.

If the **U**ndo command is enabled, you can choose the /**Edit U**ndo command, and Quattro Pro brings back columns A and B. If you opted against enabling the Undo feature to conserve RAM, however, choosing the /Edit Undo command has no effect on the deleted columns.

In this event, choose Undo Last Command on the Transcript menu to reverse the last operation you made. Undo Last Command doesn't actually reverse the last operation like /Edit Undo does. Instead, Quattro Pro plays back all the commands in your Transcript, beginning at the last checkpoint and through the command preceding the one you want to undo ({/ Column;Delete}, highlighted in fig. 15.15).

When executed, Quattro Pro takes control of your notebook, replaying all the keystrokes and menu command selections until your notebook appears just as it did before issuing the /Edit Delete Columns command.

To use this command properly, you must enter the Transcript menu immediately and choose Undo Last Command. If you issue other keystrokes before doing so, you create a new "last command" in the Transcript. To abort an Undo Last Command operation, press Ctrl+Break; Quattro Pro stops the playback as soon as the current command finishes.

Restoring Parts of the Transcript

The Restore To Here command plays back portions of a transcript. In this operation, Quattro Pro replays your command history, beginning at the last checkpoint and concluding with the command highlighted in the Transcript window. During a replay, Quattro Pro re-enacts all the selector movements and the menu and command selections that you originally used to create the transcript.

> The Restore To Here command replays your transcript only for the active notebook. If you have multiple windows open in Quattro Pro's memory, this command doesn't replay the transcripts for the other notebooks simultaneously.

TIP

The Restore To Here command provides the security and flexibility not available with the Undo Last Command option. Now suppose that you make the same delete column error described in the preceding section; this time, however, rather than choose Undo Last Command immediately, you continue to work with the active notebook. Later, you realize your mistake.

To replay a portion of your transcript and undelete the column, follow these steps:

1. Highlight the transcript line containing the command immediately preceding the /**E**dit **D**elete **C**olumns command.

2. Call up the Transcript menu (press /) and choose **R**estore To Here.

Quattro Pro replays your transcript history up to the point before the delete operation.

Another benefit of the **R**estore To Here command is that this command can protect your notebook data in case you experience a system crash or power failure. Although the **R**estore To Here command cannot restore commands appearing before the last checkpoint, this command is extremely useful.

In either event, follow these steps:

1. Highlight the last command line in your transcript.

2. Activate the Transcript menu and choose **R**estore To Here.

Quattro Pro replays your transcript history from the last checkpoint to the point of failure. To abort this command, press Ctrl+Break. Quattro Pro stops the replay operation at the end of the current command.

Playing Back a Transcript Block

The **P**layback Block command, like the **R**estore To Here command, plays back portions of a transcript. This command replays all commands appearing inside a block in the transcript that you specify.

To use this command, follow these steps:

1. Highlight the first command you want to play back, and then press / to activate the Transcript menu.

2. Choose **B**egin Block.

3. Highlight the last command line you want to play back, press / to activate the Transcript menu, and then choose **E**nd Block. Quattro Pro puts arrowheads next to each command line in the block (see fig. 15.16).

4. Press / to activate the Transcript menu and choose **P**layback Block. Quattro Pro replays the commands marked in the block.

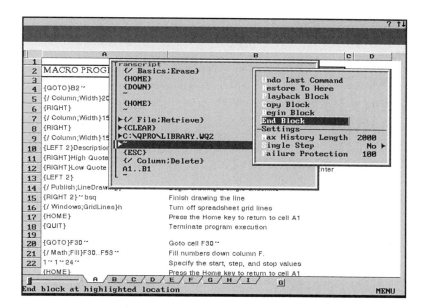

Fig. 15.16

Selecting a transcript block.

When you choose **P**layback Block, Quattro Pro plays back the marked command block. To abort this operation, press Ctrl+Break. Quattro Pro stops the playback at the end of the current command.

Copying a Transcript Block

The commands appearing in the transcript are exactly the same as the instructions that appear in a macro. By copying commands from the transcript into a notebook, you can turn the commands into macro instructions.

A **C**opy Block operation is similar to a **P**layback Block operation—you specify the beginning and end blocks in the transcript on which to perform an operation. To copy a block to a notebook, follow these steps:

1. Highlight the first command you want to play back, and then press / to activate the Transcript menu.

2. Choose **B**egin Block.

3. Highlight the last command line you want to play back, press / to activate the Transcript menu, and then choose **E**nd Block. Quattro Pro puts arrowheads next to each command line in the block.

4. Choose **C**opy Block. Quattro Pro prompts you to create/modify a macro name.

5. Type a name and press Enter to record the macro name.

6. When prompted, type the cell address into which you want to copy the transcript commands.

7. Press Enter to copy the transcript commands into the active notebook.

To copy the block to another notebook open in memory, you can use one of the following methods:

■ When Quattro Pro prompts you for a destination block, press Alt+0, the Pick Window key, to display a list of open notebooks. Highlight a notebook name and press Enter to load the notebook into the active window. Position the selector on the notebook and press Enter to copy the block to that location.

■ You can type the standard link syntax when prompted for a destination block. Figure 15.17 shows the syntax that was used to copy the block from the transcript onto NOTEBK4.WQ2 beginning at cell D2.

You can choose the /**T**ools **M**acro **N**ame command to assign a macro name to the block, and choose the /**T**ools **M**acro **P**aste command to copy the block into NOTEBK4.WQ2.

Fig. 15.17

Using the standard link syntax to copy a transcript command block to another notebook.

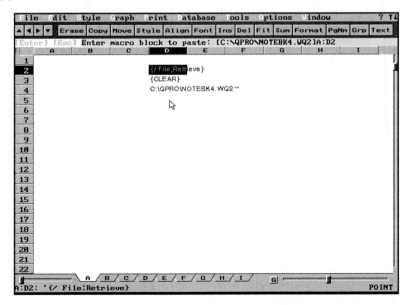

Defining the Maximum History Length

The Transcript utility records your keystrokes and menu command selections in a file called QUATTRO.LOG. When you load Quattro Pro into your PC, the program opens this file and begins appending to it.

Quattro Pro enables you to establish the number of keystrokes the program stores in QUATTRO.LOG. By default, this setting is 2,000 keystrokes. When the file reaches this maximum, Quattro Pro renames the file QUATTRO.BAK and opens a new, empty QUATTRO.LOG file. When Quattro Pro updates QUATTRO.LOG, the program overwrites the QUATTRO.BAK file.

You can use the **M**ax History Length setting to increase the maximum number of keystrokes recorded in the log. The maximum value permitted for this setting is 25,000 keystrokes. To increase the **M**ax History Length setting to 7,500 keystrokes, for example, follow these steps:

1. Choose **M**ax History Length from the Transcript menu.

2. When prompted, type **7500** (see fig. 15.18).

3. Press Enter to record the new setting.

> Be careful of the value you enter here; if you enter **0** as the setting, Quattro Pro disables the Transcript facility altogether.

CAUTION

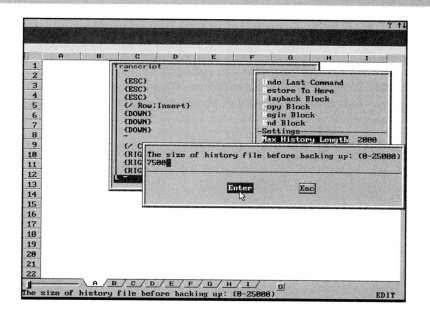

Fig. 15.18

Choose a higher maximum history length setting.

Defining the Playback Mode

Choose the **S**ingle Step command to determine the speed with which Quattro Pro replays a transcript command history when prompted.

By default, this command is set to **N**o, which causes Quattro Pro to replay a transcript command history without any delay. The **Y**es setting pauses the replay until you press any key on the keyboard; the **T**imed setting pauses the replay operation momentarily between each transcript command line (see fig. 15.19).

Fig. 15.19

Pausing the steps in a replay operation.

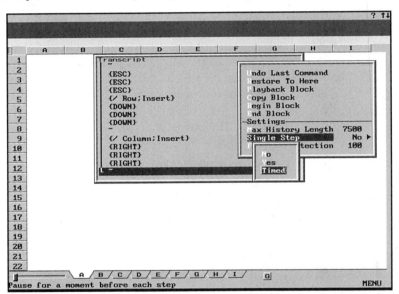

Now choose a replay operation. When executed, Quattro Pro replays the transcript one command line at a time, pausing for a moment between commands. Press Ctrl+Break during a replay operation to stop the operation.

Defining Failure Protection

By default, Quattro Pro writes the transcript to disk after every 100 keystrokes. The **F**ailure Protection facility ensures that you can recover most or all of your work in case of a power failure.

When you lower this setting, Quattro Pro writes to disk more often and increases the likelihood that the transcript will slow down your work sessions. If you are comfortable with increasing the risk of data loss, choose the **F**ailure Protection command and enter a higher setting.

To set this command to 500 keystrokes, for example, follow these steps:

1. Choose **F**ailure Protection from the Transcript menu.

2. When prompted, type **500** (see fig. 15.20).

3. Press Enter to record the new setting.

At higher settings, Quattro Pro stores your keystrokes and menu command selections in a memory buffer and writes the keystrokes to disk at less frequent intervals.

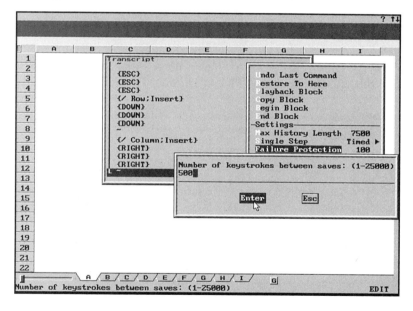

Fig. 15.20

Increasing the number of keystrokes to be stored before writing a transcript to disk.

Exiting Transcript

Press Esc to leave the Transcript menu and return to the Transcript window. To return to the active notebook, press Esc again.

> **TIP**
>
> To disable the Transcript facility altogether and free RAM for use in other areas of Quattro Pro, set the **M**ax History Length setting to 0.

Questions & Answers

This chapter introduces you to the /**Tools M**acro menu of commands. If you have questions concerning particular situations that aren't addressed in the examples given, look through this section.

Recording a Macro

Q: I pressed Alt+F2 R to begin recording a macro, but nothing happened. Did I do something wrong?

A: When Quattro Pro is recording a macro, the program displays REC on the status line at the bottom of your screen. If this mode indicator doesn't appear, choose /**Tools M**acro **R**ecord **Y**es and try again. Note that Quattro Pro does nothing spectacular to indicate that it's recording a macro.

Q: Why doesn't Quattro Pro give me an instant replay of a macro I just recorded?

A: You may not have turned on the macro recorder, and Quattro Pro hasn't recorded anything. Make sure that the REC mode indicator is showing on the status line while you are recording.

You also may have exited the active notebook before choosing the Instant Replay command, and Quattro Pro erased the recorded macro from memory. To replay a macro properly, be sure to choose /**Tools M**acro Instant Replay when you finish recording.

Also, be sure you didn't select your menu commands with your mouse.

Executing a Macro

Q: Why doesn't Quattro Pro execute my instant macro?

A: Quattro Pro accepts only letters as valid instant macro names. If you named your macro \5, for example, choose /**T**ools **M**acro **N**ame and rename the macro with a letter.

Q: Why doesn't Quattro Pro execute the instant macro I named /a?

A: When you name an instant macro, you must use the backslash (\), not the forward slash (/). If your macro name contains the forward slash, Quattro Pro does nothing when you press Alt+a. Choose /**T**ools **M**acro **N**ame and rename the macro.

Q: Why doesn't my autoload macro work when I load a linked notebook application?

A: Look at your macro. Is the first command in the macro {ESC}? If not, type {**ESC**} above the first command—this command is necessary to back Quattro Pro out of the linking options prompt. Choose /**T**ools **M**acro **N**ame and rename the macro, defining the cell that contains {ESC} as the first cell in the macro block.

Q: I don't want my autoload macro to affect every notebook that I load. What should I do?

A: Choose /**O**ptions **S**tartup **S**tartup Macro, press Backspace until you delete the autoload name, and press Enter to record no autoload name. Choose /**O**ptions **U**pdate to save the new setting.

You must rename the macro if you originally named it \0 to correspond to the default setting for the **S**tartup Macro command.

Q: When I execute a macro, Quattro Pro modifies the notebook that the macro is on and not the notebook that I want modified. What's happening?

A: You didn't define the first notebook as a macro library. Choose /**T**ools **M**acro **L**ibrary **Y**es. Press Alt+0 and activate the target notebook. Execute the macro again.

Using the Transcript

Q: Why is the Transcript window empty when plenty of command history should appear?

A: Quattro Pro disables the Transcript facility when the /**T**ools **M**acro Transcript **M**ax History Length setting is 0. Enter a larger number if you want Quattro Pro to maintain a transcript history of your work sessions.

Summary

In this chapter you learned how to create, debug, edit, and execute macro programs. You also were introduced to the Transcript facility, a tool that helps you maintain the integrity of your Quattro Pro work sessions.

Having completed this chapter, you should understand the following Quattro Pro concepts:

- Recording, pasting, naming, editing, and executing basic macro programs

- Using the Macro Debugger to ferret out macro commands that cause execution errors

- Applying the commands on the Transcript menu to view your command history, replay transcript blocks, and undo notebook mistakes

- Copying a transcript block to a notebook, naming the block as a macro, and then replaying the block on-screen

- Defining parameters that determine the size of the transcript, how often the transcript is updated, and the transcript's replay mode

In Chapter 16, you learn how to customize and streamline your Quattro Pro work sessions by creating default settings tailor-made to your specific needs, using Quattro Pro's **O**ptions menu. By using the commands on this menu, you can modify how Quattro Pro interacts with your system hardware, select complementary screen colors for your display, change the cell format default settings, and configure and then store start-up options for the next work session.

Customizing Quattro Pro

This chapter introduces you to the **O**ptions menu commands, which enable you to fine-tune Quattro Pro's global, notebook, and page default settings. These three types of settings are important to your daily work sessions because they control how Quattro Pro interacts with your computer hardware and your active notebook. If you don't change the options, Quattro Pro uses its default settings.

The **O**ptions menu commands aren't so much operating commands as they are a set of rules that Quattro Pro follows each time it loads into your computer. Without these settings, Quattro Pro doesn't know whether to display in text or WYSIWYG display mode, cannot properly use your computer's expanded memory, has no idea how to color the various parts of its screen display, and cannot send data to the correct printer port.

Global defaults go into effect immediately, but others have an effect only when Quattro Pro loads into your computer. Notebook options affect only the active notebook, and page defaults affect only the active page. In this chapter, you learn the domain of each option type as it's discussed.

The first part of Chapter 16 is devoted to reviewing the commands on the **O**ptions menu. As in previous chapters, you come to understand the organization of the commands on this menu. A quick preview of Quattro Pro's coloring palette concludes this section.

The next section shows you how to set and reset options that you use to define Quattro Pro's global default settings. These settings remind Quattro Pro about your printer and screen, as well as which display mode to use on start-up. You also learn how to create your own set of "start-up rules" for Quattro Pro to follow the next time it loads.

This chapter also reviews the Update command. Using the Update command saves your current system settings as global defaults, which become the defaults for all future Quattro Pro work sessions.

The last part of this chapter teaches you about defining notebook format settings, selecting recalculation modes, and invoking global, notebook, and formula protection. Remember, these final settings affect only individual notebooks and pages. Update doesn't store the settings for each new notebook you create.

Reviewing the Options Menu

Use the 15 Options menu commands to set, reset, and save the global, notebook, and page defaults for using Quattro Pro. The Options menu contains three types of commands: global, notebook, and page defaults (see fig. 16.1). Quattro Pro displays the current settings for certain commands at the right margin of this menu.

The first 10 commands tell Quattro Pro how to interact with your screen display and printer, what colors to display, and where and how to store files. If Quattro Pro seems to perform well and you are comfortable with its on-screen appearance, you may not have to change many of the default system settings.

The Update command saves the current Options menu settings, which become the defaults for every Quattro Pro work session from now on. Quattro Pro stores the default menu settings on your hard disk drive in two files: RSC.RF and QUATTRO.MU. (If you are on a network, you are using the QUATTRO.MP file, not the QUATTRO.MU file.)

The Update command saves only global default options—not any of the notebook or page options—for future work sessions. All other options (WYSIWYG Zoom %, Formats, Recalculation, and Protection) are saved only with the active notebook when you choose /File Save, /File Save As, or /File Save All.

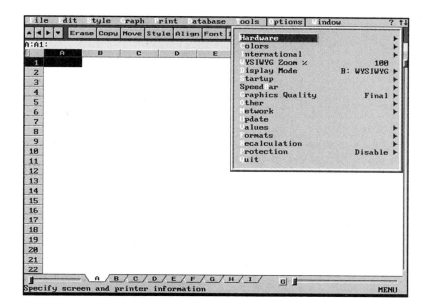

Fig. 16.1

The **O**ptions menu commands.

TIP

Choosing **U**pdate saves all system defaults that can be updated, including those defaults set on the **S**tyle, **G**raph, and **P**rint menus.

The /**O**ptions **V**alues command displays a settings window that summarizes all system defaults for the current work session. By using this command, you quickly can review all current default settings. When you choose this command, Quattro Pro displays the status box shown in figure 16.2. Each time you choose /**O**ptions **U**pdate, Quattro Pro updates the settings information that appears in the status box.

The next three commands on the menu are default format options that affect only individual notebooks and/or pages. These commands store default numeric formats, enable you to choose the formula recalculation method, and turn global notebook and formula protection on and off.

Table 16.1 explains the purpose of the **O**ptions menu commands. As with most other Quattro Pro commands, these commands are intuitive. Choose **C**olors to set color options, for example, **D**isplay Mode to change the display mode, or Speed**B**ar to reconfigure the SpeedBar.

Fig. 16.2

Reviewing the status of a Quattro Pro work session.

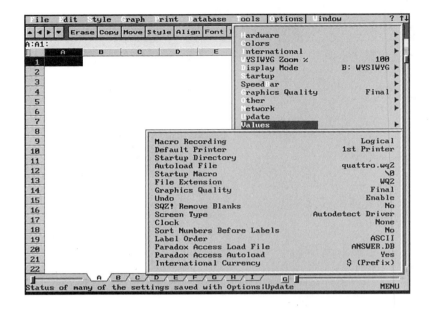

Table 16.1 The Options Menu Commands

Command	Description
Hardware	Configures screen and printer settings and shows memory status
Colors	Customizes colors for all Quattro Pro screens
International	Configures currency, date, and time settings according to international standards
WYSIWYG Zoom %	Sets the percent zoom factor used to enlarge and reduce the notebook area shown in one screen
Display Mode	Sets the display mode between WYSIWYG and text
Startup	Displays current start-up and default options
Speed**B**ar	Changes the macro key button assignments on the EDIT mode and READY mode SpeedBars
Graphics Quality	Toggles between final and draft graphics quality
Other	Sets **U**ndo, **M**acro, **E**xpanded Memory, **C**lock, and **P**aradox options

Command	Description
Network	Configures the network operating environment options, such as drive mappings
Update	Updates and saves all current default settings
Values	Displays a settings menu that summarizes all current defaults saved with the **Update** command
Formats	Sets the global display formats
Recalculation	Sets the recalculation mode
Protection	Enables and disables global notebook protection and adds or removes formula password protection

Setting Hardware Options

When you choose /**O**ptions **H**ardware, Quattro Pro displays a submenu with three command options and three non-interactive fields that display only system data (see fig. 16.3). Table 16.2 describes the options available on the **H**ardware submenu.

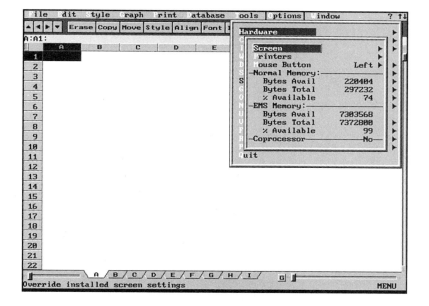

Fig. 16.3

The **H**ardware submenu.

Table 16.2 Choosing Hardware Options

Command	Description
Screen	Sets characteristics for the screen display
Printers	Reconfigures and installs printers
Mouse Button	Determines which mouse button is used to choose commands
Normal Memory	Displays conventional memory statistics
EMS Memory	Displays expanded memory statistics
Coprocessor	Indicates whether a math coprocessor is installed

The **S**creen and **P**rinters commands enable you to change the system settings for your screen and printer. The **M**ouse Button command enables you to choose the mouse button (**L**eft or **R**ight) that's used to choose commands and highlight cells on a notebook.

The final three commands, distinguished by a line through their names (and no available boldfaced letter shortcut key), display information about how Quattro Pro is using your hardware. You cannot execute these commands. When you add memory or a coprocessor to your system, however, Quattro Pro updates the information in these three fields. (For more details, see the section "Reviewing Normal Memory, EMS, and Coprocessor Data" later in this chapter.)

Choosing a New Screen Display Setting

During installation, Quattro Pro detects your screen display and installs the proper screen driver file. This file contains special codes that tell Quattro Pro how to display itself. Depending on your display model—and therefore the contents of this file—you may be able to modify certain display characteristics directly from the **O**ptions menu.

To change these stored specifications without reinstalling the program, choose /**O**ptions **H**ardware **S**creen. Quattro Pro displays the submenu shown in figure 16.4.

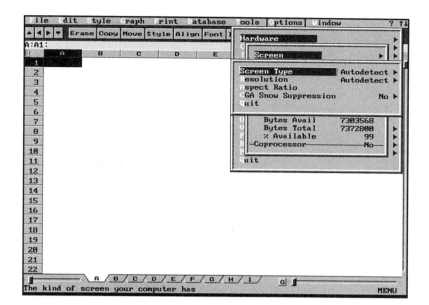

Fig. 16.4

The **S**creen submenu commands.

Screen Type

The **S**creen Type option enables you to choose a different screen driver for your display when you aren't in WYSIWYG mode. The default setting, **A**utodetect, causes Quattro Pro to evaluate your screen type on its own.

TIP

BAR **Text** During the installation of Quattro Pro, you may have selected WYSIWYG display mode, the default start-up display mode that Quattro Pro suggested that you use. If you selected a non-WYSIWYG display mode and now want to switch to WYSIWYG, click the BAR button on the SpeedBar and then click the WYS button. (You also can choose /**O**ptions **D**isplay Mode **B**: WYSIWYG to exit text display mode.) To switch back to 80x25 text display mode, click the Text button or choose /**O**ptions **D**isplay Mode **A**: 80x25.

You should have Quattro Pro autodetect your screen type except in special cases, such as when you want to choose a special display setting such as **F**. Monochrome EGA. If you choose a driver that's incompatible with your type of screen, Quattro Pro may not display correctly.

To choose a new screen type, choose **S**creen Type. Then choose a different driver from the list that is displayed, as shown in figure 16.5.

Fig. 16.5

Selecting a new driver from the **S**creen Type list.

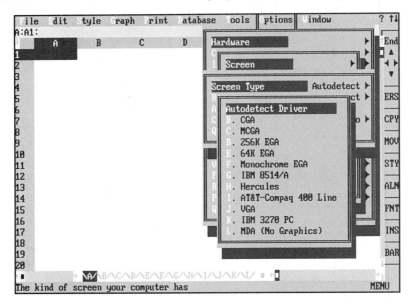

NOTE

Quattro Pro doesn't execute the **S**creen Type or **R**esolution command when your display is in WYSIWYG display mode. To modify the display mode so that you can change the screen type, choose /**O**ptions **D**isplay Mode **A**: 80x25 before you execute either command.

Resolution

The number of pixels (or dots) your screen can display determines the clarity, or *resolution*, of a graphics image. A resolution of 640x480, for example, means that a screen can illuminate 640 dots horizontally and 480 dots vertically. The more dots a screen can display, the crisper the resolution of a graphics image. Some VGA screens can display a resolution of 1280x1024—an ideal resolution for computer-aided design (CAD) applications.

Many display adapter cards support multiple resolution modes. In this case, you can choose one resolution mode for notebook text and another for notebook graphics. To choose a different screen resolution (if this option is available with your screen adapter card), choose **R**esolution and then choose a resolution setting from the list Quattro Pro displays. Quattro Pro supports resolution settings up to a maximum of 640x480.

> **TIP**
>
> Because Quattro Pro automatically chooses the highest resolution available for your display, you probably don't need to change this value.

Aspect Ratio

Each screen display has a height-to-width measurement called the *aspect ratio*. A properly adjusted aspect ratio ensures that the shape of a graph is correct so that a pie graph looks like a pie and not like an egg or a pancake.

To adjust the aspect ratio, choose the **A**spect Ratio command from the **S**creen Type submenu. Quattro Pro displays a circular shape. Press the up- and down-arrow keys to mold the figure until it appears as a near-perfect circle. Press Enter to accept that height-to-width ratio or Esc to cancel the operation.

CGA Snow Suppression

If your computer has a Color Graphics Adapter (CGA), your screen may flicker when you scroll about the notebook window. Use the **C**GA Snow Suppression command to eliminate this problem. To enable snow suppression, choose **Y**es on the submenu that appears when you choose this command.

Choosing Printers

During the initial program installation, you supplied Quattro Pro with your printer's brand name and model number. Quattro Pro used this information to create a driver file containing special codes that tell Quattro Pro how to print notebooks and graphs on your particular printer.

To make changes to the printer driver file without reinstalling the program, choose /**O**ptions **H**ardware **P**rinters. Quattro Pro displays the submenu pictured in figure 16.6.

Fig. 16.6

The **P**rinters submenu.

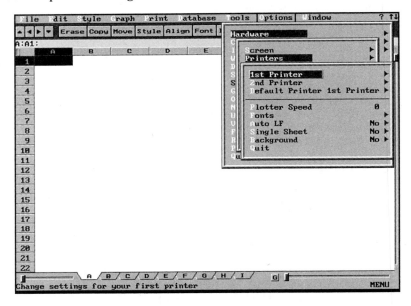

This submenu is divided into two sections. The top section contains commands for installing two printers and choosing one of them as the default printer. The bottom section contains printer setup commands that enable you to record plotter speed, choose printer fonts, adjust line feeds, toggle between continuous and single-sheet paper feeding, and invoke background printing.

Notice that the current settings for many of these commands appear in the right margin of the menu.

Configuring a Second Printer

With the first three options on the **P**rinters submenu, you can record configuration data for one or two printers. If you own only one printer, this printer must be the default. If you own two printers, you can configure both and toggle between them with the **D**efault Printer command.

Follow these steps to configure a second printer:

1. Choose /**O**ptions **H**ardware **P**rinters **2**nd Printer.

2. Choose **T**ype of printer. Quattro Pro displays a scrollable list of printer manufacturers.

3. Choose the correct printer manufacturer from the list. Quattro Pro displays a scrollable list of printer models.

4. Choose the appropriate printer model from the list. Quattro Pro displays a list of possible print resolution settings.

5. Choose a resolution mode setting. Quattro Pro returns to the 2nd Printer submenu.

   The next two steps are necessary only when you own a serial printer or when you don't have a standard parallel printer connected to port LPT1, the default printer port for most PCs.

6. Choose **D**evice and specify the port to which the printer is connected.

7. If you own a serial printer, enter the appropriate data for **B**aud rate, **P**arity, and **S**top bits.

The 2nd Printer submenu now should reflect the new printer settings under the Make, Model, and Mode headings (see fig. 16.7).

Fig. 16.7

Quattro Pro updates the
2nd Printer submenu.

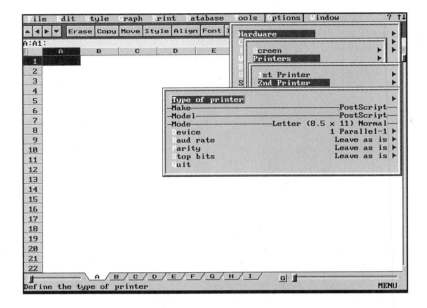

To choose the new printer as the default printer, follow these steps:

1. Press Esc to return to the **P**rinters submenu.

2. Choose **D**efault Printer.

3. Choose the number of the printer you want to be the default printer. (This printer is the one to which Quattro Pro will print unless otherwise instructed.)

> **TIP**
>
> Quattro Pro Versions 3.0, 4.0, and 5.0 print faster on Hewlett-Packard (HP) laser printers than previous versions. If you prefer high-resolution printing, try the following two tricks for exploiting this speed improvement. First, configure your laser printer as a more recent model. (If you own a LaserJet model, for example, configure it as a LaserJet II.) Second, indicate that you have more printer memory than you actually do. If you get a memory error, switch back to the original setting.

Setting Plotter Speed

The **P**lotter Speed option enables you to specify the print speed for a color plotter. The fastest speed is 9, and the slowest is 1. The default setting, 0, tells Quattro Pro to run at the plotter's fastest speed.

Experiment with the **P**lotter Speed setting; you may want to slow down the plotter speed intentionally when using older pens. Slowing down a plotter that uses old pens helps improve the quality of your plotter's printouts.

Installing Fonts

You can install special printer fonts by choosing the **F**onts command from the /**O**ptions **H**ardware **P**rinters menu. The first choice on this submenu, **C**artridge Fonts, enables you to install font cartridges for a Hewlett-Packard LaserJet printer or Canon Laser Printer. After you choose this command, you need to tell Quattro Pro which fonts you have and in which port, or cartridge slot, on the printer (**R**ight Cartridge or **L**eft Cartridge) they are installed (see fig. 16.8).

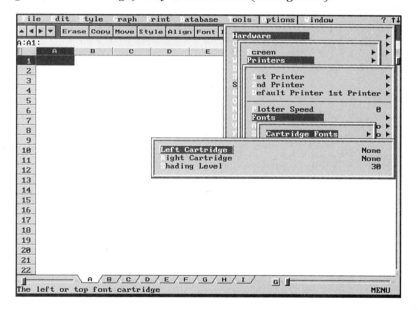

Fig. 16.8

Selecting the **F**onts command to install special printer fonts.

The **C**artridge Fonts command displays Canon or LaserJet cartridge fonts only when the /**O**ptions **H**ardware **P**rinters **D**efault Printer setting is a Canon or LaserJet printer.

NOTE

The **S**hading Level command on the **C**artridge Fonts submenu enables you to specify shading levels to use for cell shading. This command affects only the intensity of shaded cells on an HP LaserJet printout; it doesn't affect the appearance of shaded cells on the notebook when you are in WYSIWYG display mode. (To change the colors that Quattro Pro uses to shade cells, choose the /**O**ptions **C**olors **S**preadsheet **S**hading command.)

When you choose the **S**hading Level command, you specify a percent value, corresponding to one of the eight levels of shading available on an HP LaserJet printer (see table 16.3). The default shading level percentage is 30.

Table 16.3 HP LaserJet Shading Levels

Shading %	HP LaserJet Shading Level #	Shading Contrast
1-2	1	Lightest
3-10	2	
11-20	3	
21-35	4	Medium
36-55	5	
56-80	6	
81-99	7	
100	8	Darkest

The second option on the **F**onts submenu, **A**utoscale Fonts, enables you to decide how Quattro Pro scales fonts when printing graphs. The way in which Quattro Pro scales fonts normally depends on the size of the area in which you choose to display a graph. The less space Quattro Pro has to work in, the smaller the actual font size. If you prefer that Quattro Pro not scale your fonts in this manner, set **A**utoscale Fonts to **N**o.

Controlling Line Feeds

Using the /**O**ptions **H**ardware **P**rinters **A**uto LF option tells Quattro Pro whether to issue a line-feed character and carriage return after each line. Most printers have automatic line feed, so the default setting is **No**. If your printouts are double-spaced, try choosing the **Yes** option. If the printer crams several lines of text onto one line, try choosing **No**.

Printing on Single Sheets

Quattro Pro assumes that you are using continuous-feed (tractor-fed) paper to print your notebooks. When you choose /**O**ptions **H**ardware **P**rinters **S**ingle Sheet, the setting is **No**, the normal setting for dot-matrix printers that use tractor feeding.

If you want to feed paper into your printer one sheet at a time, set the **S**ingle Sheet option to **Yes**. This technique is useful when your second printer is a letter-quality printer. Set the option to **No** when printing to an ASCII file so that Quattro Pro doesn't ask you for the next sheet.

Printing in the Background

With Quattro Pro's print spooler feature, you can continue to work with your notebooks after sending multiple print jobs to the printer. The Borland Print Spooler program, BPS.COM, collects print jobs, temporarily saves them to your hard disk drive, and then releases control of Quattro Pro back to you. While you continue to work with the current notebook, the print spooler sends data to the printer *in the background* without impairing the performance of Quattro Pro on your computer.

To print jobs in the background with Quattro Pro, you must do two things: type **bps** at the DOS prompt to load the BPS.COM program into your PC's memory, and enable background printing with the /**O**ptions **H**ardware **P**rinters **B**ackground **Y**es command. This command tells Quattro Pro that if the BPS.COM is loaded into memory, the program should send all print jobs to the Borland Print Spooler.

> **NOTE**
>
> You must load these two programs in the exact order listed. Don't load Quattro Pro, shell out to DOS with the /**F**ile **U**tilities **D**OS Shell command, and then try to load BPS.COM.

CAUTION

The print spooler doesn't replace—and may conflict with—a network print spooler. If you choose to use the print spooler on a network, load the print spooler before loading the network shell. If you encounter problems, use the network spooler or the print spooler—not both. (See Appendix B, "Installing Quattro Pro on a Network," for more information.)

Reviewing Normal Memory, EMS, and Coprocessor Data

The /Options Hardware menu gives you access to some of Quattro Pro's knowledge of your computer system. The bottom three entries on this submenu indicate the amount of memory in use and memory available to Quattro Pro (in bytes and as a percent of total available); the amount of expanded memory in use and available (in bytes and as a percent of total available); and whether a math coprocessor is installed. All three values are detected by Quattro Pro from DOS and displayed here for your convenience.

Figure 16.3 earlier in the chapter shows the current hardware status on the Hardware submenu. Quattro Pro indicates that the computer has 220,404 bytes (or 74%) of free conventional memory, 297,232 bytes of total conventional memory, 7,303,568 bytes (or 99%) of free expanded memory, 7,372,800 bytes of total expanded memory, and no coprocessor available.

Using Quattro Pro's Coloring Palette

You can change the colors for each part of Quattro Pro's display by choosing the /Options Colors command. When you choose this command, you see a submenu listing areas of the program that you may color. Table 16.4 describes the choices that appear on this submenu.

Table 16.4 Changing Color Options

Command	Description
Menu	Changes colors on the pull-down menus
Desktop	Changes colors located behind a notebook
Spreadsheet	Changes colors on a notebook and those colors used in WYSIWYG display mode
Conditional	Sets colors for special numbers and formulas
Help	Changes colors on the help windows
File Manager	Sets colors for the File Manager
Palettes	Resets all default Quattro Pro colors

With the **Colors** command, you can choose the colors for Quattro Pro
to use in all parts of its program display. Feel free to experiment with
new combinations; you always can reinstate the original scheme with
the **P**alettes command.

After you choose a command from the **Colors** submenu, Quattro Pro
displays a special coloring tool called the *coloring palette* (see fig. 16.9).
Look closely and notice the tiny rotating bar positioned on one of the
color pairs in this box. This bar indicates the current color combination setting for the Quattro Pro screen area selected. Figure 16.9, for
example, shows this palette's setting when you choose /**O**ptions **C**olors
Menu **K**ey Letter. Each time you want to alter one of Quattro Pro's display colors, this coloring tool appears. Use the arrow keys or click to
choose a different color combination.

> **NOTE**
>
> The **C**olors command is a notebook default, which means that changes
> made with this command affect all pages in the active notebook only.
> The exceptions to this rule are the /**O**ptions **C**olors **C**onditional and
> /**O**ptions **C**olors **S**preadsheet **C**ells options, which are page defaults.
> Changes made with these commands affect only the active page in the
> active notebook.

Fig. 16.9

Changing Quattro Pro's colors.

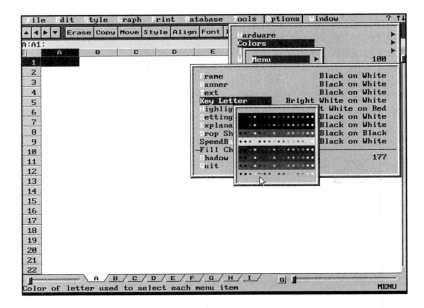

Note that a few screen elements require you to enter ASCII character codes (such as the /**O**ptions **C**olors **M**enu **S**hadow option). These ASCII codes enable Quattro Pro to display graphics characters in various parts of the screen when you are in text display mode. Consult the ASCII table in Appendix C, "Using ASCII Characters," for sensible values in these instances.

Choosing Menu Colors

The **M**enu command on the **C**olors submenu enables you to choose new color combinations for Quattro Pro's pull-down menus (see fig. 16.10).

On the **M**enu submenu, Quattro Pro lists the parts of a menu that may be colored. Choose a part to color, and Quattro Pro displays the coloring palette with the rotating bar (refer to fig. 16.9). Choose a new color, and Quattro Pro immediately refreshes the screen display to show the new color combination. If you want to change the color of the Speed-Bar, for example, choose /**O**ptions **C**olors **M**enu **S**peedB**a**r.

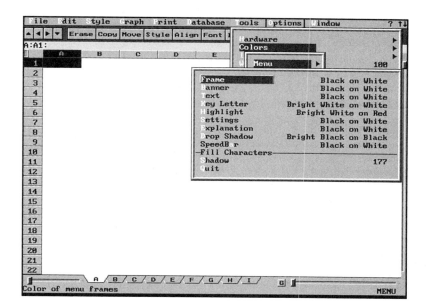

Fig. 16.10

The **M**enu submenu commands.

Choosing Desktop Colors

By using the **Desktop** command, you can choose new color combinations for Quattro Pro's desktop. The desktop is the part of the display not filled with a notebook window. Here, you also may specify ASCII characters for Quattro Pro to use as background shading.

When you choose /**O**ptions **C**olors **D**esktop, Quattro Pro displays a list of the parts of the desktop that may be colored, including the status line, the modes and status indicators on the status line, error messages, and the area below notebook windows. Choose a part to color, and Quattro Pro displays the coloring palette with the rotating bar. Choose a new color, and Quattro Pro immediately refreshes the screen display to reflect the new color combination.

Choosing Notebook Colors

The next command on the **Colors** submenu enables you to color various portions of a notebook window, such as the frame around a notebook window, locked titles text, unprotected cell data, drawn lines, and the WYSIWYG display mode window. When you choose /**O**ptions **C**olors **S**preadsheet, Quattro Pro displays a list of the parts of the notebook window that may be colored. Choose a part to color, and Quattro Pro displays the coloring palette with the rotating bar. Choose a new color, and Quattro Pro immediately refreshes the screen display to reflect the new color combination.

TIP

> The **C**ells option under /**O**ptions **C**olors **S**preadsheet is a page default setting, so you can specify different cell colors for different pages within the same notebook.

To change the colors used to create Quattro Pro's WYSIWYG display mode, choose the **W**YSIWYG Colors option on the **S**preadsheet submenu. Quattro Pro displays a list of the parts of the WYSIWYG notebook window that may be colored. Choose a part to color, and Quattro Pro displays the coloring palette with the rotating bar. Choose a new color, and Quattro Pro immediately reflects the new color combination.

Choosing Conditional Colors

The /**O**ptions **C**olors **C**onditional command displays the submenu pictured in figure 16.11. With the **C**onditional submenu options, you can specify the color your data will have when certain conditions are met.

The most common use for this option is to specify an acceptable range for a set of data and require Quattro Pro to show values outside that range in a different color. The **O**n/Off command tells Quattro Pro whether to display conditional colors, enabling the conditional coloring that you set up with commands on this submenu.

ERR enables you to specify the color to use when ERR and NA values appear on a notebook. **S**mallest Normal Value and **G**reatest Normal Value define the range of values that are considered "normal." (Normal, in this case, is whatever you need it to be in light of the numbers contained in your notebook report.)

The next three command options enable you to define colors to be used when notebook values fall below, equal, or are greater than a certain value. Define the colors using the **B**elow Normal Color, **N**ormal Cell Color, and **A**bove Normal Color options.

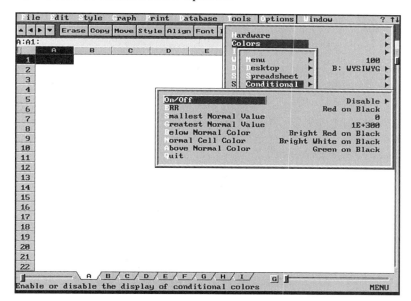

Fig. 16.11

The **C**onditional submenu commands.

Remember, in addition to specifying the normal range and colors, you must enable the conditional color option by choosing the **O**n/Off command.

Another good use for the **C**onditional color settings is to set negative numbers apart from positive numbers. In financial applications, for example, you may need to know whether a business is operating in the red or the black. By assigning the color red to negative numbers on a notebook, you provide conclusive and easy-to-find evidence.

The **C**onditional command is a page default setting, so you can specify different conditional settings for different pages within the same notebook.

Choosing Help Colors

With the **Help** command, you can choose different color combinations for Quattro Pro's help windows. After you choose /**O**ptions **C**olors **H**elp, Quattro Pro displays a list of the parts of the help window that may be colored. These parts include the frame around a help window, the text, and the highlighter in the window.

Choose a part to color, and Quattro Pro displays the coloring palette with the rotating bar. Choose a new color, and the color takes effect immediately.

Because Quattro Pro doesn't show help windows as part of its normal display, press F1 to make sure that your color selection is acceptable before saving the changes.

Choosing File Manager Colors

The **F**ile Manager command enables you to change the color display of Quattro Pro's File Manager. When you choose /**O**ptions **C**olors **F**ile Manager, Quattro Pro displays a list of the parts of the screen that may be colored. These parts include the active cursor, inactive cursor (highlight bar), and marked text. Choose a part to color, and Quattro Pro displays the coloring palette with the rotating bar. Choose a new color, and the color takes effect immediately.

Because Quattro Pro doesn't show the File Manager as part of its normal notebook display, choose /**F**ile Utilities **F**ile Manager to load the File Manager and make sure that your color selection is acceptable before saving the changes.

Choosing Palette Colors

The **P**alettes command on the **C**olors submenu enables you to recall Quattro Pro's original color scheme, even if you previously saved custom color combinations with the Update command. To recall Quattro Pro's default color settings, follow these steps:

1. Choose /**O**ptions **C**olors **P**alettes.

2. Choose the **C**olor option.

3. Choose /**O**ptions **U**pdate to save the change.

Your other palette options include **M**onochrome, **B**lack & White, **G**ray Scale, and **V**ersion 3 Color.

Setting International Options

Quattro Pro offers excellent foreign-language compatibility. If you are using a non-English copy of the program, you can enter @function commands in your native language or in English. All other commands must be entered in your local language.

When you retrieve Lotus 1-2-3 worksheets (or any other compatible spreadsheet) into Quattro Pro, the program translates the @function commands into your language.

Quattro Pro supports the LaserJet III printer and some printers that are more common in Europe. If you want to print text using Hershey or Bitstream characters from the international character set, Borland recommends that you contact Borland Technical Support at 408-461-9000 (the number used at this writing) to obtain a special set of fonts containing additional international characters.

By default, Quattro Pro uses the United States conventions for the currency symbol, numerical punctuation, dates, and times. To change the default to international standards for displaying currency symbols, punctuation, dates, and times, choose /**O**ptions **I**nternational.

Businesses with an international clientele may find the **I**nternational command particularly helpful. By using this command, you can create a contract bid, for example, containing the date format, punctuation style, and currency symbol of your client's country.

Many international settings that you create with this command are accessed with the /**S**tyle **N**umeric Format command. If you enter a new currency symbol, for example, Quattro Pro attaches that symbol to monetary values on your notebook when you format the values with the /**S**tyle **N**umeric Format **C**urrency command. The same holds true for international punctuation, dates, and times. Figure 16.12 shows the current **I**nternational command settings in the right margin of the submenu; table 16.5 describes the commands.

Fig. 16.12

The International default settings.

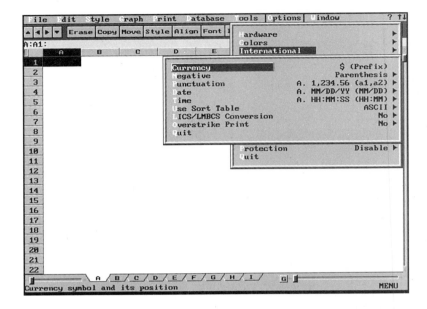

Table 16.5 The International Submenu Commands

Command	Description
Currency	Assigns location and style of the currency symbol
Negative	Puts parentheses around or a negative sign in front of negative values
Punctuation	Assigns the type of punctuation used in numbers
Date	Sets long and short international date formats
Time	Sets long and short international time formats
Use Sort Table	Specifies a set of sort rules to use
LICS/LMBCS Conversion	Converts LICS or LMBCS characters into uppercase ASCII characters
Overstrike Print	Enables the printing of accented characters

The International submenu commands enable you to specify the format in which values are displayed, as well as where in a cell the values are placed when you enter them.

Choosing a Currency Symbol

With the Currency command on the International submenu, you can choose the symbol that Quattro Pro attaches to monetary values on a notebook. This symbol is the character that appears when you choose the /Style Numeric Format Currency command. By default, Quattro Pro shows the dollar sign ($) as a prefix to a number.

To choose a different currency and symbol setting, follow these steps:

1. Choose /Options International Currency.

2. Press the Backspace key until the current currency symbol is erased.

3. Enter the ASCII code that corresponds to the currency symbol. Press Enter to store them or Esc to cancel the operation. (Appendix C lists the ASCII characters available.)

> **TIP**
>
> Entering an ASCII code to create a currency symbol is different than entering a code for a shadow on the Colors submenu. In this case, you must press Alt+*Code*, in which *Code* is the ASCII code equivalent for the currency symbol. To enter the symbol for the Japanese yen (¥), for example, hold down the Alt key and type **157** on the numeric keypad to create the ¥ symbol.

4. Choose Suffix or Prefix to set the orientation for the new currency symbol. (Suffix puts the symbol after the number; Prefix puts the symbol before the number.)

Attaching Symbols to Negative Values

Use the /Options International Negative Parentheses command to put parentheses around all negative values in your notebook. This style of displaying negative values is popular in financial and accounting applications.

Use the /**O**ptions International **N**egative **S**ign command to place a negative sign in front of all negative values in your notebook. This style of
displaying negative values is popular in scientific and mathematical
applications.

Choosing the Punctuation

The **P**unctuation command enables you to specify how Quattro Pro
displays decimal points, separates arguments in @functions, and segre-
gates zeros in numbers larger than 999. The default style is **A**. 1,234.56
(a1,a2).

To choose a new punctuation style, follow these steps:

1. Choose /**O**ptions International **P**unctuation.

2. Choose a punctuation style from the submenu shown in figure 16.13.

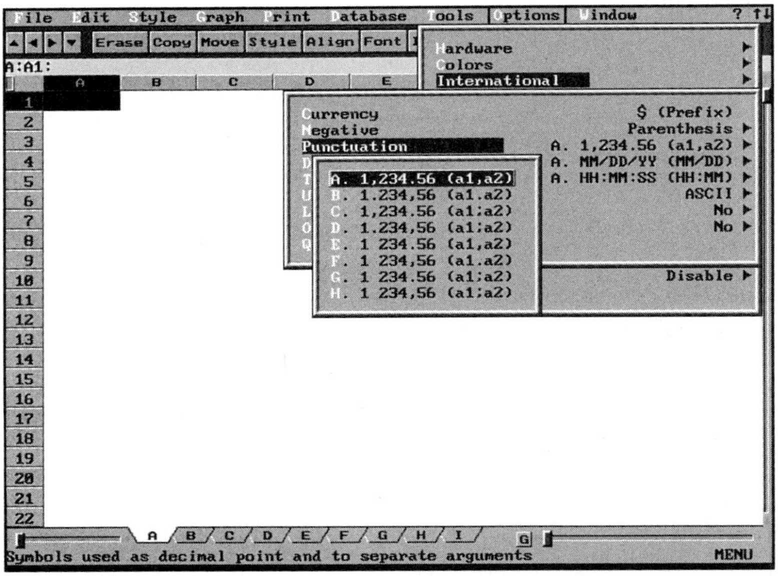

Fig. 16.13

Choosing an interna-
tional punctuation
setting.

Choosing Date Formats

The **D**ate command can display dates in several popular international
formats. The date formats you choose with this command become

available as the long and short international date formats when you choose /**O**ptions **F**ormats **N**umeric Format **D**ate. The default style is **A**. MM/DD/YY (MM/DD).

To choose a new international date format, follow these steps:

1. Choose /**O**ptions **I**nternational **D**ate.

2. Choose a date format from the submenu displayed in figure 16.14.

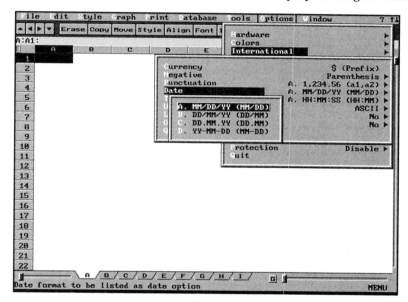

Fig. 16.14

Selecting an international date setting.

Choosing Time Formats

The /**O**ptions **I**nternational **T**ime command can display times in several popular international formats. The time formats you choose with this command become available as the long and short international time formats when you choose /**O**ptions **F**ormats **N**umeric Format **T**ime. The default style is **A**. HH:MM:SS (HH:MM).

To choose a new international time format, follow these steps:

1. Choose /**O**ptions **I**nternational **T**ime.

2. Choose a time format from the submenu shown in figure 16.15.

Fig. 16.15

Selecting an interna-
tional time setting.

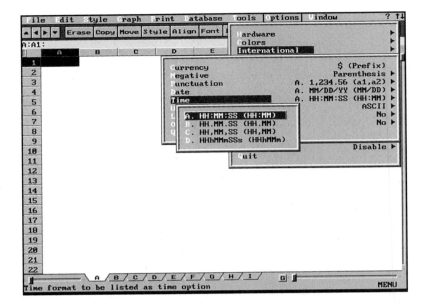

Choosing New Sort Rules

When you choose /**O**ptions International Use Sort Table, Quattro
Pro displays a submenu offering six sort rule options: **A**SCII.SOR,
INTL.SOR, **I**NTL850.SOR, **N**ORDAN.SOR, **N**ORDAN40.SOR, and
SWEDFIN.SOR.

NOTE

The **U**se Sort Table command names contain a SOR extension that identifies the name of the file that Quattro Pro uses to manage each type of
sort operation. These files are standard Borland files and may be used
with Paradox.

The ASCII sort rule option (**A**SCII.SOR) tells Quattro Pro to sort data so
that uppercase letters appear before lowercase and accented letters
appear after the letter z. See Appendix C for a complete list of ASCII
characters.

The international sort rule option (**I**NTL.SOR) tells Quattro Pro to sort
uppercase, lowercase, and accented characters according to the dictionary method (AaBbCc and so on). With this method, letter c with a
cedilla (ç) appears among the C's rather than after the letter z, as with

the ASCII sort order. If you are using code page 850, use the INTL850.SOR option instead of INTL.SOR.

The Norwegian/Danish (**NORDAN.SOR**) and Swedish/Finnish (**SWEDFIN.SOR**) sort rule options are like the international sort rule option, except that Quattro Pro sorts characters unique to these countries at the end of the regular alphabet. The NORDAN40.SOR option provides compatibility with the revised version of NORDAN.SOR that comes with Paradox.

> Any file in the default Quattro Pro directory with an SOR extension appears on the **U**se Sort Table submenu. If you have Russian and Japanese SOR files, for instance, the files also appear on this submenu.
>
> **NOTE**

Choosing LICS/LMBCS Conversion

Lotus 1-2-3 worksheets use proprietary character sets called the Lotus International Character Set (LICS) and the Lotus Multibyte Character Set (LMBCS). The LICS character set is the same as the ASCII character set, until you reach character 128. The characters in positions 128 through 255 in the LICS table aren't the standard IBM international and graphics characters.

Before you load a 1-2-3 worksheet into Quattro Pro, choose the /Options International LICS/LMBCS Conversion **Yes** command to convert all LICS and LMBCS characters (128 through 255) to the normal ASCII characters. This procedure ensures that Quattro Pro's sort rules work properly on your 1-2-3 worksheets. Then, when you save a file in a 1-2-3 worksheet format, Quattro Pro converts characters to match the LICS or LMBCS character set specifications.

Choosing Overstrike Print

The **Overstrike Print** command on the **International** submenu ensures that Quattro Pro places the proper accent symbol over an international character when you use a 7-bit printer. Choose **Yes** to enable the command. The default setting is **No**. The Diablo 630, Qume Sprint, Epson FX-80, and Epson LQ-1500 are examples of common 7-bit printers.

Using WYSIWYG Zoom %

The **W**YSIWYG Zoom % command enables you to enlarge or shrink proportionately the active notebook area—the area that Quattro Pro displays one screen at a time. This command is ideal for same-screen viewing of a large notebook that has many rows and columns.

After you choose /**O**ptions **W**YSIWYG Zoom %, Quattro Pro prompts you for a zoom percentage (%) factor. Enter any value between 25 and 200 and press Enter. (The default percentage is 100.) To enlarge the displayed notebook area, enter a percentage greater than 100; to shrink the displayed notebook area, enter a percentage lower than 100. Quattro Pro immediately resizes the notebook area according to the zoom percentage.

NOTE

> The **W**YSIWYG Zoom % command works only when Quattro Pro is displaying in WYSIWYG display mode. Changing the zoom percentage factor for this command from text display mode has no observable effect. If you switch back to WYSIWYG display mode, however, the notebook reflects the change.

Setting Display Mode Options

The **D**isplay Mode command enables you to change the overall on-screen appearance of Quattro Pro. Normally, Quattro Pro displays in 80x25 text mode. If you have the right display adapter card, however, you can display Quattro Pro in WYSIWYG display mode or in several different extended text modes. Use WYSIWYG display mode when you want to display an inserted graph on a notebook.

When you choose /**O**ptions **D**isplay Mode, Quattro Pro presents you with display mode alternatives, as listed in the following table. Choose the mode you want. After you choose a new display mode, Quattro Pro immediately refreshes the screen display to reflect the new mode. Experiment with each mode available for your screen type.

Command	Description
A: 80x25	Sets display mode to 80 by 25 characters (the default)
B: WYSIWYG	Switches to WYSIWYG display mode
C: EGA: 80x43	Sets display mode to 80 by 43 characters
D: VGA: 80x50	Sets display mode to 80 by 50 characters

Version 5.0 also has an extensive list of extended text display modes. When you choose /**O**ptions **D**isplay Mode, Quattro Pro also shows a list of 17 extended text display mode settings (options **C** through **S** in fig. 16.16). The submenu initially shows only 14 settings; you have to scroll down to see the rest.

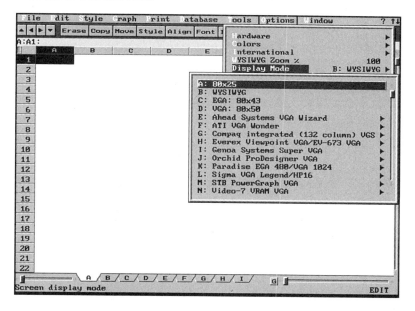

Fig. 16.16

Quattro Pro's extended text mode settings.

Version 5.0 takes full advantage of EGA and VGA graphics cards that support extended text mode. (Most graphics cards do; check your owner's manual.) If your graphics card isn't on the list, experiment with some of the others. If you have an EGA graphics display card, for example, try the **K**: Paradise EGA 480/VGA 1024 option. When you choose this option, Quattro Pro prompts you to choose a 132x25 or 132x43 (vertical characters by horizontal characters) display mode.

TIP

If your screen blanks or displays garbled information, press Enter twice to reset your display mode to the default setting. This action chooses **D**isplay Mode on the **O**ptions menu and then chooses the first choice on the list, **A**: 80x25. Certain systems may require a reset or cold boot to restore the proper video mode.

In extended text mode, you can view up to 132 by 75 characters per screen at the same time—ideal for reviewing large financial notebooks with many years of data.

Setting Start-Up Options

When you choose /**O**ptions **S**tartup, Quattro Pro displays the submenu shown in figure 16.17. The commands on this submenu enable you to specify start-up information that Quattro Pro uses each time you load the program into your system or when you create a new notebook file.

Fig. 16.17

The **S**tartup submenu.

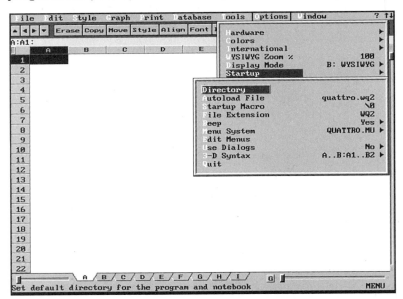

Because the **S**tartup options are system options, you must execute /**O**ptions **U**pdate to store the **S**tartup settings permanently for the next work session. The default settings for these commands appear at the right margin of the submenu.

Setting the Default Directory

With the **D**irectory command on the **S**tartup submenu, you can choose the directory in which Quattro Pro will store notebook files. The /**F**ile **S**ave and /**F**ile **R**etrieve commands enable you to access a file on any drive and directory available to your system, not just the default directory. Even so, setting a default directory is useful when you find that you frequently use the same drive and directory.

Although you literally can store your notebook files anywhere on your hard disk drive, you should create a special directory to hold all your Quattro Pro notebooks. If you want to store your files in a directory called C:\QPRO\FILES, for example, follow these steps:

1. Choose /**O**ptions **S**tartup **D**irectory.

2. Press the Backspace key until you erase the current directory name.

3. Type **c:\qpro\files** (or another valid directory name).

4. Press Enter to record the new name or Esc to cancel the operation.

> The directory name that you enter with the **D**irectory command already must exist on your hard disk drive; Quattro Pro doesn't create it for you. When you specify a directory name that doesn't exist, Quattro Pro displays an error message. You can use the File Manager to make a directory; see Chapter 8 for more details.

NOTE

Using an Autoload File

With the **A**utoload File command on the **S**tartup submenu, you can designate a notebook file for Quattro Pro to open automatically each time you load the program. If the file isn't in the directory named with the **D**irectory option, be sure to enter the full path name here.

The default autoload file name is QUATTRO.WQ2. If a file with that name appears in the default directory, Quattro Pro automatically loads that notebook file instead of NOTEBK1.WQ2. If you want to autoload a file named QUARTER1 in a directory named C:\SALES, follow these steps:

1. Choose /Options Startup Autoload File.

2. Press the Backspace key until you erase the current file name.

3. Type **c:\sales\quarter1.wq2** (or another valid autoload file).

4. Press Enter to record the new file name or Esc to cancel the operation.

A second method of autoloading a file doesn't require the use of this command. Type the file name on the DOS command line after Quattro Pro's program file name but before you press Enter to load the program. Type **q quarter2** at the DOS prompt, for example, and press Enter to load a notebook file named QUARTER2.WQ2.

NOTE ▶ Quattro Pro assumes that this file name's extension is WQ2; if the extension is different, type that extension after the file name and before pressing Enter. The file must be in the default or program directory, or in the subdirectory from which you are loading Quattro Pro.

You also can enter other command-line options—called *switches*—as you load the program. For these switches, use the following syntax and press Enter:

Q *filename macroname /switches*

NOTE ▶ In this syntax, *macroname* is the name of the macro that Quattro Pro will execute as soon as Quattro Pro opens the notebook specified by *filename*. This macro must be in the autoloaded notebook.

The switches, shown in table 16.6, tell Quattro Pro how to configure certain parts of itself as it loads into your system.

Table 16.6 Command-Line Switches

Switch	Description
/D	Tells Quattro Pro to load a specific resource file with an RF extension; if the resource file isn't in the current directory, you also must specify the directory and path name
/I	Tells Quattro Pro to autodetect the screen display and other hardware as it's loading

Switch	Description
/IC	Tells Quattro Pro to load with a color palette
/IM	Tells Quattro Pro to load with a monochrome palette
/IB	Tells Quattro Pro to load with a black-and-white palette
/Ex	Tells Quattro Pro to load with LIM 4.0 Expanded Memory Specification (EMS). The x specifies the numbers range from 0 (no EMS used) to 65355; each number represents one logical page, each page being 16,000 bytes.
/X	Tells Quattro Pro to load with up to 512K extended-memory code-swapping enabled (recommended if you have a 286-based AT computer with 1M of RAM)
/K	Tells Quattro Pro to load and use the PenDOS operating system

Choosing a Start-Up Macro

The **Startup Macro** command on the **Startup** submenu enables you to run a macro automatically each time you retrieve a new notebook. This command is useful if, for example, you normally use a macro to format your notebooks before entering data into them. (See Chapter 15, "Creating Macros," for complete coverage of macros.)

To execute a macro named \m each time you create a new notebook, follow these steps:

1. Choose /**O**ptions **S**tartup **S**tartup Macro.

2. Press the Backspace key until you erase \0, the default start-up macro name.

3. Type **\m** (or another valid macro file name).

4. Press Enter to record the new name or Esc to cancel the operation.

Selecting a New Default File Extension

The **File Extension** command on the **Startup** submenu tells Quattro Pro the three-letter file extension that it should put on the end of each note-book file name. By default, Quattro Pro uses the extension WQ2.

This process enables you to specify other applications for Quattro Pro, such as Paradox or 1-2-3, to which Quattro can write files. If you are in an office in which 1-2-3 and Quattro Pro are used, you probably want to change the extension to WK1. To do so, follow these steps:

1. Choose /Options Startup File Extension.
2. Press the Backspace key until the current extension is erased.
3. Type **WK1** (or another valid three-character extension).
4. Press Enter to record the new extension or Esc to cancel the operation.

Specifying Beep Tones

Use the **Beep** command on the /Options **Startup** menu to turn Quattro Pro's error tone on and off. This beep sounds each time you make an illegal entry or incorrectly execute a command. If you prefer not to hear the error tone, choose **No**. The default setting is **Yes**.

Choosing a Menu Tree

The **Menu System** command on the **Startup** submenu enables you to load alternate custom menu trees that you have created. When you choose this command, Quattro Pro displays a list of all available menu trees. By default, Quattro Pro shows **QUATTRO** (the standard Quattro Pro tree). When you choose a new menu tree, Quattro Pro's menu bar immediately reflects the new menu tree structure.

To switch to a custom tree named BOB, for example, follow these steps:

1. Choose /Options **Startup** **Menu System**.
2. Choose BOB.

Quattro Pro immediately displays the custom menu tree.

To create custom menu trees, choose /Options **Startup** **Edit Menus**. The **Edit Menus** command accesses the Menu Editor tool. With this tool, you can reorganize and customize menu trees in the Menu Editor window.

Using Dialog Boxes

Quattro Pro can display several menu commands as dialog boxes. A *dialog box* is a tool for setting options that normally appear on a command's submenu.

A dialog box makes viewing and setting options much easier because all the information needed to define a command appears on one screen. Quattro Pro dialog boxes eliminate the need to move up and down layers of menus and submenus to choose commands and options.

The following Quattro Pro commands offer dialog boxes:

> /**Graph C**ustomize Series
>
> /**Graph O**verall
>
> /**Graph X**-Axis
>
> /**Graph Y**-Axis
>
> /**Print L**ayout

> For more details about how to use the dialog boxes associated with these commands, refer to the sections in Chapters 9 and 11 where these commands are covered.

NOTE

Choose /**O**ptions **S**tartup **U**se Dialogs to define whether Quattro Pro displays dialog boxes rather than menus. The **Y**es option (the default) turns on the display of dialog boxes. To suppress the display of dialog boxes so that you can use the menus instead, choose /**O**ptions **S**tartup **U**se Dialogs **N**o.

Remember to choose /**O**ptions **U**pdate if you want to save the current setting for this command for all future work sessions.

Changing 3-D Cell Block Notation Style

Two notation styles exist for expressing 3-D blocks in Quattro Pro. Both styles perform equally well, but one or the other may seem more intuitive to you. The default style shows the beginning and ending page name followed by the block address, as in A..C:A1..G10. Throughout this book, you have seen this notation style used when Quattro Pro operates on a 3-D cell block.

The second notation style shows the beginning page name and upper-left corner of the cell block followed by the ending page name and lower-right corner of the cell block, as in A:A1..C:G10. To use the second notation style, choose the /**O**ptions **S**tartup **3**-D Syntax command; then choose the A:A1..**B**:B2 option.

When you switch notation styles, all formulas in all open notebooks switch to the new 3-D cell block notation style. The formulas in unopened notebooks will change the next time you open them into Quattro Pro. To revert to the default notation style, choose /**O**ptions **S**tartup **3**-D Syntax **A**..**B**:A1..B2.

Customizing the SpeedBar

The SpeedBar is the horizontal bar of sculpted buttons appearing at the top of Quattro Pro's WYSIWYG display mode screen or the vertical bar appearing at the right side of Quattro Pro's text display mode screen. You can customize any or all of the buttons on the READY or EDIT mode SpeedBars, as well as add additional buttons (up to a maximum of 15) to each SpeedBar. (The four arrows at the left edge of the SpeedBar aren't user-assignable.)

NOTE

The SpeedBar and the mouse pointer appear on-screen only if you have a mouse attached to your system. Quattro Pro recognizes when a mouse is present. If you have a mouse but no SpeedBar appears, make sure that a mouse driver has been installed before running Quattro Pro.

Reassigning the SpeedBar buttons is useful if you find that you frequently execute a keystroke sequence. If you frequently press Ctrl+Break, for example, to cancel a menu command and return to the active notebook, you can assign {BREAK} to one of the macro buttons.

Afterwards, when you need to press Ctrl+Break, you instead can click the button assigned to that task.

To assign a new function to one of the SpeedBar buttons, follow these steps:

1. Choose /**O**ptions Speed**B**ar.

2. A submenu listing the **READY** mode SpeedBar and **E**DIT mode SpeedBar options appears. For this example, choose **RE**ADY mode SpeedBar.

3. Choose the button you want to customize. (By default, on the READY mode SpeedBar, **A** Button corresponds to Erase, **B** Button to Copy, **C** Button to Move, and so on.) For this example, choose **O** Button, a blank button.

4. Choose **S**hort name. Type a name of up to three characters and then press Enter. For example, you can type **BRK** for Break. The short name appears on the SpeedBar when you use text display mode.

5. Choose **L**ong name. Type in a name of up to 10 characters and then press Enter. For example, type **Break** for the name. The long name appears on a SpeedBar when you display Quattro Pro in WYSIWYG display mode.

6. Choose **M**acro. Enter any valid macro command and press Enter. For this example, type **{BREAK}** for the command.

7. Choose **Q**uit twice to return to the /**O**ptions Speed**B**ar menu.

Quattro Pro enables you to assign up to 15 button entries per SpeedBar (buttons A through O). When no more SpeedBar buttons can fit within the width of your screen display, Quattro Pro replaces the rightmost button on the WYSIWYG display mode SpeedBar with the BAR button. Click the BAR button to display additional button assignments for the current SpeedBar.

The SpeedBar shown in the upper half of figure 16.18 illustrates the appearance of a notebook window when more buttons are defined than can fit onto the READY mode SpeedBar. Notice that the BAR button at the right end of the SpeedBar has replaced the Text button that normally appears in that position.

Fig. 16.18

A SpeedBar when more buttons are defined than can fit in a spreadsheet window.

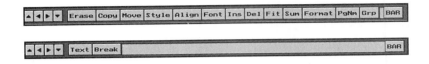

To reveal additional buttons for the READY mode SpeedBar, click the BAR button once; Quattro Pro shows the SpeedBar pictured in the lower half of figure 16.18. On this SpeedBar, notice that the Text button now appears in the first position, and the Break button—the button responsible for extending the length of this SpeedBar—appears in the second position. To return to the READY mode SpeedBar shown in the upper half of this figure, click the BAR button again.

To remove a button from a SpeedBar, delete the button's settings from the **R**EADY mode SpeedBar or **E**DIT mode SpeedBar submenus. If, for example, you choose **/O**ptions Speed**B**ar **R**EADY mode SpeedBar and then delete the **S**hort name, **L**ong name, and **M**acro definitions for **M** Button (used to define the Group button), Quattro Pro updates the READY mode SpeedBar so that the button no longer appears in its default slot.

TIP

Place the {BREAK} macro command in front of each READY mode SpeedBar button assignment. {BREAK} ensures that Quattro Pro is in READY mode before executing the action called for by the **M**acro command entry.

Figure 16.19 shows the **M**acro command entry for the Erase button. Notice that {BREAK} precedes the {/ Block;Erase} command. (The {/ Block;Erase} command is the menu equivalent of the /**E**dit **E**rase Block command, so clicking the Erase button has the effect of choosing the **E**rase Block command.)

Setting Graphics Quality Options

The /**O**ptions **G**raphics **Q**uality command enables you to choose the quality of Quattro Pro's printing graphics. Specify **D**raft or **F**inal quality.

Quattro Pro takes time to render the required font files before the program can display or print a font. Each time you choose a new font, Quattro Pro may pause to render these font files. After Quattro Pro creates a font file, the program can access that particular font the next time without making you wait.

To save time, you can choose **D**raft graphics quality to have Quattro Pro substitute Hershey fonts for Bitstream fonts. That way, Quattro Pro doesn't need to stop and render fonts. When you want to look in more detail at your file, return to **F**inal quality graphics.

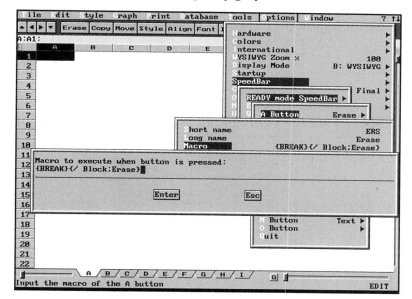

Fig. 16.19

The macro command assigned to the Erase SpeedBar button.

Using Other Options

Choosing the **O**ther command from the **O**ptions menu displays a submenu of miscellaneous system options (see fig. 16.20). Some of these options, such as the **U**ndo and **M**acro functions, become invaluable to you as you continue working with Quattro Pro. Notice that the current settings for some of the commands appear at the right margin of this submenu.

Fig. 16.20

The /**O**ptions **O**ther commands.

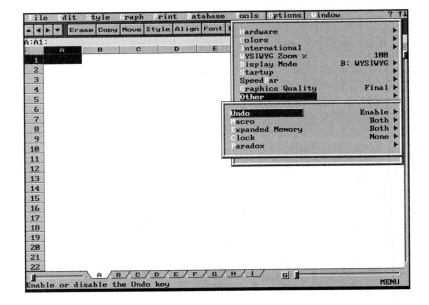

Undo

Choose /**O**ptions **O**ther **D**isable or **E**nable to control the status of the /**E**dit Undo command. Remember, this command can undo many—but not all—Quattro Pro operations.

Disabling this function speeds up Quattro Pro's operation a bit. If you are at all prone to mistakes, however, leave the **U**ndo command enabled; it's well worth the minor loss in operating speed.

Macro Redraw

The **M**acro setting on the /**O**ptions **O**ther menu enables you to specify which parts of the screen to avoid redrawing during macro execution. The default setting, **B**oth, suppresses redrawing of menus and notebook windows until macro execution is completed. This suppression speeds up the execution of macros. You can specify that Quattro Pro suppress redrawing of a notebook **P**anel or **W**indow, or you can turn off redraw suppression altogether (**N**one).

TIP

Setting /**O**ptions **R**ecalculation **M**ode to **M**anual enables your macros to execute more quickly. If necessary, press F9 (Calc) to recalculate notebook formulas after a macro finishes executing.

Expanded Memory

If your computer has Expanded Memory Specification (EMS), Quattro Pro detects and uses this memory area to store notebook data. Although this memory enables you to work with more notebooks at a time or with larger notebooks, using expanded memory exclusively for notebook information slows down performance.

Quattro Pro tries to balance speed and space considerations by storing only some of your notebooks in EMS. To influence this balance, you can specify the use of EMS with the **E**xpanded Memory option on the /**O**ptions **O**ther menu (see fig. 16.21).

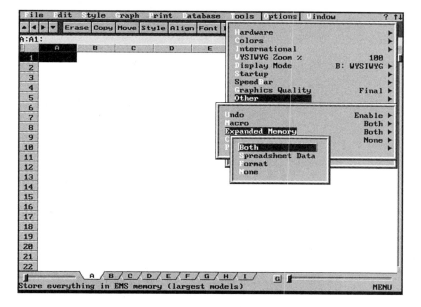

Fig. 16.21

The **E**xpanded Memory submenu.

If you are working with large files and need more memory, you may want to have Quattro Pro store notebook and format data in EMS by choosing the **B**oth option. If you need more speed from Quattro Pro, choose **S**preadsheet Data or **F**ormat. These two commands restrict

EMS usage to formulas and labels, or just formats, respectively. Choose None to ensure that Quattro Pro operates at the fastest possible speed.

TIP

If you have trouble loading large notebooks when the **E**xpanded Memory command is set to **N**one, try using the **F**ormat setting. **F**ormat enables you to load parts of the notebook into expanded memory while retaining much of the operation speed gains possible with the **N**one option.

Clock Display

The **C**lock option on the **O**ther submenu enables you to specify whether to display the time on the status line in **S**tandard format, International format, or not at all (None, the default). To specify in detail the sort of international format you want, use the /**O**ptions International Time option.

To change the clock display, follow these steps:

1. Choose /**O**ptions **O**ther **C**lock.

2. Choose one of the three options on the clock submenu: **S**tandard, International, or None.

3. Choose Update to save this setting for future work sessions.

As soon as you return to the notebook, the date and time appears on the status line (see fig. 16.22).

Fig. 16.22

Displaying the date and time on the status line.

Paradox

The **P**aradox option on the /**O**ptions **O**ther menu enables you to set options for using Paradox files on a local area network (LAN). If you are working on a LAN, you need to specify more information: the type of network you have, and the directory in which the PARADOX.NET file resides. The **P**aradox submenu provides these options through the Network Type and **D**irectory options.

Setting Network Options

The /**O**ptions **N**etwork command enables you to configure options that control how Quattro Pro operates on a network running Novell NetWare Version 2.15c or later. These options include defining drive mappings, printing jobs with an identifying banner, setting a refresh interval, and monitoring the status of print jobs in the network queue.

◀ CAUTION

Before you try to modify any network options, consult with your network administrator to make sure that you have the appropriate access rights to make such changes on your network.

Drive Mappings

To create drive mappings for a network drive, choose /**O**ptions **N**etwork **D**rive mappings. Quattro Pro prompts you to supply several pieces of information about the network: the drive letter, the file server name, the volume name, the directory path name, and the user name. You may create up to eight drive mappings to drive letters G through Z with this command.

Figure 16.23 shows two drive mappings created for users CATHY and PATRICK in the SYS volume on the B&A network drive.

◀ NOTE

Be sure to load the NetWare IPX shell before you try to create drive mappings for a network drive. Otherwise, Quattro Pro displays the error message `Network shell not loaded`. Press Esc to continue.

Fig. 16.23

Creating drive mappings to a network drive.

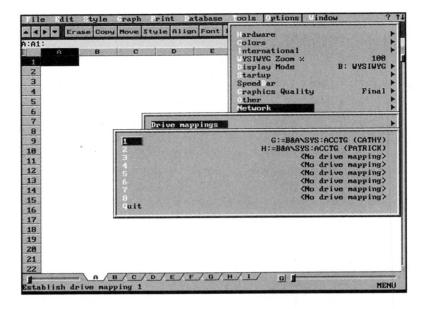

After you establish drive mappings to a network drive through Quattro Pro, you can use any of the **F**ile menu commands to read and write data to and from a network drive. To save a file named BUDGETS.WQ2 to the ACCTG directory on network drive H, for example, use the following steps:

1. Choose /**F**ile **S**ave.

2. In the file selection dialog box, click the DRV button to view a list of all local and mapped drives.

3. Click the H drive letter. Quattro Pro writes the drive letter and path (\ACCTG) on the input line and prompts you for a file name.

4. Type the file name **budgets** and press Enter.

Print Job Banners

If you want to print an identifying banner before each print job, choose /**O**ptions **N**etwork **B**anner **Y**es. Choose the **N**o option to cancel network banner printing.

The **No** setting is the same as specifying the NB command-line option to the NetWare CAPTURE command.

NOTE

Refresh Interval

The /**O**ptions Network **R**efresh Interval command determines how often Quattro Pro updates queue information in the Print Manager window and on the status line while the Queue Monitor is engaged. Valid settings range from 1 to 300 seconds. You should choose a setting that doesn't burden the network workload; your network administrator can provide this information for you.

Queue Monitor

The Queue Monitor enables you to track the progress and status of print jobs that you send to the network print queue. Choose /**O**ptions Network **Q**ueue Monitor **Y**es to turn on this feature.

When engaged, the Queue Monitor displays three pieces of information on the status line: the number of print jobs you have sent from Quattro Pro not yet printed, the number of jobs ahead of the first job you sent, and the status of the first of your uncompleted print jobs. Queue Monitor information displays atop all other status-line information for as long as your print jobs are in the network queue.

If your print job is ready to be printed, Quattro Pro displays Actv on the status line. If you have suspended your print job in the Print Manager, Quattro Pro displays Held. After your jobs finish printing, Quattro Pro displays Complete.

User Name

To set the default user name for network access and logging on, choose /**O**ptions Network **U**ser Name. When Quattro Pro prompts you for a user name, type a name of up to 32 characters and press Enter.

Updating the Options

With the exception of the **Colors** and **WYSIWYG** Zoom % commands, all the options discussed so far in this chapter are global default options. If you change your system settings but don't update Quattro Pro's resource file, you lose the new settings when you quit Quattro Pro. In this case, Quattro Pro reverts to the old default settings the next time you load the program into your computer.

To update new system settings so that they are active the next time you begin a Quattro Pro work session, choose /**O**ptions Update.

Specifying Format Options

With the **Formats** command on the **O**ptions menu, you can change how Quattro Pro displays formatted data on your notebooks (see fig. 16.24). Setting the **Formats** command options affects the current notebook window. These settings become the default settings for that notebook. The following sections discuss each option in detail.

Fig. 16.24

The **F**ormats submenu.

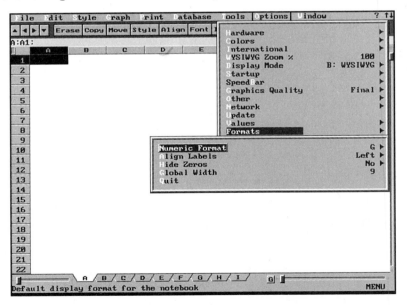

Numeric Format

The **N**umeric Format option enables you to specify the default format for displaying the values within every page in your notebook. All values are changed to the format you specify except those that have been specified with the /**S**tyle **N**umeric Format command as a block of values. Initially, the default format is **G**eneral, which right-aligns values and dates and aligns labels according to the /**O**ptions **F**ormats **A**lign Labels setting.

To change the global numeric format, follow these steps:

1. Choose /**O**ptions **F**ormats **N**umeric Format.

2. Choose a format from the submenu. (These formats are the same ones available with the /**S**tyle **N**umeric Format command.)

If you choose **D**ate, Quattro Pro presents a list of format choices for date and time options.

Align Labels

The **A**lign Labels option on the /**O**ptions **F**ormats menu enables you to specify how Quattro Pro aligns labels in a cell in every page in your notebook. Initially, alignment is set to **L**eft, but you also can choose **C**enter or **R**ight alignment.

Hide Zeros

With the **H**ide Zeros option on the /**O**ptions **F**ormats menu, you can suppress the display of any cell whose value equals zero, whether the zero was entered directly or returned as the result of a formula calculation. This setting affects only the active notebook page, so if you want to hide zeros on other pages in the same notebook, you must activate the pages one by one and choose the **H**ide Zeros option.

When zero suppression is on, you easily can assume that a zero cell is empty and then accidentally write over cells that contain needed formulas.

CAUTION

Global Width

The **G**lobal Width option enables you to specify the width of all columns on the active page at one time. The initial default width is 9 character spaces. To change the column width, choose /**O**ptions **F**ormats **G**lobal Width and type the value for the new default for the current notebook.

To change the column width globally for a different page in the active notebook, activate that page and choose the **G**lobal Width option.

Controlling Recalculation

The /**O**ptions **R**ecalculation menu options enable you to specify how Quattro Pro updates formula results when you change cell values on which those formulas depend (see fig. 16.25). These options affect every page in the active notebook.

Fig. 16.25

The **R**ecalculation submenu.

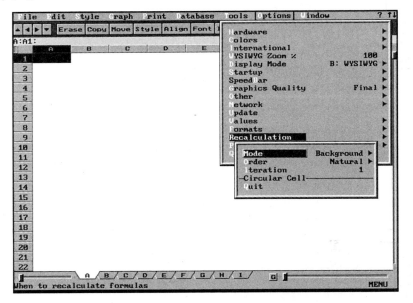

Mode

The **Mode** option enables you to specify whether Quattro Pro calculates formulas behind the scenes (**Background**), while you wait (**Automatic**), or on request (**Manual**). Choose /**O**ptions **R**ecalculation **M**ode and then choose the mode you want.

If you choose **M**anual, your notebook occasionally may need to be recalculated. When a notebook requires formula recalculation, Quattro Pro displays CALC on the status line at the bottom of the notebook window. Press F9 (the Calc key) when you want to recalculate all the formulas in a notebook.

Order of Recalculation

You can use the **O**rder option on the /**O**ptions **R**ecalculation menu to specify one of three available orders in which the set of formulas is calculated. The order in which formulas update cells can affect the resulting values.

In **N**atural order (the default), before a formula is calculated, all the cells the formula references first are recalculated. The two other options are **C**olumn-wise and **R**ow-wise. In **C**olumn-wise recalculation, Quattro Pro starts in cell A1 and proceeds down column A. When the formulas in column A are recalculated, Quattro Pro begins at the top of column B. **R**ow-wise calculation also starts at cell A1 but proceeds row by row.

Number of Iterations

Quattro Pro enables the specification of formulas that are circular in nature. A circular formula contains a cell or block address reference that includes the location of the formula. Each time you recalculate a circular formula, the formula adds itself to the resulting value. Only in the most complex of engineering or financial situations are circular references desirable.

The Iteration option enables you to specify the number of cycles of recalculation Quattro Pro should perform each time the notebook is recalculated. To specify the number of recalculation iterations if circular references exist, follow these steps:

1. Choose /Options Recalculation Iteration.

2. Enter any number up to 255 iterations.

Circular Cell

Circular Cell is a non-interactive menu field. If your notebook contains a formula with a circular reference, the address of the cell containing the formula is displayed in this field. After you correct a circular reference, this field again displays the heading Circular Cell.

Setting Protection Options

Use the /Options Protection setting to Enable and Disable protection for the active page. When enabled, this feature prevents cells that haven't been protected otherwise (with /Style Protection Unprotect) from being overwritten.

You also can assign a password to your notebook to prevent formulas from being accidentally erased or overwritten. With formula protection in place, the only way to edit cells containing formulas is to enter a password and remove the protection.

To password-protect your formulas, follow these steps:

1. Choose /Options Protection Formulas Protect (see fig. 16.26).

2. Type a password. This password is required to remove protection so that cells containing formulas can be edited.

3. Press Enter. Quattro Pro prompts you to verify the password you just entered.

4. Retype the password exactly, matching cases. Press Enter.

    If you enter the password differently the second time, you see the message Passwords do not match. Press Enter to return to the Options menu.

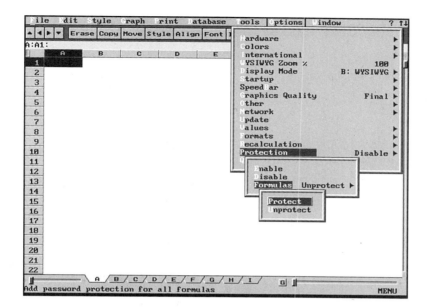

Fig. 16.26

Assigning a password to protect formulas in the active notebook page.

Any user trying to edit a formula-protected cell receives the message Formula protection is enabled. To be able to edit the formula, the user must supply the appropriate password.

CAUTION

Passwords are case-sensitive. If you type a word in all uppercase, all lowercase, or mixed format when you set your password, you must re-type it exactly when you want to remove protection; otherwise, you have no way to regain access to the formulas.

As you invest time and energy into a notebook, you may want to ensure that a simple error on your part doesn't result in the loss of valuable data. To avoid data loss, enable protection and/or formula protection.

Questions & Answers

This chapter introduces you to the **O**ptions menu commands. If you have questions concerning particular situations not addressed in the examples given, this section may provide the answers.

Hardware Options

Q: Quattro Pro seems to run slower than it should, yet my notebook applications aren't all that big. What's going on?

A: In general, Quattro Pro slows down because you are running out of system memory. Limited or fragmented hard disk space, however, also can affect Quattro Pro's speed. The VROOMM utility periodically writes part of the program onto your hard disk. If you have limited or fragmented space on your hard disk, the VROOMM utility becomes less efficient. To correct this situation, try deleting any unnecessary file from your hard disk drive. Then run a disk defragmentation program (such as Norton Utilities' Speed Disk) to organize the remaining files in the most efficient manner.

See how much memory is available to Quattro Pro on the **Hard-ware** submenu and then check to see how much space is free on your hard disk drive. If you have free memory and disk space, consider making the following changes on the **O**ptions menu:

- Choose /**O**ptions **D**isplay Mode and choose a text display.

- Choose /**O**ptions **C**olors **C**onditional **O**n/Off **D**isable.

- Choose /**O**ptions **O**ther **U**ndo **D**isable.

- Choose /**O**ptions **O**ther Expanded Memory **N**one, if you don't have expanded memory in your computer.

Making some or all of these changes improves Quattro Pro's operating speed. You must weigh for yourself the loss of each feature, however, against a gain in operating speed.

Q: I installed a second printer on my computer system. I also have an AB switch box so that I can change quickly from one printer to the other. Do I need to tell Quattro Pro that I have two printers?

A: Using an AB switch box isn't a substitute for configuring a second printer. Quattro Pro creates a printer driver file for each printer you configure. Not all printers use the same codes; therefore, using an AB switch box doesn't guarantee that one printer's driver file will work with a second printer.

To configure the second printer, choose /**O**ptions **H**ardware **P**rint-ers **2**nd Printer and specify the manufacturer, model, printing mode, and port connection. Next, choose /**O**ptions **U**pdate to store this information permanently. Finally, choose /**O**ptions **H**ardware **P**rinters **D**efault Printer to define this printer as the default printer.

Q: I'm getting garbled printer output. What should I check?

A: First, make sure that the definition file contains the correct configuration information. (Choose /**O**ptions **H**ardware **P**rinters and then **1**st Printer or **2**nd Printer.)

Second, if you are using a serial printer, make sure that the parity, baud rate, and stop bits match those set on your printer's configuration panel. If you don't know these values, check your printer manual.

Third, choose /**O**ptions **H**ardware **P**rinters Auto LF **N**o. Quattro Pro may be printing the data correctly but all on the same line.

Q: When I choose /**O**ptions **D**isplay Mode and choose an extended text display mode, why does Quattro Pro lock up? I can't control the selector or input commands.

A: Make sure that you have selected the correct screen driver with the /**O**ptions **H**ardware **S**creen **S**creen Type command. When in doubt, set this option to Autodetect and have Quattro Pro take over.

Q: Why does nothing happen when I choose /**O**ptions **U**pdate?

A: You don't see the effects of your system settings changes immediately, although the settings no doubt have been saved. To see whether the new system specifications are in effect, choose /**O**ptions **V**alues. Alternately, you can try out some of the affected commands to see whether the changes you made are in effect.

Default Format Options

Q: When I choose /**O**ptions **F**ormats **H**ide Zeros, Quattro Pro doesn't remove the trailing zeros from a block of values I have marked. Why?

A: This option doesn't remove trailing zeros; it enables you to suppress only the display of entries with a numeric value that equals exactly zero.

To remove trailing zeros from a value, choose one of the formats on the /**St**yle **N**umeric Format menu and reduce the number of displayed decimal places.

Q: Why isn't Quattro Pro recalculating my formulas when I enter new data into a notebook?

A: Check the mode indicator on the status line at the bottom of your notebook. If it says CALC, press F9, and Quattro Pro recalculates your formulas.

If you want Quattro Pro to recalculate formulas as the referenced data changes, choose /**O**ptions **R**ecalculation **M**ode **A**utomatic.

Summary

Chapter 16 showed you how to change many of the system settings Quattro Pro uses to interact with your computer and screen display. This chapter also discussed how Quattro Pro calculates values and sets global formats for the active notebook.

You now should understand that you may store system settings permanently by choosing the /**O**ptions **U**pdate command, and that the global format settings apply only to the active notebook.

Having completed this chapter, you should understand the following Quattro Pro concepts:

- Reconfiguring installed printers, displays, and your mouse

- Changing Quattro Pro's screen colors

- Defining formats for displaying currency symbols, numerical punctuation, and dates and times

- Changing screen display modes

- Choosing your own "start-up rules"

- Setting the miscellaneous system settings

- Renaming and redefining the function of the SpeedBar buttons

- Choosing between slower but high-quality on-screen fonts, or faster but low-quality on-screen fonts

- Defining the network environment settings

- Storing the current system settings in Quattro Pro's resource files as the new defaults

- Reviewing all current system settings in the status box

- Changing the default global notebook settings

- Specifying a recalculation mode and enabling global notebook and formula protection

The rest of *Using Quattro Pro 5.0*, Special Edition, is devoted to topics crucial to advancing your user skills. If you haven't glanced through the appendixes, do so now.

Appendix A addresses hardware, operating system, and installation issues that help you create the most efficient operating environment for Quattro Pro.

Appendix B shows you how to install and manage Quattro Pro on a local area network (LAN). Because Version 5.0 arrives "network-ready," the discussion concentrates on preparing your network for program installation.

Appendix C contains an ASCII table and instructions for using ASCII characters and decimal-equivalent codes with three commands on the Options menu. Appendix C also discusses how to convert printer codes into setup strings using the ASCII table.

Appendixes

P A R T

IV

O U T L I N E

Installing and Configuring Quattro Pro

Creating an ideal hardware and operating system environment is critical to installing and using Quattro Pro. Many possible hardware and operating system combinations exist for Quattro Pro because the program can run on an IBM PC, an 80486 system, and everything in between.

Appendix A begins by discussing how to create the ideal operating environment. Issues covered include obtaining peak performance from your computer's microprocessor, managing random-access memory (RAM), managing your disk effectively, selecting an appropriate video display and printer, and using peripherals.

Throughout the discussion, you can take stock of your computer equipment. You may discover a need for additional hardware. Because Quattro Pro can use your equipment effectively, however, you may find that your computer system is sufficient to install Quattro Pro.

The next section offers step-by-step instructions for installing your copy of Quattro Pro.

CAUTION

If you now use an earlier version of Quattro Pro, read "Upgrading from a Previous Version of Quattro Pro" in this appendix before you install Version 5.0 on your computer. The upgrading section tells you to delete certain files from the existing Quattro Pro directory before you install the new version so that files from two different versions of Quattro Pro aren't mixed together.

After Quattro Pro is installed, you can reconfigure many hardware settings from the Options menu. The commands on this menu enable you to fine-tune your copy of Quattro Pro until you attain the most productive operating environment.

This appendix concludes with a look at some common questions and answers about installing the program. Scan the last section for quick solutions to questions concerning system configuration or program installation.

Setting Up the Ideal System Configuration

The ideal system configuration depends on your computer equipment. Unless you can afford to purchase a fully loaded 80486 system with a great deal of RAM, a math coprocessor chip, a VGA display, and so on, you are in the same boat as most Quattro Pro users. Most users can benefit from knowing several tricks for getting the best performance from their computer equipment.

Program Requirements

To operate Quattro Pro, you must have at least the following hardware and operating system software available:

Hardware

- IBM XT, AT compatible, or PS/2
- 512K of RAM (640K recommended)

- 6M of free space on your hard disk drive

- A monochrome graphics display system

Operating system

- DOS 2.0 or later

The following configuration is an example of an ideal operating environment for using Quattro Pro:

Hardware

- 80486-based computer

- 2M of RAM

- 10M of free space on your hard disk drive

- Super VGA graphics display system

- Microsoft or Logitech mouse or compatible

Operating systems

- DOS 6.0

- Microsoft Windows 3.1

Quattro Pro's performance improves noticeably when you can improve the recommended minimum hardware configuration. Not all users have access to 80486-based computers and have to make the best of what they have. Fortunately, even with the minimum recommended configuration, Quattro Pro performs well.

Microprocessor Clock Speed and Math Coprocessor Chip

Your computer's microprocessor clock speed determines how fast Quattro Pro processes commands. The original IBM PC and XT systems use the 8086 or 8088 chip, running at 4.77 MHz (megahertz). A *hertz* is a unit of frequency equal to one cycle per second. A *megahertz* equals 1 million cycles per second.

The AT systems use an 80286 chip with clock speeds ranging from 6 to 25 MHz. The 80386 chips process data from 16 to 33 MHz. The 80486 chips process data from 16 to 66 MHz. The processing speed difference between the first PC and today's powerful 80486 is truly remarkable. In some instances, the processing speed of an 80486 is 60 times faster than the speed of the original IBM PC.

Unless you want to upgrade your microprocessor chip—which may mean purchasing a new computer system—only two methods exist for speeding up Quattro Pro execution with the microprocessor. First, if your current chip has an adjustable clock speed, make sure that the clock speed is on the highest setting.

Second, you can purchase a math coprocessor chip. These add-on chips decrease your microprocessor's workload by assuming many of the number-crunching responsibilities. Best of all, math chips are relatively inexpensive—$70-$400 in most cases. Quattro Pro detects the presence of a math coprocessor chip—no special installation is necessary.

Random-Access Memory Management

To use Quattro Pro, your personal computer must have a minimum of 512K of random-access memory (RAM). Quattro Pro can operate more efficiently with more RAM. Gains in efficiency come in two forms: the capability to create bigger notebooks with more complex formulas, and increased program execution speed.

Most PC systems come with a minimum of 640K of RAM. DOS uses this first 640K of RAM—otherwise known as *conventional memory*—to store program code and other data while your computer is on. When your computer has 640K of RAM, DOS uses what memory is available to store Quattro Pro program code; the rest is available for building and temporarily storing notebooks.

When you have other software programs running on your system, they also require some of the 640K. Terminate-and-stay-resident (TSR) programs such as SideKick, Superkey, RAM drives, print spoolers, and mouse drivers, for example, load into your system's RAM and remain there during Quattro Pro work sessions. The RAM that your computer allocates to these programs decreases the memory available to Quattro Pro for building notebooks.

You can add two types of memory beyond the 640K of RAM: *extended memory* and *expanded memory*. The first extra 384K of RAM that you add to the basic 640K is *high memory*, which is used primarily to store CPU instructions and video display data. Neither DOS nor Quattro Pro can use this memory as is to store program code or notebook data.

Memory beyond 1M is extended memory, which is used by RAM disks, print spoolers, and Microsoft Windows applications. DOS and Quattro Pro cannot access and use extended memory for notebook data. Fortunately, however, memory drivers enable you to configure extended memory as expanded memory.

Quattro Pro can use expanded memory to store notebook labels, values, and formatting. This memory usually comes on a card that you plug into an expansion slot inside your computer. Expanded-memory cards are sold with software driver programs that enable you to install the cards for use with your computer (the names of four cards that Quattro Pro supports are listed later in this section). You add the driver name to your CONFIG.SYS file.

> **TIP**
>
> Quattro Pro 5.0 provides an expanded memory utility, EMSTEST.COM, for detecting and testing basic EMS functions. Run this program after you finish installing the program on your computer.

Regardless of how your memory is configured, recognize that all RAM has the same purpose—to store data while your computer is on. What differentiates one type of memory from the other is that DOS can recognize and use only the first 640K of RAM. Although Quattro Pro recognizes and uses expanded memory, the program cannot use extended memory. Remember the following rule of thumb: if your computer has more than 640K of RAM, configure the additional memory as expanded memory so that Quattro Pro can use it.

One of Quattro Pro's most unique features is the *Virtual Real-Time Object-Oriented Memory Manager (VROOMM)*. Borland created this RAM-management utility to enable Quattro Pro to work on a wide range of PCs. VROOMM technology takes into account the different memory allocation schemes used by different systems. With VROOMM, you can manage your memory better by allocating as much RAM as possible to notebook operations. VROOMM accomplishes this allocation by loading small portions of program code on an as-needed basis.

VROOMM works no matter what memory configuration your computer has. If your computer system has less than 1M of RAM, and all memory above 640K is configured as extended memory, you can invoke a special start-up parameter to tell Quattro Pro to set up a cache for VROOMM objects in extended memory.

To use VROOMM in this way, type **q /x** at the DOS prompt and press Enter to load Quattro Pro. If you are using Microsoft Windows, enter **/x** into the **O**ptional Parameters text box inside Quattro Pro's PIF file. (Quattro Pro copies a PIF file named Q.PIF into the program directory during installation.) Similarly, you can enter **q /x** as the final line in the AUTOEXEC.BAT file. Each time you boot your system, Quattro Pro loads with VROOMM object caching in place.

This start-up parameter isn't recommended for systems with more than 1M of RAM. Remember, always configure memory above 1M as expanded memory. Quattro Pro operates with any LIM 3.2 or 4.0 card and supports the following expanded memory cards:

    Intel Above Board

    AST RAMpage!

    Quadram Liberty

    STB Memory Champion

External features such as operating systems, memory-resident utilities, and application drivers affect the amount of RAM available to Quattro Pro. You can maximize the memory available to Quattro Pro by removing unused peripheral driver programs and TSR applications from your system's memory. These programs consume RAM that Quattro Pro otherwise can use for storing notebook data. To free up RAM used by a TSR application or set aside for peripheral driver programs, remove the program name from the CONFIG.SYS or AUTOEXEC.BAT file and reboot your system.

The simplest way to remove a program name from a CONFIG.SYS file or an AUTOEXEC.BAT file is to create a new, streamlined CONFIG.SYS or AUTOEXEC.BAT file. To create a new, streamlined CONFIG.SYS file, for example, follow these steps:

NOTE

Make a copy of your original CONFIG.SYS file before creating a new file, in case you later want to revert back to the original file. To make a copy, rename CONFIG.SYS to CONFIG.OLD before you proceed with these steps.

1. At the DOS command prompt, type the following and press Enter:

   copy con config.sys

2. Type the following information into the file (press Enter after each line):

   files=20
   buffers=20

3. Press Ctrl+Z to save the file CONFIG.SYS on your hard disk.

4. Reboot the system to place the new CONFIG.SYS file into effect.

Entering data into a notebook, building a graph, and opening multiple notebooks are examples of internal activities that consume your computer's RAM. You can maximize the memory available to Quattro Pro by building efficient notebooks. Quattro Pro activities such as cell formatting, using the Undo feature, and opening multiple notebooks consume system memory. To minimize this memory loss, follow these rules:

■ *Regain unused memory blocks.* Quattro Pro uses system memory in blocks. The larger the active area of a notebook, the more memory Quattro Pro needs. When you erase areas of your notebook, memory remains allocated but unused. First, save your notebook. Then, erase the notebook from memory and recall the notebook. Quattro Pro recalls the notebook into a smaller memory block.

■ *Review the number of open notebook files.* Keep open only those notebook files that must be open for the Quattro Pro session at hand. Close unneeded documents to recover system memory.

■ *Recover memory by erasing unneeded data and cell formats from the current notebook.* Quattro Pro uses memory to retain the data and cell formats for the current notebook(s).

■ *Build streamlined notebooks.* Rather than create huge notebooks to assimilate large volumes of data, try using several smaller linked notebooks. You can recall and update several smaller notebooks faster—and with less memory used—than struggling with large notebooks. If, however, you are using several notebooks, each containing a small amount of data, combine them into one larger notebook. The idea is to find the happy medium between using one large, memory-intensive notebook and several small notebooks, which, when loaded into memory at the same time, can be equally memory-intensive.

Hard Disk Drive Management

Borland recommends a minimum of 6M of free space on your hard disk for Quattro Pro. This figure is based on the total disk storage space necessary for the program files, font files, and several notebook and graph files.

If you don't have this much free space on your hard disk drive, you must delete files until you do have enough free space before you can install Quattro Pro.

Video Displays and Printers

Quattro Pro supports all the video display types available in today's market and the following graphics cards:

- IBM Color/Graphics Adapter
- Hercules Graphics Card (monochrome)
- IBM Enhanced Graphics Adapter (monochrome or color)
- IBM Video Graphics Array (monochrome or color)
- IBM 3270/PC and 3270/AT with APA
- AT&T 6300 640x640
- MCGA (IBM Model 30)
- IBM 8514 Graphics Adapter

Quattro Pro also supports most dot-matrix, daisywheel, laser, inkjet, and PostScript printers.

The Super VGA graphics display system is the current state of the art in video displays. This display type offers superior color graphics and unsurpassed resolution. If you can afford one, a Super VGA display system is the ideal way to display Quattro Pro graphs on-screen.

Fortunately, Quattro Pro enables you to build and annotate graphs with just a graphics card and a monochrome display capable of high-resolution graphics. If you don't have a graphics card, you can build and print graphs, but you cannot see them on-screen.

You also can display Quattro Pro in text or graphics display modes. You can toggle between the two modes from the Quattro Pro **O**ptions menu or by clicking the Text and WYS buttons on the SpeedBar.

Mice

If you never have used a mouse, you are missing out on a great productivity tool. Building Quattro Pro notebooks is easier and more efficient when you use a mouse and a keyboard together. Quattro Pro supports all mice compatible with the Microsoft mouse interface, including the Microsoft serial and bus mice, the Mouse Systems mouse (with the MSMOUSE driver), and the Logitech mouse.

Installing the Program

Quattro Pro's installation utility is self-explanatory and mostly self-running. Before you begin installing Quattro Pro, review the following list to ensure that you have the correct system configuration for using Quattro Pro:

- IBM-XT, IBM-AT, or PS/2-compatible computer with at least 512K of RAM

- IBM DOS Version 2.0 or later, or MS-DOS Version 2.0 or later

- Hard disk drive with at least 6M of available storage space

- RAM exceeding 1M defined as expanded memory

Your CONFIG.SYS file must contain the following statements:

```
BUFFERS=20
FILES=20
```

TIP

The Quattro Pro installation utility can make the necessary changes to your CONFIG.SYS and AUTOEXEC.BAT files. During installation, the program will ask whether you want to have Quattro Pro change the files for you. Choose Yes. For complete details, see the section "Entering Your Name and Serial Number" later in this appendix.

Using the installation utility is the easiest way to change those files. To change the files yourself—for example, to add the driver name for an expanded memory card—use a word processing program in non-document or DOS text file mode.

The AUTOEXEC.BAT file path statement should contain C:\QPRO, the name of the directory in which Quattro Pro resides. This statement enables you to start Quattro Pro from the DOS prompt at any directory on your hard disk. Without C:\QPRO in the path statement, you can start Quattro Pro only from the QPRO directory.

Copying Files

During the first part of the installation process, Quattro Pro copies program files to the default directory. To start the installation, place installation disk 1 into any available floppy drive (drive A, for example). From your DOS C:\ prompt, type **a:\install** and press Enter. After a moment or two, the screen shown in figure A.1 appears.

Fig. A.1

The initial installation screen.

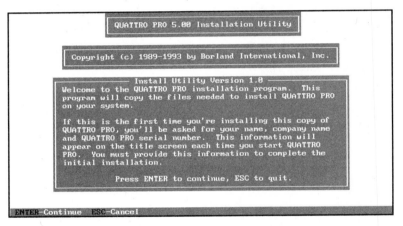

> **NOTE**
>
> If your screen is unreadable, press Esc to quit the installation, type **a:\install /b**, and then press Enter. The installation utility will load in black and white.

Figure A.1 shows that Quattro Pro first requires your name, company name, and the serial number from installation disk 1. Because you cannot complete the installation without this information, gather it before continuing. Press Enter to begin the installation or Esc to quit.

Quattro Pro can install itself from any drive you specify. When you press Enter at the initial installation screen, Quattro Pro displays the screen shown in figure A.2. Note that the program knows which drive you have started from, and suggests that drive letter as the default source drive to use (drive B in fig. A.2). Generally, drive A or drive B is the source drive from which you copy the Quattro Pro files. If you copy the Quattro Pro files onto your hard disk before installing the program, that drive's letter (for example, C or D) will appear as the source drive.

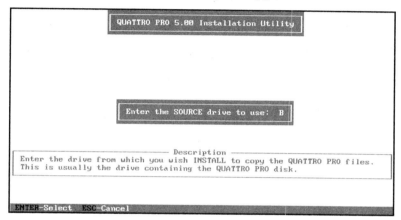

Fig. A.2

Selecting the source drive from which to install Quattro Pro.

The installation utility ensures that you have enough free storage space on your computer's hard disk drive and displays the directory to which files are copied (see fig. A.3). To install Quattro Pro into a different path on your hard disk drive, press F2 to change the default selection, use the arrow keys to move to your selection, and press Enter. When you're finished, press Enter to continue or press Esc to quit.

You cannot use a mouse at any time during the installation of Quattro Pro.

NOTE

If you don't have at least 6M of free storage space, Quattro Pro displays an error message telling you so. If you see this error message, press Esc three times to exit the installation program and delete files from your hard disk drive until you free up at least 6M of storage space.

The installation utility copies the Quattro Pro files to the default path, \QPRO (or to the path you specified in the preceding section). During this process, Quattro Pro prompts you to change disks and press a key until the files are copied from all disks (see fig. A.4).

Fig. A.3

Choosing the destination
drive and Quattro Pro
directory name.

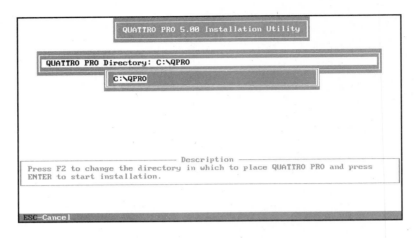

Fig. A.4

Copying Quattro Pro
files.

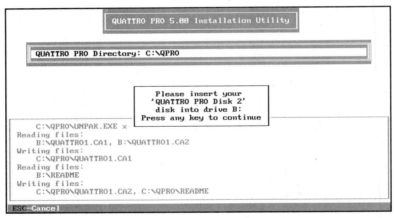

You see the progress of the installation on-screen as the installation
utility reads and writes files. After all the files are transferred, Quattro
Pro displays the message shown in figure A.5.

When you see the screen pictured in figure A.5, you have completed
phase one of the installation process. If your screen doesn't look like
the one shown in figure A.5, you must start the installation again. As
long as you swapped disks correctly when prompted by Quattro Pro,
you are ready to move on to phase two of the installation procedure.

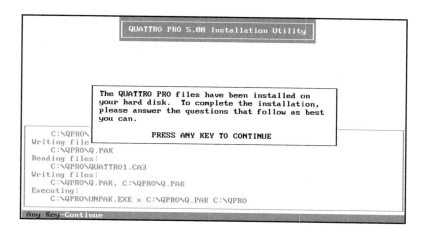

Fig. A.5

A successful file transfer.

Selecting Your Equipment

You must tell Quattro Pro about your equipment. In the second phase of installation, you select a monitor type, determine whether you will operate Quattro Pro on a network, and define how Quattro Pro will display notebooks, printouts, and graphs.

Selecting a Monitor Type

The installation utility detects whether you have a color graphics display card installed in your computer. You must tell Quattro Pro, however, whether your monitor is color, monochrome, or gray scale (see fig. A.6).

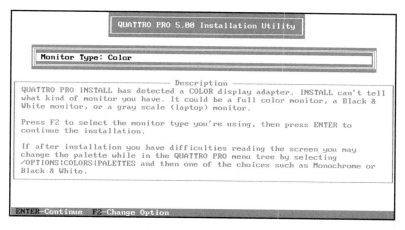

Fig. A.6

Specifying a color, monochrome, or gray-scale monitor.

To change the default selection, press F2, use the arrow keys to move to your selection, and press Enter. When finished, press Enter to continue or press Ctrl+X to quit.

Entering Your Name and Serial Number

The installation program next displays a screen prompting you to enter your company name, your name, and the serial number that appears on disk 1. You must supply this information to complete the installation.

The program then asks whether you want to install Quattro Pro on a network server. The default setting is No. To install Quattro Pro 5.0 on a network server, press F2, choose Yes, and press Enter. (Refer to Appendix B, "Installing Quattro Pro on a Network," for instructions on installing Quattro Pro on a network server.) After you finish, press Enter to continue or Ctrl+X to quit.

The installation program next asks whether you want to edit the AUTOEXEC.BAT and CONFIG.SYS files. The default setting is Yes. Press Enter to have the program add C:\QPRO to the path statement in the AUTOEXEC.BAT file and also set the FILES and BUFFERS values in your CONFIG.SYS file. If you prefer to modify the AUTOEXEC.BAT and CONFIG.SYS files yourself, press F2, choose No, and press Enter.

Selecting a Printer

Select a printer manufacturer and model from the Printer Manufacturer screen (see fig. A.7). Press F2, use the arrow keys to highlight the appropriate manufacturer, and then press Enter. If your printer manufacturer isn't listed, check your printer manual for information on the types of printers your printer can emulate. Many printers emulate Epson and IBM printers.

After you select a printer manufacturer, Quattro Pro displays the Printer Model screen (see fig. A.8). To choose a printer model, highlight the appropriate name on the list and press Enter. Press Enter again to continue.

After you select a printer model, Quattro Pro asks you to choose an initial mode at which to print notebooks and graphs. Figure A.9 displays a high-resolution mode in which the dots per inch (dpi) setting is 240x216, and the paper size setting is 8 1/2 by 11 inches.

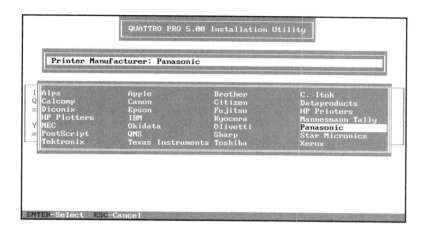

Fig. A.7

Selecting Panasonic as
a printer manufacturer.

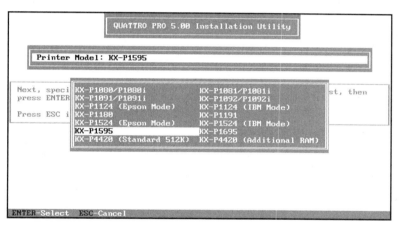

Fig. A.8

Selecting KX-P1595 as
a printer model.

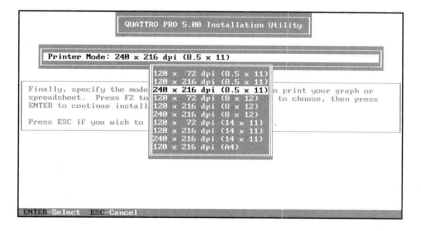

Fig. A.9

Selecting a default
printer mode.

By default, Quattro Pro highlights the first mode setting on the Printer Mode screen. The first setting always selects the lowest resolution supported by your printer. You can select a medium or high mode by pressing F2 and selecting a different option.

The actual dpi ratings available on this menu depend on the individual printer. If you select an Epson LQ-2500 printer, for example, the dpi rating in high mode is 360x180.

Selecting the Default Display Mode

You next decide whether or not to use WYSIWYG as the default display mode. WYSIWYG display mode offers the highest resolution and crispest display of all available Quattro Pro display modes. To use this mode, you must have installed in your PC an EGA or VGA graphics display card that supports at least 640x350 resolution.

TIP

WYSIWYG, or "what you see is what you get," is a common computer term that describes a state-of-the-art design capability. With WYSIWYG, what you create on-screen in Quattro Pro is what you get when you print a notebook to the printer.

If you choose Yes (see fig. A.10), Quattro Pro uses WYSIWYG as the default display mode each time you begin a work session.

Fig. A.10

Choosing WYSIWYG as the default display mode.

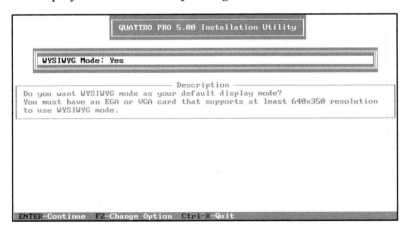

```
                  QUATTRO PRO 5.00 Installation Utility

     WYSIWYG Mode: Yes

                              Description
     Do you want WYSIWYG mode as your default display mode?
     You must have an EGA or VGA card that supports at least 640x350 resolution
     to use WYSIWYG mode.




 ENTER-Continue   F2-Change Option   Ctrl-X-Quit
```

Installing for Use with Microsoft Windows

Quattro Pro asks whether you want to install Quattro Pro to work with Microsoft Windows. The default setting is No. If you use Windows on your computer, press F2, highlight Yes, and then press Enter (see fig. A.11). Press Enter once more to continue.

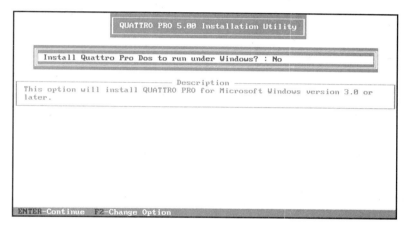

Fig. A.11

Installing Quattro Pro for use with Microsoft Windows.

Quattro Pro then asks you for the path to the Windows directory. Press F2, type the drive letter and path name, and press Enter. Press Enter again to continue. The next time you load Windows, Quattro Pro creates and stores a special icon inside a group window called QPRO (see fig. A.12). This icon-creation procedure occurs only once. To start the Quattro Pro program from Windows, double-click the Quattro Pro 5.0 icon.

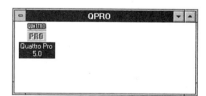

Fig. A.12

The Windows program icon for Quattro Pro 5.0.

Selecting the Character Set

Next, choose the character set used by Quattro Pro. Quattro Pro uses the character set definition when displaying the default Bitstream-SC fonts. The choices on this menu are Standard U.S. (the default) and Standard European (see fig. A.13).

Fig. A.13

Selecting the character
set to use with Quattro
Pro.

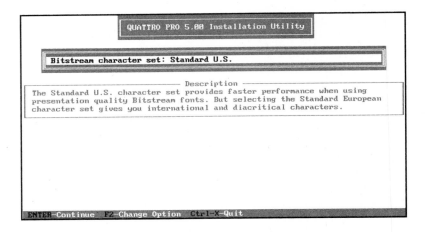

If you want to display any special characters or diacritical marks that
are part of the international character set, press F2, choose Standard
European, and press Enter. When finished, press Enter to continue.

Completing the Installation

After the installation utility successfully installs Quattro Pro, the screen
shown in figure A.14 appears. Press Enter to leave the installation utility and return to DOS. Next, press Ctrl+Alt+Del to reboot your machine
to place all changes made to your AUTOEXEC.BAT and CONFIG.SYS
files into effect.

Fig. A.14

The Successful
Installation screen.

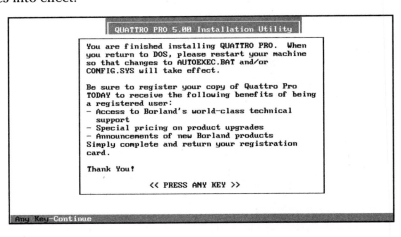

If Quattro Pro fails to transfer all configuration files successfully, you must begin the process again. Installation can fail for a number of reasons. The most common reason for failure is because the hard disk drive is full. Make sure that you have 6M of space on your hard disk before attempting to install Quattro Pro.

Upgrading from a Previous Version of Quattro Pro

Upgrading from Version 1.0, 2.0, 3.0, or 4.0 to Quattro Pro Version 5.0 is simple. Be careful, however, when you perform the steps outlined in this section, because you will delete many Quattro Pro files from at least two directories on your hard disk drive.

The Quattro Pro Version 5.0 Installation Facility doesn't upgrade all your Version 1.0, 2.0, 3.0, or 4.0 files automatically. The only files that you may use with Version 5.0 are spreadsheet files (WQ*), workspace files (WSP), clip-art files (CLP), and custom menu tree files (MU). Copy these files to another directory (outside the \QPRO directory) before you install Version 5.0.

> Make sure that you don't have any of your spreadsheet files in the QPRO directory, because you will be deleting the remaining files from this directory in an upcoming step.

CAUTION

The following procedure shows you how to prepare a hard disk drive for upgrading to Version 5.0. You should have two Quattro Pro directories: \QPRO, in which files from previous versions reside, and \QPRO\FONTS, the subdirectory in which all previous versions of the font files reside.

You must remove all Version 1.0, 2.0, 3.0, and 4.0 program files and font files from your hard disk drive before installing Version 5.0. Don't intermingle program and font files from the versions because you may get unpredictable results during your work sessions.

To prepare a hard disk drive for installation, follow these steps:

1. At the DOS command prompt, type **cd\qpro\fonts** and press Enter to go to the FONTS subdirectory.

2. Type **del *.*** and press Enter to delete all Version 1.0, 2.0, 3.0, or 4.0 font files from the FONTS subdirectory.

3. Type **cd..** and press Enter to go to the QPRO directory.

4. Type **del *.*** and press Enter to delete all Version 1.0, 2.0, 3.0, or 4.0 program files from the QPRO directory.

NOTE

The DOS DEL command deletes only files that have read-write status. If you originally changed the attributes of your program files to read-only, you must make your files read-write before you try to delete them. Otherwise, the installation procedure fails when Quattro Pro tries to install the new program files.

If you used the BSINST.EXE or SPDINST.EXE programs to convert third-party Bitstream fonts for use with earlier versions of Quattro Pro, you must rebuild those fonts using the same Bitstream font installation program. You can rebuild these fonts after you complete the installation of Version 5.0.

TIP

To rebuild Bitstream typefaces with a BCO extension, use the BSINST.EXE program. To rebuild Bitstream typefaces with a SPD extension, use the SPDINST.EXE program.

To start a Bitstream font installation program, place the diskette that contains the fonts into a floppy drive. At the DOS prompt, type the name of the font installation program, press the space bar to insert a space, and then type the drive letter where you placed the font disk. Type, for example, **bsinst a:** to install BCO-type fonts on a diskette in your A drive, or **spdinst b:** to install SPD-type fonts on a diskette in your B drive.

Press Enter and follow the screen prompts as they appear to rebuild those fonts for use with Quattro Pro Version 5.0. After you complete these steps, load Quattro Pro. The Bitstream fonts you installed are available on the /**S**tyle **F**ont **T**ypeface menu.

Finally, if you are using Borland's Pro View, Pro Show Value Pack, or Presentation Pack, you must reinstall them for use with Quattro Pro 5.0.

You must translate custom menu trees from earlier versions of Quattro Pro before you can use them in Version 5.0. To translate a custom menu tree created in Quattro Pro Version 1.0, 2.0, 3.0, or 4.0, first copy your custom menu tree files back into the newly installed \QPRO directory. Then run the NEWMU.BAT program to convert each custom menu tree file into a Version 5.0 menu tree file. To convert a custom Version 4.0 menu tree named CUSTOM4.MU into a Version 5.0 menu tree, for example, type the following at the DOS command prompt and then press Enter:

newmu c:\qpro\custom4 c:\qpro\custom5

You must supply a different name for the converted menu tree. Quattro Pro does not convert a menu tree using the same name.

Loading and Quitting Quattro Pro

To load Quattro Pro, type **q** at the DOS prompt and then press Enter.

To quit the program, choose **F**ile **E**xit (type **/FX**) or press Ctrl+X. Quattro Pro returns to the operating system.

Reconfiguring and Enhancing Quattro Pro

You never should have to install Quattro Pro 5.0 on the same computer again. Many software companies require that you reinstall their programs when you want to alter the way your computer equipment interacts with the software.

You easily can reconfigure your copy of Quattro Pro. You can add new printers, customize the SpeedBar buttons, and switch the display mode directly from Quattro Pro's **O**ptions menu (see Chapter 16, "Customizing Quattro Pro").

Questions & Answers

This section deals with commonly asked questions and start-up problems and solves glitches encountered when creating the ideal system configuration and installing Quattro Pro.

Ideal System Configuration

Q: Why does Quattro Pro operate slowly on my system?

A: If you have expanded memory, make sure that the EMS driver is included in the CONFIG.SYS file.

If your system has between 640K and 1,024K bytes of RAM, load Quattro Pro by typing **q /x** at the DOS prompt. The /x option enables Borland's VROOMM memory manager to use extended memory for object caching.

Q: Why doesn't my mouse work properly when I use Quattro Pro's graphics display mode?

A: Older mouse drivers support only 80x24 screen displays. Quattro Pro supports EGA 80x43, VGA 80x50, and EGA/VGA graphics modes. To display Quattro Pro in a mode other than 80x24, your mouse driver version must conform to the following specifications:

Brand	Version
Microsoft Mouse	6.11 or higher
Mouse Systems	6.01 or higher
Logitech	4.0 or higher
PC Mouse	6.01 or higher

Installation Utility

Q: The text of the installation utility is difficult to read. What can I do?

A: Press Ctrl+X to exit INSTALL. Then type **a:install /b** and press Enter to force Quattro Pro to display in a black-and-white mode (type **a:install /m** for monochrome).

Q: The computer displays the message Not enough disk space to install Quattro Pro when I try to install the program. What can I do?

A: Exit the installation utility. Erase nonessential files from your hard disk drive until you have at least 6M of free storage space on your hard disk drive. (Keep in mind that 6M is equal to 6,144,000 bytes of disk space, not 6,000,000 bytes.)

Q: I am upgrading from a previous version of Quattro Pro and noticed that during installation, I wasn't prompted to install any fonts. Did I do something wrong?

A: No. Quattro Pro Version 5.0 uses faster Bitstream-SC fonts in place of the Bitstream fonts that came in Version 3.0.

In previous versions of the program, prebuilding a single bit-mapped font file (.FON) for each point size within a particular typeface file (.SFO) was necessary; in Version 4.0 and Version 5.0, the Bitstream-SC fonts use a single typeface file (.SPO) and a single bit-mapped font file (.FN2). This improvement in Quattro Pro's font management technology has eliminated the need for building fonts in advance during installation.

Q: The computer displays the message Not enough memory to run Quattro Pro when I try to load the program. What can I do?

A: Erase all TSR programs from your CONFIG.SYS and AUTOEXEC.BAT files. Reboot your system and try again.

If your computer has expanded memory that conforms to the LIM 3.2 or 4.0 standard, the memory card may not be Quattro Pro-compatible. Run EMSTEST.COM (in the QPRO directory) from DOS to test whether your EMS memory is configured correctly. If the EMSTEST.COM utility encounters errors, contact the manufacturer of your expanded memory board.

Try loading Quattro Pro without loading the EMS driver through the CONFIG.SYS file. Load CONFIG.SYS into a word processing program as a DOS text file. Delete the name of the driver program, save the file, and then reboot your computer so that the new CONFIG.SYS settings take effect.

Create an alternate, streamlined CONFIG.SYS file by following these steps:

1. Rename the CONFIG.SYS file to CONFIG.OLD.

2. At the DOS command prompt, type the following and press Enter:

    COPY CON CONFIG.SYS

3. Now type the following information into the file (press Enter after each line):

> **files=20**
> **buffers=20**

4. Press Ctrl+Z to save the file CONFIG.SYS on your hard disk.

5. Press Ctrl+Alt+Del to reboot the system and place the new CONFIG.SYS file into effect.

Installing Quattro Pro on a Network

With a few notable exceptions, installing Quattro Pro on a network is similar to installing the program on a single PC. (Appendix A covers single PC installation.) This appendix contains information that shows network administrators how to install Quattro Pro successfully on a local area network (LAN).

This appendix begins by discussing the hardware and software required to install and operate Quattro Pro on a network server. The second section shows how to prepare a network server for installation. To prepare the network server, you create special directories to store program files, shared data files, and each user's private files. The third section contains step-by-step instructions for installing Quattro Pro on a network server.

After installing Quattro Pro on the network server, you prepare each workstation to use Quattro Pro. A section of the appendix shows how to prepare each workstation and create start-up defaults for each user. Then you learn how to add additional users after you install Quattro

Pro on a network server. For each Quattro Pro user you want to add to the network, you must purchase a Quattro Pro LAN Pack from Borland.

This appendix also includes a step-by-step explanation of the procedure to follow if you need to upgrade a Quattro Pro Version 3.0 or 4.0 network configuration to Version 5.0.

CAUTION

If you now use Version 3.0 or 4.0 on a network, read the section "Upgrading a Network from Version 3.0 or 4.0 to Version 5.0" later in this appendix before you install Version 5.0 on your computer. The upgrading section instructs you to delete certain files from the existing Quattro Pro directory before you install the new version so that files from two different versions of Quattro Pro are not mixed together.

One section of the appendix discusses the difference between using Quattro Pro on a single PC and concurrently on multiple workstations.

This appendix concludes with a look at some common questions and answers about installing and managing the program on a network. Scan through this last section if you need a quick solution to questions concerning system configuration or program installation issues.

What You Need To Run Quattro Pro on a Network

To install and operate Quattro Pro on a network server, you must have at least the following hardware and operating system software available:

Hardware

- A network server (preferably a dedicated server) with at least 6M of free hard disk space

- One or more 100% IBM-PC compatible workstations, each with at least 640K of RAM

- A monochrome or color graphics display system

Operating systems

- Novell Advanced NetWare Version 2.0A or higher

- 3Com 3+ Version 1.0 or higher

- Banyan Vines network

- A network that is 100% compatible with Novell, 3Com, or Banyan Vines

- DOS 3.1 or higher

The performance of Quattro Pro improves noticeably when you can improve the recommended minimum hardware configuration. For suggestions about how to achieve optimum performance from Quattro Pro—whether you are using the program on a single PC or on multiple workstations—see the section "Setting Up the Ideal System Configuration" in Appendix A.

Preparing for Installation

The network administrator is the person best qualified to install Quattro Pro on a network server. The network administrator has the network rights necessary to copy files, create directories, and modify each workstation's operating environment. If you don't have the appropriate rights for your network, consult with the person who does.

Before installing Quattro Pro, prepare the network server by creating special directories to store program files, shared data files, and each user's private files. You must create a minimum of three directories to complete the installation preparation:

- Create a system file directory named QPRO. This directory stores the Quattro Pro program files.

- Create a shared directory named QPRODATA. This directory stores all notebook files that users can share.

- Create a private directory named QPROPRIV. Under this directory, create private subdirectories for each user (\QPROPRIV\ JEAN, for example, for a user named Jean). Each user's private subdirectory stores the user's unique Quattro Pro defaults and private data files.

■ Optionally, create a subdirectory named FONTS under the QPRO directory. The FONTS directory stores the font files that Quattro Pro creates. Note that Quattro Pro will create this directory during installation if it doesn't already exist. You may want to create it at the same time you create the system file, shared, and private directories, however, particularly if you are assigning access rights to these directories. If you do decide to create it, you must use the name FONTS so that Quattro Pro knows where to place the fonts that it renders.

For full details about assigning directory access rights, see "Assigning Access Rights to the Quattro Pro Directories" later in this appendix.

TIP

You may place the private directories on any drive that users can access from their workstations. A user may want to store all private files, for example, on the workstation's hard disk drive.

The directory names QPRO, QPRODATA, and QPROPRIV are only suggested directory names—you may call them anything you want. If you opted against creating the FONTS directory when you created the directory file, shared data, and private directories, Quattro Pro creates it as a subdirectory that appears under the system file directory (generally QPRO).

NOTE

Don't restrict access rights to the directories before installing the program. The directories all must have full read-write network rights so that Quattro Pro can copy files into the directories.

Installing the Program

Quattro Pro's installation utility is self-explanatory and mostly self-running. Before you begin, review the following checklist to ensure that you have prepared the network server correctly for installation:

■ Created a system file directory called QPRO

■ Created a private directory called QPROPRIV

■ Created one or more private subdirectories under the private directory (such as \QPROPRIV\JEAN for user Jean)

■ Assured that all aforementioned directories have read-write network rights

To begin the installation, log onto the network server from any workstation that has at least one floppy drive. Place installation disk 1 into drive A at that workstation. Type **a:\install** and then press Enter to begin the installation.

Choosing the Source Drive and Destination Directory

When prompted for the source drive, press Enter to accept the default setting (drive A).

When prompted for the Quattro Pro directory, verify that the default setting includes the correct network drive letter and system file directory name. If the default setting isn't correct, press F2 to display an edit box. Type the correct drive letter and directory path name and then press Enter to store that setting. To install Quattro Pro in a system file directory named QPRO on network drive F, for example, type **f:\qpro** (see fig. B.1).

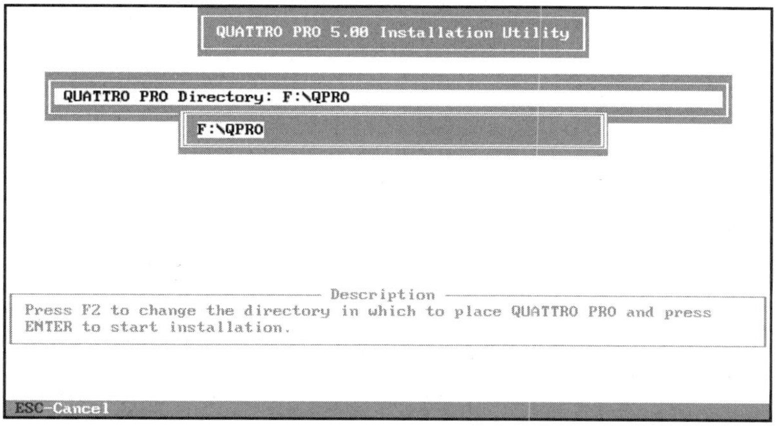

```
┌─────────────────────────────────────────────────────────────┐
│          ┌─────────────────────────────────────────┐         │
│          │ QUATTRO PRO 5.00 Installation Utility    │         │
│          └─────────────────────────────────────────┘         │
│  ┌─────────────────────────────────────────────────────────┐ │
│  │ QUATTRO PRO Directory: F:\QPRO                           │ │
│  │      ┌──────────────────────────────────────────┐       │ │
│  │      │ F:\QPRO                                   │       │ │
│  │      └──────────────────────────────────────────┘       │ │
│  └─────────────────────────────────────────────────────────┘ │
│                                                               │
│                                                               │
│  ┌──────────────────── Description ──────────────────────┐   │
│  │ Press F2 to change the directory in which to place     │   │
│  │ QUATTRO PRO and press ENTER to start installation.     │   │
│  └───────────────────────────────────────────────────────┘   │
│                                                               │
│ ESC-Cancel                                                    │
└─────────────────────────────────────────────────────────────┘
```

Fig. B.1

Choosing the drive and directory where program files will be copied.

Copying Files

Press Enter to begin copying the program files. Quattro Pro prompts you to swap disks until all files are copied into the system file directory on your network server.

Entering the Personal Signature Data

Quattro Pro next prompts you to identify your monitor type so that the program can correctly display the remaining installation screens. The program also asks you to enter information about yourself: your company name, your name, and the serial number stamped on disk 1. You must supply this personal signature data to continue the installation.

Each time you start Quattro Pro, the program displays your personal signature data on the start-up screen.

Specifying a Network Installation

Quattro Pro asks Are you installing Quattro Pro on a network server? The default setting is No for single PC installations. Press F2 and choose the Yes option (see fig. B.2).

Fig. B.2

Specifying that installation is taking place on a network server.

```
               QUATTRO PRO 5.00 Installation Utility

   Are you installing Quattro Pro on a network server?: No

                            Description
   If you're installing QUATTRO PRO for shared use on a File Server, answer
   Yes.
                                 No
                                 Yes




   ENTER-Select  ESC-Cancel
```

Quattro Pro then asks you to enter the directory for the QPRO.NET file. The QPRO.NET file controls the Quattro Pro user count on the network and must reside in a directory that has read-write network rights (use the FONTS or the QPRODATA directory, for example). Press F2 and type **f:\qprodata** (see fig. B.3). Press Enter twice to continue the installation.

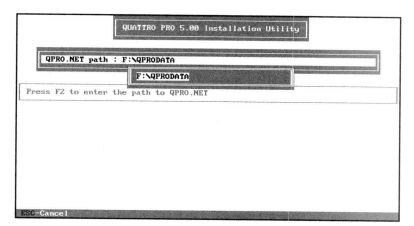

Fig. B.3

Selecting the location for the QPRO.NET file.

Selecting Your Equipment

Quattro Pro asks about the hardware you are using. Answer for the workstation from which you are installing Quattro Pro. You later can customize the hardware settings for other workstations connected to the network.

> Refer to Appendix A for comprehensive coverage of this part of the installation process.

NOTE

Recording Personal Signature Data

After you select your equipment, you must perform one final step to conclude the installation of Quattro Pro on the network server. Execute the QPUPDATE.EXE program to record your personal signature data and network name in a file called QPRO.SOM. To acquire documentation for additional users, you must purchase an appropriate number of Quattro Pro LAN Packs from Borland.

Quattro Pro copies the QPUPDATE.EXE program and the QPRO.SOM file into your system file directory (QPRO) during installation. Change to this directory now, and then execute the QPUPDATE.EXE program. Type **cd\qpro** at the DOS prompt and then press Enter.

Next, type **qpupdate** and press Enter.

The first screen that appears verifies that the QPRO.SOM file exists in your system file directory. Press Enter to continue.

The second screen displays the personal signature data you entered during the installation. You can change the name of the network administrator on this screen, but you cannot change the company name (see fig. B.4). Press F2 to continue.

Fig. B.4

Reviewing your personal signature data.

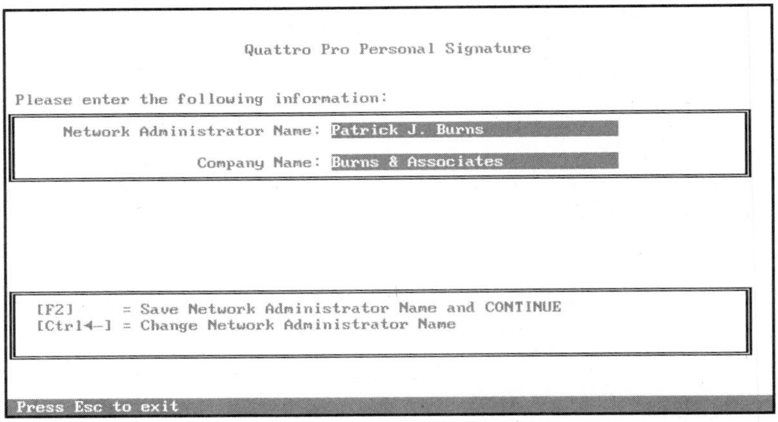

The third and final screen enables you to specify the type of network and verify the directory location for the QPRO.NET file (see fig. B.5). To specify a Novell network, for example, press 1. Then press F3 to save all information in the QPRO.SOM file and exit.

You now are ready to prepare individual workstations to operate Quattro Pro from the network server.

Preparing the Workstations

Before you operate Quattro Pro on a network server, you must prepare each workstation connected to the network server. This process involves modifying the AUTOEXEC.BAT and CONFIG.SYS files,

establishing menu tree and program defaults for each user, assigning
network access rights to all Quattro Pro directories, and updating each
user's log-on script.

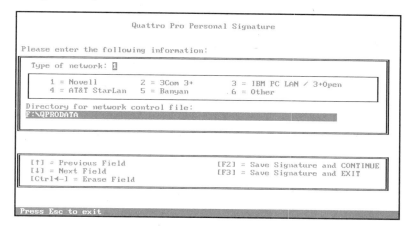

Fig. B.5

Specifying the network
type.

Before you begin, review the following checklist to ensure that each
workstation is ready for preparation:

- One private directory has been created as a subdirectory of
QPROPRIV for each Quattro Pro network user. Each private directory has full read-write-create rights.

- Each workstation has AUTOEXEC.BAT and CONFIG.SYS files.

- Each workstation has available a copy of DOS 3.1 or later (with the
DOS SHARE.EXE program).

> Each user's private directory can reside on the workstation hard disk. For
> diskless workstations, however, the private directory must reside on the
> network server.

TIP

Creating a Menu Preference File

During installation, Quattro Pro copies the default user interface file—
called a *menu tree*—that the program displays when loaded. In a network configuration, users need their own menu preference (.MP) file.
Users who created custom menu trees in an earlier version of Quattro
Pro can continue to use those menu preference files by converting

them with the MPMAKE.EXE program. Menu preference files belong in a user's private directory; don't store .MP files in the QPRO directory.

To create a menu preference file for each user, change to the system file (QPRO) directory. Type **cd\qpro**, for example, and press Enter.

Execute the MPMAKE.EXE program using the following syntax:

MPMAKE *name.mu dirname*

Here, *name.mu* is the name of the menu file to create, and *dirname* is the name of the directory in which Quattro Pro copies the .MP file. Supply a drive letter and a full directory path name for both arguments. Valid .MP files include the following:

QUATTRO.MP   A menu preference file that uses the standard Quattro Pro menu tree

CUSTOM.MP   A menu preference file that uses a custom menu tree that you created

To create an .MP file for user Jean that displays the standard Quattro Pro menu tree, for example, type the following and press Enter:

mpmake f:\qpro\quattro.mu f:\qpropriv\jean

Repeat this process for each network user who will use Quattro Pro.

TIP

Only the menu trees for which you create .MP files appear on the users' selection list when the users choose the /**O**ptions **S**tartup **M**enu System command.

Creating a Default Resource File

Each user also needs one default resource file (.RF) in his or her private directory. This file stores information about each user's preferred Quattro Pro defaults—items that users may change by using the /**O**ptions menu. This file includes screen and printer configurations, screen colors, start-up directory, default file name extension, and so on. Suppose that the custom menu tree that you have created in Quattro Pro 5.0 is named 123.MP, and you want to make that menu tree available to other users on the network. To do so, each user needs a copy of the 123.RF file.

To create a default resource file for each user, change to the system file (QPRO) directory. Type **cd\qpro** and press Enter.

Copy the RSC.RF file into each user's private directory using the DOS COPY command. To copy the RSC.RF file into user Jean's private directory, for example, type the following and then press Enter:

>   **copy rsc.rf f:\qpropriv\jean**

After a copy of the RSC.RF file exists in each user's private directory, delete the RSC.RF file from the system file directory (QPRO).

> If you forget to delete the RSC.RF file from the QPRO directory, Quattro Pro uses that as the default file for the first user that loads Quattro Pro at a workstation. Subsequent users will be unable to load Quattro Pro from their workstations.

CAUTION

Creating a Private Named Styles File

In a single PC installation, Quattro Pro stores all named styles in a single file called QUATTRO.STY. In a network environment, all Quattro Pro users share the named styles available in QUATTRO.STY. When one user changes a named style using the /Style Define Style command, those changes go into effect for every workstation on the network.

To create a private named style file for each Quattro Pro user on a network, copy the QUATTRO.STY file into each user's private directory. This directory is the same one in which their private .RF and .MP files are stored. Each user may then modify the named styles without affecting the named styles used by other users on the same network.

Modifying the AUTOEXEC.BAT and CONFIG.SYS Files

The AUTOEXEC.BAT and CONFIG.SYS files at each workstation also require some changes. The CONFIG.SYS file should contain at least the following statement:

>   FILES=20

TIP

Set FILES=40 if you intend to access Paradox database files using
Quattro Pro's /**D**atabase **P**aradox Access command.

Modify the DOS PATH statement at each workstation to reflect, in the
order shown, the following information:

- The name of a user's private directory

- The name of the system file directory (QPRO)

- The DOS SHARE command

The AUTOEXEC.BAT file for user Jean, for example, may look like the
following:

```
PATH F:\QPROPRIV\JEAN;F:\QPRO
SHARE
```

CAUTION

Don't forget to include the DOS SHARE command in each user's
AUTOEXEC.BAT file. You need the SHARE.EXE program to be able to
use Quattro Pro notebook files concurrently.

If you want to add a log-on command to an AUTOEXEC.BAT file—a command that automatically logs a user onto the network server—place
the command before the DOS PATH statement. This statement will determine which directories are part of the search path and not the path
specified in the network login script. See your network documentation
for details about coordinating search paths using the DOS PATH statement and the network login script.

The AUTOEXEC.BAT file for a user on a Novell network, for example,
may look like the following:

```
IPX
NET3
F:
LOGIN JEAN
PATH F:\QPROPRIV\JEAN;F:\QPRO
SHARE
```

In this file, the IPX command loads a network card driver, the NET3
command loads the Novell Workstation Shell, and F: switches the user
to drive F. The line LOGIN JEAN is a Novell-specific command that logs
in user Jean to the network. Now that the network-workstation connection is complete, the PATH statement containing references to the network server drive (such as F:\QPRO) is valid.

When the PATH statement appears after the LOGIN line, your network login script may supersede the DOS PATH statement. See your network documentation for details.

The DOS SHARE command is critical to the use of Quattro Pro on a network. This command loads a memory-resident DOS module that enables file sharing and file locking on a network. To use SHARE.EXE, first verify that it exists in the DOS directory on the network server. If the program doesn't exist, copy it into the DOS directory from a master DOS floppy disk. Add the name of the DOS directory (probably \DOS) to the PATH statement in each user's AUTOEXEC.BAT file.

Assigning Access Rights to the Quattro Pro Directories

Table B.1 contains a list of the suggested directory names and suggested access rights. Use the information in this table as a guide for setting up user access rights on your network. (See your network manuals for information about assigning access rights on your network.) You may want to assign different levels of access rights to different users on your network.

Table B.1 Network Directories and their Access Rights

Directory Contents	Suggested Name	Suggested Rights
System files	QPRO	Read-open-search
Fonts	FONTS (\QPRO\FONTS)	Read-write-create-modify (required)
Shared data	QPRODATA	Read-write-create-modify
Private data	QPROPRIV*username*	Full rights except Supervisor and Parental

After you assign network rights, each workstation is ready to operate Quattro Pro. Now, you should reboot each workstation to place into effect all changes made to the workstation start-up files.

Starting Quattro Pro from a Workstation

Start Quattro Pro at each workstation. If you have dedicated four serial numbers for network use, you may operate Quattro Pro concurrently at four workstations. To start Quattro Pro from DOS, switch to the user's private directory, press Q, and then press Enter.

After the program loads into each workstation, users may want to modify further the default settings for their own workstations. This process may involve selecting a different menu tree or modifying any of the Quattro Pro environment defaults using the commands found on the /Options menu. After finishing this customization process, each user must choose /Options Update to save those settings (in the RSC.RF file located in his or her private directory) for all future work sessions.

Adding Users to the Network

To increase the number of concurrent Quattro Pro users permitted on a network, purchase additional Quattro Pro LAN packs from Borland. Each Quattro Pro LAN Pack provides you with one serial number.

Prepare the new workstation to operate Quattro Pro as described in the preceding section. Remember, because each Quattro Pro user must have a private directory, be sure to create a new private directory for a new user. To add user Sara to the network, for example, create a subdirectory called SARA (QPROPRIV\SARA) and copy a set of .MP and .RF files to this directory.

Finally, check that the new users' /Options menu settings match the network hardware and the hardware in use at that particular workstation. The following checklist suggests the items you should check before starting Quattro Pro on a new workstation:

- Check the printer definition setting by choosing /Options Hardware Printers 1st Printer Type of Printer.

- Verify that the user's printer device setting matches the port connection on the network using the /Options Hardware Printers 1st (or 2nd) Printer Device command. The appropriate setting for this command is N Network Queue if the user will be printing on a shared network printer.

- Select a screen type setting that matches the user's display system using the /Options Hardware Screen Screen Type command.

- Change the Quattro Pro default directory setting to the user's private data directory with /**O**ptions **S**tartup **D**irectory command.

- Choose /**O**ptions **U**pdate to save all changes.

Upgrading a Network from Version 3.0 or 4.0 to Version 5.0

Upgrading from a Version 3.0 or 4.0 to a Version 5.0 network configuration is simple. Be careful when you perform the steps outlined in this section, however; you will be deleting many Quattro Pro files from your system file (QPRO) and font file (FONTS) directories. If these directories contain any spreadsheet files (WQ*), workspace files (WSP), clip-art files (CLP), and custom menu tree files (MU) that you want to keep, copy those files to another directory before proceeding.

Keep the following things in mind as you prepare to upgrade your network installation:

- If you originally installed additional Bitstream fonts for use with those program versions, you must reinstall the fonts after completing your installation of Quattro Pro. Be sure to reinstall the Version 3.0 or 4.0 fonts using the same, original installation utility (BSINST.EXE or SPDINST.EXE). Then, after you load Quattro Pro, your fonts appear beside the 5.0 fonts on the **T**ypeface menu when you choose the /**S**tyle **F**ont command.

- The QPRO and FONTS directories must have read-write-delete network rights before you can upgrade the Quattro Pro files.

- You must translate custom menu trees from earlier versions of Quattro Pro before they can be used in Version 5.0. To translate a custom menu tree, first copy your custom menu tree file back into the newly installed /QPRO directory. Run the NEWMU.BAT batch file to convert a custom menu tree file into a Version 5.0 menu tree file. To convert a custom Version 4.0 menu tree named CUSTOM4.MU into a Version 5.0 menu tree, for example, type the following at the DOS command prompt and then press Enter:

    newmu c: \qpro\custom4 c: \qpro\custom5

You must supply a different name for the converted menu tree. Quattro Pro does not convert a menu tree using the same name.

■ If you are using Borland's ProView, ProShow Value Pack, or Presentation Pack, you must reinstall them for use with Quattro Pro 5.0.

To upgrade to Version 5.0, follow these steps:

1. At the DOS command prompt, type **cd\qpro\fonts** and press Enter to log onto the FONTS subdirectory.

2. Type **del *.*** and press Enter to delete all font files from the FONTS subdirectory.

3. Type **cd\qpro** and then press Enter to log onto the QPRO directory.

4. Type **del *.*** and press Enter to delete all program files from the QPRO directory.

5. Run the INSTALL.EXE program on disk 1 as described in "Installing the Program" earlier in this appendix.

6. Copy a set of Version 5.0 .MP and .RF files to each user's private directory.

What's Different about Using Quattro Pro on a Network

One significant difference exists between using Quattro Pro on a single PC and on a network. On a single PC, a user has full, unrestricted access rights to all files on the PC hard disk. On a network, the network administrator assigns access rights to each user and to each directory. (For a list of suggested directory rights, see table B.1 earlier in this appendix.) Some users may be given free rein to copy, modify, delete, and create files on the network; others may have these rights only in shared data and private directories.

On a network, when several users want to modify Quattro Pro notebook files simultaneously, access-priority rules govern this activity. Basically, the first user to open a Quattro Pro data file from a shared network directory has full read-write network rights to that file. A second user may open the same file, but Quattro Pro prevents that user from saving the file under the same name in the same directory—as long as the first user continues to work with the file. As soon as the first user closes the notebook file, the second user is given full read-write network rights to that file. If a third user wants to save the same file, that user must wait for the second user to close the notebook file before saving.

In Quattro Pro, attempts to retrieve an open file cause the program to display a message asking if the user wants to open the file in read-only status. Respond **Yes** to open the file. A user can read and edit the file but cannot save it under the same name in the same directory. If the user tries to do so, Quattro Pro displays a prompt asking the user to rename the file or save it in a different directory. Choose /**F**ile Save **As** and enter the new file name or new directory name.

> **NOTE**
>
> Quattro Pro displays a sharing violation message when a user tries to save a read-only file without first changing the file name or the directory. Press Esc or Enter to remove the message and then save the file under a different name or in a different directory.

Quattro Pro Version 5.0 provides better support for network installations than previous versions of the program do. Table B.2 summarizes the Version 5.0 network features and references the chapter where you can locate more specific information about a feature.

Table B.2 Quattro Pro Version 5.0 Network Features

Feature	Command	Chapter
Create/edit a drive mapping	/**O**ptions Network **D**rive mappings	16
Show a drive mapping	/**F**ile **O**pen and click the NET button	8
Set up a user name	/**O**ptions Network **U**ser Name	16
Control banner printing	/**O**ptions Network **B**anner	16
Set up a network printer	/**O**ptions **H**ardware **P**rinters **1**st Printer **D**evice **N** Network Queue	16
Access a network drive	/**F**ile **O**pen and click the DRV button	8
View jobs in a network queue	/**P**rint **P**rint Manager and then /**Q**ueue **N**etwork	9
Monitor progress of network queue	/**O**ptions Network **Q**ueue Monitor **Y**es	16

Questions & Answers

The following sections deal with commonly asked questions and start-up problems. Here, you learn how to solve glitches encountered when installing and using Quattro Pro on a network server.

Installing the Program

Q: When I tried to install the program onto my network server drive, Quattro Pro displayed an error message saying that the drive is invalid. Why?

A: The workstation from which Quattro Pro is being installed must be physically wired to the network server and must be logged onto the network drive before you start installation. Return to DOS and use the appropriate network logon procedure to connect to the network server. Restart the installation.

Q: After I installed Quattro Pro and tried to load the program, I received the error message Cannot open QPRO.NET file. What do I do?

A: Quattro Pro couldn't find the QPRO.NET file. Make sure that QPRO.NET is located on the path specified in QPRO.SOM and that you have read-write access to that directory.

Q: I am upgrading from Quattro Pro Version 3.0 to Version 5.0 on my network. I have a system file directory named QPRO but don't have a private directory named QPROPRIV or QPRODATA. Will the installation work?

A: Yes. The only directory name that Quattro Pro requires for a successful installation is FONTS, a subdirectory it automatically creates under the system file directory. You may choose different names for the other directories or accept Quattro Pro's defaults.

Q: I accidentally installed QPRO.NET in the QPRO directory when I meant to specify QPRODATA. If I just copy the QPRO.NET file into the QPRODATA directory, will Quattro Pro load?

A: No. After you specify the path for the QPRO.NET file, you cannot change it except by updating the directory path field in the QPUPDATE.EXE program (refer to fig. B.6). Remember, the QPRO.NET file must reside in a directory with read-write network rights (hence the suggestion to use QPRODATA). If you accidentally install the file in a different directory and want to use that directory, to load Quattro Pro you must rerun QPUPDATE.EXE, specify that directory, and then assign read-write rights to that directory.

Using Quattro Pro on a Network

Q: One user on our network created a custom menu tree in Version 5.0 that we want to adopt for the entire Quattro Pro 5.0 user base on our network. Is there an easy way to adopt this customized menu tree?

A: The user who created the custom menu tree has an .MU and an .MP (menu preference) file in a private directory. Move the .MU file to the Quattro Pro system file directory (QPRO), and then copy the .MP file into each user's private directory. After each user restarts Quattro Pro, the user must choose /**O**ptions **S**tartup **M**enu System and choose the custom menu from the list. Choose /**O**ptions Update to use the custom menu tree as the default for future work sessions.

Printing on a Network Printer

Q: When I print a notebook to a shared network printer, Quattro Pro first prints a title, then prints the notebook, and then feeds a blank page out of the printer. Can I control this problem in any way?

A: Each network has its own methods for managing print jobs. On a Novell network, the CAPTURE command is useful for controlling your print jobs. Borland recommends that you use the following syntax when printing to a shared printer on a Novell network:

    CAPTURE /TI=50 /NB /NT /NFF /P=0 /NA

In this syntax, /TI=50 sets the timeout option to 50 seconds, /NB tells the network to omit the banner page, /NT and /NFF tells the network to leave all tabs and form feeds unchanged, /P=0 indicates that the name of the shared network printer is 0, and /NA disables the Autoendcap feature. See your network manuals for more specific information about controlling print jobs on a shared network printer.

Q: When I choose the /**P**rint **S**preadsheet Print command to print a notebook, nothing happens. What should I check for?

A: Choose the /**O**ptions **H**ardware **P**rinters **1**st (or **2**nd) Printer **De**vice command, which should be set to **N** Network Queue. If this setting doesn't solve the problem, try using one of the LPT settings or the Parallel setting. Experiment with each setting until you find one that works.

Using ASCII Characters

Table C.1 lists the American Standard Code for Information Interchange (ASCII) character table. The table lists 255 characters and their decimal and hexadecimal equivalents.

Entering ASCII Characters in Notebook Cells

Quattro Pro accepts all ASCII characters in notebook cells. When you create a graph from a notebook containing ASCII characters, some characters display as text in the graph.

The ASCII characters of particular importance are the international characters (such as é, £, and ¯), mathematical characters (such as π and √), and border characters.

To enter an ASCII character into a notebook cell, hold down the Alt key as you type the decimal-code equivalent on your numeric keypad. (Remember, the Num Lock key must be toggled on for your keystroke to work properly.) When you release the Alt key, the character appears on the input line.

To enter the mathematical symbol for a square root into a notebook cell, for example, follow these steps:

1. Press and hold down the Alt key.

2. Type **251** as the decimal code.

3. Release the Alt key. Quattro Pro reproduces the square root symbol on the input line at the top of your screen.

4. Press Enter to store the symbol in the cell.

Table C.1 ASCII Codes

Decimal	Hex	Graphic Character	Decimal	Hex	Graphic Character
0	0		24	18	↑
1	1	☺	25	19	↓
2	2	☻	26	1A	→
3	3	♥	27	1B	←
4	4	♦	28	1C	∟
5	5	♣	29	1D	↔
6	6	♠	30	1E	▲
7	7	•	31	1F	▼
8	8	◘	32	20	
9	9	○	33	21	!
10	A	◙	34	22	"
11	B	♂	35	23	#
12	C	♀	36	24	$
13	D	♪	37	25	%
14	E	♫	38	26	&
15	F	☼	39	27	'
16	10	►	40	28	(
17	11	◄	41	29	)
18	12	↕	42	2A	*
19	13	‼	43	2B	+
20	14	¶	44	2C	,
21	15	§	45	2D	-
22	16	▬	46	2E	.
23	17	↨	47	2F	/

Decimal	Hex	Graphic Character	Decimal	Hex	Graphic Character
48	30	0	96	60	`
49	31	1	97	61	a
50	32	2	98	62	b
51	33	3	99	63	c
52	34	4	100	64	d
53	35	5	101	65	e
54	36	6	102	66	f
55	37	7	103	67	g
56	38	8	104	68	h
57	39	9	105	69	i
58	3A	:	106	6A	j
59	3B	;	107	6B	k
60	3C	<	108	6C	l
61	3D	=	109	6D	m
62	3E	>	110	6E	n
63	3F	?	111	6F	o
64	40	@	112	70	p
65	41	A	113	71	q
66	42	B	114	72	r
67	43	C	115	73	s
68	44	D	116	74	t
69	45	E	117	75	u
70	46	F	118	76	v
71	47	G	119	77	w
72	48	H	120	78	x
73	49	I	121	79	y
74	4A	J	122	7A	z
75	4B	K	123	7B	{
76	4C	L	124	7C	|
77	4D	M	125	7D	}
78	4E	N	126	7E	~
79	4F	O	127	7F	Δ
80	50	P	128	80	Ç
81	51	Q	129	81	ü
82	52	R	130	82	é
83	53	S	131	83	â
84	54	T	132	84	ä
85	55	U	133	85	à
86	56	V	134	86	á
87	57	W	135	87	ç
88	58	X	136	88	ê
89	59	Y	137	89	ë
90	5A	Z	138	8A	è
91	5B	[	139	8B	ï
92	5C	\	140	8C	î
93	5D	]	141	8D	ì
94	5E	^	142	8E	Ä
95	5F	_	143	8F	À

(continues)

Table C.1 Continued

Decimal	Hex	Graphic Character	Decimal	Hex	Graphic Character
144	90	É	192	C0	└
145	91	æ	193	C1	┴
146	92	Æ	194	C2	┬
147	93	ô	195	C3	├
148	94	ö	196	C4	─
149	95	ò	197	C5	┼
150	96	û	198	C6	╞
151	97	ù	199	C7	╟
152	98	ÿ	200	C8	╚
153	99	Ö	201	C9	╔
154	9A	Ü	202	CA	╩
155	9B	¢	203	CB	╦
156	9C	£	204	CC	╠
157	9D	¥	205	CD	═
158	9E	₧	206	CE	╬
159	9F	ƒ	207	CF	╧
160	A0	á	208	D0	╨
161	A1	í	209	D1	╤
162	A2	ó	210	D2	╥
163	A3	ú	211	D3	╙
164	A4	ñ	212	D4	╘
165	A5	Ñ	213	D5	╒
166	A6	ª	214	D6	╓
167	A7	º	215	D7	╫
168	A8	¿	216	D8	╪
169	A9	⌐	217	D9	┘
170	AA	¬	218	DA	┌
171	AB	½	219	DB	█
172	AC	¼	220	DC	▄
173	AD	¡	221	DD	▌
174	AE	«	222	DE	▐
175	AF	»	223	DF	▀
176	B0	░	224	E0	α
177	B1	▒	225	E1	β
178	B2	▓	226	E2	Γ
179	B3	│	227	E3	π
180	B4	┤	228	E4	Σ
181	B5	╡	229	E5	σ
182	B6	╢	230	E6	µ
183	B7	╖	231	E7	τ
184	B8	╕	232	E8	Φ
185	B9	╣	233	E9	Θ
186	BA	║	234	EA	Ω
187	BB	╗	235	EB	δ
188	BC	╝	236	EC	∞
189	BD	╜	237	ED	φ
190	BE	╛	238	EE	∈
191	BF	┐	239	EF	∩

Decimal	Hex	Graphic Character	Decimal	Hex	Graphic Character
240	F0	≡	248	F8	°
241	F1	±	249	F9	·
242	F2	≥	250	FA	·
243	F3	≤	251	FB	√
244	F4	⌠	252	FC	n
245	F5	⌡	253	FD	²
246	F6	÷	254	FE	∎
247	F7	≈	255	FF	

Entering ASCII Characters in Dialog Boxes

You also enter ASCII characters into Quattro Pro dialog boxes. When you choose /Options International Currency, Quattro Pro displays a dialog box and prompts you to enter a new currency symbol. To enter the British pound currency symbol (£), for example, follow these steps:

1. Press the Backspace key to delete the dollar sign (the default currency symbol).

2. Press and hold down the Alt key.

3. Type the decimal code **156** on the numeric keypad.

4. Release the Alt key. Quattro Pro reproduces the British pound symbol in the dialog box.

5. Press Enter to store the British pound symbol setting.

When you choose /**S**tyle **N**umeric Format **C**urrency and format a value, the British pound symbol appears instead of the dollar sign. To keep the British pound symbol as the global default, choose /**O**ptions Update.

> **NOTE**
>
> Some terminate-and-stay-resident (TSR) programs, such as SuperKey, assign special operations to the Alt key. If you have such programs on your PC, pressing Alt plus a decimal code doesn't display the ASCII character. Instead, press Alt+Shift and then type the decimal code.

You can use other special characters with Quattro Pro. The /Options Colors Menu Shadow command, for example, prompts you to enter the decimal code equivalent for the ASCII character that Quattro Pro uses to create menu shadows. ASCII decimal code 2 displays smiling faces in the menu shadows.

The /Options Colors Desktop command prompts you to enter the decimal code equivalent for the ASCII character that Quattro Pro uses to create fill characters when no windows are displayed. ASCII decimal code 14 displays musical note symbols in the background area.

Notice that these two commands require you to enter the decimal code equivalents for the ASCII character. Don't enter the actual symbols by pressing Alt plus the decimal code. If you do, Quattro Pro doesn't interpret the command settings correctly.

NOTE
> These last two techniques for displaying special symbols on-screen are operable only when you are in text display mode.

Converting ASCII Codes into Printer Setup Strings

Another use for the ASCII table is to create printer setup strings that you supply at the /Print Layout Setup String command prompt.

As discussed in Chapter 9, the control panel on a printer enables you to invoke various print modes such as draft printing, boldface printing, and compressed printing. Other print modes that your printer supports often don't appear as hardware options on the control panel (italic mode is a good example).

You can create and issue software commands that invoke special print modes. You first must review your printer manual. In the manual, you should find a table of software commands such as CTRL+F or ESC+4.

Printing modes generally are set through the use of control codes, which consist of one or more ASCII characters. These control codes, which vary from printer to printer, fall into two categories: control sequences and escape sequences.

In a *control sequence*, each code begins with the control character and is followed by a hexadecimal character. CTRL+F, for example, invokes the compressed printing mode for a Panasonic printer. To use this software command, convert the command to a code that your printer understands. The printer code that signifies a CTRL sequence is \0. The decimal equivalent for the hexadecimal F is 15.

To invoke compressed mode, do the following:

1. Choose /**P**rint **L**ayout **S**etup String.

2. When prompted, type **\015** and press Enter.

The next time you print a notebook, the text prints in compressed type.

In an *escape sequence*, each code begins with the ASCII code for the ESCAPE character (ESC). Don't confuse this character with the Escape (Esc) key on your keyboard—the character and the key aren't the same thing. ESC+4, for example, invokes the italic printing mode for a standard IBM printer. To use this software command, convert the command to a code that your printer understands. The code that signifies an ESC sequence is \027.

To invoke the italic printing mode, do the following:

1. Choose /**P**rint **L**ayout **S**etup String.

2. When prompted, type **\0274** and press Enter.

The next time you print a notebook, the text appears in italic. Consult your printer manual for the appropriate control and escape sequences. Some printer manuals even list setup strings that can be used with several popular software products.

After Quattro Pro sends a setup string to your printer, that printing mode remains the default until you issue a setup string that cancels it.

You also can turn your printer off and then back on to clear the setup string settings from your printer's memory. If you use this technique, you must delete the setup string entered at the /**P**rint **L**ayout **S**etup String prompt before you print another notebook.

Symbols

D

G

A Powerful Dose of DOS for the Everyday User!

Teach Yourself
with QuickStarts from Que!

Count on Que for the Latest in DOS Information!

Improve with Hot Tips!

These unique guides teach readers shortcuts as well as powerful techniques—improving the proficiency of both novice and experienced users.

Excel for the Mac Hot Tips

Ron Person

Version 4

$12.99 USA
1-56529-162-X, 224pp., 5½ X 8½

Excel for Windows Hot Tips

Ron Person

Version 4.0

$12.99 USA
1-56529-164-6, 224pp., 5½ X 8½

OS/2 2.1 Hot Tips

Que Development

Latest Version

$12.99 USA
1-56529-265-0, 224pp., 5½ X 8½

Windows Hot Tips

Steve Konicki

Version 3.1

$12.99 USA
1-56529-179-4, 224pp., 5½ X 8½

Word for Windows Hot Tips

George Beinhorn

Latest Version

$12.99 USA
1-56529-163-8, 224pp., 5½ X 8½